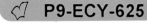

Second Edition

FUNDAMENTALS OF
Data Structures
in Pascal

ELLIS HOROWITZ · SARTAJ SAHNI

University of Southern California   *University of Minnesota*

COMPUTER SCIENCE PRESS

Computer Science Press
1803 Research Boulevard
Rockville, Maryland 20850

3 4 5 6 Printing   Year 90 89 88 87

Fundamentals of Data Structures in Pascal is another version of *Fundamentals of Data Structures* by Horowitz and Sahni. In the earlier work, all of the algorithms are written in the SPARKS language while in this work all the algorithms are written in the Pascal language.
Copyright © 1984 Computer Science Press, Inc.

Fundamentals of Data Structures
Copyright © 1982 Computer Science Press, Inc.

Fundamentals of Data Structures
Copyright © 1976 Computer Science Press, Inc.

Fundamentals of Data Structures in Pascal is the result of the combined efforts of the authors. Their names have been listed in alphabetical order with no implication that one is senior and the other junior.

Library of Congress Cataloging-in-Publication Data

Horowitz, Ellis.
    Fundamentals of data structures in Pascal.

    Bibliography: p.
    Includes index.
    1. Data structures (Computer science) 2. PASCAL
(Computer program language) I. Sahni, Sartaj.
II. Title.
QA76.9.D35H67 1986   005.7'3   86-13679
ISBN 0-88175-165-0
ISSN 0888-2088

in fond memory of our fathers
Irving Horowitz and Dharam Nath Sahni

CONTENTS

CHAPTER 5   TREES

CHAPTER 6   GRAPHS

CHAPTER 7   INTERNAL SORTING

CHAPTER 8   EXTERNAL SORTING

PREFACE TO
THE SECOND EDITION

This second edition incorporates numerous suggestions for improvements as well as corrections for errata which we have received from the many users of the previous edition.

For many years a data structures course has been taught in computer science programs. Often it is regarded as a central course of the curriculum. It is fascinating and instructive to trace the history of how the subject matter for this course has changed. Back in the middle 1960's the course was not entitled Data Structures but perhaps List Processing Languages. The major subjects were systems such as SLIP (by J. Weizenbaum), IPL-V (by A. Newell, C. Shaw, and H. Simon), LISP 1.5 (by J. McCarthy) and SNOBOL (by D. Farber, R. Griswold, and I. Polonsky). Then, in 1968, volume I of the Art of Computer Programming by D. Knuth appeared. His thesis was that list processing was not a magical thing that could only be accomplished within a specially designed system. Instead, he argued that the same techniques could be carried out in almost any language and he shifted the emphasis to efficient algorithm design. SLIP and IPL-V faded from the scene, while LISP and SNOBOL moved to the programming languages course. The new strategy was to explicitly construct a representation (such as linked lists) within a set of consecutive storage locations and to describe the algorithms by using English plus assembly language.

Progress in the study of data structures and algorithm design has continued. Out of this recent work has come many good ideas which we believe should be presented to students of computer science. It is our purpose in writing this book to emphasize those trends which we see as especially valuable and long lasting.

The most important of these new concepts is the need to distinguish between the specification of a data structure and its realization within an available programming language. This distinction has been mostly blurred in previous books where the primary emphasis has either been on a programming language or on representational techniques. Our attempt here has been to separate out the specification of the data structure from its realization and to show how both of these processes can be successfully accomplished. The specification stage requires one to concentrate on describing the functioning of the data structure without concern for its implementation. This can be done using English and mathematical notation, but here we introduce a programming notation called axioms. The resulting implementation independent specification is valuable in two ways: (i) to help prove that a program which uses this data structure is correct, and (ii) to prove that a particular implementation of the data structure is correct. To describe a data structure in a representation independent way one needs a syntax. This can be seen at the end of section 1.1 where we also precisely define the notions of data object and data structure.

This book also seeks to teach the art of analyzing algorithms but not at the cost of undue mathematical sophistication. The value of an implementation ultimately relies on its resource utilization: time and space. This implies that the student needs to be capable of analyzing these factors. A great many analyses have appeared in the literature, yet from our perspective most students don't attempt to rigorously analyze their programs. The data structures course comes at an opportune time in their training to advance and promote these ideas. For every algorithm that is given here we supply a simple, yet rigorous worst case analysis of its behavior. In some cases the average computing time is also derived.

The growth of data base systems has put a new requirement on data structures courses, namely to cover the organization of large files. Also, many instructors like to treat sorting and searching because of the richness of its examples of data structures and its practical application. The choice of our later chapters reflects this growing interest.

One especially important consideration is the choice of an algorithm description language. Such a choice is often complicated by the practical matters of student background and language availability. But today the programming language Pascal has become pervasive as the language of instruction in Computer Science departments. With that fact in mind we decided to alter our book *Fundamentals of Data Structures*, rewriting all of the algorithms into Pascal.

The basic audience for this book is either the computer science major with at least one year of courses or a beginning graduate student with prior training in a field other than computer science. This book contains more than one semester's worth of material and several of its chapters may be skipped without harm. The following are two scenarios which may help in deciding what chapters should be covered.

The first author has used this book with sophomores who have had one semester of Pascal and one semester of assembly language. He would cover chapters one through five skipping sections 2.2, 2.3, 3.2, 4.7, 4.11, and 5.8. Then, in whatever time was left chapter seven on sorting was covered. The second author has taught the material to juniors who have had one quarter of FORTRAN or PASCAL and two quarters of introductory courses which themselves contain a potpourri of topics. In the first quarter's data structure course, chapters one through three are lightly covered and chapters four through six are completely covered. The second quarter starts with chapter seven which provides an excellent survey of the techniques which were covered in the previous quarter. Then the material on external sorting, symbol tables and files is sufficient for the remaining time. Note that the material in chapter 2 is largely mathematical and can be skipped without harm.

The paradigm of class presentation that we have used is to begin each new topic with a problem, usually chosen from the computer science arena. Once defined, a high level design of its solution is made and each data structure is axiomatically specified. A tentative analysis is done to determine which operations are critical. Implementations of the data structures are then given followed by an attempt at verifying that the representation and specifications are consistent. The finished algorithm in the book is examined followed by an argument concerning its correctness. Then an analysis is done by determining the relevant parameters and applying some straightforward rules to obtain the correct computing time formula.

In summary, as instructors we have tried to emphasize the following notions to our students: (i) the ability to define at a sufficiently high level of abstraction the data structures and algorithms that are needed; (ii) the ability to devise alternative implementations of a data structure; (iii) the ability to synthesize a correct algorithm; and (iv) the ability to analyze the computing time of the resultant program. In addition there are two underlying currents which, though not explicitly emphasized, are covered throughout. The first is the notion of writing nicely structured programs. For all of the programs contained herein we have tried our best to structure them appropriately. We hope that by reading programs with good style the students will pick up good writing habits. A nudge on the instructor's part will also prove useful. The second current is the choice of examples. We have tried to use those examples which prove a point well, have application to computer programming, and exhibit some of the brightest accomplishments in computer science.

At the close of each chapter there is a list of references and selected readings. These are not meant to be exhaustive. They are a subset of those books and papers that we found to be the most useful. Otherwise, they are either historically significant or develop the material in the text somewhat further.

Many people have contributed their time and energy to improve our original book *Fundamentals of Data Structures* and we would like to thank them here again. We wish to thank Arvind [sic], T. Gonzalez, L. Landweber, J. Mistra, and D. Wilczynski, who used the book in their own classes and gave us detailed reactions. Thanks are also due to A. Agrawal,

M. Cohen, A. Howells, R. Istre, D. Ledbetter, D. Musser and to our students in CS 202, CSci 5121 and 5122 who provided many insights. For administrative and secretarial help we thank M. Eul, G. Lum, J. Matheson, S. Moody, K. Pendleton, and L. Templet. To the referees for their pungent yet favorable comments we thank S. Gerhart, T. Standish, and J. Ullman. Finally, we would like to thank our institutions, the University of Southern California and the University of Minnesota, for encouraging in every way our efforts to produce this book.

We would also like to express our thanks for the enthusiastic and helpful feedback we have received from the numerous users of the previous edition.

Ellis Horowitz
Sartaj Sahni
June 1986

Chapter 1

INTRODUCTION

1.1 OVERVIEW

The field of *computer science* is so new that one feels obliged to furnish a definition before proceeding with this book. One often quoted definition views computer science as the *study of algorithms*. This study encompasses four distinct areas:

(i) *machines for executing algorithms*—this area includes everything from the smallest pocket calculator to the largest general purpose digital computer. The goal is to study various forms of machine fabrication and organization so that algorithms can be effectively carried out.

(ii) *languages for describing algorithms*—these languages can be placed on a continuum. At one end are the languages which are closest to the physical machine and at the other end are languages designed for sophisticated problem solving. One often distinguishes between two phases of this area: language design and translation. The first calls for methods for specifying the syntax and semantics of a language. The second requires a means for translation into a more basic set of commands.

(iii) *foundations of algorithms*—here people ask and try to answer such questions as: is a particular task accomplishable by a computing device; or what is the minimum number of operations necessary for any algorithm which performs a certain function? Abstract models of computers are devised so that these properties can be studied.

(iv) *analysis of algorithms*—whenever an algorithm can be specified it makes sense to wonder about its behavior. This was realized as far back as 1830 by Charles Babbage, the father of computers. An algorithm's behavior pattern or *performance profile* is measured in terms of the computing time and space that are consumed while the algorithm is processing. Questions such as the worst and average time and how often they occur are typical.

We see that in this definition of computer science, "algorithm" is a fundamental notion. Thus it deserves a precise definition. The dictionary's

1

definition, "any mechanical or recursive computational procedure," is not entirely satisfying since these terms are not basic enough.

Definition: An *algorithm* is a finite set of instructions which, if followed, accomplish a particular task. In addition every algorithm must satisfy the following criteria:

(i)   *input:* there are zero or more quantities which are externally supplied;

(ii)   *output:* at least one quantity is produced;

(iii) *definiteness:* each instruction must be clear and unambiguous;

(iv)   *finiteness:* if we trace out the instructions of an algorithm, then for all cases the algorithm will terminate after a finite number of steps;

(v)   *effectiveness:* every instruction must be sufficiently basic that it can in principle be carried out by a person using only pencil and paper. It is not enough that each operation be definite as in (iii), but it must also be feasible.

In formal computer science, one distinguishes between an algorithm, and a program. A program does not necessarily satisfy condition (iv). One important example of such a program for a computer is its operating system which never terminates (except for system crashes) but continues in a wait loop until more jobs are entered. In this book we will deal strictly with programs that always terminate. Hence, we will use these terms interchangeably.

An algorithm can be described in many ways. A natural language such as English can be used but we must be very careful that the resulting instructions are definite (condition iii). An improvement over English is to couple its use with a graphical form of notation such as flowcharts. This form places each processing step in a "box" and uses arrows to indicate the next step. Different shaped boxes stand for different kinds of operations. All this can be seen in figure 1.1 where a flowchart is given for obtaining a Coca-Cola from a vending machine. The point is that algorithms can be devised for many common activities.

Have you studied the flowchart? Then you probably have realized that it isn't an algorithm at all! Which properties does it lack?

Returning to our earlier definition of computer science, we find it extremely unsatisfying as it gives us no insight as to why the computer is revolutionizing our society nor why it has made us re-examine certain basic assumptions about our own role in the universe. While this may be an unrealistic demand on a definition even from a technical point of view it is unsatisfying. The definition places great emphasis on the concept of algo-

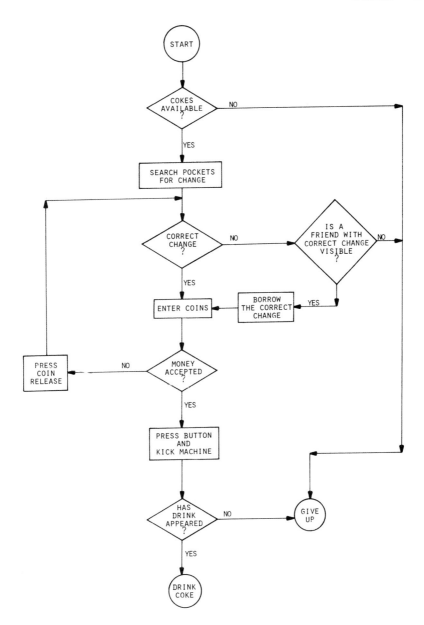

Figure 1.1 Flowchart for obtaining a Coca-Cola.

rithm, but never mentions the word "data". If a computer is merely a means to an end, then the means may be an algorithm but the end is the transformation of data. That is why we often hear a computer referred to as a data processing machine. Raw data is input and algorithms are used to transform it into refined data. So, instead of saying that computer science is the study of algorithms, alternatively, we might say that computer science is the *study of data:*

(i)   machines that hold data;
(ii)   languages for describing data manipulation;
(iii)   foundations which describe what kinds of refined data can be produced from raw data;
(iv)   structures for representing data.

There is an intimate connection between the structuring of data, and the synthesis of algorithms. In fact, a data structure and an algorithm should be thought of as a unit, neither one making sense without the other. For instance, suppose we have a list of n pairs of names and phone numbers $(a_1, b_1)(a_2, b_2), \ldots, (a_n, b_n)$, and we want to write a program which when given any name, prints that person's phone number. This task is called searching. Just how we would write such an algorithm critically depends upon how the names and phone numbers are stored or structured. One algorithm might just forge ahead and examine names, $a_1, a_2, a_3, \ldots$ etc., until the correct name was found. This might be fine in Oshkosh, but in Los Angeles, with hundreds of thousands of names, it would not be practical. If, however, we knew that the data was structured so that the names were in alphabetical order, then we could do much better. We could make up a second list which told us for each letter in the alphabet, where the first name with that letter appeared. For a name beginning with, say, S, we would avoid having to look at names beginning with other letters. So because of this new structure, a very different algorithm is possible. Other ideas for algorithms become possible when we realize that we can organize the data as we wish. We will discuss many more searching strategies in Chapters 7 and 9.

Therefore, computer science can be defined as the study of data, its representation and transformation by a digital computer. The goal of this book is to explore many different kinds of data objects. For each object, we consider the class of operations to be performed and then the way to represent this object so that these operations may be efficiently carried out. This implies a mastery of two techniques: the ability to devise alternative forms of data representation, and the ability to analyze the algorithm which operates on that structure. The pedagogical style we have chosen is to consider problems which have arisen often in computer applications. For each problem we will specify the data object or objects and what is to be accomplished. After we have decided upon a representation of the objects, we will give a complete algorithm and analyze its computing time. After reading through several of these examples you should be confident enough to try one on your own.

There are several terms we need to define carefully before we proceed. These include data structure, data object, data type and data representation. These four terms have no standard meaning in computer science circles, and they are often used interchangeably.

A *data type* is a term which refers to the kinds of data that variables may "hold" in a programming language. In FORTRAN the data types are INTEGER, REAL, LOGICAL, COMPLEX, and DOUBLE PRECISION. In PL/I there is the data type CHARACTER. The fundamental data type of SNOBOL is the character string and in LISP it is the list (or S-expression). Some of the standard data types in Pascal are: integer, real, boolean, char, and array. With every programming language there is a set of built-in data types. This means that the language allows variables to name data of that type and provides a set of operations which meaningfully manipulate these variables. Some data types are easy to provide because they are already built into the computer's machine language instruction set. Integer and real arithmetic are examples of this. Other data types require considerably more effort to implement. In some languages, there are features which allow one to construct combinations of the built-in types. In COBOL and PL/I this feature is called a STRUCTURE while in PASCAL it is called a RECORD. However, it is not necessary to have such a mechanism.

Data object is a term referring to a set of elements, say D. For example the data object *integers* refers to $D = \{0, \pm 1, \pm 2, \ldots\}$. The data object *alphabetic character strings of length less than thirty one* implies $D = \{'','A','B',\ldots,'Z','AA', \ldots\}$. Thus, D may be finite or infinite and if D is very large we may need to devise special ways of representing its elements in our computer.

The notion of a data structure as distinguished from a data object is that we want to describe not only the set of objects, but the way they are related. Saying this another way, we want to describe the set of operations which may legally be applied to elements of the data object. This implies that we must specify the set of operations and show how they work. For integers we would have the arithmetic operations $+, -, *, /$ and perhaps many others such as mod, ceil, floor, greater than, less than, etc. The data object integers plus a description of how $+, -, *, /$, etc. behave constitutes a data structure definition.

To be more precise let's examine a modest example. Suppose we wan to define the data structure natural number (abbreviated natno) where natno $= \{0,1,2,3,\ldots\}$ with the three operations being a test for zero, addition and equality. The following notation can be used:

```
          structure NATNO
  1         declare ZERO()  →  natno
  2                 ISZERO(natno)  →  boolean
  3                 SUCC(natno)  →  natno
  4                 ADD(natno, natno)  →  natno
  5                 EQ(natno, natno)  →  boolean
  6         for all x, y ∈ natno let
  7                 ISZERO(ZERO) ::= true; ISZERO(SUCC(x)) ::= false
  8                 ADD(ZERO, y) ::= y, ADD(SUCC(x), y) ::=
                    SUCC(ADD(x, y))
  9                 EQ(x, ZERO) ::= if ISZERO(x) then true else false
 10                 EQ(ZERO, SUCC(y)) ::= false
 11                 EQ(SUCC(x), SUCC(y)) ::= EQ(x, y)
 12         end
 13       end NATNO
```

In the declare statement five functions are defined by giving their names, inputs and outputs. ZERO is a constant function which means it takes no input arguments and its result is the natural number zero, written as ZERO. ISZERO is a boolean function whose result is either **true** or **false**. SUCC stands for successor. Using ZERO and SUCC we can define all of the natural numbers as: ZERO, 1 = SUCC(ZERO), 2 = SUCC(SUCC-(ZERO)), 3 = SUCC(SUCC(SUCC(ZERO))), ... etc. The rules on line 8 tell us exactly how the addition operation works. For example if we wanted to add two and three we would get the following sequence of expressions:

$$ADD(SUCC(SUCC(ZERO)),SUCC(SUCC(SUCC(ZERO))))$$

which, by line 8 equals

$$SUCC(ADD(SUCC(ZERO),SUCC(SUCC(SUCC(ZERO)))))$$

which, by line 8 equals

$$SUCC(SUCC(ADD(ZERO),SUCC(SUCC(SUCC(ZERO)))))$$

which, by line 8 equals

$$SUCC(SUCC(SUCC(SUCC(ZERO)))))$$

Of course, this is not the way to implement addition. In practice we use bit strings which is a data structure that is usually provided on our computers. But however the ADD operation is implemented, it must obey these rules. Hopefully, this motivates the following definition.

Definition: A *data structure* is a set of domains $\mathscr{D}$, a designated domain $d \in \mathscr{D}$, a set of functions $\mathscr{F}$ and a set of axioms $\mathscr{A}$. The triple $(\mathscr{D}, \mathscr{F}, \mathscr{A})$ denotes the data structure d and it will usually be abbreviated by writing d.

In the previous example

d = natno, $\mathscr{S}$ = {natno, boolean}
$\mathscr{F}$ = {ZERO,ISZERO,SUCC,ADD}
$\mathscr{A}$ = {lines 7 thru 10 of the structure NATNO}

The set of axioms describes the semantics of the operations. The form in which we choose to write the axioms is important. Our goal here is to write the axioms in a representation independent way. Then, we discuss ways of implementing the functions using a conventional programming language.

An *implementation of a data structure d* is a mapping from d to a set of other data structures e. This mapping specifies how every object of d is to be represented by the objects of e. Secondly, it requires that every function of d must be written using the functions of the implementing data structures e. Thus we say that integers are represented by bit strings, boolean is represented by zero and one, an array is represented by a set of consecutive words in memory.

In current parlance the triple ($\mathscr{S}$, $\mathscr{F}$, $\mathscr{A}$) is referred to as an *abstract data type*. It is called abstract precisely because the axioms do not imply a form of representation. Another way of viewing the implementation of a data structure is that it is the process of refining an abstract data type until all of the operations are expressible in terms of directly executable functions. But at the first stage a data structure should be designed so that we know *what* it does, but not necessarily *how* it will do it. This division of tasks, called specification and implementation, is useful because it helps to control the complexity of the entire process.

1.2   HOW TO CREATE PROGRAMS

Now that you have moved beyond the first course in computer science, you should be capable of developing your programs using something better than the seat-of-the-pants method. This method uses the philosophy: write something down and then try to get it working. Surprisingly, this method is in wide use today, with the result that an average programmer on an average job turns out only between five to ten lines of correct code per day. We hope your productivity will be greater. But to improve requires that you apply some discipline to the process of creating programs. To understand this process better, we consider it as broken up into five phases: requirements, design, analysis, coding, and verification.

(i) *Requirements.* Make sure you understand the information you are given (the input) and what results you are to produce (the output). Try to write down a rigorous description of the input and output which covers all cases.

You are now ready to proceed to the design phase. Designing an algorithm is a task which can be done independently of the programming language you eventually plan to use. In fact, this is desirable because it means you can postpone questions concerning *how* to represent your data and *what* a particular statement looks like and concentrate on the order of processing.

(ii) *Design*. You may have several data objects (such as a maze, a polynomial, or a list of names). For each object there will be some basic operations to perform on it (such as print the maze, add two polynomials, or find a name in the list). Assume that these operations already exist in the form of procedures and write an algorithm which solves the problem according to the requirements. Use a notation which is natural to the way you wish to describe the order of processing.

(iii) *Analysis*. Can you think of another algorithm? If so, write it down. Next, try to compare these two methods. It may already be possible to tell if one will be more desirable than the other. If you can't distinguish between the two, choose one to work on for now and we will return to the second version later.

(iv) *Refinement and coding*. You must now choose representations for your data objects (a maze as a two dimensional array of zeros and ones, a polynomial as a one dimensional array of degree and coefficients, a list of names possibly as an array) and write algorithms for each of the operations on these objects. The order in which you do this may be crucial, because once you choose a representation, the resulting algorithms may be inefficient. Modern pedagogy suggests that all processing which is independent of the data representation be written out first. By postponing the choice of how the data is stored we can try to isolate the operations that depend on the choice of data representation. You should consider alternatives, note them down and review them later. Finally you produce a complete version of your first program.

It is often at this point that one realizes that a much better program could have been built. Perhaps you should have chosen the second design alternative or perhaps you have spoken to a friend who has done it better. This happens to industrial programmers as well. If you have been careful about keeping track of your previous work it may not be too difficult to make changes. One of the criteria of a good design is that it can absorb changes relatively easily. It is usually hard to decide whether to sacrifice this first attempt and begin again or just continue to get the first version working. Different situations call for different decisions, but we suggest you eliminate the idea of working on both at the same time. If you do decide to scrap your work and begin again, you can take comfort in the fact that it will probably be easier the second time. In fact you may save as much debugging time later on by doing a new version now. This is a phenomenon which has been observed in practice.

The graph in figure 1.2 shows the time it took for the same group to build 3 FORTRAN compilers (A, B and C). For each compiler there is the time they estimated it would take them and the time it actually took. For each subsequent compiler their estimates became closer to the truth, but in every case they underestimated. Unwarranted optimism is a familiar disease in computing. But prior experience is definitely helpful and the time to build the third compiler was less than one fifth that for the first one.

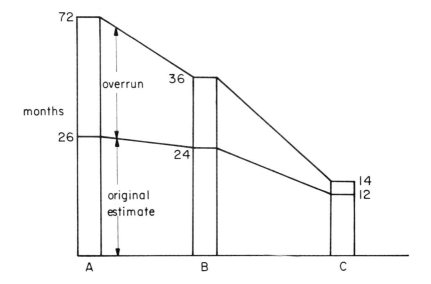

Figure 1.2   History of three FORTRAN compilers.

(v) *Verification.* Verification consists of three distinct aspects: program proving, testing and debugging. Each of these is an art in itelf. Before executing your program you should attempt to prove it is correct. Proofs about programs are really no different from any other kind of proof, only the subject matter is different. If a correct proof can be obtained, then one is assured that for all possible combinations of inputs, the program and its specification agree. Testing is the art of creating sample data upon which to run your program. If the program fails to respond correctly then debugging is needed to determine what went wrong and how to correct it. One proof tells us more than any finite amount of testing, but proofs can be hard to obtain. Many times during the proving process errors are discovered in the code. The proof can't be completed until these are eliminated. This is another use of program proving, namely as a methodology for discovering errors. Finally there may be tools available at your computing center to aid in the testing process. One such tool instruments your source code and then tells you for every data set: (i) the number of times a statement was executed, (ii) the number of times a branch was taken, (iii) the smallest and largest values of all variables. As a minimal requirement, the test data you construct should force every statement to execute and every condition to assume the value true and false at least once.

One thing you have forgotten to do is to document. But why bother to document until the program is entirely finished and correct? Because for each procedure you made some assumptions about its input and output. If you have written more than a few procedures, then you have already begun to forget what those assumptions were. If you note them down with the code, the problem of getting the procedures to work together will be easier to solve. The larger the software, the more crucial is the need for documentation.

The previous discussion applies to the construction of a single procedure as well as to the writing of a large software system. Let us concentrate for a while on the question of developing a single procedure which solves a specific task. This shifts our emphasis away from the management and integration of the various procedures to the disciplined formulation of a single, reasonably small and well-defined task. The design process consists essentially of taking a proposed solution and successively refining it until an executable program is obtained. The initial solution may be expressed in English or some form of mathematical notation. At this level the formulation is said to be abstract because it contains no details regarding how the objects will be represented and manipulated in a computer. If possible the designer attempts to partition the solution into logical subtasks. Each subtask is similarly decomposed until all tasks are expressed within a programming language. This method of design is called the *top-down* approach. Inversely, the designer might choose to solve different parts of the problem directly in his programming language and then combine these pieces into a complete program. This is referred to as the *bottom-up* approach. Experience suggests that the top-down approach should be followed when creating a program. However, in practice it is not necessary to unswervingly follow the method. A look ahead to problems which may arise later is often useful.

Underlying all of these strategies is the assumption that a language exists for adequately describing the processing of data at several abstract levels. For this purpose we use the language Pascal coupled with carefully chosen English narrative. Such a language might be called pseudo-Pascal. Let us examine two examples of top-down program development.

Suppose we devise a program for sorting a set of $n \geq 1$ integers. One of the simplest solutions is given by the following

"from those integers which remain unsorted, find the smallest and place it next in the sorted list"

This statement is sufficient to construct a sorting program. However, several issues are not fully specified such as where and how the integers are initially stored and where the result is to be placed. One solution is to store the values in an array in such a way that the i-th integer is stored in the i-th array position, $a[i]$ $1 \leq i \leq n$. Program 1.1 is a refinement of the solution.

for $i := 1$ **to** n **do**
begin
    examine $a[i]$ to $a[n]$ and suppose the smallest integer is at $a[j]$;
    interchange $a[i]$ and $a[j]$;
end;

Program 1.1 Selection Sort

Note how we have begun to use Pascal pseudo-code. There now remain two clearly defined subtasks: (i) to find the minimum integer and (ii) to interchange it with $a[i]$. This latter problem can be solved by the code

$$t := a[i]; \quad a[i] := a[j]; \quad a[j] := t;$$

The first subtask can be solved by assuming the minimum is $a[i]$, checking $a[i]$ with $a[i + 1]$, $a[i + 2]$, ... and whenever a smaller element is found, regarding it as the new minimum. Eventually $a[n]$ is compared to the current minimum and we are done. Putting all these observations together we get the procedure *sort* (Program 1.2). *elementlist* is an array of integers.

```
1    procedure sort (var a: elementlist; n: integer);
2    {sort the n integers a[1..n] into nondecreasing order}
3    var i, j, k, t: integer;
4    begin
5         for i := 1 to n do
6         begin
7              j := i;
8              {find smallest integer in a[j..n]}
9              for k := j + 1 to n do
10                  if a[k] < a[j] then j := k;
11             {interchange}
12             t := a[i]; a[i] := a[j]; a[j] := t;
13        end; {of for i}
14   end; {of sort}
```

Program 1.2 Selection Sort

The obvious question to ask at this point is: "does this procedure work correctly?"

Theorem: Procedure *sort(a,n)* correctly sorts a set of $n \geq 1$ integers; the result remains in $a[1..n]$ such that $a[1] \leq a[2] \leq \ldots \leq a[n]$.

Proof: We first note that for any i, say $i = q$, following the execution of lines 7-12, it is the case that $a[q] \leq a[r]$, $q < r \leq n$. Also, observe that when i becomes greater than q, $a[1..q]$ is unchanged. Hence, following the last execution of these lines (i.e., $i = n$), we have $a[1] \leq a[2] \leq \ldots \leq a[n]$. ∎

We observe at this point that the upper limit of the **for**-loop in line 5 can be changed to $n - 1$ without damaging the correctness of the algorithm.

Let us develop another program. We assume that we have $n \geq 1$ distinct integers which are already sorted and stored in the array $a[1..n]$. Our task is to determine if the integer x is present and if so to return j such that $x = a[j]$; otherwise return $j = 0$. By making use of the fact that the set is sorted we conceive of the following efficient method:

"let $a[mid]$ be the middle element. There are three possibilities. Either $x < a[mid]$ in which case x can only occur as $a[1]$ to $a[mid - 1]$; or $x > a[mid]$ in which case x can only occur as $a[mid + 1]$ to $a[n]$; or $x = a[mid]$ in which case set j to mid and return. Continue in this way by keeping two pointers, *lower* and *upper*, to indicate the range of elements not yet tested."

At this point you might try the method out on some sample numbers. This method is referred to as *binary search*. Note how at each stage the number of elements in the remaining set is decreased by about one half. Note also that at each stage, x is compared with $a[mid]$ and depending on whether $x > a[mid]$, or $x < a[mid]$, or $x = a[mid]$, we do a different thing. To implement this in Pascal we could use the **if-then-else** construct:

if $x > a[mid]$ **then** ....
    else if $x < a[mid]$ **then** ..
        else ..

From this construct it isn't readily apparent that we are considering the three cases that can result from the comparison between x and $a[i]$. To make the program more transparent, we introduce a compare function that has value '>', '<' or '=' depending on the outcome of the comparison. This function is given in Program 1.3.

```
function compare (x, y: element): char;
begin
  if x > y then compare := '>'
          else if x < y then compare := '<'
                        else compare := '='
end; {of compare}
```

Program 1.3 Compare

We can now refine the description of binary search to get a pseudo-Pascal procedure. The result is given in Program 1.4.

```
procedure binsrch (a:elementlist; x:element; var n,j:integer);
{search the sorted array a[1..n] for x}
initialize lower and upper
begin
    while there are more elements and x not found do
    begin
        let a[mid] be the middle element;
        case compare (x, a[mid]) of
            '>': set lower to mid + 1;
            '<': set upper to mid - 1;
            '=': found x;
        end; {of case}
    end; {of while}
    not found;
end; {of binsrch}
```

Program 1.4 Algorithm for binary search

Another refinement yields the Pascal procedure of Program 1.5.

```
1   procedure binsrch (a:elementlist; x:element; var n,j:integer);
2   {search the sorted array a[1..n] for x}
3   var lower, upper, mid: integer; found : boolean;
4   begin
5       lower := 1; upper := n; found := false; j := 0;
6       while (lower <= upper) and (not found) do {while more elements}
7       begin
8           mid := (lower + upper) div 2;
9           case compare (x, a[mid]) of
10              '>': lower := mid + 1; {x > a[mid]}
11              '<': upper := mid - 1; {x < a[mid]}
12              '=': begin j := mid; found := true; end; {x = a[mid]}
13          end; {of case}
14      end; {of while}
15  end; {of binsrch}
```

Program 1.5 Pascal procedure for binary search

To prove this program correct we make assertions about the relationship between variables before and after the **while** loop of lines 6-14. As we enter this loop and as long as x is not found the following holds:

lower ≤ *upper* **and** $a[lower]$ ≤ x ≤ $a[upper]$ **and** *SORTED* (a,n)

Now, if control passes out of the **while** loop past line 14, then we know the condition of line 6 is false, so either *lower* > *upper* or x has been found. If *lower* > *upper*, then the above assertion implies that x is not present.

Unfortunately a complete proof takes us beyond our scope but those who wish to pursue program proving should consult our references at the end of this chapter. An analysis of the computing time for *binsrch* is carried out in section 7.1.

Recursion

We have tried to emphasize the need to structure a program to make it easier to achieve the goals of readability and correctness. Actually one of the most useful syntactical features for accomplishing this is the procedure. Given a set of instructions which perform a logical operation, perhaps a very complex and long operation, they can be grouped together as a procedure. The procedure name and its parameters are viewed as a new instruction which can be used in other programs. Given the input-output specifications of a procedure, we don't even have to know how the task is accomplished, only that it is available. This view of the procedure implies that it is invoked, executed and returns control to the appropriate place in the calling procedure. What this fails to stress is the fact that procedures may call themselves (direct recursion) before they are done or they may call other procedures which again invoke the calling procedure (indirect recursion). These recursive mechanisms are extremely powerful, but even more importantly, many times they can express an otherwise complex process very clearly. For these reasons we introduce recursion here.

Most students of computer science view recursion as a somewhat mystical technique which is useful only for some very special class of problems (such as computing factorials or Ackermann's function). This is unfortunate because any program that can be written using assignment, the **if-then-else** statement and the **while** statement can also be written using assignment, **if-then-else** and recursion. Of course, this does not say that the resulting program will necessarily be easier to understand. However, there are many instances when this will be the case. When is recursion an appropriate mechanism for algorithm exposition? One instance is when the problem itself is recursively defined. Factorial fits this category, also binomial coefficients where

$$\binom{n}{m} = \frac{n!}{m!(n-m)!}$$

can be recursively computed by the formula

$$\binom{n}{m} = \binom{n-1}{m} + \binom{n-1}{m-1}$$

Another example is reversing a character string, $s = $ '$x_1 \ldots x_n$'. Let us assume that the **type** string has been declared as:

type *string* = **record**
                       length: **integer**; {length of string}
                       c: **array**[1..100] **of char**;
        end;

and that the following functions have already been defined;

(1) *substring* (s,i,j) ... this yields the string made up of the ith through jth characters in s; for appropriately defined i and j. Thus if $0 < i \leq j \leq s.length$, then the string $s.c[i] \ldots s.c[j]$ is the desired substring.

(2) *concat*$(s1,s2)$ ... this function yields a string of length $s1.length + s2.length$ obtained by concatenating $s1$ and $s2$ with $s1$ preceding $s2$.

Using these functions, a recursive function (Program 1.6) to reverse the string s is easily obtained.

```
function reverse (s: string): string;
{reverse the string s}
var n: integer;
begin
  n := s.length;
  if n <= 1
  then reverse := s
  else reverse := concat(reverse(substring(s,2,n)),s.c[1]);
end; {of reverse}
```

Program 1.6 String reversal

If this looks too simple let us develop a more complex recursive procedure. Given a set of $n \geq 1$ elements the problem is to print all possible permutations of this set. For example if the set is $\{a,b,c\}$, then the set of permutations is $\{(a,b,c), (a,c,b), (b,a,c,), (b,c,a), (c,a,b), (c,b,a)\}$. It is easy to see that given n elements there are $n!$ different permutations. A simple algorithm can be constructed by looking at the case of four elements (a,b,c,d). The answer is obtained by writing

(i) a followed by all permutations of (b,c,d)
(ii) b followed by all permutations of (a,c,d)
(iii) c followed by all permutations of (a,b,d)
(iv) d followed by all permutations of (a,b,c)

The expression "followed by all permutations" is the clue to recursion. It implies that we can solve the problem for a set with n elements if we have an algorithm which works on $n - 1$ elements. These considerations lead to Program 1.7 which is invoked by *perm*(a,1,n).

```
procedure perm (a: elementlist; k,n: integer);
{generate all the permutations of a[k..n]}
var t: element; {type of entries in a}
    i: integer;
begin
  if k = n
  then begin {output permutation}
              for i := 1 to n do
                  write(a[i]);
              writeln;
       end
  else begin
       {a[k..n] has more than one permutation.
       Generate these recursively.}
       for i := k to n do
       begin
         {interchange a[k] and a[i]}
         t := a[k]; a[k] := a[i]; a[i] := t;
         perm (a, k+1, n); {all permutations of a[k+1..n]}
       end;
       end; {of else}
end; {of perm}
```

Program 1.7 Permutation

Try this algorithm out on sets of length one, two, and three to ensure that you understand how it works. Then try to do one or more of the exercises at the end of this chapter which ask for recursive procedures.

Another time when recursion is useful is when the data structure that the algorithm is to operate on is recursively defined. We will see several important examples of such structures, especially lists in section 4.9 and binary trees in section 5.4. Another instance when recursion is invaluable is when we want to describe a backtracking procedure.

1.3 HOW TO ANALYZE PROGRAMS

One goal of this book is to develop skills for making evaluative judgements about programs. There are many criteria upon which we can judge a program, for instance:

(i)   Does it do what we want it to do?

(ii)   Does it work correctly according to the original specifications of the task?

(iii)   Is there documentation which describes how to use it and how it works?

(iv)   Are **procedures** created in such a way that they perform logical sub-functions?

(v)   Is the code readable?

The above criteria are all vitally important when it comes to writing software, most especially for large systems. Though we will not be discussing how to reach these goals, we will try to achieve them throughout this book with the programs we write. Hopefully this more subtle approach will gradually infect your own program writing habits so that you will automatically strive to achieve these goals.

There are other criteria for judging programs which have a more direct relationship to performance. These have to do with computing time and storage requirements of the algorithms. Performance evaluation can be loosely divided into 2 major phases: (a) a priori estimates and (b) a posteriori testing. Both of these are equally important.

First consider a priori estimation. Suppose that somewhere in one of your programs is the statement

$$x := x + 1.$$

We would like to determine two numbers for this statement. The first is the amount of time a single execution will take; the second is the number of times it is executed. The product of these numbers will be the total time taken by this statement. The second statistic is called the *frequency count*, and this may vary from data set to data set. One of the hardest tasks in estimating frequency counts is to choose adequate samples of data. It is impossible to determine exactly how much time it takes to execute any command unless we have the following information:

(i)   the machine we are executing on;
(ii)   its machine language instruction set;
(iii) the time required by each machine instruction;
(iv)   the translation a compiler will make from the source to the machine language.

It is possible to determine these figures by choosing a real machine and an existing compiler. Another approach would be to define a hypothetical machine (with imaginary execution times), but make the times reasonably close to those of existing hardware so that resulting figures would be representative. Neither of these alternatives seems attractive. In both cases the exact times we would determine would not apply to many machines or to any machine. Also, there would be the problem of the compiler, which could vary from machine to machine. Moreover, it is often difficult to get reliable timing figures because of clock limitations and a multi-programming or time sharing environment. Finally, the difficulty of learning another machine language outweighs the advantage of finding "exact" fictitious times. All these considerations lead us to limit our goals for an a priori analysis. Instead, we will concentrate on developing only the frequency count for all statements. The anomalies of machine configuration and language will be lumped together when we do our experimental studies. Parallelism will not be considered.

Consider the three examples of Figure 1.3 below.

–		**for** $i := 1$ **to** n **do**
–	**for** $i := 1$ **to** n **do**	
–		**for** $j := 1$ **to** n **do**
$x := x + 1$	$x := x + 1;$	
–		$x := x + 1;$
–		
–		
(a)	(b)	(c)

Figure 1.3: Three simple programs for frequency counting.

In program (a) we assume that the statement $x := x + 1$ is not contained within any loop either explicit or implicit. Then its frequency count is one. In program (b) the same statement will be executed n times and in program (c) n^2 times (assuming $n \geq 1$). Now 1, n, and n^2 are said to be different and increasing orders of magnitude just like 1, 10, 100 would be if we let $n = 10$. In our analysis of execution we will be concerned chiefly with determining the order of magnitude of an algorithm. This means determining those statements which may have the greatest frequency count.

To determine the order of magnitude, formulas such as

$$\sum_{1 \leq i \leq n} 1, \ \sum_{1 \leq i \leq n} i, \ \sum_{1 \leq i \leq n} i^2$$

often occur. In the program segment of figure 1.3(c) the statement $x := x + 1$ is executed

$$\sum_{1 \leq i \leq n} \ \sum_{1 \leq j \leq n} 1 = \sum_{1 \leq i \leq n} n = n^2 \text{ times}$$

Simple forms for the above three formulas are well known, namely,

$$n, \ \frac{n(n + 1)}{2}, \ \frac{n(n + 1)(2n + 1)}{6}$$

In general

$$\sum_{1 \leq i \leq n} i^k = \frac{n^{k + 1}}{k + 1} + \text{ terms of lower degree}, \ k \geq 0.$$

To clarify some of these ideas, let us look at a simple program for computing the n-th Fibonacci number. The Fibonacci sequence starts as

$$0, \ 1, \ 1, \ 2, \ 3, \ 5, \ 8, \ 13, \ 21, \ 34, \ 55, \ \ldots$$

Each new term is obtained by taking the sum of the two previous terms. If we call the first term of the sequence F_0 then $F_0 = 0$, $F_1 = 1$ and in general

$$F_n = F_{n-1} + F_{n-2}, \ n \geq 2.$$

The program *fibonacci* (Program 1.8) inputs any non-negative integer n and prints the value F_n.

```
1    program fibonacci (input, output);
2    {compute the Fibonacci number Fₙ}
3    type natural = 0..maxint;
4    var fnm1,fnm2,fn,n,i : natural;
5    begin
6        readln(n)
7        if n <= 1 then writeln(n) {F₀ = 0 and F₁ = 1}
8                  else
9                  begin { compute Fₙ }
10                       fnm2 := 0; fnm1 := 1;
11                       for i := 2 to n do
12                       begin
13                            fn := fnm1 + fnm2;
14                            fnm2 := fnm1;
15                            fnm1 := fn;
16                       end; {of for}
17                       writeln(fn);
18                  end; {of else}
19    end. {of fibonacci}
```

Program 1.8 Fibonacci Numbers

To analyze the time complexity of this program, we need to consider the two cases: (i) $n = 0$ or 1, and (ii) $n > 1$. We shall count the total number of statement executions and use this as a measure of the time complexity of the program. Further, we note that only executable statements contribute to the complexity of the program. Thus, lines 3 and 4 do not add to the time needed to compute a Fibonacci number. Also, **begin** statements will not be counted as they simply designate the start of statement blocks.

When $n = 0$ or 1, lines 6, 7, and 19 get executed once each. We shall give line 7 a count of 2 (one for the conditional and one for the **then** clause). The total statement count for this case is therefore 4. When $n > 1$, the **for** loop of lines 11-16 gets executed. Line 11 gets executed n times while lines 12-16 get executed $n-1$ times each (note that the last time line 11 is executed, i is incremented to $n + 1$ and the loop exited). Each execution of line 10 counts as 2 towards the statement count as line 10 contains two statements. The contribution of each line of the program to the total statement count is summarized in figure 1.4. The contribution of the remaining lines is zero. Line 7a refers to the conditional of line 7 and 7b refers to the **then** clause.

line	count	line	count
6	1	14	n-1
7a	1	15	n-1
7b	1	16	n-1
10	2	17	1
11	n	18	1
13	n-1	19	1

Figure 1.4 Statement counts for computing F_n, $n > 1$.

Clearly, the actual time taken by each statement will vary. The **for** statement is really a combination of several statements, but we will count it as one. The total count then is $5n + 3$. We will often write this as $O(n)$, ignoring the two constants 5 and 3. This notation means that the order of magnitude is proportional to n.

The notation $f(n) = O(g(n))$ (read as f of n equals big-oh of g of n) has a precise mathematical definition.

Definition: $f(n) = O(g(n))$ iff there exist two constants c and n_o such that $|f(n)| \le c|g(n)|$ for all $n \ge n_o$.

$f(n)$ will normally represent the computing time of some algorithm. When we say that the computing time of an algorithm is $O(g(n))$ we mean that its execution takes no more than a constant times $g(n)$. n is a parameter which characterizes the inputs and/or outputs. For example n might be the number of inputs or the number of outputs or their sum or the magnitude of one of them. For the Fibonacci program n represents the magnitude of the input and the time for this program is written as $T(fibonacci) = O(n)$.

We write $O(1)$ to mean a computing time which is a constant. $O(n)$ is called linear, $O(n^2)$ is called quadratic, $O(n^3)$ is called cubic, and $O(2^n)$ is called exponential. If an algorithm takes time $O(\log n)$ it is faster, for sufficiently large n, than if it had taken $O(n)$. Similarly, $O(n \log n)$ is better than $O(n^2)$ but not as good as $O(n)$. These seven computing times, $O(1)$, $O(\log n)$, $O(n)$, $O(n \log n)$, $O(n^2)$, $O(n^3)$, and $O(2^n)$ are the ones we will see most often in this book.

If we have two algorithms which perform the same task, and the first has a computing time which is $O(n)$ and the second $O(n^2)$, then we will usually take the first as superior. The reason for this is that as n increases the time for the second algorithm will get far worse than the time for the first. For example, if the constant for algorithms one and two are 10 and 1/2 respectively, then we get the following table of computing times:

n	10n	$n^2/2$
1	10	1/2
5	50	12-1/2
10	100	50
15	150	112-1/2
20	200	200
25	250	312-1/2
30	300	450

For $n \le 20$, algorithm two has a smaller computing time but once past that point algorithm one becomes better. This shows why we choose the algorithm with the smaller order of magnitude, but we emphasize that this is not the whole story. For small data sets, the respective constants must be carefully determined. In practice these constants depend on many factors, such as the language and the machine one is using. Thus, we will usually postpone the establishment of the constant until after the program has been written. Then a performance profile can be gathered empirically.

Figures 1.5 and 1.6 show how the computing times (counts) grow with a constant equal to one. Notice how the times $O(n)$ and $O(n \log n)$ grow much more slowly than the others. For large data sets, algorithms with a complexity greater than $O(n \log n)$ are often impractical. An algorithm which is exponential will work only for very small inputs. For exponential

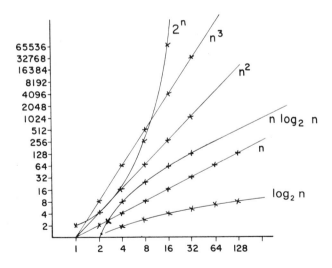

Figure 1.5   Rate of Growth of Common Computing Time Functions.

$\log_2 n$	n	$n \log_2 n$	n^2	n^3	2^n
0	1	0	1	1	2
1	2	2	4	8	4
2	4	8	16	64	16
3	8	24	64	512	256
4	16	64	256	4096	65536
5	32	160	1024	32768	2,147,483,648

Figure 1.6: Values for Computing Functions

algorithms, even if we improve the constant, say by $1/2$ or $1/3$, we will not improve the amount of data we can handle by very much.

Given an algorithm, we analyze the frequency count of each statement and total the sum. This may give a polynomial

$$P(n) = c_k n^k + c_{k-1} n^{k-1} + \ldots + c_1 n + c_o$$

where the c_i are constants, $c_k \neq 0$ and n is a parameter. Using big-oh notation, $P(n) = O(n^k)$. On the other hand, if any step is executed 2^n times or more the expression

$$c2^n + P(n) = O(2^n).$$

Another valid performance measure of an algorithm is the space it requires. Often one can trade space for time, getting a faster algorithm that uses more space. We shall see instances of this in subsequent chapters.

We end this chapter with a problem from recreational mathematics. A magic square is an $n \times n$ matrix of the integers 1 to n^2 such that the sum of every row, column and diagonal is the same. For example, if $n = 5$ we have

15	8	1	24	17
16	14	7	5	23
22	20	13	6	4
3	21	19	12	10
9	2	25	18	11

where the common sum is 65. When n is odd H. Coxeter has given a simple rule for generating a magic square:

"Start with 1 in the middle of the top row; then go up and left assigning numbers in increasing order to empty squares; if you fall off the square imagine the same square as tiling the plane and continue; if a square is occupied, move down instead and continue."

The magic square above was formed using this rule. We now write a Pascal program for creating an $n \times n$ magic square for n odd.

```pascal
program magic(input, output);
{create a magic square of size n}
label 999;
const maxsize = 50; {maximum square size − 1}
var square : array [0..maxsize , 0..maxsize] of integer;
    i, j, k, l : integer; {indices}
    key : integer; {counter}
    n : integer; {square size}
begin
  readln(n); {input square size}
  if (n > maxsize+1) or (n < 1)
  then
  begin
       writeln('error..n out of range'); goto 999;
  end
  else
  if n mod 2 = 0 then begin
                      writeln('error..n is even');
                      goto 999;
               end;
  {n is odd}
  for i := 0 to n − 1 do{initialize square to zero}
    for j := 0 to n − 1 do square[i, j] := 0;
  square [0,(n − 1) div 2] := 1; {middle of first row}
  {i and j are current position}
  key := 2; i := 0; j := (n −1) div 2;
  while key <= n * n do
  begin
    {move up and left. The next two if statements may
    be replaced by the mod operator if − 1 mod n is
    implemented to have value n − 1}
    if i − 1 < 0 then k := n − 1
                else k := i − 1;
    if j − 1 < 0 then l := n − 1
                else l := j − 1;
    if square[k, l] <> 0
    then i := (i + 1) mod n {square occupied, move down}
    else begin {square [k, l] is unoccupied}
           i := k
```

{the **mod** operator may be used here
   if −1 **mod** $n = n - 1$}
   if $j - 1 < 0$ **then** $j := n - 1$
                      else $j := j - 1$;
   end;
   $square[i, j] := key$;
   $key := key + 1$;
 end; {of **while**}
 {output the magic square}
 writeln('magic square of size ', n);
 for $i := 0$ **to** $n - 1$ **do**
 begin
   for $j := 0$ **to** $n - 1$ **do**
     write($square[i,j]$);
   writeln;
   end; {of **for**}
999: **end** {of *magic*}

Program 1.9 Magic Square

The magic square is represented using a two dimensional array having n rows and n columns. For this application it is convenient to number the rows (and columns) from zero to $n - 1$ rather than from one to n. Thus, when the program "falls off the square," the **mod** operator sets i and/or j back to zero or $n - 1$.

The **while** loop is governed by the variable *key* which is an integer variable initialized to 2 and increased by one each time through the loop. Thus each statement within the **while** loop will be executed no more than $n^2 - 1$ times and hence the computing time for *magic* is $O(n^2)$. Since there are n^2 positions in which the algorithm must place a number, we see that $O(n^2)$ is the best bound an algorithm for the magic square problem can have.

REFERENCES AND SELECTED READINGS

For a discussion of algorithms and how to analyze them see

The Art of Computer Programming: Fundamental Algorithms, by D. E. Knuth, vol. 1, chapter 1, 2nd edition, Addison-Wesley, 1973.

For a discussion of good programming techniques see

Structured Programming by O. J. Dahl, E. W. Dijkstra, and C. A. R. Hoare, Academic Press, 1972.

The Elements of Programming Style by B. W. Kernighan and P. J. Plauger, McGraw-Hill, 1974.

ACM Computing Surveys, Special Issue: Programming, vol. 6, no. 4, December, 1974.
For a discussion of tools and procedures for developing very large software systems see

Practical Strategies for Developing Large Software Systems, by E. Horowitz, Addison-Wesley, May, 1975.

For a discussion of the more abstract formulation of data structures see

"Toward an understanding of data structures" by J. Earley, *CACM*, vol. 14, no. 10, October, 1971, pp. 617-627.

"Another look at data," by G. Mealy, *Proc. AFIPS Fall Joint Computer Conference*, vol. 31, 1967, pp. 525-534.

For a further discussion of program proving see

"Assigning meaning to programs," by R. W. Floyd, *Proc. of a Symposium in Applied Mathematics*, vol. 19, J. T. Schwartz, ed., American Mathematical Society, Providence, 1967, pp. 19-32.

"An interactive program verification system," by D. I. Good, R. L. London, W. W. Bledsoe, *IEEE Transactions on Software Engineering*, SE-1, vol. 1, March, 1975, pp. 59-67.

The text *Concepts in discrete mathematics*, by S. Sahni, Camelot Publishing Company, Fridley, Minnesota, 1981, contains a detailed study of techniques for algorithm analysis.

EXERCISES

1. Look up the word *algorithm* or its older form *algorism* in the dictionary.

2. Consider the two statements: (i) Is $n = 2$ the largest value of n for which there exists positive integers x, y and z such that $x^n + y^n = z^n$ has a solution; (ii) Store 5 divided by zero into X and go to statement 10. Both do not satisfy one of the five criteria of an algorithm. Which criteria do they violate?

3. Describe the flowchart in figure 1.1. by using a combination of Pascal and English. Can you do this without using the **goto** statement?

4. Discuss how you would actually represent the list of name and telephone number pairs in a real machine. How would you handle people with the same last name?

5. Determine the frequency counts for all statements in the following two program segments:

    ```
    1 for i := 1 to n do          1  i := 1
    2    for j := 1 to i do       2  while i <= n do
    3       for k := 1 to j do    3  begin
    4          x := x + 1 ;        4     x := x + 1 ;
                                   5     i := i + 1 ;
                                   6  end;
              (a)                        (b)
    ```

6. Horner's Rule is a means for evaluating a polynomial $A(x) = a_n x^n + a_{n-1} x^{n-1} + \ldots + a_1 x + a_0$ at a point x_o using a minimum number of multiplications. This rule is:

    $$A(x) = (\ldots((a_n x_o + a_{n-1})x_o + \ldots + a_1) x_o + a_0$$

    Write a Pascal program to evaluate a polynomial using Horner's Rule. Determine how many times each statement is executed.

7. Given n boolean variables $x_1, \ldots, x_n$ we wish to print all possible combinations of truth values they can assume. For instance, if $n = 2$, there are four possibilities: true, true; true, false; false, true; false, false. Write a Pascal program to accomplish this and do a frequency count.

8. Compare the two functions n^2 and $2^n/4$ for various values of n. Determine when the second becomes larger than the first.

9. Write a Pascal program which prints out the integer values of x, y, z in nondecreasing order. What is the computing time of your method?

10. Write a Pascal procedure which searches an array $a[1..n]$ for the element x. If x occurs, then set j to its position in the array else set j to zero. Try writing this without using the **goto** statement.

11. One useful facility we might add to Pascal is the ability to manipulate character strings. Suppose we choose to implement the data **type** string as a **record** as below:

    type *string* = **record**
                    length: **integer**; {number of characters}
                    c : **array**[1..100] **of char**;
                end;

    (i) Write the functions *concat*, *substring*, and *reverse* described in section 1.2.

(ii) Write a function *index(x,y)* which searches string x for the first occurrence of string y. If y does not appear in x, then *index* equals zero. Otherwise, *index* is the starting position in x of the first occurrence of y.

Test these functions out using suitable test data.

12. Suppose that strings are represented as in Exercise 11. Write a function *compact(s)* that replaces each sequence of blanks in s by a single blank. Test your function using suitable data.

13. Write a program that accepts as input a string s (see Exercise 11) and determines the frequency of occurrence of each of the distinct characters in s. Test your program using suitable test data.

14. Trace the action of the procedure below on the elements 2, 4, 6, 8, 10, 12, 14, 16, 18, 20 searching for x = 1, 3, 13 or 21.

$i := 1; j := n$
repeat
$k := (i + j)/2$
if $a[k] < = x$ **then** $i := k + 1$
               else $j := k - 1$
until $i > j$

What is the computing time for this segment in terms of n?

15. Prove by induction:

a) $\sum_{1 \leq i \leq n} i = n(n + 1)/2, \quad n \geq 1$

b) $\sum_{1 \leq i \leq n} i^2 = n(n + 1)(2n + 1)/6, \quad n \geq 1$

c) $\sum_{0 \leq i \leq n} x^i = (x^{n+1} - 1)/(x - 1), \quad x \neq 1, n \geq 0$

16. List as many rules of style in programming that you can think of that you would be willing to follow yourself.

17. Using the notation introduced at the end of section 1.1, define the structure Boolean with operations AND, OR, NOT, IMP and EQV (equivalent) using only the **if-then-else** statement. e.g. NOT $(X) :: =$ **if** X **then false else true.**

18. Give a version of a binary search procedure which initializes *lower* to zero and *upper* to $n + 1$.

19. Take any version of binary search, express it using assignment, **if-then-else** and **goto** and then give an equivalent recursive program.

20. Analyze the computing time of procedure *sort* as given in section 1.2.

21. Write a recursive procedure for computing the binomial coefficient $\binom{n}{m}$ as defined in section 1.2, where $\binom{n}{0} = \binom{n}{n} = 1$. Analyze the time and space requirements of your algorithm.

22. Ackermann's function $A(m,n)$ is defined as follows:

$$A(m,n) = \begin{cases} n + 1 & , \text{ if } m = 0 \\ A(m - 1, 1) & , \text{ if } n = 0 \\ A(m - 1, A(m,n - 1)) & , \text{ otherwise} \end{cases}$$

This function is studied because it grows very fast for small values of m and n. Write a recursive procedure for computing this function. Then write a nonrecursive algorithm for computing Ackermann's function.

23. (Tower of Hanoi) There are three towers and sixty four disks of different diameters placed on the first tower. The disks are in order of decreasing diameter as one scans up the tower. Monks were reputedly supposed to move the disks from tower 1 to tower 3 obeying the rules: (i) only one disk can be moved at any time; (ii) no disk can be placed on top of a disk with smaller diameter. Write a recursive procedure which prints the sequence of moves which accomplish this task.

24. Write an equivalent recursive version of program *magic* as given in section 1.3.

25. The *pigeon hole principle* states that if a function f has n distinct inputs but less than n distinct outputs then there exist two inputs a **and** b such that $a \neq b$ and $f(a) = f(b)$. Write a program to find the values a and b for which the range values are equal.

26. Given n, a positive integer, determine if n is the sum of all of its divisors; i.e. if n is the sum of all t such that $1 \leq t < n$ and t divides n.

27. Consider the function $F(x)$ defined by
    if x is even **then** $F := x$ **div** 2
                    else $F := F (F(3x + 1))$

    Prove that $F(x)$ terminates for all integers x. (Hint: consider integers of the form $(2i + 1)2^k - 1$ and use induction.)

28. If S is a set of n elements, the *powerset* of S is the set of all possible subsets of S. For example if $S = (a,b,c)$, then *powerset* $(S) = \{(\ ), (a), (b), (c), (a,b), (a,c), (b,c), (a,b,c),\}$. Write a recursive procedure to compute *powerset* (S).

Chapter 2

ARRAYS

2.1 AXIOMATIZATION

It is appropriate that we begin our study of data structures with the array. The array is often the only means for structuring data which is provided in a programming language. Therefore it deserves a significant amount of attention. If one asks a group of programmers to define an array, the most often quoted saying is: *a consecutive set of memory locations*. This is unfortunate because it clearly reveals a common point of confusion, namely the distinction between a data structure and its representation. It is true that arrays are almost always implemented by using consecutive memory, but not always. Intuitively, an array is a set of pairs, index and value. For each index which is defined, there is a value associated with that index. In mathematical terms we call this a correspondence or a mapping. However, as computer scientists we want to provide a more functional definition by giving the operations which are permitted on this data structure. For arrays this means we are concerned with only two operations, one that retrieves and the other that stores values. Using our notation this structure can be defined as:

structure *ARRAY (value, index)*
  declare *CREATE( )* → *array*
          RETRIEVE(array,index) → *value*;
          STORE *(array,index,value)* → array;
  for all *A* ϵ *array*, *i,j* ϵ *index*, *x* ϵ *value* **let**
    RETRIEVE(CREATE,i) :: = **error**
    RETRIEVE(STORE(A,i,x),j) :: =
      if *EQUAL(i,j)* **then** *x* **else** *RETRIEVE(A,j)*
  end
end *ARRAY*

The function CREATE produces a new, empty array. RETRIEVE takes as input an array and an index, and either returns the appropriate value or an error. STORE is used to enter new index-value pairs. The second axiom is read as "to retrieve the j-th item where x has already been stored at index i in A is equivalent to checking if i and j are equal and if so, x, or search for the j-th value in the remaining array, A." This axiom was originally given by J. McCarthy. Notice how the axioms are independent of any representation scheme. Also, i and j need not necessarily be integers, but we assume only that an EQUAL function can be devised.

If we restrict the index values to be integers, then assuming a conventional random access memory we can implement STORE and RETRIEVE so that they operate in a constant amount of time. If we interpret the indices to be n-dimensional, $(i_1, i_2, \ldots, i_n)$, then the previous axioms apply immediately and define n-dimensional arrays. In section 2.4 we will examine how to implement RETRIEVE and STORE for multi-dimensional arrays using consecutive memory locations.

2.2   ORDERED LISTS

One of the simplest and most commonly found data object is the ordered or linear list. Examples are the days of the week

(MONDAY, TUESDAY, WEDNESDAY, THURSDAY, FRIDAY, SATURDAY, SUNDAY)

or the values in a card deck

(2, 3, 4, 5, 6, 7, 8, 9, 10, Jack, Queen, King, Ace)

or the floors of a building

(basement, lobby, mezzanine, first, second, third)

or the years the United States fought in World War II

(1941, 1942, 1943, 1944, 1945).

If we consider an ordered list more abstractly, we say that it is either empty or it can be written as

$$(a_1, a_2, a_3, \ldots, a_n)$$

where the a_i are atoms from some set S.

There are a variety of operations that are performed on these lists. These operations include:

(i)   find the length of the list, n;

(ii)   read the list from left-to-right (or right-to-left);

(iii) retrieve the i-th element, $1 \leq i \leq n$;

(iv)   store a new value into the i-th position, $1 \leq i \leq n$;

(v)   insert a new element at position i, $1 \leq i \leq n + 1$ causing elements numbered $i, i + 1 ..., n$ to become numbered $i + 1, i + 2, ..., n + 1$;

(vi)   delete the element at position i, $1 \leq i \leq n$ causing elements numbered $i + 1, ..., n$ to become numbered $i, i + 1, ..., n - 1$.

See exercise 22 for a set of axioms which uses these operations to abstractly define an ordered list. It is not always necessary to be able to perform all of these operations; many times a subset will suffice. In the study of data structures we are interested in ways of representing ordered lists so that these operations can be carried out efficiently.

Perhaps the most common way to represent an ordered list is by an array where we associate the list element a_i with the array index i. This we will refer to as a *sequential mapping*, because using the conventional array representation we are storing a_i and a_{i+1} into consecutive locations i and $i + 1$ of the array. This gives us the ability to retrieve or modify the values of random elements in the list in a constant amount of time, essentially because a computer memory has random access to any word. We can access the list element values in either direction by changing the subscript values in a controlled way. It is only operations (v) and (vi) which require real effort. Insertion and deletion using sequential allocation forces us to move some of the remaining elements so that sequential mapping is preserved in its proper form. It is precisely this overhead which leads us to consider nonsequential mappings of ordered lists in Chapter 4.

Let us jump right into a problem requiring ordered lists which we will solve by using one dimensional arrays. This problem has become the classical example for motivating the use of list processing techniques which we will see in later chapters. Therefore, it makes sense to look at the problem and see why arrays offer only a partially adequate solution. The problem calls for building a set of subroutines which allow for the manipulation of symbolic polynomials. By "symbolic," we mean the list of coefficients and exponents which accompany a polynomial, e.g. two such polynomials are

$$A(x) = 3x^2 + 2x + 4 \text{ and } B(x) = x^4 + 10x^3 + 3x^2 + 1$$

For a start, the capabilities we would include are the four basic arithmetic operations: addition, subtraction, multiplication, and division. We will also need input and output routines and some suitable format for preparing polynomials as input. The first step is to consider how to define polynomials as a computer structure. For a mathematician a polynomial is a sum of terms where each term has the form ax^e; x is the variable, a is the coefficient and e is the exponent. However this is not an appropriate definition for our purposes. When defining a data object one must decide what functions will be available, what their input is, what their output is and exactly what it is that they do. A complete specification of the data structure polynomial is now given.

structure *POLYNOMIAL*
   declare *ZERO( )* → *poly;ISZERO(poly)* → *Boolean*
        COEF(poly,exp) → *coef;*
        ATTACH(poly,coef,exp) → *poly*
        REM(poly,exp) → *poly*
        SMULT(poly,coef,exp) → *poly*
        ADD(poly,poly) → *poly; MULT(poly,poly)* → *poly;*
   for all *P,Q* ε *poly*, *c,d* ε *coef* *e,f* ε *exp* **let**
     REM(ZERO,f) :: = *ZERO*
     REM(ATTACH(P,c,e),f) :: =
        if $e = f$ **then** *REM(P,f)* **else** *ATTACH(REM(P,f),c,e)*
     ISZERO(ZERO) :: = **true**
     ISZERO(ATTACH(P,c,e)) :: =
        if *COEF(P,e)* $= -c$ **then** *ISZERO(REM(P,e))* **else false**
     COEF(ZERO,e) :: = 0
     COEF(ATTACH(P,c,e),f) :: =
        if $e = f$ **then** $c +$ *COEF(P,f)* **else** *COEF(P,f)*
     SMULT(ZERO,d,f) :: = *ZERO*
     SMULT(ATTACH(P,c,e),d,f) :: =
     ATTACH(SMULT(P,d,f),c ⋆ *d,e + f)*
     ADD(P,ZERO) :: = *P*
     ADD(P,ATTACH(Q,d,f)) :: = *ATTACH(ADD(P,Q),d,f)*
     MULT(P,ZERO) :: = *ZERO*
     MULT(P,ATTACH(Q,d,f)) :: = *ADD(MULT(P,Q),SMULT(P,d,f))*
   end
end *POLYNOMIAL*

In this specification every polynomial is either ZERO or constructed by applying ATTACH to a polynomial. For example the polynomial $P = 10x - 12x^3 - 10x + 0x^2$ is represented by the string

$$\text{ATTACH(ATTACH(ATTACH(ATTACH(ZERO,10,1),}-12,3),$$
$$-10,1),0,2).$$

Notice the absence of any assumptions about the order of exponents, about nonzero coefficients, etc. These assumptions are decisions of representation. Suppose we wish to remove from P those terms having exponent one. Then we would write REM(P,1) and by the axioms the above string would be transformed into

$$\text{ATTACH(REM(ATTACH(ATTACH(ATTACH(ZERO,10,1),}-12,3),$$
$$-10,1),1),0,2)$$

which is transformed into

$$\text{ATTACH(REM(ATTACH(ATTACH(ZERO,10,1),}-12,3),1),0,2)$$

which becomes

$$\text{ATTACH(ATTACH(REM(ATTACH(ZERO,10,1),1),}-12,3),0,2)$$

which becomes

$$\text{ATTACH(ATTACH(REM(ZERO,1),}-12,3),0,2)$$

which becomes finally

$$\text{ATTACH(ATTACH(ZERO,}-12,3),0,2)$$

or $-12x^3 + 0x^2$.

These axioms are valuable in that they describe the meaning of each operation concisely and without implying an implementation. Note how trivial the addition and multiplication operations have become.

Now we can make some representation decisions. Exponents should be unique and in decreasing order is a very reasonable first decision. This considerably simplifies the operations ISZERO, COEF and REM while ADD, SMULT and MULT remain unchanged. Now assuming a new function EXP(*poly*) → *exp* which returns the leading exponent of poly, we can write a version of ADD which is expressed more like a program, but is still representation independent.

{$c := a + b$ where a and b are the input polynomials}
$c := ZERO$;
while not $ISZERO(a)$ **and not** $ISZERO(b)$ **do**
begin
  case *compare* $(EXP(a), EXP(b))$ **of**
    '<': **begin**
        $c := ATTACH(c, COEF(b, EXP(b)), EXP(b))$;
        $b := REM(b, EXP(b))$;
    end;
  '=': **begin**
        $c := ATTACH(c, COEF(a, EXP(a)) + COEF(b, EXP(b)), EXP(a))$;
        $a := REM(a, EXP(a))$; $b := REM(b, EXP(b))$;
    end;
  '>': **begin**
        $c := ATTACH(c, COEF(a, EXP(a)), EXP(a))$;
        $a := REM(a, EXP(a))$;
    end
  end; {of **case**}
end; {of **while**}
insert any remaining terms of a or b into c

The basic loop of this algorithm consists of merging the terms of the two polynomials, depending upon the result of comparing the exponents. The **case** statement determines how the exponents are related and performs the proper action. Since the tests within the **case** statement require two terms, if one polynomial gets exhausted we must exit and the remaining terms of the other can be copied directly into the result. With these insights, suppose we now consider the representation question more carefully.

A general polynomial $A(x)$ can be written as

$$a_n x^n + a_{n-1} x^{n-1} + ... + a_1 x + a_0$$

where $a_n \neq 0$ and we say that the degree of A is n. Each $a_i x^i$ is a *term* of the polynomial. If $a_i = 0$ then it is a *zero term*, otherwise it is a *nonzero* term.

One way to represent polynomials in Pascal is to define the data type *poly*:

```
type poly = record
                degree : 0..maxdegree;
                coef : array[0..maxdegree] of real;
            end;
```

where *maxdegree* is a constant representing the largest degree polynomial that is to be represented. Now, if *a* is of type *poly* and $n \leq maxdegree$, then the polynomial $A(x)$ above would be represented as:

a.degree $= n$
a.coef $[i] = a_{n-i},\ 0 \leq i \leq n$

Note that a.coef$[i]$ is the coefficient of x^{n-i} and the coefficients are stored in order of decreasing exponents. This representation leads to very simple algorithms for many of the operations one wishes to perform on polynomials (addition, subtraction, evaluation, multiplication, etc.). It is, however, quite wasteful in its use of computer memory. For instance, if a.degree $\ll$ maxdegree, then most of the positions in a.coef $[0..maxdegree]$ are unused. To avoid this wastage, we would like to be able to define the data type *poly* using variable sized records as below:

type *poly* $=$ **record**
        degree : 0.. **maxint**;
        coef : **array**[0..*degree*] **of real**;
       end;

Such a declaration is, of course, not permitted in standard Pascal. While such a type definition solves the problem mentioned earlier, it does not yield a desirable representation. To see this, let us consider polynomials that have many zero terms. Such polynomials are called *sparse*. For instance, the polynomial $x^{1000} + 1$ has two nonzero terms and 999 zero terms. Using variable sized records as above, 999 of the entries in *coef* will be zero.

Suppose we take the polynomial $A(x)$ above and keep only its nonzero coefficients. Then we will really have the polynomial

$$b_{m-1}x^{e_{m-1}} + b_{m-2}x^{e_{m-2}} + ... + b_0x^{e_0} \qquad (1)$$

where each b_i is a nonzero coefficient of A and the exponents e_i are decreasing $e_{m-1} > e_{m-2} > ... > e_0 \geq 0$. If all of A's coefficients are nonzero, then $m = n + 1$, $e_i = i$, and $b_i = a_i$ for $0 \leq i \leq n$. Alternatively, only a_n may be nonzero, in which case $m = 1$, $b_0 = a_n$, and $e_0 = n$.

All our polynomials will be represented in a global array called *terms* that is defined as below:

```
type term = record
            coef : real; {coefficient}
            exp : 0..maxint; {exponent}
         end;
var terms : array[1..maxterms] of term;
```

where *maxterms* is a constant.

Consider the two polynomials $A(x) = 2x^{1000} + 1$ and $B(x) = x^4 + 10x^3 + 3x^2 + 1$. These could be stored in the array *terms* as shown in figure 2.1. Note that *af* and *bf* give the location of the first term of A and B, respectively, while *al* and *bl* give the location of the last term of A and B. *free* gives the location of the next free location in the array *terms*. For our example, $af = 1$, $al = 2$, $bf = 3$, $bl = 6$, and $free = 7$.

	af ↓	al ↓	bf ↓			bl ↓	free ↓
coef	2	1	1	10	3	1	
exp	1000	0	4	3	2	0	

Figure 2.1

This representation scheme does not impose any limit on the number of polynomials that can be stored in *terms*. Rather, the total number of non-zero terms in all the polynomials together cannot exceed *maxterms*.

Is this representation any better than the one that used variable sized records? Well, it certainly solves our problem when many zero terms are present. $A(x) = 2x^{1000} + 1$ uses only 6 units of space (one for *af*, one for *al*, two for the coefficients, and two for the exponents). However, when all terms are nonzero as in $B(x)$ above, the new scheme uses about twice as much space as the one that used variable sized records. Unless we know beforehand that each of our polynomials has very few zero terms in it, the representation using the array *terms* will be preferred over the one using variable sized records.

When the global array *terms* is used, a polynomial $D(x) = 0$ with no nonzero terms will have *df* and *dl* such that $dl = df - 1$. In general, a polynomial E that has n nonzero terms will have *ef* and *el* such that $el = ef + n - 1$.

Let us now write a Pascal procedure to add two polynomials A and B represented as above to obtain the sum $C = A + B$. Procedure *padd* (Program 2.1) adds $A(x)$ and $B(x)$ term by term to produce $C(x)$. The terms of C are entered into the array *terms* starting at the position *free* (procedure *newterm*, Program 2.2). In case there isn't enough space in *terms* to accommodate C, an error message is printed and the program terminates. 999 is the label of the last statement in the program (i.e., the statement **end**.). Hence, a **goto** 999 terminates the program.

```
 1  procedure padd(af,al,bf,bl : integer; var cf,cl : integer);
 2  {add A(x) and B(x) to get C(x)}
 3  var p,q : integer; c : real;
 4  begin
 5    p := af ; q := bf ; cf := free;
 6    while (p <= al) and (q <= bl) do
 7      case compare (terms[p].exp, terms[q].exp) of
 8        '=': begin
 9               c := terms[p].coef + terms[q].coef ;
10               if c <> 0 then newterm(c, terms[p].exp);
11               p := p + 1; q := q + 1;
12             end;
13        '<': begin
14               newterm (terms[q].coef, terms[q].exp);
15               q := q + 1
16             end;
17        '>': begin
18               newterm (terms[p].coef, terms[p].exp);
19               p := p + 1 ;
20             end;
21      end; {of case and while}
22    {add in remaining terms of A(x)}
23    while p <= al do
24    begin
25      newterm(terms[p].coef, terms[p].exp);
26      p := p + 1;
27    end;
28    {add in remaining terms of B(x)}
29    while q <= bl do
30    begin
31      newterm(terms[q].coef, terms[q].exp);
32      q := q + 1;
33    end;
34    cl := free -1;
35  end; {of padd}
```

Program 2.1   Procedure *padd*

```
procedure newterm (c : real; e : integer);
{add a new term to C(x)}
begin
  if free > maxterms then begin
                        writeln('too many terms in polynomials');
                        goto 999; {terminate program}
                        end;
  terms[free].coef := c;
  terms[free].exp := e;
  free := free + 1;
end; {of newterm}
```

Program 2.2   Procedure *newterm*

Let us now analyze the computing time of this algorithm. It is natural to carry out this analysis in terms of the number of nonzero terms in A and B. Let m and n be the number of nonzero terms in A and B respectively. The assignments of line 5 are made only once and hence contribute $O(1)$ to the overall computing time. If either $n = 0$ or $m = 0$, the **while** loop of line 6 is not executed.

In case neither m nor n equals zero, the **while** loop of line 6 is entered. Each iteration of this **while** loop requires $O(1)$ time. At each iteration, either the value of p or q or both increases by 1. Since the iteration terminates when either p or q exceeds al or bl respectively, the number of iterations is bounded by $m + n - 1$. This worst case is achieved, for instance, when $A(x) = \Sigma_{i=0}^{n} x^{2i}$ and $B(x) = \Sigma_{i=0}^{n} x^{2i+1}$. Since none of the exponents are the same in A and B, *terms* $[p].exp \neq terms[q].exp$. Consequently, on each iteration the value of only one of p or q increases by 1. So, the worst case computing time for this **while** loop is $O(n + m)$. The total computing time for the **while** loops of lines 23 and 29 is bounded by $O(n + m)$, as the first cannot be iterated more than m times and the second more than n. Taking the sum of all of these steps, we obtain $O(n + m)$ as the asymptotic computing time of this algorithm.

As we create polynomials, *free* is continually incremented until it tries to exceed *maxterms*. When this happens must we quit? We must unless there are some polynomials which are no longer needed. There may be several such polynomials whose space can be reused. We could write a procedure which would compact the remaining polynomials, leaving a large, consecutive free space at one end. But this may require much data movement. Even worse, if we move a polynomial we must change its start and end pointers. This demands a sophisticated compacting routine coupled with a disciplined use of names for polynomials. In Chapter 4, we will see an elegant solution to these problems.

2.3 SPARSE MATRICES

A matrix is a mathematical object which arises in many physical problems. As computer scientists, we are interested in studying ways to represent matrices so that the operations to be performed on them can be carried out efficiently. A general matrix consists of m rows and n columns of numbers as in figure 2.2.

$$
\begin{array}{c c}
\begin{array}{ccc}
\text{col 1} & \text{col 2} & \text{col 3}
\end{array} & \\
\begin{array}{l}
\text{row 1} \\ \text{row 2} \\ \text{row 3} \\ \text{row 4} \\ \text{row 5}
\end{array}
\begin{bmatrix}
-27, & 3, & 4 \\
6, & 82, & -0.3 \\
109, & -64, & 4 \\
.12, & 8, & 9 \\
3.4, & 36, & 27
\end{bmatrix}
\end{array}
$$

(a)

$$
\begin{array}{c}
\begin{array}{cccccc}
\text{col 1} & \text{col 2} & \text{col 3} & \text{col 4} & \text{col 5} & \text{col 6}
\end{array} \\
\begin{bmatrix}
15, & 0, & 0, & 22, & 0, & -15 \\
0, & 11, & 3, & 0, & 0, & 0 \\
0, & 0, & 0, & -6, & 0, & 0 \\
0, & 0, & 0, & 0, & 0, & 0 \\
91, & 0, & 0, & 0, & 0, & 0 \\
0, & 0, & 28, & 0, & 0, & 0
\end{bmatrix}
\end{array}
$$

row 6

(b)

Figure 2.2 Example of 2 matrices.

The first matrix has five rows and three columns, the second six rows and six columns. In general, we write $m \times n$ (read m by n) to designate a matrix with m rows and n columns. Such a matrix has mn elements. When m is equal to n, we call the matrix *square*.

It is very natural to store a matrix in a two dimensional array, say $A[1..m, 1..n]$. Then we can work with any element by writing $A[i, j]$; and this element can be found very quickly, as we will see in the next section. Now if we look at the second matrix of figure 2.2, we see that it has many zero entries. Such a matrix is called *sparse*. There is no precise definition of when a matrix is sparse and when it is not, but it is a concept which we can all recognize intuitively. Above, only 8 out of 36 possible elements are non-zero and that is sparse! A sparse matrix requires us to consider an alternate form of representation. This comes about because in practice many of the matrices we want to deal with are large, e.g., 1000×1000, but at the same time they are sparse: say only 1000 out of one million possible elements are nonzero. On most computers today it would be impossible to store a full 1000×1000 matrix in the memory at once. Therefore, we ask for an alternative representation for sparse matrices. The alternative representation will explicitly store only the nonzero elements.

Each element of a matrix is uniquely characterized by its row and column position, say i,j. We might then store a matrix as a list of 3-tuples of the form

$$(i,j,\text{value}).$$

Also it might be helpful to organize this list of 3-tuples in some way, perhaps placing them so that the row numbers are increasing. We can go one step farther and require that all the 3-tuples of any row be stored so that the columns are increasing. Thus, we might store the second matrix of figure 2.2 in the array $A[0..t, 1..3]$ where $t = 8$ is the number of nonzero terms.

	1,	2,	3
A[0,	6,	6,	8
[1,	1,	1,	15
[2,	1,	4,	22
[3,	1,	6,	-15
[4,	2,	2,	11
[5,	2,	3,	3
[6,	3,	4,	-6
[7,	5,	1,	91
[8,	6,	3,	28

Figure 2.3 Sparse matrix stored as triples.

The elements $A[0,1]$ and $A[0,2]$ contain the number of rows and columns of the matrix. $A[0,3]$ contains the number of nonzero terms.

Now what are some of the operations we might want to perform on these matrices? One operation is to compute the transpose matrix. This is where we move the elements so that the element in the i,j position gets put in the j,i position. Another way of saying this is that we are interchanging rows and columns. The elements on the diagonal will remain unchanged, since $i = j$.

The transpose of the example matrix looks like

	1,	2,	3
B[0,	6,	6,	8
[1,	1,	1,	15
[2,	1,	5,	91
[3,	2,	2,	11
[4,	3,	2,	3
[5,	3,	6,	28
[6,	4,	1,	22
[7,	4,	3,	−6
[8,	6,	1,	−15

Since A is organized by row, our first idea for a transpose algorithm might be

for each row i **do**
  take element (i,j,val) and
  store it in (j,i,val) of the transpose;

The difficulty is in not knowing where to put the element (j,i,val) until all other elements which precede it have been processed. In our example of figure 2.3, for instance, we have item

$$(1,1,15) \text{ which becomes } (1,1,15)$$

$$(1,4,22) \text{ which becomes } (4,1,22)$$

$$(1,6, -15) \text{ which becomes } (6,1, -15).$$

If we just place them consecutively, then we will need to insert many new triples, forcing us to move elements down very often. We can avoid this data movement by finding the elements in the order we want them, which would be as

for all elements in column j **do**
  place element (i,j,val) in position (j,i,val);

This says find all elements in column 1 and store them into row 1, find all elements in column 2 and store them in row 2, etc. Since the rows are originally in order, this means that we will locate elements in the correct column order as well.

Define the data type *sparsematrix* as below:

type *sparsematrix* = **array**[0..*maxterms*, 1..3] **of integer**;

where *maxterms* is a constant. The procedure *transpose* (Program 2.3) computes the transpose of A. A is initially stored as a sparse matrix in the array *a* and its transpose is obtained in the array *b*.

```
1    procedure transpose (a : sparsematrix; var b : sparsematrix);
2    {b is set to be the transpose of a}
3    var m,n,p,q,t,col : integer;
4    {m : number of rows in a
5     n : number of columns in a
6     t : number of terms in a
7     q : position of next term in b
8     p : current term in a}
9    begin
10       m := a[0,1]; n := a[0.2]; t := a[0,3];
11       b[0,1] := n; b[0,2] := m; b[0,3] := t;
12       if t > 0 then {nonzero matrix}
13       begin
14          q := 1;
15          for col := 1 to n do {transpose by columns}
16             for p := 1 to t do
17                if a[p,2] = col then
18                begin
19                   b[q,1] := a [p,2]; b[q,2] := a[p,1];
20                   b[q,3] := a [p,3]; q := q + 1;
21                end;
22       end; {of if}
23    end; {of transpose}
```

Program 2.3 Procedure *transpose*

It is not too difficult to see that the procedure is correct. The variable q always gives us the position in b where the next term in the transpose is to be inserted. The terms in b are generated by rows. Since the rows of B are the columns of A, row i of B is obtained by collecting all the nonzero terms in column i of A. This is precisely what is being done in lines 15–21. On the first iteration of the **for** loop of lines 15–21 all terms from column 1 of A are collected, then all terms from column 2 and so on until eventually, all terms from column n are collected.

How about the computing time of this algorithm? For each iteration of the loop of lines 15–21, the **if** clause of line 17 is tested t times. Since the number of iterations of the loop of lines 15–21 is n, the total time for line 17 becomes nt. The assignments in lines 19 and 20 take place exactly t times as there are only t nonzero terms in the sparse matrix being generated. Lines 10–14 take a constant amount of time. The total time for the algorithm is therefore $O(nt)$. In addition to the space needed for a and b, the algorithm requires only a fixed amount of additional space, i.e. space for the variables m, n, t, q, col and p.

We now have a matrix transpose algorithm which we believe is correct and which has a computing time of $O(nt)$. This computing time is a little disturbing since we know that in case the matrices had been represented as two dimensional arrays, we could have obtained the transpose of an $n \times m$ matrix in time $O(nm)$. The algorithm for this takes the form:

```
for j := 1 to n do
  for i := 1 to m do
    B[j,i] := A[i,j];
```

The $O(nt)$ time for procedure *transpose* becomes $O(n^2m)$ when t is of the order of nm. This is worse than the $O(nm)$ time using arrays. Perhaps, in an effort to conserve space, we have traded away too much time. Actually, we can do much better by using some more storage. We can in fact transpose a matrix represented as a sequence of triples in time $O(n + t)$. This algorithm, *fasttranspose* (program 2.4), proceeds by first determining the number of elements in each column of A. This gives us the number of elements in each row of B. From this information, the starting point in b of each of its rows is easily obtained. We can now move the elements of a one by one into their correct position in b. *maxcol* is a constant such that the number of columns in A never exceeds *maxcol*.

```
1  procedure fasttranspose (a : sparsematrix; var b : sparsematrix);
2  {The transpose of a is placed in b and is found in O(n + t) time where
3   n is the number of columns and t the number of terms in a}
4  var s,t : array[1..maxcol] of integer;
5    i,j,n,terms : integer;
6  begin
7    n := a[0,2]; terms := a[0,3];
8    b[0,1] := n; b[0,2] := a[0,1]; b[0,3] := terms;
9    if terms > 0 then {nonzero matrix}
10   begin
11     {compute s[i] = number of terms in row i of b}
12     for i := 1 to n do s[i] := 0; {initialize}
13     for i := 1 to terms do s[a[i,2]] := s [a[i,2]] + 1;
14     {t[i] = starting position of row i in b}
15     t[1] := 1;
16     for i := 2 to n do t[i] := t[i − 1] + s[i − 1];
17     for i := 1 to terms do {move from a to b}
18     begin
19       j := t [a[i,2]];
20       b[j,1] := a[i,2]; b[j,2] := a[i,1]; b[j,3] := a[i,3];
21       t[a[i,2]] := j + 1;
22     end;
23   end; {of if}
24 end; {of fasttranspose}
```

Program 2.4   Procedure *fasttranspose*

The correctness of procedure *fasttranspose* follows from the preceding discussion and the observation that the starting point of row i, $i > 1$ of B is $t[i − 1] + s[i − 1]$ where $s[i − 1]$ is the number of elements in row $i − 1$ of B and $t[i − 1]$ is the starting point of row $i − 1$. The computation of s and t is carried out in lines 12-16. In lines 17-22 the elements of a are examined one by one starting from the first and successively moving to the t-th element. $t[j]$ is maintained so that it is always the position in b where the next element in row j is to be inserted.

There are four loops in *fasttranspose* which are executed n, t, $n − 1$, and t times respectively. Each iteration of the loops takes only a constant amount of time, so the order of magnitude is $O(n + t)$. The computing time of $O(n + t)$ becomes $O(nm)$ when t is of the order of nm. This is the same as when two dimensional arrays were in use. However, the constant factor associated with *fasttranspose* is bigger than that for the array algorithm. When t is sufficiently small compared to its maximum of nm, *fasttranspose* will be faster. Hence in this representation, we save both space and time! This was not true of *transpose* since t will almost always be greater than $\max\{n,m\}$ and nt will therefore always be at least nm. The constant factor associated with *transpose* is also bigger than the one in the array algorithm. Finally, one should note that *fasttranspose* requires more space than does *transpose*. The space required by *fasttranspose* can be reduced by utilizing the same space to represent the two arrays s and t.

If we try the algorithm on the sparse matrix of figure 2.3 then after execution of the third **for** loop the values of s and t are

	[1]	[2]	[3]	[4]	[5]	[6]
$s =$	2	1	2	2	0	1
$t =$	1	3	4	6	8	8

$s[i]$ is the number of entries in row i of the transpose. $t[i]$ points to the position in the transpose where the next element of row i is to be stored.

Suppose now you are working for a machine manufacturer who is using a computer to do inventory control. Associated with each machine that the company produces, say MACH[1] to MACH[m], there is a list of parts that it is comprised of. This information could be represented in a two dimensional table

	PART[1]	PART[2]	PART[3]	...	PART[n]
MACH[1]	0,	5,	2,	...,	0
MACH[2]	0,	0,	0,	...,	3
MACH[3]	1,	1,	0,	...,	8
.	.	.	.		.
.	.	.	.		.
.	.	.	.		.
MACH[m]	6,	0,	0,	...,	7

array MACHPT[m,n]

The table will be sparse and all entries will be non-negative integers, MACHPT[i,j] is the number of units of PART[j] in MACH[i]. Each part is itself composed of smaller parts called microparts. This data will also be encoded in a table whose rows are PART[1] to PART[n] and whose columns are MICPT[1] to MICPT[p]. We want to determine the number of microparts that are necessary to make up each machine.

Observe that the number of MICPT[*j*] making up MACH[*i*] is
MACHPT[*i*,1] * MICPT[1,*j*]+ MACHPT[*i*,2] * MICPT[2,*j*]

$$+ \ldots + \text{MACHPT}[i,n] * \text{MICPT}[n,j]$$

where the arrays are named MACHPT[*m*,*n*] and MICPT[*n*,*p*]. This sum is more conveniently written as

$$\sum_{k=1}^{n} \text{MACHPT}[i,k] * \text{MICPT}[k,j].$$

If we compute these sums for each machine and each micropart then we will have a total of *mp* values which we might store in a third table MACHSUM[*m*,*p*]. Regarding these tables as matrices this application leads to the general definition of matrix product:

Given *A* and *B* where *A* is $m \times n$ and *B* is $n \times p$, the product matrix *C* has dimension $m \times p$. Its *i*,*j* element is defined as

$$c_{ij} = \sum_{1 \leq k \leq n} a_{ik} b_{kj}$$

for $1 \leq i \leq m$ and $1 \leq j \leq p$. The product of two sparse matrices may no longer be sparse, for instance,

$$\begin{bmatrix} 1, & 0, & 0 \\ 1, & 0, & 0 \\ 1, & 0, & 0 \end{bmatrix} \begin{bmatrix} 1, & 1, & 1 \\ 0, & 0, & 0 \\ 0, & 0, & 0 \end{bmatrix} = \begin{bmatrix} 1 & 1 & 1 \\ 1 & 1 & 1 \\ 1 & 1 & 1 \end{bmatrix}$$

Consider an algorithm which computes the product of two sparse matrices represented as an ordered list instead of an array. To compute the elements of *C* row-wise so we can store them in their proper place without moving previously computed elements, we must do the following: fix a row of *A* and find all elements in column *j* of *B* for $j = 1,2,\ldots,p$. Normally, to find all the elements in column *j* of *B* we would have to scan all of *B*. To avoid this, we can first compute the transpose of *B* which will put all column elements consecutively. Once the elements in row *i* of *A* and column *j* of *B* have been located, we just do a merge operation similar to the polynomial addition of section 2.2. An alternative approach is explored in the exercises.

Before we write a matrix multiplication procedure, it will be useful to define a sub-procedure as in Program 2.5.

```
procedure storesum (var c: sparsematrix; var q: integer;
                            row, col: integer; var sum: integer);
{If sum ≠ 0, then it along with its row and column position
is stored as the q + 1th entry in c}
begin
   if sum < > 0 then
      if q < maxterms then begin
                              q := q + 1;
                              c[q,1] := row;
                              c[q,2] := col;
                              c[q,3] := sum;
                              sum := 0;
                           end
                    else begin
                              writeln('Number of terms in product exceeds
                              maxterms');
                              goto 999; {terminate program}
                           end ;
end; {of storesum}
```

Program 2.5 Storesum

The procedure *mmult* (Program 2.6) multiplies the matrices A and B to obtain the product matrix C using the strategy outlined above. A, B, and C are stored as sparse matrices in the arrays a, b, and c respectively. Procedure *mmult* makes use of variables i,j,q,r,col and *rowbegin*. The variable r is the row of A that is currently being multiplied with the columns of B. *rowbegin* is the position in a of the first element of row r. *col* is the column of B that is currently being multiplied with row r of A. q is the position in c for the next element generated. i and j are used to successively examine elements of row r and column *col* of A and B respectively. In addition to all this, line 20 of the algorithm introduces a dummy term into each of a and d. This enables us to handle end conditions (i.e., computations involving the last row of A or last column of B) in an elegant way. The label 999 is assumed to be the label attached to the last statement in the program.

We leave the correctness proof of this algorithm as an exercise. Let us examine its complexity. In addition to the space needed for a, b, c and some simple variables, space is also needed for the transpose matrix d.

Algorithm *fasttranspose* also needs some additional space. The exercises explore a strategy for *mmult* which does not explicitly compute *d* and the only additional space needed is the same as that required by *fasttranspose*. Turning our attention to the computing time of *mmult*, we see that lines 6-21 require only $O(p + tb)$ time. The **while** loop of lines 22-54 is executed at most *m* times (once for each row of *A*). In each iteration of the **while** loop of lines 25-50 either the value of *i* or of *j* or of both increases by 1 or *i* and *col* are reset. The maximum total increment in *j* over the whole loop is *tb*. If d_r is the number of terms in row *r* of *A* then the value of *i* can increase at most d_r times before *i* moves to the next row of *A*.

```
 1  procedure mmult (a,b : sparsematrix; var c : sparsematrix);
 2  {c = a * b ; a is m × n and b is n × p}
 3  var i,j,m,n,p,q,r,ta,tb,col,sum,rowbegin: integer;
 4      d : sparsematrix;
 5  begin
 6      m := a[0,1]; n := a[0,2]; ta := a[0,3];
 7      if n <> b[0,1] then begin
 8                          writeln('Incompatible matrices');
 9                          goto 999; {terminate program}
10                          end ;
11      p := b[0,2]; tb := b[0,3];
12      if (ta = maxterms) or (tb = maxterms) then
13                  begin
14                      writeln('Too many terms in a or b');
15                      goto 999; {terminate program}
16                  end;
17  fasttranspose(b,d);
18      i := 1; q := 0; rowbegin := 1; r := a[1,1];
19      {set boundary conditions}
20      a[ta + 1,1] := m + 1; d[tb + 1,1] := p + 1;
21      d[tb + 1,2] := 0; sum := 0;
22      while i <= ta do {generate row r of c}
23      begin
24          col := d[1,1]; j := 1;
25          while j <= tb + 1 do {multiply row r of a by column col of b}
26          begin
27              if a[i,1] <> r
28              then begin {end of row r}
29                      storesum (c,q,r,col,sum);
30                      i := rowbegin;
```

```
31                    {go to next column}
32                    while d[j,1] = col do j := j + 1;
33                    col := d[j,1];
34                 end
35            else if d[j,1] <> col
36                 then begin {end of column col of b}
37                         storesum (c,q,r,col,sum);
38                         {set to multiply row r with next column}
39                         i := rowbegin; col := d[j,1];
40                     end
41            else if a[i,2] < d[j,2];
42                 then i := i + 1 {advance to next term in row}
43                 else if a[i,2] = d[j,2]
44                     then begin {add to sum}
45                         sum := sum + a[i,3] * d[j,3];
46                         i := i + 1; j := j + 1;
47                     end
48                 else {advance to next term in column col}
49                     j := j + 1;
50        end; {of while j <= tb + 1}
51        while a[i,1] = r do {advance to next row}
52            i := i + 1;
53        rowbegin := i; r := a[i,1];
54        end; {end of while i <= ta}
55        c[0,1] := m; c[0,2] := p; c[0,3] := q;
56    end; {of mmult}
```

Program 2.6 Procedure *mmult*

When this happens, i is reset to *rowbegin* in line 30. At the same time *col* is advanced to the next column. Hence, this resetting can take place at most p times (there are only p columns in B). The total maximum increments in i is therefore pd_r. The maximum number of iterations of the **while** loop of lines 25-50 is therefore $p + pd_r + tb$. The time for this loop while multiplying with row r of A is $O(pd_r + tb)$. Lines 51-53 take only $O(d_r)$ time. Hence, the time for the outer **while** loop, lines 22-54, for the iteration with row r of A is $O(pd_r + tb)$. The overall time for this loop is then $O(\Sigma_r(pd_r + tb)) = O(pta + mtb)$

Once again, we may compare this computing time with the time to multiply matrices when arrays are used. The classical multiplication algorithm is:

```
for i := 1 to m do
  for j := 1 to p do
  begin
    sum := 0;
    for k := 1 to n do
      sum := sum + a[i,k] * b[k,j];
    c[i,j] := sum;
  end ;
```

The time for this is $O(mnp)$. Since $ta \leq nm$ and $tb \leq np$, the time for *mmult* is at most $O(mnp)$. However, its constant factor is greater than that for matrix multiplication using arrays. In the worst case when $ta = nm$ or $tb = np$, *mmult* will be slower by a constant factor. However, when ta and tb are sufficiently smaller than their maximum values, i.e., A and B are sparse, *mmult* will outperform the above multiplication algorithm for arrays.

The above analysis for *mmult* is nontrivial. It introduces some new concepts in algorithm analysis and you should make sure you understand the analysis.

This representation for sparse matrices permits one to perform operations such as addition, transpose and multiplication efficiently. There are, however, other considerations which make this representation undesirable in certain applications. Since the number of terms in a sparse matrix is variable, we would like to represent all our sparse matrices in one array (as we did for polynomials in section 2.2) rather than using a separate array for each matrix. This would enable us to make efficient utilization of space. However, when this is done, we run into difficulties in allocating space from this array to any individual matrix. These difficulties also arise with the polynomial representation of the previous section and will become apparent when we study a similar representation for multiple stacks and queues in section 3.4.

2.4 REPRESENTATION OF ARRAYS

Even though multidimensional arrays are provided as a standard data object in most high level languages, it is interesting to see how they are represented in memory. Recall that memory my be regarded as one dimensional with words numbered from 1 to m. So, we are concerned with representing n dimensional arrays in a one dimensional memory. While many representations might seem plausible, we must select one in which the location in memory of an arbitrary array element, say $A[i_1, i_2, ..., i_n]$, can be determined efficiently. This is necessary since programs using arrays may, in general, use array elements in a random order. In addition to being able to retrieve array elements easily, it is also necessary to be able to determine the amount of memory space to be reserved for a particular array. Assuming that each array element requires only one word of memory, the number of words needed is the number of elements in the array. If an array is declared $A[l_1..u_1, l_2..u_2, ..., l_n..u_n]$, then it is easy to see that the number of elements is

$$\prod_{i=1}^{n} (u_i - l_i + 1).$$

One of the common ways to represent an array is in row major order. If we have the declaration

$$A[4..5, \ 2..4, \ 1..2, \ 3..4]$$

then we have a total of $2 \cdot 3 \cdot 2 \cdot 2 = 24$ elements. Then using row major order these elements will be stored as

$$A[4,2,1,3], \ A[4,2,1,4], \ A[4,2,2,3], \ A[4,2,2,4]$$

and continuing

$$A[4,3,1,3], \ A[4,3,1,4], \ A[4,3,2,3], \ A[4,3,2,4]$$

for 3 more sets of four until we get

$$A[5,4,1,3], \ A[5,4,1,4], \ A[5,4,2,3], \ A[5,4,2,4].$$

We see that the subscript at the right moves the fastest. In fact, if we view the subscripts as numbers, we see that they are, in some sense, increasing:

$$4213, 4214, \ ..., 5423, 5424.$$

Another synonym for row major order is lexicographic order.

From the compiler's point of view, the problem is how to translate from the name $A[i_1, i_2, ..., i_n]$ to the correct location in memory. Suppose $A[4,2,1,3]$ is stored at location 100. Then $A[4,2,1,4]$ will be at 101 and $A[5,4,2,4]$ at location 123. These two addresses are easy to guess. In general, we can derive a formula for the address of any element. This formula makes use of only the starting address of the array plus the declared dimensions.

To simplify the discussion we shall assume that the lower bounds on each dimension l_i are 1. The general case when l_i can be any integer is discussed in the exercises. Before obtaining a formula for the case of an n-dimensional array, let us look at the row major representation of 1, 2 and 3 dimensional arrays. To begin with, if A is declared $A[1..u_1]$, then assuming one word per element, it may be represented in sequential memory as in figure 2.4. If α is the address of $A[1]$, then the address of an arbitrary element $A[i]$ is just $\alpha + (i - 1)$.

array element: $A[1]$, $A[2]$, $A[3]$, ..., $A[i]$, ..., $A[u_1]$
address: $\alpha, \alpha + 1, \alpha + 2, ..., \alpha + i - 1, ..., \alpha + u_1 - 1$
total number of elements $= u_1$

Figure 2.4: Sequential representation of $A[1..u_1]$

The two dimensional array $A[1..u_1, 1..u_2]$ may be interpreted as u_1 rows: $row_1, row_2, ..., row u_1$, each row consisting of u_2 elements. In a row major representation, these rows would be represented in memory as in figure 2.5.

	col 1	col 2	...	col u_2
row 1	X	X	...	X
row 2	X	X	...	X
row 3	X	X	...	X
		⋮		
row u_1	X	X	...	X

(a)

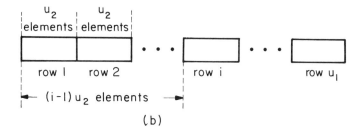

(b)

Figure 2.5 Sequential representation of A $[1..u_1, 1..u_2]$.

Again, if α is the address of $A[1,1]$, then the address of $A[i,1]$ is $\alpha + (i - 1)u_2$, as there are $i - 1$ rows each of size u_2 preceding the first element in the i-th row. Knowing the address of $A[i,1]$, we can say that the address of $A[i,j]$ is then simply $\alpha + (i - 1)u_2 + (j - 1)$.

Figure 2.6 shows the representation of the 3 dimensional array $A[1..u_1, 1..u_2, 1..u_3]$. *This array is interpreted as* u_1 2 dimensional arrays of dimension $u_2 \times u_3$. To locate $A[i,j,k]$, we first obtain $\alpha + (i - 1)u_2u_3$ as the address for $A[i,1,1]$ since there are $i - 1$ 2 dimensional arrays of size $u_2 \times u_3$ preceding this element. From this and the formula for addressing a 2 dimensional array, we obtain $\alpha + (i - 1)u_2u_3 + (j - 1)u_3 + (k - 1)$ as the address of $A[i,j,k]$.

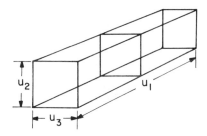

(a) 3-dimensional array $A[1..u_1, 1..u_2, 1..u_3]$ regarded as u_1 2-dimensional arrays.

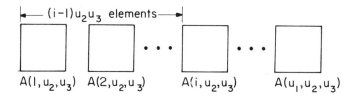

(b) Sequential row major representation of a 3-dimensional array. Each 2-dimensional array is represented as in Figure 2.5.

Figure 2.6   Sequential representation of $A[1..u_1, 1..u_2, 1..u_3]$.

Generalizing on the preceding discussion, the addressing formula for any element $A[i_1, i_2, ..., i_n]$ in an n-dimensional array declared as $A[1..u_1, 1..u_2, ..., 1..u_n]$ may be easily obtained. If α is the address for $A[1,1, ...,1]$ then $\alpha + (i_1 - 1)u_2u_3 \ ... \ u_n$ is the address for $A[i_1,1, ...,1]$. The address for $A[i_1,i_2,1, ..., 1]$ is then $\alpha + (i_1 - 1)u_2u_3 \ ... \ u_n + (i_2 - 1)u_3u_4 \ ... \ u_n$.

Repeating in this way the address for $A[i_1,i_2, ...,i_n]$ is

$$\alpha + (i_1 - 1)u_2u_3 \dots u_n$$
$$+ (i_2 - 1)u_3u_4 \dots u_n$$
$$+ (i_3 - 1)u_4u_5 \dots u_n$$
$$\vdots$$
$$+ (i_{n-1} - 1)u_n$$
$$+ (i_n - 1)$$

$$= \alpha + \sum_{j=1}^{n} (i_j - 1)a_j \quad \text{with} \quad \begin{cases} a_j = \prod_{k=j+1}^{n} u_k & 1 \leq j < n \\ \\ a_n = 1 \end{cases}$$

Note that a_j may be computed from a_{j+1}, $1 \leq j < n$ using only one multiplication as $a_j = u_{j+1}a_{j+1}$. Thus, a compiler will initially take the declared bounds $u_1, \dots, u_n$ and use them to compute the constants $a_1, \dots, a_{n-1}$ using $n - 2$ multiplications. The address of $A[i_1, \dots, i_n]$ can then be found using the formula, requiring $n - 1$ more multiplications and n additions.

An alternative scheme for array representation, column major order, is considered in exercise 19.

To review, in this chapter we have used arrays to represent ordered lists of polynomials and sparse matrices. In all cases we have been able to move the values around, accessing arbitrary elements in a fixed amount of time, and this has given us efficient algorithms. However several problems have been raised. By using a sequential mapping which associates a_i of $(a_1, \dots, a_n)$ with the i-th element of the array, we are forced to move data around whenever an insert or delete operation is used. Secondly, once we adopt one ordering of the data we sacrifice the ability to have a second ordering simultaneously.

EXERCISES

1. Write a Pascal procedure which multiplies two polynomials represented using the array *terms* of section 2.2. What is the computing time of your procedure?

2. Write a Pascal procedure which evaluates a polynomial at a value x_o using the representation above. Try to minimize the number of operations.

3. If $A = (a_1, ...,a_n)$ and $B = (b_1, ..., b_m)$ are ordered lists, then $A < B$ if $a_i = b_i$ for $1 \leq i < j$ and $a_j < b_j$ or if $a_i = b_i$ for $1 \leq i \leq n$ and $n < m$. Write a procedure which returns $-1, 0, +1$ depending upon whether $A < B$, $A = B$ or $A > B$. Assume you can compare atoms a_i and b_i.

4. Assume that n lists, $n > 1$, are being represented sequentially in the one dimensional array *space* $[1..m]$. Let *front*$[i]$ be one less than the position of the first element in the i-th list and let *rear*$[i]$ point to the last element in the i-th list, $1 \leq i \leq n$. Further assume that *rear*$[i] \leq$ *front*$[i + 1]$, $1 \leq i \leq n$ with *front*$[n + 1] = m$. The functions to be performed on these lists are insertion and deletion.
   a) Obtain suitable initial and boundary conditions for *front*$[i]$ and *rear*$[i]$
   b) Write a procedure *insert(i,j,item* : **integer**) to insert *item* after the $(j - 1)$st element in list i. This procedure should fail to make an insertion only if there are already m elements in *space*.

5. Using the assumptions of exercise 4 write a procedure *delete(i,j* : **integer; var** *item* : **integer**) which sets *item* to the j-th element of the i-th list and removes it. The i-th list should be maintained as sequentially stored.

6. The polynomials $A(x) = x^{2n} + x^{2n-2} + ... + x^2 + x^0$ and $B(x) = x^{2n+1} + x^{2n-1} + ... + x^3 + x$ cause *padd* to work very hard. For these polynomials determine the exact number of times each statement will be executed.

7. Analyze carefully the computing time and storage requirements of algorithm *fasttranspose*. What can you say about the existence of an even faster algorithm?

8. Using the idea in *fasttranspose* of m row pointers, rewrite algorithm *mmult* to multiply two sparse matrices A and B represented as in §2.3 without transposing B. What is the computing time of your algorithm?

9. When all the elements either above or below the main diagonal of a square matrix are zero, then the matrix is said to be triangular. Figure 2.7 shows a lower and upper triangular matrix.

   In a lower triangular matrix, A, with n rows, the maximum number of non-zero terms in row i is i. Hence, the total number of nonzero terms is $\sum_{i=1}^{n} i = n(n + 1)/2$. For large n it would be worthwhile to save the space taken by the zero entries in the upper triangle. Obtain an addressing formula for elements a_{ij} in the lower triangle if this lower triangle is stored by rows in an array $B[1 .. n(n + 1)/2)]$ with $A[1,1]$ being stored in $B[1]$. What is the relationship between i and j for elements in the zero part of A?

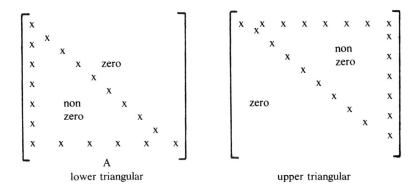

Figure 2.7

10. Let A and B be two lower triangular matrices, each with n rows. The total number of elements in the lower triangles is $n(n + 1)$. Devise a scheme to represent both the triangles in an array $c[1 .. n, 1 .. n+ 1]$. [Hint: represent the triangle of A as the lower triangle of c and the tranpose of B as the upper triangle of c.] Write algorithms to determine the values of $A[i,j]$, $B[i,j]$, $1 \leq i$, $j \leq n$ from the array c.

11. Another kind of sparse matrix that arises often in numerical analysis is the tridiagonal matrix. In this square matrix, all elements other than those on the major diagonal and on the diagonals immediately above and below this one are zero (figure 2.8).

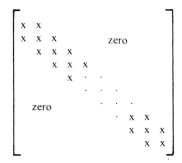

Figure 2.8 Tridiagonal matrix A.

If the elements in the band formed by these three diagonals are represented rowwise in an array, b, with $A[1,1]$ being stored in $b[1]$, obtain an algorithm to determine the value of $A[i,j]$, $1 \leq i, j \leq n$ from the array b.

12. Define a square band matrix $A_{n,a}$ to be an $n \times n$ matrix in which all the non-zero terms lie in a band centered around the main diagonal. The band includes $a - 1$ diagonals below and above the main diagonal and also the main diagonal (figure 2.9).

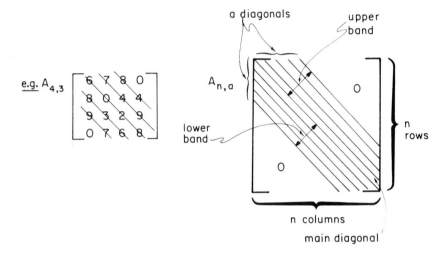

Figure 2.9 Square band matrix.

a) How many elements are there in the band of $A_{n,a}$?
b) What is the relationship between i and j for elements a_{ij} in the band of $A_{n,a}$?
c) Assume that the band of $A_{n,a}$ is stored sequentially in an array b by diagonals starting with the lowermost diagonal. Thus $A_{4,3}$ above would have the following representation:

b[1]	b[2]	b[3]	b[4]	b[5]	b[6]	b[7]	b[8]	b[9]	b[10]	b[11]	b[12]	b[13]	b[14]
9	7	8	3	6	6	0	2	8	7	4	9	8	4
a_{31}	a_{42}	a_{21}	a_{32}	a_{43}	a_{11}	a_{22}	a_{33}	a_{44}	a_{12}	a_{23}	a_{34}	a_{13}	a_{24}

Obtain an addressing formula for the location of an element a_{ij} in the lower band of $A_{n,a}$.
e.g. $LOC(a_{31}) = 1$, $LOC(a_{42}) = 2$ in the example above.

13. A generalized band matrix $A_{n,a,b}$ is an $n \times n$ matrix A in which all the nonzero terms lie in a band made up of $a - 1$ diagonals below the main diagonal, the main diagonal and $b - 1$ diagonals above the main diagonal (figure 2.10)
a) How many elements are there in the band of $A_{n,a,b}$?
b) What is the relationship between i and j for elements a_{ij} in the band of $A_{n,a,b}$?

c) Obtain a sequential representation of the band of $A_{n,a,b}$ in the one dimensional array c. For this representation write a Pascal procedure *value* (n,a,b,i,j,c) which determines the value of element a_{ij} in the matrix $A_{n,a,b}$. The band of $A_{n,a,b}$ is represented in the array c.

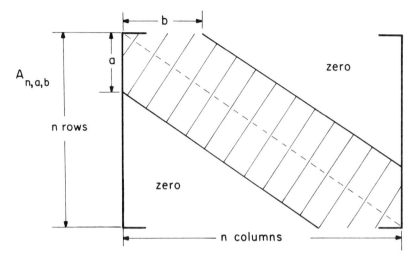

Figure 2.10 Generalized band matrix.

14. How much time does it take to locate an arbitrary element $A[i,j]$ in the representation of §2.3 and to change its value?

15. A variation of the scheme discussed in §2.3 for sparse matrix representation involves representing only the nonzero terms in a one dimensional array v in the order described. In addition, a strip of $n \times m$ bits, $bits[1..n, 1..m]$ is also kept. $bits[i,j] = 0$ if $A[i,j] = 0$ and $bits[i,j] = 1$ if $A[i,j] \neq 0$. The figure below illustrates the representation for the sparse matrix of figure 2.4.

$$\begin{bmatrix} 1 & 0 & 0 & 1 & 0 & 1 \\ 0 & 1 & 1 & 0 & 0 & 0 \\ 0 & 0 & 0 & 1 & 0 & 0 \\ 0 & 0 & 0 & 0 & 0 & 0 \\ 1 & 0 & 0 & 0 & 0 & 0 \\ 0 & 0 & 1 & 0 & 0 & 0 \end{bmatrix} \qquad \begin{bmatrix} 15 \\ 22 \\ -15 \\ 11 \\ 3 \\ -6 \\ 91 \\ 28 \end{bmatrix}$$

$$bits \qquad\qquad\qquad v$$

   (i) On a computer with w bits per word, how much storage is needed to represent a sparse matrix $A_{n \times m}$ with t nonzero terms?

  (ii) Write an algorithm to add two sparse matrices A and C represented as above to obtain $D = A + C$. How much time does your algorithm take?

 (iii) Discuss the merits of this representation versus the representation of §2.3. Consider space and time requirements for such operations as random access, add, multiply, and transpose. Note that the random access time can be improved somewhat by keeping another array ra such that $ra[i] =$ number of nonzero terms in rows 1 through $i - 1$.

16. A complex-valued matrix X is represented by a pair of matrices (A,B) where A and B contain real values. Write a program which computes the product of two complex valued matrices (A,B) and (C,D), where

$$(A,B) * (C,D) = (A + iB) * (C + iD) = (AC - BD) + i (AD + BC)$$

Determine the number of additions and multiplications if the matrices are all $n \times n$.

17. How many values can be held by an array with dimensions $a[0..n]$, $b[-1.. n, 1..m]$, $c[-n..0, 1..2]$?

✓18. Obtain an addressing formula for the element $A[i_1, i_2, ...,i_n]$ in an array declared as $A[l_1..u_1, l_2..u_2, ..., l_n..u_n]$. Assume a row major representation of the array with one word per element and α the address of $A[l_1, l_2, ...,l_n]$.

19. Do exercise 18 assuming a column major representation. In this representation, a 2 dimensional array is stored sequentially by columns rather than by rows.

20. An $m \times n$ matrix is said to have a *saddle point* if some entry $A(i,j)$ is the smallest value in row i and the largest value in column j. Write a Pascal program which determines the location of a saddle point if one exists. What is the computing time of your method?

21. Given an array $a[1..n]$ produce the array $z[1..n]$ such that $z[1] = a[n]$, $z[2] = a[n - 1]$, ..., $z[n - 1] = a[2]$, $z[n] = a[1]$. Use a minimal amount of storage.

22. One possible set of axioms for an ordered list comes from the six operations of section 2.2.

```
    structure ORDERED_LIST(atoms)
      declare MTLST( ) → list
             LEN(list) → integer
             RET(list,integer) → atom
             STO(list,integer,atom) → list
             INS(list,integer,atom) → list
             DEL(list, integer) → list;
       for all L ε list, i,jε integer a,b ε atom let
         LEN(MTLST) :: = 0;  LEN(STO(L,i,a)) :: = 1 + LEN(L)
         RET(MTLST,j) :: = error
         RET(STO(L,i,a),j) :: =
           if i = j then a else RET (L,j)
         INS(MTLST, j,b) :: = STO(MTLST, j,b)
         INS(STO(L,i,a),j,b) :: =
           if i ≥ j then STO(INS(L,j,b), i + 1,a)
                     else STO(INS(L,j,b),i,a)
         DEL(MTLST,j) :: = MTLST
         DEL(STO(L,i,a),j) :: =
           if i = j then DEL(L,j)
                     else if i > j then STO(DEL(L,j),i − 1,a)
                                   else STO(DEL(L,j),i,a)
      end
    end ORDERED_LIST
```

Use these axioms to describe the list $A = (a,b,c,d,e)$ and show what happens when $DEL(A,2)$ is executed.

23. There are a number of problems, known collectively as "random walk" problems, which have been of longstanding interest to the mathematical community. All but the most simple of these are extremely difficult to solve and for the most part they remain largely unsolved. One such problem may be stated as follows:

A (drunken) cockroach is placed on a given square in the middle of a tile floor in a rectangular room of size $n \times m$ tiles. The bug wanders (possibly in search of an aspirin) randomly from tile to tile throughout the room. Assuming that he may move from his present tile to any of the eight tiles surrounding him (unless he is against a wall) *with equal probability*, how long will it take him to touch every tile on the floor at least once?

Hard as this problem may be to solve by pure probability theory techniques, the answer is quite easy to solve using the computer. The technique for doing so is called "simulation" and is of wide-scale use in industry to predict traffic-flow, inventory control and so forth. The problem may be simulated using the following method:

An $n \times m$ array *count* is used to represent the number of times our cockroach has reached each tile on the floor. All the cells of this array are initialized to zero. The position of the bug on the floor is represented by the coordinates (*ibug,jbug*). The 8 possible moves of the bug are represented by the tiles located at (*ibug* + *imove*[*k*], *jbug* + *jmove*[*k*]) where $1 \leq k \leq 8$ and:

imove[1] = −1	jmove[1] = 1
imove[2] = 0	jmove[2] = 1
imove[3] = 1	jmove[3] = 1
imove[4] = 1	jmove[4] = 0
imove[5] = 1	jmove[5] = −1
imove[6] = 0	jmove[6] = −1
imove[7] = −1	jmove[7] = −1
imove[8] = −1	jmove[8] = 0

A *random* walk to one of the 8 given squares is simulated by generating a random value for *k* lying between 1 and 8. Of course the bug cannot move outside the room, so that coordinates which lead up a wall must be ignored and a new random combination formed. Each time a square is entered, the count for that square is incremented so that a nonzero entry shows the number of times the bug has landed on that square so far. When every square has been entered at least once, the experiment is complete.

Write a program to perform the specified simulation experiment. Your program *MUST:*

1) Handle all values of *n* and *m*, $2 < n \leq 40$, $2 \leq m \leq 20$.
2) Perform the experiment for
   a) *n* = 15, *m* = 15   starting point: (20,10)
   b) *n* = 39, *m* = 19   starting point: (1,1)
3) Have an iteration limit, that is, a maximum number of squares the bug may enter during the experiment. This assures that your program does not get "hung" in an "infinite" loop. A maximum of 50,000 is appropriate for this lab.
4) For each experiment print: a) the total number of legal moves which the cockroach makes; b) the final *count* array. This will show the "density" of the walk, that is, the number of times each tile on the floor was touched during the experiment.

(Have an aspirin). This exercise was contributed by Olson.

24. Chess provides the setting for many fascinating diversions which are quite independent of the game itself. Many of these are based on the strange "L-shaped" move of the knight. A classical example is the problem of the knight's tour, which has captured the attention of mathematicians and puzzle enthusiasts since the beginning of the eighteenth century. Briefly stated, the problem is to move the knight, beginning from any given square on the chessboard, in such a manner that it travels successively to all 64 squares, touching each square once and only once. It is convenient to represent a solution by placng the numbers 1,2 ...,64 in the squares of the chessboard indicating the order in which the squares are reached. Note that it is not required that the knight be able to reach the initial

position by one more move; if this is possible the knight's tour is called re-entrant. One of the more ingenious methods for solving the problem of the knight's tour is that given by J. C. Warnsdorff in 1823. His rule is that the knight must always be moved to one of the squares from which there are the fewest exits to squares not already traversed.

The goal of this exercise is to write a computer program to implement Warnsdorff's rule. The ensuing discussion will be much easier to follow, however, if you first try to construct a particular solution to the problem by hand before reading any further.

The most important decisions to be made in solving a problem of this type are those concerning how the data is to be represented in the computer. Perhaps the most natural way to represent the chessboard is by an 8×8 array *board* as shown in the figure below. The eight possible moves of a knight on square (5,3) are also shown in the figure.

board

	1	2	3	4	5	6	7	8
1								
2								
3		8		1				
4	7				2			
5			K					
6	6				3			
7		5		4				
8								

In general a knight at (i,j) may move to one of the squares $(i-2, j+1), (i-1, j+2), (i+1, j+2), (i+2, j+1), (i+2, j-1), (i+1, j-2), (i-1, j-2), (i-2, j-1)$. Notice, however that if (i,j) is located near one of the edges of the board, some of these possibilities could move the knight off the board, and of course this is not permitted. The eight possible knight moves may conveniently be represented by two arrays *ktmov1* and *ktmov2* as shown below.

ktmov1	*ktmov2*
−2	1
−1	2
1	2
2	1
2	−1
1	−2
−1	−2
−2	−1

Then a knight at (i,j) may move to $(i + ktmov1[k], j + ktmov2[k])$, where k is some value between 1 and 8, provided that the new square lies on the chessboard.

Below is a description of an algorithm for solving the knight's tour problem using Warnsdorff's rule. The data representation discussed in the previous section is assumed.

a) [Initialize chessboard] For $1 \le i,j \le 8$ set *board* $[i,j] = 0$.

b) [Set starting position] Read and print i,j and then set *board*$[i,j]$ to 1.

c) [Loop] For $2 \le m \le 64$ do steps d through g.

d) [Form set of possible next squares] Test each of the eight squares one knight's move away from (i,j) and form a list of the possibilities for the next square $(nexti[l], nextj[l])$. Let *npos* be the number of possibilities. (That is, after performing this step we will have $nexti[l] = i + ktmov1[k]$ and $nextj[l] = j + ktmov2[k]$, for certain values of k between 1 and 8. Some of the squares $(i + ktmov1[k], j + ktmov2[k])$ may be impossible for the next move either because they lie off the chessboard or because they have been previously occupied by the knight—i.e., they contain a nonzero number. In every case we will have $0 \le npos \le 8$.)

e) [Test special cases] If $npos = 0$ the knight's tour has come to a premature end; report failure and then go to step h. If $npos = 1$ there is only one possibility for the next move; set $min = 1$ and go right to step g.

f) [Find next square with minimum number of exits] For $1 \le l \le npos$ set *exits*$[l]$ to the number of exits from square $(nexti[l], nextj[l])$. That is, for each of the values of l examine each of the next squares $(nexti[l] + ktmov1[k], nextj[l] + ktmov2[k])$ to see if it is an exit from $nexti[l], nextj[l]$, and count the number of such exits in *exits*$[l]$. (Recall that a square is an exit if it lies on the chessboard and has not been previously occupied by he knight.) Finally, set *min* to the location of the minimum value of *exits*. (There may be more than one occurrence of the minimum value of *exits*. If this happens, it is convenient to let *min* denote the first such occurrence, although it is important to realize that by so doing we are not actually guaranteed of finding a solution. Nevertheless, the chances of finding a complete knight's tour in this way are remarkably good, and that is sufficient for the purposes of this exercise.)

g) [Move knight] Set $i = nexti[min]$, $j = nextj[min]$ and *board*$[i,j] = m$. (Thus, (i,j) denotes the new position of the knight, and *board*$[i,j]$ records the move in proper sequence.)

h) [Print] Print out *board* showing the solution to the knight's tour, and then terminate the algorithm.

The problem is to write a program which corresponds to this algorithm. This exercise was contributed by Legenhausen and Rebman.

Chapter 3

STACKS AND QUEUES

3.1 FUNDAMENTALS

Two of the more common data objects found in computer algorithms are stacks and queues. They arise so often that we will discuss them separately before moving on to more complex objects. Both these data objects are special cases of the more general data object, an ordered list which we considered in the previous chapter. Recall that $A = (a_1, a_2, \ldots, a_n)$, is an ordered list of $n \geq 0$ elements. The a_i are referred to as atoms or elements which are taken from some set. The null or empty list has $n = 0$ elements.

A *stack* is an ordered list in which all insertions and deletions are made at one end, called the *top*. A *queue* is an ordered list in which all insertions take place at one end, the *rear*, while all deletions take place at the other end, the *front*. Given a stack $S = (a_1, \ldots, a_n)$, we say that a_1 is the *bottommost* element and element a_i is on *top* of element a_{i-1}, $1 < i \leq n$. When viewed as a queue with a_n as the rear element one says that a_{i+1} is behind a_i, $1 \leq i < n$.

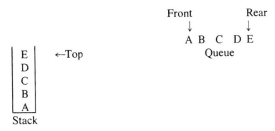

Figure 3.1.

The restrictions on a stack imply that if the elements A, B, C, D, E are added to the stack, in that order, then the first element to be removed/deleted must be E. Equivalently we say that the last element to be inserted into the

65

stack will be the first to be removed. For this reason stacks are sometimes referred to as *Last In First Out* (LIFO) lists. The restrictions on a queue require that the first element which is inserted into the queue will be the first one to be removed. Thus A is the first letter to be removed, and queues are known as *First In First Out* (FIFO) lists. Note that the data object queue as defined here need not necessarily correspond to the mathematical concept of queue in which the insert/delete rules may be different.

One natural example of stacks which arises in computer programming is the processing of procedure calls and their terminations. Suppose we have four procedures as below:

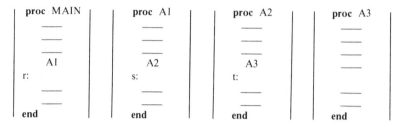

Figure 3.2 Sequence of subroutine calls.

The MAIN procedure invokes procedure $A1$. On completion of $A1$ execution of MAIN will resume at location r. The address r is passed to $A1$ which saves it in some location for later processing. $A1$ then invokes $A2$ which in turn invokes $A3$. In each case the invoking procedure passes the return address to the invoked procedure. If we examine the memory while $A3$ is computing there will be an implicit stack which looks like

$$(q,r,s,t).$$

The first entry, q, is the address to which MAIN returns control. This list operates as a stack since the returns will be made in the reverse order of the invocations. Thus t is removed before s, s before r and r before q. Equivalently, this means that $A3$ must finish processing before $A2$, $A2$ before $A1$, and $A1$ before MAIN. This list of return addresses need not be maintained in consecutive locations. For each procedure there is usually a single location associated with the machine code which is used to retain the return address. This can be severely limiting in the case of recursive and re-entrant procedures, since every time we invoke a procedure the new return address wipes out the old one. For example, if we inserted a call to $A1$ within procedure $A3$ expecting the return to be at location u, then at execution time the stack would become (q,u,s,t) and the return address r would be lost. When recursion is allowed, it is no longer adequate to reserve one location for the return address of each procedure. Since returns are made in the reverse order of calls, an elegant and natural solution to this procedure return problem is afforded through the explicit use of a stack of return addresses. Whenever a return is made, it is to the top address in the stack. Implementing recursion using a stack is discussed in Section 4.9.

Associated with the object stack there are several operations that are necessary:

CREATE(S)   which creates S as an empty stack;

ADD(i,S)   which inserts the element i onto the stack S and returns the new stack;

DELETE(S)   which removes the top element of stack S and returns the new stack;

TOP(S)   which returns the top element of stack S;

ISEMTS(S)   which returns true if S is empty else false;

These five functions constitute a working definition of a stack. However we choose to represent a stack, it must be possible to build these operations. But before we do this let us describe formally the structure STACK.

```
     structure STACK (item)
1      declare CREATE( )  →  stack
2              ADD(item,stack)  →  stack
3              DELETE(stack)  →  stack
4              TOP(stack)  →  item
5              ISEMTS(stack)  →  boolean;
6      for all S ∈ stack, i ∈ item let
7          ISEMTS(CREATE)         ::=  true
8          ISEMTS(ADD(i,S))       ::=  false
9          DELETE(CREATE)         ::=  error
10         DELETE(ADD(i,S))       ::=  S
11         TOP(CREATE)            ::=  error
12         TOP(ADD(i,S))          ::=  i
13     end
     end STACK
```

The five functions with their domains and ranges are declared in lines 1 through 5. Lines 6 through 13 are the set of axioms which describe how the functions are related. Lines 10 and 12 are the essential ones which define the last-in-first-out behavior. The above definitions describe an infinite stack for no upper bound on the number of elements is specified. This will be dealt with when we represent this structure in a computer.

The simplest way to represent a stack is by using a one dimensional array, say $stack[1..n]$, where n is the maximum number of allowable entries. The first or bottom element in the stack will be stored at $stack[1]$, the second at $stack[2]$ and the i-th at $stack[i]$. Associated with the array will be a variable, *top*, which points to the top element in the stack. With this decision made the following implementations result:

$$CREATE(stack) ::= \textbf{var } stack: \textbf{array}[1..n] \textbf{ of } items; top: 0..n;$$
$$top := 0;$$
$$ISEMTS(stack) ::= \textbf{if } top = 0 \textbf{ then true}$$
$$\textbf{else false};$$
$$TOP(stack) ::= \textbf{if } top = 0 \textbf{ then } error$$
$$\textbf{else } stack[top];$$

The implementations of these three operations using an array are so short that we needn't make them separate procedures but can just use them directly whenever we need to. The ADD and DELETE operations are only a bit more complex. The corresponding procedures have been written assuming that *stack*, *top*, and *n* are global.

```
procedure add(item : items);
{add item to the global stack stack;
 top is the current top of stack
 and n is its maximum size}
begin
  if top = n then stackfull;
  top := top + 1;
  stack[top] := item;
end; {of add}
```

Program 3.1 Add to a stack

```
procedure delete(var item : items);
{remove top element from the stack stack and put it in item}
begin
  if top = 0 then stackempty;
  item := stack[top];
  top := top − 1;
end; {of delete}
```

Program 3.2 Delete from a stack

Programs 3.1 and 3.2 are so simple that they perhaps need no more explanation. Procedure *delete* actually combines the functions TOP and DELETE, *stackfull* and *stackempty* are procedures which we leave unspecified since they will depend upon the particular application. Often a *stackfull* condition will signal that more storage needs to be allocated and the program re-run. *Stackempty* is often a meaningful condition. In Section 3.3 we will see a very important computer application of stacks where *stackempty* signals the end of processing.

The correctness of the stack implementation above may be established by showing that in this implementation, the stack axioms of lines 7-12 of the stack structure definition are true. Let us show this for the first three rules. The remainder of the axioms can be shown to hold similarly.

(i)   line 7: *ISEMTS(CREATE)* ::= **true**

Since CREATE results in top being initialized to zero, it follows from the implementation of ISEMTS that *ISEMTS(CREATE)* :: = **true**.

(ii)   line 8: *ISEMTS(ADD(i,S))* ::= **false**

The value of *top* is changed only in procedures CREATE, *add* and *delete*. CREATE initializes *top* to zero while *add* increments it by 1 so long as *top* is less than n (this is necessary because we can implement only a finite stack). *delete* decreases *top* by 1 but never allows its value to become less than zero. Hence, $add(i)$ either results in an error condition (*stackfull*), or leaves the value of $top > 0$. This then implies that *ISEMTS(ADD(i,s))* ::= **false**.

(iii)   line 9: *DELETE(CREATE)* ::= *error*

This follows from the observation that CREATE sets $top = 0$ and the procedure *delete* signals the error condition *stackempty* when $top = 0$.

Queues, like stacks, also arise quite naturally in the computer solution of many problems. Perhaps the most common occurrence of a queue in computer applications is for the scheduling of jobs. In batch processing the jobs are "queued-up" as they are read-in and executed, one after another in the order they were received. This ignores the possible existence of priorities, in which case there will be one queue for each priority.

As mentioned earlier, when we talk of queues we talk about two distinct ends: the front and the rear. Additions to the queue take place at the rear. Deletions are made from the front. So, if a job is submitted for execution, it joins at the rear of the job queue. The job at the front of the queue is the next one to be executed. A minimal set of useful operations on a queue includes the following:

CREATEQ(Q) which creates Q as an empty queue;
ADDQ(i,Q)   which adds the element i to the rear of a queue and returns the new queue;
DELETEQ(Q) which removes the front element from the queue Q and returns the resulting queue;
FRONT(Q)   which returns the front element of Q;
ISEMTQ(Q)   which returns true if Q is empty else false.

A complete specification of this data structure is

```
     structure QUEUE (item)
1       declare CREATEQ( )  → queue
2               ADDQ(item,queue)  → queue
3               DELETEQ(queue)  → queue
4               FRONT(queue)  → item
5               ISEMTQ(queue)  → boolean;
6       for all Q ∈ queue, i ∈ item let
7           ISEMTQ(CREATEQ)       ::= true
8           ISEMTQ(ADDQ(i,Q))     ::= false
9           DELETEQ(CREATEQ)   ::= error
10          DELETEQ(ADDQ(i,Q))  ::=
11            if ISEMTQ(Q) then CREATEQ
12                          else ADDQ(i, DELETEQ(Q))
13          FRONT(CREATEQ)      ::= error
14          FRONT(ADDQ(i,Q))    ::=
15            if ISEMTQ(Q) then i else FRONT(Q)
16      end
17    end QUEUE
```

The axiom of lines 10-12 shows that deletions are made from the front of the queue.

The representation of a finite queue in sequential locations is somewhat more difficult than a stack. In addition to a one dimensional array $q[1..n]$, we need two variables, *front* and *rear*. The conventions we shall adopt for these two variables are that *front* is always 1 less than the actual front of the queue and *rear* always points to the last element in the queue. Thus, *front* = *rear* if and only if there are no elements in the queue. The initial condition then is *front* = *rear* = 0. With these conventions, let us try an example by inserting and deleting jobs, J_i, from a job queue.

front	rear	Q[1]	[2]	[3]	[4]	[5]	[6]	[7]	... Remarks
0	0		queue		empty				Initial
0	1	J1							Job 1 joins Q
0	2	J1	J2						Job 2 joins Q
0	3	J1	J2	J3					Job 3 joins Q
1	3		J2	J3					Job 1 leaves Q
1	4		J2	J3	J4				Job 4 joins Q
2	4			J3	J4				Job 2 leaves Q

With this scheme, the following implementation of the CREATEQ, ISEMTQ, and FRONT operations results for a queue with capacity *n*:

$CREATEQ(q)$ ::= **var** q: **array**$[1..n]$ **of** *items*; *front, rear*: $0..n$;
$\qquad\qquad\qquad$ *front* := 0; *rear* := 0;
$ISEMTQ(q)$ $\quad$ ::= **if** *front* $=$ *rear* **then true**
$\qquad\qquad\qquad\qquad\qquad$ **else false**;
$FRONT(q)$ $\quad$ ::= **if** $ISEMTQ(q)$ **then error**
$\qquad\qquad\qquad\qquad\qquad$ **else** $q[front + 1]$;

The procedures for ADDQ and DELETEQ are given as Programs 3.3 and 3.4.

procedure *addq* (*item* : *items*);
{add *item* to the queue *q*}
begin
$\quad$ **if** *rear* $= n$ **then** *queuefull*
$\qquad\qquad\qquad$ **else begin**
$\qquad\qquad\qquad\qquad\qquad$ *rear* := *rear* + 1;
$\qquad\qquad\qquad\qquad\qquad$ *q*[*rear*] := *item*;
$\qquad\qquad\qquad\qquad$ **end**;
end; {of *addq*}

Program 3.3 Add to a queue

procedure *deleteq* (**var** *item* : *items*);
{delete from the front of *q* and put into *item*}
begin
$\quad$ **if** *front* $=$ *rear* **then** *queueempty*
$\qquad\qquad\qquad$ **else begin**
$\qquad\qquad\qquad\qquad\qquad$ *front* := *front* + 1;
$\qquad\qquad\qquad\qquad\qquad$ *item* := *q*[*front*];
$\qquad\qquad\qquad\qquad$ **end**;
end; {of *deleteq*}

Program 3.4 Delete from a queue

The correctness of this implementation may be established in a manner akin to that used for stacks. With this set up, notice that unless the front regularly catches up with the rear and both pointers are reset to zero, then the *queuefull* signal does not necessarily imply that there are *n* elements in the queue. That is, the queue will gradually move to the right. One obvious thing to do when *queuefull* is signaled is to move the entire queue to the left so that the first element is again at $q[1]$ and *front* $= 0$. This is time consuming, especially when there are many elements in the queue at the time of the *queuefull* signal.

Let us look at an example which shows what could happen, in the worst case, if each time the queue becomes full we choose to move the entire queue left so that it starts at $q[1]$. To begin, assume there are n elements J_1, ..., J_n in the queue and we next receive alternate requests to delete and add elements. Each time a new element is added, the entire queue of $n - 1$ elements is moved left.

front	rear	$q[1]$	[2]	[3]	.....	[n]	next operation
0	n	J_1	J_2	J_3	.....	J_n	initial state
1	n		J_2	J_3	.....	J_n	delete J_1
0	n	J_2	J_3	J_4	.....	J_{n+1}	add J_{n+1} (jobs J_2 through J_n are moved)
1	n		J_3	J_4	.....	J_{n+1}	delete J_2
0	n	J_3	J_4	J_5	.....	J_{n+2}	add J_{n+2}

Figure 3.3.

A more efficient queue representation is obtained by regarding the array $q[1..n]$ as circular. It now becomes more convenient to declare the array as $q[0..n-1]$. When $rear = n - 1$, the next element is entered at $q[0]$ in case that spot is free. Using the same conventions as before, *front* will always point one position counterclockwise from the first element in the queue. Again, *front* = *rear* if and only if the queue is empty. Initially we have *front* = *rear* = 1. Figure 3.4 illustrates some of the possible configurations for a circular queue containing the four elements $J1$-$J4$ with $n > 4$. The assumption of circularity changes the *addq* and *deleteq* procedures slightly. In order to add an element, it will be necessary to move *rear* one position clockwise, i.e.,

if *rear* = $n - 1$ **then** *rear* := 0
         else *rear* := *rear* + 1.

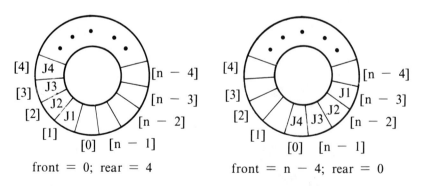

front = 0; rear = 4   front = n − 4; rear = 0

Figure 3.4 Circular queue of n elements and four jobs $J1$, $J2$, $J3$, $J4$.

Using the modulo operator which computes remainders, this is just $rear :=$ $(rear + 1)\textbf{mod } n$. Similarly, it will be necessary to move *front* one position clockwise each time a deletion is made. Again, using the modulo operator, this can be accomplished by $front := (front + 1)\textbf{mod } n$. An examination of the algorithms (Programs 3.5 and 3.6) indicates that addition and deletion can now be carried out in a fixed amount of time or $O(1)$.

procedure *addq* (*item* : *items*);
{insert *item* into the circular queue stored in $q[0..n - 1]$}
begin
    rear := (*rear* + 1)**mod** *n*; {advance *rear* clockwise}
    if *front* = *rear* **then** *queuefull*;
    q[*rear*] := *item*; {insert}
end; {of *addq*}

Program 3.5 Add to a circular queue

procedure *deleteq* (**var** *item* : *items*);
{remove front element from *q* and put into *item*}
begin
    if *front* = *rear* **then** *queueempty*;
    front := (*front* + 1)**mod** *n*; {advance *front* clockwise}
    item := *q*[*front*];
end; {of *deleteq*}

Program 3.6 Delete from a circular queue

One surprising point in the two algorithms is that the test for queue full in *addq* and the test for queue empty in *deleteq* are the same. In the case of *addq*, however, when *front* = *rear* there is actually one space free, i.e. *q*[*rear*], since the first element in the queue is not at *q*[*front*] but is one position clockwise from this point. However, if we insert an item here, then we will not be able to distinguish between the cases full and empty, since this insertion would leave *front* = *rear*. To avoid this, we signal *queuefull*, thus permitting a maximum of $n - 1$ rather than n elements to be in the queue at any time. One way to use all n positions would be to use another variable, *tag*, to distinguish between the two situations, i.e. *tag* = 0 if and only if the queue is empty. This would, however, slow down the two procedures. Since the *addq* and *deleteq* procedures will be used many times in any problem involving queues, the loss of one queue position will be more than made up for by the reduction in computing time.

The procedures *queuefull* and *queueempty* have been used without explanation, but they are similar to *stackfull* and *stackempty*. Their function will depend on the particular application.

3.2   A MAZING PROBLEM

The rat-in-a-maze experiment is a classical one from experimental psychology. A rat (or mouse) is placed through the door of a large box without a top. Walls are set up so that movements in most directions are obstructed. The rat is carefully observed by several scientists as it makes its way through the maze until it eventually reaches the exit. There is only one way out, but at the end is a nice hunk of cheese. The idea is to run the experiment repeatedly until the rat will zip through the maze without taking a single false path. The trials yield his learning curve.

We can write a computer program for getting through a maze and it will probably not be any smarter than the rat on its first try through. It may take many false paths before finding the right one. But the computer can remember the correct path far better than the rat. On its second try it should be able to go right to the end with no false paths taken, so there is no sense re-running the program. Why don't you sit down and try to write this program yourself before you read on and look at our solution. Keep track of how many times you have to go back and correct something. This may give you an idea of your own learning curve as we re-run the experiment throughout the book.

Let us represent the maze by a two dimensional array, $maze[1..m, 1..p]$, where a value of 1 implies a blocked path, while a 0 means one can walk right on through. We assume that the rat starts at $maze[1,1]$ and the exit is at $maze[m,p]$.

entrance →

0	1	0	0	0	1	1	0	0	0	1	1	1	1	1
1	0	0	0	1	1	0	1	1	1	0	0	1	1	1
0	1	1	0	0	0	0	1	1	1	1	0	0	1	1
1	1	0	1	1	1	1	0	1	1	0	1	1	0	0
1	1	0	1	0	0	1	0	1	1	1	1	1	1	1
0	0	1	1	0	1	1	1	0	1	0	0	1	0	1
0	1	1	1	1	0	0	1	1	1	1	1	1	1	1
0	0	1	1	0	1	1	0	1	1	1	1	1	0	1
1	1	0	0	0	1	1	0	1	1	0	0	0	0	0
0	0	1	1	1	1	1	0	0	0	1	1	1	1	0
0	1	0	0	1	1	1	1	1	0	1	1	1	1	0

→ exit

Figure 3.5.

With the maze represented as a two dimensional array, the location of the rat in the maze can at any time be described by the row, i, and the column, j, of its position. Now let us consider the possible moves the rat can make at some point $[i,j]$ in the maze. Figure 3.6 shows the possible moves from any point $[i,j]$. The position $[i,j]$ is marked by an X. If all the surrounding squares have a 0 then the rat can choose any of these eight squares as its next position. We call these eight directions by the names of

the points on a compass: north, northeast, east, southeast, south, southwest, west and northwest, or N, NE, E, SE, S, SW, W, NW.

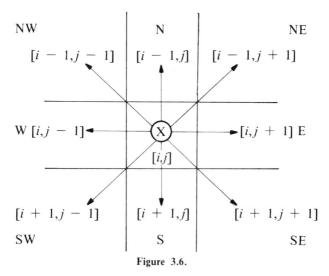

Figure 3.6.

We must be careful here because not every position has eight neighbors.
If $[i,j]$ is on a border where either $i = 1$ or m, or $j = 1$ or p, then less than
eight and possibly only three neighbors exist. To avoid checking for these
border conditions we can surround the maze by a border of ones. The
array will therefore be declared as $maze[0..m+1, 0..p+1]$.

Another device that will simplify the problem is to predefine the possible
directions to move in a table, *move*, as below:

type *offsets* = **record**
                    a: −1..1;
                    b: −1..1;
                end;
      directions = (N, NE, E, SE, S, SW, W, NW);
var *move*: **array** [*directions*] **of** *offsets*;

q	$move[q].a$	$move[q].b$
N	−1	0
NE	−1	1
E	0	1
SE	1	1
S	1	0
SW	1	−1
W	0	−1
NW	−1	−1

If we are at position $[i,j]$ in the maze and we wish to find the position $[g,h]$ that is southwest of us, then we set:

$$g := i + move[SW].a; \quad h := j + move[SW].b;$$

For example, if we are at position [3,4], then position $[3 + 1 = 4, 4 + (-1) = 3]$ is southwest.

As we move through the maze we may have the chance to go in several directions. Not knowing which one to choose, we pick one but save our current position and the direction of the last move in a list. This way if we have taken a false path we can return and try another direction. With each new location we will examine the possibilities, starting from the north and looking clockwise. Finally, in order to prevent us from going down the same path twice we use another array $mark[0:m + 1,0:p + 1]$ which is initially zero. $mark[i,j]$ is set to 1 once we arrive at that position. We assume $maze[m,p] = 0$ as otherwise there is no path to the exit. Program 3.7 is a first pass at an algorithm.

```
initialize list to the maze entrance coordinates and direction north;
while list is not empty do
begin
  (i,j,mov) := coordinates and direction from front of list;
  while there are more moves do
  begin
    (g,h) := coordinates of next move;
    if (g = m) and (h = p) then success;
    if maze[g,h] = 0 {legal move}
       and (mark[g,h] = 0) {haven't been here before}
    then begin
           mark[g,h] := 1;
           add (i,j,mov) to front of list;
           i := g; j := h; mov := 0;
         end;
  end;
end;
writeln('no path found');
```

Program 3.7 First pass at maze algorithm

This is not a Pascal program and yet it describes the essential processing without too much detail. The use of indentation for delineating important blocks of code plus the use of Pascal reserved words make the looping and conditional tests transparent.

What remains to be pinned down? Using the three arrays *maze*, *mark* and *move* we need only specify how to represent the list of new triples. Since the algorithm calls for removing first the most recently entered triple, this list should be a stack. We can use the sequential representation we saw before. All we need to know now is a reasonable bound on the size of this stack. Since each position in the maze is visited at most once, at most *mp* elements can be placed into the stack. Thus *mp* locations is a safe but somewhat conservative bound. In the following maze the only path has at most $\lceil m/2 \rceil (p + 1)$ positions.

$$\begin{bmatrix} 0 & 0 & 0 & 0 & 0 & 0 \\ 1 & 1 & 1 & 1 & 1 & 0 \\ 0 & 0 & 0 & 0 & 0 & 0 \\ 0 & 1 & 1 & 1 & 1 & 1 \\ 0 & 0 & 0 & 0 & 0 & 0 \\ 1 & 1 & 1 & 1 & 1 & 0 \\ 0 & 0 & 0 & 0 & 0 & 0 \\ 0 & 1 & 1 & 1 & 1 & 1 \\ 0 & 0 & 0 & 0 & 0 & 0 \end{bmatrix}$$

Thus *mp* is not too crude a bound. We are now ready to give a precise maze algorithm [Program 3.8].

While using nonnumeric indices for *move* keeps the correspondence with direction transparent, it makes the resulting Pascal program somewhat cumbersome. This is so because the predecessor of N and the successor of NW are not defined. For this reason, in writing procedure *path* we assume that *move* is actually declared as:

var *move* : **array**[1..8] **of** *offsets*;

The correspondence is *move*[1] = *move*[N], ..., *move*[8] = *move*[NW].

The arrays *maze*, *mark*, *move*, and *stack* along with the variables or constants *top*, *m*, *p*, and *n* are assumed global to *path*. Further, it is assumed that *stack*[1..*n*] is an array of *items* where the type *items* is defined as:

type *items* = **record**
        x:1..*m*;
        y:1..*p*;
        dir:1..9;
     end;

If *n* is at least *mp*, then the *stackfull* condition will never occur.

procedure *path*
{output a path (if any) in the maze. *maze*[0,*i*] = *maze*[*m* + 1,*i*] = *maze*[*j*,0] = *maze*[*j*,*p* +1] = 1, 0 ≤ *i* ≤ *p*+1, 0 ≤ *j* ≤ *m*+1}
label 99;
var *position*: *items*; *d,g,h,i,j,q*: **integer**;
begin
  {start at (1,1)}
  mark[1,1] := 1; *top* := 1;
  with *stack*[1] **do begin** *x* := 1; *y* := 1; *dir* := 2; **end**;
  while *top* > 0 **do** {stack not empty}
  begin
   delete(*position*); {unstack}
   with *position* **do begin** *i* := *x*; *j* := *y*; *d* := *dir*; **end**;
   while *d* <= 8 **do** {move forward}
   begin
    g := *i* + *move*[*d*].*a*;   *h* := *j* + *move*[*d*].*b*;
    if (*g* = *m*) **and** (*h* = *p*) **then** {reached exit}
    begin {output *path*}
     for *q* := 1 **to** *top* **do**
        writeln(*stack*[*q*]);
     writeln(*i,j*); **writeln**(*m,p*);
     goto 99; {end of procedure}
    end; {of **if**}
    if (*maze*[*g,h*] = 0) **and** *mark*[*g,h*] = 0)
    then begin {new position}
        mark[*g,h*] := 1;
        with *position* **do** *x* := *i*; *y* := *j*; *dir* := *d* + 1; **end**;
        add(*position*); {stack it}
        i := *g*; *j* := *h*; *d* := 1; {move to (*g,h*)}
      end
    else *d* := *d* + 1; {try next direction}
   end; {of **while** *d* <= 8}
  end; {of *top* > 0}
  writeln('no path in maze');
99: **end**; {of *path*}

Program 3.8 Procedure *path*

Now, what can we say about the computing time of this procedure? It is interesting that even though the problem is easy to grasp, it is difficult to make any but the most trivial statement about the computing time. The reason for this is because the number of iterations of the main **while** loop is entirely dependent upon the given maze. What we can say is that each new position $[i,j]$ that is visited gets marked, so paths are never taken twice. There are at most eight iterations of the inner **while** loop for each marked position. Each iteration of the inner **while** loop takes a fixed amount of time, $O(1)$, and if the number of zeros in *maze* is z then at most z positions can get marked. Since z is bounded above by mp, the computing time is $O(mp)$. (In actual experiments, however, the rat may be inspired by the watching psychologists and the invigorating odor from the cheese at the exit. It might reach its goal by examining far fewer paths than those examined by algorithm *path*. This may happen despite the fact that the rat has no pencil and only a very limited mental stack. It is difficult to incorporate the effect of the cheese odor and the cheering of the psychologists into a computer algorithm.) The array *mark* can be eliminated altogether and *maze*[*g,h*] changed to 1 instead of setting *mark*[*g,h*] to 1, but this will destroy the original maze.

3.3 EVALUATION OF EXPRESSIONS

When pioneering computer scientists conceived the idea of higher level programming languages, they were faced with many technical hurdles. One of the biggest was the question of how to generate machine language instructions which would properly evaluate any arithmetic expression. A complex assignment statement such as

$$X := A/B ** C + D * E - A * C \tag{3.1}$$

might have several meanings (note that the exponentiation operator ** is not a standard Pascal operator); and even if it were uniquely defined, say by a full use of parentheses, it still seemed a formidable task to generate a correct and reasonable instruction sequence. Fortunately the solution we have today is both elegant and simple. Moreover, it is so simple that this aspect of compiler writing is really one of the more minor issues.

An expression is made up of operands, operators and delimiters. The expression above has five operands: $A,B,C,D,$ and E. Though these are all one letter variables, operands can be any legal variable name or constant in our programming language. In any expression the values that variables take must be consistent with the operations performed on them. These operations are described by the operators. In most programming languages there are several kinds of operators which correspond to the different kinds of data a variable can hold. First, there are the basic arithmetic operators: plus, minus, times, divide, and exponentiation $(+, -, *, /, **)$. Other arithemetic operators include unary plus, unary minus and **mod, ceil,** and **floor.** The latter three may sometimes be library subroutines rather than predefined operators. A second class are the relational operators: $<, <=, =, <>,$

$>=, >$. These are usually defined to work for arithmetic operands, but they can just as easily work for character string data. ('CAT' is less than 'DOG' since it precedes 'DOG' in alphabetical order.) The result of an expression which contains relational operators is one of the two constants: **true** or **false**. Such an expression is called Boolean, named after the mathematician George Boole, the father of symbolic logic.

The first problem with understanding the meaning of an expression is to decide in what order the operations are carried out. This means that every language must uniquely define such an order. For instance, if $A = 4, B = C = 2, D = E = 3$, then in eq. 3.1 we might want X to be assigned the value

$$
\begin{aligned}
& 4/(2 ** 2) + (3 * 3) - (4 * 2) \\
= {} & (4/4) + 9 - 8 \\
= {} & 2.
\end{aligned}
$$

However, the true intention of the programmer might have been to assign X the value

$$
\begin{aligned}
& (4/2) ** (2 + 3) * (3 - 4) * 2 \\
= {} & (4/2) ** 5 * -1 * 2 \\
= {} & (2 ** 5)* -2 \\
= {} & 32 * -2 \\
= {} & -64.
\end{aligned}
$$

Of course, he could specify the latter order of evaluation by using parentheses:

$$
X := ((((A/B) ** (C + D)) * (E - A)) * C).
$$

To fix the order of evaluation, we assign to each operator a priority. Then within any pair of parentheses we understand that operators with the highest priority will be evaluated first. A set of sample priorities from Pascal (including the nonstandard **) is given in Figure 3.7.

operator	priority
, unary−, unary+, **not	4
*, /, **div**, **mod**, **and**	3
+, −, **or**	2
<, <=, =, <>, >=, >	1

Figure 3.7 Priority of arithmetic, Boolean, and relational operators in Pascal.

Notice that all of the relational operators have the same priority. Similarly, exponentiation, unary minus, unary plus and Boolean negation all have top priority. When we have an expression where two adjacent operators have the same priority, we need a rule to tell us which one to perform first. For example, do we want the value of $-A ** B$ to be understood as $(-A) ** B$ or $-(A ** B)$? Convince yourself that there will be a difference by trying $A = -1$ and $B = 2$. From algebra we normally consider $A ** B ** C$ as $A ** (B ** C)$ and so we rule that operators in priority 4 are evaluated right-to-left. However, for expressions such as $A * B/C$ we generally execute left-to-right or $(A * B)/C$. So we rule that for all other priorities, evaluation of operators of the same priority will proceed left to right. Remember that by using parentheses we can override these rules, and such expressions are always evaluated with the innermost parenthesized expression first.

Now that we have specified priorities and rules for breaking ties we know how $X := A/B ** C + D * E - A * C$ will be evaluated, namely as

$$X := ((A/(B ** C)) + (D * E)) - (A * C).$$

How can a compiler accept such an expression and produce correct code? The answer is given by reworking the expression into a form we call postfix notation. If e is an expression with operators and operands, the conventional way of writing e is called *infix*, because the operators come *in*-between the operands. (Unary operators precede their operand.) The *postfix* form of an expression calls for each operator to appear *after* its operands. For example,

$$\text{infix: } A * B/C \text{ has postfix: } AB * C/.$$

If we study the postfix form of $A * B/C$ we see that the multiplication comes immediately after its two operands A and B. Now imagine that $A * B$ is computed and stored in T. Then we have the division operator, $/$, coming immediately after its two operands T and C.

Let us look at our previous example

$$\text{infix: } A/B ** C + D * E - A * C$$

$$\text{postfix: } ABC ** /DE * + AC * -$$

and trace out the meaning of the postfix.

Every time we compute a value let us store it in the temporary location T_i, $i \geq 1$. Reading left to right, the first operation is exponentiation:

Operation	Postfix
$T_1 := B ** C$	$AT_1/DE * + AC * -$
$T_2 := A/T_1$	$T_2DE * + AC * -$
$T_3 := D * E$	$T_2T_3 + AC * -$
$T_4 := T_2 + T_3$	$T_4AC * -$
$T_5 := A * C$	$T_4 T_5 -$
$T_6 := T_4 - T_5$	T_6

So T_6 will contain the result. Notice that if we had parenthesized the expression, this would change the postfix only if the order of normal evaluation were altered. Thus, $A/(B ** C) + (D * E) - A * C$ will have the same postfix form as the previous expression without parentheses. But $(A/B) ** (C + D) * (E - A) * C$ will have the postfix form $AB/CD + ** EA - * C *$.

Before attempting an algorithm to translate expressions from infix to postfix notation, let us make some observations regarding the virtues of postfix notation that enable easy evaluation of expressions. To begin with, the need for parentheses is eliminated. Secondly, the priority of the operators is no longer relevant. The expression may be evaluated by making a left to right scan, stacking operands, and evaluating operators using as operands the correct number from the stack and finally placing the result onto the stack (see Program 3.9). This evaluation process is much simpler than attempting a direct evaluation from infix notation.

procedure *eval* (*e* : *expression*);
{evaluate the postfix expression *e*. It is assumed that the last
character in *e* is '#'. A procedure *nexttoken* is used
to extract from *e* the next token (a token is either an operator,
operand, or '#'). A one dimensional array *stack* [1..*n*] is used
as a stack.}
var *x* : *token*;
begin
   top := 0; {initialize *stack*}
   x := *nexttoken* (*e*);
   while *x* <> '#' **do**
   begin
     if *x* is an operand
     then *add* (*x*) {add to *stack*}
     else begin {operator}
          remove the correct number of operands for operator
          x from *stack*; perform the operation *x* and store the
          result (if any) onto the stack;
       end;
     x := *nexttoken* (*e*);
   end; {of **while**}
end; {of *eval*}

Program 3.9   Algorithm to evaluate postfix expressions

To see how to devise an algorithm for translating from infix to postfix, note that the order of the operands in both forms is the same. In fact, it is simple to describe an algorithm for producing postfix from infix:

1) fully parenthesize the expression;
2) move all operators so that they replace their corresponding right parentheses;
3) delete all parentheses.

For example, $A / B ** C + D * E - A * C$ when fully parenthesized yields

$$(((A / (B ** C)) + (D * E)) - (A * C)).$$

The arrows point from an operator to its corresponding right parenthesis. Performing steps 2 and 3 gives

$$ABC ** / DE * + AC * -.$$

The problem with this as an algorithm is that it requires two passes: the first one reads the expression and parenthesizes it while the second actually moves the operators. As we have already observed, the order of the operands is the same in infix and postfix. So as we scan an expression for the first time, we can form the postfix by immediately passing any operands to the output. Then it is just a matter of handling the operators. The solution is to store them in a stack until just the right moment and then to unstack and pass them to the output.

For example, since we want $A + B * C$ to yield $ABC * +$ our algorithm should perform the following sequence of stacking (these stacks will grow to the right):

Next Token	Stack	Output
none	empty	none
A	empty	A
+	+	A
B	+	AB

At this point the algorithm must determine if * gets placed on top of the stack or if the + gets taken off. Since * has greater priority we should stack * producing

*	+ *	AB
C	+ *	ABC

Now the input expression is exhausted, so we output all remaining operators in the stack to get

$$ABC * +$$

For another example, $A * (B + C) * D$ has the postfix form $ABC + * D *$, and so the algorithm should behave as

Next Token	Stack	Output
none	empty	none
A	empty	A
*	*	A
(	* (	A
B	* (	AB
+	* (+	AB
C	* (+	ABC

At this point we want to unstack down to the corresponding left parenthesis, and then delete the left and right parentheses; this gives us:

)	*	ABC +
*	*	ABC + *
D	*	ABC + * D
done	empty	ABC + * D *

These examples should motivate the following hierarchy scheme for binary arithmetic operators and delimiters. The general case involving all the operators of figure 3.7 is left as an exercise.

Symbol	In-Stack Priority	In-Coming Priority
)	—	—
**	3	4
*,/	2	2
binary +, −	1	1
(	0	4

Figure 3.8 Priorities of Operators for Producing Postfix.

The rule will be that *operators are taken out of the stack as long as their in-stack priority, isp, is greater than or equal to the in-coming priority, icp, of the new operator. isp[x] and icp[x]* are arrays which reflect the table of figure 3.8. Our algorithm to transform from infix to postfix is given in Program 3.10.

procedure *postfix* (*e* : *expression*);
{output the postfix form of the infix expression *e*.
nexttoken and *stack* are as in procedure *eval*. It is
assumed that the last token in *e* is '#'. '−#' is used
at the bottom of the stack and *isp* ['−#] = −1.}
var *x,y* : *token*;
begin
  stack [1] := '−#'; *top* := 1; {initialize *stack*}
  x := *nexttoken*(*e*);
  while *x* <> '#' **do**
  begin
    if *x* is an operand
    then write(*x*)
    else if *x* = ')'
      then begin {unstack until '('}
          while *stack*[*top*] <> '(' **do**
          begin *delete*(*y*); **write**(*y*); **end**;
          delete(*y*); {delete '('}
        end
      else begin
          while *isp* [*stack* [*top*]] > = *icp* [*x*] **do**
          begin *delete*(*y*); **write**(*y*); **end**;
          add(*x*);
        end;
    x := *nexttoken*(*e*);
  end; {of **while**}
  {end of expression; empty stack}
  while *top* > 1 **do**
  begin *delete*(*y*); **write**(*y*); **end**;
  writeln('#');
end; {of *postfix*}

Program 3.10   Convert from infix to postfix form

As for the computing time, the algorithm makes only one pass across the
input. If the expression has *n* symbols, then the number of operations is
proportional to some constant times *n*. The stack cannot get any deeper than
the number of operators plus 1, but it may achieve this bound as it does for *A*
+ *B* * *C* ** *D*.

3.4   MULTIPLE STACKS AND QUEUES

Up to now we have been concerned only with the representation of a single stack or a single queue in the memory of a computer. For these two cases we have seen efficient sequential data representations. What happens when a data representation is needed for several stacks and queues? Let us once again limit ourselves to sequential mappings of these data objects into an array $v[1..m]$. If we have only 2 stacks to represent, then the solution is simple. We can use $v[1]$ for the bottommost element in stack 1 and $v[m]$ for the corresponding element in stack 2. Stack 1 can grow towards $v[m]$ and stack 2 towards $v[1]$. It is therefore possible to utilize efficiently all the available space. Can we do the same when more than 2 stacks are to be represented? The answer is no, because a one dimensional array has only two fixed points $v[1]$ and $v[m]$ and each stack requires a fixed point for its bottommost element. When more than two stacks, say n, are to be represented sequentially, we can initially divide out the available memory $v[1..m]$ into n segments and allocate one of these segments to each of the n stacks. This initial division of $v[1..m]$ into segments may be done in proportion to expected sizes of the various stacks if the sizes are known. In the absence of such information, $v[1..m]$ may be divided into equal segments. For each stack i we shall use $b[i]$ to represent a position one less than the position in v for the bottommost element of that stack. $t[i]$, $1 \le i \le n$ will point to the topmost element of stack i. We shall use the boundary condition $b[i] = t[i]$ iff the i-th stack is empty. If we grow the i-th stack in lower memory indexes than the $(i + 1)$-th, then with roughly equal initial segments we have

$$b[i] = t[i] = \lfloor m/n \rfloor (i - 1), 1 \le i \le n$$

as the initial values of $b[i]$ and $t[i]$ (see figure 3.9). Stack i, $1 \le i \le n$ can grow from $b[i] + 1$ up to $b[i + 1]$ before it catches up with the $(i + 1)$-th stack. It is convenient both for the discussion and the algorithms to define $b[n + 1] = m$. Using this scheme, the add and delete algorithms of Programs 3.11 and 3.12 result.

procedure *add* (*i* : **integer**; *x* : *items*);
{add *x* to the *i*-th *stack*}
begin
   if $t[i] = b[i + 1]$ **then** *stackfull(i)*;
   $t[i] := t[i] + 1$;
   $v[t[i]] := x$; {add to *i*-th stack}
end; {of *add*}

Program 3.11   Add to *i*-th stack

procedure *delete* (*i* : **integer**; **var** *x* : *items*);
{*delete* topmost item of stack *i*}
begin
  if *t*[*i*] = *b*[*i*] **then** *stackempty*(*i*);
  x := *v*[*t*[*i*]];
  t[*i*] := *t*[*i*] − 1;
end; {of *delete*}

Program 3.12   Delete from *i*-th stack

The algorithms to add and delete appear to be as simple as in the case of only 1 or 2 stacks. This really is not the case since the *stackfull* condition in algorithm *add* does not imply that all *m* locations of *v* are in use. In fact, there may be a lot of unused space between stacks *j* and *j* + 1 for $1 \le j \le n$ and $j \ne i$ (figure 3.10). The procedure *stackfull* (*i*) should therefore determine whether there is any free space in *v* and shift stacks around so as to make some of this free space available to the *i*-th stack.

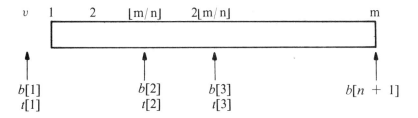

Figure 3.9   Initial configuration for *n* stacks in *v*[1..*m*]. All stacks are empty and memory is divided into roughly equal segments.

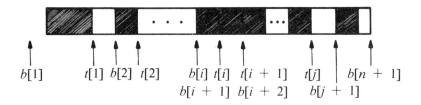

Figure 3.10   Configuration when stack *i* meets with stack *i* + 1 but there is still free space elsewhere in *v*.

Several strategies are possible for the design of algorithm *stackfull*. We shall discuss one strategy in the text and look at some others in the exercises. The primary objective of algorithm *stackfull* is to permit the adding of elements to stacks so long as there is some free space in v. One way to guarantee this is to design *stackfull* along the following lines:

a) determine the least j, $i < j \leq n$ such that there is free space between stacks j and $j + 1$, i.e., $t[j] < b[j + 1]$. If there is such a j, then move stacks $i + 1$, $i + 2$, ...,j one position to the right (treating $v[1]$ as leftmost and $v[m]$ as rightmost), thereby creating a space between stacks i and $i + 1$.

b) if there is no j as in a), then look to the left of stack i. Find the largest j such that $1 \leq j < i$ and there is space between stacks j and $j + 1$, i.e., $t[j] < b[j + 1]$. If there is such a j, then move stacks $j + 1$, $j + 2$, ...,i one space left creating a free space between stacks i and $i + 1$.

c) if there is no j satisfying either the conditions of a) or b), then all m spaces of v are utilized and there is no free space.

The writing of algorithm *stackfull* using the above strategy is left as an exercise. It should be clear that the worst case performance of this representation for the n stacks together with the above strategy for *stackfull* would be rather poor. In fact, in the worst case $O(m)$ time may be needed for each insertion (see exercises). In the next chapter we shall see that if we do not limit ourselves to sequential mappings of data objects into arrays, then we can obtain a data representation for m stacks that has a much better worst case performance than the representation described here. Sequential representations for n queues and other generalizations are discussed in the exercises.

EXERCISES

1. Consider a railroad switching network as below

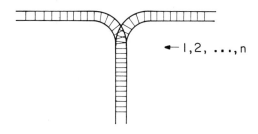

$\leftarrow 1,2, \ldots, n$

Railroad cars numbered 1,2,3 ...,n are at the right. Each car is brought into the stack and removed at any time. For instance, if $n = 3$, we could move 1 in, move 2 in, move 3 in and then take the cars out producing the new order 3,2,1. For $n = 3$ and 4 what are the possible permutations of the cars that can be obtained? Are any permutations not possible?

2. Using a Boolean variable to distinguish between a circular queue being empty or full, write insert and delete procedures.

3. Complete the correctness proof for the stack implementation of section 3.1.

4. Use the queue axioms to prove that the circular queue representation of section 3.1 is correct.

5. A double ended queue (deque) is a linear list in which additions and deletions may be made at either end. Obtain a data representation mapping a deque into a one dimensional array. Write algorithms to add and delete elements from either end of the deque.

6. [Mystery function] Let f be an operation whose argument and result is a queue and which is defined by the axioms:

    $f(CREATEQ)$ $::=$ $CREATEQ$
    $f(ADDQ(i,q))$ $::=$ **if** $ISEMTQ(q)$ **then** $ADDQ(i,q)$
                               else $ADDQ(FRONT(q), f(DELETEQ(ADDQ(i,q))))$

    What does f do?

7. A linear list is being maintained circularly in an array $c[0..n-1]$ with *front* and *rear* set up as for circular queues.

    a) Obtain a formula in terms of *front*, *rear* and n for the number of elements in the list.
    b) Write an algorithm to delete the k-th element in the list.
    c) Write an algorithm to insert an element y immediately after the k-th element.

    What is the time complexity of your algorithms for b) and c)?

8. Let $L = (a_1, a_2, ..., a_n)$ be a linear list represented in the array $v[1..n]$ using the mapping: the i-th element of L is stored in $v[i]$. Write an algorithm to make an inplace reversal of the order of elements in v. I.e., the algorithm should transform v such that $v[i]$ contains the $(n-i+1)$-th element of L. The only additional space available to your algorithm is that for simple variables. The input to the algorithm is v and n. How much time does your algorithm take to accomplish the reversal?

9. a) Find a path through the maze of figure 3.5.
    b) Trace out the action of procedure *path* on the maze of figure 3.5. Compare this to your own attempt in a).

10. What is the maximum path length from start to finish in any maze of dimensions $n \times m$?

11. Write the postfix form of the following expressions:
   a) $A ** B ** C$
   b) $- A + B - C + D$
   c) $A ** -B + C$
   d) $(A + B) * D + E/(F + A * D) + C$
   e) A **and** B **or** C **or** **not** $(E > F)$ (assuming Pascal precedence)
   f) **not** $(A$ **and** **not** $((B < C)$ **or** $(C > D)))$ **or** $(C < E)$

12. Obtain *isp* and *icp* priorities for all the operators of figure 3.7 together with the delimiters '(', and ')'. These priorities should be such that algorithm *postfix* correctly generates the postfix form for all expressions made up of operands and these operators and delimiters.

13. Use the *isp* and *icp* priorities obtained in exercise 12 to answer the following:
   a) In algorithm *postfix* what is the maximum number of elements that can be on the stack at any time if the input expression e has n operators and delimiters?
   b) What is the answer to a) if e contains no operators of priority 4 (cf. Fig. 3.7), has n operators and the depth of nesting of parentheses is at most 6?

14. Another expression form that is easy to evaluate and is parenthesis free is known as *prefix*. In this way of writing expressions, the operators precede their operands. For example:

infix	prefix
$A * B/C$	$/* ABC$
$A/B ** C + D * E - A * C$	$- + /A ** BC * DE * AC$
$A * (B + C)/D - G$	$-/* A + BCDG$

   Notice that the order of operands is not changed in going from infix to prefix.
   a) What is the prefix form of the expressions in exercise 11?
   b) Write an algorithm to evaluate a prefix expression, e. (Hint: Scan e right to left and assume that the leftmost token of e is '#'.)
   c) Write an algorithm to transform an infix expression e into its prefix equivalent. Assume that the input expression e begins with a '#' and that the prefix expression should begin with a '#'.
   What is the time complexity of your algorithms for b) and c)? How much space is needed by each of these algorithms?

15. Write an algorithm to transform from prefix to postfix. Carefully state any assumptions you make regarding the input. How much time and space does your algorithm take?

16. Do exercise 15 but this time for a transformation from postfix to prefix.

17. Write an algorithm to generate fully parenthesized infix expressions from their postfix form. What is the complexity (time and space) of your algorithm?

18. Do exercise 17 starting from prefix form.

19. Two stacks are to be represented in an array $v[1..m]$ as described in §3.4. Write algorithms $add(i,x)$ and $delete(i)$ to add x and delete an element from stack i, $1 \leq i \leq 2$. Your algorithms should be able to add elements to the stacks so long as there are fewer than m elements in both stacks together.

20. Obtain a data representation mapping a stack s and a queue q into a single array $v[1..n]$. Write algorithms to add and delete elements from these two data objects. What can you say about the suitability of your data representation?

21. Write a Pascal procedure implementing the strategy for $stackfull(i)$ outlined in §3.4.

22. For the add and $delete$ algorithms of §3.4 and the $stackfull(i)$ algorithm of exercise 21 produce a sequence of adds and deletes that will require $O(m)$ time for each add. Use $n = 2$ and start from a configuration representing a full utilization of $v[1..m]$.

23. It has been empirically observed that most programs that get close to using all available space eventually run out of space. In the light of this observation, it seems futile to move stacks around providing space for other stacks to grow in if there is only a limited amount of space that is free. Rewrite the algorithm of exercise 21 so that the algorithm terminates if there are fewer than c free spaces. c is an empirically determined constant and is provided to the algorithm.

24. Another strategy for the $stackfull(i)$ condition of §3.4 is to redistribute all the free space in proportion to the rate of growth of individual stacks since the last call to $stackfull$. This would require the use of another array $lt[1..n]$ where $lt[j]$ is the value of $t[j]$ at the last call to $stackfull$. Then the amount by which each stack has grown since the last call is $t[j] - lt[j]$. The figure for stack i is actually $t[i] - lt[i] + 1$, since we are now attempting to add another element to i.

Write algorithm $stackfull(i)$ to redistribute all the stacks so that the free space between stacks j and $j + 1$ is in proportion to the growth of stack j since the last call to $stackfull$. $stackfull(i)$ should assign at least 1 free location to stack i.

25. Design a data representation sequentially mapping n queues into an array $v[1..m]$. Represent each queue as a circular queue within v. Write procedures *addq*, *deleteq* and *queuefull* for this representation.

26. Design a data representation, sequentially mapping n data objects into an array $v[1..m]$. n_1 of these data objects are stacks and the remaining $n_2 = n - n_1$ are queues. Write algorithms to add and delete elements from these objects. Use the same *spacefull* algorithm for both types of data objects. This algorithm should provide space for the i-th data object if there is some space not currently being used. Note that a circular queue with space for r elements can hold only $r - 1$.

27. [Landweber]
People have spent so much time playing card games of solitaire that the gambling casinos are now capitalizing on this human weakness. A form of solitaire is described below. Your assignment is to write a computer program to play the game thus freeing hours of time for people to return to more useful endeavors.

To begin the game, 28 cards are dealt into 7 piles. The leftmost pile has 1 card, the next two cards, and so forth up to 7 cards in the rightmost pile. Only the uppermost card of each of the 7 piles is turned face up. The cards are dealt left to right, one card to each pile, dealing to one less pile each time, and turning the first card in each round face up.

On the topmost face-up card of each pile you may build in descending sequences red on black or black on red. For example, on the 9 of spades you may place either the 8 of diamonds or the 8 of hearts. All face-up cards on a pile are moved as a unit and may be placed on another pile according to the bottommost face-up card. For example, the 7 of clubs on the 8 of hearts may be moved as a unit onto the 9 of clubs or the 9 of spades.

Whenever a face-down card is uncovered, it is turned face up. If one pile is removed completely, a face-up King may be moved from a pile (together with all cards above it) or the top of the waste pile (see below)) into the vacated space. There are four output piles, one for each suit, and the object of the game is to get as many cards as possible into the output piles. Each time an Ace appears at the top of a pile or the top of the stack it is moved into the appropriate output pile. Cards are added to the output piles in sequence, the suit for each pile being determined by the Ace on the bottom.

From the rest of the deck, called the stock, cards are turned up one by one and placed face up on a waste pile. You may always play cards off the top of the waste pile, but only one at a time. Begin by moving a card from the stock to the top of the waste pile. If there is ever more than one possible play to be made, the following order must be observed:

i) Move a card from the top of a playing pile or from the top of the waste pile to an output pile. If the waste pile becomes empty, move a card from the stock to the waste pile.

ii) Move a card from the top of the waste pile to the leftmost playing pile to which it can be moved. If the waste pile becomes empty move a card from the stock to the waste pile.

iii) Find the leftmost playing pile which can be moved and place it on top of the leftmost playing pile to which it can be moved.

iv) Try i), ii) and iii) in sequence, restarting with i) whenever a move is made.

v) If no move is made via (i) - (iv) move a card from the stock to the waste pile and retry (i).

Only the topmost card of the playing piles or the waste pile may be played to an output pile. Once played on an output pile, a card may not be withdrawn to help elsewhere. The game is over when either

i) all the cards have been played to the output or

ii) the stock pile has been exhausted and no more cards can be moved.

When played for money, the player pays the house $52 at the beginning, and wins $5 for every card played to the output piles.

Write your program so that it will play several games, and determine your net winnings. Use a random number generator to shuffle the deck.

Output a complete record of two games in easily understood form. Include as output the number of games played and the net winnings (+ or −).

Chapter 4

LINKED LISTS

4.1 SINGLY LINKED LISTS

In the previous chapters, we studied the representation of simple data structures using an array and a sequential mapping. These representations had the property that successive nodes of the data object were stored a fixed distance apart. Thus, (i) if the element a_{ij} of a table was stored at location L_{ij}, then $a_{i,j+1}$ was at the location $L_{ij} + c$ for some constant c; (ii) if the i-th node in a queue was at location L_i, then the $(i + 1)$-th node was at location $L_i + c$ mod n for the circular representation; (iii) if the topmost node of a stack was at location L_T, then the node beneath it was at location $L_T - c$, etc. These sequential storage schemes proved adequate given the functions one wished to perform (access to an arbitrary node in a table, insertion or deletion of nodes within a stack or queue).

However, when a sequential mapping is used for ordered lists, operations such as insertion and deletion of arbitrary elements become expensive. For example, consider the following list of three - letter English words ending in AT:

(BAT, CAT, EAT, FAT, HAT, JAT, LAT MAT,

OAT, PAT, RAT, SAT, TAT, VAT, WAT)

To make this list complete we naturally want to add the word GAT, which means gun or revolver. If we are using an array to keep this list, then the insertion of GAT will require us to move elements already in the list either one location higher or lower. We must either move HAT, JAT, LAT, ..., WAT or else move BAT, CAT, EAT and FAT. If we have to do many such insertions into the middle, then neither alternative is attractive because of the amount of data movement. On the other hand, suppose we decide to remove the word LAT which refers to the Latvian monetary unit. Then again, we have to move many elements so as to maintain the sequential representation of the list.

When our problem called for several ordered lists of varying sizes, sequential representation again proved to be inadequate. By storing each list in a different array of maximum size, storage may be wasted. By maintaining the lists in a single array a potentially large amount of data movement is needed. This was explicitly observed when we represented several stacks, queues, polynomials and matrices. All these data objects are examples of ordered lists. Polynomials are ordered by exponent while matrices are ordered by rows and columns. In this chapter we shall present an alternate representation for ordered lists which will reduce the time needed for arbitrary insertion and deletion.

An elegant solution to this problem of data movement in *sequential* representations is achieved by using *linked* representations. Unlike a sequential representation where successive items of a list are located a fixed distance apart, in a linked representation these items may be placed anywhere in memory. Another way of saying this is that in a sequential representation the order of elements is the same as in the ordered list, while in a linked representation these two sequences need not be the same. To access elements in the list in the correct order, with each element we store the address or location of the next element in that list. Thus, associated with each data item in a linked representation is a pointer to the next item. This pointer is often referred to as a link. In general, a *node* is a collection of data, *data*1, ..., *datan* and links *link*1, ..., *linkm*. Each item in a node is called a *field*. A field contains either a data item or a link.

Figure 4.1 shows how some of the nodes of the list we considered before may be represented in memory by using pointers. The elements of the list are stored in a one dimensional array called *data*. But the elements no longer occur in sequential order, BAT before CAT before EAT, etc. Instead we relax this restriction and allow them to appear anywhere in the array and in any order. In order to remind us of the real order, a second array, *link*, is added. The values in this array are pointers to elements in the *data* array. Since the list starts at *data*[8] = BAT, let us set a variable $f = 8$. *link*[8] has the value 3, which means it points to *data*[3] which contains CAT. The third element of the list is pointed at by *link*[3] which is EAT. By continuing in this way we can list all the words in the proper order. We recognize that we have come to the end when *link* has a value of zero.

Some of the values of *data* and *link* are undefined such as data[2], link[2], data[5], link[5], etc. We shall ignore this for the moment.

It is customary to draw linked lists as an ordered sequence of nodes with links being represented by arrows as in figure 4.2. We shall use the name of the pointer variable that points to the list as the name of the entire list.

	data	link
1	HAT	15
2		
3	CAT	4
4	EAT	9
5		
6		
7	WAT	0
8	BAT	3
9	FAT	1
10		
11	VAT	7
	.	.
	.	.
	.	.

Figure 4.1 Non-Sequential List Representation.

Thus the list of figure 4.2 is the list f. Notice that we do not explicitly put in the values of the pointers but simply draw arrows to indicate they are there. This is so that we reinforce in our own mind the facts that (i) the nodes do not actually reside in sequential locations, and that (ii) the locations of nodes may change on different runs. Therefore, when we write a program which works with lists, we almost never look for a specific address except when we test for zero.

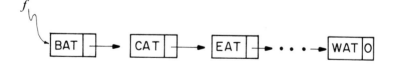

Figure 4.2 Usual Way to Draw a Linked List.

Let us now see why it is easier to make arbitrary insertions and deletions using a linked list rather than a sequential list. To insert the data item GAT between FAT and HAT the following steps are adequate:

(i)   get a node which is currently unused; let its address be x;
(ii)   set the *data* field of this node to GAT;

(iii) set the *link* field of *x* to point to the node after FAT which contains HAT;

(iv) set the *link* field of the node containing FAT to *x*.

Figure 4.3a shows how the arrays *data* and *link* will be changed

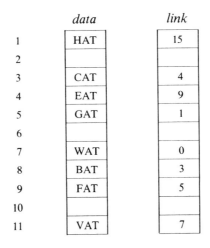

Figure 4.3(a) Insert GAT Into *data*[5].

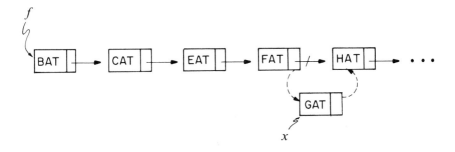

Figure 4.3(b) Insert Node GAT Into List.

after we insert GAT. Figure 4.3(b) shows how we can draw the insertion using our arrow notation. The new arrows are dashed. The important thing to notice is that when we insert GAT we do not have to move any elements which are already in the list. We have overcome the need to move data at the expense of the storage needed for the second field, *link*. But we will see that this is not too severe a penalty.

Now suppose we want to delete GAT from the list. All we need to do is find the element which immediately precedes GAT, which is FAT, and set *link*[9] to the position of HAT which is 1. Again, there is no need to move the data around. Even though the *link* field of GAT still contains a pointer to HAT, GAT is no longer in the list (see figure 4.4).

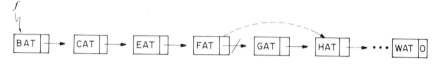

Figure 4.4   Delete GAT from List.

From our brief discussion of linked lists, we see that the following capabilities are needed to make linked representations possible:

(i)   A mechanism to define the structure of a node (i.e., the fields that it is composed of).

(ii)   A means to create nodes as needed.

(iii)   A way to free nodes that are no longer in use.

These capabilities are provided in the programming language Pascal. To define a node structure, we need to know the **type** of each of its fields. The data field in the above example is simply an array of characters while the *link* field is a pointer to another node. In Pascal, pointer types are defined as below:

type *pointertype* = ↑*nodetype*;

where *nodetype* refers to the type of nodes that the pointer may point to. So, if the type of the nodes in our earlier example is denoted by *threeletternode* then *ptr*, defined below, gives the type of the *link* field of the nodes.

type *ptr* = ↑*threeletternode*;

The data type *threeletternode* may itself be defined as a record as below:

type *threeletternode* = **record**
                    data: **array**[1..3] **of char**;
                    link: *ptr*;
                end;

Note that the variable *f* in the *threeletternode* example is also a pointer and its type is to be declared as below:

var *f* : *ptr*;

The fields of the node pointed to by *f* may be referenced in the following way:

f↑.*data*, *f*↑.*data*[1], *f*↑.*data*[2], *f*↑.*data*[3], *f*↑.*link*

This is shown diagramatically in figure 4.5.

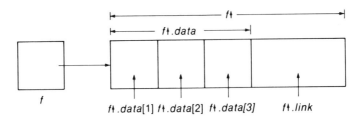

Figure 4.5.

Example 4.1: If a linked list is to consist of nodes that have a *data* field of type integer and a *link* field, the following type definition can be used:

type *pointer* = ↑*listnode*;
    listnode = **record**
                data: **integer**;
                link: *pointer*;
              end;

The type definition:

type *ptra* = ↑*nodea*;
    ptrb = ↑*nodeb*;
    nodea = **record**
                *data*1: **integer**;
                *data*2: **char**;
                *data*3: **real**;
                linka: *ptra*;
                linkb: *ptrb*;
              end;
    nodeb = **record**
                data: **integer**;
                link: *ptrb*;
                end;

defines the type *nodea* to consist of three data fields and two link fields while nodes of type *nodeb* will consist of one data field and one link field. Note that the *linkb* field of nodes of type *nodea* must point to nodes of type *nodeb*. □

Nodes of a predefined type may be created using the procedure *new*. If *f* is of type *ptr* then following the call *new(f)*, *f*↑ denotes the node (or variable) of type *threeletternode* that is created. Similarly, if *x*, *y*, and *z* are, respectively, of type *pointer*, *ptra*, and *ptrb* (cf. example 4.1), then following the sequence of calls:

new(x); *new(y)*; *new(z)*;

x↑, *y*↑, and *z*↑ will, respectively, denote the nodes of type *listnode*, *nodea*, and *nodeb* that are created. These nodes may be disposed as below:

dispose(f); *dispose(x)*; *dispose(y)*; *dispose(z)*;

Note that some implementations of Pascal do not provide a *dispose* function.

Pascal also provides a special constant **nil** that may be assigned to any pointer variable, regardless of type. This is generally used to denote a pointer field that points to no node (for example, the link field in the last node of figure 4.3b) or an empty list (as in $f = $ **nil**).

Arithmetic on pointer variables is not permitted. However, two pointer variables of the same type may be compared to see if both point to the same node. Thus if x and y are pointer variables of the same type then the expressions:

$x = y$, $x <> y$, $x = $ **nil**, and $x <> $ **nil**

are valid while the expressions:

$x + 1$ and $y * 2$

are invalid.

The effect of the assignments:

$x := y$ and $x↑ := y↑$

on the initial configuration of figure 4.6(a) is given in figures 4.6(b) and (c). Note also that pointer values may neither be input nor output. In many applications, these restrictions on the use of pointers create no difficulties.

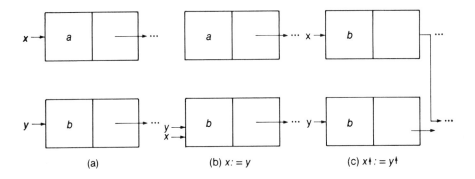

Figure 4.6.

In fact, in most applications, it does not even make sense to perform arithmetic on pointers. However, there are applications where we will want to perform arithmetic and/or input/output on pointers. We shall see applications where arithmetic on pointers is required in sections 4.7 and 4.9. Applications requiring input/output of pointer values will be seen in Chapters 8 and 10. When arithmetic and/or input/output on pointers is to be performed, we can implement our own pointer type by using integers. This is discussed in section 4.7.

Example 4.2: Procedure *create2* creates a linked list with two nodes of type *listnode* (cf. example 4.1). The *data* field of the first node is set to 10 and that of the second to 20. *first* is a pointer to the first node.

The resulting list structure is:

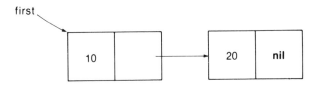

procedure *create2*(**var** *first : pointer*);
var *second: pointer*;
begin
  new(first);
  new(second);
  first↑.link := *second*; {link first node to second}
  second↑.link := **nil**; {last node}
  first↑.data := 10; {set data of first node}
  second↑.data := 20; {set data of second node}
end; {of create2}

Program 4.1   Create2

Example 4.3: Let *first* be a pointer to a linked list as in example 4.2. *first* = **nil** if the list is empty (i.e., there are no nodes on the list). Let *x* be a pointer to some arbitrary node in the list. The following procedure (Program 4.2) inserts a node with data field 50 following the node pointed at by *x*.

procedure *insert*(**var** *first : pointer*; *x : pointer*);
var *t: pointer*;
begin
  new(t); {get a new node}
  t↑.data := 50; {set its data field}
  if *first* = **nil**
  then begin {insert into empty list}
       first := *t*;
       t↑.link := **nil**;
    end
  else begin {insert after *x*}
      t↑.link := *x↑.link*;
      x↑.link := *t*;
    end;
end; {of insert}

Program 4.2   Insert

The resulting list structure for the two cases *first* = **nil** and *first* ≠ **nil** is:

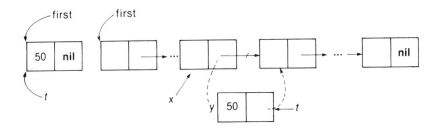

Example 4.4: Let *first* and *x* be as in example 4.3. Let *y* point to the node (if any) that precedes *x* and let *y* = **nil** if *x* = *first*. Procedure *delete* (Program 4.3) deletes node *x* from the list.

procedure *delete(x,y : pointer;* **var** *first : pointer);*
begin
  if *y* = **nil then** *first := first↑.link*
           else *y↑.link := x↑.link;*
  dispose(x); {return the node}
end; {of *delete*}

Program 4.3   Delete

4.2 LINKED STACKS AND QUEUES

We have already seen how to represent stacks and queues sequentially. Such a representation proved efficient if we had only one stack or one queue. However, when several stacks and queues co-exist, there was no efficient way to represent them sequentially. In this section we present a good solution to this problem using linked lists. Figure 4.7 shows a linked stack and a linked queue.

Notice that the direction of links for both the stack and queue are such as to facilitate easy insertion and deletion of nodes. In the case of figure 4.7(a), one can easily add a node at the top or delete one from the top. In figure 4.7(b), one can easily add a node at the rear and both addition and deletion can be performed at the front, though for a queue we normally would not wish to add nodes at the front. If we wish to represent *n* stacks

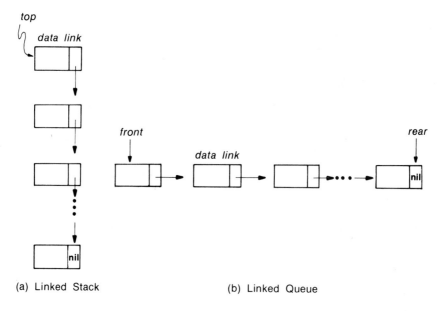

(a) Linked Stack   (b) Linked Queue

Figure 4.7.

and m queues simultaneously, then the set of algorithms (Programs 4.4-4.7) and initial conditions given below will serve our purpose.

Node and *pointer* are as defined below:

type *pointer* = ↑*node*;
     node = **record**
            data: **integer**;
            link: *pointer*;
        end;

The following global arrays of type *pointer* are used:

$top[i]$ = node at top of i-th stack, $1 \leq i \leq n$
$front[i]$ = node at front of i-th queue, $1 \leq i \leq m$
$rear[i]$ = last node in i-th queue, $1 \leq i \leq m$.

The initial conditions are:

$top[i]$ = **nil**, $1 \leq i \leq n$
$front[i]$ = **nil**, $1 \leq i \leq m$

and the boundary conditions are:

$top[i] = $ **nil** iff the i-th stack is empty
$front[i] = $ **nil** iff the i-th queue is empty

procedure $addstack(i,y : $ **integer**);
{add y to the i-th stack, $1 \leq i \leq n$}
var $x: pointer$;
begin
  $new(x)$; {get a node}
  $x\uparrow.data := y$; {sets its $data$ field}
  $x\uparrow.link := top[i]$; {attach to top of i-th stack}
  $top[i] := x$; {update stack $pointer$}
end; {of $addstack$}

Program 4.4 Add to a linked stack

procedure $deletestack(i : $ **integer**; **var** $y : $ **integer**);
{delete the top node from stack i and set y
to be its $data$ field, $1 \leq i \leq n$}
var $x: pointer$;
begin
  if $top[i] = $ **nil then** $stackempty$;
  $x := top[i]$;
  $y := x\uparrow.data$; {data field of top node}
  $top[i] := x\uparrow.link$; {remove top node}
  $dispose(x)$; {free the node}
end; {of $deletestack$}

Program 4.5 Delete from a linked stack

procedure $addqueue(i,y : $ **integer**);
{add y to queue i, $1 \leq i \leq m$}
var $x: pointer$;
begin
  $new(x)$;
  $x\uparrow.data := y$; $x\uparrow.link := $ **nil**;
  if $front[i] = $ **nil**
  then $front[i] := x$ {empty queue}
  else $rear[i]\uparrow.link := x$;
  $rear[i] := x$;
end; {of $addqueue$}

Program 4.6 Add to a linked queue

procedure *deletequeue*(*i* : **integer**; **var** *y* : **integer**);
{delete the first node in queue *i* and set *y*
to its *data* field, $1 \leq i \leq m$}
var *x*: *pointer*;
begin
  if *front*[*i*] = **nil then** *queueempty*;
  x := *front*[*i*];
  front[*i*] := *x*↑.*link*; {delete first node}
  y := *x*↑.*data*;
  dispose(*x*); {free the node}
end; {of *deletequeue*}

Program 4.7 Delete from a linked queue

The solution presented above to the *n*-stack, *m*-queue problem is seen to be both computationally and conceptually simple. There is no need to shift stacks or queues around to make space. Computation can proceed so long as there are free nodes. Though additional space is needed for the link fields, the cost is no more than a factor of 2. Sometimes the *data* field does not use the whole word and it is possible to pack the *link* and *data* fields into the same word. In such a case the storage requirements for sequential and linked representations would be the same. For the use of linked lists to make sense, the overhead incurred by the storage for the links must be overridden by: (i) the virtue of being able to represent complex lists in a simple way, and (ii) the computing time for manipulating the lists is less than for a sequential representation.

4.3 POLYNOMIAL ADDITION

Let us tackle a reasonable size problem using linked lists. This problem, the manipulation of symbolic polynomials, has become a classical example of the use of list processing. As in chapter 2, we wish to be able to represent any number of different polynomials as long as their combined size does not exceed our block of memory. In general, we want to represent the polynomial

$$A(x) = a_m x^{e_m} + \ldots + a_1 x^{e_1}$$

where the a_i are non-zero coefficients with exponents e_i such that $e_m > e_{m-1} > \ldots > e_2 > e_1 \geq 0$. Each term will be represented by a node. A node will be of fixed size having 3 fields which represent the coefficient and exponent of a term plus a pointer to the next term.

Assuming that all coefficients are integer, the required type declarations are:

type *polypointer* = ↑*polynode*;
  polynode = **record**
        coef: **integer**; {coefficient}
        exp: **integer**; {exponent}
        link: *polypointer*;
      end;

Polynodes will be drawn as below:

For instance, the polynomial $a = 3x^{14} + 2x^8 + 1$ would be stored as

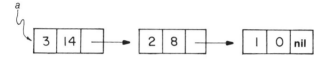

while $b = 8x^{14} - 3x^{10} + 10x^6$ would look like

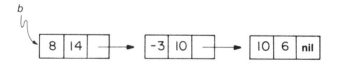

In order to add two polynomials together we examine their terms starting at the nodes pointed to by a and b. Two pointers p and q are used to move along the terms of a and b. If the exponents of two terms are equal, then the coefficients are added and a new term created for the result. If the exponent of the current term in a is less than the exponent of the current term of b, then a duplicate of the term of b is created and attached to c. The pointer q is advanced to the next term. Similar action is taken on a if $p\uparrow.exp > q\uparrow.exp$. Figure 4.8 illustrates this addition process on the polynomials a and b above.

Each time a new node is generated its *coef* and *exp* fields are set and it is appended to the end of the list c. In order to avoid having to search for the last node in c each time a new node is added, we keep a pointer d which points to the current last node in c. The complete addition algorithm is specified by the procedure *padd* (Program 4.9). *padd* makes use of a proce-

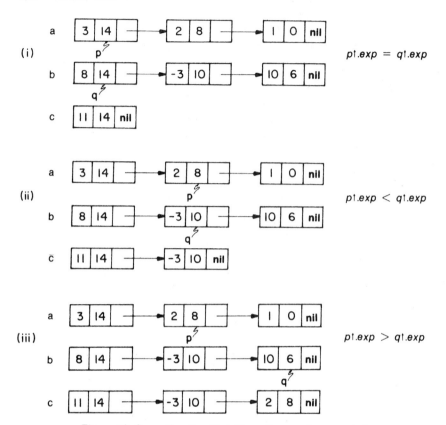

Figure 4.8 Generating the First Three Terms of $c = a + b$.

dure *attach* (Program 4.8), which creates a new node and appends it to the end of c. To make things work out neatly, c is initially given a single node with no values which is deleted at the end of the algorithm. Though this is somewhat inelegant, it avoids more computation. As long as its purpose is clearly documented, such a tactic is permissible.

```
procedure attach(c,e : integer; var d : polypointer);
{create a new node with coef = c, and exp = e and attach it to the node
pointed at by d. d is updated to point to this new node.}
var x: polypointer;
begin
    new(x);
    with x↑ do begin coef := c; exp := e; end;
    d↑.link := x;
    d := x; {d points to new last node}
end; {of attach}
```

Program 4.8 Attach a node to the end of a list

```
 1  procedure padd(a,b : polypointer; var c : polypointer);
 2  {polynomials a and b represented as singly linked lists
 3  are summed to form the new polynomial named c}
 4  var p,q,d: polypointer; x : integer;
 5  begin
 6    p := a; q := b; {p,q point to next term of a and b}
 7    new(c); d := c; {initial node for c, returned later}
 8    while (p <> nil) and (q <> nil) do
 9      case compare (p↑.exp, q↑.exp) of
10        '=': begin
11              x := p↑.coef + q↑.coef;
12              if x <> 0 then attach (x,p↑.exp,d);
13              p := p↑.link; q := q↑.link; {advance to next term}
14            end;
15        '<': begin
16              attach(q↑.coef, q↑.exp, d);
17              q := q↑.link; {next term of b}
18            end;
19        '>': begin
20              attach(p↑.coef, p↑.exp, d);
21              p := p↑.link; {next term of a}
22            end;
23      end; {of case and while}
24    while p <> nil do {copy rest of a}
25    begin
26      attach(p↑.coef, p↑.exp, d);
27      p := p↑.link;
28    end;
29    while q <> nil do {copy rest of b}
30    begin
31      attach(q↑.coef, q↑.exp, d);
32      q := q↑.link;
33    end;
34    d↑.link := nil; {last node}
35    {delete extra initial node}
36    p := c; c := c↑.link; dispose(p);
37  end; {of padd}
```

Program 4.9 Procedure to add two polynomials.

This is our first really complete example of the use of list processing, so it should be carefully studied. The basic algorithm is straightforward, using a merging process which streams along the two polynomials either copying terms or adding them to the result. Thus, the main **while** loop of lines 8-23 has 3 cases depending upon whether the next pair of exponents are $=$, $<$, or $>$. Notice that there are 5 places where a new term is created, justifying our use of the procedure *attach*.

Finally, some comments about the computing time of this algorithm. In order to carry out a computing time analysis it is first necessary to determine which operations contribute to the cost. For this algorithm there are several cost measures:

(i)   coefficient additions;
(ii)   coefficient comparisons;
(iii) additions/deletions to available space;
(iv)   creation of new nodes for c.

Let us assume that each of these four operations, if done once, takes a single unit of time. The total time taken by algorithm *padd* is then determined by the number of times these operations are performed. This number clearly depends on how many terms are present in the polynomials a and b. Assume that a and b have m and n terms respectively.

$$a(x) = a_m x^{e_m} + \ldots + a_1 x^{e_1}, \ b(x) = b_n x^{f_n} + \ldots + b_1 x^{f_1}$$

where

$$a_i, \ b_i \neq 0 \quad \text{and} \quad e_m > \ldots > e_1 \geq 0, \ f_n > \ldots > f_1 \geq 0.$$

Then clearly the number of coefficient additions can vary as

$$0 \leq \text{coefficient additions} \leq \min \ \{m, n\}.$$

The lower bound is achieved when none of the exponents are equal, while the upper bound is achieved when the exponents of one polynomial are a subset of the exponents of the other.

As for exponent comparisons, one comparison is made on each iteration of the **while** loop of lines 8-23. On each iteration either p or q or both move to the next term in their respective polynomials. Since the total number of terms is $m + n$, the number of iterations and hence the number of exponent comparisons is bounded by $m + n$. One can easily construct a case when $m + n - 1$ comparisons will be necessary: e.g. $m = n$ and

$$e_m > f_n > e_{m-1} > f_{n-1} > \ldots > f_2 > e_{n-m+2} > \ldots > e_1 > f_1.$$

The maximum number of terms in c is $m + n$, and so no more than $m + n$ new nodes are created (this excludes the additional node which is attached to the front of c and later returned). In summary then, the maximum number of executions of any of the statements in *padd* is bounded above by $m + n$. Therefore, the computing time is $O(m + n)$. This means that if the algorithm is implemented and run on a computer, the time taken will be $c_1m + c_2n + c_3$ where c_1,c_2,c_3 are constants. Since any algorithm that adds two polynomials must look at each nonzero term at least once, every algorithm must have a time requirement of $c'_1m + c'_2n + c'_3$. Hence, algorithm *padd* is optimal to within a constant factor.

The use of linked lists is well suited to polynomial operations. We can easily imagine writing a collection of procedures for input, output, addition, subtraction and multiplication of polynomials using linked lists as the means of representation. A hypothetical user wishing to read in polynomials $a(x)$, $b(x)$ and $c(x)$ and then compute $d(x) = a(x) * b(x) + c(x)$ would write in his main program:

read(a);
read(b);
read(c);
$t := pmul(a,b)$;
$d: = padd(t,c)$;
print(d);

Now our user may wish to continue computing more polynomials. At this point it would be useful to reclaim the nodes which are being used to represent $t(x)$. This polynomial was created only as a partial result towards the answer $d(x)$. By returning the nodes of $t(x)$, they may be used to hold other polynomials.

Procedure *erase* (Program 4.10) frees up the nodes in t one by one. It is possible to free all the nodes in t in a more efficient way by modifying the list structure in such a way that the *link* field of the last node points to the first node in t (see figure 4.9). A list in which the last node points back to the *first* is called a *circular* list. A singly linked list in which the last node has a **nil** link is called a *chain*.

```
procedure erase(var t : polypointer);
{free all the nodes in the chain t}
var x: polypointer;
begin
  while t <> nil do
  begin
    x := t↑.link;
    dispose(t);
    t := x;
  end;
end; {of erase}
```

Program 4.10: Erasing a chain.

Figure 4.9 Circular list representation of $t = 3x^{14} + 2x^8 + 1$.

The reason we dispose of nodes that are no longer in use is so that these nodes may be reused later. This objective, together with an efficient erase algorithm for circular lists, may be met by maintaining our own list (as a chain) of nodes that have been 'disposed.' When a new node is needed, we may examine this list. If this list is not empty, then one of the nodes on it may be made available for use. Only when this list is empty do we need to use procedure *new* to create a new node.

Let *av* be a variable of type *polypointer* that points to the first node in our list of nodes that have been 'disposed.' This list will henceforth be called the *available space list* or *av list*. Initially, *av* = **nil**. Instead of using the procedures *new* and *dispose*, we shall now use the procedures *getnode* (Program 4.11) and *ret* (Program 4.12).

```
procedure getnode(var x : polypointer);
{provide a node for use}
begin
  if av = nil
  then new(x)
  else begin x := av; av := av↑.link; end;
end; {of getnode}
```

Program 4.11 Getnode

```
procedure ret(x: polypointer);
{free the node pointed to by x}
begin
  x↑.link := av;
  av := x;
end; {of ret}
```

Program 4.12 Ret

A circular list may now be erased in a fixed amount of time independent of the number of nodes on the list. Procedure *cerase* (Program 4.13) does this.

procedure *cerase*(**var** *t* : *polypointer*);
{erase the circular list *t*}
var *x* : *polypointer*;
begin
  if *t* <> **nil**
  then begin
        x := *t↑.link*; {second node}
        t↑.link := *av*; {first node linked to *av*}
        av := *x*; {second node of *t* becomes front of *av* list}
        t := **nil** ;
      end;
end; {of *cerase*}

Program 4.13   Erasing a circular list

Figure 4.10 is a schematic showing the link changes involved in erasing a circular list.

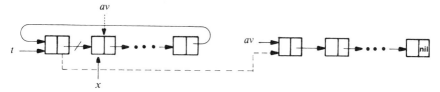

Figure 4.10   Dashes Indicate Changes Involved in Erasing a Circular List.

A direct changeover to the structure of figure 4.9, however, causes some problems during addition, etc., as the zero polynomial has to be handled as a special case. To avoid such special cases one may introduce a head node into each polynomial; i.e., each polynomial, zero or nonzero, will contain one additional node. The *exp* and *coef* fields of this node will not be relevant. Thus, the zero polynomial will have the representation:

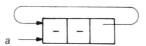

while $a = 3x^{14} + 2x^8 + 1$ will have the representation

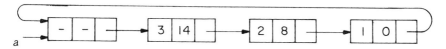

For this circular list with head node representation the test for *t* = **nil** may be removed from *cerase*. The only changes to be made to algorithm *padd* are:

(i)   change line 6 to: $p := a\uparrow.link$; $q := b\uparrow.link$;
(ii)   change line 8 to: **while** $(p <> a)$ **and** $(q <> b)$ **do**
(iii) change line 24 to: **while** $p <> a$ **do**
(iv)   change line 29 to: **while** $q <> b$ **do**
(v)   change line 36 to: $d\uparrow.link := c$;

Thus the algorithm stays essentially the same. Zero polynomials are now handled in the same way as nonzero polynomials.

A further simplification in the addition algorithm is possible if the *exp* field of the head node is set to -1. Now when all nodes of *a* have been examined $p = a$ and $exp(p) = -1$. Since $-1 \le exp(q)$ the remaining terms of *b* can be copied by further executions of the case statement. The same is true if all nodes of *b* are examined before those of *a*. This implies that there is no need for additional code to copy the remaining terms as in *padd*. The final algorithm (*cpadd*) takes the simple form given in Program 4.14.

```
procedure cpadd(a,b : polypointer; var c : polypointer);
{polynomials a and b are represented as circular lists with head nodes so
that a↑.exp = b↑.exp = −1. Their sum, c, is returned as a circular list.}
var p,q,d : polypointer; x : integer; done : boolean;
begin
  p := a↑.link; q := b↑.link;
  getnode (c); c↑.exp := −1; {head node for c}
  d := c; {last node in c}; done := false;
  repeat
    case compare(p↑.exp, q↑.exp) of
    '=': if p = a then done := true
         else begin
                x := p↑.coef + q↑.coef;
                if x <> 0 then attach(x, p↑.exp, d);
                p := p↑.link; q := q↑.link;
              end;
    '<': begin
           attach(q↑.coef, q↑.exp, d);
           q := q↑.link;
         end;
    '>': begin
           attach(p↑.coef, p↑.exp, d);
           p := p↑.link;
         end;
    end; {of case}
  until done;
  d↑.link := c; {link last node to first}
end; {of cpadd}
```

Program 4.14   Adding circularly represented polynomials

Let us review what we have done so far. We have introduced the notions of a singly linked list, a chain, and a singly linked circular list. Each node on one of these lists consists of exactly one link field and some number of other fields. In all of our examples, all nodes on any given list had the same fields. The concept of a singly linked list does not require this and in subsequent sections, we shall see lists that violate this property.

In dealing with polynomials, we found it convenient to use circular lists. This use required us to introduce the notion of an available space list. Such a list consists of all nodes that have been used at least once and are currently not in use. By using the available space list and the procedures *getnode*, *ret*, and *cerase*, it became possible to erase circular lists in constant time and also to reuse all nodes currently not in use. As we continue, we shall see more problems that call for variations in node structure and list representation because of the operations we wish to perform.

4.4   MORE ON LINKED LISTS

It is often necessary and desirable to build a variety of routines for manipulating singly linked lists. Some that we have already seen are: 1) *getnode* and 2) *ret* which get and return nodes to *av*. Another useful operation is one which inverts a chain. This routine is especially interesting because it can be done "in place" if we make use of 3 pointers.

procedure *invert*(**var** x : *pointer*);
{a chain pointed at by x is inverted so that if $x = (a_1, \ldots, a_n)$ then after execution $x = (a_n, \ldots, a_1)$}
var p,q,r : *pointer*;
begin
    $p := x$; $q := $ **nil**; {q trails p}
    while $p <> $ **nil do**
    begin
        $r := q$; $q := p$; {r trails q}
        $p := p\uparrow.link$; {p moves to next node}
        $q\uparrow.link := r$; {link q to preceding node}
    end;
    $x := q$;
end; {of *invert*}

Program 4.15   Invert a list

The reader should try this algorithm out on at least 3 examples: the empty list, and lists of length 1 and 2, to convince himself that he understands the mechanism. For a list of $m \geq 1$ nodes, the **while** loop is executed m times and so the computing time is linear or $O(m)$.

Another useful procedure is one which concatenates two chains x and y.

```
procedure concatenate(x,y : pointer; var z : pointer);
{x = (a₁,..., aₘ) and y = (b₁,..., bₙ), m,n ≥0
produces the new chain z = (a₁, ..., aₘ,b₁,..., bₙ)}
var p : pointer;
begin
  if x = nil
  then z := y
  else begin
         z := x;
         if y <> nil
         then begin {find last node in x}
                p := x;
                while p↑.link <> nil do p := p↑.link;
                p↑.link := y; {link last of x to first of y}
              end;
       end;
end; {of cancatenate}
```

Program 4.16 Concatenate

The complexity of this algorithm is also linear in the length of the list x.
Now let us take another look at circular lists like the one below:

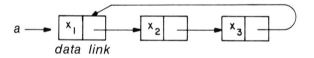

data link

$a = (x_1,x_2,x_3)$. Suppose we want to insert a new node at the front of this list. We have to change the *link* field of the node containing x_3. This requires that we move down the entire length of a until we find the last node. It is more convenient if the name of a circular list points to the last node rather than the first, for example:

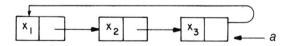

Now we can write procedures which insert a node at the front or at the rear of a circular list and take a fixed amount of time.

```
procedure insertfront(var a : pointer; x : pointer);
{insert the node pointed at by x at the front of the circular list a, where a
points to the last node in the list}
begin
  if a = nil
  then begin {empty list}
          a := x;
          x↑.link := x;
        end
  else begin
          x↑.link := a↑.link;
          a↑.link := x;
        end;
end; {of insertfront}
```

Program 4.17   Insert at the front

To insert x at the rear, one only needs to add the additional statement
$a := x$ to the **else** clause of *insertfront*.

As a last example of a simple procedure for circular lists, we write a function
which determines the length of such a list.

```
function length(a : pointer) : integer;
{find the length of the circular list a}
var x: pointer;
begin
  length := 0;
  if a <> nil
  then begin
          x := a;
          repeat
            length := length + 1;
            x := x↑.link;
          until x =a;
        end;
end; {of length}
```

Program 4.18   Length

4.5   EQUIVALENCE RELATIONS

Let us put together some of these ideas on linked and sequential representations to solve a problem which arises in the translation of computer languages,

the processing of equivalence relations. In FORTRAN one is allowed to share the same storage among several program variables through the use of the EQUIVALENCE statement. For example, the following pair of Fortran statements

DIMENSION $A(3)$, $B(2,2)$, $C(6)$

EQUIVALENCE $(A(2)$, $B(1,2)$, $C(4))$, $(A(1),D)$, (D,E,F), (G,H)

would result in the following storage assignment for these variables:

MEMORY

1			$C(1)$			
2		$B(1,1)$	$C(2)$			
3		$A(1)$	$B(2,1)$	$C(3)$	D	E	F
4		$A(2)$	$B(1,2)$	$C(4)$			
5		$A(3)$	$B(2,2)$	$C(5)$			
6			$C(6)$			
7		G	H			

As a result of the equivalencing of $A(2)$, $B(1,2)$ and $C(4)$, these were assigned the same storage word 4. This in turn equivalenced $A(1)$, $B(2,1)$ and $C(3)$, $B(1,1)$ and $C(2)$, and $A(3)$, $B(2,2)$ and $C(5)$. Because of the previous equivalence group, the equivalence pair $(A(1), D)$ also resulted in D sharing the same space as $B(2,1)$ and $C(3)$. Hence, an equivalence of the form $(D, C(5))$ would conflict with previous equivalences, since $C(5)$ and $C(3)$ cannot be assigned the same storage. Even though the sum of individual storage requirements for these variables is 18, the memory map shows that only 7 words are actually required because of the overlapping specified by the equivalence groups in the EQUIVALENCE statement. The functions to be performed during the processing of equivalence statements, then, are:
(i)   determine whether there are any conflicts;
(ii)   determine the total amount of storage required;
(iii) determine the relative address of all variables (i.e., the address of $A(1)$, $B(1,1)$, $C(1)$, D, E, F, G and H in the above example).
    In the text we shall solve a simplified version of this problem. The extension to the general FORTRAN equivalencing problem is fairly straightforward and appears as an exercise. We shall restrict ourselves to the case in which only

simple variables are being equivalenced and no arrays are allowed. For ease in processing, we shall assume that all equivalence groups are pairs of numbers (i,j) where if EQUIVALENCE(A,F) appears then i,j are the integers representing A and F. These can be thought of as the addresses of A and F in a symbol table. Furthermore, it is assumed that if there are n variables, then they are represented by the numbers 1 to n.

The FORTRAN statement EQUIVALENCE specifies a relationship among addresses of variables. This relation has several properties which it shares with other relations such as the conventional mathematical equals. Suppose we denote an arbitrary relation by the symbol $\equiv$ and suppose that:

(i)   For any variable x, $x \equiv x$, e.g. x is to be assigned the same location as itself. Thus $\equiv$ is *reflexive*.

(ii)   For any two variables x and y, if $x \equiv y$ then $y \equiv x$, e.g. assigning y the same location as x is the same as assigning x the same location as y. Thus, the relation $\equiv$ is *symmetric*.

(iii)   For any three variables x, y and z, if $x \equiv y$ and $y \equiv z$ then $x \equiv z$, e.g. if x and y are to be assigned the same location and y and z are also to be assigned the same location, then so also are x and z. The relation $\equiv$ is *transitive*.

Definition: A relation, $\equiv$, over a set S, is said to be an *equivalence relation* over S iff it is symmetric, reflexive and transitive over S.

Examples of equivalence relations are numerous. For example, the "equal to" ($=$) relationship is an equivalence relation since: (i) $x = x$, (ii) $x = y$ implies $y = x$, and (iii) $x = y$ and $y = z$ implies $x = z$. One effect of an equivalence relation is to partition the set S into equivalence classes such that two members x and y of S are in the same equivalence class iff $x \equiv y$. For example, if we have 12 variables numbered 1 through 12 and the following equivalences were defined via the EQUIVALENCE statement:

$$1 \equiv 5,\ 4 \equiv 2,\ 7 \equiv 11,\ 9 \equiv 10,\ 8 \equiv 5,\ 7 \equiv 9,\ 4 \equiv 6,\ 3 \equiv 12 \text{ and } 12 \equiv 1$$

then, as a result of the reflexivity, symmetry and transitivity of the relation $\equiv$, we get the following partitioning of the 12 variables into 3 equivalence classes:

$$\{1,\ 3,\ 5,\ 8,\ 12\};\ \{2,\ 4,\ 6\};\ \{7,\ 9,\ 10,\ 11\}.$$

So, only three words of storage are needed for the 12 variables. In order to solve the FORTRAN equivalence problem over simple variables, all one has to do is determine the equivalence classes. The number of equivalence classes is the number of words of storage to be allocated and the members of the same equivalence class are allocated the same word of storage.

The algorithm to determine equivalence classes works in essentially two phases. In the first phase the equivalence pairs (i,j) are read in and stored somewhere. In phase two we begin at one and find all pairs of the form $(1,j)$. The values 1 and j are in the same class. By transitivity, all pairs of the form (j,k) imply k is in the same class. We continue in this way until the entire equivalence class containing one has been found, marked and printed. Then we continue on.

The first design for this algorithm might go as in Program 4.19.

```
procedure equivalence;
begin
   initialize;
   while more pairs do
   begin
      read the next pair (i,j);
      process this pair;
   end;
   initialize for output;
   repeat
      output a new equivalence class;
   until done;
end; {of equivalence}
```

Program 4.19 First pass at equivalence algorithm

Let m and n represent the number of related pairs and the number of objects respectively. Now we need to determine which data structure should be used to hold these pairs. To determine this we examine the operations that are required. The pair (i,j) is essentially two random integers in the range 1 to n. Easy random access would dictate an array, say *pairs* $[1..n,1..m]$. The i-th row would contain the elements j which are paired directly to i in the input. However, this would potentially be very wasteful of space since very few of the array elements would be used. It might also require considerable time to insert a new pair, (i,k), into row i since we would have to scan the row for the next free location or use more storage.

These considerations lead us to consider a linked list to represent each row. Each node on the list requires only a *data* and a *link* field. However, we still need random access to the i-th row so a one dimensional array, *seq*$[1..n]$ can be used as the headnodes of the n lists. Looking at the second phase of the algorithm we need a mechanism which tells us whether or not object *i* has yet to be printed. A boolean array, *out*[1..*n*] can be used for this. Now we have the next refinement of the algorithm. This refinement assumes that *n* is a global constant.

```
procedure equivalence;
declare seq, out, and other local variables;
begin
    initialize seq to nil and out to true;
    while more pairs do {input pairs}
    begin
        read the next pair (i,j);
        put j on the seq[i] list;
        put i on the seq[j] list;
    end
    for i := 1 to n do {output equivalence classes}
        if out[i] then begin
                    out[i] := false;
                    output this equivalence class;
                  end;
end; {of equivalence}
```

Program 4.20 A more detailed version of equivalence algorithm

Let us simulate the algorithm as we have it so far, on the previous data set. After the **while** loop is completed the lists will look like this.

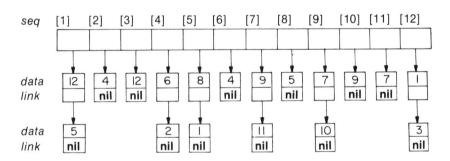

For each relation *i* ≡ *j*, two nodes are used. *seq*[*i*] points to a list of nodes which contains every number which is directly equivalenced to *i* by an input relation.

In phase two we can scan the *seq* array and start with the first *i*, 1 ≤ *i* ≤ *n* such that *out*[*i*] = **true**. Each element in the list *seq*[*i*] is printed. In order to process the remaining lists which, by transitivity, belong in the same class as *i*, a stack of their nodes is created. This is accomplished by changing the *link* fields so they point in the reverse direction. The complete procedure is given in program 4.21.

```
procedure equivalence;
{input the equivalence pairs and output the equivalence classes}
type pointer = ↑node;
     node = record
                data : 1..n;
                link : pointer;
            end;
var seq : array [1..n] of pointer;
    out : array [1..n] of boolean;
    i,j : integer;
    x,y,top : pointer;
    done: boolean;
begin
  {initialize seq and out}
  for i := 1 to n do begin seq[i] := nil; out[i] := true; end;
  {Phase 1: input equivalence pairs}
  while not eof(input) do
  begin
    readln(i,j);
    new(x); {add j to list seq[i]}
    x↑.data := j; x↑.link := seq[i]; seq[i] := x;
    new(x); {add i to list seq[j]}
    x↑.data := i; x↑.link := seq[j]; seq[j] := x;
  end;
  {Phase 2: output the equivalence classes}
  for i := 1 to n do
  if out [i] {needs to be output}
  then begin
          writeln('A new class:',i);
          out[i] := false;
          x := seq[i]; top := nil; {init stack} done := false;
          repeat {find rest of class}
            while x <> nil do {process the list}
            begin
              j := x↑.data;
              if out [j]
              then begin
```

```
            writeln(j);  out[j]  :=  false;
            y  :=  x↑.link;  x↑.link  :=  top;
            top  :=  x;  x  :=  y;
          end
      else  x  :=  x↑.link;
    end;  {of while  x <> nil}
    if  top  =  nil then  done  :=  true
    else  begin
            x  :=  seq[top↑.data];
            top  :=  top↑.link;  {unstack}
          end;
        until  done;
      end;  {of if}
end;  {of equivalence}
```

Program 4.21   Procedure to find equivalence classes

Analysis of Procedure *equivalence*

The initialization of *seq* and *out* takes $O(n)$ time. The processing of each input pair in phase 1 takes a constant amount of time. Hence, the total time for this phase is $O(m)$ where m is the number of pairs input. In phase 2 each node is put onto the linked stack at most once. Since there are only $2m$ nodes and the **for** loop is executed n times, the time for this phase is $O(m + n)$. Hence, the overall computing time is $O(m + n)$. Any algorithm which processes equivalence relations must look at all the m equivalence pairs and also at all the n variables at least once. Thus, there can be no algorithm with a computing time less than $O(m + n)$. This means that procedure *equivalence* is optimal to within a constant factor. Unfortunately, the space required by the algorithm is also $O(m + n)$. In chapter 5 we shall see an alternate solution to this problem which requires only $O(n)$ space.

4.6 SPARSE MATRICES

In Chapter 2, we saw that when matrices were sparse (i.e. many of the entries were zero), then much space and computing time could be saved if only the nonzero terms were retained explicitly. In the case where these nonzero terms did not form any "nice" pattern such as a triangle or a band, we devised a sequential scheme in which each nonzero term was represented by a node with three fields: row, column and value. These nodes were sequentially organized. However, as matrix operations such as addition, subtraction and multiplication are performed, the number of nonzero terms in matrices will vary, matrices representing partial computations (as in the case of polynomials) will be created and will have to be destroyed later on to make space for further matrices. Thus, sequential schemes for representing sparse matrices suffer from the same inadequacies as similar schemes for polynomials. In this section we shall study a very general linked list scheme for sparse matrix representation. As we have already seen, linked schemes facilitate efficient representation of varying size structures and here, too, our scheme will overcome the aforementioned shortcomings of the sequential representation studied in Chapter 2.

In the data representation we shall use, each column of a sparse matrix will be represented by a circularly linked list with a head node. In addition, each row will also be a circularly linked list with a head node.

Each node will have a field called *head*. This field will be used to distinguish between head nodes and nodes representing nonzero matrix elements. Each head node has three additional fields: *down*, *right*, and *next*. The total number of head nodes is max {number of rows, number of columns}. The head node for row i is also the head node for column i. The *down* field of a head node is used to link into a column list while the *right* field is used to link into a row list. The *next* field links the head nodes together.

Every other node has five additional fields: *row*, *col*, *down*, *right*, and *value* (figure 4.11). The *down* field is used to link to the next nonzero term in the same column and the *right* field links to the next nonzero term in the same row. Thus if $a_{ij} \neq 0$, then there is a node with *head* = **false**, *value* = a_{ij}, *row* = i, and *col* = j. This node is linked into the circular linked lists for row i and column j. Hence, it is simultaneously in two different lists.

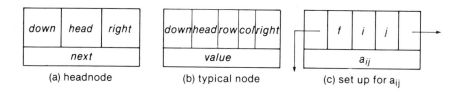

(a) headnode   (b) typical node   (c) set up for a_{ij}

Figure 4.11 Node structure for sparse matrices.

As remarked earlier, each head node is in three lists: a row list, a column list, and a list of head nodes. The list of head nodes itself has a head node which is identical to the six field nodes used to represent nonzero elements. The *row* and *col* fields of this node are used to store the matrix dimensions.

Figure 4.13 shows the linked structure obtained for the 6×7 matrix, A, of figure 4.12.

$$\begin{bmatrix} 0, & 0, & 11, & 0, & 0, & 13, & 0 \\ 12, & 0, & 0, & 0, & 0, & 0, & 14 \\ 0, & -4, & 0, & 0, & 0, & -8, & 0 \\ 0, & 0, & 0, & 0, & 0, & 0, & 0 \\ 0, & 0, & 0, & 0, & 0, & 0, & 0 \\ 0, & -9, & 0, & 0, & 0, & 0, & 0 \end{bmatrix}$$

Figure 4.12 6×7 sparse matrix A.

While figure 4.13 does not show the value of the *head* fields, these values are readily determined from the node structure shown. For each nonzero term of A, we have one six field node which is in exactly one column list and one row list. The head nodes are marked H1-H7. As can be seen from the figure, the *right* field of the head node list header is used to link into the list of head nodes. Notice that the whole matrix may be referenced through the head node, *a*, of the list of head nodes.

If we wish to represent an $n \times m$ sparse matrix with r nonzero terms, then the number of nodes needed is $\max\{n,m\} + r + 1$. While each node may require several words of memory, the total storage needed will be less than nm for sufficiently small r.

Having arrived at this representation for sparse matrices, let us see how to manipulate it to perform efficiently some of the common operations on matrices. But first, let us see how the required node structure may be defined in Pascal. This time, we need to use variant records as below:

```
type matrixpointer = ↑matrixnode
     matrixnode = record
                       down: matrixpointer;
                       right: matrixpointer;
                       case head: boolean of
                          true: (next : matrixpointer);
                          false: (value : integer;
                                  row: integer;
                                  col: integer);
                  end;
```

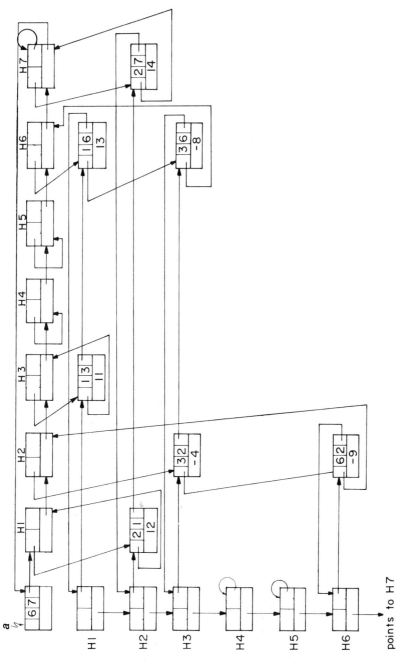

Figure 4.13 Linked Representation of the Sparse Matrix A. The *head* field of a node is not shown. Its value for each node should be clear from the node structure.

The first operation we shall consider is that of reading in a sparse matrix and obtaining its linked representation. We shall assume that the first input line consists of n (the number of rows), m (the number of columns), and r (the number of nonzero terms). This line is followed by r lines of input; each of these is a triple of the form (i,j,a_{ij}). These triples consist of the *row*, *col*, and *value* of the nonzero terms of the matrix. It is further assumed that these triples are ordered by rows and within rows by columns.

For example, the input for the 6×7 sparse matrix of figure 4.11, which has 7 nonzero terms, would take the form: 6,7,7;1,3,11;1,6,13;2,1,12;2,7,14; 3,2,–4;3,6,–8;6,2,–9. We shall not concern ourselves here with the actual format of this input on the input media (cards, disk, etc.) but shall just assume we have some mechanism to get the next triple (see the exercises for one possible input format). The procedure *mread* will also make use of an auxiliary array *hdnode*, which will be assumed to be at least as large as the largest dimensioned matrix to be input. *hdnode[i]* will be a pointer to the head node for column i, and hence also for row i. This will permit us to efficiently access columns at random while setting up the input matrix. Procedure *mread* (Program 4.22) proceeds by first setting up all the head nodes and then setting up each row list, simultaneously building the column lists. The *next* field of headnode i is initially used to keep track of the last node in column i. Eventually, in line 39, the headnodes are linked together through this field.

Analysis of Algorithm MREAD

Since *new* works in a constant amount of time, all the head nodes may be set up in $O(\max\{n,m\})$ time, where n is the number of rows and m the number of columns in the matrix being input. Each nonzero term can be set up in a constant amount of time because of the use of the variable *last* and a random access scheme for the bottommost node in each column list. Hence, the **for** loop of lines 19–33 can be carried out in $O(r)$ time. The rest of the algorithm takes $O(\max\{n,m\})$ time. The total time is therefore $O(\max\{n,m\} + r) = O(n + m + r)$. Note that this is asymptotically better than the input time of $O(nm)$ for an $n \times m$ matrix using a two dimensional array, but slightly worse than the sequential sparse method of section 2.3.

Before closing this section, let us take a look at an algorithm to return all nodes of a sparse matrix. These nodes may be returned one at a time using *dispose*. A faster way to return the nodes is to set up an available space list as was done in section 4.3 for polynomials. Assume that *av* points to the front of this list and that this list is linked through the field *right*. Procedure *merase* (Program 4.23) solves our problem in an efficient way.

```
 1  procedure mread (var a : matrixpointer);
 2  {read in a matrix and set up its linked representation.
 3   An auxiliary global array hdnode is used}
 4  var i,m,n,p,r,rrow,ccol,val,currentrow : integer;
 5      x,last : matrixpointer;
 6  begin
 7    readln(n,m,r); {matrix dimensions}
 8    if m > n then p := m else p := n;
 9    {set up head node for list of head nodes}
10    new(a); a↑.head := false; a↑.row := n; a↑.col := m;
11    if p = 0 then a↑.right := a
12            else begin
13    for i := 1 to p do {initialize head nodes}
14    begin
15      new(x); hdnode [i] := x;
16      with x↑  do begin head := true; right := x; next := x; end;
17    end;
18    currentrow := 1; last := hdnode [1]; {last node in current row}
19    for i := 1 to r do {input triples}
20    begin
21      readln(rrow,ccol,val);
22      if rrow > currentrow
23      then begin {close current row}
24              last↑.right := hdnode[currentrow];
25              currentrow := rrow; last := hdnode[rrow];
26          end;
27      new (x); {node for new triple}
28      with x↑ do begin head := false; row :=rrow; col := ccol; value := val;
29              end;
30      last↑.right :=x; last := x; {link into row list}
31      {link into column list}
32      hdnode[ccol]↑.next↑.down := x; hdnode[ccol]↑.next := x;
33    end; {of input triples}
34    {close last row}
35    if r > 0 then last↑.right := hdnode[currentrow];
36    for i := 1 to m do {close all column lists}
37      hdnode[i]↑.next↑.down := hdnode[i];
38    {link the head nodes together}
39    for i := 1 to p − 1 do hdnode[i]↑.next := hdnode [i + 1];
40    hdnode[p]↑.next := a;
41    a↑.right := hdnode[1];
42  end; {of mread}
```

Program 4.22   Read in a sparse matrix.

procedure *merase* (**var** *a* : *matrixpointer*);
{Return all nodes of *a* to the *av* list. This list is a chain linked
via the *right* field. *av* points to its first node.}
var *x,y* : *matrixpointer*;
begin
   x := *a↑.right*; *a↑.right* := *av*; *av* := *a*; {return *a*}
   while *x* <> *a* **do** {erase by rows}
   begin
     y := *x↑.right*;
     x↑.right := *av*;
     av := *y*;
     x := *x↑.next*; {next row}
   end;
  a := **nil**;
end; {of *merase*}

Program 4.23 Erasing a sparse matrix.

Analysis of Procedure *merase*

Since each node is in exactly one row list, it is sufficient to just return all the row lists of the matrix *a*. Each row list is circularly linked through the field *right*. Thus, nodes need not be returned one by one as a circular list can be erased in a constant amount of time. The computing time for the algorithm is readily seen to be $O(n + m)$. Note that even if the available space list had been linked through the field *down*, then erasing could still have been carried out in $O(n + m)$ time. The subject of manipulating these matrix structures is studied further in the exercises. The representation studied here is rather general. For most applications this generality is not needed. A simpler representation resulting in simpler algorithms is discussed in the exercises.

4.7 DOUBLY LINKED LISTS AND DYNAMIC STORAGE MANAGEMENT

So far we have been working chiefly with singly linked linear lists. For some problems these would be too restrictive. One difficulty with these lists is that if we are pointing to a specific node, say p, then we can easily move only in the direction of the links. The only way to find the node which precedes p is to start back at the beginning of the list. The same problem arises when one wishes to delete an arbitrary node from a singly linked list. As can be seen from example 4.4, in order to easily delete an arbitrary node one must know the preceding node. If we have a problem where moving in either direction is often necessary, then it is useful to have doubly linked lists. Each node now has two link fields, one linking in the forward direction and one in the backward direction.

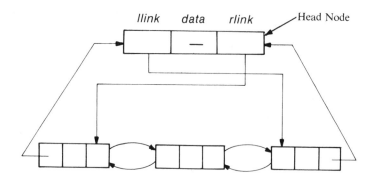

Figure 4.14 Doubly Linked Circular List with Head Node.

A node in a doubly linked list has at least 3 fields, say *data*, *llink* (left link) and *rlink* (right link). A doubly linked list may or may not be circular. A sample doubly linked circular list with 3 nodes is given in figure 4.14. Besides these three nodes a special node has been added called a head node. As was true in the earlier sections, head nodes are again convenient for the algorithms. The *data* field of the head node will not usually contain information. Now suppose that p points to any node in a doubly linked list. Then it is the case that

$$p = p\uparrow.llink\uparrow.rlink = p\uparrow.rlink\uparrow.llink$$

This formula reflects the essential virtue of this structure, namely, that one can go back and forth with equal ease. An empty list is not really empty since it will always have its head node and it will look like

Now to work with these lists we must be able to insert and delete nodes. Procedure *ddelete* (Program 4.24) deletes node x from list l. x now points to a node which is no longer part of the list l. Figure 4.15 shows how the method works on a doubly linked list with only a single node. Even though the *rlink* and *llink* fields of node x still point to the head node, this node has effectively been removed as there is no way to access x through l.

procedure *ddelete* (*x,l* : *dpointer*);
begin
   if *x* = *l* **then** *nomorenodes*; {empty list}
   x↑.llink↑.rlink := *x↑.rlink*;
   x↑.rlink↑.llink := *x↑.llink*;
   dispose(*x*);
end; {of *ddelete*}

Program 4.24   Deleting from a doubly linked circular list.

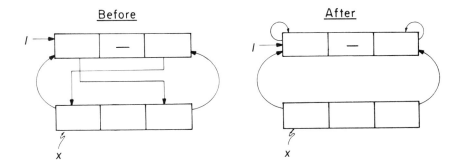

Figure 4.15.

Insertion is only slightly more complex (Program 4.25).

procedure *dinsert* (*p*, *x* : *dpointer*);
{insert node *p* to the right of node *x*}
begin
   p↑.llink := *x*; *p↑.rlink* := *x↑.rlink*;
   x↑.rlink↑.llink := *p* ; *x↑.rlink* := *p*;
end; {of *dinsert*}

Program 4.25   Insertion into a doubly linked circular list.

We shall now see an important problem from operating systems which is
nicely solved by the use of doubly linked lists.

Dynamic Storage Management

In a multiprocessing computer environment, several programs reside in memory at the same time. Different programs have different memory requirements. Thus, one program may require 60K of memory, another 100K, and yet another program may require 300K. Whenever the operating system needs to request memory, it must be able to allocate a block of contiguous storage of the right size. When the execution of a program is complete, it releases or frees the memory block allocated to it and this freed block may now be allocated to another program. In a dynamic environment the request sizes that will be made are not known ahead of time. Moreover, blocks of memory will, in general, be freed in some order different from that in which they were allocated. At the start of the computer system no jobs are in memory and so the whole memory, say of size m words, is available for allocation to programs. Now, jobs are submitted to the computer and requests are made for variable size blocks of memory. Assume we start off with 100,000 words of memory and five programs, $P1$, $P2$, $P3$, $P4$, and $P5$ make requests of size 10,000, 15,000, 6,000, 8,000 and 20,000, respectively. Figure 4.16 indicates the status of memory after storage for $P5$ has been allocated. The unshaded area indicates the memory that is currently not in use. Assume that programs $P4$ and $P2$ complete execution, freeing the memory used by them. Figure 4.17 shows the status of memory after the blocks for $P2$ and $P4$ are freed. We now have three blocks of contiguous memory that are in use and another three that are free. In order to make further allocations, it is necessary to keep track of those blocks that are not in use. This problem is similar to the one encountered in the previous sections where we had to maintain a list of all free nodes. The difference between the situation then and the one we have now is that the free space consists of variable size blocks or nodes and that a request for a block of memory may now require allocation of only a portion of a node rather than the whole node. One of the functions of an operating system is to maintain a list of all blocks of storage currently not in use and then to allocate storage from this unused pool as required. One can once again adopt the chain structure used earlier to maintain the available sapce list. Now, in addition to linking all the free blocks together, it is necessary to retain information regarding the size of each block in this list of free nodes. Thus, each node on the free list has two fields in its first word, i.e., *size* and *link*. Figure 4.18 shows the free list corresponding to figure 4.17. The use of a head node simplifies later algorithms.

Note, however, that the storage management problem cannot be solved by defining a data type *block* with the fields *size*, *link*, and *usablespace*. This is so for the following reasons:

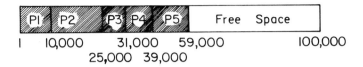

Figure 4.16 Memory after Allocation to P1-P5

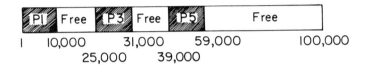

Figure 4.17 Status of Memory After Completion of P2 and P4.

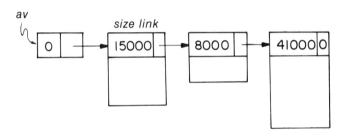

Figure 4.18 Free List with Head Node Corresponding to figure 4.17.

1. Different blocks are of different size.
2. We do not know how the usable space in each block is to be used. In general, this space will hold programs as well as data of varying type.
3. The use of a particular word in memory will change with time as this word will be a part of several different blocks as blocks continue to get allocated and freed.

Furthermore, the *link* field cannot be implemented as a Pascal pointer because the location of these fields in memory is not known and changes in time. In addition, we shall shortly see that in this application it does make sense to perform arithmetic on the link fields. In fact, without this capability, we shall have to sacrifice performance significantly.

Thus, the available memory to be managed is regarded simply as a one dimensional array of words. The array is indexed 1 through m. Each word is just a sequence of bits. We shall use the following procedures and functions to set and extract the *size* and *link* field of words:

setsize(i,j) .. set the *size* field of word *i* to *j*
setlink(i,j) .. set the *link* field of word *i* to *j*
size(i) .. extract the value in the *size* field of word *i*
link(i) .. extract the value in the *link* field of word *i*

Note that the *link* field contains an integer which is the index of the first word in the next block on the available space list. If there is no next block, then *link* = 0.

If we now receive a request for a block of memory of size *n*, then it is necessary to search down the list of free blocks finding the first block of size $\geq$ *n* and allocating *n* words out of this block. Such an allocation strategy is called *first fit*. Procedure *firstfit* (Program 4.26) makes storage allocations using the first fit strategy. An alternate strategy, *best fit*, calls for finding a free block whose size is as close to *n* as possible, but not less than *n*. This strategy is examined in the exercises.

```
procedure firstfit (n : integer; var p : integer);
{Allocate a block of size n using first fit. p is set to 0
 if there is no block large enough, otherwise p is the
 start of the allocated block.}
var q : integer; notdone : boolean;
begin
   p := link(av); q := av; {q trails p} notdone := true;
   while (p <> 0) and notdone  do {examine free blocks}
      if size(p) > = n {block large enough}
      then begin {allocate from this block}
              setsize(p, size(p) − n);
              if size(p) = 0 {allocate whole block}
              then setlink(q, link(p))
              else p := p + size(p); {allocate last n words}
              notdone := false;
           end
      else begin
              q := p; p := link(p); {next block}
           end; {of if and while}
end; {of firstfit}
```

Program 4.26   First fit allocation.

This procedure is simple enough to understand. In case only a portion of a free block is to be allocated, the allocation is made from the bottom of the block. This avoids changing any links in the free list unless an entire block is allocated. There are, however, two major problems with *firstfit*. First, experiments have shown that after some processing time many small nodes are left in the available space list, these nodes being smaller than any requests that would be made. Thus, a request for 9900 words allocated from a block of size 10,000 would leave behind a block of size 100, which may be smaller than any requests that will be made to the system. Retaining these small nodes on the available space list tends to slow down the allocation process as the time needed to make an allocation is proportional to the number of nodes on the available space list. To get around this, we choose some suitable constant ϵ such that if the allocation of a portion of a node leaves behind a node of size $<_\epsilon$, then the entire node is allocated. I.e., we allocate more storage than requested in this case. The second problem arises from the fact that the search for a large enough node always begins at the front of the list. As a result of this, all the small nodes tend to collect at the front so that it is necessary to examine several nodes before an allocation for larger blocks can be made. In order to distribute small nodes evenly along the list, one can begin searching for a new node from a different point in the list each time a request is made. To implement this, the available space list is maintained as a circular list with a head node of size zero. *av* now points to the last node from which an allocation was made. We shall see what the new allocation algorithm looks like after we discuss what has to be done to free a block of storage.

The second operation is the freeing of blocks or returning nodes to *av*. Not only must we return the node but we also want to recognize if its neighbors are also free so that they can be coalesced into a single block. Looking back at figure 4.18, we see that if *P3* is the next program to terminate, then rather than just adding this node onto the free list to get the free list of figure 4.19, it would be better to combine the adjacent free blocks corresponding to *P2* and *P4*, obtaining the free list of figure 4.20. This combining of adjacent free blocks to get bigger free blocks is necessary. The block allocation algorithm splits big blocks while making allocations. As a result, available block sizes get smaller and smaller. Unless recombination takes place at some point, we will no longer be able to meet large requests for memory.

With the structure we have for the available space list, it is not easy to determine whether blocks adjacent to the block (n,p) (n = size of block and p = starting location) being returned are free. The only way to do this, at present, is to examine all the nodes in *av* to determine whether:

(i) the left adjacent block is free, i.e., the block ending at $p - 1$;

(ii) the right adjacent block is free, i.e., the block beginning at $p + n$.

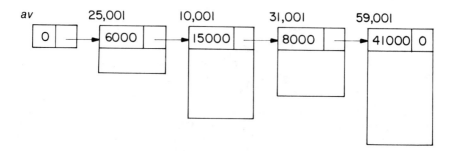

Figure 4.19   Available Space List When Adjacent Free Blocks Are Not Coalesced.

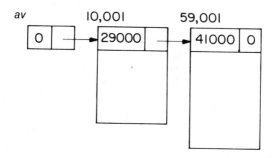

Figure 4.20   Available Space List When Adjacent Free Blocks are Coalesced.

In order to determine (i) and (ii) above without searching the available space list, we adopt the node structure of figure 4.21 for allocated and free nodes.

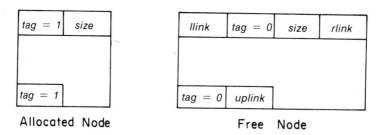

Figure 4.21.

The first and last words of each block are reserved for allocation information. The first word of each free block has four fields: *llink, rlink, tag* and *size*. Only the *tag* and *size* field are important for a block in use. The last word in each free block has two fields: *tag* and *uplink*. Only the *tag* field is important for a block in use. Now by just examining the tags at $p - 1$ and $p + n$ one can determine whether the adjacent blocks are free. The *uplink* field of a free block points to the start of the block. The available space list will now be a doubly linked circular list, linked through the fields *llink* and *rlink*. It will have a head node with *size* = 0. A doubly linked list is needed, as the return block algorithm will delete nodes at random from *av*. The need for *uplink* will become clear when we study the freeing algorithm. Since the first and last nodes of each block have *tag* fields, this system of allocation and freeing is called the *Boundary Tag method*. It should be noted that the *tag* fields in allocated and free blocks occupy the same bit position in the first and last words, respectively. This is not obvious from figure 4.21 where the *llink* field precedes the *tag* field in a free node. The labeling of fields in this figure has been done so as to obtain clean diagrams for the available space list. The algorithms we shall obtain for the boundary tag method will assume that memory is numbered 1 to m and that $tag\,(0) = tag\,(m + 1) = 1$. This last requirement will enable us to free the block beginning at 1 and the one ending at m without having to test for these blocks as special cases. Such a test would otherwise have been necessary as the first of these blocks has no left adjacent block while the second has no right adjacent block. While the *tag* information is all that is needed in an allocated block, it is customary to also retain the size in the block. Hence, figure 4.21 also includes a *size* field in an allocated block.

Before presenting the allocate and free algorithms let us study the initial condition of the system when all of memory is free. Assuming memory begins at location 1 and ends at m, the *av* list initially looks as in figure 4.22.

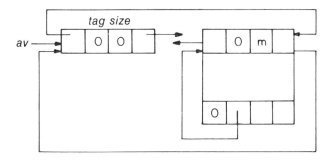

Figure 4.22.

The allocate and free procedures (Programs 4.27 and 4.28) use the following functions and procedures. The implementation of these is left unspecified.

setxyz(i,j)...set the *xyz* field of word *i* to *j*
xyz(i)...extract the value in the *xyz* field of word *i*

```
1   procedure allocate(n : integer; var p : integer);
2   {Use next fit to allocate a block of size at least n.
3    No blocks of size < eps are retained on the av list.
4    p is set as in procedure firstfit.}
5   label 99;
6   var diff: integer;
7   begin
8       p := rlink(av); {start search at p}
9       repeat
10          if size(p) >= n {block large enough} then
11          begin
12              diff := size(p) - n;
13              if diff < eps {allocate whole block}
14              then begin
15                      setrlink(llink(p), rlink(p)); {delete from list}
16                      setllink(rlink(p), llink(p));
17                      settag(p,1); settag(p + size(p) - 1,1);
18                      av := llink(p); {start next search here}
19                      goto 99;
20                  end
21              else begin {allocate last n words}
22                      setsize(p,diff); setuplink(p + diff - 1, p);
23                      settag(p + diff - 1,0); av := p;
24                      p := p + diff; setsize(p,n);
25                      settag(p, 1); settag(p + n - 1,1);
26                      goto 99;
27                  end;
28          end;
29          p := rlink(p); {examine next block}
30      until p = rlink(av);
31      p := 0; {no block large enough}
32  99: end; {of allocate}
```

Program 4.27   Allocate using next fit.

While the allocate and free procedures (Programs 4.27 and 4.28) may appear complex, they are a direct consequence of the doubly linked list structure of the available space list and also of the node structure in use. Notice that the use of a head node eliminates the test for an empty list in both algorithms and hence simplifies them. The use of circular linking makes it easy to start the search for a large enough node at any point in the available space list. The *uplink* field in a free block is needed only when returning a block whose left adjacent block is free (see lines 16 and 37 of procedure *free*). In lines 31 and 40 *av* is changed so that it always points to the start of a free block rather than into the middle of a free block. One may readily verify that the algorithms work for special cases such as when the available space list contains only the head node.

The best way to understand the algorithms is to simulate an example. Let us start with a memory of size 5000 from which the following allocations are made: $r_1 = 300$, $r_2 = 600$, $r_3 = 900$, $r_4 = 700$, $r_5 = 1500$ and $r_6 = 1000$. At this point the memory configuration is as in figure 4.23. This figure also depicts the different blocks of storage and the available space list. Note that when a portion of a free block is allocated, the allocation is made from the bottom of the block so as to avoid unnecessary link changes in the *av* list. First block r_1 is freed. Since $tag(5001) = tag(4700) = 1$, no coalescing takes place and the block is inserted into the *av* list (figure 4.24(a)). Next, block r_4 is returned. Since both its left adjacent block (r_5) and its right adjacent block (r_3) are in use at this time ($tag(2500) = tag(3201) = 1$), this block is just inserted into the free list to get the configuration of figure 4.24(b). Block r_3 is next returned. Its left adjacent block is free, $tag(3200) = 0$; but its right adjacent block is not, $tag(4101) = 1$. So this block is just attached to the end of its adjacent free block without changing any link fields (figure 4.24(c)). Block r_5 next becomes free. $tag(1000) = 1$ and $tag(2501) = 0$ and so this block is coalesced with its right adjacent block which is free and inserted into the spot previously occupied by this adjacent free block (figure 4.24(d)). r_2 is freed next. Both its upper and lower adjacent blocks are free. The upper block is deleted from the free space list and combined with r_2. This bigger block is now just appended to the end of the free block made up of r_3, r_4 and r_5 (figure 4.24(e)).

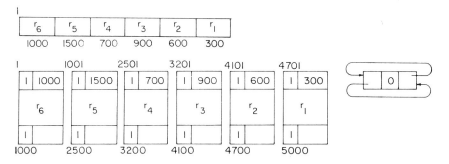

Figure 4.23.

```
 1  procedure free(p : integer);
 2  {return a block beginning at p and of size size(p)}
 3  var n,q : integer;
 4  begin
 5      n := size(p);
 6      if (tag(p − 1) = 1) and (tag(p + n) = 1)
 7      then begin {both adjacent blocks in use}
 8              settag(p,0); settag(p+ n − 1,0); {free the block}
 9              setuplink(p + n − 1,p);
10              {insert at right of av}
11              setllink(p, av); setrlink(p,rlink(av));
12              setllink(rlink(p),p); setrlink(av,p);
13          end
14      else if (tag(p + n) = 1) and (tag(p − 1) = 0)
15          then begin {only left block free}
16                  q := uplink(p − 1); {start of left block}
17                  setsize(q, size(q) + n);
18                  setuplink(p + n − 1,q); settag(p + n − 1,0);
19              end
20          else if (tag(p + n) = 0) and (tag(p − 1) = 1)
21              then begin {only right block free}
22                      {replace block beginning at p + n by
23                      one beginning at p}
24                      setrlink(llink(p + n), p);
25                      setlink(rlink(p + n), p);
26                      setllink(p, llink(p + n));
27                      setrlink(p, rlink(p + n));
28                      setsize(p,n + size(p + n));
29                      setuplink(p + size(p) − 1, p);
30                      settag(p,0);
31                      av := p;
32                  end
33              else begin {both adjacent blocks free}
34                      {delete right block from av list}
35                      setrlink(llink(p + n),rlink(p + n));
36                      setllink(rlink(p + n),llink(p + n));
37                      q := uplink(p − 1);
38                      setsize(q, size(q) + n + size(p +n)):
39                      setuplink(q + size(q) − 1,q);
40                      av := llink(p + n);
41                  end;
42  end; {of free}
```

Program 4.28   Free a block using boundary tags.

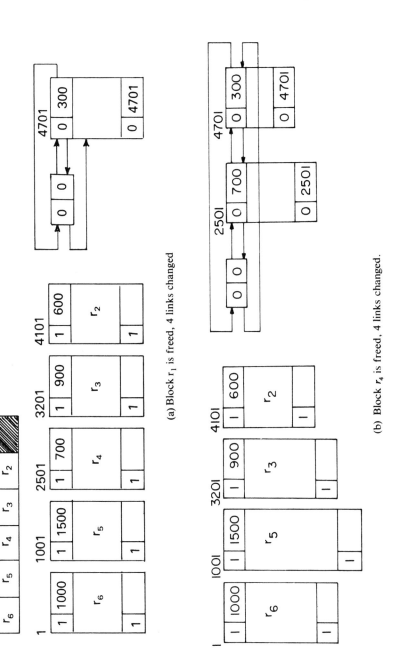

(a) Block r_1 is freed, 4 links changed

(b) Block r_4 is freed, 4 links changed.

Figure 4.24 Freeing of Blocks in Boundary Tag System.

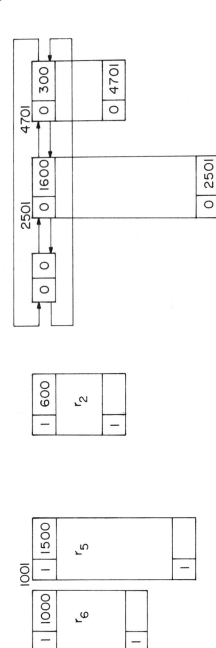

(c) Block r_3 is freed, no links changed.

Figure 4.24   Freeing of Block in Boundary Tag System (contd.).

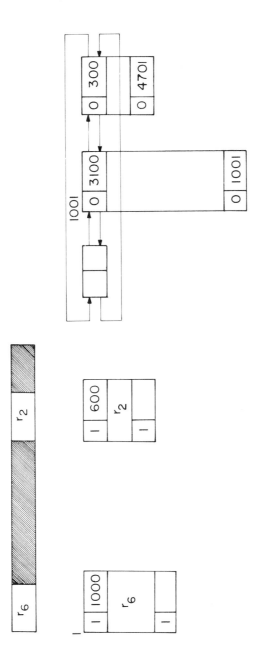

(d) Block r_5 freed, 4 links set

Figure 4.24   Freeing of Block in Boundary Tag System (contd.).

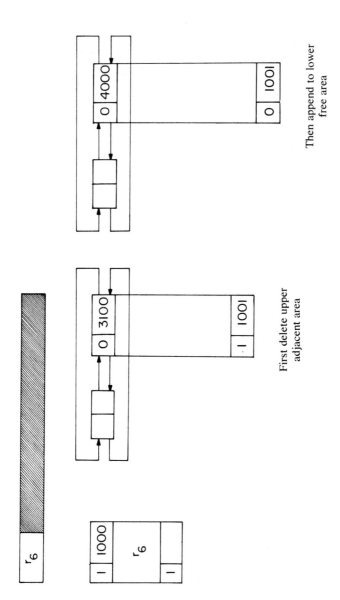

First delete upper
adjacent area

Then append to lower
free area

(e) Block r_2 is freed, 2 links changed

Figure 4.24 Freeing of Blocks in Boundary Tag System (contd.).

As for the computational complexity of the two algorithms, one may readily verify that the time required to free a block of storage is independent of the number of free blocks in *av*. Freeing a block takes a constant amount of time. In order to accomplish this we had to pay a price in terms of storage. The first and last words of each block in use are reserved for *tag* information. Though additional space is needed to maintain *av* as a doubly linked list, this is of no consequence as all the storage in *av* is free in any case. The allocation of a block of storage still requires a search of the *av* list. In the worst case all free blocks may be examined.

An alternative scheme for storage allocation, the Buddy System, is investigated in the exercises.

4.8   GENERALIZED LISTS

In Chapter 3, a linear list was defined to be a finite sequence of $n \geq 0$ elements, $\alpha_1, \ldots, \alpha_n$, which we write as $A = (\alpha_1, \ldots, \alpha_n)$. The elements of a linear list are restricted to be atoms and thus the only structural property a linear list has is the one of position, i.e. α_i precedes α_{i+1}, $1 \leq i < n$. It is sometimes useful to relax this restriction on the elements of a list, permitting them to have a structure of their own. This leads to the notion of a generalized list in which the elements α_i, $1 \leq i \leq n$ may be either atoms or lists.

Definition: A *generalized list, A,* is a finite sequence of $n \geq 0$ elements, $\alpha_1, \ldots, \alpha_n$ where the α_i are either atoms or lists. The elements α_i, $1 \leq i \leq n$ which are not atoms are said to be the *sublists* of *A*.

The list *A* itself is written as $A = (\alpha_1, \ldots, \alpha_n)$. *A* is the *name* of the list $(\alpha_1, \ldots, \alpha_n)$ and *n* its *length*. By convention, all list names will be represented by capital letters. Lower case letters will be used to represent atoms. If $n \geq 1$, then α_1 is the *head* of *A* while $(\alpha_2, \ldots, \alpha_n)$ is the *tail* of *A*.

The above definition is our first example of a recursive definition so one should study it carefully. The definition is recursive because within our description of what a list is, we use the notion of a list. This may appear to be circular, but it is not. It is a compact way of describing a potentially large and varied structure. We will see more such definitions later on. Some examples of generalized lists are:

(i) $D = (\ )$ the null or empty list; its length is zero.
(ii) $A = (a, (b,c))$ a list of length two; its first element is the atom '*a*' and its second element is the linear list (b,c).

(iii) $B = (A,A,(\ ))$ a list of length three whose first two elements are the list A, the third element the null list.

(iv) $C = (a,\ C)$ a recursive list of length two. C corresponds to the infinite list $C = (a,(a,(a,\dots))$.

Example one is the empty list and is easily seen to agree with the definition. For list A, we have

$$head(A) = \text{'}a\text{'},\ tail(A) = ((b,c)).$$

The *tail* (A) also has a head and tail which are (b,c) and $(\ )$ respectively. Looking at list B we see that

$$head(B) = A,\ tail(B) = (A,(\ ))$$

Continuing, we have

$$head(tail(B)) = A,\ tail(tail(B)) = ((\ ))$$

both of which are lists.

Two important consequences of our definition for a list are: (i) lists may be shared by other lists as in example iii, where list A makes up two of the sublists of list B; and (ii) lists may be recursive as in example iv. The implications of these two consequences for the data structures needed to represent lists will become evident as we go along.

First, let us restrict ourselves to the situation where the lists being represented are neither shared nor recursive. To see where this notion of a list may be useful, consider how to represent polynomials in several variables. Suppose we need to devise a data representation for them and consider one typical example, the polynomial $P(x,y,z) =$

$$x^{10}y^3z^2 + 2x^8y^3z^2 + 3x^8y^2z^2 + x^4y^4z + 6x^3y^4z + 2yz$$

One can easily think of a sequential representation for P, say using nodes with four fields: *coef*, *expx*, *expy*, and *expz*. But this would mean that polynomials in a different number of variables would need a different number of fields, adding another conceptual inelegance to other difficulties we have already seen with the sequential representation of polynomials. If we used linear lists, we might conceive of a node of the form

coef	expx	expy
expz	link	

These nodes would have to vary in size depending on the number of variables, causing difficulties in storage management. The idea of using a general list structure with fixed size nodes arises naturally if we consider rewriting $P(x,y,z)$ as

$$((x^{10} + 2x^8)y^3 + 3x^8y^2)z^2 + ((x^4 + 6x^3)y^4 + 2y)z$$

Every polynomial can be written in this fashion, factoring out a main variable z, followed by a second variable y, etc. Looking carefully now at $P(x,y,z)$ we see that there are two terms in the variable z, $Cz^2 + Dz$, where C and D are polynomials themselves but in the variables x and y. Looking closer at $C(x,y)$, we see that it is of the form $Ey^3 + Fy^2$, where E and F are polynomials in x. Continuing in this way we see that every polynomial consists of a variable plus coefficient exponent pairs. Each coefficient is itself a polynomial (in one less variable) if we regard a single numerical coefficient as a polynomial in zero variables.

From the preceding discussion, we see that every polynomial, regardless of the number of variables in it, can be represented using nodes of the type *polynode* defined below:

```
type triple = (variable, ptr, no);
     polypointer = ↑polynode;
     polynode = record
                   link : polypointer;
                   exp: integer;
                   case trio : triple of
                      variable: (vble : char);
                      ptr: (dlink : polypointer);
                      no: (coef : integer);
                end;
```

Note that the type of the field *vble* can be changed to **integer** in case all variables are kept in a table and *vble* just gives the corresponding table index.

The polynomial $P = 3x^2y$ now takes the representation given in figure 4.26 while $P(x,y,z)$ defined above has the list representation shown in figure 4.25. For simplicity, the *trio* field is omitted from figure 4.25. The value of this field for each node is self evident.

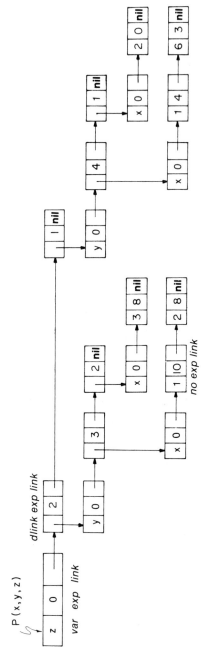

Figure 4.25 Representation of $P(x,y,z)$ using three fields per node. The *trio* field has not been shown. Its value should be evident from the node structure.

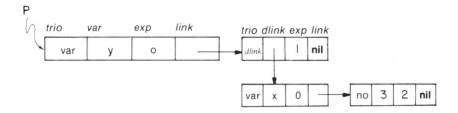

Figure 4.26.

It is a little surprising that every generalized list can be represented using the node structure:

tag = true/false	*data/dlink*	*link*

This structure may be defined in Pascal as below:

type *listpointer* = ↑*listnode*;
    listnode = **record**
                link : *listpointer*;
                case *tag* : **boolean of**
                false: (*data* : **char**);
                true: (*dlink* : *listpointer*);
            end;

where the type of the *data* field will change from one application to the next. The reader should convince himself that this node structure is adequate for the representation of any list A. The *link* field may be used as a pointer to the tail of the list while the *data/dlink* field can hold an atom in case *head* (A) is an atom or be a pointer to the list representation of *head* (A) in case it is a list. Using this node structure, the example lists i-iv have the representation shown in figure 4.27. In these examples, the data field is of type **char**.

Recursive Algorithms for Lists

Now that we have seen a particular example where generalized lists are useful, let us return to their definition again. Whenever a data object is defined recursively, it is often easy to describe algorithms which work on these objects recursively. To see how recursion is useful, let us write a procedure (Program 4.29) which produces an exact copy of a nonrecursive list p in which no sublists are shared. We will assume the nodes of p are of type *listnode* as defined earlier.

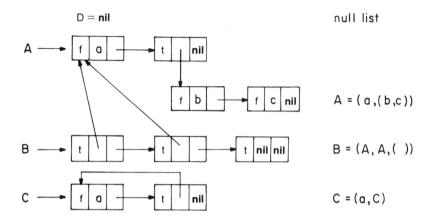

Figure 4.27   Representation of Lists i-iv. An *f* in the *tag* field represents the value false while a *t* represents the value true.

```
function copy(p : listpointer): listpointer;
{copy the nonrecursive list with no shared sublists
 pointed at by p}
var q : listpointer;
begin
    q := nil
    if p <> nil
    then begin
            new(q); q↑.tag := p↑.tag;
            if not p↑.tag then q↑.data := p↑.data
                          else q↑.dlink := copy(p↑.dlink);
            q↑.link := copy(p↑.link);
        end;
    copy := q;
end; {of copy}
```

Program 4.29   Copy a list.

The above procedure reflects exactly the definition of a list. We immediately see that *copy* works correctly for an empty list. A simple proof using induction will verify the correctness of the entire procedure. Once we have established that the program is correct we may wish to remove the recursion for efficiency. This can be done using some straightforward rules. The following rules assume that the recursive procedure does not use the labels 1, 2,..., k where k is one more than the number of places from which a recursive call is made.

(i)   At the beginning of the procedure or function, code is inserted which declares a stack (called recursion stack) and initializes it to be empty. In the most general case, the stack will be used to hold the values of parameters, local variables, and a return address for each recursive call. We might prefer to use a separate stack for each value.

(ii)   The label 1 is attached to the first executable statement.

(iii) If this is a function, then replace all appearances of the function name on the left hand side of assignment statements by a new variable, say z, of the same type as the function.

Now, each recursive call is replaced by a set of instructions which do the following:

(iv)   Store the values of all pass by value parameters and local variables in the stack. The pointer to the top of the stack can be treated as global.

(v)   Create the i-th new label, i, and store i in the stack. The value i of this label will be used as the return address. This label is placed in the program as described in rule (vii).

(vi)   Evaluate the arguments of this call that correspond to pass by value parameters (they may be expressions) and assign these values to the appropriate formal parameters.

(vii) Insert an unconditional branch to the beginning of the procedure.

(viii) If this is a procedure, add the label created in (v) to the statement immediately following the unconditional branch. In case this statement already has a label, change it and all references to it to the label created in (v). If this is a function then follow the unconditional branch by code to use the value of the variable z in the same way the function value was used earlier. The first statement of this code is given the label that was created in (v).

These steps are sufficient to remove all recursive calls from the procedure or function. Finally, we need to precede the last **end** statement of the procedure or function by code to do the following:

(ix)   If the recursion stack is empty, then assign the value of z to the function name and execute a normal **end** of function in case this is a function. In the case of a procedure, we simply execute a normal **end** of procedure.

(x)   If the stack is not empty, then restore the value of all pass by value parameters and of all local variables that are not pass by reference actual parameters. These are at the top of the stack. Use the return label from the top of the stack and execute a branch to this label. This can be done using a **case** statement as shown in the following example.

(xi)   In addition, the label (if any) attached to the **end** of the procedure or function statement is moved to the first statement of the code for (ix) and (x).

By following these rules carefully one can take any recursive program and produce a program which works in exactly the same way, yet which uses only iteration to control the flow of the program. On many compilers this resultant program will be much more efficient than its recursive version. On other compilers the times may be fairly close. Once the transformation to iterative form has been accomplished, one can often simplify the program even further thereby producing even more gains in efficiency. These rules have been used to produce the iterative version of *copy* which appears in Program 4.30.

```
function copy(p : listpointer): listpointer;
{copy the nonrecursive list with no shared sublists
pointed at by p}
label 1, 2, 3;
constant stacksize = 100;
var stackpointer: 0..100;
        qstack : array[1..stacksize] of listpointer;
        pstack : array[1..stacksize] of listpointer;
        labelstack : array[1..stacksize] of integer;
        returnlabel : integer;
        q : listpointer;
        z : listpointer;
begin
   stackpointer := 0; {initialize stacks}
1 : q := nil;
   if p <> nil
   then begin
           new(q); q↑.tag := p↑.tag;
           if not p↑.tag then q↑.data := p↑.data
           else begin
                   stackpointer := stackpointer + 1;
                   if stackpointer > stacksize then stackfull;
                   qstack[stackpointer] := q;
                   pstack[stackpointer] := p;
                   labelstack[stackpointer] := 2;
                   p := p↑.dlink;
                   goto 1;
                   2: q↑.dlink := z;
               end; {of if not p↑.tag}
           stackpointer := stackpointer + 1;
           if stackpointer > stacksize then stackfull;
           qstack[stackpointer] := q;
           pstack[stackpointer] := p;
```

```
            labelstack[stackpointer] := 3;
            p := p↑.link;
            goto 1;
            3: q↑.link := z;
        end; {of if p <> nil}
    z := q;
    if stackpointer <> 0
    then begin {simulate an end of function}
            q := qstack[stackpointer];
            p := pstack[stackpointer];
            returnlabel := labelstack[stackpointer];
            stackpointer := stackpointer − 1;
            case returnlabel of
                2: goto 2;
                3: goto 3;
            end; {of case}
        end; {of if stackpointer <> 0}
    copy := z;
    end; {of copy}
```

Program 4.30 Nonrecursive version of *copy*

It is hard to believe that the nonrecursive version is any more intelligible than the recursive one. But it does show explicitly how to implement such an algorithm in, say, FORTRAN. The non-recursive version does have some virtues, namely, it is more efficient. The overhead of parameter passing on most compilers is heavy. Moreover, there are optimizations that can be made on the latter version, but not on the former. Thus, both of these forms have their place. We will often use the recursive version for descriptive purposes.

Now let us consider the computing time of this algorithm. The null list takes a constant amount of time. For the list

$$A = ((a,b),((c,d),e))$$

which has the representation of figure 4.28, p takes on the values given in figure 4.29. The sequence of values should be read down the columns, b, r, s, t, u, v, w, x are the addresses of the eight nodes of the list. From this particular example one should be able to see that nodes with $tag =$ **false** will be visited twice, while nodes with $tag =$ **true**, will be visited three times. Thus, if a list has a total of m nodes, no more than $3m$ executions of any statement will occur. Hence, the algorithm is $O(m)$ or linear which is the

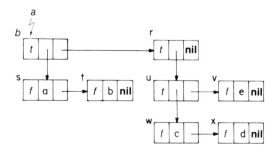

Figure 4.28   Linked Representation for A.

Levels of recursion	Value of p	Continuing Levels	p	Continuing Levels	p
1	b	2	r	3	u
2	s	3	u	4	v
3	t	4	w	5	o
4	o	5	x	4	v
3	t	6	o	3	u
2	s	5	x	2	r
1	b	4	w	3	o
				2	r
				1	b

Figure 4.29   Values of Parameter in Execution of *copy(a)*.

best we could hope to achieve. Another factor of interest is the maximum depth of recursion or, equivalently, how many locations one will need for the recursion stack. Again, by carefully following the algorithm on the previous example one sees that the maximum depth is a combination of the lengths and depths of all sublists. However, a simple upper bound to use is m, the total number of nodes. Though this bound will be extremely large in many cases, it is achievable, for instance, if

$$A = (((((a))))).$$

Another procedure which is often useful is one which determines whether two lists are identical. This means they must have the same structure and the same data in corresponding fields. Again, using the recursive definition of a list we can write a short recursive procedure (Program 4.31) which accomplishes this task.

```
function equal(s, t : listpointer): boolean;
{s and t are nonrecursive lists. This function has value
 true iff the two lists are identical}
var x : boolean;
begin
  equal := false;
  if (s = nil) and (t = nil)
  then equal := true
  else if (s <> nil) and (t <> nil)
        then if s↑.tag = t↑.tag
              then begin
                    if not s↑.tag
                    then if s↑.data = t↑.data then x := true
                                               else x := false
                    else x := equal(s↑.dlink,t↑.dlink)
                    if x then equal := equal(s↑.link,t↑.link)
                  end;
end; {of equal}
```

Program 4.31 Equal

Procedure *equal* is a function which returns either the value **true** or **false**. Its computing time is clearly no more than linear when no sublists are shared since it looks at each node of *s* and *t* no more than three times· For unequal lists the procedure terminates as soon as it discovers that the lists are not identical.

Another handy operation on nonrecursive lists is the function which computes the depth of a list. The depth of the empty list is defined to be zero and in general

$$depth(s) = \begin{cases} 0, \text{ if } s \text{ is an atom} \\ 1 + \max\{depth(x_1),\ldots,depth(x_n)\}, \text{ if } s \text{ is the list} \\ \qquad\qquad (x_1,\ldots,x_n), \ n \geq 1. \end{cases}$$

Procedure *depth* (Program 4.32) is a very close transformation of the definition which is itself recursive.

```
function depth(s : listpointer): integer;
{compute the depth of the nonrecursive list s}
var p : listpointer; m,n: integer;
begin
  if s <> nil
  then begin
          p := s; m := 0;
          while p <> nil do
          begin
            if p↑.tag
            then begin
                    n := depth(p↑.dlink);
                    if m < n then m := n;
                  end;
              p := p↑.link;
          end;
          depth := m + 1;
        end
  else depth := 0;
end; {of depth}
```

Program 4.32   Depth

By now you have seen several programs of this type and you should be feeling more comfortable both reading and writing recursive algorithms. To convince yourself that you understand the way these work, try exercises 36, 37, and 38.

Reference Counts, Shared and Recursive Lists

In this section we shall consider some of the problems that arise when lists are allowed to be shared by other lists and when recursive lists are permitted. Sharing of sublists can in some situations result in great savings in storage used, as identical sublists occupy the same space. In order to facilitate ease in specifying shared sublists, we extend the definition of a list to allow for naming of sublists. A sublist appearing within a list definition may be named through the use of a list name preceding it. For example, in the list $A = (a,(b,c))$, the sublist (b,c) could be assigned the name Z by writing $A = (a,Z(b,c))$. In fact, to be consistent we would then write $A(a,Z(b,c))$ which would define the list A as above.

Lists that are shared by other lists, such as list A of figure 4.27, create problems when one wishes to delete the first node. If the first node of A is deleted, it is necessary to change the pointers from the list B to point to the second node. However, one normally does not know all the points from which a particular list is being referenced. (Even if we did have this information, the deletion of the first node could require a large amount of time.) Addition at the front can be accomplished by inserting a new node after the first node; moving the contents of the first node to this new node; adding the new data into the old first node. This solution requires us to treat addition at the front differently from addition else-where. An elegant and efficient solution results when each list and sublist has a head node. If each list is to have a head node, then lists i-iv are represented as in figure 4.30. Even in situations where one does not wish to dynamically add or delete nodes from lists, as in the case of multi-variate polynomials, head nodes prove useful in determining when the nodes of a particular structure may be returned to the storage pool. For example, let t and u be program variables pointing to the two poly-nomials $(3x^4 + 5x^3 + 7x)y^3$ and $(3x^4 + 5x^3 + 7x)y^6 + (6x)y$ of figure 4.31. If $perase$ is to erase a polynomial, then the invocation $perase(t)$ should not return the nodes corresponding to the coefficient $3x^4 + 5x^3 + 7x$ since this sublist is also part of u.

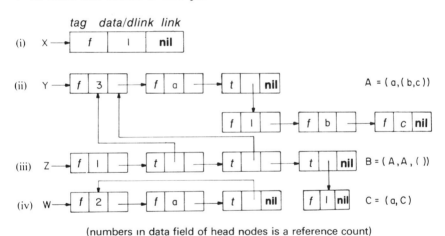

(numbers in data field of head nodes is a reference count)

Figure 4.30   Structure with Head Nodes for Lists i-iv.

Thus, whenever lists are being shared by other lists, we need a mechanism to help determine whether or not the list nodes may be physically returned to the available space list. This mechanism is generally provided through the use of a reference count maintained in the head node of each list. Since the *data* field of the head nodes is free, the reference count is maintained in this field (alterna-tively a third variant may be introduced with tag having three possible values 0,1,2). This reference count of a list is the number of pointers (either program variables or pointers from other lists) to that list. If the lists i-iv of figure 4.30 are accessible via the program variables x, y, z and w, then the reference counts

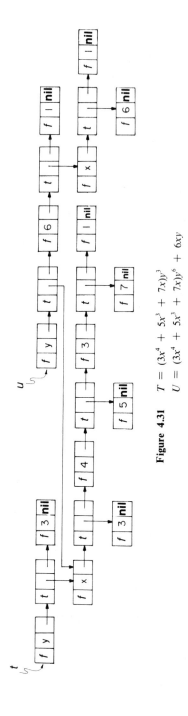

Figure 4.31 $T = (3x^4 + 5x^3 + 7x)y^3$
$U = (3x^4 + 5x^3 + 7x)y^6 + 6xy$

for the lists are:

(i) $ref(x) = 1$ accessible only via x
(ii) $ref(y) = 3$ pointed to by y and two points from z
(iii) $ref(z) = 1$ accessible only via z
(iv) $ref(w) = 2$ two pointers to list c

Now a call to *lerase(t)* (list erase) should result only in a decrementing by 1 of the reference counter of t. Only if the reference count becomes zero are the nodes of t to be physically returned to the available space list. The same is to be done to the sublists of t.

Assume that the data type *listpointer* is defined as:

```
type listpointer = ↑listnode;
     three = 0..2;
     listnode = record
                    link: listpointer;
                    case tag: three of
                      0: (data: integer);
                      1: (dlink: listpointer);
                      2: (ref: integer);
                  end;
```

An algorithm to erase a list x could proceed by examining the top level nodes of a list whose reference count has become zero. Any sublists encountered are erased and finally, the top level nodes are linked into the available space list. The list erase algorithm is given in Program 4.33.

```
procedure lerase(var x : listpointer);
{recursively erase a nonrecursive list. Each
 head node has a reference count.}
var y : listpointer;
begin
   x↑.ref := x↑.ref −1; {decrement reference count}
   if x↑.ref = 0
   then begin
           y := x; {y traverses top level of x}
           while y↑.link <> nil do
           begin
              y := y↑.link;
              if y↑.tag = 1 then lerase(y↑.dlink);
           end;
           y↑.link := av; {attach top level nodes to av list}
           av := x; x := nil;
        end;
end; {of lerase}
```

Program 4.33   Lerase

A call to *lerase(y)* will now only have the effect of decreasing the reference count of *y* to 2. Such a call followed by a call to *lerase(z)* will result in:

(i)   reference count of *z* becomes zero;

(ii) next node is processed and $y\uparrow.ref$ reduces to 1;

(iii) $y\uparrow.ref$ becomes zero and the five nodes of list $A(a,(b,c))$ are returned to the available space list;

(iv) the top level nodes of *z* are linked into the available space list.

The use of head nodes with reference counts solves the problem of determining when nodes are to be physically freed in the case of shared sublists. However, for recursive lists, the reference count never becomes zero. *lerase(w)* just results in $w\uparrow.ref$ becoming one. The reference count does not become zero even though this list is no longer accessible either through program variables or through other structures. The same is true in the case of indirect recursion (figure 4.32). After calls to *lerase(r)* and *lerase(s)*, $r\uparrow.ref = 1$ and $s\uparrow.ref = 2$ but the structure consisting of *r* and *s* is no longer being used and so it should have been returned to the available space list.

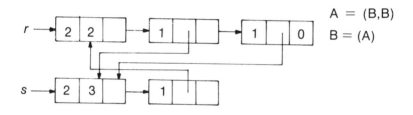

Figure 4.32   Indirect Recursion of Lists *A* and *B* Pointed to by Program Variables *r* and *s*.

Unfortunately, there is no simple way to supplement the list structure of figure 4.32 so as to be able to determine when recursive lists may be physically erased. It is no longer possible to return all free nodes to the available space list when they become free. So when recursive lists are being used, it is possible to run out of available space even though not all nodes are in use. When this happens, it is possible to collect unused nodes (i.e., garbage nodes) through a process known as garbage collection. This will be described in the next section.

4.9   GARBAGE COLLECTION AND COMPACTION

As remarked at the close of the last section, garbage collection is the process of collecting all unused nodes and returning them to available space.

This process is carried out in essentially two phases. In the first phase, known as the marking phase, all nodes in use are marked. In the second phase all unmarked nodes are returned to the available space list. This second phase is trivial when all nodes are of the same size. In this case, the second phase requires only the examination of each node to see whether or not it has been marked. If there are a total of n nodes, then the second phase of garbage collection can be carried out in $O(n)$ steps. In this situation it is only the first or marking phase that is of any interest in designing an algorithm. When variable size nodes are in use, it is desirable to compact memory so that all free nodes form a contiguous block of memory. In this case the second phase is referred to as memory compaction. Compaction of disk space to reduce average retrieval time is desirable even for fixed size nodes. In this section we shall study two marking algorithms and one compaction algorithm.

Marking

In order to be able to carry out the marking, we need a mark field in each node. It will be assumed that this mark field can be changed at any time by the marking algorithm. Marking algorithms mark all directly accessible nodes (i.e., nodes accessible through program variables referred to as pointer variables) and also all indirectly accessible nodes (i.e., nodes accessible through link fields of nodes in accessible lists). It is assumed that a certain set of variables has been specified as pointer variables and that these variables at all times are either **nil** (i.e., point to nothing) or are valid pointers to lists. It is also assumed that the link fields of nodes always contain valid link infomation.

Knowing which variables are pointer variables, it is easy to mark all directly accessible nodes. The indirectly accessible nodes are marked by systematically examining all nodes reachable from these directly accessible nodes. Before examining the marking algorithms let us review the node structure in use. Each node regardless of its usage will have two Boolean fields: *mark* and *tag*. If *tag* = **false**, then the node contains only atomic information in a field called *data*. If *tag* = **true**, then the node has two link fields: *dlink* and *rlink*. Atomic information can be stored only in nodes that have *tag* = **false**. Such nodes are called *atomic* nodes. All other nodes are list nodes. This node structure is slightly different from the one used in the previous section where a node with *tag* = **false** contained atomic information as well as a *link*. With this new node structure, the list $(a,(b))$ is represented as in figure 4.33. The type definition for the new nodes is given below:

type *listpointer* = ↑*listnode*;
    listnode = **record**
                    mark: **boolean**;
                    case *tag*: **boolean of**
                    true: (*dlink*: *listpointer*;
                              rlink: *listpointer*);
                    false: (*data*: **char**)
                end;

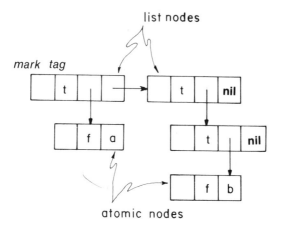

Figure 4.33.

Both of the marking algorithms we shall discuss will require that all nodes be initially unmarked (i.e., *x↑.mark* = **false** for every node *x↑*). Procedure *driver* (Program 4.34) will repeatedly call a marking algorithm to mark all nodes accessible from each of the pointer variables being used. In line 6, procedure *mark1* is invoked. If we wish to use the second marking algorithm, then we need merely invoke *mark2* instead of *mark1*. Both the marking algorithms have been written to work on arbitrary list structures (not just generalized lists as described here).

```
1  procedure driver
2  begin
3    for each pointer variable x that points to an unmarked node do
4    begin
5      x↑.mark := true;
6      if x↑.tag then mark1(x); {x is a list node}
7    end;
8  end; {of driver}
```

Program 4.34 Driver

The first marking algorithm *mark*1 will start from the list node *x* and mark all nodes that can be reached from *x* via a sequence of *rlink's* and *dlink's*; examining all such paths will result in the examination of all reachable nodes. While examining any node of type list we will have a choice as to whether to move to the *dlink* or to the *rlink*. *mark*1 will move to the *dlink* but will at the same time place the *rlink* on a stack in case the *rlink* is a list node not yet marked. The use of this stack will enable us to return at a later point to the *rlink* and examine all paths from there. This strategy is similar to the one used in the previous section for *lerase*.

```
1   procedure mark1(x : listpointer);
2   {mark all nodes accessible from the list node x. add and delete
3    are the standard stack procedures. top points to the stack top.}
4   var p,q : listpointer; done : boolean;
5   begin
6     top := 0; add(x); {put x on the stack}
7     while top > 0 do {stack not empty}
8     begin
9       delete(p); {unstack}; done := false;
10      repeat {move down stacking rlinks as needed}
11        q := p↑.rlink;
12        if q <> nil
13        then begin
14              if q↑.tag and not q↑.mark then add(q); {unmarked list node}
15              q↑.mark := true; {mark q}
16            end;
17        p := p↑.dlink;
18        if p <> nil then
19          {a marked or atomic node cannot lead to new nodes}
20          if p↑.mark or not p↑.tag then done := true
21                                   else p↑.mark := true
22                            else done := true;
23      until done;
24      if p <> nil then p↑.mark := true;
25    end; {of while}
26  end; {of mark1}
```

Program 4.35   First marking algorithm.

Analysis of *mark*1

In lines 12-14 of *mark*1 we check to see if $q = p↑.rlink$ can lead to other unmarked accessible nodes. If so, *q* is stacked. The examination of nodes continues with the node at $p↑.dlink$. When we have moved downwards as far as is possible, we exit from the loop of lines 10-23. At this point we try out one of the alternative moves from the stack, line 9.

One may readily verify that *mark*1 does indeed mark all previously unmarked nodes which are accessible from x.

In analyzing the computing time of this algorithm we observe that on each iteration (except for the last) of the loop of lines 10–23, at least one previously unmarked node gets marked (line 21). Thus, if the **while** loop, lines 7–25, is iterated r times and the total number of iterations of the **repeat** loop, lines 10–23, is u then at least $w = u - r$ previously unmarked nodes get marked by the algorithm. Let m be the number of new nodes marked. Then $m \geq w = u - r$. Also, the number of iterations of the loop of lines 7–25 is one plus the number of nodes that get stacked. The only nodes that can be stacked are those previously unmarked (line 14). Once a node is stacked it gets marked (line 15). Hence $r \leq m + 1$. From this and the knowledge that $m \geq u - r$, we conclude that $u \leq 2m + 1$. The computing time of the algorithm is $O(u + r)$. Substituting for u and r we obtain $O(m)$ as the computing time. The time is linear in the number of new nodes marked! Since any algorithm to mark nodes must spend at least one unit of time on each new node marked, it follows that there is no algorithm with a time less than $O(m)$. Hence *mark*1 is optimal to within a constant factor (recall that $2m = O(m)$ and $10m = O(m)$).

Having observed that *mark*1 is optimal to within a constant factor you may be tempted to sit back in your arm chair and relish a moment of smugness. There is, unfortunately, a serious flaw with *mark*1. This flaw is sufficiently serious as to make the algorithm of little use in many garbage collection applications. Garbage collectors are invoked only when we have run out of space. This means that at the time *mark*1 is to operate, we do not have an unlimited amount of space available in which to maintain the stack. In some applications each node might have a free field which can be used to maintain a linked stack. In fact, if variable size nodes are in use and storage compaction is to be carried out then such a field will be available (see the compaction algorithm *compact*). When fixed size nodes are in use, compaction can be efficiently carried out without this additional field and so we will not be able to maintain a linked stack (see exercises for another special case permitting the growth of a linked stack). Realizing this deficiency in *mark*1, let us proceed to another marking algorithm *mark*2. *mark*2 will not require any additional space in which to maintain a stack. Its computing time is also $O(m)$ but the constant factor here is larger than that for *mark*1.

Unlike *mark*1 which does not alter any of the links in the list x, the algorithm *mark*2 will modify some of these links. However, by the time it finishes its task the list structure will be restored to its original form. Starting from a list node x, *mark*2 traces all possible paths made up of *dlink*'s and *rlink*'s. Whenever a choice is to be made the *dlink* direction is explored first. Instead of maintaining a stack of alternative choices (as was done by *mark*1) we now maintain the path taken from x to the node p that is currently being examined. This path is maintained by changing some of the links along the path from x to p.

Consider the example list of figure 4.34(a). Initially, all nodes except node A are unmarked and only node E is atomic. From node A we can either move down to node B or right to node I. $mark2$ will always move down when faced with such an alternative. We shall use p to point to the node currently being examined and t to point to the node preceding p in the path from x to p. The path t to x will be maintained as a chain comprised of the nodes on this $t - x$ path. If we advance from node p to node q then either $q = p\uparrow.rlink$ or $q = p\uparrow.dlink$ and q will become the node currently being examined. The node preceding q on the $x - q$ path is p and so the path list must be updated to represent the path from p to x. This is simply done by adding node p to the $t - x$ (read as "t to x") path already constructed. Nodes will be linked onto this path either through their $dlink$ or $rlink$ field. Only list nodes will be placed onto this path chain. When node p is being added to the path chain, p is linked to t via its $dlink$ field if $q = p\uparrow.dlink$. When $q = p\uparrow.rlink$, p is linked to t via its $rlink$ field. In order to be able to determine whether a node on the $t - x$ path list is linked through its $dlink$ or $rlink$ field we make use of the tag field. Notice that since the $t - x$ path list will contain only list nodes, the tag on all these nodes will be **true**. When the $dlink$ field is used for linking, this tag will be changed to **false**. Thus, for nodes on the $t - x$ path we have:

$$tag = \begin{cases} \textbf{false} & \text{if the node is linked via its } dlink \text{ field} \\ \textbf{true} & \text{if the node is linked via its } rlink \text{ field} \end{cases}$$

The tag will be reset to **true** when the node gets off the $t - x$ path list. (While this use of the tag field represents a slight abuse of the language, it is preferable to introducing an additional field.)

Figure 4.34(b) shows the $t - x$ path list when node p is being examined. Nodes A, B and C have a tag of zero (for false) indicating that linking on these nodes is via the $dlink$ field. This also implies that in the original list structure, $B = A\uparrow.dlink$, $C = B\uparrow.dlink$ and $D = p = C\uparrow.dlink$. Thus, the link information destroyed while creating the $t - x$ path list is present in the path list. Nodes B, C, and D have already been marked by the algorithm. In exploring p we first attempt to move down to $q = p\uparrow.dlink = E$. E is an atomic node so it gets marked and we then attempt to move right from p. Now, $q = p\uparrow.rlink = F$. This is an unmarked list node. So, we add p to the path list and proceed to explore q. Since p is linked to q by its $rlink$ field, the linking of p onto the $t - x$ path is made through its $rlink$ field. Figure 4.34(c) shows the list structure at the time node G is being examined. Node G is a dead end. We cannot move further either down or right. At this time we move backwards on the $x - t$ path resetting links and tags until we reach a node whose $rlink$ has not yet been examined. The marking con-

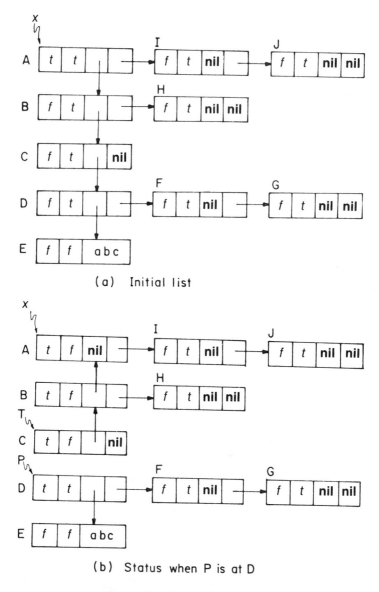

(a)   Initial list

(b)   Status when P is at D

Figure 4.34   Example list for *mark2*.

tinues from this node. Because nodes are removed from the $t - x$ path list in the reverse order in which they were added to it, this list behaves as a stack. The remaining details of *mark2* are spelled out in Program 4.36. The same driver as for *mark1* is assumed.

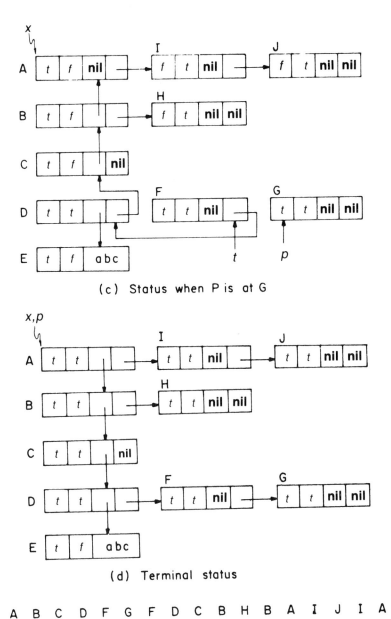

(c) Status when P is at G

(d) Terminal status

A B C D F G F D C B H B A I J I A

(e) Path taken by P

Figure 4.34   Example List for *mark2* (contd.).

The procedure *mark2* given in Program 4.36(a) makes use of three other procedures which are given in Programs 4.36(b)–(d). These latter are to be physically placed between the **var** and first **begin** statement of *mark2*. Procedure *mark2* first attempts to move *p* one node down. If it cannot, then an attempt is made to move *p* one node to the right. If even this cannot be done, then we attempt to backup on the $t-x$ list and move *p* to a node from which a downward move may be possible. When even this backup is not possible, *mark2* terminates. The correctness of the procedures of Programs 4.36(a)–(d) is easily established.

```
 1   procedure mark2(x : listpointer);
 2   {same function as mark1}
 3   var p,q,t : listpointer; failure : boolean;
 4   begin
 5      p := x; t := nil; {initialize t − x path list}
 6      repeat
 7         movedown;
 8         if failure then begin
 9                        moveright;
10                           if failure then backup;
11                        end;
12      until failure;
13   end; {of mark2}
```
Program 4.36(a)   Second marking algorithm

```
 1   procedure movedown;
 2   {Attempt to move p one node down}
 3   begin
 4      q := p↑.dlink; {go down list}; failure := true;
 5      if q <> nil
 6      then if not q↑.mark and q↑.tag
 7           then begin {unmarked list node}
 8                   q↑.mark := true; p↑.tag := false;
 9                   p↑.dlink := t; t := p; {add p to t − x path list}
10                   p := q; failure := false;
11                end
12           else q↑.mark := true;
13   end; {of movedown}
```
Program 4.36(b)   Procedure to move down one node

```
 1   procedure moveright;
 2   {Attempt to move p one node right}
 3   begin
 4      q := p↑.rlink; {move right}; failure := true;
 5      if q <> nil
 6      then if not q↑.mark and q↑.tag
 7           then begin {unmarked list node}
```

```
8                q↑.mark := true;  p↑.rlink := t;
9                t := p; p := q; failure := false;
10              end
11          else  q↑.mark := true;
12  end; {of moveright}
```

Program 4.36(c)   Procedure to move right one node

```
1  procedure backup;
2  {Attempt to backup on t − x list}
3  begin
4    failure := true;
5    while (t <> nil) and failure do
6    begin
7      q := t;
8      if not q↑.tag
9      then begin {linked via dlink}
10            t := q↑.dlink;  q↑.dlink := p;
11            q↑.tag := true; p := q;
12            moveright;
13         end
14      else begin {linked via rlink}
15            {p is to right of q}
16            t := q↑.rlink;  q↑.rlink := p;
17            p := q;
18         end;
19    end; {of while}
20  end; {of backup}
```

Program 4.36(d)   Procedure to back up on the t − x list

Analysis of mark2

Figure 4.34(e) shows the path taken by p on the list of 4.34(a). It should be clear that a list node previously unmarked gets visited at most three times. Except for node x, each time a node already marked is reached at least one previously unmarked node is also examined (i.e. the one that led to this marked node). Hence the computing time of mark2 is $O(m)$ where m is the number of newly marked nodes. The constant factor associated with m is, however, larger than that for mark1 but mark2 does not require the stack space needed by mark1. A faster marking algorithm can be obtained by judiciously combining the strategies of mark1 and mark2 (see the exercises).

When the node structure of section 4.8 is in use, an additional Boolean field in each node is needed to implement the strategy of mark2. This field is used to distinguish between the case when a dlink is used to link into the path list and when an rlink is used. The existing tag field cannot be used as some of the nodes on the $t − x$ path list will originally have tag =

true while others will have *tag* = **false** and so it will not be possible to correctly reset tag values when nodes are removed from the $t - x$ list.

Storage Compaction

When all requests for storage are of a fixed size, it is enough to just link all unmarked (i.e. free) nodes together into an available space list. However, when storage requests may be for blocks of varying sizes, it is desirable to compact storage so that all the free space forms one contiguous block. Consider the memory configuration of figure 4.35. Nodes in use have a *mark* field = t (for true) while free nodes have their *mark* field = f (for false). The nodes are labeled 1 through 8, with n_i, $1 \le i \le 8$ being the size of the *i-th node*.

The free nodes could be linked together to obtain the available space list of figure 4.36. While the total amount of memory available is $n_1 + n_3 + n_5 + n_8$, a request for this much memory cannot be met since the memory is

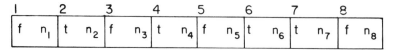

Figure 4.35 Memory Configuration After Marking. Free Nodes Have mark field = f.

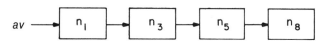

Figure 4.36 Available Space List Corresponding to figure 4.35.

fragmented into 4 nonadjacent nodes. Further, with more and more use of these nodes, the size of free nodes will get smaller and smaller. Ultimately, it will be impossible to meet requests for all but the smallest of nodes. In order to overcome this, it is necessary to reallocate the storage of the nodes in use so that the used part of memory (and hence also the free portion) forms a contiguous block at one end as in figure 4.37. This reallocation of storage resulting in a partitioning of memory into two contiguous blocks (one used, the other free) is referred to as storage compaction. Since there will, in general, be links from one node to another, storage compaction must update these links to point to the relocated address of the respective node. If node n_i starts at location l_i before compaction and at l'_i after compaction, then all link references to l_i must also be changed to l'_i in order not to disrupt the linked list structures existing in the system. Figure 4.38(a) shows a possible link configuration at the time the garbage collection process is invoked. Links are shown only for those nodes that were marked during the marking phase. It is assumed that there are only two links per node. Figure 4.38(b) shows the configuration following compaction. Note that the list structure is unchanged even though the actual addresses represented by the links have been changed. With storage compaction we may identify three tasks: (i) determine new addresses for nodes in use; (ii) update all links in nodes in use; and (iii) relocate nodes to new addresses. Our storage compaction algorithm, *compact* (Program 4.37), is fairly straightforward, implementing each of these three tasks in a separate scan of memory. The algorithm assumes that each node, free or in use, has a *size* field giving the length of the node and an additional field, *newaddr*, which may be used to store the relocated address of the node. Further, it is assumed that each node has two link fields *link*1 and *link*2. The extension of the algorithm to the most general situation in which nodes have a variable number of links is simple and requires only a modification of phase II. As in the case of the dynamic storage management algorithms of section 4.7, the link fields contain integer values that give us the index of the first word in the node pointed at. 0 denotes a **nil** link. The fields in a node may be set and extracted using appropriate procedures and functions, respectively. In addition, we assume that the memory to be compacted is the array *memory*[1..*m*].

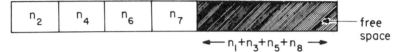

Figure 4.37 Memory Configuration After Reallocating Storage to Nodes in Use.

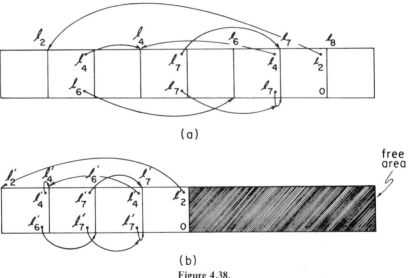

(a)

(b)

Figure 4.38.

In analyzing this algorithm we see that if the number of nodes in memory is n, then phases I and II each require n iterations of their respective **while** loops. Since each iteration of these loops takes a fixed amount of time, the time for these two phases is $O(n)$. Phase III, however, will in general be more expensive. Though the **while** loop of this phase is also executed only n times, the time per iteration depends on the size of the node being relocated. If s is the amount of memory in use, then the time for this phase is $O(n + s)$. The overall computing time is, therefore, $O(n + s)$. The value of

```
procedure compact;
{compact the array memory[1..m]. Every node that is in
use has mark = true; a newaddr field, and two link fields.
size(i) = number of words in the node.}
var i,j,k : integer;
begin
  {phase I: Scan memory left to right assigning new
  addresses to nodes in use. av points to the next available word.}
  av := 1; i := 1;
  while i <= m do
  begin
    if mark(i)
    then begin {assign new address}
            setnewaddr(i, av);
            av := av + size (i);
         end;
    i := i + size(i); {next node}
  end;
  {phase II: Update all links. Assume that newaddr(0) = 0}
  i := 1;
  while i <=m do
  begin
    if mark(i)
    then begin
            setlink1 (i, newaddr(link1 (i)));
            setlink2 (i, newaddr(link2 (i)));
         end;
    i := i + size(i);
  end;
  {phase III: relocate nodes}
  i := 1;
  while i <= m do
    if mark(i)
    then begin
            k := i - newaddr(i); l := newaddr(i);
            for j := i to i + size(i) - 1 do
              memory[j - k] := memory[j];
            i := i + size(l);
         end
    else i := i + size(i);
end; {of compact}
```

Program 4.37   Memory compaction.

av at the end of phase I marks the beginning of the free space. At the termination of the algorithm the space *memory*[*av*] to *memory*[*m*] is free space. Finally, the physical relocation of nodes in phase III can be carried out using a long shift in case your computer has this facility.

In conclusion, we remark that both marking and storage compaction are slow processes. The time for the former is O(number of nodes) while the time for the latter is O(number of nodes $+$ Σ (size of nodes relocated)). In the case of generalized lists, garbage collection is necessitated by the absence of any other efficient means to free storage when needed. Garbage collection has found use in some programming languages where it is desirable to free the user from the task of returning storage. In both situations, a disciplined use of pointer variables and link fields is required. Clever coding tricks involving illegal use of link fields could result in chaos during marking and compaction. While compaction has been presented here primarily for use with generalized list systems using nodes of variable size, compaction can also be used in other environments such as the dynamic storage allocation environment of section 4.7. Even though coalescing of adjacent free blocks takes place in algorithm *free* of section 4.7, it is still possible to have several small nonadjacent blocks of memory free. The total size of these blocks may be large enough to meet a request and it may then be desirable to compact storage. The compaction algorithm in this case is simpler than the one described here. Since all addresses used within a block will be relative to the starting address rather than the absolute address, no updating of links within a block is required. Phases I and III can, therefore, be combined into one phase and phase II eliminated altogether. Since compaction is very slow, one would like to minimize the number of times it is carried out. With the introduction of compaction, several alternative schemes for dynamic storage management become viable. The exercises explore some of these alternatives.

4.10 STRINGS—A CASE STUDY

Suppose we have two character strings $S =$ '$x_1 \ldots x_m$' and $T =$ '$y_1 \ldots y_n$'. The characters x_i, y_j come from a set usually referred to as the *character set* of the programming language. The value n (or m) is the length of the character string T and is an integer which is greater than or equal to zero. If $n = 0$ then T is called the empty or *null string*. In this section we will discuss several alternate ways of implementing strings using the techniques of this chapter.

We begin by defining the data structure STRING using the axiomatic notation. For a set of operations we choose to model this structure after the string operations of *PL/I*. These include:

(i)   NULL produces an instance of the null string;

(ii)   ISNULL returns **true** if the string is null else **false**;

(iii) IN takes a string and a character and inserts it at the end of the string;

(iv)   LEN returns the length of a string;

(v)   CONCAT places a second string at the end of the first string;

(vi)   SUBSTR returns any length of consecutive characters;

(vii) INDEX determines if one string is contained within another.

We now formally describe the string data structure.

structure *STRING*
    declare *NULL* ( ) → *string; ISNULL (string)* → *boolean*
           IN (string, char) → *string; LEN (string)* → *integer*
           CONCAT (string, string) → *string*
           SUBSTR (string, integer, integer) → *string*
           INDEX (string, string) → *integer;*
    for all *S,T* ϵ *string, i,j* ϵ *integer, c,d* ϵ *char* **let**
    ISNULL (NULL) :: = **true;** *ISNULL (IN(S,c))* ::= **false**
    LEN(NULL) ::= 0; *LEN(IN(S,c))* ::= 1 + *LEN(S)*
    CONCAT(S,NULL) ::= *S*
    CONCAT(S,IN(T,c)) ::= *IN(CONCAT(S,T),c)*
    SUBSTR(NULL,i,j) ::= *NULL*
    SUBSTR(IN(S,c),i,j) ::=
       if $(j = 0)$ **or** $(i + j - 1 > LEN(IN(S,c)))$ **then** *NULL*
         else if $(i + j - 1 = LEN(IN(S,c)))$
              then *IN(SUBSTR(S,i,j − 1),c)*
              else *SUBSTR(S,i,j)*
    INDEX(S,NULL) ::= *LEN(S)* + 1
    INDEX(NULL,IN(T,d)) ::= 0
    INDEX(IN(S,c),IN(T,d)) ::=
       if $(c = d)$ **and** $(INDEX(S,T) = LEN(S) - LEN(T) + 1)$
       then *INDEX(S,T)*
       else *INDEX(S,IN (T,d))*
  end
end *STRING*

As an example of how these axioms work, let $S = \text{'}abcd\text{'}$. This will be represented as

$$IN(IN(IN(IN(NULL,a),b),c),d).$$

Now suppose we follow the axioms as they apply to SUBSTR(S,2,1). By the SUBSTR axioms we get

$$\begin{aligned}
\text{SUBSTR}(S,2,1) &= \text{SUBSTR}(\text{IN}(\text{IN}(\text{IN}(\text{NULL},a),b),c),2,1) \\
&= \text{SUBSTR}(\text{IN}(\text{IN}(\text{NULL},a),b),2,1) \\
&= \text{IN}(\text{SUBSTR}(\text{IN}(\text{NULL},a),2,0),b) \\
&= \text{IN}(\text{NULL},b) \\
&= \text{`}b\text{'}
\end{aligned}$$

Suppose we try another example, SUBSTR(S,3,2)

$$\begin{aligned}
&= \text{IN}(\text{SUBSTR}(\text{IN}(\text{IN}(\text{IN}(\text{NULL},a),b),c),3,1),d) \\
&= \text{IN}(\text{IN}(\text{SUBSTR}(\text{IN}(\text{IN}(\text{NULL},a),b),3,0),c),d) \\
&= \text{IN}(\text{IN}(\text{NULL},c),d) \\
&= \text{`}cd\text{'}
\end{aligned}$$

For your amusement try to simulate the steps taken for INDEX(S,T) where $T = $ 'bc' = IN(IN(NULL,b),c).

4.10.1 Data Representations for STRINGS

In deciding on a data representation for a given data object one must take into consideration the cost of performing different operations using that representation. In addition, a hidden cost resulting from the necessary storage management operations must also be taken into account. For strings, all three types of representation: sequential, linked list with fixed size nodes, and linked list with variable size nodes, are possible candidates. Let us look at the first two of these schemes and evaluate them with respect to storage management as well as efficiency of operation.

Sequential. In this representation successive characters of a string will be placed in consecutive character positions in the array $c[1..m]$ (of type **char**). The string $s = $ '$x_1, ...,x_n$' could then be represented as in figure 4.39 with s a

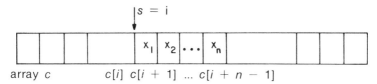

Figure 4.39   Sequential Representation of $s = $ '$x_1 ...x_n$'.

pointer to the first character. In order to facilitate easy length determination, the length of string s could be kept in another variable, sl. Thus, we would have $sl = n$. $SUBSTR(s,j,k - j + 1)$ could be done now by copying over the characters $x_j,...,x_k$ from locations $c[s + j - 1]$ through $c[s + k - 1]$ into a free space. The length of the string created would be $k - j + 1$ and the time required $O(k - j + 1)$ plus the time needed to locate a free space big enough to hold the string. CONCAT(s,t) could similarly be carried out; the length of the resulting string would be $sl + tl$. For storage management two possibilities exist. The boundary tag scheme of section 4.7 could be used in conjunction with the storage compaction strategies of section 4.9. The storage overhead would be enormous for small strings. Alternatively, we could use garbage collection and compaction whenever more free space was needed. This would eliminate the need to return free spaces to an available space list and hence simplify the storage allocation process (see exercises).

While a sequential representation of strings might be adequate for the functions discussed above, such a representation is not adequate when insertions and deletions into and from the middle of a string are carried out. An insertion of '$y_1, ...,y_n$' after the i-th character of s will, in general require copying over the characters $x_1, ...,x_i$ followed by $y_1, ..., y_m$ and then $x_{i+1}, ...,x_n$ into a new free area (see figure 4.40). The time required for this is $O(n + m)$. Deletion of a substring may be carried out by either replacing the deleted characters by a special symbol, $\sim$, or by compacting the space originally occupied by this substring (figure 4.41). The former entails storage waste while the latter in the worst case takes time proportional to LENGTH(s). The replacement of a substring of s by another string t is efficient only if the length of the substring being replaced is equal to LENGTH(t). If this is not the case, then some form of string movement will be required.

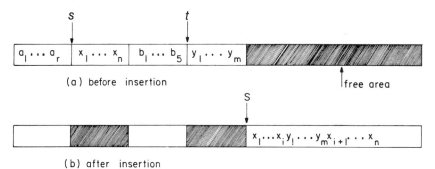

Figure 4.40   Insertion Into a Sequential String.

Linked List—Fixed Size Nodes.   An alternative to sequential string representation is a linked list representation in which each node has two fields: *data* and *link*. The size of the node is the number of characters that can be stored in the *data* field. Let us assume that a link field need only be two characters long. Thus on a computer that uses 6 bits per character, the link field will be 12 bits long. This permits link values in the range [0, 2^{12}-1]. So, up to 2^{12} nodes may be referenced. In the purest form of a linked list representation of strings, each node is of size 1 (i.e., the data field can hold only one character). Normally, this would represent extreme wastage of

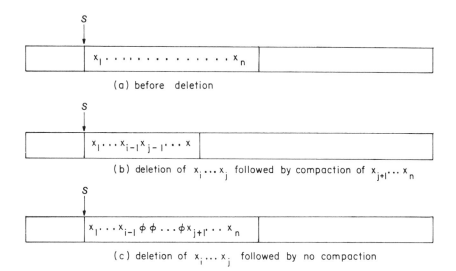

Figure 4.41   Deletion of a Substring.

space. With a link field of size two characters, this would mean that only 1/3 of available memory would be available to store string information while the remaining 2/3 will be used only for link information. With a node size of 8, 80% of available memory could be used for string information. When using nodes of size > 1, it is possible that a string may need a fractional number of nodes. With a node size of 4, a string of length 13 will need only 3-1/4 nodes. Since fractional nodes cannot be allocated, 4 full nodes may be used with the last three characters of the last node set to $\sim$ (figure 4.42(a)). An in place insertion might require one node to be split into two as in figure 4.42(b). Deletion of a substring can be carried out by replacing all characters in this substring by $\sim$ and freeing nodes in which the *data* field consists only of $\sim$'s. In place replacement can be performed similarly. Storage compaction may be carried out when there are no free nodes. Strings containing many occurrences of $\sim$ could be compacted freeing several nodes. String representation with variable sized nodes is similar.

When the node size is 1 things work out very smoothly. Insertion, deletion and concatenation are particularly easy. The length may be determined easily by retaining a head node with this information. Let us look more closely at the operations of insertion and concatenation when the node size is one and no head node is maintained. First, let us write a procedure, sinsert (Program 4.38) which takes two character strings and inserts the second after the i-th character of the first. Procedure *sinsert* assumes that the label 999 has been assigned to the last statement in the program. So a **goto** 999 terminates the program.

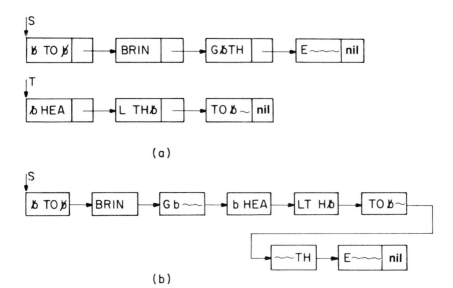

(a)

(b)

Figure 4.42.

```
1  procedure sinsert (var s: stringpointer; t: stringpointer; i: integer);
2  {Insert string t after the i-th character of s.
3  A new string s is created and t is destroyed.}
4  var iptr, q : stringpointer; j : integer;
5  begin
6    if (i < 0) or (i > length(s)) then begin
7                                writeln('string length error');
8                                goto 999; {999 is program end}
9                              end;
10   if s = nil then s := t
11   else if t < > nil
12        then begin {0 ≤ i ≤ length(s) and length(t) > 0}
13              iptr := s;
14              for j := 1 to i − 1 do {find the i-th node of s}
15               iptr := iptr↑.link;
16              {find last node q in t}
17              q := t;
18              while q↑.link < > nil do q := q↑.link;
19              if i = 0 then begin q↑.link := s; s := t; end
20                   else begin q↑.link := iptr↑.link; iptr↑.link :=t; end;
21           end; {of if t <> nil}
22   end; {of sinsert}
```

Program 4.38   String insertion.

Examine how the algorithm works on the strings below.

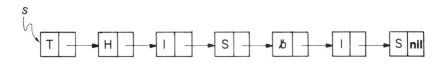

t is to be inserted after the fifth character of s to give the result 'THIS NOW IS.' The fifth character in s and the last character of t are blanks. After line 18 is executed in *sinsert* the following holds.

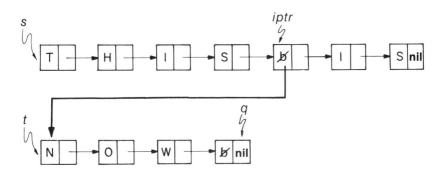

In line 20, the last node of t is linked to the node pointed at by *iptr↑.link* and *iptr↑.link* is changed so as to point to node t.

The computing time of *sinsert* is proportional to $i + length(t)$. We can produce a more efficient algorithm by altering the data structure only slightly. If we use singly linked circular lists, then s and t will be represented as in Figure 4.43. The new version of *sinsert* is obtained by replacing lines 12–21 by the code given in Program 4.39.

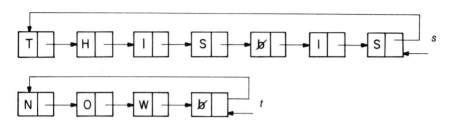

Figure 4.43 Circular Representation of *s* and *t*.

```
then begin
     iptr := s;
     for j := 1 to i do iptr := iptr↑.link;
     if i = 0
     then begin
          q := s↑.link; s↑.link := t↑.link; t↑.link := q;
          end
     else begin
          q := t↑.link; t↑.link := iptr↑.link; iptr↑.link := q;
          end;
if (iptr = s) and (i <> 0) then s := t;
```

Program 4.39 Replacement code for *sinsert*

By using circular lists we avoided the need to find the end of list *t*. The computing time for this version is $O(i)$ and is independent of the length of *t*.

4.10.2 Pattern Matching in STRINGS

Now let us develop an algorithm for a more sophisticated application of strings. Given two strings *s* and *pat* we regard the value of *pat* as a pattern to be searched for in *s*. If it occurs, then we want to know the node in *s* where *pat* begins.

Procedure *find* (Program 4.40) is a straightforward consequence of the data representation. Unfortunately, it is not very efficient. Suppose

$$s = \text{`aaa} \dots a\text{'}; \; pat = \text{`aaa} \dots ab\text{'}$$

where $length(s) = m$, $length(pat) = n$ and m is much larger than n. Then the first $n - 1$ letters of *pat* will match with the *a*'s in string *s* but the *n*-th letter of *pat* will not. The pointer *p* will be moved to the second occurrence of '*a*' in *s* and the $n - 1$ *a*'s of *pat* will match with *s* again. Proceeding in this way we see there will be $m - n + 1$ times that *s* and *pat* have $n - 1$ *a*'s in common. Therefore, algorithm *find* will require at least $(m - n + 1)$ $(n - 1) = O(mn)$ operations. This makes the cost of *find* proportional to the product of the lengths of the two lists or quadratic rather than linear.

```
procedure find(s,pat : stringpointer; var i : stringpointer);
{i is set to nil if pat does not occur in s; otherwise i
 is set to point to the first node in s where pat begins.}
label 99:
var p,q : stringpointer;
begin
    if (pat <> nil) and (s <> nil)
    then begin
            i := s; p := s; q := pat; {i is starting point}
            repeat
              if p↑.data = q↑.data
              then begin {characters match}
                      q := q↑.link;
                      if q = nil then goto 99; {match found}
                      p := p↑.link; {next char in s}
                   end
              else begin {no match}
                      i := i↑.link; p := i; q := pat;
                   end;
            until p = nil;
        end;
    i := nil; {pat is nil or does not occur in s}
99: end; {of find}
```

Program 4.40   Find

There are several improvements that can be made. One is to avoid the situation where *length*(*pat*) is greater than the remaining length of *s* but the algorithm is still searching for a match. Another improvement would be to check that the first and last characters of *pat* are matched in *S* before checking the remaining characters. Of course, these improvements will speed up processing on the average. Procedure *nfind* (Program 4.41) incorporates these improvements.

procedure *nfind(s, pat : stringpointer*; **var** *i : stringpointer)*;
{pattern matching by first matching first and last
 characters of *pat*}
label 99:
var *p,q,j,r : stringpointer*; *t :* **integer;**
begin
   if *(pat* $<>$ **nil) and** *(s* $<>$ **nil)**
   then begin
        p := pat; q := p; t := 0;
        while *q↑.link* $<>$ **nil do** {find end and *length* $-$ 1 of *pat* }
        begin *q := q↑.link; t := t +* 1; **end;**
        j := s; r := s; i := s;
        for *k :=* 1 **to** *t* **do** {find *t +* 1st node of *s*}
          if *j* $<>$ **nil then** *j := j↑.link*;
        while *j* $<>$ **nil do** {*j* is *t* char from *i*}
        begin
            p := pat; r := i;
            if *q↑.data = j↑.data* {check last char of *pat*}
            then begin {check preceding char of *pat*}
                while *(p↑.data = r↑.data)* **and** *(p* $<>$ *q)* **do**
                begin *p := p↑.link; r := r↑.link;* **end;**
                if *p = q* **then goto** 99; {success}
                end;
            i := i↑.link; j := j↑.link;
        end; {of **while**}
      end; {of **if**}
   i := **nil;** {*pat =* **nil** or no match}
99: **end;** {of *nfind*}

Program 4.41 Nfind

If we apply *nfind* to the strings *s =* '*aa ... a*' and *pat =* '*a ... ab*', then the computing time for these inputs is $O(m)$ where $m = lengths(s)$ which is far better than *find* which required $O(mn)$ time . However, the worst case computing time for *nfind* is still $O(mn)$.

nfind is a reasonably complex program employing linked lists and it should be understood before one reads on. The use of pointers like *p, q, j, r* is very typical for programs using this data representation.

It would be far better if we could devise an algorithm which works in time $O(length(s) + length(pat))$, which is optimal for this problem since we must certainly look at all of *pat* and potentially all of *s*. Another desirable feature of any pattern finding algorithm is to avoid rescanning the string *s*.

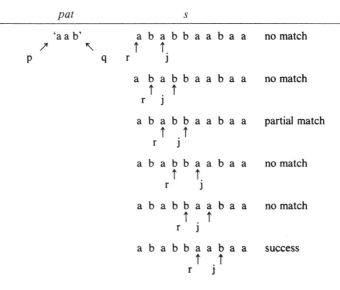

pat   *s*

'a a b'   a b a b b a a b a a   no match

a b a b b a a b a a   no match

a b a b b a a b a a   partial match

a b a b b a a b a a   no match

a b a b b a a b a a   no match

a b a b b a a b a a   success

Figure 4.44 Action of *nfind* on *s* and *pat*.

If *s* is so large that it cannot conveniently be stored in memory, then rescanning adds complications to the buffering operations. Such an algorithm
has been developed by Knuth, Morris and Pratt. Using their example
suppose

$$pat = `a \ b \ c \ a \ b \ c \ a \ c \ a \ b'$$

Let $s = s_1 \ s_2 \ ... \ s_m$ and assume that we are currently determining whether or
not there is a match beginning at s_i. If $s_i \neq a$ then, clearly, we may proceed
by comparing s_{i+1} and a. Similarly if $s_i = a$ and $s_{i+1} \neq b$ then we may
proceed by comparing s_{i+1} and a. If $s_i \ s_{i+1} = ab$ and $s_{i+2} \neq c$ then we have the
situation:

$$s = ` - a \ b \ ? \ ? \ ? \ . \ . \ . \ . \ ? \ '$$
$$pat = \quad ` \ a \ b \ c \ a \ b \ c \ a \ c \ a \ b \ '$$

The ? implies we do not know what the character in *s* is. The first ? in *s*
represents s_{i+2} and $s_{i+2} \neq c$. At this point we know that we may continue the
search for a match by comparing the first character in *pat* with s_{i+2}. There is
no need to compare this character of *pat* with s_{i+1} as we already know that
s_{i+1} is the same as the second character of *pat*, *b*, and so $s_{i+1} \neq a$. Let us try

this again assuming a match of the first four characters in *pat* followed by a non-match, i.e. $s_{i+4} \neq b$. We now have the situation:

$$s = ' - a \; b \; c \; a \; ? \; ? \; \ldots \; ? \; '$$
$$pat = ' \; a \; b \; c \; a \; b \; c \; a \; c \; a \; b \; '$$

We observe that the search for a match can proceed by comparing s_{i+4} and the second character in *pat*, *b*. This is the first place a partial match can occur by sliding the pattern *pat* towards the right. Thus, by knowing the characters in the pattern and the position in the pattern where a mismatch occurs with a character in *s* we can determine where in the pattern to continue the search for a match without moving backwards in *s*. To formalize this, we define a failure function for a pattern.

Definition: If $p = p_1 p_2 \ldots p_n$ is a pattern, then its *failure function, f,* is defined as:

$$f(j) = \begin{cases} \text{largest } i < j \text{ such that } p_1 p_2 \cdots p_i = p_{j-i+1} p_{j-i+2} \cdots p_j \\ \text{if such an } i \geq 1 \text{ exists} \\ 0 \text{ otherwise} \end{cases}$$

For the example pattern above, *pat* = abcabcacab, we have

j	1	2	3	4	5	6	7	8	9	10
pat	a	b	c	a	b	c	a	c	a	b
f	0	0	0	1	2	3	4	0	1	2

From the definition of the failure function we arrive at the following rule for pattern matching: *If a partial match is found such that $s_{i-j+1} \ldots s_{i-1} = p_1 p_2 \ldots p_{j-1}$ and $s_i \neq p_j$ then matching may be resumed by comparing s_i and $p_{f(j-1)+1}$ if $j \neq 1$. If $j = 1$, then we may continue by comparing s_{i+1} and p_1.*

In order to use the above rule when the pattern is represented as a linked list as per our earlier discussion, we include in every node representing the pattern, an additional field called *next*. If $loc(j)$ is the node representing p_j, $1 \leq j \leq n$, then we define

$$loc(j)\uparrow. \; next = \begin{cases} 0 & \text{if } j = 1 \\ loc(f(j-1)+1) & \text{if } j \neq 1 \end{cases}$$

Figure 4.45 shows the pattern *pat* with the *next* field ·included.

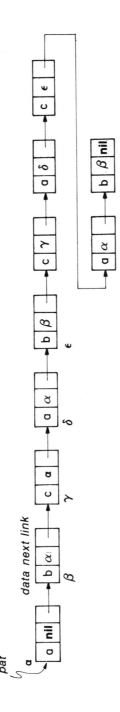

Figure 4.45 Augmented Pattern *pat* with *next* Field.

With this definition for *next*, the pattern matching rule translates to procedure *pmatch* (Program 4.42).

```
 1   procedure pmatch(s, pat : stringpointer;var found:boolean
 2   determine if pat is a substring of s
 3   var p,q : stringpointer;
 4   begin
 5     found := true; p := s; q := pat;
 6     while (p <> nil) and (q <> nil) do
 7       if p↑.data = q↑.data
 8       then begin {character match}
 9               p := p↑.link; q := q↑.link;
10            end
11       else if q := pat
12         then p := p    .link
13         else q := q    .next;
14     if q <> nil then found := false {no match}
15   end; {of pmatch}
```

Program 4.42   Pmatch

The correctness of *pmatch* follows from the definitions of the failure function and of *next*. To determine the computing time, we observe that lines 9 and 12 can be executed for a total of at most $m = length(s)$ times as in each iteration p moves right on s but p never moves left in the algorithm. As a result q can move right on *pat* at most m times (line 9). Since each execution of the **else** clause in line 13 moves q left on *pat*, it follows that this clause can be executed at most m times as otherwise q must fall off the left end of *pat*. As a result, the maximum number of iterations of the **while** loop of lines 6–13 is m and the computing time of *pmatch* is $O(m)$. The performance of the algorithm may be improved by starting with a better failure function (see exercise 56).

The preceding discussion shows that *nfind* can be improved to an $O(m)$ algorithm provided we are either given the failure function or *next*. We now look into the problem of determining f. Once f is known, it is easy to get *next*. From exercise 55 we know that the failure function for any pattern $p_1p_2 \ldots p_n$ is given by:

$$f(j) = \begin{cases} 0 & \text{if } j = 0, 1 \\ f^m(j - 1) + 1 & \text{where } m \text{ is the least integer } k \text{ for which} \\ & p_{f^k(j-1)+1} = p_j \\ 0 & \text{if there is no } k \text{ satisfying the above} \end{cases}$$

(note that $f^1(j) = f(j)$ and $f^m(j) = f(f^{m-1}(j))$)

This directly yields the procedure of Program 4.43 to compute f.

```
1   procedure fail(p : pattern; var f : failure);
2   {compute the failure function for the pattern p[1..n]}
3   var i,j : integer;
4   begin
5     f[1] := 0;
6     for j := 2 to n do {compute f[j]}
7     begin
8       i := f[j- 1];
9       while (p[j] <> p[i + 1]) and (i > 0) do i := f[i];
10      if p[j] = p[i+1] then f[j] := i + 1
11                       else f[j] := 0;
12    end;
13  end; {of fail}
```

Program 4.43   Fail

In analyzing the computing time of this algorithm we note that in each iteration of the **while** loop of line 9 the value of i decreases (by the definition of f). The variable i is reset at the beginning of each iteration of the **for** loop. However, it is either reset to 0 (when $j = 2$ or when the previous iteration went through line 11) or it is reset to a value 1 greater than its terminal value on the previous iteration (i.e. when the previous iteration went through line 10). Since only n executions of line 8 are made, the value of i therefore has a total increment of at most n. Hence it cannot be decremented more than n times. Consequently the **while** loop of line 9 is iterated at most n times over the whole algorithm and the computing time of *fail* is $O(n)$.

Even if we are not given the failure function for a pattern, pattern matching can be carried out in time $O(n + m)$. This is an improvement over *nfind*.

REFERENCES AND SELECTED READINGS

A general reference for the topics discussed here is *The Art of Computer Programming: Fundamental Algorithms* by D. Knuth, volume I 2nd edition, Addison-Wesley, Reading, 1973.

For a discussion of early list processing systems see "Symmetric list processor" by J. Weizenbaum, *CACM*, vol. 6, no. 9, Sept. 1963, pp. 524-544.

"A comparison of list processing computer languages," by Bobrow and B. Raphael, *CACM*, vol. 7, no. 4, April 1964, pp. 231-240.

"An introduction to IPL-V" by A. Newell and F. M. Tonge, *CACM*, vol. 3, no. 4, April 1960, pp. 205-211.

"Recursive functions of symbolic expressions and their computation by machine: I," by J. McCarthy, *CACM*, vol. 3, no. 4, April 1960, pp. 184-195.

For a survey of symbol manipulation systems see *Proceedings of the Second Symposium on Symbolic and Algebraic Manipulation,* ed. S. R. Petrick, March, 1971, available from ACM.

For further articles on dynamic storage allocation see "An estimate of the store size necessary for dynamic storage allocation" by J. Robson, *JACM*, vol. 18, no. 3, July 1971, pp. 416-423.

"Multiword list items" by W.T. Comfort, *CACM*, vol. 7, no. 6, June 1964, pp. 357-362.

"A weighted buddy method for dynamic storage allocation" by K. Shen and J. Peterson, *CACM*, vol. 17, no. 10, October 1974, pp. 558-562.

"Statistical properties of the buddy system," by P. Purdom and S. Stigler, *JACM*, vol. 14, no. 4, October 1970, pp. 683-697.

"A class of dynamic memory allocation algorithms," by D. Hirschberg, *CACM*, vol. 16, no. 10, October 1973, pp. 615-618.

The reference count technique for lists was first given in "A method for overlapping and erasure of lists," by G. Collins, *CACM*, vol. 3, no. 12, December 1960, pp. 655-657.

The algorithm *mark2* is adapted from: "An efficient machine-independent procedure for garbage collection in various list structures," by H. Schorr and W. Waite, *CACM*, vol. 10, no. 8, Aug. 1967, pp. 501-506.

More list copying and marking algorithms may be found in "Copying list structures using bounded workspace," by G. Lindstrom, *CACM*, vol. 17, no. 4, April 1974, pp. 198-202; "A nonrecursive list moving algorithm," by E. Reingold, *CACM*, vol. 16, no. 5, May 1973, p. 305-307; "Bounded workspace garbage collection in an address-order preserving list processing environment," by D. Fisher, *Information Processing Letters*, vol. 3, no. 1, July 1974, pp. 29-32.

For string processing systems see the early works "COMIT," by V. Yngve, *CACM*, vol. 6, no. 3, March 1963, pp. 83–84; SNOBOL, A String Manipulation Language, by D. Farber, R. Griswold and I. Polonsky, *JACM*, vol. 11, no. 1, 1964, pp. 21–30; "String processing techniques," by S. Madnick, *CACM*, vol. 10, no. 7, July 1967, pp. 420–427; "Fast Pattern Matching in Strings," by D. Knuth, J. Morris and V. Pratt, Stanford Technical Report #74-440, August 1974.

EXERCISES

Exercises 1–6 assume that each node has two fields: *data* and *link*.

1. Write an algorithm *length* to count the number of nodes in a singly linked list p, where p points to the first node in the list. The last node has link field **nil**.

2. Let p be a pointer to the first node in a singly linked list and x an arbitrary node in this list. Write an algorithm to delete this node from the list. If $x = p$, then p should be reset to point to the new first node in the list.

3. Let $x = (x_1, x_2, ..., x_n)$ and $y = (y_1, y_2, ..., y_m)$ be two linked lists. Write an algorithm to merge the two lists together to obtain the linked list $z = (x_1, y_1, x_2, y_2, ..., x_m, y_m, x_{m+1}, ..., x_n)$ if $m \leq n$ and $z = (x_1, y_1, x_2, y_2, ..., x_n, y_n, y_{n+1}, ..., y_m)$ if $m > n$. No additional nodes may be used.

4. Do exercise 1 for the case of circularly linked lists.

5. Do exercise 2 for the case of circularly linked lists.

6. Do exercise 3 for the case of circularly linked lists.

7. Devise a representation for a list where insertions and deletions can be made at either end. Such a structure is called a deque. Write a procedure for inserting and deleting at either end.

8. Consider the hypothetical data object $X2$. $X2$ is a linear list with the restriction that while additions to the list may be made at either end, deletions can be made from one end only. Design a linked list representation for $X2$. Write addition and deletion algorithms for $X2$. Specify initial and boundary conditions for your representation.

9. Give an algorithm for a singly linked circular list which reverses the direction of the links.

10. Let p be a pointer to a circularly linked list. Show how this list may be used as a queue. I.e., write algorithms to add and delete elements. Specify the value for p when the queue is empty.

11. It is possible to traverse a singly linked list in both directions (i.e., left to right and a restricted right to left traversal) by reversing the links during the left to right traversal. A possible configuration for a list p under this scheme would be:

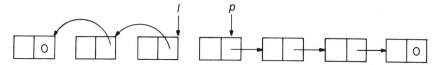

p points to the node currently being examined and l to the node on its left. Note that all nodes to the left of p have their links reversed.

  i)   Write an algorithm to move p, n nodes to the right from a given position (l,p).

 ii)   Write an algorithm to move p, n nodes left from any given position (l,p).

12. Write an algorithm $pread(x)$ to read in n pairs of coefficients and exponents, (c_i, e_i) $1 \leq i \leq n$ of a univariate polynomial, x, and to convert the polynomial into the circular linked list structure of section 4.3. Assume $e_i > e_{i+1}$, $1 \leq i < n$, and that $c_i \neq 0$, $1 \leq i \leq n$. Your algorithm should leave x pointing to the head node. Show that this operation can be performed in time $O(n)$.

13. Let a and b be pointers to the head nodes of two polynomials represented as in exercise 12. Write an algorithm to compute the product polynomial $c = a * b$. Your algorithm should leave a and b unaltered and create c as a new list. Show that if n and m are the number of terms in a and b respectively, then this multiplication can be carried out in time $O(nm^2)$ or $O(mn^2)$. If a, b are dense show that the multiplication takes $O(mn)$.

14. Let a be a pointer to the head node of a univariate polynomial as in section 4.3. Write an algorithm, $peval$ (a,x) to evaluate the polynomial a at the point x, where x is some real number.

15. Extend the equivalence algorithm of section 4.5 to handle the case when the variables being equivalenced may be subscripted. The input now consists of 4-tuples $(i, ioff, j, joff)$ where i and j, as before, represent the variables. $Ioff$ and $joff$ give the position in i or j being equivalenced relative to the start of i or j. For example, if i represents the array A dimensioned $A(-6:10)$ and j the array B dimensioned $B(1:20)$, the equivalence EQUIVALENCE($A(5),B(6)$) will be represented by the 4-tuple $(i, 12, j, 6)$. Your algorithm will begin by reading in these 4-tuples and setting them up in lists as in section 4.5. Each node on a list will have three fields $ioff, jvar, joff$. Thus, for the equivalence 4-tuple above, the node $\boxed{12 \mid j \mid 6}$ will be put onto the list for i and the node $\boxed{6 \mid i \mid 12}$ onto the list for j. Now process these lists outputting equivalence classes. With each class, output the relative position of each member of the class and check for conflicting equivalences.

In exercises 16–20 the sparse matrices are represented as in section 4.6.

16. Let a and b be two sparse matrices represented as in section 4.6. Write an algorithm, $madd(a,b,c)$ to create the matrix $c = a + b$. Your algorithm should leave the matrices a and b unchanged and set up c as a new matrix in accordance with this data representation. Show that if a and b are $n \times m$ matrices with r_A and r_B nonzero terms, then this addition can be carried out in $O(n + m + r_A + r_B)$ time.

17. Let a and b be two sparse matrices. Write an algorithm $mmul(a,b,c)$ to set up the structure for $c = a * b$. Show that if a is an $n \times m$ matrix with r_A nonzero terms and if b is an $m \times p$ matrix with r_B nonzero terms, then c can be computed in time $O(pr_A + nr_B)$. Can you think of a way to compute c in $O(min\{ pr_A, nr_B\})$?

18. Write an algorithm to write out the terms of a sparse matrix a as triples (i,j,a_{ij}). The terms are to be output by rows and within rows by columns. Show that this operation can be performed in time $O(n + r_A)$ if there are r_A nonzero terms in a and a is an $n \times m$ matrix.

19. Write an algorithm $mtrp(a,b)$ to compute the matrix $b = a^T$, the transpose of the sparse matrix a. What is the computing time of your algorithm?

20. Design an algorithm to copy a sparse matrix. What is the computing time of your algorithm?

21. A simpler and more efficient representation for sparse matrices can be obtained when one is restricted to the operations of addition, subtraction and multiplication. In this representation, nodes have the fields: *down*, *right*, *row*, *col*, and *value*. Each nonzero term is representated by a node. These nodes are linked together to form two circular lists. The first list, the rowlist, is made up by linking nodes by rows and within rows by columns. This is done via the *right* field. The second list, the column list, is made up by linking nodes via the *down* field. In this list, nodes are linked by columns and within columns by rows. These two lists share a common head node. In addition, a node is added to contain the dimensions of the matrix. The matrix a of figure 4.12 has the representation shown in figure 4.46.

    Using the same assumptions as for algorithm *mread* of section 4.6 write an algorithm to read in a matrix and set up its internal representation as above. How much time does your algorithm take? How much additional space is needed?

22. For the representation of exercise 21 write algorithms to
    (i)   erase a matrix
    (ii) add two matrices

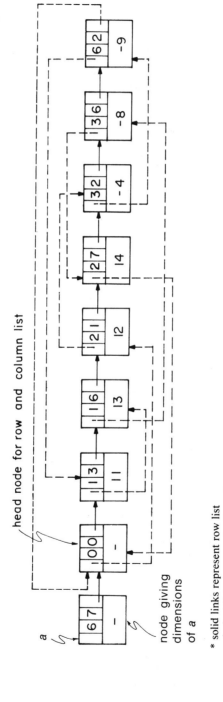

head node for row and column list

node giving
dimensions
of a

* solid links represent row list
dashed links represent column list

Figure 4.46 Representation of matrix A of figure 4.12 using the scheme of exercise 21.

(iii) multiply two matrices
(iv) print out a matrix
For each of the above obtain computing times. How do these times compare with the corresponding times for the representation of section 4.6?

23. Compare the sparse representations of exercise 21 and section 4.6 with respect to some other operations. For example, how much time is needed to output the entries in an arbitrary row or column?

24. (a) Write an algorithm *bestfit(n,p)* similar to algorithm *firstfit* of section 4.7 to allocate a block of size n using a best fit strategy. Each block in the chain of available blocks has a *size* field giving the number of words in that block. The chain has a head node, *av* (see figure 4.18). The best fit strategy examines each block in this chain. The allocation is made from the smallest block of size $\geq n$. p is set to the starting address of the space allocated.
(b) Which of the algorithms *bestfit* and *firstfit* takes less time?
(c) Give an example of a sequence of requests for memory and memory freeing that can be met by *bestfit* but not by *firstfit*.
(d) Do (c) for a sequence that can be met by *firstfit* but not by *bestfit*.

25. Which of the two algorithms *allocate* and *free* of section 4.7 require the condition $tag[0] = tag[m + 1] = 1$ in order to work right? Why?

26. Consider the operation XOR (exclusive OR, also written as ⊕) defined as below (for i,j binary):

$$i \oplus j = \begin{cases} 0 & \text{if } i \text{ and } j \text{ are identical} \\ 1 & \text{otherwise} \end{cases}$$

This differs from the usual OR of logic in that

$$i \text{ OR } j = \begin{cases} 0 & \text{if } i = j = 0 \\ 1 & \text{otherwise} \end{cases}$$

The definition can be extended to the case where i and j are binary strings (i.e., take the XOR of corresponding bits of i and j). So, for example, if $i = 10110$ and $j = 01100$, then $i \text{ XOR } j = i \oplus j = 11010$.

Note that $a \oplus (a \oplus b) = (a \oplus a) \oplus b = b$
and that $(a \oplus b) \oplus b = a \oplus (b \oplus b) = a$

This gives us a space saving device for storing the right and left links of a doubly linked list. The nodes will now have only two fields: *info* and *link*. If l is to the left of node x and r to its right, then $link(x) = l \oplus r$ (as in the case of the storage management algorithms, we assume that available memory is an array *memory* $[1..n]$ and that the *link* field just gives us the next node's position in this array). For the leftmost node $l = 0$ and for the rightmost node $r = 0$.

Let (l,r) be a doubly linked list so represented. l points to the leftmost node and r to the right most node in the list.

   i)   Write an algorithm to traverse the doubly linked list (l,r) from left to right listing out the contents of the *info* field of each node.

   ii) Write an algorithm to traverse the list right to left listing out the contents of the *info* field of each node.

27. Design a storage management scheme for the case when all requests for memory are of the same size, say k. Is it necessary to coalesce adjacent blocks that are free? Write algorithms to free and allocate storage in this scheme.

28. Consider the dynamic storage management problem in which requests for memory are of varying sizes as in section 4.7. Assume that blocks of storage are freed according to the LAFF discipline (Last Allocated First Freed).

   (i)   Design a structure to represent the free space.

   (ii) Write an algorithm to allocate a block of storage of size n.

   (iii) Write an algorithm to free a block of storage of size n beginning at p.

29. In the case of static storage allocation all the requests are known in advance. If there are n requests $r_1, r_2, ..., r_n$ and $\Sigma r_i \leq M$ where M is the total amount of memory available, then all requests can be met. So, assume $\Sigma r_i > M$.

   i)   Which of these n requests should be satisfied if we wish to maximize the number of satisfied requests?

   ii) Under the maximization criterion of (i), how small can the ratio $\dfrac{\text{storage allocated}}{M}$ get?

   iii) Would this be a good criterion to use if jobs are charged a flat rate, say \$3 per job, independent of the size of the request?

   iv) The pricing policy of (iii) is unrealistic when there can be much variation in request size. A more realistic policy is to charge say x cents per unit of request. Is the criterion of (i) a good one for this pricing policy? What would be a good maximization criterion for storage allocation now?

Write an algorithm to determine which requests are to be satisfied now. How much time does your algorithm take as a function of n, the number of requests? [If your algorithm takes a polynomial amount of time, and works correctly, take it to your instructor immediately. You have made a major discovery.]

30. [Buddy System] The text examined the boundary tag method for dynamic storage management. The next 6 exercises will examine an alternative approach in which only blocks of size a power of 2 will be allocated. Thus if a request for a block of size n is made, then a block of size $\lceil \log_2 n \rceil$ is allocated. As a result of this, all free blocks are also of size a power of 2. If the total memory size is 2^m addressed from 0 to $2^m - 1$, then the possible sizes for free blocks are 2^k, $0 \leq k \leq m$. Free blocks of the same size will be maintained in the same available space list. Thus, this system will have $m+1$ available space lists.

Each list is a doubly linked circular list and has a head node $avail[i]$, $0 \leq i \leq$ m. Every free node has the following structure:

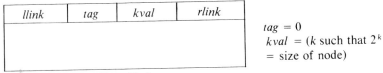

llink	tag	kval	rlink

$tag = 0$
$kval = (k$ such that 2^k
$= $ size of node)

Free Node

Initially all of memory is free and consists of one block beginning at 0 and of size 2^m. Write an algorithm to initialize all the available space lists.

31. [Buddy System Allocation] Using the available space list structure of exercise 30 write an algorithm to meet a request of size n if possible. Note that a request of size n is to be met by allocating a block of size 2^k, $k = \lceil \log_2 n \rceil$. To do this examine the available space lists $avail[i]$, $k \leq i \leq m$ finding the smallest i for which $avail[i]$ is not empty. Remove one block from this list. Let p be the starting address of this block. If $i > k$, then the block is too big and is broken into two blocks of size 2^{i-1} beginning at p and $p + 2^{i-1}$ respectively. The block beginning at $p + 2^{i-1}$ is inserted into the corresponding available list. If $i - 1 > k$, then the block is to be further split and so on. Finally, a block of size 2^k beginning at p is allocated. A block in use has the form:

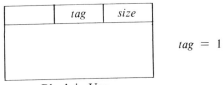

	tag	size

$tag = 1$

Block in Use

(i) Write an algorithm using the strategy outlined above to allocate a block of storage to meet a request for n units of memory.

(ii) For a memory of size $2^m = 16$ draw the binary tree representing the splitting of blocks taking place in satisfying 16 consecutive requests for memory of size 1. (Note that the use of the tag in the allocated block does not really create a problem in allocations of size 1 since memory would be allocated in units where 1 unit may be a few thousand words.) Label each node in this tree with its starting address and present $kval$, i.e., power of 2 representing its size.

32. [Locating Buddies] Two nodes in the tree of exercise 31 are said to be buddies if they are sibling nodes. Prove that two nodes starting at x and y, respectively, are buddies iff:

(i) the $kvals$ for x and y are the same; and

(ii) $x = y \oplus 2^k$ where $\oplus$ is the exclusive OR (XOR) operation defined in exercise 26. The $\oplus$ is taken pairwise bitwise on the binary representation of y and 2^k.

33.   [Freeing and Coalescing Blocks] When a block with $kval$ k becomes free it is to be returned to the available space list. Free blocks are combined into bigger free blocks iff they are buddies. This combining follows the reverse process adopted during allocation. If a block beginning at p and of size k becomes free, it is to be combined with its buddy $p \oplus 2^k$ if the buddy is free. The new free block beginning at $l = \min \{p,p \oplus 2^k\}$ and of size $k + 1$ is to be combined with its buddy $l \oplus 2^{k+1}$ if free and so on. Write an algorithm to free a block beginning at p and having $kval = k$ combining buddies that are free.

34.   (i)   Does the freeing algorithm of exercise 33 always combine adjacent free blocks? If not, give a sequence of allocations and freeings of storage showing this to be the case.

(ii)   How small can the ratio $\dfrac{\text{storage requested}}{\text{storage allocated}}$ be for the Buddy System?
Storage requested $= \Sigma n_i$ where n_i is the actual amount requested. Give an example approaching this ratio.

(iii)   How much time does the allocation algorithm take in the worst case to make an allocation if the total memory size is 2^m?

(iv)   How much time does the freeing algorithm take in the worst case to free a block of storage?

35.   [Buddy system when memory size is not a power of 2]
(i)   How are the available space lists to be initialized if the total storage available is not a power of 2?

(ii)   What changes are to be made to the block freeing algorithm to take care of this case? Do any changes have to be made to the allocation algorithm?

36.   Write a nonrecursive version of algorithm $lerase(x)$ of section 4.8.

37.   Write a nonrecursive version of algorithm $equal(s,t)$ of section 4.8.

38.   Write a nonrecursive version of algorithm $depth(s)$ of section 4.8.

39.   Write a procedure which takes an arbitrary nonrecursive list l with no shared sublists and inverts it and all of its sublists. For example, if $l = (a, (b,c))$, then inverse $(l) = ((c,b),a)$.

40.   Devise a procedure that produces the list representation of an arbitrary list given its linear form as a string of atoms, commas, blanks and parentheses.

For example, for the input $l = (a,(b,c))$, your procedure should produce the structure:

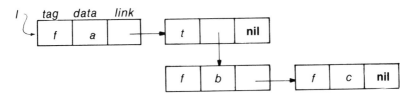

41. One way to represent generalized lists is through the use of two field nodes and a symbol table which contains all atoms and list names together with pointers to these lists. Let the two fields of each node be named *alink* and *blink*. Then *blink* either points to the next node on the same level, if there is one, or is **nil**. The *alink* field either points to a node at a lower level or, in the case of an atom or list name, to the appropriate entry in the symbol table. For example, the list $B(A,(D,E),(\ ),B)$ would have the representation:

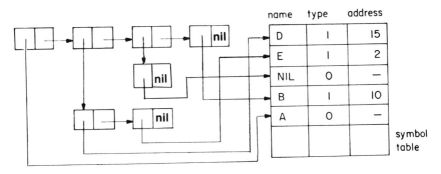

(The list names D and E were already in the table at the time the list B was input. A was not in the table and so is assumed to be an atom.)

The symbol table retains a type bit for each entry. Type $= 1$ if the entry is a list name and type $= 0$ for atoms. The NIL atom may either be in the table or *alink* can be set to **nil** to represent the NIL atom. Write an algorithm to read in a list in parentheses notation and to set up its linked representation as above with x set to point to the first node in the list. Note that no head nodes are in use. The following subalgorithms may be used by *lread*.

  (i)   *get(a,p)* ... searches the symbol table for the name a. p is set to 0 if a is not found in the table, otherwise, p is set to the position of a in the table.

  (ii)   *put(a,t,p)* ... enters a into the table. p is the position at which a was entered. If a is already in the table, then the type and address fields of the old entry are changed. $t = $ **nil** to enter an atom or $t <>$ **nil** to enter a list with first node *t*. (*Note*: this permits definition of lists using indirect recursion). The diagram is for the case when the addresses *t* are integers.

(iii)   *nexttoken* ... gets next token in input list. (A token may be a list name, atom, '(' ')' or ','. A '#' is returned if there are no more tokens.)

(iv)   *new(x)* ... gets a node for use.

You may assume that the input list is syntactically correct. In case a sublist is labeled as in the list $C(D,E(F,G))$ the structure should be set up as in the case $C(D,(F,G))$ and E should be entered into the symbol table as a list with the appropriate storing address.

42.   Rewrite algorithm *mark*1 of section 4.9 using the conventions of section 4.8 for the tag field.

43.   Rewrite algorithm *mark*1 of section 4.9 for the case when each list and sublist has a head node. Assume that the *dlink* field of each head node is free and so may be used to maintain a linked stack without using any additional space. Show that the computing time is still $O(m)$.

44.   When the *dlink* field of a node is used to retain atomic information as in section 4.8, implementing the marking strategy of *mark*2 requires an additional bit in each node. In this exercise we shall explore a marking strategy which does not require this additional bit. Its worst case computing time will however be $O(mn)$ where *m* is the number of nodes marked and *n* the total number of nodes in the system. Write a marking algorithm using the node structure and conventions of section 4.8. Each node has the fields: *mark*, *tag*, *dlink* and *rlink*. Your marking algorithm will use variable *p* to point to the node currently being examined and *next* to point to the next node to be examined. If *l* is the address of the as yet unexplored list node with least address and *p* the address of the node currently being examined then the value of *next* will be min $\{l,p + 1\}$. Show that the computing time of your algorithm is $O(mn)$.

45.   Prove that *mark*2(*x*) marks all unmarked nodes accessible from *x*.

46.   Write a composite marking algorithm using *mark*1, *mark*2 and a fixed amount *m* of stack space. Stack nodes as in *mark*1 until the stack is full. When the stack becomes full, revert to the strategy of *mark*2. On completion of *mark*2, pick up a node from the stack and explore it using the composite algorithm. In case the stack never overflows, the composite algorithm will be as fast as *mark*1. When $m = 0$, the algorithm essentially becomes *mark*2. The computing time will in general be somewhere in between that of *mark*1 and *mark*2.

47.   Write a storage compaction algorithm to be used following the marking phase of garbage collection. Assume that all nodes are of a fixed size and can be addressed *node[i]*, $1 \le i \le m$. Show that this can be done in two phases, where

in the first phase a left to right scan for free nodes and a right to left scan for nodes in use is carried out. During this phase, used nodes from the right end of memory are moved to free positions at the left end. The relocated address of such nodes is noted in one of the fields of the old address. At the end of this phase all nodes in use occupy a contiguous chunk of memory at the left end. In the second phase links to relocated nodes are updated.

48. Write a compaction algorithm to be used in conjunction with the boundary tag method for storage management. Show that this can be done in one left to right scan of memory blocks. Assume that memory blocks are independent and do not reference each other. Further assume that all memory references within a block are made relative to the start of the block. Assume the start of each in-use block is in a table external to the space being allocated.

49. Design a dynamic storage management system in which blocks are to be returned to the available space list only during compaction. At all other times, a *tag* is set to indicate the block has become free. Assume that initially all of memory is free and available as one block. Let memory be addressed 1 through m. For your design, write the following algorithms:
    (i)   *allocate(n,p)* ... allocates a block of size n; p is set to its starting address. Assume that size n includes any space needed for control fields in your design.
    (ii) *free(n,p)* ... free a block of size n beginning at p.
    (iii) *compact* ... compact memory and reinitialize the available space list. You may assume that all address references within a block are relative to the start of the block and so no link fields within blocks need be changed. Also, there are no interblock references.

50. Write an algorithm to make an in-place replacement of a substring of x by the string y. Assume that strings are represented using fixed size nodes and that each node in addition to a link field has space for 4 characters. Use $\sim$ to fill up any unused space in a node.

51. Using the definition of STRING given in section 4.10, simulate the axioms as they would apply to (i) CONCAT(S,T) (ii) SUBSTR(S,2,3), (iii) INDEX(S,T) where S = 'abcde' and T = 'cde'.

52. If $x = (x_1, ...,x_m)$ and $y = (y_1, ...,y_n)$ are strings where x_i and y_i are letters of the alphabet, then x is less than y if $x_i = y_i$ for $1 \le i \le j$ and $x_j < y_j$ or if $x_i = y_i$ for $1 \le i \le m$ and $m < n$. Write an algorithm which takes two strings x,y and returns either $-1, 0, +1$ if $x < y$, $x = y$ or $x > y$, respectively.

53. Let x and y be strings represented as singly linked lists. Write a procedure which finds the first character of x that does not occur in the string y.

54. Show that the computing time for procedure *nfind* is still $O(mn)$. Find a string and a pattern for which this is true.

55. (a) Compute the failure function for each of the following patterns:

(i) $a\ a\ a\ a\ b$

(ii) $a\ b\ a\ b\ a\ a$

(iii) $a\ b\ a\ a\ b\ a\ a\ b\ b$

(b) For each of the above patterns obtain the linked list representations including the field *next* as in figure 4.44.

(c) Let $p_1 p_2 \ldots p_n$ be a pattern of length n. Let f be its failure function. Define $f^1(j) = f(j)$ and $f^m(j) = f(f^{m-1}(j))$, $1 \le j \le n$ and $m > 1$. Show using the definition of f that:

$$f(j) = \begin{cases} 0 & \text{if } j = 1 \\ f^m(j-1) + 1 & \text{where } m \text{ is the least integer } k \text{ for which} \\ & p_{f^k(j-1)+1} = p_j \\ 0 & \text{if there is no } k \text{ satisfying the above} \end{cases}$$

56. The definition of the failure function may be strengthened to

$$f(j) = \begin{cases} \text{largest } i < j & \text{such that } p_1 p_2 \ldots p_i = p_{j-i+1}\, p_{j-i+2} \ldots p_j \\ & \text{and } p_{i+1} \ne p_{j+1} \\ 0 & \text{if there is no } i \ge 1 \text{ satisfying above} \end{cases}$$

(a) Obtain the new failure function for the pattern *pat* of the text.

(b) Show that if this definition for f is used in the definition of *next* then algorithm *pmatch* still works correctly.

(c) Modify algorithm *fail* to compute f under this definition. Show that the computing time is still $O(m)$.

(d) Are there any patterns for which the observed computing time of *pmatch* is more with the new definition of f than with the old one? Are there any for which it is less? Give examples.

57. [Programming Project]

Design a linked allocation system to represent and manipulate univariate polynomials with integer coefficients (use circular linked lists with head nodes). Each term of the polynomial will be represented as a node. Thus, a node in this system will have three fields as below:

Exponent	Link
Coefficient	

In order to erase polynomials efficiently, we shall need to use an available space list and associated procedures as described in section 4.3. The external (i.e., for input or output) representation of a univariate polynomial will be assumed to be a sequence of integers of the form: $ne_1c_1e_2c_2e_3c_3 \ldots e_nc_n$, where the e_i represent the exponents and the c_i the coefficients. n gives the number of terms in the polynomial. The exponents are in decreasing order, i.e., $e_1 > e_2 > \ldots > e_n$.

Write and test the following procedures:

  (i)   *pread(x)* ... read in an input polynomial and convert it to its circular list representation using a head node. *x* is set to point to the head node of this polynomial.

  (ii)   *pwrite(x)* ... convert the polynomial *x* from its linked list representation to its external representation and output it.

  (iii)   *padd(x,y,z)* ... $z = x + y$

  (iv)   *psub(x,y,z)* ... $z = x - y$

  (v)   *pmul(x,y,z)* ... $z = x * y$

  (vi)   *peval(x,a,v)* ... *a* is a real constant and the polynomial *x* is evaluated at the point *a*. *v* is set to this value.

  Note: Procedures iii-vi should leave the input polynomials unaltered after completion of their respective tasks.

  (vii)   *perase(x)* ... return the circular list *x* to the available space list.

58. [Programming Project] In this project, we shall implement a complete linked list system to perform arithmetic on sparse matrices using the representation of section 4.6. First, design a convenient node structure assuming *value* is an integer.

Since we shall need to erase circular lists, we shall utilize the available space list concept introduced in section 4.3. So, we may begin by writing and testing the procedures associated with this list. Next, write and test the following procedures for matrix operations:

a) *mread(a)* ... read matrix *a* and set up according to the representation of section 4.6. The input has the following format:

  line 1:   *n m r* n = # or rows
                             m = # or columns
                             r = # of nonzero terms

  line 2 ⎫
    . ⎬ triples of (row, column, value)
    . ⎭

These triples are in increasing order by rows. Within rows, the triples are in increasing order of columns. The data is to be read in one line at a time and converted to internal representation. The variable *a* is set to point to the head node of the circular list of head nodes (as in the text).

b) *mwrite(a)* ... print out the terms of *a*. To do this, you will have to design a suitable output format. In any case, the output should be ordered by rows and within rows by columns.

c) *merase(a)* ... return all nodes of the sparse matrix *a* to the available space list.

d) *madd(a,b,c)* ... create the sparse matrix $c = a + b$. *a* and *b* are to be left unaltered.

e) *msub(a,b,c)* ... $c = a - b$. *a* and *b* are to be left unaltered.

f) *mmul(a,b,c,)* ... create the sparse matrix $c = a * b$. a and b are to be left unaltered.

g) *mtrp(a,b)* ... create the sparse matrix $b = a^t$. a is to be left unaltered.

59. [Programming Project] Do the project of exercise 58 using the matrix representation of exercise 21.

60. (Landweber)

This problem is to simulate an airport landing and takeoff pattern. The airport has 3 runways, runway 1, runway 2 and runway 3. There are 4 landing holding patterns, two for each of the first two runways. Arriving planes will enter one of the holding pattern queues, where the queues are to be as close in size as possible. When a plane enters a holding queue, it is assigned an integer *id* number and an integer giving the number of time units the plane can remain in the queue before it must land (because of low fuel level). There is also a queue for takeoffs for each of the three runways. Planes arriving in a takeoff queue are also assigned an integer *id*. The takeoff queues should be kept approximately the same size.

At each time 0–3 planes may arrive at the landing queues and 0–3 planes may arrive at the takeoff queues. Each runway can handle one takeoff or landing at each time slot. Runway 3 is to be used for takeoffs except when a plane is low on fuel. At each time unit, planes in either landing queue whose air time has reached zero must be given priority over other landings and takeoffs. If only one plane is in this category, runway 3 is to be used. If more than one, then the other runways are also used (at each time at most 3 planes can be serviced in this way).

Use successive even (odd) integers for *id*'s of planes arriving at takeoff (landing) queues. At each time unit assume that arriving planes are entered into queues before takeoffs or landings occur. Try to design your algorithm so that neither landing nor takeoff queues grow excessively. However, arriving planes must be placed at the ends of queues. Queues cannot be reordered.

The output should clearly indicate what occurs at each time unit. Periodically output (a) the contents of each queue; (b) the average takeoff waiting time; (c) the average landing waiting time; (d) the average flying time remaining on landing; and (e) the number of planes landing with no fuel reserve. (b) and (c) are for planes that have taken off or landed, respectively. The output should be self explanatory and easy to understand (and uncluttered).

The input can be from cards (terminal, file) or it can be generated by a random number generator. For each time unit the input is of the form:

col1: 0-3   indicating the number of planes arriving at takeoff queues.
col2: 0-3   indicating # of planes arriving at landing queues
col4-5 1-20 ⎫
col6-7 1-20 ⎬ units of flying time for planes arriving in landing queues
col8-9 1-20 ⎭ (from col2)

Chapter 5

TREES

5.1 BASIC TERMINOLOGY

In this chapter we shall study a very important data object, trees. Intuitively, a tree structure means that the data are organized so that items of information are related by branches. One very common place where such a structure arises is in the investigation of genealogies. There are two types of genealogical charts which are used to present such data: the *pedigree* and the *lineal* chart. Figure 5.1 gives an example of each.

The pedigree chart shows someone's ancestors, in this case those of Dusty, whose two parents are Honey Bear and Brandy. Brandy's parents are Nuggett and Coyote, who are Dusty's grandparents on her father's side. The chart continues one more generation farther back to the great-grandparents. By the nature of things, we know that the pedigree chart is normally two-way branching, though this does not allow for inbreeding. When that occurs we no longer have a tree structure unless we insist that each occurrence of breeding is separately listed. Inbreeding may occur frequently when describing family histories of flowers or animals.

The lineal chart of figure 5.1(b), though it has nothing to do with people, is still a genealogy. It describes, in somewhat abbreviated form, the ancestry of the modern European languages. Thus, this is a chart of descendants rather than ancestors and each item can produce several others. Latin, for instance, is the forebear of Spanish, French, Italian and Rumanian. Proto Indo-European is a prehistoric language presumed to have existed in the fifth millenium B.C. This tree does not have the regular structure of the pedigree chart, but it is a tree structure nevertheless.

With these two examples as motivation let us define formally what we mean by a tree.

Definition: A *tree* is a finite set of one or more nodes such that: (i) there is a specially designated node called the *root*; (ii) the remaining nodes are parti-

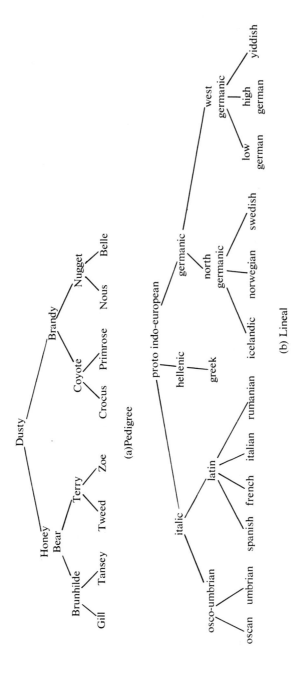

(a) Pedigree

(b) Lineal

Figure 5.1 Two Types of Geneological Charts.

tioned into $n \geq 0$ disjoint sets T_1, ..., T_n where each of these sets is a tree. T_1, ..., T_n are called the *subtrees* of the root.

Again we have an instance of a recursive definition (compare this with the definition of a generalized list in section 4.8). If we return to figure 5.1 we see that the roots of the trees are Dusty and Proto Indo-European. Tree (a) has two subtrees whose roots are Honey Bear and Brandy while tree (b) has 3 subtrees with roots Italic, Hellenic, and Germanic. The condition that T_1, ..., T_n be disjoint sets prohibits subtrees from ever connecting together (no cross breeding). It follows that every item in a tree is the root of some subtree of the whole. For instance, West Germanic is the root of a subtree of Germanic which itself has three subtrees with roots: Low German, High German and Yiddish. Yiddish is a root of a tree with no subtrees.

There are many terms which are often used when referring to trees. A *node* stands for the item of information plus the branches to other items. Consider the tree in figure 5.2. This tree has 13 nodes, each item of data being a single letter for convenience. The root is A and we will normally draw trees with the root at the top. The number of subtrees of a node is called its *degree*. The degree of A is 3, of C is 1 and of F is zero. Nodes that have degree zero are called *leaf* or *terminal* nodes. $\{K,L,F,G,M,I,J\}$ is the set of leaf nodes. Alternatively, the other nodes are referred to as *nonterminals*. The roots of the subtrees of a node, X, are the *children* of X. X is the *parent* of its children. Thus, the children of D are H, I, J; the parent of D is A.

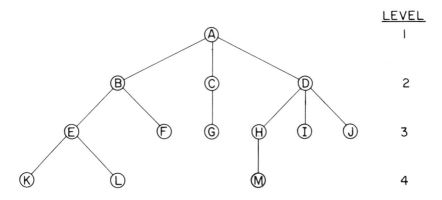

Figure 5.2   A Sample Tree.

Children of the same parent are said to be *siblings*. H, I and J are siblings. We can extend this terminology if we need to so that we can ask for the grandparent of M which is D, etc. The *degree of a tree* is the maximum degree of the nodes in the tree. The tree of figure 5.2 has degree 3. The *ancestors* of a node are all the nodes along the path from the root to that node. The ancestors of M are A, D and H.

The *level* of a node is defined by initially letting the root be at level one. If a node is at level l, then its children are at level $l + 1$. Figure 5.2 shows the levels of all nodes in that tree. The *height* or *depth* of a tree is defined to be the maximum level of any node in the tree.

A *forest* is a set of $n \geq 0$ disjoint trees. The notion of a forest is very close to that of a tree because if we remove the root of a tree we get a forest. For example, in figure 5.2 if we remove A we get a forest with three trees.

There are other ways to draw a tree. One useful way is as a list. The tree of figure 5.2 could be written as the list

$$(A(B(E(K,L),F),C(G),D(H(M),I,J)))$$

The information in the root node comes first followed by a list of the subtrees of that node.

Now, how do we represent a tree in memory? If we wish to use linked lists, then a node must have a varying number of fields depending upon the number of branches.

DATA	LINK 1	LINK 2	•••	LINK n

However, it is often simpler to write algorithms for a data representation where the node size is fixed. Using data and pointer fields we can represent a tree using the fixed node size list structure we devised in Chapter 4. The list representation for the tree of figure 5.2 is on page 207. We can now make use of many of the general procedures that we originally wrote for handling lists. Thus, the data object tree is a special instance of the data object list and we can specialize the list representation scheme to them. In a later section we will see that another data object which can be used to represent a tree is the data object binary tree.

5.2 BINARY TREES

A binary tree is an important type of tree structure which occurs very often. It is characterized by the fact that any node can have at most two branches, i.e., there is no node with degree greater than two. For binary trees we distinguish between the subtree on the left and on the right, whereas for trees the order of the subtrees was irrelevant. Also a binary tree may have zero nodes. Thus a binary tree is really a different object than a tree.

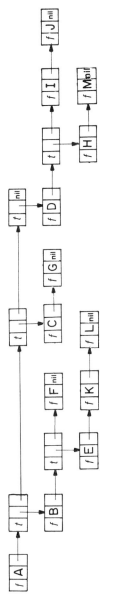

List representation for the tree of figure 5.2

Definition: A *binary tree* is a finite set of nodes which is either empty or consists of a root and two disjoint binary trees called the *left subtree* and the *right subtree*.

Using the notation introduced in Chapter 1 we can define the data structure binary tree as follows:

structure *BTREE*
  declare *CREATE*( ) → *btree*
           ISMTBT(*btree*) → *boolean*
           MAKEBT(*btree,item,btree*) → *btree*
           LCHILD(*btree*) → *btree*
           DATA(*btree*) → *item*
           RCHILD(*btree*) → btree
  for all *p,r* ϵ *btree*, *d* ϵ *item* **let**
    ISMTBT(*CREATE*) :: = **true**
    ISMTBT(*MAKEBT*(*p,d,r*)) :: = **false**
    LCHILD(*MAKEBT*(*p,d,r*)) :: = *p*; *LCHILD*(*CREATE*) :: = *error*
    DATA(*MAKEBT*(*p,d,r*)) :: = *d*; *DATA*(*CREATE*) :: = *error*
    RCHILD(*MAKEBT*(*p,d,r*)) :: = *r*; *RCHILD*(*CREATE*) :: = *error*
  end
end *BTREE*

This set of axioms defines only a minimal set of operations on binary trees. Other operations can usually be built in terms of these. See exercise 35 for an example.

The distinctions between a binary tree and a tree should be analyzed. First of all there is no tree having zero nodes, but there is an empty binary tree. The two binary trees below

are different. The first one has an empty right subtree while the second has an empty left subtree. If the above are regarded as trees, then they are the same despite the fact that they are drawn slightly differently.

Figure 5.3 shows two sample binary trees. These two trees are special kinds of binary trees. The first is a *skewed* tree, skewed to the left, and there is a corresponding one which skews to the right. Tree 5.3(b) is called a *complete* binary tree. This kind of binary tree will be defined formally later on. Notice that all terminal nodes are on adjacent levels. The terms

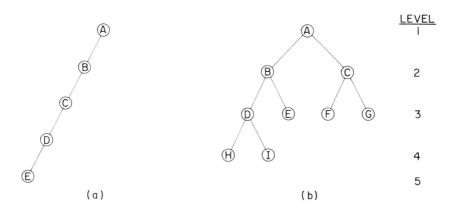

Figure 5.3   Two Sample Binary Trees.

that we introduced for trees such as degree, level, height, leaf, parent, and child all apply to binary trees in the natural way. Before examining data representations for binary trees, let us first make some relevant observations regarding such trees. First, what is the maximum number of nodes in a binary tree of depth k?

Lemma 5.1   (i)   The maximum number of nodes on level i of a binary tree is 2^{i-1}, $i \geq 1$ and

(ii)   The maximum number of nodes in a binary tree of depth k is $2^k - 1$, $k \geq 1$.

Proof: (i) The proof is by induction on i.

Induction Base: The root is the only node on level $i = 1$. Hence the maximum number of nodes on level $i = 1$ is $2^0 = 2^{i-1}$.

Induction Hypothesis: For all j, $1 \leq j < i$, the maximum number of nodes on level j is 2^{j-1}.

Induction Step: The maximum number of nodes on level $i - 1$ is 2^{i-2}, by the induction hypothesis. Since each node in a binary tree has maximum degree 2, the maximum number of nodes on level i is 2 times the maximum number on level $i - 1$ or 2^{i-1}.

(ii)   The maximum number of nodes in a binary tree of depth k is $\Sigma_{i=1}^{k}$ (maximum number of nodes on level i)

$$= \sum_{i=1}^{k} 2^{i-1} = 2^k - 1. \quad \square$$

Next, let us examine the relationship between the number of terminal nodes and the number of nodes of degree 2 in a binary tree.

Lemma 5.2: For any nonempty binary tree, T, if n_0 is the number of terminal nodes and n_2 the number of nodes of degree 2, then $n_0 = n_2 + 1$.
Proof: Let n_1 be the number of nodes of degree 1 and n the total number of nodes. Since all nodes in T are of degree ≤ 2 we have:

$$n = n_0 + n_1 + n_2 \qquad (5.1)$$

If we count the number of branches in a binary tree, we see that every node except for the root has a branch leading into it. If B is the number of branches, then $n = B + 1$. All branches emanate either from a node of degree one or from a node of degree 2. Thus, $B = n_1 + 2n_2$. Hence, we obtain

$$n = 1 + n_1 + 2n_2 \qquad (5.2)$$

Subtracting (5.2) from (5.1) and rearranging terms we get

$$n_0 = n_2 + 1 \qquad \square$$

In figure 5.3(a) $n_0 = 1$ and $n_2 = 0$ while in figure 5.3(b) $n_0 = 5$ and $n_2 = 4$.
As we continue our discussion of binary trees, we shall derive some other interesting properties.

5.3 BINARY TREE REPRESENTATIONS

A *full* binary tree of depth k is a binary tree of depth k having $2^k - 1$ nodes. By lemma 5.1, this is the maximum number of nodes such a binary tree can have. Figure 5.4 shows a full binary tree of depth 4. A very elegant sequential representation for such binary trees results from sequentially numbering the nodes, starting with nodes on level 1, then those on level 2 and so on. Nodes on any level are numbered from left to right (see figure 5.4). This numbering scheme gives us the definition of a complete binary tree. A binary tree with n nodes and a depth k is *complete* iff its nodes correspond to the nodes which are numbered one to n in the full binary tree of depth k. The nodes may now be stored in a one dimensional array *tree*, with the node numbered i being stored in *tree*[i]. Lemma 5.3 enables us to easily determine the locations of the parent, left child and right child of any node i in the binary tree.

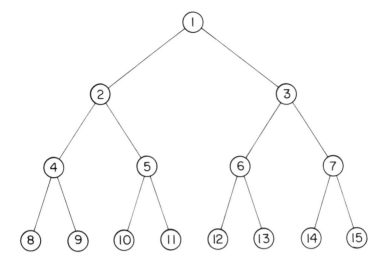

Figure 5.4 Full Binary Tree of Depth 4 with Sequential Node Numbers.

Lemma 5.3: If a complete binary tree with n nodes (i.e., depth $= \lfloor \log_2 n \rfloor +$ 1) is represented sequentially as above then for any node with index i, $1 \leq i$ $\leq n$ we have:

  (i)   *parent*(i) is at $\lfloor i/2 \rfloor$ if $i \neq 1$. When $i = 1$, i is the root and has no parent.

  (ii) *lchild*(i) is at $2i$ if $2i \leq n$. If $2i > n$, then i has no left child.

  (iii) *rchild*(i) is at $2i + 1$ if $2i + 1 \leq n$. If $2i + 1 > n$, then i has no right child.

Proof: We prove (ii). (iii) is an immediate consequence of (ii) and the numbering of nodes on the same level from left to right. (i) follows from (ii) and (iii). We prove (ii) by induction on i. For $i = 1$, clearly the left child is at 2 unless $2 > n$ in which case 1 has no left child. Now assume that for all j, $1 \leq j \leq i$, *lchild*(j) is at $2j$. Then, the two nodes immediately preceding *lchild*($i + 1$) in the representation are the right child of i and the left child of i. The left child of i is at $2i$. Hence, the left child of $i + 1$ is at $2i + 2 = 2(i + 1)$ unless $2(i + 1) > n$ in which case $i + 1$ has no left child.   □

This representation can clearly be used for all binary trees though in most cases there will be a lot of unutilized space. For complete binary trees the representation is ideal as no space is wasted. For the skewed tree of figure 5.3(a), however, less than half the array is utilized. In the worst case a skewed tree of depth k will require $2^k - 1$ spaces. Of these only k will be occupied.

	tree		*tree*
[1]	A		A
[2]	B		B
[3]	—		C
[4]	C		D
[5]	—		E
[6]	—		F
[7]	—		G
[8]	D		H
[9]	—		I
.	.		
.	.		
.	.		
[16]	E		

Figure 5.5   Array Representation of the Binary Trees of figure 5.3.

While the above representation appears to be good for complete binary trees it is wasteful for many other binary trees. In addition, the representation suffers from the general inadequacies of sequential representations. Insertion or deletion of nodes from the middle of a tree requires the movement of potentially many nodes to reflect the change in level number of these nodes. These problems can be easily overcome through the use of a linked representation. Each node will have three fields *leftchild*, *data* and *rightchild* and is defined in Pascal as

type *treepointer* = ↑*treerecord*;
　　treerecord = **record**
　　　　　　　　leftchild : *treepointer*;
　　　　　　　　data : **char**;
　　　　　　　　rightchild : *treepointer*;
　　　　　　　end;

We shall draw such a node using either of the representations below:

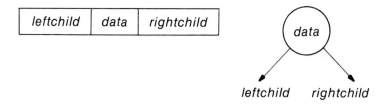

While this node structure will make it difficult to determine the parent of a node, we shall see that for most applications, it is adequate. In case it is necessary to be able to determine the parent of random nodes, then a fourth field *parent* may be included. The representation of the binary tree of figure 5.3 using this node structure is given in figure 5.6. A tree is referred to by the variable that points to its root.

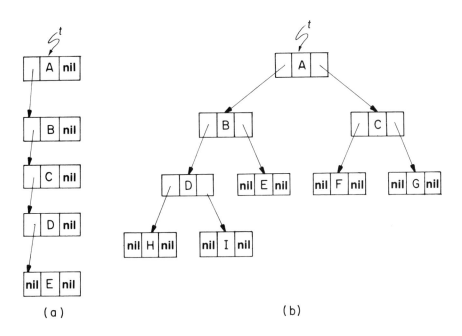

(a)   (b)

Figure 5.6   Linked Representation for the Binary Trees of Figure 5.3.

5.4 BINARY TREE TRAVERSAL

There are many operations that we often want to perform on trees. One notion that arises frequently is the idea of traversing a tree or visiting each node in the tree exactly once. A full traversal produces a linear order for the information in a tree. This linear order may be familiar and useful. When traversing a binary tree we want to treat each node and its subtrees in the same fashion. If we let *L*, *D*, *R* stand for moving left, printing the data, and moving right when at a node then there are six possible combinations of traversal: *LDR*, *LRD*, *DLR*, *DRL*, *RDL*, and *RLD*. If we adopt the convention that we traverse left before right then only three traversals remain: *LDR*, *LRD* and *DLR*. To these we assign the names inorder, postorder and preorder because there is a natural correspondence between these traversals and producing the infix, postfix and prefix forms of an expression. Consider the binary tree of figure 5.7. This tree contains an arithmetic expression with binary operators: add(+), multiply(*), divide(/), exponentiation(**) and variables A, B, C, D, and E. We will not worry for now how this binary tree was formed, but assume that it is available. We will define three types of traversals and show the results for this tree.

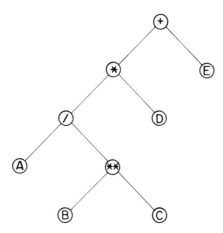

Figure 5.7   Binary Tree with Arithmetic Expression.

Inorder Traversal: informally this calls for moving down the tree towards the left until you can go no farther. Then you "visit" the node, move one node to the right and continue again. If you cannot move to the right, go back one more node. A precise way of describing this traversal is to write it as a recursive procedure.

```
1   procedure inorder(currentnode:treepointer);
2   {currentnode is a pointer to a node in a binary tree. For full
3    tree traversal, pass inorder the pointer to the top of the tree}
4   begin {inorder}
5     if currentnode < > nil
6     then
7     begin
8       inorder(currentnode↑.leftchild);
9       write(currentnode↑.data);
10      inorder(currentnode↑.rightchild);
11    end
12  end; {of inorder}
```

Program 5.1   Inorder

Recursion is an elegant device for describing this traversal. Let us trace how **procedure** *inorder* (program 5.1) works on the tree of figure 5.7.

Call of *inorder*	value in root	Action
MAIN	+	
1	*	
2	/	
3	A	
4	**nil**	write ('A')
4	**nil**	write ('/')
3	**	
4	B	
5	**nil**	write ('B')
5	**nil**	write ('**')
4	C	
5	**nil**	write ('C')
5	**nil**	write ('*')
2	D	
3	**nil**	write ('D')
3	**nil**	write ('+')
1	E	
2	**nil**	write ('E')
2	**nil**	

The elements get output in the order

$$A / B ** C * D + E$$

which is the *in*fix form of the expression.

A second form of traversal is *preorder*:

```
1  procedure preorder(currentnode:treepointer);
2  {currentnode is a pointer to a node in a binary tree. For full
3   tree traversal, pass preorder the pointer to the top of the tree}
4  begin {preorder}
5    if currentnode < > nil
6    then
7    begin
8      write(currentnode↑.data);
9      preorder(currentnode↑.leftchild);
10      preorder(currentnode↑.rightchild);
11    end {of if}
12  end; {of preorder}
```

Program 5.2 Preorder

In words we would say "visit a node, traverse left and continue again. When you cannot continue, move right and begin again or move back until you can move right and resume." The nodes of figure 5.7 would be output in *pre*order as

$$+ * / A ** B\ C\ D\ E$$

which we recognize as the *pre*fix form of the expression.

At this point it should be easy to guess the next traversal method which is called *postorder*:

```
1   procedure postorder(currentnode:treepointer);
2   {currentnode is a pointer to a node in a binary tree. For full
3    tree traversal, pass postorder the pointer to the top of the tree}
4   begin {postorder}
5     if currentnode < > nil
6     then
7     begin
8       postorder(currentnode↑.leftchild);
9       postorder(currentnode↑.rightchild);
10      write(currentnode↑.data);
11    end {of if}
12  end; {of postorder}
```

Program 5.3   Postorder

The output produced by **procedure** *postorder* (program 5.3) is

$$A\ B\ C ** / D * E +$$

which is the *post*fix of our expression.

Though we have written these three algorithms using recursion, it is very easy to produce an equivalent nonrecursive procedure. Let us take inorder as an example. To simulate the recursion we need two stacks, one which will hold values of *pointer* where *pointer* points to a node in the tree and one which holds return addresses to the place where the algorithm should resume after an end is encountered. We replace every recursive call by a mechanism which places the new pair (*pointer, returnad*) onto the stacks and goes to the beginning; and where there is a return or end we insert code which deletes the top pair from the stacks if possible and either ends or branches to *returnad* (see section 4.9 for the exact details). Program 5.4 describes this algorithm fully.

```
1   procedure inorder1 (currentnode:treepointer);
2   {a nonrecursive version of inorder using two stacks of size
3    maxstacksize}
4   label 1,2,3;
5   const maxstacksize  = 100;
6   var stackpointer : 0 .. maxstacksize + 1;
7       returnaddressstack : array [1 .. maxstacksize] of 2 .. 3;
8       nodestack : array [1 .. maxstacksize] of treepointer;
9       addresstoreturnto : integer;
10  begin
11    stackpointer := 0; {initialize the stacks}
12  1: if currentnode < > nil
13    then
14    begin
15      stackpointer := stackpointer + 1;
16      if stackpointer > maxstacksize then stackfull;
17      nodestack[stackpointer] := currentnode;
18      returnaddressstack[stackpointer] := 2;
19      currentnode := currentnode↑.leftchild;
20      goto 1;           {traverse left subtree}
21  2:  write (currentnode↑.data);
22      stackpointer := stackpointer + 1;
23      if stackpointer > maxstacksize then stackfull;
24      nodestack[stackpointer] := currentnode;
25      returnaddressstack[stackpointer] := 3;
26      currentnode := currentnode↑.rightchild;
27      goto 1;           {traverse right subtree}
28    end; {of if}
29  3:if stackpointer <> 0
30    then
31    begin {stack not empty, simulate a return}
32      currentnode := nodestack[stackpointer];
33      addresstoreturnto := returnaddressstack[stackpointer];
34      stackpointer := stackpointer - 1;
35      case addresstoreturnto of
36        2 : goto 2;
37        3 : goto 3;
38      end; {of case}
39    end; {of if}
40  end; {of inorder1}
```

Program 5.4   Inorder1

Though this procedure seems highly unstructured its virtue is that it is semi-automatically produced from the recursive version using a fixed set of rules. Our faith in the correctness of this program can be justified if we first prove the correctness of the original version and then prove that the transformation rules result in a correct and equivalent program. Also we can simplify this program after we make some observations about its behavior. For every pair (*current-node*,3) in the two stacks when we come to label 3 this pair will be removed. All such consecutive pairs will be removed until either *stackpointer* gets set to zero or we reach a pair (*currentnode*,2). Therefore, the presence of label 3 pairs is useful in no way and we can delete that part of the algorithm. This means we can eliminate the lines 22-25. We next observe that this leaves us with only one return address, label 2, so we need not place that on the stack either. Our new version now looks like:

```
1   procedure inorder2(currentnode:treepointer);
2   {simpler, nonrecursive version using one stack of size maxstacksize}
3   const maxstacksize = 100;
4   label 1,2;
5   var stackpointer : integer;
6        nodestack : array [1 .. maxstacksize] of treepointer;
7   begin
8    stackpointer := 0; {initialize the stack}
9   1: if currentnode < > nil
10     then
11     begin
12      stackpointer := stackpointer + 1;
13      if stackpointer > maxstacksize then stackfull;
14      nodestack[stackpointer] := currentnode;
15      currentnode := currentnode↑.leftchild;
16      goto 1;              {traverse left subtree}
17   2: write(currentnode↑.data);
18      currentnode := currentnode↑.rightchild;
19      goto 1;              {traverse right subtree}
20     end;
21     if stackpointer <> 0
22     then
23     begin {stack not empty}
24      currentnode := nodestack[stackpointer];
25      stackpointer := stackpointer − 1;
26      goto 2;
27     end {of if}
28   end; {of inorder2}
```

Program 5.5 Inorder2

This program is considerably simpler than the previous version, but it may still offend some people because of the seemingly undisciplined use of **goto**'s. A structured Pascal version would be:

```
1   procedure inorder3 (currentnode:treepointer);
2   {a nonrecursive, no goto version using a stack of size
3    maxstacksize}
4   const maxstacksize = 100;
5   var done : boolean;
6       stackpointer : integer;
7       nodestack : array[1 .. maxstacksize] of treepointer;
8   begin
9     stackpointer := 0; {initialize the stack}
10    done := false; {initialize loop condition}
11    repeat
12      while currentnode <> nil do {move down leftchild fields}
13      begin
14        stackpointer := stackpointer + 1;
15        if stackpointer > maxstacksize then stackfull;
16        nodestack[stackpointer] := currentnode;
17        currentnode := currentnode↑.leftchild;
18      end; {of while}
19      if stackpointer <> 0
20      then
21      begin
22        currentnode := nodestack[stackpointer];
23        stackpointer := stackpointer - 1;
24        write(currentnode↑.data);
25        currentnode := curentnode↑.rightchild;
26      end
27      else done := true;
28    until done;
29  end; {of inorder3}
```

Program 5.6   Inorder3

What are the computing time and storage requirements of *inorder3*? Let n be the number of nodes in the tree. If we consider the action of the above algorithm, we note that every node of the tree is placed on the stack once. Thus, the statements on lines 14-17 and 22-25 are executed n times. Moreover, *currentnode* will equal **nil** once for every **nil** link in the tree which is exactly

$$2n_0 + n_1 = n_0 + n_1 + n_2 + 1 = n + 1.$$

So every step will be executed no more than some small constant times n or $O(n)$. With some further modifications we can lower the constant (see exercises). The space required for the stack is equal to the depth of the tree. This is at most n.

Before we leave the topic of tree traversal, we shall consider one final question. Is it possible to traverse binary trees without the use of extra space for a stack? One simple solution is to add a *parent* field to each node. Then we can trace our way back up to any root and down again. Another solution which requires two bits per node is given in section 5.6. If the allocation of this extra space is too costly then we can use the method of algorithm *mark*2 of section 4.9. No extra storage is required since during processing the *leftchild* and *rightchild* fields are used to maintain the paths back to the root. The stack of addresses is stored in the leaf nodes. The exercises examine this algorithm more closely.

5.5   MORE ON BINARY TREES

Using the definition of a binary tree and the recursive version of the traversals, we can easily write other routines for working with binary trees. For instance, if we want to produce an exact copy of a given binary tree we can modify the postorder traversal algorithm only slightly to get:

```
1   function copy(originaltree:treepointer): treepointer;
2   {for a binary tree originaltree, copy returns a pointer to an exact
3    copy of originaltree}
4   var temptree : treepointer;
5   begin
6     if originaltree <> nil
7     then
8     begin
9       new(temptree);
10      temptree↑.leftchild := copy(originaltree↑.leftchild);
11      temptree↑.rightchild := copy(originaltree↑.rightchild);
12      temptree↑.data := originaltree↑.data;
13      copy := temptree;
14    end
15    else copy := nil;
16  end {of copy}
```

Program 5.7   Copy

Another problem that is especially easy to solve using recursion is determining the equivalence of two binary trees. Binary trees are equivalent if they have the same topology and the information in corresponding nodes is identical. By the same topology we mean that every branch in one tree corresponds to a branch in the second in the same order. Algorithm *equal*, program 5.8, traverses the binary trees in preorder, though any order could be used.

```
1   function equal(firsttree, secondtree:treepointer): boolean;
2   {this procedure returns false if the binary trees firsttree and
3    secondtree are not equivalent. Otherwise, it will return true}
4   begin
5     equal := false; {initialize answer}
6     if ((firsttree =nil) and (secondtree = nil))
7     then equal := true
8     else
9       if ((firsttree < > nil) and (secondtree < > nil))
10      then
11        if firsttree↑.data = secondtree↑.data
12        then
13          if equal (firsttree↑.leftchild, secondtree↑.leftchild)
14          then
15            equal := equal(firsttree↑.rightchild, secondtree↑.rightchild);
16  end; {of equal}
```

Program 5.8 Equal

We have seen that binary trees arise naturally with genealogical information and further that there is a natural relationship between the tree traversals and various forms of expressions. There are many other instances when binary trees are important, and we will look briefly at two of them now. The first problem has to do with processing a list of alphabetic data, say a list of variable names such as

$$X1, \ I, \ J, \ Z, \ FST, \ X2, \ K.$$

We will grow a binary tree as we process these names in such a way that for each new name we do the following: compare it to the root and if the new name alphabetically precedes the name at the root then move left or else move right; continue making comparisons until we fall off an end of the tree; then create a new node and attach it to the tree in that position. The sequence of binary trees obtained for the above data is given in figure 5.8. Given the tree in figure 5.8(g) consider the order of the identifiers if they were output using an inorder traversal

$$FST, \ I, \ J, \ K, \ X1, \ X2, \ Z$$

So by growing the tree in this way we turn inorder into a sorting method. In Chapter 9 we shall prove that this method works in general.

As a second example of the usefulness of binary trees, consider the set of formulas one can construct by taking variables $x_1, x_2, x_3, \ldots$ and the operators $\wedge$ (**and**), $\vee$ (**or**) and $\neg$ (**not**). These variables can only hold one of two possible values, true or false. The set of expressions which can be formed using these variables and operators is defined by the rules: (i) a variable is an expression; (ii) if x, y are expressions then $x \wedge y$, $x \vee y$, $\neg x$ are expressions. Parentheses can be used to alter the normal order of evaluation which is **not** before **and** before **or**. This comprises the formulas in the *propositional calculus* (other operations such as implication can be expressed using $\wedge$, $\vee$, $\neg$). The expression

$$x_1 \vee (x_2 \wedge \neg x_3)$$

is a formula (read "x_1 or x_2 and not x_3"). If x_1 and x_3 are false and x_2 is true, then the value of this expression is

$$\text{false} \vee (\text{true} \wedge \neg \text{false})$$
$$= \text{false} \vee \text{true}$$
$$= \text{true}$$

The *satisfiability problem* for formulas of the propositional calculus asks if there is an assignment of values to the variables which causes the value of the expression to be true. This problem is of great historical interest in computer science. It was originally used by Newell, Shaw and Simon in the late 1950's to show the viability of heuristic programming (the Logic Theorist).

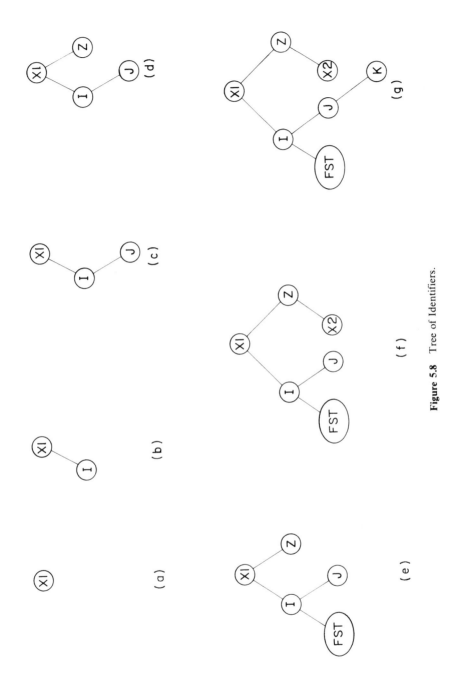

Figure 5.8 Tree of Identifiers.

Again, let us assume that our formula is already in a binary tree, say

$$(x_1 \wedge \neg x_2) \vee (\neg x_1 \wedge x_3) \vee \neg x_3$$

in the tree

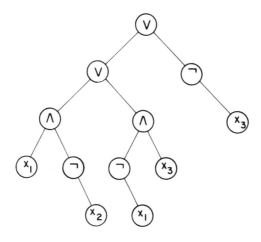

Figure 5.9 Propositional Formula in a Binary Tree.

The inorder of this tree is $x_1 \wedge \neg x_2 \vee \neg x_1 \wedge x_3 \vee \neg x_3$, the infix form of the expression. The most obvious algorithm to determine satisfiability is to let (x_1, x_2, x_3) take on all possible combinations of truth and falsity and to check the formula for each combination. For n variables there are 2^n possible combinations of true $= t$ and false $= f$, e.g. for $n = 3$ (t,t,t), (t,t,f), (t,f,t), (t,f,f), (f,t,t), (f,t,f), (f,f,t), (f,f,f). The algorithm will take at least $O(g2^n)$ or exponential time where g is the time to substitute values for x_1, x_2, x_3 and evaluate the expression.

To evaluate an expression one method would traverse the tree in postorder, evaluating subtrees until the entire expression is reduced to a single value. This corresponds to the postfix evaluation of an arithmetic expression that we saw in section 3.3. Viewing this from the perspective of the tree representation, for every node we reach, the values of its arguments (or children) have already been computed. So when we reach the $\vee$ node on level two, the values of $x_1 \wedge \neg x_2$ and $\neg x_1 \wedge x_3$ will already be available to us and we can apply the rule for **or**. Notice that a node containing $\neg$ has only a single right branch since **not** is a unary operator.

For the purposes of this algorithm we assume each node has four fields:

leftchild	data	value	rightchild

where *leftchild, data, rightchild* are as before and *value* is of type Boolean. This node structure may be defined in Pascal as below

type *typesofdata* = (*logicalnot, logicaland, logicalor, logicaltrue,*
                              logicalfalse);
   treepointer = ↑*treerecord*;
   treerecord = **record**
                leftchild : *treepointer*;
                data   : *typesofdata*;
                value   : **boolean**;
                rightchild : *treepointer*;
          end;

Also we assume that for leaf nodes *t↑.data* contains the current value of the variable represented at this node. With these preparations and assuming an expression with n variables pointed at by *tree* we can now write a first pass at our algorithm for satisfiability:

for all 2^n possible combinations **do**
begin
   generate the next combination;
   replace the variables by their values
   evaluate *tree* by traversing it in postorder;
   if *tree↑.value*
     then output *combination* and **stop**
end
writeln ('*no satisfiable combination*')

Now let us concentrate on this modified version of postorder. Changing the original recursive version seems the simplest thing to do. We obtain the procedure of program 5.9.

```
1  procedure postordereval(tree : treepointer);
2  begin
3    if tree <> nil
4    then
5    begin
6      postordereval(tree↑.leftchild);
7      postordereval(tree↑.rightchild);
8      case tree↑.data of
9        logicalnot  : tree↑.value := not tree↑.rightchild↑.value;
10       logicaland  : tree↑.value := tree↑.leftchild↑.value and
11                       tree↑.rightchild↑.value;
12       logicalor   : tree↑.value := tree↑.leftchild↑.value or
13                       tree↑.rightchild↑.value;
14       logicaltrue : tree↑.value := true;
15       logicalfalse : tree↑.value := false;
16     end; {of case}
17   end; {of if}
18 end; {of postordereval}
```

Program 5.9   Postordereval

5.6 THREADED BINARY TREES

If we look carefully at the linked representation of any binary tree, we notice that there are more null links than actual pointers. As we saw before, there are $n + 1$ null links and $2n$ total links. A clever way to make use of these null links has been devised by A. J. Perlis and C. Thornton. Their idea is to replace the null links by pointers, called threads, to other nodes in the tree. If $p↑.rchild$ is normally equal to **nil**, we will replace it *by a pointer to the node which would be printed after p when traversing the tree in inorder*. A null *leftchild* link at node p is replaced *by a pointer to the node which immediately precedes node p* in inorder. Figure 5.10 shows the binary tree of figure 5.3(b) with its new threads drawn in as dotted lines.

The tree t has 9 nodes and 10 null links which have been replaced by threads. If we traverse t in inorder the nodes will be visited in the order $H\ D\ I\ B\ E\ A\ F\ C\ G$. For example node E has a predecessor thread which points to B and a successor thread which points to A.

In the memory representation we must be able to distinguish between threads and normal pointers. This is done by adding two boolean fields to the record, *leftthread* and *rightthread*.

If $tree↑.leftthread =$ true, then $tree↑.leftchild$ contains a thread and otherwise it contains a pointer to the leftchild. Simularly if $tree↑.rightthread =$

true, then *tree↑.rightchild* contains a thread and otherwise it contains a pointer to the rightchild.

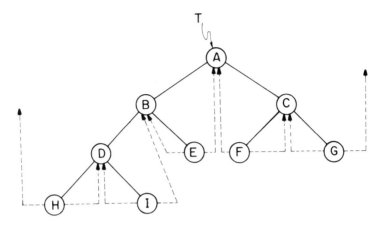

Figure 5.10 Threaded Tree Corresponding to Figure 5.3(b).

This node structure is now given by the following Pascal type declaration:

type *threadedpointer* = ↑*threadedtree*;
      threadedtree = **record**
                    leftthread : **boolean**;
                    leftchild : *threadedpointer*;
                    data : **char**;
                    rightchild : *threadedpointer*;
                    rightthread: **boolean**;
             end;

In figure 5.10 we see that two threads have been left dangling in *leftchild* of H and *rightchild* of G. In order that we leave no loose threads we will assume a head node for all threaded binary trees. Then the complete memory representation for the tree of figure 5.10 is shown in figure 5.11. The tree *t* is the left subtree of the head node. We assume that an empty binary tree is represented by its head node as

leftthread	*leftchild*	*data*	*rightchild*	*rightthread*
true				*false*

This assumption will permit easy algorithm design. Now that we have made use of the old null links we will see that the algorithm for inorder traversal is simplified. First, we observe that for any node x in a binary tree, if $x\uparrow.rightthread$ = true, then the inorder successor of x is $x\uparrow.rightchild$ by definition of threads. Otherwise the inorder successor of x is obtained by following a path of left child links from the right child of x until a node with $leftthread$ = true is reached. The algorithm $insuc$ (program 5.10) finds the inorder successor of any node x in a threaded binary tree.

```
1  function insuc(tree : threadedpointer) : threadedpointer;
2  {find the inorder successor of tree in a threaded binary tree}
3  var temp : threadedpointer;
4  begin
5    temp := tree↑.rightchild;
6    if not tree↑.rightthread
7    then while not temp↑.leftthread do
8         temp := temp↑.leftchild;
9    insuc := temp;
10 end; {of insuc}
```

Program 5.10   Insuc

The interesting thing to note about procedure $insuc$ is that it is now possible to find the inorder successor of an arbitrary node in a threaded binary tree without using an additional stack. If we wish to list in inorder all the nodes in a threaded binary tree, then we can make repeated calls to the procedure $insuc$. Since the tree is the left subtree of the head node and because of the choice of $rightthread$ = false for the head node, the inorder sequence of nodes for tree t is obtained by the procedure $tinorder$ (program 5.11).

```
1  procedure tinorder(tree : threadedpointer);
2  {traverse the threaded binary tree in inorder}
3  var temp : threadedpointer;
4  begin
5    temp := tree;
6    repeat
7      temp := insuc(temp);
8      if temp <> tree
9      then write(temp↑.data);
10   until temp = tree;
11 end; {of tinorder}
```

Program 5.11   Tinorder

The computing time is still $O(n)$ for a binary tree with n nodes. The constant here will be somewhat smaller than for procedure $inorder3$.

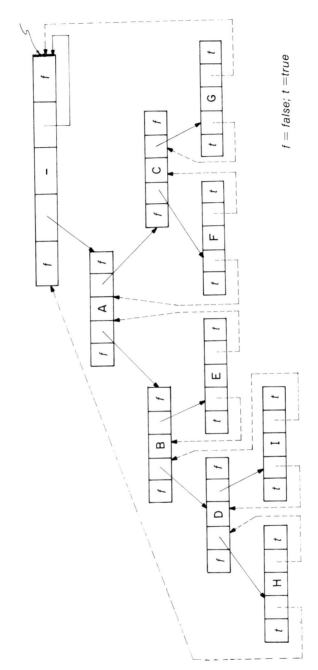

$f = false; t = true$

Figure 5.11 Memory Representation of Threaded Tree.

We have seen how to use the threads of a threaded binary tree for inorder traversal. These threads also simplify the algorithms for preorder and postorder traversal. Before closing this section let us see how to make insertions into a threaded tree. This will give us a procedure for growing threaded trees. We shall study only the case of inserting a node t as the right child of a node s. The case of insertion of a left child is given as an exercise. If s has an empty right subtree, then the insertion is simple and diagrammed in figure 5.12(a). If the right subtree of s is non-empty, then this right subtree is made the right subtree of t after insertion. When this is done, t becomes the inorder predecessor of a node which has a *leftthread* $=$ *true* field and consequently there is a thread which has to be updated to point to t. The node containing this thread was previously the inorder successor of s. Figure 5.12(b) illustrates the insertion for this case. In both cases s is the inorder predecessor of t. The details are spelled out in algorithm *insertright*, program 5.12.

```
1  procedure insertright(s, t : threadedpointer);
2  {insert node t as the right child of s in a threaded binary
3  tree}
4  var temp : threadedpointer;
5  begin
6      t↑.rightchild := s↑.rightchild;
7      t↑.rightthread := s↑.rightthread;
8      t↑.leftchild := s;
9      t↑.leftthread := true; {leftchild is a thread}
10     s↑.rightchild := t {attach t to s}
11     s↑.rightthread := false;
12     if not t↑.rightthread
13     then                         {s had a right child}
14     begin
15         temp := insuc(t);
16         temp↑.leftchild := t;
17     end;
18  end; {of insertright}
```

Program 5.12   Insertright

5.7 BINARY TREE REPRESENTATION OF TREES

We have seen several representations for and uses of binary trees. In this section we will see that every tree can be represented as a binary tree. This is important because the methods for representing a tree as suggested in section 5.1 had some undesirable features. One form of representation used variable size nodes. While the handling of nodes of variable size is not

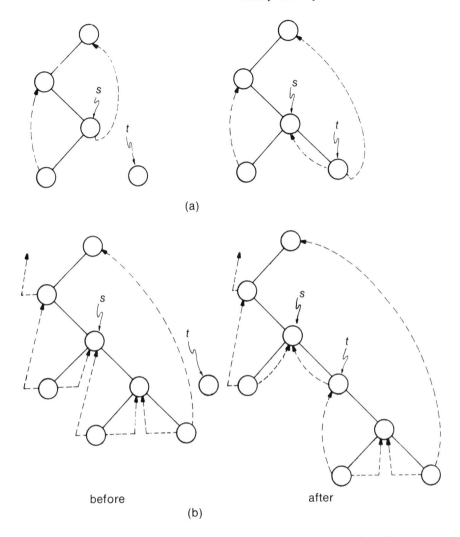

before   after

(b)

Figure 5.12   Insertion of t as a Right Child of s in a Threaded Binary Tree.

impossible, in section 4.7 we saw that it was considerably more difficult than the handling of fixed size nodes An alternative would be to use fixed size nodes, each node having k child fields, if k is the maximum degree of any node. As Lemma 5.4 shows, this would be very wasteful in space.

Lemma 5.4: If T is a k-ary tree (i.e., a tree of degree k) with n nodes, each having a fixed size as in figure 5.13, then $n(k-1)+1$ of the nk link fields are nil, $n \geq 1$.

Proof: Since each non-nil link points to a node and exactly one link points to each node other than the root, the number of non-nil links in an n node tree is exactly $n - 1$. The total number of link fields in a k-ary tree with n nodes is nk. Hence, the number of null links is $nk - (n - 1) = n(k - 1) + 1$.   □

DATA			
CHILD 1	CHILD 2	· · · · · · ·	CHILD k

Figure 5.13   Possible Node Structure for a k-ary Tree.

Lemma 5.4 implies that for a 3-ary tree more than $2/3$ of the link fields are nil! The proportion of nil links approaches 1 as the degree of the tree increases. The importance of using binary trees to represent trees is that for binary trees only about $1/2$ of the link fields are nil.

In arriving at the binary tree representation of a tree we shall implicitly make use of the fact that the order of the children of a node is not important. Suppose we have the tree of figure 5.14.

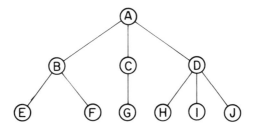

Figure 5.14   A Sample Tree.

Then, we observe that the reason we needed nodes with many link fields is that the prior representation was based on the parent-child relationship and a node can have any number of children. To obtain a binary tree representation, we need a relationship, between the nodes, that can be characterized by at most two quantities. One such relationship is the leftmost-child-next-right-sibling relationship. Every node has at most one leftmost child and at most one next right sibling. In the tree of figure 5.14, the leftmost child of B is E and the next right sibling of B is C. Strictly speaking, since the order of children in a tree is not important, any of the children of a node could be its leftmost child and any of its siblings could be its next right sibling. For the sake of definiteness, we choose the nodes based upon how the tree is drawn. The binary tree corresponding to the tree of figure 5.14 is thus obtained by connecting together all siblings of a node and deleting all links from a node to its children except for the link to its leftmost child. The node structure corresponds to that of

DATA	
CHILD	SIBLING

Using the transformation described above, we obtain the following representation for the tree of figure 5.14.

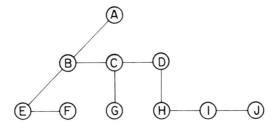

This does not look like a binary tree, but if we tilt it roughly 45° clockwise we get

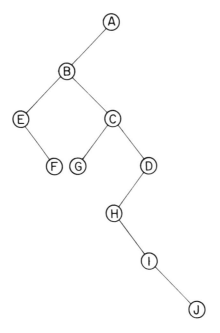

Figure 5.15   Associated Binary Tree for Tree of figure 5.14.

Let us try this transformation on some simple trees just to make sure we've got it.

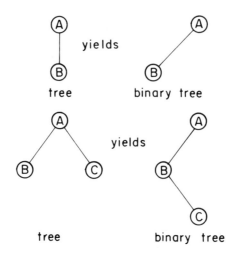

One thing to notice is that the *rchild* of the root node of every resulting binary tree will be empty. This is because the root of the tree we are transforming has no siblings. On the other hand, if we have a forest then these can all be transformed into a single binary tree by first obtaining the binary tree representation of each of the trees in the forest and then linking all the binary trees together through the *sibling* field of the root nodes. For instance, the forest with three trees

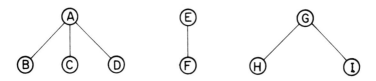

yields the binary tree

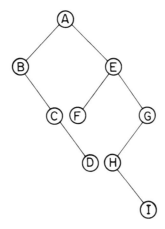

We can define this transformation in a formal way as follows:

If $T_1, ..., T_n$ is a forest of trees, then the binary tree corresponding to this forest, denoted by $B(T_1, ..., T_n)$:

(i)   is empty if $n = 0$

(ii)   has root equal to root(T_1); has left subtree equal to $B(T_{11}, T_{12}, ..., T_{1m})$ where $T_{11}, ..., T_{1m}$ are the subtrees of root(T_1); and has right subtree $B(T_2, ..., T_n)$.

Preorder and inorder traversals of the corresponding binary tree T of a forest F have a natural correspondence with traversals on F. Preorder traversal of T is equivalent to visiting the nodes of F in *tree preorder* which is defined by:

(i)   if F is empty then return;

(ii)   visit the root of the first tree of F;

(iii)   traverse the subtrees of the first tree in tree preorder;

(iv)   traverse the remaining trees of F in tree preorder.

Inorder traversal of T is equivalent to visiting the nodes of F in *tree inorder* as defined by:

(i)   if F is empty then return;

(ii)   traverse the subtrees of the first tree in tree inorder;

(iii)   visit the root of the first tree;

(iv)   traverse the remaining trees in tree inorder.

The above definitions for forest traversal will be referred to as preorder and inorder. The proofs that preorder and inorder on the corresponding binary tree are the same as preorder and inorder on the forest are left as exercises. There is no natural analog for postorder traversal of the corresponding binary tree of a forest. Nevertheless, we can define the *postorder traversal*

of a forest as:
   (i)   if *F* is empty then return;
   (ii)   traverse the subtrees of the first tree of *F* in tree postorder;
   (iii) traverse the remaining trees of *F* in tree postorder;
   (iv)   visit the root of the first tree of *F*.
This traversal is used later on in section 5.8.3 for describing the minimax procedure.

5.8   APPLICATIONS OF TREES

5.8.1   Set Representation

In this section we study the use of trees in the representation of sets. We shall assume that the elements of the sets are the numbers 1,2,3, ...,n. These numbers might, in practice, be indices into a symbol table where the actual names of the elements are stored. We shall assume that the sets being represented are pairwise disjoint; i.e., if S_i and S_j, $i \neq j$, are two sets then there is no element which is in both S_i and S_j. For example, if we have 10 elements numbered 1 through 10, they may be partitioned into three disjoint sets $S_1 = \{1, 7, 8, 9\}$; $S_2 = \{2, 5, 10\}$ and $S_3 = \{3, 4, 6\}$. The operations we wish to perform on these sets are:
   (i)   Disjoint set union ... if S_i and S_j are two disjoint sets, then their union $S_i \cup S_j = \{$all elements x such that x is in S_i or $S_j\}$. Thus, $S_1 \cup S_2 = \{1, 7, 8, 9, 2, 5, 10\}$. Since we have assumed that all sets are disjoint, following the union of S_i and S_j we can assume that the sets S_i and S_j no longer exist independently, i.e., they are replaced by $S_i \cup S_j$ in the collection of sets.
   (ii)   Find(i) ... find the set containing element i. Thus, 4 is in set S_3 and 9 is in set S_1.
   The sets will be represented by trees. One possible representation for the sets S_1, S_2 and S_3 is:

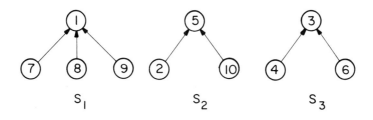

Note that the nodes are linked on the parent relationship, i.e. each node other than the root is linked to its parent. The advantage of this will become apparent when we present the *union* and *find* algorithms. First, to take the union of S_1 and S_2 we simply make one of the trees a subtree of the other. $S_1 \cup S_2$ could then have one of the following representations:

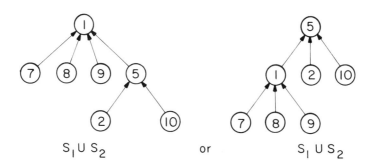

In order to find the union of two sets, all that has to be done is to set the parent field of one of the roots to the other root. This can be accomplished easily if, with each set name, we keep a pointer to the root of the tree representing that set. If, in addition, each root has a pointer to the set name, then to determine which set an element is currently in, we follow parent links to the root of its tree and use the pointer to the set name. The data representation for S_1, S_2 and S_3 may then take the form:

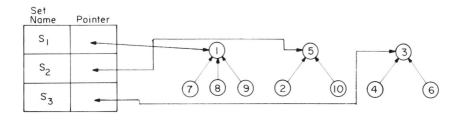

In presenting the *union* and *find* algorithms we shall ignore the actual set names and just identify sets by the roots of the trees representing them. This will simplify the discussion. The transition to set names is easy. If we determine that element i is in a tree with root j and j has a pointer to entry k in the set name table, then the set name is just *name*[k]. If we wish to union sets S_i and S_j, then we wish to union the trees with roots *pointer*(S_i) and *pointer*(S_j). As we shall see, in many applications the set name is just the element at the root. The operation of *find*(i) now becomes: determine the root of the tree containing element i. *union*(i,j) requires two trees with roots i and j to be joined. We shall assume that the nodes in the trees are numbered 1 through n so that the node index corresponds to the element index. Thus, element 6 is represented by the node with index 6. Consequently, each node needs only one field: the *parent* field to link to its parent. Root nodes have a *parent* field of zero. Based on the above discussion we see that the only data structure needed is an array, *parent* [1 .. *maxsets*] of type integer. *maxsets* is an upper bound on the number of elements we might have. Our first attempt at arriving at *union*, *find* algorithms would result in the algorithms u and f given in program 5.13.

```
1   procedure u(i,j : integer);
2   {replace the disjoint sets with roots i and j, i ≠ j with
3     their union}
4   begin
5     parent[i] := j;
6   end; {of u}


7   function f(i : integer) : integer;
8   {find the root of the tree containing element i}
9   var temp : integer;
10  begin
11    temp := i;
12    while parent[temp] > 0 do
13        temp := parent[temp];
14    f := temp;
15  end; {of f}
```

Program 5.13 u and f

While these two algorithms are very easy to state, their performance characteristics are not very good. For instance, if we start off with p elements each in a set of its own, i.e., $S_i = \{i\}$, $1 \le i \le p$, then the initial configuration consists of a forest with p nodes and *parent*[i] = 0, $1 \le i \le p$. Now let us process the following sequence of *union-find* operations.

$$u(1,2), \ f(1), \ u(2,3), \ f(1), \ u(3,4)$$
$$f(1), \ u(4,5), \ \ldots, \ f(1), \ u(n - 1,n)$$

This sequence results in the degenerate tree:

Since the time taken for a union is constant, all the $n - 1$ unions can be processed in time $O(n)$. However, each *find* requires following a chain of *parent* links from one to the root. The time required to process a *find* for an element at level i of a tree is $O(i)$. Hence, the total time needed to process the $n - 2$ finds is $O(\sum_{i=1}^{n-2} i) = O(n^2)$. We can do much better if care is taken to avoid the creation of degenerate trees. In order to accomplish this we shall make use of a *Weighting Rule* for *union* (i,j). *If the number of nodes in tree i is less than the number in tree j, then make j the parent of i, otherwise make i the parent of j.* Using this rule on the sequence of set unions given before we obtain the trees on page 240. Remember that the arguments of *union* must both be roots. The time required to process all the n finds is only $O(n)$ since in this case the maximum level of any node is 2. This, however, is not the worst case. In lemma 5.5 we show that using the weighting rule, the maximum level for any node is $\lfloor \log n \rfloor + 1$. First, let us see how easy it is to implement the weighting rule. We need to know how many nodes there are in any tree. To do this easily, we maintain a count field in the root of every tree. If i is a root node, then $count[i] = $ number of nodes in that tree. The count can be maintained in the *parent* field as a negative number. This is equivalent to using a one bit field to distinguish a count from a pointer. No confusion is created as for all other nodes the *parent* is positive.

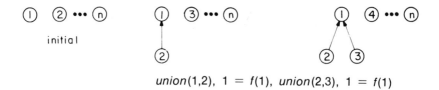

$$union(1,2), \ 1 = f(1), \ union(2,3), \ 1 = f(1)$$

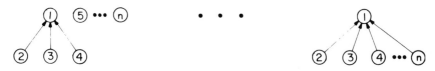

$$union(1,4), \ 1 = f(1), \ \ldots, \ 1 = f(1), \ union(1,n)$$

Trees obtained using the weighting rule

```
1  procedure union(i,j : integer);
2  {union sets with roots i and j, i ≠ j, using the
3   weighting rule. parent[i] = − count[i] and parent[j]
4   = −count[j]}
5  var temp : integer;
6  begin
7    temp : = parent[i] + parent[j]
8    if parent[i] > parent[j]
9    then
10   begin      {i has fewer nodes}
11     parent[i] := j;
12     parent[j] := temp;
13   end
14   else
15   begin      {j has fewer nodes}
16     parent[j] := i;
17     parent[i] := temp;
18   end;
19 end; {of union}
```

Program 5.14 Union

The time required to perform a union has increased somewhat but is still bounded by a constant, i.e. it is $O(1)$. The *find* algorithm remains unchanged. The maximum time to perform a find is determined by lemma 5.5.

Lemma 5.5: Let T be a tree with n nodes created as a result of algorithm *union*. No node in T has level greater $\lfloor \log_2 n \rfloor + 1$.

Proof: The lemma is clearly true for $n = 1$. Assume it is true for all trees with i nodes, $i \leq n - 1$. We shall show that it is also true for $i = n$. Let T be a tree with n nodes created by the *union* algorithm. Consider the last union operation performed, *union*(k,j). Let m be the number of nodes in tree j and $n - m$ the number in k. Without loss of generality we may assume $1 \leq m \leq n/2$. Then the maximum level of any node in T is either the same as that in k or is one more than that in j. If the former is the case, then the maximum level in T is $\leq \lfloor \log_2 (n - m) \rfloor + 1 \leq \lfloor \log_2 n \rfloor + 1$. If the latter is the case then the maximum level in T is $\leq \lfloor \log_2 m \rfloor + 2 \leq \lfloor \log_2 n/2 \rfloor + 2 \leq \lfloor \log_2 n \rfloor + 1$. □

Example 5.1 shows that the bound of lemma 5.5 is achievable for some sequence of unions.

Example 5.1: Consider the behavior of algorithm *union* on the following sequence of unions starting from the initial configuration $parent[i] = -count[i] = -1$, $1 \leq i \leq n = 2^3$

$union(1,2)$, $union(3,4)$, $union(5,6)$, $union(7,8)$,
$union(1,3)$, $union(5,7)$, $union(1,5)$.

The following trees are obtained:

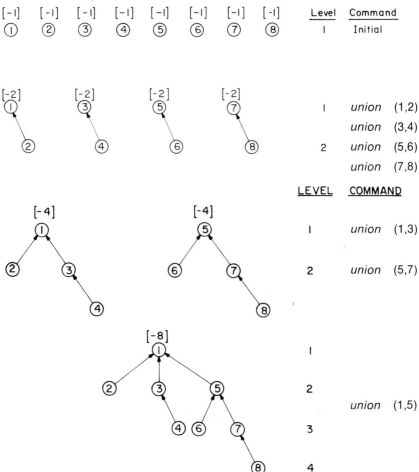

Level	Command
I	Initial
I	union (1,2)
	union (3,4)
2	union (5,6)
	union (7,8)

LEVEL	COMMAND
I	union (1,3)
2	union (5,7)
I	
2	
	union (1,5)
3	
4	

As is evident, the maximum level in any tree is $\lfloor \log_2 m \rfloor + 1$ if the tree has m nodes.   ☐

As a result of lemma 5.5, the maximum time to process a find is at most $O(\log n)$ if there are n elements in a tree. If an intermixed sequence of $n - 1$ *union* and m *find* operations is to be processed, then the worst case time becomes $O(n + m \log n)$. Surprisingly, further improvement is possible. This time the modification will be made in the find algorithm using the *Collapsing Rule: If j is a node on the path from i to its root and parent*[i] $\neq$

root(*i*) then set *parent*[*j*] to *root*(*i*). The new algorithm then becomes program 5.15. This modification roughly doubles the time for an individual find. However, it reduces the worst case time over a sequence of finds.

```
1    function find(i : integer) : integer;
2    {find the root of the tree containing element i. Use
3     the collapsing rule to collapse all nodes from i to
4     the root temp.}
5    var temp : integer;
6         temp1 : integer;
7         temp2 : integer;
8    begin
9      temp := i;
10     while parent[temp] > 0 do {find root}
11        temp := parent[temp];
12     temp2 := i;
13     while temp2 <> temp do
14     begin
15        temp1 := parent[temp2];
16        parent[temp2] := temp;
17        temp2 := temp1;
18     end
19     find := temp;
20   end; {of find}
```

Program 5.15   Find

Example 5.2: Consider the tree created by algorithm *union* on the sequence of unions of example 5.1. Now process the following 8 finds:

$$find(8), \; find(8), \; ... \; find(8)$$

Using the old version *f* of algorithm *find*, *find*(8) requires going up 3 parent link fields for a total of 24 moves to process all 8 finds. In algorithm *find*, the first *find*(8) requires going up 3 links and then resetting 2 links. Each of the remaining 7 finds requires going up only 1 link field. The total cost is now only 12 moves.

The worst case behavior of the *union-find* algorithms while processing a sequence of unions and finds is stated in lemma 5.6. Before stating this lemma, let us introduce a very slow growing function $\alpha(m,n)$ which is related to a functional inverse of Ackermann's function $A(p,q)$. We have the following definition for $\alpha(m,n)$:

$$\alpha(m,n) = \min\{z \geq 1 \mid A(z,4\lceil m/n \rceil) > \log_2 n\}$$

The definition of Ackermann's function used here is:

$$A(p,q) = \begin{cases} 2q & p = 0 \\ 0 & q = 0 \text{ and } p \geq 1 \\ 2 & p \geq 1 \text{ and } q = 1 \\ A(p-1, A(p,q-1)) & p \geq 1 \text{ and } q \geq 2 \end{cases}$$

The function $A(p,q)$ is a very rapidly growing function. One may prove the following three facts:

$$\left. A(3,4) = 2^{2^{\cdot^{\cdot^{\cdot^{2}}}}} \right\} \quad 65,536 \text{ two's} \quad \ldots \text{(a)}$$

$$A(p,q+1) > A(p,q) \qquad \ldots \text{(b)}$$

$$A(p+1,q) \geq A(p,q) \qquad \ldots \text{(c)}$$

If we assume $m \neq 0$ then (b) and (c) together with the definition of $\alpha(m,n)$ imply that $\alpha(m,n) \leq 3$ for $\log_2 n < A(3,4)$. But from (a), $A(3,4)$ is a very large number indeed! In lemma 5.6 n will be the number of *unions* performed. For all practical purposes we may assume $\log_2 n < A(3,4)$ and hence $\alpha(m,n) \leq 3$.

Lemma 5.6: [Tarjan] Let $T(m,n)$ be the maximum time required to process any intermixed sequence of $m \geq n$ *find*s and $n - 1$ *union*s. Then $k_1 m \alpha(m,n) \leq T(m,n) \leq k_2 m \alpha(m,n)$ for some positive constants k_1 and k_2. $\square$

Even though the function $\alpha(m,n)$ is a very slowly growing function, the complexity of *union-find* is not linear in m, the number of *find*s. As far as the space requirements are concerned, the space needed is one node for each element.

Let us look at an application of algorithms *union* and *find* to processing the equivalence pairs of section 4.5. The equivalence classes to be generated may be regarded as sets. These sets are disjoint as no variable can be in two equivalence classes. To begin with all n variables are in an equivalence class of their own; thus $parent[i] = -1$, $1 \leq i \leq n$. If an equivalence pair, $i \equiv j$, is to be processed, we must first determine the sets containing i and j. If these are different, then the two sets are to be replaced by their union. If the two sets are the same, then nothing is to be done as the relation $i \equiv j$ is redundant; i and j are already in the same equivalence class. To process each equivalence pair we need to perform at most two finds and one union. Thus, if we have n variables and $m \geq n$ equivalence pairs, the total processing time is at most $O(m\alpha(2m,m))$. While for very large n this is slightly worse than the algorithm of section 4.5, it has the advantage of needing less space and also of being "on line."

In Chapter 6 we shall see another application of the *union-find* algorithms.

Example 5.3: We shall use the *union-find* algorithms to process the set of equivalence pairs of section 4.5. Initially, there are 12 trees, one for each variable. $parent[i] = -1$, $1 \leq i \leq 12$.

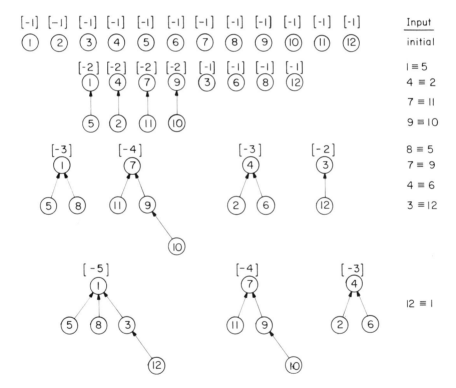

Each tree represents an equivalence class. It is possible to determine if two elements are currently in the same equivalence class at each stage of the processing by simply making two finds.   □

5.8.2   Decision Trees

Another very useful application of trees is in decision making. Consider the well-known *eight coins* problem. Given coins a,b,c,d,e,f,g,h, we are told that one is a counterfeit and has a different weight than the others. We want to determine which coin it is, making use of an equal arm balance. We want to do so using a minimum number of comparisons and at the same time determine whether the false coin is heavier or lighter than the rest. The tree below represents a set of decisions by which we can get the answer to our problem. This is why it is called a decision tree. The use of capital H or L means that the counterfeit coin is *h*eavier or *l*ighter. Let us trace through one possible sequence. If $a + b + c < d + e + f$, then we know that the false coin is present among the six and is neither g nor h. If on our next measurement we find that $a + d < b + e$, then by interchanging d and b we have no change in the inequality. This tells us two things: (i) that c or f is not the culprit, and (ii) that b or d is also not the culprit. If $a + d$ was equal to $b + e$, then c or f would be the counterfeit coin. Knowing at this point that either a or e is the counterfeit, we compare a with a good coin, say b. If $a = b$, then e is heavy, otherwise a must be light.

By looking at this tree we see that all possibilities are covered, since there are 8 coins which can be heavy or light and there are 16 terminal nodes. Every path requires exactly 3 comparisons. Though viewing this problem as a decision tree is very useful it does not immediately give us an algorithm. To solve the 8 coins problem with a program, we must write a series of tests which mirror the structure of the tree. Moreover we must be sure that a single comparison yields one of three possibilities: $=, >$ or $<$. To perform the last comparison we will use the procedure *comp*:

```
1  procedure comp(x,y,z : integer);
2  {x is compared against the standard coin z}
3  begin
4    if x > z then writeln (x, 'heavy')
5             else writeln (y, 'light');
6  end; {of comp}
```

Program 5.16   Comp

To assure a three way branch we assume the function *compare(a,b: integer)* : **char** where the result is either '$<$', '$=$', or '$>$' with the obvious interpretations. The procedure *eightcoins* (program 5.17) is now transparent and clearly mirrors the decision tree of figure 5.16.

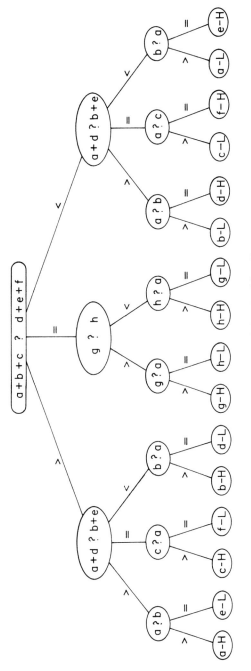

Figure 5.16 Eight Coins Decision Tree.

```
1  procedure eightcoins;
2  {eight weights of coins are input; the illegal one
3   is discovered using only three comparisons}
4  var a,b,c,d,e,f,g,h : integer;
5  begin
6    read(a,b,c,d,e,f,g,h);
7    case compare(a + b + c, d + e + f) of
8      '=' : if g > h then comp(g,h,a)
9                     else  comp(h,g,a);
10     '>' : case compare(a + d, b + e) of
11                        '=' : comp(c,f,a);
12                        '>' : comp(a,e,b);
13                        '<' : comp(b,d,a);
14           end; {of case}
15     '<' : case compare(a + d, b + e) of
16                        '=' : comp(f,c,a);
17                        '>' : comp(d,b,a);
18                        '<' : comp(e,a,b);
19           end; {of case}
20     end; {of case}
21  end; {of eightcoins}
```

Program 5.17 Eightcoins

5.8.3 Game Trees

Another interesting application of trees is in the playing of games such as tic-tac-toe, chess, nim, kalah, checkers, go, etc. As an example, let us consider the game of nim. This game is played by two players A and B. The game itself is described by a *board* which initially contains a pile of n toothpicks. The players A and B make moves alternately with A making the first move. A *legal move* consists of removing either 1, 2, or 3 of the toothpicks from the pile. However, a player cannot remove more toothpicks than there are on the pile. The player who removes the last toothpick loses the game and the other player wins. The *board configuration* at any time is completely specified by the number of toothpicks remaining in the pile. At any time the game status is determined by the board configuration together with the player whose turn it is to make the next move. A *terminal board configuration* is one which represents either a *win*, *lose* or *draw* situation. All other configurations are *nonterminal*. In nim there is only one terminal configuration: there are no toothpicks in the pile. This configuration is a win for player A if B made the last move, otherwise it is a win for B. The game of nim cannot end in a draw.

A sequence C_1, ...,C_m of board configurations is said to be *valid* if:

(i) C_1 is the starting configuration of the game;

(ii) C_i, $0 < i < m$, are nonterminal configurations;

(iii) C_{i+1} is obtained from C_i by a legal move made by player A if i is odd and by player B if i is even. It is assumed that there are only finitely many legal moves.

A valid sequence C_1, ...,C_m of board configurations with C_m a terminal configuration is an *instance* of the game. The *length* of the sequence C_1, C_2, ...,C_m is m. A *finite game* is one in which there are no valid sequences of infinite length. All possible instances of a finite game may be represented by a *game tree*. The tree of figure 5.17 is the game tree for nim with $n = 6$. Each node of the tree represents a board configuration. The root node represents the starting configuration C_1. Transitions from one level to the next are made via a move of A or B. Transitions from an odd level represent moves made by A. All other transitions are the result of moves made by B. Square nodes have been used in figure 5.17 to represent board configurations when it was A's turn to move. Circular nodes have been used for other configurations. The edges from level 1 nodes to level 2 nodes and from level 2 nodes to level 3 nodes have been labeled with the move made by A and B respectively (for example, an edge labeled 1 means 1 toothpick is to be removed). It is easy to figure out the labels for the remaining edges of the tree. Terminal configurations are represented by leaf nodes. Leaf nodes have been labeled by the name of the player who wins when that configuration is reached. By the nature of the game of nim, player A can win only at leaf nodes on odd levels while B can win only at leaf nodes on even levels. The degree of any node in a game tree is at most equal to the number of distinct legal moves. In nim there are at most 3 legal moves from any configuration. By definition, the number of legal moves from any configuration is finite. The *depth* of a game tree is the length of a longest instance of the game. The depth of the nim tree of figure 5.17 is 7. Hence, from start to finish this game involves at most 6 moves. It is not difficult to see how similar game trees may be constructed for other finite games such as chess, tic-tac-toe, kalah, etc. (Strictly speaking, chess is not a finite game as it is possible to repeat board configurations in the game. We can view chess as a finite game by disallowing this possibility. We could, for instance, define the repetition of a board configuration as resulting in a draw.)

Now that we have seen what a game tree is, the next question is "of what use are they?" Game trees are useful in determining the next move a player

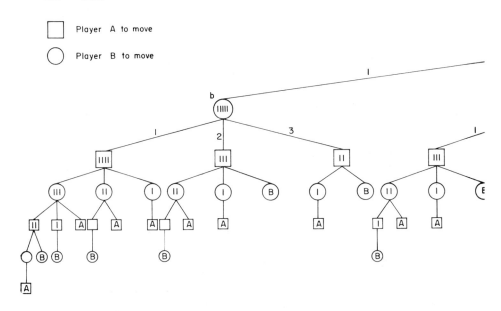

Figure 5.17   Complete Game Tree for Nim with $n = 6$.

should make. Starting at the initial configuration represented by the root of figure 5.17 player A is faced with the choice of making any one of three possible moves. Which one should he make? Assuming that player A wants to win the game, he should make the move that maximizes his chances of winning. For the simple tree of figure 5.17 this move is not too difficult to determine. We can use an evaluation function $E(X)$ which assigns a numeric value to the board configuration X. This function is a measure of the value or worth of configuration X to player A. So, $E(X)$ is high for a configuration from which A has a good chance of winning and low for a configuration from which A has a good chance of losing. $E(X)$ has its maximum value for configurations that are either winning terminal configurations for A or configurations from which A is guaranteed to win regardless of B's countermoves. $E(X)$ has its minimum value for configurations from which B is guaranteed to win.

For a game such as nim with $n = 6$, whose game tree has very few nodes, it is sufficient to define $E(X)$ only for terminal configurations. We could define $E(X)$ as:

$$E(X) = \begin{cases} 1 \text{ if } X \text{ is a winning configuration for } A \\ -1 \text{ if } X \text{ is a losing configuration for } A \end{cases}$$

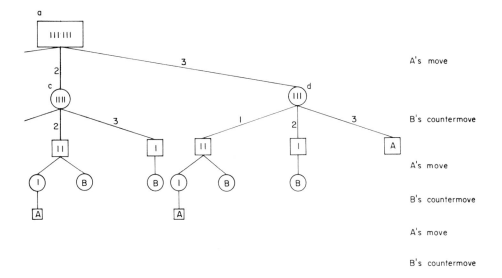

Using this evaluation function we wish to determine which of the configurations b, c, d player A should move the game into. Clearly, the choice is the one whose value is max $\{V(b), V(c), V(d)\}$ where $V(x)$ is the value of configuration x. For leaf nodes x, $V(x)$ is taken to be $E(x)$. For all other nodes x let $d \geq 1$ be the degree of x and let $c_1, c_2, ..., c_d$ be the configurations represented by the children of x. Then $V(x)$ is defined by:

$$V(x) = \begin{cases} \displaystyle\max_{1 \leq i \leq d} \{V(c_i)\} & \text{if } x \text{ is a square node} \\[2ex] \displaystyle\min_{1 \leq i \leq d} \{V(c_i)\} & \text{if } x \text{ is a circular node} \end{cases} \qquad (5.3)$$

The justification for (5.3) is fairly simple. If x is a square node, then it is at an odd level and it will be A's turn to move from here if the game ever reaches this node. Since A wants to win he will move to that child node with maximum value. In case x is a circular node it must be on an even level and if the game ever reaches this node, then it will be B's turn to move. Since B is out to win the game for himself, he will (barring mistakes) make a move that will minimize A's chances of winning. In this case the next configuration will be $\min_{1 \le i \le d} \{V(c_i)\}$. Equation (5.3) defines the *minimax* procedure to determine the value of a configuration x. This is illustrated on the hypothetical game of figure 5.18. P_{11} represents an arbitrary board configuration from which A has to make a move. The values of the leaf nodes are obtained by evaluating the function $E(x)$. The value of P_{11} is obtained by starting at the nodes on level 4 and computing their values using eq. (5.3). Since level 4 is a level with circular nodes all unknown values on this level may be obtained by taking the minimum of the children values. Next, values on levels 3, 2 and 1 may be computed in that order. The resulting value for P_{11} is 3. This means that starting from P_{11} the best A can hope to do is reach a configuration of value 3. Even though some nodes have value greater than 3, these nodes will not be reached, as B's countermoves will prevent the game from reaching any such configuration (assuming B's countermoves are optimal for B with respect to A's evaluation function). For example, if A made a move to P_{21}, hoping to win the game at P_{31}, A would indeed be surprised by B's countermove to P_{32} resulting in a loss to A. Given A's evaluation function and the game tree of figure 5.18, the best move for A to make is to configuration P_{22}. Having made this move, the game may still not reach configuration P_{52} as B would, in general, be using a different evaluation function, which might give different values to various board configurations. In any case, the *minimax* procedure can be used to determine the best move a player can make given his evaluation function. Using the minimax procedure on the game tree for nim (figure 5.17) we see that the value of the root node is $V(a) = 1$. Since $E(X)$ for this game was defined to be 1 iff A was guaranteed to win, this means that if A makes the optimal move from node a then no matter what B's countermoves A will win. The optimal move is to node b. One may readily verify that from b A can win the game independent of B's countermove!

For games such as nim with $n = 6$, the game trees are sufficiently small that it is possible to generate the whole tree. Thus, it is a relatively simple matter to determine whether or not the game has a winning strategy. Moreover, for such games it is possible to make a decision on the next move by looking ahead all the way to terminal configurations. Games of this type are not very interesting since assuming no errors are made by either player, the outcome of the game is predetermined and both players should use similar evaluation functions, i.c., $E_A(X) = 1$ for X a winning configuration and $E_A(X) = -1$ for X a losing configuration for A; $E_B(X) = -E_A(X)$.

Of greater interest are games such as chess where the game tree is too large to be generatated in its entirety. It is estimated that the game tree for chess has $> 10^{100}$ nodes. Even using a computer which is capable of generating 10^{11} nodes a second, the complete generation of the game tree for

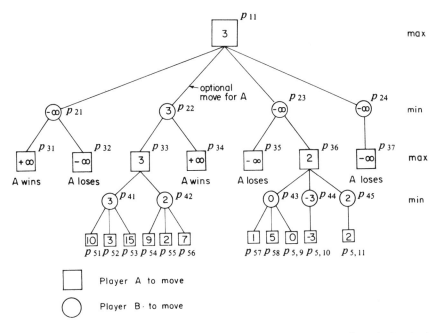

Figure 5.18 Portion of Game Tree for a Hypothetical Game. The value of terminal nodes is obtained from the evaluation function $E(x)$ for player A.

chess would require more than 10^{80} years. In games with large game trees the decision as to which move to make next can be made only by looking at the game tree for the next few levels. The evaluation function $E(X)$ is used to get the values of the leaf nodes of the subtree generated and then eq. (5.3) can be used to get the values of the remaining nodes and hence to determine the next move. In a game such as chess it may be possible to generate only the next few levels (say 6) of the tree. In such situations both the quality of the resulting game and its outcome will depend upon the quality of the evaluating functions being used by the two players as well as of the algorithm being used to determine $V(X)$ by minimax for the current game configuration. The efficiency of this algorithm will limit the number of nodes of the search tree that can be generated and so will have an effect on the quality of the game.

Let us assume that player A is a computer and attempt to write an algorithm that A can use to compute $V(X)$. It is clear that the procedure to compute $V(X)$ can also be used to determine the next move that A should make. A fairly simple recursive procedure to evaluate $V(X)$ using minimax can be obtained if we recast the definition of minimax into the following form:

$$
V'(X) = \begin{cases} e(X) & \text{if } X \text{ is a leaf of the subtree generated} \\[2ex] \max_{1 \le i \le d} \{-V'(c_i)\} & \text{If } X \text{ is not a leaf of the subtree generated and } c_i, \\ & 1 \le i \le d \text{ are the children of } X. \end{cases}
$$

(5.4)

where $e(X) = E(X)$ if X is a position from which A is to move and $e(X) = -E(X)$ otherwise.

Starting at a configuration X from which A is to move, one can easily prove that eq. (5.4) computes $V'(X) = V(X)$ as given by eq. (5.3). In fact, values for all nodes on levels from which A is to move are the same as given by eq. (5.3) while values on other levels are the negative of those given by eq. (5.3).

The recursive procedure to evaluate $V'(X)$ based on eq. (5.4) is then $ve(X,l)$ (program 5.18). This algorithm evaluates $V'(X)$ by generating only l levels of the game tree beginning with X as root. One may readily verify that this algorithm traverses the desired subtree of the game tree in postorder.

```
1   function ve(x:node; l : integer) : integer;
2   {compute V'(n) by looking at most l moves ahead. e(x)
3    is the evaluation function for player A. For convenience,
4    it is assumed that starting from any board configuration x
5    the legal moves of the game permit a transition only to the
6    configurations c[1 .. d] if x is not a terminal
7    configuration.}
8   var ans : integer;
9       temp, i : integer;
10  begin
11    if terminal(x) or (l = 0)
12    then ve := e(x)
13    else
14    begin
15      ans := -ve(c[1], l - 1);
16      for i := 2 to d do
17      begin
18        temp := -ve(c[i], l - 1)
19        if ans < temp then ans := temp
20      end;
21      ve := ans;
22    end; {of if}
23  end; {of ve}
```

Program 5.18   Ve

An initial call to algorithm *ve* with $x = P_{11}$ and $l = 4$ for the hypothetical game of figure 5.18 would result in the generation of the complete game tree. The values of various configurations would be determined in the order: P_{31}, P_{32}, P_{21}, P_{51}, P_{52}, P_{53}, P_{41}, P_{54}, P_{55}, P_{56}, P_{42}, P_{33}, ..., P_{37}, P_{24}, P_{11}. It is possible to introduce, with relative ease, some heuristics into algorithm *ve* that will in general result in the generation of only a portion of the possible configurations while still computing $V'(X)$ accurately.

Consider the game tree of figure 5.18. After $V(P_{41})$ has been computed, it is known that $V(P_{33})$ is at least $V(P_{41}) = 3$. Next, when $V(P_{55})$ is determined to be 2, then we know that $V(P_{42})$ is at most 2. Since P_{33} is a max position, $V(P_{42})$ cannot affect $V(P_{33})$. Regardless of the values of the remaining children of P_{42}, the value of P_{33} is not determined by $V(P_{42})$ as $V(P_{42})$ cannot be more than $V(P_{41})$. This observation may be stated more formally as the following rule: The *alpha* value of a max position is defined to be the minimum possible value for that position. *If the value of a min position is determined to be less than or equal to the alpha value of its parent, then we may stop generation of the remaining children of this min position.* Termination of node generation under this rule is known as *alpha cutoff*. Once $V(P_{41})$ in figure 5.18 is determined, the alpha value of P_{33} becomes 3. $V(P_{55})$ $\leq$ alpha value of P_{33} implies that P_{56} need not be generated.

A corresponding rule may be defined for min positions. The *beta* value of a min position is the maximum possible value for that position. *If the value of a max position is determined to be greater than or equal to the beta value of its parent node, then we may stop generation of the remaining children of this max position.* Termination of node generation under this rule is called *beta cutoff*. In figure 5.18, once $V(P_{35})$ is determined, the beta value of P_{23} is known to be at most $-\infty$. Generation of P_{57}, P_{58}, P_{59} gives $V(P_{43}) = 0$. Thus, $V(P_{43})$ is greater than or equal to the beta value of P_{23} and we may terminate the generation of the remaining children of P_{36}. The two rules stated above may be combined together to get what is known as *alpha-beta pruning*. When alpha-beta pruning is used on figure 5.18, the subtree with root P_{36} is not generated at all! This is because when the value of P_{23} is being determined the alpha value of P_{11} is 3. $V(P_{35})$ is less than the alpha value of P_{11} and so an alpha cutoff takes place. It should be emphasized that the alpha or beta value of a node is a dynamic quantity. Its value at any time during the game tree generation depends upon which nodes have so far been generated and evaluated.

In actually introducing alpha-beta pruning into algorithm *ve* it is necessary to restate this rule in terms of the values defined by eq. (5.4). Under eq. (5.4) all positions are max positions since the values of the min positions of eq. (5.3) have been multiplied by -1. The alpha-beta pruning rule now reduces to the following rule: let the *B*-value of a position be the minimum value that that position can have.

For any position X, let B be the B-value of its parent and let mb = − B. Then, if the value of X is determined to be greater than or equal to mb, we may terminate generation of the remaining children of X. Incorporating this rule into algorithm *ve* is fairly straightforward and results in algorithm *veb*. This algorithm has the additional parameter *mb* which is the negative of the *B*-value of the parent of *X*.

```
1    function  veb(x : node; l,mb : integer):integer;
2    {determine V'(x) as in eq. (5.4) using the B-rule and looking
3     only l moves ahead. Remaining assumptions and notations
4     are the same as for algorithm ve. Configurations c[1..d] are global}
5    var ans : integer;
6        temp, i : integer;
7    begin
8    if terminal(x) or (l = 0)
9      then  veb := e(x)
10     else
11     begin
12         ans := −maxint
13         i := 1;
14         while (i <= d) and (ans < mb) do
15         begin
16             temp := −veb(c[i], l − 1, −ans);
17             if ans < temp then ans := temp;
18             i := i + 1;
19         end; {of while}
20         veb := ans;
21     end; {of if}
22   end; {of veb}
```

Program 5.19   Veb

If Y is a position from which A is to move, then the initial call $veb(Y,l,maxinteger)$ correctly computes $V'(Y)$ with an l move look ahead. Further pruning of the game tree may be achieved by realizing that the B-value of a node X places a lower bound on the value grandchildren of X must have in order to affect X's value. Consider the subtree of figure 5.19(a). If $V'(GC(X)) \leq B$ then $V'(C(X)) \geq − B$. Following the evaluation of $C(X)$, the B-value of X is max $\{B, − V'(C(X))\} = B$ as $V'(C(X)) \geq − B$. Hence unless $V'(GC(X)) > B$, it cannot affect $V'(X)$ and so B is a lower bound on the value $GC(X)$ should have. Incorporating this lower bound into algorithm *veb* yields algorithm *ab* (program 5.20). The additional parameter *lb* is a lower bound on the value X should have.

```
1   function ab(x : node; l,lb,mb : integer):integer;
2   {same as algorithm veb. lb is a lower bound on V'(x)}
3   var ans : integer;
4        temp,i : integer;
5   begin
6     if terminal(x) or (l = 0)
7     then ab := e(x)
8     else
9     begin
10      ans := lb;
11      i := 1;
12      while (i <= d) and (ans < mb) do
13      begin
14        temp := −ab(c[i], l − 1, −mb, −ans);
15        if ans < temp then ans := temp;
16        i := i + 1;
17      end; {of while}
18      ab := ans;
19    end; {of if}
20  end; {of ab}
```

Program 5.20   Ab

One may easily verify that the initial call $ab(Y,l,mininteger, maxinteger)$ gives the same result as the call $ve(Y,l)$.

Figure 5.19(b) shows a hypothetical game tree in which the use of algorithm *ab* results in greater pruning than achieved by algorithm *veb*. Let us first trace the action of *veb* on the tree of figure 5.19(b). We assume the initial call to be *veb* $(P_1,l,\textbf{maxint})$ where l is the depth of the tree. After examining the left subtree of P_1, the B value of P_1 is set to 10 and nodes P_3, P_4, P_5 and P_6 are generated. Following this, $V'(P_6)$ is determined to be 9 and then the B-value of P_5 becomes −9. Using this, we continue to evaluate the node P_7. In the case of *ab*, however, since the B-value of P_1 is 10, the lower bound for P_4 is 10 and so the effective B-value of P_4 becomes 10. As a result the node P_7 is not generated since no matter what its value $V'(P_5) \geq$ −9 and this will not enable $V'(P_4)$ to reach its lower bound.

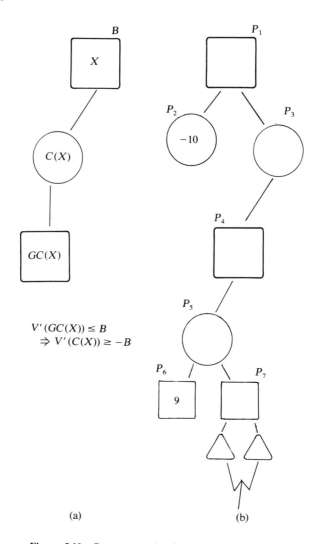

$$V'(GC(X)) \le B$$
$$\Rightarrow V'(C(X)) \ge -B$$

(a)   (b)

Figure 5.19   Game trees showing lower bounding.

5.9   COUNTING BINARY TREES

As a conclusion to our chapter on trees, we determine the number of distinct binary trees having n nodes. We know that if $n = 0$ or $n = 1$ there is one such tree. If $n = 2$, then there are two distinct binary trees

and if $n = 3$, there are five

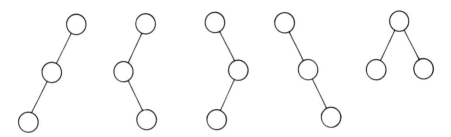

How many distinct binary trees are there with n nodes?

Before solving this problem let us look at some other counting problems that are equivalent to this one.

In section 5.4 we introduced the notion of preorder, inorder and post-order traversals. Suppose we are given the preorder sequence

$$A \; B \; C \; D \; E \; F \; G \; H \; I$$

and the inorder sequence

$$B \; C \; A \; E \; D \; G \; H \; F \; I$$

of the same binary tree. Does such a pair of sequences uniquely define a binary tree? Asked another way, can the above pair of sequences come from more than one binary tree? We can construct the binary tree which has these sequences by noticing that the first letter in preorder, A, must be the root and by the definition of inorder all nodes preceding A must occur in the left subtree and the remaining nodes occur in the right subtree.

This gives us

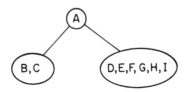

as our first approximation to the correct tree. Moving right in the preorder sequence we find B as the next root and from the inorder we see B has an empty left subtree and C is in its right subtree. This gives

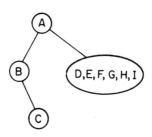

as the next approximation. Continuing in this way we arrive at the binary tree

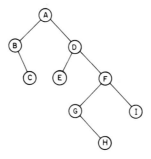

By formalizing this argument (see the exercises) we can verify that every binary tree has a unique pair of preorder-inorder sequences.

Let the nodes of an n node binary tree be numbered 1 to n. The *inorder permutation* defined by such a binary tree is the order in which its nodes are visited during an inorder traversal of the tree. A *preorder permutation* is similarly defined.

As an example, consider the binary tree above with the following numbering of nodes:

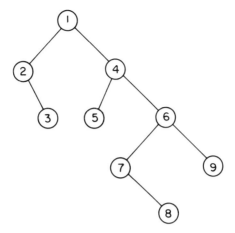

Its preorder permutation is 1,2, ...,9 and its inorder permutation is 2,3,1,5, 4,7,8,6,9.

If the nodes of a binary tree are numbered such that its preorder permutation is 1,2, ...,n, then from our earlier discussion it follows that distinct binary trees define distinct inorder permutations. The number of distinct binary trees is thus equal to the number of distinct inorder permutations obtainable from binary trees having the preorder permutation 1,2, ...,n.

Using this concept of an inorder permutation, it is possible to show that the number of distinct permutations obtainable by passing the numbers 1 to n through a stack and deleting in all possible ways is equal to the number of distinct binary trees with n nodes (see the exercises). If we start with the numbers 1,2,3 then the possible permutations obtainable by a stack are

$$1,2,3; \quad 1,3,2; \quad 2,1,3; \quad 2,3,1; \quad 3,2,1;$$

It is not possible to obtain 3,1,2. Each of these five permutations corresponds to one of the five distinct binary trees with 3 nodes

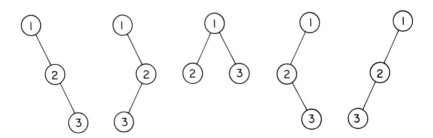

Another problem which surprisingly has connection with the previous two is the following: we have a product of n matrices

$$M_1 * M_2 * M_3 * \ldots * M_n$$

that we wish to compute. We can perform these operations in any order because multiplication of matrices is associative. We ask the question: how many different ways can we perform these multiplications? For example, if $n = 3$, there are two possibilities

$$(M_1 * M_2) * M_3 \text{ and } M_1 * (M_2 * M_3)$$

and if $n = 4$, there are five ways

$$((M_1 * M_2) * M_3) * M_4, (M_1 * (M_2 * M_3)) * M_4,$$
$$M_1 * ((M_2 * M_3) * M_4)$$
$$(M_1 * (M_2 * (M_3 * M_4))), ((M_1 * M_2) * (M_3 * M_4))$$

Let b_n be the number of different ways to compute the product of n matrices. Then $b_2 = 1$, $b_3 = 2$, $b_4 = 5$. Let M_{ij}, $i \leq j$, be the product $M_i * M_{i+1} * \ldots * M_j$. The product we wish to compute is M_{1n}. M_{1n} may be computed by computing any one of the products $M_{1i} * M_{i+1,n}$ $1 \leq i < n$. The number of ways to obtain M_{1i} and $M_{i+1,n}$ is b_i and b_{n-i} respectively. Therefore, letting $b_1 = 1$ we have:

$$b_n = \sum_{1 \leq i \leq n-1} b_i b_{n-i}, \quad n > 1.$$

If we can determine an expression for b_n only in terms of n, then we have a solution to our problem. Now instead let b_n be the number of distinct binary trees with n nodes. Again an expression for b_n in terms of n is what we want. Then we see that b_n is the sum of all possible binary trees formed in the following way, a root and two subtrees with b_i and b_{n-i-1} nodes,

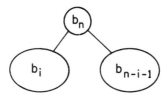

for $0 \leq i \leq n - 1$. This says that

$$b_n = \sum_{0 \leq i \leq n-1} b_i \, b_{n-i-1}, \quad n \geq 1 \text{ and } b_0 = 1 \tag{5.5}$$

This formula and the previous one are essentially the same.

So, *the number of binary trees with n nodes, the number of permutations of 1 to n obtainable with a stack, and the number of ways to multiply n + 1 matrices are all equal to the same number!*

To obtain this number we must solve the recurrence of eq. (5.5). To begin we let

$$B(x) = \sum_{i \geq 0} b_i x^i \tag{5.6}$$

which is the generating function for the number of binary trees. Next, observe that by the recurrence relation we get the identity

$$x \, B^2(x) = B(x) - 1$$

Using the formula to solve quadratics and the fact (eq. (5.5)) that $B(0) = b_0 = 1$ we get:

$$B(x) = \frac{1 - \sqrt{1 - 4x}}{2x}$$

It is not clear at this point that we have made any progress but by using the binomial theorem to expand $(1 - 4x)^{1/2}$ we get

$$B(x) = \frac{1}{2x} \left(1 - \sum_{n \geq 0} \binom{1/2}{n} (-4x)^n \right)$$

$$= \sum_{m \geq 0} \binom{1/2}{m+1} (-1)^m 2^{2m+1} x^m \tag{5.7}$$

Comparing eqs. (5.6) and (5.7) we see that b_n, which is the coefficient of x^n in $B(x)$, is:

$$\binom{1/2}{n+1}(-1)^n 2^{2n+1}$$

Some simplification yields the more compact form

$$b_n = \frac{1}{n+1}\binom{2n}{n}$$

which is approximately

$$b_n = O(4^n/n^{3/2})$$

REFERENCES AND SELECTED READINGS

For other representations of trees see:

The Art of Computer Programming: Fundamental Algorithms, by D. Knuth, second edition, Addison-Wesley, Reading, 1973.

For the use of trees in generating optimal compiled code see:

"The generation of optimal code for arithmetic expressions," by R. Sethi and J. Ullman, *JACM*, vol. 17, no. 4, October 1970, pp. 715-728.

"The generation of optimal code for a stack machine" by J. L. Bruno and T. Lassagne, *JACM*, vol. 22, no. 3, July 1975, pp. 382-396.

Algorithm *inorder*4 (program 5.21) of the exercises is adapted from:

"An improved algorithm for traversing binary trees without auxilary stack," by J. Robson, *Information Processing Letters*, vol. 2, no. 1, March 1973, pp. 12-14.

Further tree traversal algorithms may be found in:

"Scanning list structures without stacks and tag bits," by G. Lindstrom, *Information Processing Letters,* vol. 2, no. 2, June 1973, pp. 47-51.

"Simple algorithms for traversing a tree without an auxiliary stack," by B. Dwyer, *Information Processing Letters,* vol. 2, no. 5, Dec. 1973, pp. 143-145.

The use of threads in connection with binary trees is given in:

"Symbol manipulation by threaded lists," by A. Perlis and C. Thornton, *CACM*, vol. 3, no. 4, April 1960, pp. 195-204.

For a further analysis of the set representation problem see:

Fundamentals of Computer Algorithms, E. Horowitz and S. Sahni, Computer Science Press, Maryland, 1978.

The computing time analysis of the UNION-FIND algorithms may be found in:

"Efficiency of a good but not linear set union algorithm," by R. Tarjan, *JACM*, vol. 22, no. 2, April 1975, pp. 215–225.

Our discussion of alpha-beta cutoffs is from:

"An analysis of alpha beta cutoffs," by D. Knuth, Stanford Technical Report 74-441, Stanford University, 1975.

For more on game playing see:

Problem Solving Methods in Artificial Intelligence, by N. Nilsson, McGraw-Hill, New York, 1971.

Artificial Intelligence: The Heuristic Programming Approach, by J. Slagle, McGraw-Hill, York, 1971.

EXERCISES

1. For the binary tree below list the terminal nodes, the nonterminal nodes and the level of each node.

2. Draw the internal memory representation of the above binary tree using (a) sequential, (b) linked, and (c) threaded linked representations.

3. Write a procedure which reads in a tree represented as a list as in section 5.1 and creates its internal representation using nodes with 3 fields, *tag, data, link*.

4. Write a procedure which reverses the above process and takes a pointer to a tree and prints out its list representation.

5. Write a nonrecursive version of procedure *preorder*.

6. Write a nonrecursive version of procedure *postorder* without using **goto**'s.

7. Rework *inorder3* so it is as fast as possible. (Hint: minimize the stacking and the testing within the loop.)

8. Write a nonrecursive version of procedure *postorder* using only a fixed amount of additional space. (See exercise 36 for details.)

9. Do exercise 8 for the case of *preorder*.

10. Given a tree of names constructed as described in section 5.5 prove that an inorder traversal will always print the names in alphabetical order.

Exercises 11–13 assume a linked representation for a binary tree.
11. Write an algorithm to list the *data* fields of the nodes of a binary tree *T* by level. Within levels nodes are to be listed left to right.

12. Give an algorithm to count the number of leaf nodes in a binary tree *T*. What is its computing time?

13. Write an algorithm *swaptree(t)* which takes a binary tree and swaps the left and right children of every node. For example, if *t* is the binary tree

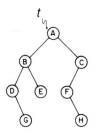
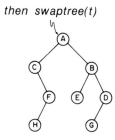

14. Devise an external representation for formulas in the propositional calculus. Write a procedure which reads such a formula and creates a binary tree representation of it. How efficient is your procedure?

15. Procedure *postordereval* must be able to distinguish between the symbols ∧, ∨, ¬ and a pointer in the *data* field of a node. How should this be done?

16. What is the computing time for *postordereval?* First determine the logical parameters.

17. Write an algorithm which inserts a new node *t* as the left child of node *s* in a threaded binary tree. The left pointer of *s* becomes the left pointer of *t*.

18. Write a procedure which traverses a threaded binary tree in postorder. What are the time and space requirements of your method?

19. Define the inverse transformation of the one which creates the associated binary tree from a forest. Are these transformations unique?

20. Prove that preorder traversal on trees and preorder traversal on the associated binary tree gives the same result.

21. Prove that inorder traversal for trees and inorder traversal on the associated binary tree give the same result.

22. Using the result of example 5.3, draw the trees after processing the instruction *union*(12,10).

23. Consider the hypothetical game tree:

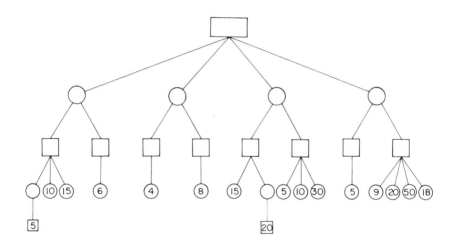

(a) Using the minimax technique (eq. (5.3)) obtain the value of the root node.
(b) What move should player A make?
(c) List the nodes of this game tree in the order in which their value is computed by algorithm *ve*.
(d) Using eq. (5.4) compute $V'(X)$ for every node X in the tree.
(e) Which nodes of this tree are not evaluated during the computation of the value of the root node using algorithm *ab* with x = root, l = **maxint**, lb = $-$**maxint** and mb = **maxint**?

24. Show that $V'(X)$ computed by eq. (5.4) is the same as $V(X)$ computed by eq. (5.3) for all nodes on levels from which A is to move. For all other nodes show that $V(X)$ computed by eq. (5.3) is the negative of $V'(X)$ computed by eq. (5.4).

25. Show that algorithm *ab* when initially called with $lb = -\text{maxint}$ and $mb = \text{maxint}$ yields the same results as *ve* does for the same X and l.

26. Prove that every binary tree is uniquely defined by its preorder and inorder sequences.

27. Do the inorder and postorder sequences of a binary tree uniquely define the binary tree? Prove your answer.

28. Answer exercise 27 for preorder and postorder.

29. Write an algorithm to construct the binary tree with a given preorder and inorder sequence.

30. Do exercise 29 for inorder and postorder.

31. Prove that the number of distinct permutations of $1, 2, ..., n$ obtainable by a stack is equal to the number of distinct binary trees with n nodes. (Hint: Use the concept of an inorder permutation of a tree with preorder permutation $1, 2, ..., n$).

32. Using Stirling's formula derive the more accurate value of the number of binary trees with n nodes,

$$b_n = (4^n / n^{3/2} \sqrt{\pi})(1 + O(1/n))$$

33. Consider threading a binary tree using preorder threads rather than inorder threads as in the text. Is it possible to traverse a binary tree in preorder without a stack using these threads?

34. Write an algorithm for traversing an inorder threaded binary tree in preorder.

35. The operation PREORD(btree) → queue returns a queue whose elements are the data items of btree in preorder. Using the operation APPENDQ(queue, queue) → queue which concatenates two queues, PREORD can be axiomatized by

PREORD(CREATE) :: = MTQ
PREORD(MAKEBT(p,d,r)) :: =
   APPENDQ(APPENDQ(ADDQ(MTQ,d),PREORD(p)),PREORD(r))

Devise similar axioms for inorder and postorder.

36. Program 5.21 performs an inorder traversal without using threads, a stack or a *parent* field. Verify that the algorithm is correct by running it on a variety of binary trees which cause every statement to execute at least once. Before attempting to study this algorithm be sure you understand *mark2* of section 4.9.

37. Extend the equivalence algorithm discussed in section 5.8.1 so it handles the equivalencing of arrays (see section 4.5). Analyze the computing time of your solution.

38. [Wilczynski] Following the conventions of LISP assume nodes with two fields $\boxed{\text{HEAD}}\ \boxed{\text{TAIL}}$. If $A = ((a(bc)))$ then $HEAD(A) = (a(bc)$, $TAIL(A) = NIL$, $HEAD(HEAD(A)) = a$, $TAIL(HEAD(A)) = ((bc))$. $CONS(A,B)$ gets a new node T, stores A in its HEAD, B in its TAIL and returns T. B must always be a list. If $L = a$, $M = (bc)$ then $CONS(L,M) = (abc)$, $CONS(M,M) = ((bc)bc)$. Three other useful functions are: $ATOM(X)$ which is true if X is an atom else false, $NULL(X)$ which is true if X is NIL else false, $EQUAL(X,Y)$ which is true if X and Y are the same atoms or equivalent lists else false.
   a) Give a sequence of HEAD, TAIL operations for extracting a from the lists:
      $((cat))$, $((a))$, $((mart))$, $(((cb))a)$.
   b) Write recursive procedures for: COPY, REVERSE, APPEND.
   c) Implement this "LISP" subsystem. Store atoms in an array, write procedures *makelist* and *listprint* for input and output of lists.

```
1   procedure inorder4 (t : treepointer);
2   {inorder traversal of binary tree t using a fixed
3   amount of additional storage}
4   label 1, 80, 99;
5   var top, lastright : treepointer;
6   p, q, r, av, r1 : treepointer;
7   begin
8   if t = nil then goto 99; {empty binary tree}
9   top := nil; lastright := nil; p := t; q := t;
10  repeat
11     repeat
12         if (p↑.leftchild = nil) and (p↑.rightchild = nil)
13             then {cannot move down}
14                 begin
15                 writeln(p↑.data); goto 1
16                 end
17             else if p↑.leftchild = nil then {move to p↑.righchild}
18                         begin
19                         writeln(p↑.data);
20                         r := p↑.rightchild; p↑.rightchild := q;
21                         q := p; p := r;
22                         end
23                                 else {move to p↑.leftchild}
24                                     begin
25                                     r := p↑.leftchild; p↑.leftchild := q;
26                                     q := p; p := r;
27                                     end
28     until false;
29  {p is a leaf node, move upwards to a node whose right
30   subtree hasn't yet been examined}
31  1: av := p;
32     repeat
33         if p = t then goto 99;
34         if q↑.leftchild = nil
35         then begin
36                 r := q↑.rightchild; q↑.rightchild := p;
37                 p : q; q := r;
38             end
39         else if q↑.rightchild = nil
40             then begin {q is linked via leftchild}
41                     r := q↑.leftchild; q↑.leftchild := p;
42                     p := q; q := r; writeln(p↑.data);
43                     end
```

```
44              else {check if p is rightchild of q}
45              if q = lastright then begin
46                      r := top; lastright := r↑.leftchild;
47                      top := r↑.rightchild;    {unstack}
48                      r↑.leftchild := nil; r↑.rightchild := nil;
49                      r := q↑.rightchild; q↑.rightchild := p;
50                      p := q; q := r; end
51          else begin {p is a leftchild of q}
52            writeln(q↑.data) {visit q}
53                      av↑.leftchild := lastright; av↑.rightchild := top;
54                      top := av; lastright := q;
55                      r := q↑.leftchild; q↑.leftchild := p; {restore
                           link to p}
56                      r1 := q↑.rightchild; q↑.rightchild := r;
57                      p := r1; goto 80;
58                      {move right}
59                          end
60      until false;
61      80: {dummy statement}
62   until false;
63   99 : end; {of inorder4}
```

Program 5.21   Inorder4

Chapter 6

GRAPHS

6.1 TERMINOLOGY AND REPRESENTATIONS

6.1.1 Introduction

The first recorded evidence of the use of graphs dates back to 1736 when Euler used them to solve the now classical Koenigsberg bridge problem. In the town of Koenigsberg (in Eastern Prussia) the river Pregal flows around the island Kneiphof and then divides into two. There are, therefore, four land areas bordering this river (figure 6.1). These land areas are interconnected by means of seven bridges *a-g*. The land areas themselves are labeled *A-D*. The Koenigsberg bridge problem is to determine whether starting at some land area it is possible to walk across all the bridges exactly once returning to the starting land area. One possible walk would be to start from land area *B;* walk across bridge *a* to island *A;* take bridge *e* to area *D;* bridge *g* to *C*; bridge *d* to *A*; bridge *b* to *B* and bridge *f* to *D*. This walk does not go across all bridges exactly once, nor does it return to the starting land area *B*. Euler answered the Koenigsberg bridge problem in the negative: The people of Koenigsberg will not be able to walk across each bridge exactly once and return to the starting point. He solved the problem by representing the land areas as vertices and the bridges as edges in a graph (actually a multigraph) as in figure 6.1(b). His solution is elegant and applies to all graphs. Defining the *degree* of a vertex to be the number of edges incident to it, Euler showed that there is a walk starting at any vertex, going through each edge exactly once and terminating at the start vertex iff the degree of each vertex is even. A walk which does this is called *Eulerian*. There is no Eulerian walk for the Koenigsberg bridge problem as all four vertices are of odd degree.

Since this first application of graphs, they have been used in a wide variety of applications. Some of these applications are: analysis of electrical circuits, finding shortest routes, project planning, identification of chemical compounds, statistical mechanics, genetics, cybernetics, linguistics, social

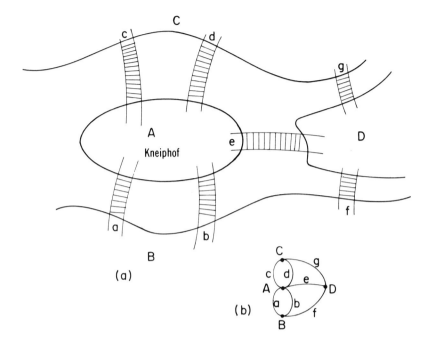

Figure 6.1 Section of the river Pregal in Koenigsberg and Euler's graph.

sciences, etc. Indeed, it might well be said that of all mathematical structures, graphs are the most widely used.

6.1.2 Definitions and Terminology

A graph, G, consists of two sets V and E. V is a finite non-empty set of *vertices*. E is a set of pairs of vertices; these pairs are called *edges*. $V(G)$ and $E(G)$ will represent the sets of vertices and edges of graph G. We will also write $G = (V,E)$ to represent a graph. In an *undirected graph* the pair of vertices representing any edge is unordered. Thus, the pairs (v_1, v_2) and (v_2, v_1) represent the same edge. In a *directed graph* each edge is represented by a directed pair $\langle v_1, v_2 \rangle$. v_1 is the *tail* and v_2 the *head* of the edge. Therefore $\langle v_2, v_1 \rangle$ and $\langle v_1, v_2 \rangle$ represent two different edges. Figure 6.2 shows three graphs G_1, G_2 and G_3.

The graphs G_1 and G_2 are undirected. G_3 is a directed graph.

$V(G_1) = \{1,2,3,4\};$ $E(G_1) = \{(1,2),(1,3),(1,4),(2,3),(2,4),(3,4)\}$
$V(G_2) = \{1,2,3,4,5,6,7\};$ $E(G_2) = \{(1,2),(1,3),(2,4),(2,5),(3,6),(3,7)\}$
$V(G_3) = \{1,2,3,\};$ $E(G_3) = \{\langle 1,2 \rangle,\langle 2,1 \rangle,\langle 2,3 \rangle\}.$

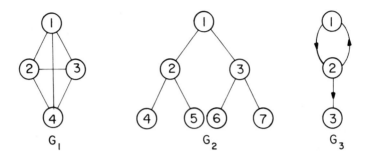

Figure 6.2   Three sample graphs.

Note that the edges of a directed graph are drawn with an arrow from the tail to the head. The graph G_2 is also a tree while the graphs G_1 and G_3 are not. Trees can be defined as a special case of graphs, but we need more terminology for that. If (v_1,v_2) or $\langle v_1,v_2 \rangle$ is an edge in $E(G)$, then we require $v_1 \neq v_2$. In addition, since $E(G)$ is a set, a graph may not have multiple occurrences of the same edge. When this restriction is removed from a graph, the resulting data object is referred to as a multigraph. The data object of figure 6.3 is a multigraph which is not a graph.

The number of distinct unordered pairs (v_i,v_j) with $v_i \neq v_j$ in a graph with n vertices is $n(n-1)/2$. This is the maximum number of edges in any n vertex undirected graph. An n vertex undirected graph with exactly $n(n-1)/2$ edges is said to be *complete*. G_1 is the complete graph on 4 vertices while G_2 and G_3 are not complete graphs. In the case of a directed graph on n vertices the maximum number of edges is $n(n-1)$.

If (v_1,v_2) is an edge in $E(G)$, then we shall say the vertices v_1 and v_2 are *adjacent* and that the edge (v_1,v_2) is *incident* on vertices v_1 and v_2. The vertices adjacent to vertex 2 in G_2 are 4, 5 and 1. The edges incident on vertex 3 in G_2 are (1,3), (3,6) and (3,7). If $\langle v_1,v_2 \rangle$ is a directed edge, then

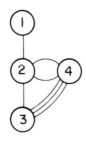

Figure 6.3   Example of a multigraph that is not a graph.

vertex v_1 will be said to be *adjacent to* v_2 while v_2 is *adjacent from* v_1. The edge $\langle v_1,v_2 \rangle$ is incident to v_1 and v_2. In G_3 the edges incident to vertex 2 are $\langle 1,2 \rangle$, $\langle 2,1 \rangle$ and $\langle 2,3 \rangle$.

A *subgraph* of G is a graph G' such that $V(G') \subseteq V(G)$ and $E(G') \subseteq E(G)$. Figure 6.4 shows some of the subgraphs of G_1 and G_3.

A *path* from vertex v_p to vertex v_q in graph G is a sequence of vertices $v_p, v_{i_1}, v_{i_2}, ..., v_{i_n}, v_q$ such that $(v_p,v_{i_1}),(v_{i_1},v_{i_2}), ..., (v_{i_n},v_q)$ are edges in $E(G)$. If G' is directed then the path consists of $\langle v_p,v_{i_1} \rangle, \langle v_{i_1},v_{i_2} \rangle, ..., \langle v_{i_n},v_q \rangle$, edges in $E(G')$. The *length* of a path is the number of edges on it. A *simple path* is a path in which all vertices except possibly the first and last are distinct. A path such as (1,2) (2,4) (4,3) we write as 1,2,4,3. Paths 1,2,4,3 and 1,2,4,2 are both of length 3 in G_1. The first is a simple path while the second is not. 1,2,3 is a simple directed path in G_3. 1,2,3,2 is not a path in G_3 as the edge $\langle 3,2 \rangle$ is not in $E(G_3)$. A *cycle* is a simple path in which the first and last vertices are the same. 1,2,3,1 is a cycle in G_1. 1,2,1 is a cycle in G_3. For the case of directed graphs we normally add on the prefix "directed" to the terms cycle and path. In an undirected graph, G, two vertices v_1 and v_2 are said to be *connected* if there is a path in G from v_1 to v_2 (since G is undi-

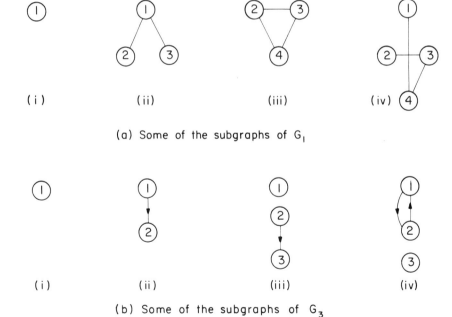

(a) Some of the subgraphs of G_1

(b) Some of the subgraphs of G_3

Figure 6.4 (a) Subgraphs of G_1 and (b) Subgraphs of G_3.

rected, this means there must also be a path from v_2 to v_1). An undirected graph is said to be connected if for every pair of distinct vertices v_i, v_j in $V(G)$ there is a path from v_i to v_j in G. Graphs G_1 and G_2 are connected while G_4 of figure 6.5 is not. A *connected component* or simply a compo-

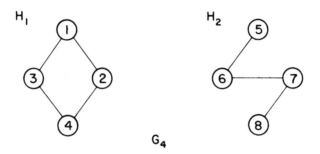

Figure 6.5   A graph with two connected components.

nent of an undirected graph is a *maximal* connected subgraph. G_4 has two components H_1 and H_2 (see figure 6.5). A *tree* is a connected acyclic (i.e., has no cycles) graph. A directed graph G is said to be *strongly connected* if for every pair of distinct vertices v_i, v_j in $V(G)$ there is a directed path from v_i to v_j and also from v_j to v_i. The graph G_3 is not strongly connected as there is no path from v_3 to v_2. A *strongly connected component* is a maximal subgraph that is strongly connected. G_3 has two strongly connected components.

Figure 6.6   Strongly connected components of G_3.

The degree of a vertex is the number of edges incident to that vertex. The degree of vertex 1 in G_1 is 3. In case G is a directed graph, we define the *in-degree* of a vertex v to be the number of edges for which v is the head. The *out-degree* is defined to be the number of edges for which v is the tail. Vertex 2 of G_3 has in-degree 1, out-degree 2 and degree 3. If d_i is the degree of vertex i in a graph G with n vertices and e edges, then it is easy to see that $e = (1/2) \sum_{i=1}^{n} d_i$.

In the remainder of this chapter we shall refer to a directed graph as a *digraph*. An undirected graph will sometimes be referred to simply as a graph.

6.1.3   Graph Representations

While several representations for graphs are possible, we shall study only the three most commonly used: adjacency matrices, adjacency lists and adjacency multilists. Once again, the choice of a particular representation will depend upon the application one has in mind and the functions one expects to perform on the graph.

Adjacency Matrix

Let $G = (V,E)$ be a graph with n vertices, $n \geq 1$. The adjacency matrix of G is a 2-dimensional $n \times n$ array, say A, with the property that $A[i,j] = 1$ iff the edge (v_i,v_j) ($\langle v_i,v_j \rangle$ for a directed graph) is in $E(G)$. $A[i,j] = 0$ if there is no such edge in G. The adjacency matrices for the graphs G_1, G_3 and G_4 are shown in figure 6.7. The adjacency matrix for an undirected graph is

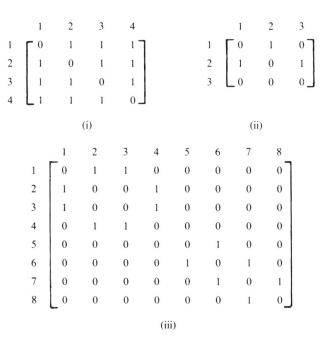

Figure 6.7   Adjacency matrices for (i) G_1, (ii) G_3 and (iii) G_4.

symmetric as the edge (v_i, v_j) is in $E(G)$ iff the edge (v_j, v_i) is also in $E(G)$. The adjacency matrix for a directed graph need not be symmetric (as is the case for G_3). The space needed to represent a graph using its adjacency matrix is n^2 bits. About half this space can be saved in the case of undirected graphs by storing only the upper or lower triangle of the matrix.

From the adjacency matrix, one may readily determine if there is an edge connecting any two vertices i and j. For an undirected graph the degree of any vertex i is its row sum $\Sigma_{j=1}^{n} A[i,j]$. For a directed graph the row sum is the out-degree while the column sum is the in-degree. Suppose we want to answer a nontrivial question about graphs such as: how many edges are there in G or is G connected. Using adjacency matrices all algorithms will require at least $O(n^2)$ time as $n^2 - n$ entries of the matrix (diagonal entries are zero) have to be examined. When graphs are sparse, i.e., most of the terms in the adjacency matrix are zero, one would expect that the former question would be answerable in significantly less time, say $O(e + n)$ where e is the number of edges in G and $e \ll n^2/2$. Such a speed up can be made possible through the use of linked lists in which only the edges that are in G are represented. This leads to the next representation for graphs.

Adjacency Lists

In this representation the n rows of the adjacency matrix are represented as n linked lists. There is one list for each vertex in G. The nodes in list i represent the vertices that are adjacent from vertex i. Each node has at least two fields: *vertex* and *link*. The *vertex* fields contain the indices of the vertices adjacent to vertex i. The adjacency lists for G_1, G_3 and G_4 are shown in figure 6.8. Each list has a headnode. The headnodes are sequential providing easy random access to the adjacency list for any particular vertex. The declarations in Pascal for the adjacency list representation would be

```
type nextnode = ↑node;
     node = record
                 vertex : integer;
                 link : nextnode;
            end;
     headnodes : array [1..n] of nextnode;
```

In the case of an undirected graph with n vertices and e edges, this representation requires n head nodes and $2e$ list nodes. Each list node has 2 fields. In terms of the number of bits of storage needed, this count should be multiplied by $\log n$ for the head nodes and $\log n + \log e$ for the list nodes

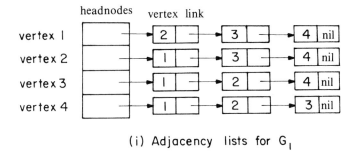

(i) Adjacency lists for G_1

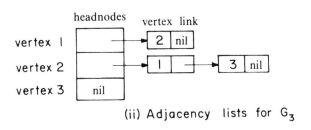

(ii) Adjacency lists for G_3

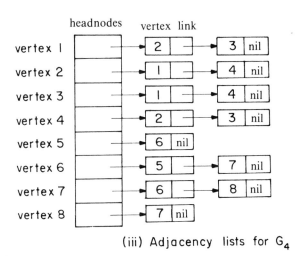

(iii) Adjacency lists for G_4

Figure 6.8   Adjacency Lists.

as it takes $O(\log m)$ bits to represent a number of value m. Often one can sequentially pack the nodes on the adjacency lists, thereby eliminating the use of records.

The array is of size $n + 2e + 1$. The vertices from vertex i are stored in $node[i]$, ..., $node[i + 1] - 1$, $1 \leq i \leq n$.

Figure 6.9 gives such a sequential representation for the graph G_4 of Figure 6.5.

var *nodes*: **array**$[1..n + 2e + 1]$ **of integer**;

[1] 10	[9] 24	[17] 3
[2] 12	[10] 2	[18] 6
[3] 14	[11] 3	[19] 5
[4] 16	[12] 1	[20] 7
[5] 18	[13] 4	[21] 6
[6] 19	[14] 1	[22] 8
[7] 21	[15] 4	[23] 7
[8] 23	[16] 2	

Figure 6.9   Sequential Representation of Graph G_4.

The degree of any vertex in an undirected graph may be determined by just counting the number of nodes in its adjacency list. The total number of edges in G may, therefore, be determined in time $O(n + e)$. In the case of a digraph the number of list nodes is only e. The out-degree of any vertex may be determined by counting the number of nodes on its adjacency list. The total number of edges in G can, therefore, be determined in $O(n + e)$. Determining the in-degree of a vertex is a little more complex. In case there is a need to repeatedly access all vertices adjacent to another vertex then it may be worth the effort to keep another set of lists in addition to the adjacency lists. This set of lists, called *inverse adjacency lists*, will contain one list for each vertex. Each list will contain a node for each vertex adjacent to the vertex it represents (see below). Alternatively, one could adopt a

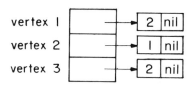

Inverse adjacency lists for G_3.

simplified version of the list structure used for sparse matrix representation in §4.5. Each node would now have four fields and would represent one edge. The node structure would be

tail	head	column link for head	row link for tail

Figure 6.10 shows the resulting structure for the graph G_3. The headnodes are stored sequentially.

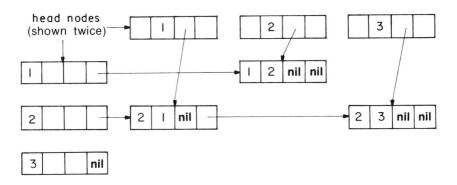

Figure 6.10 Orthogonal List Representation for G_3.

The nodes in the adjacency lists of figure 6.8 were ordered by the indices of the vertices they represented. It is not necessary that lists be ordered in this way and, in general, the vertices may appear in any order. Thus, the adjacency lists of figure 6.11 would be just as valid a representation of G_1.

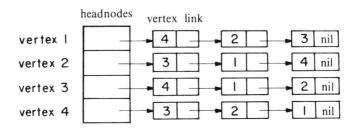

Figure 6.11 Alternate Order Adjacency List for G_1.

Adjacency Multilists

In the adjacency list representation of an undirected graph each edge (v_i, v_j) is represented by two entries, one on the list for v_i and the other on the list for v_j. As we shall see, in some situations it is necessary to be able to determine the second entry for a particular edge and mark that edge as already having been examined. This can be accomplished easily if the adjacency lists are actually maintained as multilists (i.e., lists in which nodes may be shared among several lists). For each edge there will be exactly one node, but this node will be in two lists, i.e., the adjacency lists for each of the two nodes it is incident to. The node structure now becomes

m	vertex1	vertex2	path1	path2

where m is a one bit mark field that may be used to indicate whether or not the edge has been examined. The declarations in Pascal are

```
type nextedges = ↑edge;
      edge = record
                    m : boolean;
              vertex1 : integer;
              vertex2 : integer;
                path1 : nextedge;
                path2 : nextedge;
             end;
var headnodes : array[1..n] of nextedges
```

The storage requirements are the same as for normal adjacency lists except for the addition of the mark bit m. Figure 6.12 shows the adjacency multilists for G_1. We shall study multilists in greater detail in Chapter 10.

Sometimes the edges of a graph have weights assigned to them. These weights may represent the distance from one vertex to another or the cost of going from one vertex to an adjacent vertex. In this case the adjacency matrix entries $A[i,j]$ would keep this information too. In the case of adjacency lists and multilists this weight information may be kept in the list nodes by including an additional field. A graph with weighted edges is called a *network*.

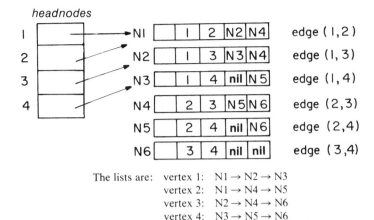

The lists are: vertex 1:   N1 → N2 → N3
                 vertex 2:   N1 → N4 → N5
                 vertex 3:   N2 → N4 → N6
                 vertex 4:   N3 → N5 → N6

Figure 6.12   Adjacency Multilists for G_1.

6.2   TRAVERSALS, CONNECTED COMPONENTS AND SPANNING TREES

Given the root node of a binary tree, one of the most common things one wishes to do is to traverse the tree and visit the nodes in some order. In the chapter on trees, we defined three ways (preorder, inorder, and postorder) for doing this. An analogous problem arises in the case of graphs. Given an undirected graph $G = (V,E)$ and a vertex v in $V(G)$ we are interested in visiting all vertices in G that are reachable from v (i.e., all vertices connected to v). We shall look at two ways of doing this: Depth First Search and Breadth First Search.

Depth First Search

Depth first search of an undirected graph proceeds as follows. The start vertex v is visited. Next an unvisited vertex w adjacent to v is selected and a depth first search from w initiated. When a vertex u is reached such that all its adjacent vertices have been visited, we back up to the last vertex visited which has an unvisited vertex w adjacent to it and initiate a depth first seach from w. The search terminates when no unvisited vertex can be reached from any of the visited ones. This procedure is best described recursively as in program 6.1. This procedure assumes a global array *visited*[1..n] of type Boolean that is initialized to **false**.

```
1   procedure dfs(v : integer);
2   {Given an undirected graph G = (V,E) with n vertices and an
3   array visited[n] initially set to false, this algorithm visits
4   all vertices reachable from v. visited is global.}
5   var w : integer;
6   begin
7     visited[v] := true;
8     for each vertex w adjacent to v do
9       if not visited[w] then dfs(w);
10  end; {of dfs}
```

Program 6.1   Dfs

In case G is represented by its adjacency lists then the vertices w adjacent to v can be determined by following a chain of links. Since the algorithm dfs would examine each node in the adjacency lists at most once and there are $2e$ list nodes, the time to complete the search is $O(e)$. If G is represented by its adjacency matrix, then the time to determine all vertices adjacent to v is $O(n)$. Since at most n vertices are visited, the total time is $O(n^2)$.

The graph G of figure 6.13(a) is represented by its adjacency lists as in figure 6.13(b). If a depth first search is initiated from vertex v_1, then the vertices of G are visited in the order: $v_1, v_2, v_4, v_8, v_5, v_6, v_3, v_7$. One may easily verify that dfs (v_1) visits all vertices connected to v_1. So, all the vertices visited, together with all edges in G incident to these vertices, form a connected component of G.

Breadth First Search

Starting at vertex v and marking it as visited, breadth first search differs from depth first search in that all unvisited vertices adjacent to v are visited next. Then unvisited vertices adjacent to these vertices are visited and so on. A breadth first search beginning at vertex v_1 of the graph in figure 6.13(a) would first visit v_1 and then v_2 and v_3. Next vertices v_4, v_5, v_6 and v_7 will be visited and finally v_8. Algorithm bfs (program 6.2) gives the details.

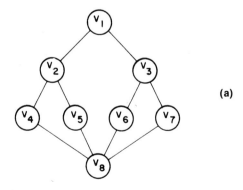

(a)

Figure 6.13   Graph G and Its Adjacency Lists.

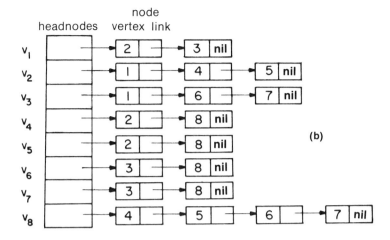

Figure 6.13   (continued)

```
1   procedure bfs(v : integer);
2   {A breadth first search of G is carried out beginning at vertex
3   v. All vertices visited are marked as visited[i] := true. The
4   graph G and array visited are global and visited is initialized
5   to false. initializequeue, addqueue, emptyqueue and deletequeue
6   are procedures/functions to handle queue operations}
7   var w : integer,
8       q : queue;
9   begin
10    visited[v] := true;
11    initializequeue(q);          {q is a queue}
12    addqueue(q,v);               {add vertex to queue}
13    while not emptyqueue(q) do
14    begin
15      deletequeue(q,v);          {remove from queue vertex v}
16      for all vertices w adjacent to v do
17        if not visited[w]
18        then
19        begin
20          addqueue(q,w);
21          visited[w] := true;
22        end; {of if and for}
23    end; {of while}
24  end; {of bfs}
```

Program 6.2   Bfs

Each vertex visited gets into the queue exactly once, so the **while** loop is iterated at most n times. If an adjacency matrix is used, then the loop takes $O(n)$ time for each vertex visited. The total time is, therefore, $O(n^2)$. In case adjacency lists are used the loop has a total cost of $d_1 + \cdots + d_n = O(e)$ where d_i = degree (v_i). Again, all vertices visited, together with all edges incident to them, form a connected component of G.

We now look at two simple applications of graph traversal: (i) finding the components of a graph, and (ii) finding a spanning tree of a connected graph.

Connected Components

If G is an undirected graph, then one can determine whether or not it is connected by simply making a call to either *dfs* or *bfs* and then determining if there is any unvisited vertex. The time to do this is $O(n^2)$ if adjacency matrices are used and $O(e)$ if adjacency lists are used. A more interesting problem is to determine all the connected components of a graph. These may be obtained by making repeated calls to either *dfs(v)* or *bfs(v)*, with *v* a vertex not yet visited. This leads to algorithm *comp* which determines all the connected components of G. The algorithm uses *dfs*. *bfs* may be used instead if desired. The computing time is not affected.

```
1   procedure comp(g : undirectedgraph);
2   {determine the connected components of g. g has n ≥ 1 vertices.
3    visited is now a local array.}
4   var visited : array [1..n] of boolean;
5        i : integer;
6   begin
7     for i := 1 to n do
8       visited[i] := false; {initialize all vertices as unvisted}
9     for i := 1 to n do
10      if not visited[i]
11      then
12      begin
13        dfs(i); {find a component}
14        outputnewvertices; {output all newly visited vertices
15                            together with all edges incident to them}
16      end; {of if and for}
17  end; {of comp}
```

Program 6.3   Comp

If G is represented by its adjacency lists, then the total time taken by *dfs* is $O(e)$. The output can be completed in time $O(e)$ if *dfs* keeps a list of all newly visited vertices. Since the **for** loops take $O(n)$ time, the total time to generate all the connected components is $O(n + e)$.

By the definition of a connected component, there is a path between every pair of vertices in the component and there is no path in G from vertex v to w if v and w are in two different components. Hence, if A is the adjacency matrix of an undirected graph (i.e., A is symmetric) then its transitive closure A^+ may be determined in $O(n^2)$ time by first determining the connected components. $A^+[i,j] = 1$ iff there is a path from vertex i to j. For every pair of distinct vertices in the same component $A^+[i,j] = 1$. On the diagonal $A^+[i,i] = 1$ iff the component containing i has at least 2 vertices. We shall take a closer look at transitive closure in section 6.3.

Spanning Trees and Minimum Cost Spanning Trees

When the graph G is connected, a depth first or breadth first search starting at any vertex visits all the vertices in G. In this case the edges of G are partitioned into two sets T (for tree edges) and B (for back edges), where T is the set of edges used or traversed during the search and B the set of remaining edges. The set T may be determined by inserting the statement $T \leftarrow T \cup \{(v,w)\}$ in the **then** clauses of *dfs* and *bfs*. The edges in T form a tree which includes all the vertices of G. Any tree consisting solely of edges in G and including all vertices in G is called a *spanning tree*. Figure 6.14 shows a graph and some of its spanning trees. When either *dfs* or *bfs* is used the edges of T form a spanning tree. The spanning tree resulting from a call to *dfs* is known as a *depth first spanning tree*. When *bfs* is used, the resulting spanning tree is called a *breadth first spanning tree*.

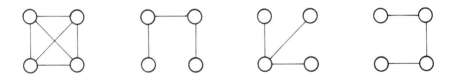

Figure 6.14   A Complete Graph and Three of Its Spanning Trees.

Figure 6.15 shows the spanning trees resulting from a depth first and breadth first search starting at vertex v_1 in the graph of figure 6.13. If any of the edges (v,w) in B (the set of back edges) is introduced into the spanning tree T, then a cycle is formed. This cycle consists of the edge (v,w) and all the edges on the path from w to v in T. If the edge $(8,7)$ is introduced

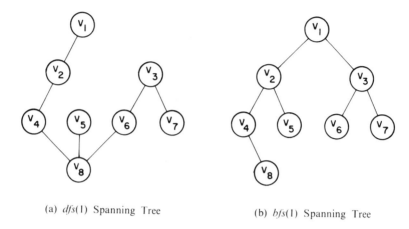

(a) *dfs*(1) Spanning Tree   (b) *bfs*(1) Spanning Tree

Figure 6.15   *dfs* and *bfs* Spanning Trees for Graph of Figure 6.13.

into the *dfs* spanning tree of figure 6.15(a), then the resulting cycle is 8,7,3,6,8.

Spanning trees find application in obtaining an independent set of circuit equations for an electrical network. First, a spanning tree for the network is obtained. Then the edges in B (i.e., edges not in the spanning tree) are introduced one at a time. The introduction of each such edge results in a cycle. Kirchoff's second law is used on this cycle to obtain a circuit equation. The cycles obtained in this way are independent (i.e, none of these cycles can be obtained by taking a linear combination of the remaining cycles) as each contains an edge from B which is not contained in any other cycle. Hence, the circuit equations so obtained are also independent. In fact, it may be shown that the cycles obtained by introducing the edges of B one at a time into the resulting spanning tree form a cycle basis and so all other cycles in the graph can be constructed by taking a linear combination of the cycles in the basis (see Harary in the references for further details). It is not difficult to imagine other applications for spanning trees. One that is of interest arises from the property that a spanning tree is a minimal subgraph G' of G such that $V(G') = V(G)$ and G' is connected (by a minimal subgraph, we mean one with the fewest number of edges). Any connected graph with n vertices must have at least $n - 1$ edges and all connected graphs with $n - 1$ edges are trees. If the nodes of G represent cities and the edges represent possible communication links connecting 2 cities, then the minimum number of links needed to connect the n cities is $n - 1$. The spanning trees of G will represent all feasible choices. In any practical situation, however, the edges will have weights assigned to them.

These weights might represent the cost of construction, the length of the link, etc. Given such a weighted graph one would then wish to select for construction a set of communication links that would connect all the cities and have minimum total cost or be of minimum total length. In either case the links selected will have to form a tree (assuming all weights are positive). In case this is not so, then the selection of links contains a cycle. Removal of any one of the links on this cycle will result in a link selection of less cost connecting all cities. We are, therefore, interested in finding a spanning tree of G with minimum cost. The cost of a spanning tree is the sum of the costs of the edges in that tree.

One approach to determining a minimum cost spanning tree of a graph has been given by Kruskal. In this approach a minimum cost spanning tree, T, is built edge by edge. Edges are considered for inclusion in T in nondecreasing order of their costs. An edge is included in T if it does not form a cycle with the edges already in T. Since G is connected and has $n > 0$ vertices, exactly $n - 1$ edges will be selected for inclusion in T. As an example, consider the graph of figure 6.16(a). The edges of this graph are considered for inclusion in the minimum cost spanning tree in the order (2,3), (2,4), (4,3), (2,6), (4,6), (1,2), (4,5), (1,5) and (5,6). This corresponds to the cost sequence 5, 6, 10, 11, 14, 16, 18, 19 and 33. The first two edges (2,3) and (2,4) are included in T. The next edge to be considered is (4,3). This edge, however, connects two vertices already connected in T and so it is rejected. The edge (2,6) is selected while (4,6) is rejected as the vertices 4 and 6 are already in T and the inclusion of (4,6) would result in a cycle. Finally, edges (1,2) and (4,5) are included. At this point, T has $n - 1$ edges and is a tree spanning n vertices. The spanning tree obtained (figure 6.16(b)) has cost 56. It is somewhat surprising that this straightforward approach should always result in a minimum spanning tree. We shall soon prove that this is indeed the case. First, let us look into the details of

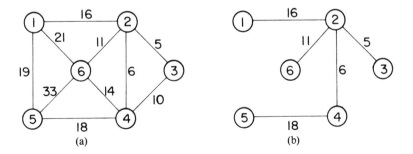

Figure 6.16   Graph and a Spanning Tree of Minimum Cost.

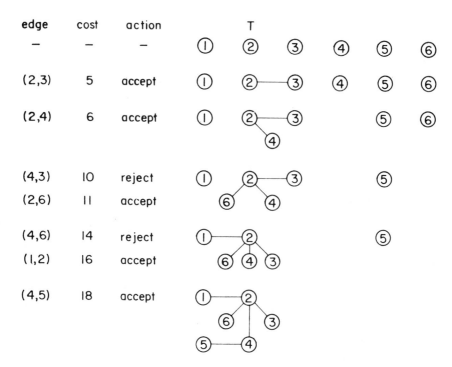

edge	cost	action
—	—	—
(2,3)	5	accept
(2,4)	6	accept
(4,3)	10	reject
(2,6)	11	accept
(4,6)	14	reject
(1,2)	16	accept
(4,5)	18	accept

Figure 6.17 Stages in Kruskal's Algorithm Leading to a Minimum Cost Spanning Tree.

the algorithm. For clarity, the Kruskal algorithm is written out more formally in figure 6.18. Initially, E is the set of all edges in G. The only functions we wish to perform on this set are: (i) determining an edge with minimum cost (line 3), and (ii) deleting that edge (line 4). Both these func-

```
1   T := φ
2   while T contains less than n − 1 edges and E not empty do begin
3       choose an edge (v,w) from E of lowest cost;
4       delete (v,w) from E;
5       if (v,w) does not create a cycle in T
6           then add (v,w) to T
7           else discard (v,w)
8   end
9   if T contains fewer than n − 1 edges then writeln ('no spanning tree')
```

Figure 6.18   Early Form of Minimum Spanning Tree Algorithm-Kruskal.

tions can be performed efficiently if the edges in E are maintained as a sorted sequential list. In Chapter 7 we shall see how to sort these edges into nondecreasing order in time $O(e \log e)$, where e is the number of edges in E. Actually, it is not essential to sort all the edges so long as the next edge for line 3 can be determined easily. It will be seen that the heap of Heapsort (section 7.6) is ideal for this and permits the next edge to be determined and deleted in $O(\log e)$ time. The construction of the heap itself takes $O(e)$ time.

In order to be able to perform steps 5 and 6 efficiently, the vertices in G should be grouped together in such a way that one may easily determine if the vertices v and w are already connected by the earlier selection of edges. In case they are, then the edge (v,w) is to be discarded. If they are not, then (v,w) is to be added to T. One possible grouping is to place all vertices in the same connected component of T into a set (all connected components of T will also be trees). Then, two vertices v,w are connected in T iff they are in the same set. For example, when the edge $(4,3)$ is to be considered, the sets would be $\{1\}, \{2,3,4\}, \{5\}, \{6\}$. Vertices 4 and 3 are already in the same set and so the edge $(4,3)$ is rejected. The next edge to be considered is $(2,6)$. Since vertices 2 and 6 are in different sets, the edge is accepted. This edge connects the two components $\{2,3,4\}$ and $\{6\}$ together and so these two sets should be unioned to obtain the set representing the new component. Using the set representation of section 5.8 and the *find* and *union* algorithms of that section we can obtain an efficient implementation of lines 5 and 6. The computing time is, therefore, determined by the time for lines 3 and 4 which in the worst case is $O(e \log e)$. We leave the writing of the resulting algorithm as an exercise. Theorem 6.1 proves that the algorithm resulting from figure 6.18 does yield a minimum spanning tree of G. First, we shall obtain a result that will be useful in the proof of this theorem.

Definition: A *spanning forest* of a graph $G = (V,E)$ is a collection of vertex disjoint trees $T_i = (V_i, E_i)$, $1 \leq i \leq k$ such that $V = \bigcup_{1 \leq i \leq k} V_i$ and $E_i \subseteq E(G)$, $1 \leq i \leq k$.

Lemma 6.1: Let $T_i = (V_i, E_i)$, $1 \leq i \leq k$, $k > 1$, be a spanning forest for the connected undirected graph $G = (V,E)$. Let w be a weighting function for $E(G)$ and let $e = (u,v)$ be an edge of minimum weight such that if $u \in V_i$ then $v \notin V_i$. Let $i = 1$ and $E' = \bigcup_{1 \leq i \leq k} E_j$. There is a spanning tree for G which includes $E' \cup \{e\}$ and has minimum weight among all spanning trees for G that include E'.

Proof: If the lemma is false, then there must be a spanning tree $T = (V,E'')$ for G such that E'' includes E' but not e and T has a weight less than the weight of the minimum spanning tree for G including $E' \cup \{e\}$. Since T is a spanning tree, it has a path from u to v. Consequently, the addition of e to E'' creates a unique cycle (exercise 22). Since $u \in V_1$ and $v \notin V_1$, it follows that there is another edge, $e' = (u',v')$ on this cycle such that $u' \in V_1$ and $v' \notin V_1$ (v' may be v). By assumption, $w(e) \leq w(e')$. Deletion of the edge e' from $E'' \cup \{e\}$ breaks this cycle and leaves behind a spanning tree T' that includes $E' \cup \{e\}$. But, since $w(e) \leq w(e')$, it follows that the weight of T' is no more than the weight of T. This contradicts the assumption on T. Hence, there is no such T and the lemma is proved.   □

Theorem 6.1: The algorithm described in figure 6.18 generates a minimum spanning tree.

Proof: The proof follows from lemma 6.1 and the fact that the algorithm begins with a spanning forest with no edges and then examines the edges of G in nondescreasing order of weight.   □

6.3   SHORTEST PATHS AND TRANSITIVE CLOSURE

Graphs may be used to represent the highway structure of a state or country with vertices representing cities and edges representing sections of highway. The edges may then be assigned weights which might be either the distance between the two cities connected by the edge or the average time to drive along that section of highway. A motorist wishing to drive from city A to city B would be interested in answers to the following questions:

(i)   Is there a path from A to B?
(ii)   If there is more than one path from A to B, which is the shortest path?

The problems defined by (i) and (ii) above are special cases of the path problems we shall be studying in this section. The length of a path is now defined to be the sum of the weights of the edges on that path rather than the number of edges. The starting vertex of the path will be referred to as the *source* and the last vertex the *destination*. The graphs will be digraphs to allow for one way streets. Unless otherwise stated, we shall assume that all weights are positive.

Single Source All Destinations

In this problem we are given a directed graph $G = (V,E)$, a weighting function $w(e), w(e) \geq 0$, for the edges of G and a source vertex v_0. The problem is to determine the shortest paths from v_0 to all the remaining vertices of G. It is assumed that all the weights are positive. As an example, consider the

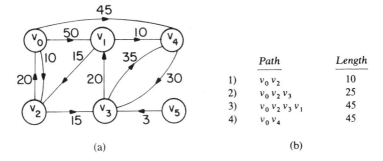

	Path	Length
1)	$v_0 v_2$	10
2)	$v_0 v_2 v_3$	25
3)	$v_0 v_2 v_3 v_1$	45
4)	$v_0 v_4$	45

(a)   (b)

Figure 6.19   Graph and Shortest Paths from v_0 to All Destinations.

directed graph of figure 6.19(a). The numbers on the edges are the weights. If v_0 is the source vertex, then the shortest path from v_0 to v_1 is $v_0 v_2 v_3 v_1$. The length of this path is $10 + 15 + 20 = 45$. Even though there are three edges on this path, it is shorter than the path $v_0 v_1$ which is of length 50. There is no path from v_0 to v_5. Figure 6.19(b) lists the shortest paths from v_0 to v_1, v_2, v_3 and v_4. The paths have been listed in nondecreasing order of path length. If we attempt to devise an algorithm which generates the shortest paths in this order, then we can make several observations. Let S denote the set of vertices (including v_0) to which the shortest paths have already been found. For w not in S, let $dist[w]$ be the length of the shortest path starting from v_0 going through only those vertices which are in S and ending at w. We observe that:

(i) If the next shortest path is to vertex u, then the path begins at v_0, ends at u and goes through only those vertices which are in S. To prove this we must show that all of the intermediate vertices on the shortest path to u must be in S. Assume there is a vertex w on this path that is not in S. Then, the v_0 to u path also contains a path from v_0 to w which is of length less than the v_0 to u path. By assumption the shortest paths are being generated in nondecreasing order of path length, and so the shorter path v_0 to w must already have been generated. Hence, there can be no intermediate vertex which is not in S.

(ii) The destination of the next path generated must be that vertex u which has the minimum distance, $dist[u]$, among all vertices not in S. This follows from the definition of $dist$ and observation (i). In case there are several vertices not in S with the same $dist$, then any of these may be selected.

(iii) Having selected a vertex u as in (ii) and generated the shortest v_0 to u path, vertex u becomes a member of S. At this point the length of the shortest paths starting at v_0, going through vertices only in S and ending at a vertex w not in S may decrease; i.e., the value of $dist[w]$ may change. If it does change, then it must be due to a shorter path starting at v_0 going to u and then to w. The intermediate vertices on the v_0 to u path and the u to w path must all be in S. Further, the v_0 to u path must be the shortest such path, otherwise $dist[w]$ is not defined properly. Also, the u to w path can be chosen so as to not contain any intermediate vertices. Therefore, we may conclude that if $dist[w]$ is to change (i.e., decrease), then it is because of the path from v_0 to u to w where the path from v_0 to u is the shortest such path and the path from u to w is the edge $\langle u,w \rangle$. The length of this path is $dist[u] = \text{length } (\langle u,w \rangle)$.

The algorithm *shortestpath* as first given by Dijkstra makes use of these observations to determine the cost of the shortest paths from v_o to all other vertices in G. The actual generation of the paths is a minor extension of the algorithm and is left as an exercise. It is assumed that the n vertices of G are numbered 1 through n. The set s is maintained as a boolean array with $s[i] = \textbf{false}$ if vertex i is not in S and $s[i] = \textbf{true}$ if it is. It is assumed that the graph itself is represented by its cost adjacency matrix with $cost[i,j]$ being the weight of the edge $\langle i,j \rangle$. $cost[i,j]$ will be set to some large number, **maxint**, in case the edge $\langle i,j \rangle$ is not in $E(G)$. For $i = j$, $cost[i,j]$ may be set to any non-negative number without affecting the outcome of the algorithm. Program 6.4 describes the algorithm completely. The data types *adjacency-matrix* and *distance* are as below.

type *adjacencymatrix* = **array** [1 .. *maxn*, 1 .. *maxn*] **of integer**;
  distance = **array** [1 .. *maxn*] **of integer**;

Analysis of Algorithm *shortestpath*

From our earlier discussion, it is easy to see that the algorithm works. The time taken by the algorithm on a graph with n vertices is $O(n^2)$. To set this note that the **for** loop of line 12 takes $O(n)$ time. The **for** loop of line 19 is executed $n - 2$ times. Each execution of this loop requires $O(n)$ time at line 21 to select the next vertex and again at lines 24–27 to update *dist*. So the total time for this loop is $O(n^2)$. In case a list of T vertices currently not in S is maintained, then the number of nodes on this list would at any time be $n - i$. This would speed up lines 21 and 24–27, but the asymptotic time would remain $O(n^2)$. This and other variations of the algorithm are explored in the exercises.

```
1    procedure shortestpath (v: integer; cost: adjacencymatrix;
2                                    var dist: distance; n : integer);
3    {dist[j], 1 ≤ j ≤ n is set to the length of the shortest path
4    from vertex v to vertex j in a digraph g with n vertices.
5    dist[v] is set to zero. g is represented by its cost adjacency
6    matrix, cost[1 .. n, 1 .. n]}
7    var s : array [1 .. maxn] of boolean;
8        i : integer;
9        u : integer;
10       w : integer;
11   begin
12     for i := 1 to   n do {initialize set S to empty}
13     begin
14       s[i] := false;
15       dist[i] := cost[v,i];
16     end;
17     s[v] := true;
18     dist[v] := 0;
19     for i := 1 to n − 2 do {determine n = 1 paths from vertex v}
20     begin
21       u := choose(dist, n); {choose returns a value u:
22                     dist[u] = minimum [dist[w]] where s[w] = false}
23       s[u] := true;
24       for w := 1 to n do
25           if not s[w] then
26               if dist[u] + cost[u,w] < dist[w]
27                       then dist[w] := dist[u] + cost[u,w];
28     end; {of for i}
29     end; {of shortestpath}
```

Program 6.4   Shortestpath

Any shortest path algorithm must examine each edge in the graph at least once since any of the edges could be in a shortest path. Hence, the minimum possible time for such an algorithm would be $O(e)$. Since cost adjacency matrices were used to represent the graph, it takes $O(n^2)$ time just to determine which edges are in G and so any shortest path algorithm using this representation must take $O(n^2)$. For this representation, then, algorithm *shortestpath* is optimal to within a constant factor. Even if a change to adjacency lists is made, only the overall time for the **for** loop of lines 24–27 can be brought down to $O(e)$ (since the *dist* can change only for those vertices adjacent from u). The total time for line 21 remains $O(n^2)$.

Example 6.1: Consider the 8 vertex digraph of Figure 6.20(a) with cost adjacency matrix as in 6.20(b). The values of *dist* and the vertices selected at each iteration of the **while** loop of line 21 for finding all the shortest paths from Boston are shown in table 6.21. Note that the algorithm terminates when only seven of the eight vertices are in S. By the definition of *dist*, the distance of the last vertex, in this case Los Angeles, is correct as the shortest path from Boston to Los Angeles can go through only the remaining six vertices.   □

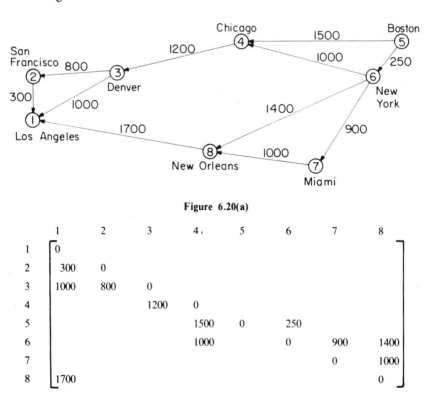

Figure 6.20(a)

	1	2	3	4 ,	5	6	7	8
1	0							
2	300	0						
3	1000	800	0					
4			1200	0				
5				1500	0	250		
6				1000		0	900	1400
7							0	1000
8	1700							0

Figure 6.20(b)   Cost Adjacency Matrix for Figure 6.20(a). All Entries Not Shown are $+\infty$.

Iteration	S	Vertex Selected	dist	LA [1]	SF [2]	D [3]	C [4]	B [5]	NY [6]	M [7]	NO [8]
Initial		—		$+\infty$	$+\infty$	$+\infty$	1500	0	250	$+\infty$	$+\infty$
1	5	6		$+\infty$	$+\infty$	$+\infty$	1250	0	250	1150	1650
2	5,6	7		$+\infty$	$+\infty$	$+\infty$	1250	0	250	1150	1650
3	5,6,7	4		$+\infty$	$+\infty$	2450	1250	0	250	1150	1650
4	5,6,7,4	8		3350	$+\infty$	2450	1250	0	250	1150	1650
5	5,6,7,4,8	3		3350	3250	2450	1250	0	250	1150	1650
6	5,6,7,4,8,3	2		3350	3250	2450	1250	0	250	1150	1650
	5,6,7,4,8,3,2										

Table 6.21   Action of *shortestpath*

All Pairs Shortest Paths

The *all pairs shortest path problem* calls for finding the shortest paths between all pairs of vertices v_i, v_j, $i \neq j$. One possible solution to this is to apply the algorithm *shortestpath* n times, once with each vertex in $V(G)$ as the source. The total time taken would be $O(n^3)$. For the all pairs problem, we can obtain a conceptually simpler algorithm which will work even when some edges in G have negative weights so long as G has no cycles with negative length. The computing time of this algorithm will still be $O(n^3)$ though the constant factor will be smaller.

The graph G is represented by its cost adjacency matrix with $cost[i,j] = 0$ and $cost[i,j] = $ **maxint** in case edge $\langle i,j \rangle$, $i \neq j$ is not in G. Define $A^k[i,j]$ to be the cost of the shortest path from i to j going through no intermediate vertex of index greater than k. Then, $A^n[i,j]$ will be the cost of the shortest i to j path in G since G contains no vertex with index greater than n. $A^0[i,j]$ is just $cost[i,j]$ since the only i to j paths allowed can have no intermediate vertices on them. The basic idea in the all pairs algorithm is to successively generate the matrices A^0, A^1, A^2, ..., A^n. If we have already generated A^{k-1}, then we may generate A^k by realizing that for any pair of vertices i,j either (i) the shortest path from i to j going through no vertex with index greater than k does not go through the vertex with index k and so its cost is $A^{k-1}[i,j]$; or (ii) the shortest such path does go through vertex k. Such a path consists of a path from i to k and another one from k to j. These paths must be the shortest paths from i to k and from k to j going through no vertex with index greater than $k - 1$, and so their costs are $A^{k-1}[i,k]$ and $A^{k-1}[k,j]$. Note that this is true only if G has no cycle with negative length containing vertex k. If this is not true, then the shortest i to j path going through no vertices of index greater than k may make several cycles from k to k and thus have a length substantially less than $A^{k-1}[i,k] + A^{k-1}[k,j]$ (see example 6.2). Thus, we obtain the following formulas for $A^k[i,j]$:

$$A^k[i,j] = \min \{A^{k-1}[i,j], A^{k-1}[i,k] + A^{k-1}[k,j]\}, \ k \geq 1$$

and

$$A^0[i,j] = \text{COST}[i,j].$$

Example 6.2:   Figure 6.22 shows a digraph together with its matrix A^0. For this graph $A^2[1,3] \neq \min \{A^1[1,3], A^1[1,2] + A^1[2,3]\} = 2$. Instead we see that $A^2[1,3] = -\infty$ as the length of the path

$$1,2,1,2,1,2, \ \ldots\ldots,1,2,3$$

can be made arbitrarily small. This is so because of the presence of the cycle 1 2 1 which has a length of -1.   □

$$\begin{bmatrix} 0, & 1, & \infty \\ -2, & 0, & 1 \\ \infty, & \infty, & 0 \end{bmatrix}$$

Figure 6.22   Graph with Negative Cycle.

The algorithm *allcosts* (program 6.5) computes $A^n[i,j]$. The computation is done in place using the array a. The reason this computation can be carried out in place is that $A^k[i,k] = A^{k-1}[i,k]$ and $A^k[k,j] = A^{k-1}[k,j]$ and so the in place computation does not alter the outcome.

```
1   procedure allcosts(cost, var a : adjacencymatrix; n : integer);
2   {cost [1 ..n, 1 .. n] is the cost adjacency matrix of a graph with n
3   vertices; a[i,j] is the cost of the shortest path between vertices
4   vi, vj. cost[i,i] = 0, 1 ≤ i ≤ n}
5   var i : integer;
6       j : integer;
7       k : integer;
8   begin
9     for i := 1 to n do
10      for j := 1 to n do
11        a[i,j] := cost [i,j]; {copy cost into a}
12      for k := 1 to n do {for a path with highest vertex index k}
13        for i := 1 to n do {for all possible pairs of vertices}
14          for j := 1 to n do
15          if a[i,k] + a[k,j]) < a[i,j]
16              then a[i,j] := a[i,k] + a[k,j];
17   end; {of allcosts}
```

Program 6.5   Allcosts

This algorithm is especially easy to analyze because the looping is independent of the data in the matrix a.

The total time for procedure *allcosts* is $O(n^3)$. An exercise examines the extensions needed to actually obtain the (i,j) paths with these lengths. Some speed up can be obtained by noticing that the innermost **for** loop need be executed only when $a[i,k]$ and $a[k,j]$ are not equal to **maxint**.

Example 6.3: Using the graph of figure 6.23(a) we obtain the cost matrix of figure 6.23(b). The initial a matrix, A^0, plus its value after 3 iterations A^1, A^2, A^3 is given in figure 6.24.   □

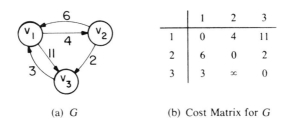

	1	2	3
1	0	4	11
2	6	0	2
3	3	∞	0

(a) *G*   (b) Cost Matrix for *G*

Figure 6.23   Directed Graph and Its Cost Matrix.

A^0	1	2	3
1	0	4	11
2	6	0	2
3	3	∞	0

A^1	1	2	3
1	0	4	11
2	6	0	2
3	3	7	0

A^2	1	2	3
1	0	4	6
2	6	0	2
3	3	7	0

A^3	1	2	3
1	0	4	6
2	5	0	2
3	3	7	0

Figure 6.24   Matrices A^k produced by *allcosts* for the digraph of figure 6.23.

Transitive Closure

A problem related to the all pairs shortest path problem is that of determining for every pair of vertices i,j in G the existence of a path from i to j. Two cases are of interest, one when all path lengths (i.e., the number of edges on the path) are required to be positive and the other when path lengths are to be nonnegative. If A is the adjacency matrix of G, then the Matrix A^+ having the property $A^+[i,j] = 1$ if there is a path of length > 0 from i to j and 0 otherwise is called the *transitive closure* matrix of G. The matrix $A*$ with the property $A*[i,j] = 1$ if there is a path of length ≥ 0 from i to j and 0 otherwise is the *reflexive transitive closure* matrix of G.

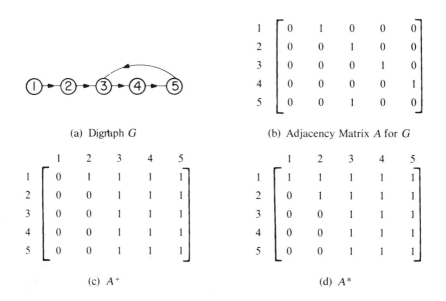

(a) Digraph G

(b) Adjacency Matrix A for G

(c) A^+

(d) $A*$

Figure 6.25 Graph G and Its Adjacency Matrix A, A^+ and $A*$.

Figure 6.25 shows A^+ and $A*$ for a digraph. Clearly, the only difference between $A*$ and A^+ is in the terms on the diagonal. $A^+[i,i] = 1$ iff there is a cycle of length > 1 containing vertex i while $A*[i,i]$ is always one as there is a path of length 0 from i to i. If we use algorithm *allcosts* with $cost[i,j] = 1$ if $\langle i,j \rangle$ is an edge in G and $cost[i,j] = +\infty$ if $\langle i,j \rangle$ is not in G, then we can easily obtain A^+ from the final matrix A by letting $A^+[i,j] = 1$ iff $A[i,j] < +\infty$. $A*$ can be obtained from A^+ by setting all diagonal elements equal to 1. The total time is $O(n^3)$. Some simplification is achieved by slightly modifying the algorithm. In this modification the computation of lines 15 and 16 of *allcosts* becomes $a[i,j] := a[i,j]$ **or** $(a[i,k]$ **and** $a[k,j])$ and $cost[i,j]$ is just the adjacency matrix of G. With this modification, a need only be a **boolean** matrix and then the final matrix A will be A^+.

6.4   ACTIVITY NETWORKS, TOPOLOGICAL SORT AND CRITICAL PATHS

Topological Sort

All but the simplest of projects can be subdivided into several subprojects called activities. The successful completion of these activities will result in the completion of the entire project. A student working towards a degree in Computer Science will have to complete several courses successfully. The project in this case is to complete the major, and the activities are the individual courses that have to be taken. Figure 6.26 lists the courses needed for a computer science major at a hypothetical university. Some of these courses may be taken independently of others while other courses have prerequisites and can be taken only if all their prerequisites have already been taken. The data structures course cannot be started until certain programming and math courses have been completed. Thus, prerequisites define precedence relations between the courses. The relationships defined may be more clearly represented using a directed graph in which the vertices represent courses and the directed edges represent prerequisites. This graph has an edge $\langle i,j \rangle$ iff course i is a prerequisite for course j.

Definition: A directed graph G in which the vertices represent tasks or activities and the edges represent precedence relations between tasks is an *activity on vertex network* or AOV-network.

Definition: Vertex i in an AOV network G is a *predecessor* of vertex j iff there is a directed path from vertex i to vertex j. i is an *immediate predecessor* of j iff $\langle i,j \rangle$ is an edge in G. If i is a predecessor of j, then j is a *successor* of i. If i is an immediate predecessor of j, then j is an *immediate successor* of i.

Figure 6.26(b) is the AOV network corresponding to the courses of figure 6.26(a). C3, C4 and C10 are the immediate predecessors of C7. C2, C3 and C4 are the immediate successors of C1. C12 is a successor of C4 but not an immediate successor. The precedence relation defined by the set of edges on the set of vertices is readily seen to be transitive. (Recall that a relation $\cdot$ is transitive iff it is the case that for all triples i,j,k, $i \cdot j$ and $j \cdot k \Rightarrow i \cdot k$.) In order for an AOV network to represent a feasible project, the precedence relation should also be irreflexive.

Definition: A relation $\cdot$ is *irreflexive* on a set S if for no element x in S it is the case that $x \cdot x$. A precedence relation which is both transitive and irreflexive is a *partial order*.

Course Number	Course Name	Prerequisites
C1	Introduction to Programming	None
C2	Numerical Analysis	C1, C14
C3	Data Structures	C1, C14
C4	Assembly Language	C1, C13
C5	Automata Theory	C15
C6	Artificial Intelligence	C3
C7	Computer Graphics	C3, C4, C10
C8	Machine Arithmetic	C4
C9	Analysis of Algorithms	C3
C10	Higher Level Languages	C3, C4
C11	Compiler Writing	C10
C12	Operating Systems	C11
C13	Analytic Geometry and Calculus I	None
C14	Analytic Geometry and Calculus II	C13
C15	Linear Algebra	C14

(a) Courses Needed for a Computer Science Degree at Some Hypothetical University

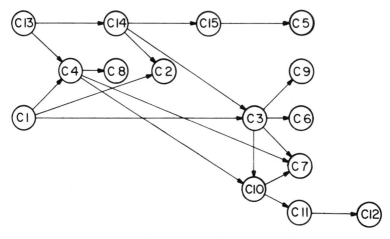

(b) AOV-Network Representing Courses as Vertices and Prerequisites as Edges

Figure 6.26 An Activity on Vertex Network.

If the precedence relation is not irreflexive, then there is an activity which is a predecessor of itself and so must be completed before it can be started. This is clearly impossible. When there are no inconsistencies of this type, the project is feasible. Given an AOV network one of our concerns would be to determine whether or not the precedence relation defined by its edges is irreflexive. This is identical to determining whether or not the network contains any directed cycles. A directed graph with no directed cycles is an *acyclic* graph. Our algorithm to test an AOV network for feasibility will also generate a linear ordering, v_{i_1}, v_{i_2}, ...,v_{i_n}, of the vertices (activities). This linear ordering will have the property that if i is a predecessor of j in the network then i precedes j in the linear ordering. A linear ordering with this property is called a *topological order*. For the network of figure 6.26(b) two of the possible topological orders are: C1, C13, C4, C8, C14, C15, C5, C2, C3, C10, C7, C11, C12, C6, C9 and C13, C14, C15, C5, C1, C4, C8, C2, C3, C10, C7, C6, C9, C11, C12. If a student were taking just one course per term, then he would have to take them in topological order. If the AOV network represented the different tasks involved in assembling an automobile, then these tasks would be carried out in topological order on an assembly line. The algorithm to sort the tasks into topological order is straightforward and proceeds by listing out a vertex in the network that has no predecessor. Then, this vertex together with all edges leading out from it is deleted from the network. These two steps are repeated until either all vertices have been listed or all remaining vertices in the network have predecessors and so none can be performed. In this case there is a cycle in the network and the project is infeasible. Figure 6.27 is a crude form of the algorithm.

```
1  input the AOV network. Let n be the number of vertices.
2  for i := 1 to n do //output the vertices//
3  begin
4    if every vertex has a predecessor
5      then [the network has a cycle and is infeasible. stop];
6    pick a vertex v which has no predecessors;
7    output v;
8    delete v and all edges leading out of v from the network;
9  end;
```

Figure 6.27   Design of a Topological Sorting Algorithm.

Trying this out on the network of figure 6.28 we see that the first vertex to be picked in line 4 is v_1, as it is the only one with no predecessors. v_1 and the edges $\langle v_1,v_2 \rangle$, $\langle v_1,v_3 \rangle$ and $\langle v_1,v_4 \rangle$ are deleted. In the resulting network (figure 6.28(b)), v_2, v_3 and v_4 have no predecessor. Any of these can be the next vertex in the topological order. Assume that v_4 is picked. Deletion of v_4 and the edges $\langle v_4, v_6 \rangle$ and $\langle v_4, v_5 \rangle$ results in the network of figure 6.28(c). Either v_2 or v_3 may next be picked. Figure 6.28 shows the progress of the algorithm on the network. In order to obtain a complete algorithm that can be easily translated into a computer program, it is necessary to

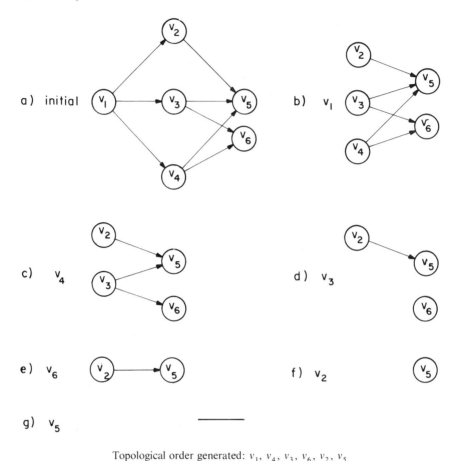

Topological order generated: $v_1, v_4, v_3, v_6, v_2, v_5$

Figure 6.28   Action of Algorithm of Figure 6.27 on an AOV Network.

specify the data representation for the AOV network. The choice of a data representation, as always, depends on the functions one wishes to perform. In this problem, the functions are: (i) decide whether a vertex has any predecessors (line 4), and (ii) delete a vertex together with all its incident edges. (i) is efficiently done if for each vertex a count of the number of its immediate predecessors is kept. (ii) is easily implemented if the network is represented by its adjacency lists. Then the deletion of all edges leading out of a vertex v can be carried out by decreasing the predecessor count of all vertices on its adjacency list. Whenever the count of a vertex drops to zero, that vertex can be placed onto a list of vertices with a zero count. Then the selection in line 6 just requires removal of a vertex from this list. Filling in these details into the algorithm of figure 6.27, we obtain the Pascal program *topologicalorder* (program 6.6).

The algorithm assumes that the network is represented by adjacency lists. But now the headnodes of these lists contain two fields: *count* and *link*.

The datatypes needed are:

type *nextnode* = ↑*node*;

$\quad\quad\quad$ *node* = **record**

$\quad\quad\quad\quad\quad\quad\quad$ *vertex* : **integer**;

$\quad\quad\quad\quad\quad\quad\quad$ *link* $\quad$: *nextnode*;

$\quad\quad\quad\quad\quad\quad$ **end**;

$\quad\quad$ *headnodes* = **record**

$\quad\quad\quad\quad\quad\quad\quad$ *count* : **integer**;

$\quad\quad\quad\quad\quad\quad\quad$ *link* $\quad$: *nextnode*;

$\quad\quad\quad\quad\quad\quad$ **end**;

$\quad$ *adjacencylists* = **array** [1 .. *n*] **of** *headnodes*;

The *count* field contains the in-degree of that vertex and *link* is a pointer to the first node on the adjacency list. Each list node has 2 fields: *vertex* and *link*. *count* fields can be easily set up at the time of input. When edge ⟨*i,j*⟩ is input, the count of vertex *j* is incremented by 1. The list of vertices with zero count is maintained as a stack. A queue could have been used but a stack is slightly simpler. The stack is linked through the *count* field of the headnodes since this field is of no use after the *count* has become zero. Figure 6.29(a) shows the input to the algorithm in the case of the network of figure 6.28(a).

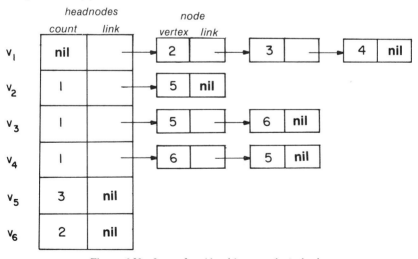

Figure 6.29 Input for Algorithm *topologicalorder*.

```
1   procedure topologicalorder (var adlist: adjacencylists; n: integer);
2   {The n vertices of an AOV-network are listed in topological order.
3    The network is represented as a set of adjacency lists with
4    adlist[i].count = the in-degree of vertex i.}
5   var i    : integer;
6       j    : integer;
7       k    : integer;
8       top  : integer;
9       ptr  : nextnode;
10      done : boolean;
11  begin
12    top := 0; {initialize stack}
13    for i := 1 to n do {create a linked stack of vertices with}
14      if adlist[i].count = 0 {no predecessors}
15      then
16      begin
17        adlist[i].count := top;
18        top := i;
19      end;
20    i := 1;
21    done := false;
22    while ((i <= n) and not done) do
23    begin {print the vertices in topological order}
24      if top = 0
25      then
26      begin
27        writeln('network has a cycle');
28        done := true;
29      end
30      else
31      j := top;
32      top := adlist[top].count; {unstack a vertex}
33      writeln (j);
34      ptr := adlist[j].link;
35      while ptr < > nil do
36      begin {decrease the count of the successor vertices of j}
37        k := ptr↑.vertex; {k is a successor of j}
38        adlist[k].count := adlist[k].count − 1; {decrease count}
39        if adlist[k].count = 0 {add vertex k to stack}
40        then
41        begin
42          adlist[k].count := top;
```

```
43              top := k;
44            end; {of if}
45            ptr := ptr↑.link;
46          end; {of while ptr < > nil}
47          i := i + 1;
48        end; {of while (i <= n) and not done}
49    end; {of topological order}
```

Program 6.6   Topological order

As a result of a judicious choice of data structures the algorithm is very efficient. For a network with n vertices and e edges, the loop of lines 13–19 takes $O(n)$ time; Lines 24–34 take $O(n)$ time over the entire algorithm; the **while** loop takes time $O(d_i)$ for each vertex i, where d_i is the out-degree of vertex i. Since this loop is encountered once for each vertex output, the total time for this part of the algorithm is $O((\Sigma_{i=1}^{n} d_i) + n) = O(e + n)$. Hence, the asymptotic computing time of the algorithm is $O(e + n)$. It is linear in the size of the problem!

Critical Paths

An activity network closely related to the AOV network is the activity on edge or AOE network. The tasks to be performed on a project are represented by directed edges. Vertices in the network represent events. Events signal the completion of certain activities. Activities represented by edges leaving a vertex cannot be started until the event at that vertex has occurred. An event occurs only when all activities entering it have been completed. Figure 6.30(a) is an AOE network for a hypothetical project with 11 tasks or activities $a_1, \ldots, a_{11}$. There are 9 events $v_1, v_2, \ldots, v_9$. The events v_1 and v_9 may be interpreted as "start project" and "finish project" respectively. Figure 6.30(b) gives interpretations for some of the 9 events. The number associated with each activity is the time needed to perform that activity. Thus, activity a_1 requires 6 days while a_{11} requires 4 days. Usually, these times are only estimates. Activities a_1, a_2 and a_3 may be carried out concurrently after the start of the project. a_4, a_5 and a_6 cannot be started until events v_2, v_3 and v_4, respectively, occur. a_7 and a_8 can be carried out concurrently after the occurrence of event v_5 (i.e., after a_4 and a_5 have been completed). In case additional ordering constraints are to be put on the activities, dummy activities whose time is zero may be introduced. Thus, if we desire that activities a_7 and a_8 not start until both events v_5 and v_6 have occurred, a dummy activity a_{12} represented by an edge $\langle v_6, v_5 \rangle$ may be introduced. Activity networks of the AOE type have proved

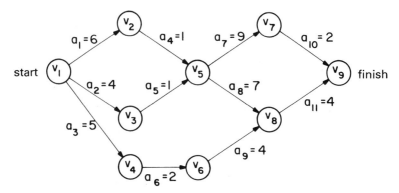

Figure 6.30(a)   AOE Network. Activity Graph of a Hypothetical Project.

event	interpretation
v_1	start of project
v_2	completion of activity a_1
v_5	completion of activities a_4 and a_5
v_8	completion of activities a_8 and a_9
v_9	completion of project

Figure 6.30(b)   Interpretation for Some of the Events in the Activity Graph of Figure 6.30(a).

very useful in the performance evaluation of several types of projects. This evaluation includes determining such facts about the project as: what is the least amount of time in which the project may be completed (assuming there are no cycles in the network); which activities should be speeded up in order to reduce completion time; etc. Several sophisticated techniques such as PERT (performance evaluation and review technique), CPM (critical path method), RAMPS (resource allocation and multi-project scheduling) have been developed to evaluate network models of projects. CPM was originally developed in connection with maintenance and construction projects. Figure 6.31 shows a network used by the Perinia Corporation of Boston in 1961 to model the construction of a floor in a multistory building. PERT was originally designed for use in the development of the Polaris Missile system.

Since the activities in an AOE network can be carried out in parallel the minimum time to complete the project is the length of the longest path from the start vertex to the finish vertex (the length of a path is the sum of the times of activities on this path). A path of longest length is a *critical path*. The path v_1,v_2,v_5,v_7,v_9 is a critical path in the network of figure 6.30(a). The length of this critical path is 18. A network may have more than one critical path (the path v_1,v_2,v_5,v_8,v_9 is also critical). The *earliest time* an event v_i can occur is the length of the longest path from the start vertex v_1 to the vertex v_i. The earliest time event v_5 can occur is 7. The earliest time an event can occur determines the *earliest start time* for all activities represented by edges leaving that vertex. Denote this time by $e(i)$ for activity a_i. For example $e(7) = e(8) = 7$. For every activity a_i we may also define the *latest time*, $l(i)$, an activity may start without increasing the project duration (i.e., length of the longest path from start to finish). In figure 6.30(a) we have $e(6) = 5$ and $l(6) = 8$, $e(8) = 7$ and $l(8) = 7$. All activities for which $e(i) = l(i)$ are called *critical activities*. The difference $l(i) - e(i)$ is a measure of the criticality of an activity. It gives the time by which an activity may be delayed or slowed without increasing the total time needed to finish the project. If activity a_6 is slowed down to take 2 extra days, this will not affect the project finish time. Clearly, all activities on a critical path are critical and speeding noncritical activities will not reduce the project duration.

The purpose of critical path analysis is to identify critical activities so that resources may be concentrated on these activities in an attempt to reduce project finish time. Speeding a critical activity will not result in a reduced project length unless that activity is on all critical paths. In figure 6.30(a) the activity a_{11} is critical but speeding it up so that it takes only three days instead of four does not reduce the finish time to seventeen days. This is so because there is another critical path v_1,v_2,v_5,v_7,v_9 that does not contain this activity. The activities a_1 and a_4 are on all critical paths. Speeding a_1 by two days reduces the critical path length to sixteen days. Critical path methods have proved very valuable in evaluating project performance and identifying bottlenecks. In fact, it is estimated that without such analysis the Polaris missile project would have taken seven instead of the five years it actually took.

Critical path analysis can also be carried out with AOV networks. The length of a path would now be the sum of the activity times of the vertices on that path. For each activity or vertex, we could analogously define the quantities $e(i)$ and $l(i)$. Since the activity times are only estimates, it is necessary to re-evaluate the project during several stages of its completion as more accurate estimates of activity times become available. These changes in activity times could make previously noncritical activities critical and vice versa. Before ending our discussion on activity networks, let us design an algorithm to evaluate $e(i)$ and $l(i)$ for all activities in an AOE-network. Once these quantities are known, then the critical activities may be easily identified. Deleting all noncritical activities from the AOE network, all critical paths may be found by just generating all paths from the start to finish vertex (all such paths will include only critical activities and

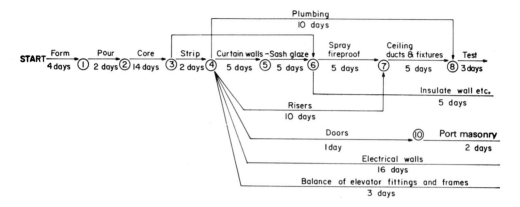

Figure 6.31   AOE network for the construction of a typical floor in a multistory building [Redrawn from Engineering News-Record (McGraw-Hill Book Company, Inc., January 26, 1961).]

so must be critical, and since no noncritical activity can be on a critical path, the network with noncritical activities removed contains all critical paths present in the original network).

In obtaining the $e(i)$ and $l(i)$ for the activities of an AOE network, it is easier to first obtain the earliest event occurrence time, $ee[j]$, and latest event occurrence time, $le[j]$, for all events, j, in the network. Then if activity a_i is represented by edge $\langle k,l \rangle$, we can compute $e(i)$ and $l(i)$ from the formulas:

$$e(i) = ee[k]$$

and

$$l(i) = le[l] - \text{duration of activity } a_i$$

(6.1)

The times $ee[j]$ and $le[j]$ are computed in two stages: a forward stage and a backward stage. During the forward stage we start with $ee[1] = 0$ and compute the remaining early start times, using the formula

$$ee[j] = \max_{i \in P(j)} \{ee[i] + \text{duration of } \langle i,j \rangle\}$$

(6.2)

where $P(j)$ is the set of all vertices adjacent to vertex j. In case this computation is carried out in topological order, the early start times of all predecessors of j would have been computed prior to the computation of $ee[j]$. The algorithm to do this is obtained easily from algorithm *topologicalorder* by inserting the step

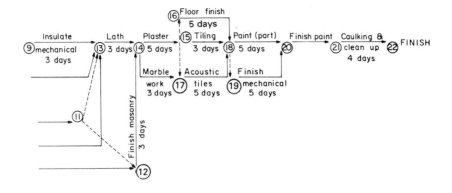

Figure 6.31   (continued)

$$\textbf{if } ee[k] < ee[j] + ptr\uparrow.dur$$
$$\textbf{then } ee[k] := ee[j] + ptr\uparrow.dur;$$

between lines 38 and 39. It is assumed that the array *ee* is initialized to zero and that *dur* is another field in the adjacency list nodes which contains the activity duration. This modification results in the evaluation of equation (6.2) in parallel with the generation of a topological order. *ee(j)* is updated each time the *ee(i)* of one of its predecessors is known (i.e., when *i* is ready for output). The step **writeln**(*j*) of line 33 may be omitted. To illustrate the working of the modified *topologicalorder* algorithm let us try it out on the network of figure 6.30(a). The adjacency lists for the network are shown in figure 6.32(a). The order of nodes on these lists determines the order in which vertices will be considered by the algorithm. At the outset the early start time for all vertices is 0, and the start vertex is the only one in the stack. When the adjacency list for this vertex is processed, the early start time of all vertices adjacent from v_1 is updated. Since vertices 2, 3 and 4 are now in the stack, all their predecessors have been processed and equation (6.2) evaluated for these three vertices. *ee*[6] is the next one determined. When vertex v_6 is being processed, *ee*[8] is updated to 11. This, however, is not the true value for *ee*[8] since equation (6.2) has not been evaluated over all predecessors of v_8 (v_5 has not yet been considered). This does not matter since v_8 cannot get stacked until all its predecessors have been processed. *ee*[5] is next updated to 5 and finally to 7. At this point *ee*[5] has been determined as all the predecessors of v_5 have been examined. The values of *ee*[7] and *ee*[8] are next obtained. *ee*[9] is ultimately determined to be 18,

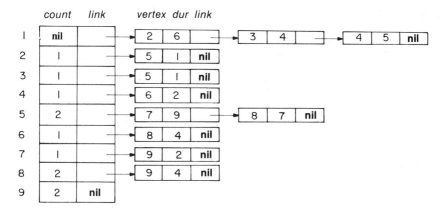

(a) Adjacency Lists for Figure 6.30(a)

ee	[1]	[2]	[3]	[4]	[5]	[6]	[7]	[8]	[9]	stack
initial	0	0	0	0	0	0	0	0	0	⌊1⌋
output v_1	0	6	4	5	0	0	0	0	0	4 / 3 / 2
output v_4	0	6	4	5	0	7	0	0	0	6 / 3 / 2
output v_6	0	6	4	5	0	7	0	11	0	3 / 2
output v_3	0	6	4	5	5	7	0	11	0	⌊2⌋
output v_2	0	6	4	5	7	7	0	11	0	⌊5⌋
output v_5	0	6	4	5	7	7	16	14	0	8 / 7
output v_8	0	6	4	5	7	7	16	14	16	⌊7⌋
output v_7	0	6	4	5	7	7	16	14	18	⌊9⌋
output v_9										

(b) Computation of ee

Figure 6.32 Action of Modified Topological Order.

the length of a critical path. One may readily verify that when a vertex is put into the stack its early time has been correctly computed. The insertion of the new statement does not change the asymptotic computing time; it remains $O(e + n)$.

In the backward stage the values of $le[i]$ are computed using a procedure analogous to that used in the forward stage. We start with $le[n] = ee[n]$ and use the equation

$$le[j] = \min_{i \in S(j)} \{le[i] - \text{duration of} \langle j,i \rangle\} \qquad (6.3)$$

where $S(j)$ is the set of vertices adjacent from vertex j. The initial values for $le[i]$ may be set to $ee[n]$. Basically, equation (6.3) says that if $\langle j,i \rangle$ is an activity and the latest start time for event i is $le[i]$, then event j must occur no later than $le[i]$ – duration of $\langle j,i \rangle$. Before $le[j]$ can be computed for some event j, the latest event time for all successor events (i.e., events adjacent from j) must be computed. These times can be obtained in a manner identical to the computation of the early times by using inverse adjacency lists and inserting the step $le[k] := \min \{le[k], le[j] - ptr\uparrow.dur\}$ at the same place as before in algorithm *topologicalorder*. The *count* field of a headnode will initially be the out-degree of the vertex. Figure 6.33 describes the process on the network of figure 6.30(a). In case the forward stage has already been carried out and a topological ordering of the vertices obtained, then the values of $le[i]$ can be computed directly, using equation (6.3), by performing the computations in the reverse topological order. The topological order generated in figure 6.32(b) is v_1, v_4, v_6, v_3, v_2, v_5, v_8, v_7, v_9. We may compute the values of $le[i]$ in the order 9,7,8,5,2,3,6,4,1 as all successors of

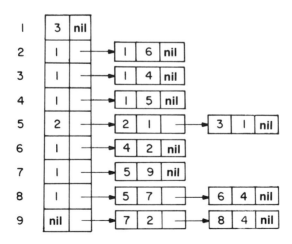

Figure 6.33(a)   Inverted Adjacency Lists for AOE Network of Figure 6.30(a).

le	[1]	[2]	[3]	[4]	[5]	[6]	[7]	[8]	[9]	stack
initial	18	18	18	18	18	18	18	18	18	9
output v_9	18	18	18	18	18	18	16	14	18	8 7
output v_8	18	18	18	18	7	10	16	14	18	6 7
output v_6	18	18	18	18	7	10	16	14	18	4 7
output v_4	3	18	18	8	7	10	16	14	18	7
output v_7	3	18	18	8	7	10	16	14	18	5
output v_5	3	6	6	8	7	10	16	14	18	3 2
output v_3	2	6	6	8	7	10	16	14	18	2
output v_2	0	6	6	8	7	10	16	14	18	1

(b) Computation of *topologicalorder* Modified to Compute Latest Event Times.

$$le[9] = ee[9] = 18$$
$$le[7] = \min\{le[9] - 2\} = 16$$
$$le[8] = \min\{le[9] - 4\} = 14$$
$$le[5] = \min\{le[7] - 9, \, le[8] - 7\} = 7$$
$$le[2] = \min\{le[5] - 1\} = 6$$
$$le[3] = \min\{le[5] - 1\} = 6$$
$$le[6] = \min\{le[8] - 4\} = 10$$
$$le[4] = \min\{le[6] - 2\} = 8$$
$$le[1] = \min\{le[2] - 6, \, le[3] - 4, \, le[4] - 5\} = 0$$

(c) Computation of *le* Directly from Equation (6.3) Using a Reverse Topological Order.

Figure 6.33

an event precede that event in this order. In practice, one would usually compute both *ee* and *le*. The procedure would then be to compute *ee* first using algorithm *topologicalorder* modified as discussed for the forward stage and to then compute *le* directly from equation (6.3) in reverse topological order.

Using the values of *ee* (figure 6.32) and of *le* (figure 6.33 and equation 6.1) we may compute the early and late times $e(i)$ and $l(i)$ and the degree of criticality of each task. Figure 6.34 gives the values. The critical activities are $a_1, a_4, a_7, a_8, a_{10}$ and a_{11}. Deleting all noncritical activities from the network we get the directed graph of figure 6.35. All paths from v_1 to v_9 in this graph are critical paths and there are no critical paths in the original network that are not paths in the graph of figure 6.35.

activity	e	l	$l - e$
a_1	0	0	0
a_2	0	2	2
a_3	0	3	3
a_4	6	6	0
a_5	4	6	2
a_6	5	8	3
a_7	7	7	0
a_8	7	7	0
a_9	7	10	3
a_{10}	16	16	0
a_{11}	14	14	0

Figure 6.34   Early, Late and Criticality Values.

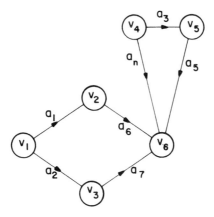

Figure 6.35   Graph Obtained After Deleting All Noncritical Activities.

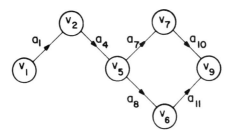

Figure 6.36   AOE-Network with Some Non-Reachable Activities.

As a final remark on activity networks we note that the algorithm *topologicalorder* detects only directed cycles in the network. There may be other flaws, such as vertices not reachable from the start vertex (figure 6.36). When a critical path analysis is carried out on such networks, there will be several vertices with $ee[i] = 0$. Since all activity times are assumed > 0 only the start vertex can have $ee[i] = 0$. Hence, critical path analysis can also be used to detect this kind of fault in project planning.

6.5   ENUMERATING ALL PATHS

In section 6.3 we looked at the problem of finding a shortest path between two vertices. In this section we will be concerned with listing all possible simple paths between two vertices in order of nondecreasing path length. Such a listing could be of use, for example, in a situation where we are interested in obtaining the shortest path that satisfies some complex set of constraints. One possible solution to such a problem would be to generate in nondecreasing order of path length all paths between the two vertices. Each path generated could be tested against the other constraints and the first path satisfying all these constraints would be the path we were looking for.

Let $G = (V,E)$ be a digraph with n vertices. Let v_1 be the source vertex and v_n the destination vertex. We shall assume that every edge has a positive cost. Let $p_1 = r[0], r[1], ..., r[k]$ be a shortest path from v_1 to v_n. I.e., p_1 starts at $v_{r[0]} = v_1$, goes to $v_{r[1]}$ and then to $v_{r[2]}, ..., v_n = v_{r[k]}$. If P is the set of all simple v_1 to v_n paths in G, then it is easy to see that every path in $P - \{p_1\}$ differs from p_1 in exactly one of the following k ways:

(1): It contains the edges $(r[1], r[2]), ..., (r[k - 1], r[k])$
but not $(r[0], r[1])$
(2): It contains the edges $(r[2], r[3]), ..., (r[k - 1], r[k])$
but not $(r[1], r[2])$

$\vdots$
$\vdots$

(k): It does not contain the edge $(r[k - 1], r[k])$.

More compactly, for every path p in $P - \{p_1\}$ there is exactly one j, $1 \le j \le k$ such that p contains the edges

$$(r[j], r[j + 1]), ..., (r[k - 1], r[k]) \text{ but not } (r[j - 1], r[j]).$$

The set of paths $P - \{p_1\}$ may be partitioned into k disjoint sets $P^{(1)}, ..., P^{(k)}$ with set $P^{(j)}$ containing all paths in $P - \{p_1\}$ satisfying condition j above, $1 \le j \le k$.

Let $p^{(j)}$ be a shortest path in $P^{(j)}$ and let q be the shortest path from v_1 to $v_{r[j]}$ in the digraph obtained by deleting from G the edges $(r[j - 1], r[j])$,

$(r[j], r[j + 1]),...,(r[k - 1], r[k])$. Then one readily obtains $p^{(j)} = q, r[j], r[j + 1]$, $...,r[k] = n$. Let $p^{(l)}$ have the minimum length among $p^{(1)}, ...p^{(k)}$. Then, $p^{(l)}$ also has the least length amongst all paths in $P - \{p_1\}$ and hence must be a second shortest path. The set $P^{(l)} - \{p^{(l)}\}$ may now be partitioned into disjoint subsets using a criterion identical to that used to partition $P - \{p_1\}$. If $p^{(l)}$ has k' edges, then this partitioning results in k' disjoint subsets. We next determine the shortest paths in each of these k' subsets. Consider the set Q which is the union of these k' shortest paths and the paths $p^{(1)}, ..., p^{(l - 1)}, ..., p^{(k)}$. The path with minimum length in Q is a third shortest path p_3. The corresponding set may be further partitioned. In this way we may successively generate the v_1 to v_n paths in nondecreasing order of path length.

At this point, an example would be instructive. Figure 6.38 shows the generation of the v_1 to v_6 path of the graph of figure 6.37. A very informal version of the algorithm appears as the procedure *mshortest*.

procedure *mshortest*(M)
{Given a digraph G with positive edge weights this procedure outputs the M shortest paths from v_1 to v_n. Q contains tuples of the form (p,C) where p is a shortest path in G satisfying constraints C. These constraints either require certain edges to be included or excluded from the path}
begin
1    $Q := \{(shortest\ v_1\ to\ v_n\ path,\ \phi)\}$;
2   **for** $i := 1$ **to** M **do begin** { generate M shortest paths }
3   let (p,C) be the tuple in Q such that path p is of minimal length;
                            {p is the i'th shortest path}
4   **writeln** path p; delete path p from Q;
5   determine the shortest paths in G under the constraints C and the additional constraints imposed by the partitioning described in the text;
6   add these shortest paths together with their constraints to Q;
7   **end**;
8 **end** {*mshortest*}

Since the number of v_1 to v_n paths in a digraph with n vertices ranges from 0 to $(n - 1)!$, a worst case analysis of the computing time of *mshortest* is not very meaningful. Instead, we shall determine the time taken to generate the first m shortest paths. Line 5 of the **for** loop may require determining $n - 1$ shortest paths in an n vertex graph. Using a modified version of algorithm *shortestpath* this would take $O(n^3)$ for each iteration of the **for** loop. The total contribution of line 5 is therefore $O(mn^3)$. In the next chapter, when we study heap sort, we shall see that it is possible to maintain Q as a heap with the result that the total contribution of lines 3

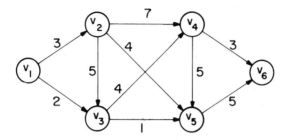

Figure 6.37 A Graph.

Shortest Path	Cost	Included Edges	Excluded Edges	New Path
$v_1v_3v_5v_6$	8	none	none	
		none	(v_5v_6)	$v_1v_3v_4v_6 = 9$
		(v_5v_6)	(v_3v_5)	$v_1v_2v_5v_6 = 12$
		$(v_3v_5)(v_5v_6)$	(v_1v_3)	$v_1v_2v_3v_5v_6 = 14$
$v_1v_3v_4v_6$	9	none	(v_5v_6)	
		none	$(v_4v_6)(v_5v_6)$	∞
		(v_4v_6)	$(v_3v_4)(v_5v_6)$	$v_1v_2v_4v_6 = 13$
		$(v_3v_4)(v_4v_6)$	$(v_1v_3)(v_5v_6)$	$v_1v_2v_3v_4v_6 = 15$
$v_1v_2v_5v_6$	12	(v_5v_6)	(v_3v_5)	
		(v_5v_6)	$(v_2v_5)(v_3v_5)$	$v_1v_3v_4v_5v_6 = 16$
		$(v_2v_5)(v_5v_6)$	$(v_1v_2)(v_3v_5)$	∞
$v_1v_2v_4v_6$	13	(v_4v_6)	$(v_3v_4)(v_5v_6)$	
		(v_4v_6)	$(v_2v_4)(v_3v_4)(v_5v_6)$	∞
		$(v_2v_4)(v_4v_6)$	$(v_1v_2)(v_3v_4)(v_5v_6)$	∞
$v_1v_2v_3v_5v_6$	14	$(v_3v_5)(v_5v_6)$	(v_1v_3)	
		$(v_3v_5)(v_5v_6)$	$(v_2v_3)(v_1v_3)$	∞
		$(v_2v_3)(v_3v_5)(v_5v_6)$	$(v_1v_2)(v_5v_6)$	
$v_1v_2v_3v_4v_6$	15	$(v_3v_4)(v_4v_6)$	$(v_1v_3)(v_5v_6)$	
		$(v_3v_4)(v_4v_6)$	$(v_2v_3)(v_1v_3)(v_5v_6)$	∞
		$(v_2v_3)(v_3v_5)(v_5v_6)$	$(v_1v_2)(v_1v_3)(v_5v_6)$	∞
$v_1v_3v_4v_5v_6$	16	(v_5v_6)	$(v_2v_5)(v_3v_5)$	
		(v_5v_6)	$(v_4v_5)(v_2v_5)(v_3v_5)$	∞
		$(v_4v_5)(v_5v_6)$	$(v_3v_4)(v_2v_5)(v_3v_5)$	$v_1v_2v_4v_5v_6 = 20$
		$(v_3v_4)(v_4v_5)(v_5v_6)$	$(v_1v_3)(v_2v_5)(v_3v_5)$	$v_1v_2v_3v_4v_5v_6 = 22$

Figure 6.38 Action of *m-shortest*.

and 6 is less than $O(mn^3)$. The total time to generate the m shortest paths is, therefore, $O(mn^3)$. The space needed is determined by the number of tuples in Q. Since at most $n-1$ shortest paths are generated at each iteration of line 5, at most $O(mn)$ tuples get onto Q. Each path has at most $O(n)$ edges and the additional constraints take less space than this. Hence, the total space requirements are $O(mn^2)$.

REFERENCES AND SELECTED READINGS

Euler's original paper on the Koenigsberg bridge problem makes interesting reading. This paper has been reprinted in:

"Leonhard Euler and the Koenigsberg Bridges," *Scientific American*, vol. 189, no. 1, July 1953, pp. 66–70.

Good general references for this chapter are:

Graph Theory, by F. Harary, Addison-Wesley, Reading, Massachsetts, 1972.

The theory of graphs and its applications, by C. Berge, John Wiley, 1962.

Further algorithms on graphs may be found in:

The design and analysis of computer algorithms, by A. Aho, J. Hopcroft and J. Ullman, Addison-Wesley, Reading, Massachusetts, 1974.

Graph theory with applications to engineering and computer science, by N. Deo, Prentice-Hall, Englewood Cliffs, New Jersey, 1974.

Combinatorial Optimization, by E. Lawler, Holt, Reinhart and Winston, 1976.

"Depth-first search and linear graph algorithms," by R. Tarjan, *SIAM Journal on Computing*, vol. 1, no. 2, 1972, pp. 146–159.

Flows in Networks, by L. Ford and D. Fulkerson, Princeton University Press, 1962.

Integer Programming and Network Flows, by T. C. Hu, Addison-Wesley, Reading, Massachusetts, 1970.

For more on activity networks and critical path analysis see:

Project Management with CPM and PERT by Moder and C. Phillips, Van Nostrand Reinhold Co., 1970.

EXERCISES

1. Does the multigraph below have an Eulerian walk? If so, find one.

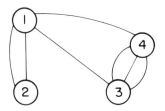

2. For the following digraph obtain:
    i) the in degree and out degree of each vertex;
    ii) its adjacency matrix;
    iii) its adjacency list representation;
    iv) its adjacency multilist representation;
    v) its strongly connected components.

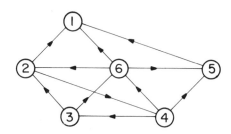

3. Devise a suitable representation for graphs so they can be stored on disk. Write an algorithm which reads in such a graph and creates its adjacency matrix. Write another algorithm which creates the adjacency lists from the disk input.

4. Draw the complete undirected graphs on one, two, three, four and five vertices. Prove that the number of edges in an n vertex complete graph is $n(n - 1)/2$.

5. Is the directed graph below strongly connected? List all the simple paths.

6. Show how the graph above would look if represented by its adjacency matrix, adjacency lists, adjacency multilist.

7. For an undirected graph G with n vertices and e edges show that $\Sigma_1^n d_i = 2e$ where d_i = degree of vertex i.

8. (a) Let G be a connected undirected graph on n vertices. Show that G must have at least $n - 1$ edges and that all connected undirected graphs with $n - 1$ edges are trees.
    (b) What is the minimum number of edges in a strongly connected digraph on n vertices? What shape do such digraphs have?

9. For an undirected graph G with n vertices prove that the following are equivalent:
    (a) G is a tree;
    (b) G is connected, but if any edge is removed the resulting graph is not connected;
    (c) For any distinct vertices $u \in V(G)$ and $v \in V(G)$ there is exactly one simple path from u to v;
    (d) G contains no cycles and has $n - 1$ edges;
    (e) G is connected and has $n - 1$ edges.

10. A *bipartite graph* $G = (V,E)$ is an undirected graph whose vertices can be partitioned into two disjoint sets V_1 and $V_2 = V - V_1$ with the properties (i) no two vertices in V_1 are adjacent in G and (ii) no two vertices in V_2 are adjacent in G. The graph G_4 of figure 6.5 is bipartite. A possible partitioning of V is: $V_1 = \{1,4,5,7\}$ and $V_2 = \{2,3,6,8\}$. Write an algorithm to determine whether a graph G is bipartite. In case G is bipartite your algorithm should obtain a partitioning of the vertices into two disjoint sets V_1 and V_2 satisfying properties (i) and (ii) above. Show that if G is represented by its adjacency lists, then this algorithm can be made to work in time $O(n + e)$ where $n = |V|$ and $e = |E|$.

11. Show that every tree is a bipartite graph.

12. Prove that a graph G is bipartite if it contains no cycles of odd length.

13. The following algorithm was obtained by Stephen Barnard to find an Eulerian circuit in an undirected graph in case there was such a circuit.

```
    function euler(v : vertex): path;
1   begin
2     path := {φ};
3     for all vertices w adjacent to v and edge (v,w) not yet used do begin
4       mark edge (v, w) as used;
5       path := {(v,w)} ∪ euler(w) ∪ path;
6     end;
7     euler := path;
8   end {euler}
```

    a) Show that if G is represented by its adjacency multilists and *path* by a linked list, then algorithm *euler* works in time $O(n + e)$.
    b) Prove by induction on the number of edges in G that the above algorithm does obtain an Euler circuit for all graphs G having such a circuit. The initial call to Euler can be made with any vertex v.
    c) At termination, what has to be done to determine whether or not G has an Euler circuit?

14. Apply depth first and breadth first search to the complete graph on four vertices. List the vertices in the order they would be visited.

15. Show how to modify algorithm *dfs* as it is used in *comp* to produce a list of all newly visited vertices.

16. Prove that when algorithm *dfs* is applied to a connected graph the edges of T form a tree.

17. Prove that when algorithm *bfs* is applied to a connected graph the edges of T form a tree.

18. Show that $A^+ = A* \times A$ where matrix multiplication of the two matrices is defined as $a_{ij}^+ = V_{k=1}^n a_{ik}^* \wedge a_{kj}$. V is the logical *or* operation and $\wedge$ is the logical *and* operation.

19. Obtain the matrices A^+ and $A*$ for the digraph of exercise 5.

20. Another way to represent a graph is by its incidence matrix, INC. There is one row for each vertex and one column for each edge. Then $INC[i,j] = 1$ if edge j is incident to vertex i. The incidence matrix for the graph of figure 6.13(a) is:

	1	2	3	4	5	6	7	8	9	10
1	1	1	0	0	0	0	0	0	0	0
2	1	0	1	1	0	0	0	0	0	0
3	0	1	0	0	1	1	0	0	0	0
4	0	0	1	0	0	0	1	0	0	0
5	0	0	0	1	0	0	0	1	0	0
6	0	0	0	0	1	0	0	0	1	0
7	0	0	0	0	0	1	0	0	0	1
8	0	0	0	0	0	0	1	1	1	1

The edges of figure 6.13(a) have been numbered from left to right, top to bottom. Rewrite algorithm *dfs* so it works on a graph represented by its incidence matrix.

21. If ADJ is the adjacency matrix of a graph $G = (V,E)$ and INC is the incidence matrix, under what conditions will $ADJ = INC \times INC^T - I$ where INC^T is the transpose of matrix INC. Matrix multiplication is defined as in exercise 18. I is the identity matrix.

22. Show that if T is a spanning tree for the undirected graph G, then the addition of an edge e, $e \notin E(T)$ and $e \in E(G)$, to T creates a unique cycle.

23. By considering the complete graph with n vertices, show that the number of spanning trees is at least $2^{n-1} - 1$.

24. The *radius* of a tree is the maximum distance from the root to a leaf. Given a connected, undirected graph write an algorithm for finding a spanning tree of minimum radius. (Hint: use breadth first search.) Prove that your algorithm is correct.

25. The *diameter* of a tree is the maximum distance between any two vertices. Given a connected, undirected graph write an algorithm for finding a spanning tree of minimum diameter. Prove the correctness of your algorithm.

26. Write out Kruskal's minimum spanning tree algorithm (figure 6.18) as a complete program. You may use as procedures the algorithms *union* and *find* of Chapter 5. Use algorithm *sort* to sort the edges into nondecreasing order by weight.

27. Using the idea of algorithm *shortestpath*, give an algorithm to find a minimum spanning tree whose worst case time is $O(n^2)$.

28. Use algorithm *shortestpath* to obtain in nondecreasing order the lengths of the shortest paths from vertex 1 to all remaining vertices in the digraph:

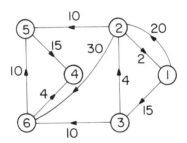

29. Rewrite algorithm *shortestpath* under the following assumptions:
    (i) G is represented by its adjacency lists, where each node has three fields: *vertex, cost,* and *link. cost* is the length of the corresponding edge and n the number of vertices in G.
    (ii) Instead of representing S, the set of vertices to which the shortest paths have already been found, the set $T = V(G) - S$ is represented using a linked list.
    What can you say about the computing time of your new algorithm relative to that of *shortestpath*?

30. Modify algorithm *shortestpath* so that it obtains the shortest paths in addition to the lengths of these paths. What is the computing time of your algorithm?

31. Using the directed graph below, explain why *shortestpath* will not work properly. What is the shortest path between vertices v_1 and v_7?

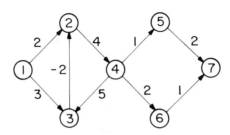

32. Modify algorithm *allcosts* so that it obtains a shortest path for all pairs of vertices i,j. What is the computing time of your new algorithm?

33. By considering the complete graph with n vertices show that the maximum number of simple paths between two vertices is $O((n - 1)!)$.

34. Use algorithm *allcosts* to obtain the lengths of the shortest paths between all pairs of vertices in the graph of exercise 31. Does *allcosts* give the right answers? Why?

35. Does the following set of precedence relations ($<$) define a partial order on the elements 1 thru 5? Why?

$1 < 2; \ 2 < 4; \ 2 < 3; \ 3 < 4; \ 3 < 5; \ 5 < 1$

36. a) For the AOE network below obtain the early, $e(\ )$, and late, $l(\ )$, start times for each activity. Use the forward-backward approach.
   b) What is the earliest time the project can finish?
   c) Which activities are critical?
   d) Is there any single activity whose speed up would result in a reduction of the project length?

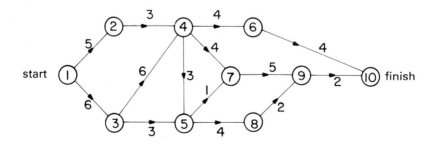

37. Define a critical AOE network to be an AOE network in which all activities are critical. Let G be the undirected graph obtained by removing the directions and weights from the edges of the network.
    a) Show that the project length can be decreased by speeding exactly one activity if there is an edge in G which lies on every path from the start vertex to the finish vertex. Such an edge is called a bridge. Deletion of a bridge from a connected graph disconnects the graph into two connected components.
    b) Write an $O(n + e)$ algorithm using adjacency lists to determine whether the connected graph G has a bridge. In case G has a bridge, your algorithm should output one such bridge.

38. Write a set of computer programs for manipulating graphs. Such a collection should allow input and **output** of arbitrary graphs, determining connected components and spanning trees. The capability of attaching weights to the edges should also be provided.

39. Make sure you can define the following terms:

    adjacent(v)   connected (v_p, v_q)
    adjacent-to(v)   connected(G)
    adjacent-from(v)   connected component
    degree(v)   strongly connected
    in-degree(v)   tree
    out-degree(v)   network
    path   spanning tree
    simple path
    cycle
    subgraph

Chapter 7

INTERNAL SORTING

7.1 SEARCHING

A file is a collection of records, each record having one or more fields. The fields used to distinguish among the records are known as *keys*. Since the same file may be used for several different applications, the key fields for record identification will depend on the particular application. For instance, we may regard a telephone directory as a file, each record having three fields: name, address, and phone number. The key is usually the person's name. However, one may wish to locate the record corresponding to a given number, in which case the phone number field would be the key. In yet another application one may desire the phone number at a particular address, so this field too could be the key. Pascal contains within it the notion of a file type, but it is much more constrained than our use of the term. In Pascal a file is assumed to be serial (a sequence of components) where the basic operations are *read, write*, and *reset*. Reading and writing of components can only be done serially (accessing one adjacent component after another). Though we will occasionally assume files can only be serially accessed, we will more generally speak of files as collections of records which, when they reside in memory, can be randomly accessed in constant time. Once we have a collection of records there are at least two ways in which to store them: sequentially or non-sequentially. For the time being let us assume we have a sequential file f and we wish to retrieve a record with a certain key value k. If f has n records with $f[i].key$ the key value for record i, then one may carry out the retrieval by examining the key values $f[n].key, ...,f[1].key$ in that order, until the correct record is located. Such a search is known as sequential search since the records are examined sequentially. Program 7.1 gives a sequential search algorithm that uses the following data types:

```
type records = record
                 key : integer;
                 other : fields;
              end;
    afile = array [0 .. n] of records;
```

```
1   procedure seqsrch( f: afile; var i: integer; n,k: integer);
2   {search a file f with key values f[1].key, ..., f[n].key for a record
3    such that f[i].key = k. If there is no such record, i is set to 0.}
4   begin
5     f[0].key := k;
6     i := n;
7     while f[i].key <> k do
8       i := i − 1;
9   end; {of seqsrch}
```

Program 7.1   Seqsrch

Note that the introduction of the dummy record 0 with key $f[0].key = k$ in f simplifies the search by eliminating the need for an end of file test ($i < 1$) in the **while** loop. While this might appear to be a minor improvement, it actually reduces the running time by 50% for large n. If no record in the file has key value k, then $i = 0$, and the above algorithm requires $n + 1$ comparisons. The number of key comparisons made in case of a successful search, depends on the position of the key in the file. If all keys are distinct and key $f[i].key$ is being searched for, then $n − i + 1$ key comparisons are made. The average number of comparisons for a successful search is, therefore, $\sum_{1 \leq i \leq n} (n − i + 1)/n = (n + 1)/2$. For large n this many comparisons is very inefficient. However, we all know that it is possible to do much better when looking up phone numbers. What enables us to make an efficient search? The fact that the entries in the file (i.e., the telephone directory) are in lexicographic order (on the name key) is what enables one to look up a number while examining only a very few entries in the file. So, if the file is ordered one should be able to search for specific records quickly.

One of the better known methods for searching an ordered sequential file is called binary search. In this method, the search begins by examining the record in the middle of the file rather than the one at one of the ends as in sequential search. Let us assume that the file being searched is ordered by nondecreasing values of the key (i.e., in alphabetical order for strings). Then, based on the results of the comparison with the middle key, $f[m].key$, one can draw one of the following conclusions:

(i)   if $k < f[m].key$ then if the record being searched for is in the file, it must be in the lower numbered half of the file;

(ii) if $k = f[m].key$ then the middle record is the one being searched for;

(iii) if $k > f[m].key$ then if the record being searched for is in the file, it must be in the higher numbered half of the file.

Consequently, after each comparison either the search terminates success-fully or the size of the file remaining to be searched is about one half of the original size (note that in the case of sequential search, after each comparison the size of the file remaining to be searched decreases by only 1). So after j key comparisons the file remaining to be examined is of size at most $\lceil n/2^j \rceil$ (n is the number of records). Hence, in the worst case, this method requires $O(\log n)$ key comparisons to search a file. Algorithm *binsrch* implements the scheme just outlined.

```
1   procedure binsrch(f : afile; var i : integer; n,k : integer);
2   {Search a file whose n records are ordered such that
3    f[1].key ≤ f[2].key ≤ ... ≤ f[n].key for a record i such that
4    f[i].key = k; i = 0 if there is no such record else f[i].key = k.
5    Throughout the algorithm, l is the smallest index such that
6    f[l].key may be k and u the largest index such
7    that f[u].key may be k.}
8   var done : boolean
9       l,u,m : integer;
10  begin
11    l := 1; u := n;  i := 0;
12    done := false;
13    while ((l <= u) and (not done)) do
14    begin
15      m := (l + u) div 2; {compute index of middle record}
16      case compare (k, f[m].key) of
17          '>' : l := m + 1 {look in upper half}
18          '=' : begin
19                  i := m;
20                  done := true;
21                end;
22          '<' : u := m - 1; {look in lower half}
23      end; {of case}
24    end; {of while}
25  end; {of binsrch}
```

Program 7.2   Binsrch

In the binary search method described above, it is always the key in the middle of the subfile currently being examined that is used for comparison. This splitting process can be described by drawing a binary decision tree in which the value of a node is the index of the key being tested. Suppose there are 31 records, then the first key tested is $f[16].key$ since $\lfloor(1 + 31)/2\rfloor$ = 16. If k is less than $f[16].key$ then $f[8].key$ is tested next as $\lfloor(1 + 15)/2\rfloor$ = 8; or if k is greater than $f[16].key$ then $f[24].key$ is tested. The binary tree describing this process is

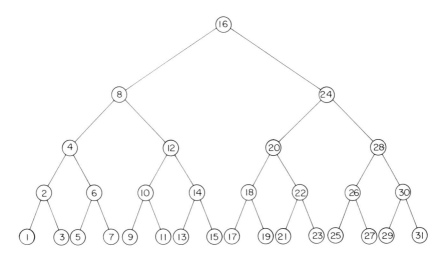

A path from the root to any node in the tree represents a sequence of comparisons made by *binsrch* to either find k or determine that it is not present. From the depth of this tree one can easily see that the algorithm makes no more than $O(\log_2 n)$ comparisons.

It is possible to consider other criteria than equal splitting for dividing the remaining file. An alternate method is Fibonacci search, which splits the subfile according to the Fibonacci sequence,

$$0, \; 1, \; 1, \; 2, \; 3, \; 5, \; 8, \; 13, \; 21, \; 34, \; ...$$

which is defined as $F_0 = 0$, $F_1 = 1$ and

$$F_i = F_{i-1} + F_{i-2}, \; i \geq 2.$$

An advantage of Fibonacci search is that it involves only addition and subtraction rather than the division in *binsrch*. So its average performance is better than that of binary search on computers for which division takes sufficiently more time than addition/subtraction.

Suppose we begin by assuming that the number of records is one less than some Fibonacci number, $n = F_a - 1$. Then, the first comparison of key k is made with $f[F_{a-1}].key$ with the following outcomes:

(i) $k < f[F_{a-1}].key$ in which case the subfile from 1 to $F_{a-1} - 1$ is searched and this file has one less than a Fibonacci number of records;

(ii) $k = f[F_{a-1}].key$ in which case the search terminates successfully;

(iii) $k > f[F_{a-1}].key$ in which case the subfile from $F_{a-1} + 1$ to $F_a - 1$ is searched and the size of this file is $F_a - 1 - (F_{a-1} + 1) + 1 = F_a - F_{a-1} - 1 = F_{a-2} - 1$.

Again it is helpful to think of this process as a binary decision tree; the resulting tree for $n = 33$ is given on page 331.

This tree is an example of a Fibonacci tree. Such a tree has $n = F_a - 1$ nodes, and its left and right subtrees are also Fibonacci trees with $F_{a-1} - 1$ and $F_{a-2} - 1$ nodes respectively. The values in the nodes show how the file will be broken up during the searching process. Note how the values of the children differ from the parent by the same amount. Moreover, this difference is a Fibonacci number. If we look at a grandparent, parent and two children where the parent is a left child, then if the difference from grandparent to parent is F_j, the next difference is F_{j-1}. If instead the parent is a right child then the next difference is F_{j-2}.

Program 7.3 implements this Fibonacci splitting idea.

Getting back to our example of the telephone directory, we notice that neither of the two ordered search methods suggested above corresponds to the one actually employed by humans in searching the directory. If we are looking for a name beginning with W, we start the search towards the end of the directory rather than at the middle. A search method based on this interpolation search would then begin by comparing key $f[i].key$ with

$$i = \frac{k - f[l].key}{f[u].key - f[l].key} n$$ ($f[l].key, f[u].key$ are the values of the smallest

and largest keys in the file). The behavior of such an algorithm will clearly depend on the distribution of the keys in the file.

We have seen that as far as the searching problem is concerned, something is to be gained by maintaining the file in an ordered manner if the file is to be searched repeatedly. Let us now look at another example where the use of ordered files greatly reduces the computational effort. The problem we are now concerned with is that of comparing two files of records containing data which is essentially the same data but has been obtained from

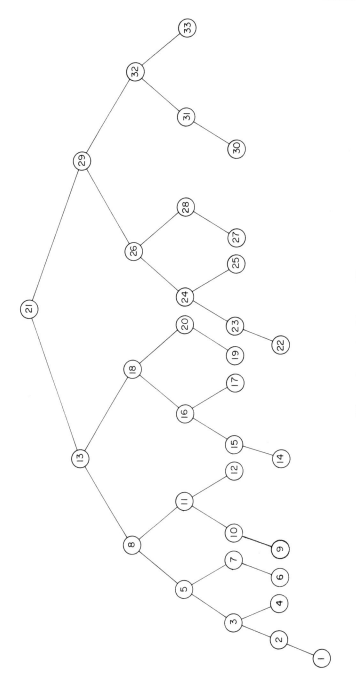

Fibonacci search with $n = 33$

```
1    procedure fibsrch(g : afile; var i : integer; n,k : integer);
2    {Search a file, g, stored in nondecreasing order by field key
3     for a record i such that f[i].key = k. Assume that
4     Fₐ + m = n + 1, m ≥ 0 and F_{a+1} > n + 1. n
5     is the number of records in g. Fₐ and F_{a+1} are consecutive
6     Fibonacci numbers. If k is not present i is set to 0.}
7    var done : boolean
8       p,q,t,a : integer;
9    began
10      a := fibindex(n + 1); {returns largest integer a: Fₐ ≤ n + 1}
11      i := fib(a - 1); {returns the a-1st Fibonacci number}
12      p := fib(a - 2);
13      q := fib(a - 3);
14      m := n + 1 - (i +p);
15      if k > g[i].key {set i so size of right subfile is p}
16      then i := i + m;
17      done := false;
18      while ((i <> 0) and (not done) do
19        case compare(k, g[i].key) of
20        '<' : if q = 0 then i := 0
21                        else
22                          begin
23                            i := i - q; t := p; p := q; q := t - q;
24                          end
25        '>' : if p = 1 then i := 0
26                        else
27                          begin
28                            i := i + q; p := p - q; q := q - p;
29                          end
30        '=' : done := true; {found a match}
31      end; {of case and while}
32    end; {of fibsrch}
```

Program 7.3 Fibsrch

two different sources. We are concerned with verifying that the two files contain the same data. Such a problem could arise, for instance, in the case of the U.S. Internal Revenue Service which might receive millions of forms from various employers stating how much they paid their employees and then another set of forms from individual employees stating how much they received. So we have two files of records, and we wish to verify that there is no discrepancy between the information on the files. Since the forms arrive at the IRS in essentially a random order, we may assume a random arrangement of the records in the files. The key here would probably be the social security numbers. Let the two files be $f1$ and $f2$ with keys $f1[i].key$ and $f2[i].key$. Let us make the following assumptions about the required verification: (i) if corresponding to a key $f1[i].key$ in the employer file there is no record in the employee file a message is to be sent to the employee; (ii) if the reverse is true, then a message is to be sent to the employer; and (iii) if there is a discrepancy between two records with the same key a message to that effect is to be output.

If one proceeded to carry out the verification directly, one would probably end up with an algorithm similar to *verify1*.

```
1   procedure verify1(f1,f2 : afile;  l,n,m : integer);
2   {Compare two unordered files f1 and f2 of size n and m respectively.
3   l is the maximum of m and n. The output is
4       (i)    all records found in f1 but not in f2
5       (ii)   all records found in f2 but not in f1
6       (iii)  all records that are in f1 and f2 with the same key
7              but have different values for other fields}
8   var i,j :integer;
9       marked : array [1 .. n] of boolean;
10  begin
11    for i := 1 to l  do marked[i] := false;
12    for i := 1 to n do
13    begin
14      seqsrch(f2,j,m,f1[i].key);
15      if j = 0 then writeln(f1[i].key, 'not in f2.') {satisfies (i)}
16      else
17      begin
18        if f1[i].other <> f2[j].other
19        then {satisfies (iii)}
20          writeln('discrepancy in ', f1[i].key,f1[i].other, f2[j].other);
21        marked[j] := true; {mark the record as being seen}
22      end;
23    end;
24    for i := 1 to m do
25      if not marked[i] then writeln (f2[i].key, 'not in f1.');
26  end; {of verify1}
```

Program 7.4   Verify1

One may readily verify that the worst case asymptotic computing time of the above algorithm is $O(mn)$. On the other hand if we first ordered the two files and then made the comparison it would be possible to carry out the verification task in time $O(t_{sort}(n) + t_{sort}(m) + n + m)$ where $t_{sort}(n)$ is the time needed to sort a file of n records. As we shall see, it is possible to sort n records in $O(n \log n)$ time, so the computing time becomes $O(\max \{n \log n, m \log m\})$. The algorithm *verify2*, program 7.5, achieves this.

```
1   procedure verify2(var f1,f2:afile; n,m:integer);
2   {Same task as verify1. However this time sort f1 and f2 so that
3    the keys are in increasing order in each file. We assume that the
4    keys in each file are distinct}
5   var i,j : integer;
6   begin
7     sort(f1, n); {sort the file by key}
8     sort(f2, m);
9     i := 1; j := 1;
10    while ((i <= n) and (j <= m)) do
11      case compare(f1[i].key, f2[j].key) of
12      '<' : begin
13              writeln(f1[i].key, 'not in f2.');
14              i := i + 1;
15            end
16      '=' : begin
17              if not (f1[i].other = f2[j].other)
18                then
19                writeln ('discrepancy in ', f1[i].other,f2[j].other);
20              i := i + 1; j := j + 1;
21            end;
22      '>' : begin
23              writeln (f2[j].key, 'not in f1.');
24              j := j + 1;
25            end;
26    end; {of case and while}
27    if i <= n then printrest (f1, i, n, 1)
28    {printrest prints the records of the file that are missing}
29    else if j <= m then printrest (f2, j, m, 2);
30  end; {of verify2}
```

Program 7.5   Verify2

We have seen two important uses of sorting: (i) as an aid in searching, and (ii) as a means for matching entries in files. Sorting also finds application in the solution of many other more complex problems, e.g., from operations research and job scheduling. In fact, it is estimated that over 25% of all computing time is spent on sorting with some installations spending more than 50% of their computing time sorting files. Consequently, the problem of sorting has great relevance in the study of computing. Unfortunately, no one method is the "best" for all initial orderings of the file being sorted. We shall therefore study several methods, indicating when one is superior to the others.

First let us formally state the problem we are about to consider. We are given a file of records $(R_1, R_2, ..., R_n)$. Each record, R_i, has key value K_i. In addition we assume an ordering relation $(<)$ on the key so that for any two key values x and y either $x = y$ or $x < y$ or $y < x$. The ordering relation $(<)$ is assumed to be transitive, i.e., for any three values x, y and z, $x < y$ and $y < z$ implies $x < z$. The sorting problem then is that of finding a permutation, σ, such that $K_{\sigma(i)} \leq K_{\sigma(i+1)}$, $1 \leq i \leq n - 1$. The desired ordering is then $(R_{\sigma(1)}, R_{\sigma(2)}, ..., R_{\sigma(n)})$.

Note that in the case when the file has several key values that are identical, the permutation, σ, defined above is not unique. We shall distinguish one permutation, σ_s, from all the others that also order the file. Let σ_s be the permutation with the following properties:

(i) $K_{\sigma_s(i)} \leq K_{\sigma_s(i+1)}$, $1 \leq i \leq n - 1$.
(ii) If $i < j$ and $K_i = K_j$ in the input file, then R_i precedes R_j in the sorted file.

A sorting method generating the permutation σ_s will be said to be *stable*.

To begin with we characterize sorting methods into two broad categories: (i) internal methods, i.e., methods to be used when the file to be sorted is small enough so that the entire sort can be carried out in main memory; and (ii) external methods, i.e., methods to be used on larger files. In this chapter we shall study the following internal sorting methods:

a) Insertion sort
b) Quick sort
c) Merge sort
d) Heap sort
e) Radix sort

External sorting methods will be studied in Chapter 8.

7.2 INSERTION SORT

The basic step in this method is to insert a record R into a sequence of ordered records, $R_1, R_2, ..., R_i$, $(K_1 \leq K_2 ... \leq K_i)$ in such a way that the resulting sequence of size $i + 1$ is also ordered. The algorithm below accomplishes this insertion. It assumes the existence of an artificial record R_0 with key $K_0 = -$**maxint** (i.e., all keys are $\geq K_0$). Also the type *afile* is defined as

type *afile* $=$ **array** $[0 \,.. \, maxn]$ **of** *records*;

```
 1   procedure insert(r : records; var list : afile; i : integer);
 2   {Insert record r with key r.key into the ordered
 3   sequence list[0], ... list[i]
 4   in such a way that the resulting sequence is
 5   also ordered on the field key.
 6   We assume that list contains a dummy record at index zero
 7   such that r.key ≥ list[0].key for all i}
 8   var j : integer;
 9   begin
10     j := i;
11     while r.key < list[j].key do
12     begin
13       list[j + 1] := list[j];
14       j := j - 1;
15     end;
16     list [j + 1] := r;
17   end; {of insert}
```

Program 7.6   Insert

Again, note that the use of R_0 enables us to simplify the **while** loop, avoiding a test for end of file, i.e., $j < 1$.

Insertion sort is carried out by beginning with the ordered sequence R_0, R_1 and then successively inserting the records $R_2, R_3, ..., R_n$ into the sequence. Since each insertion leaves the resultant sequence ordered, the file with n records can be ordered making $n - 1$ insertions. The details are given in algorithm *insort* (program 7.7).

Analysis of INSERTION SORT

In the worst case algorithm *insert(r,list,i)* makes $i + 1$ comparisons before making the insertion. Hence the computing time for the insertion is $O(i)$. *insort* invokes procedure *insert* for $i = 1,2, ..., n - 1$ resulting in an overall worst case time of $O(\sum_{i=1}^{n-1} i) = O(n^2)$.

```
1   procedure insort(var list:afile; n:integer);
2   {sort list in nondecreasing value of the file key. Assume n > 0.}
3   var j : integer;
4   begin
5     list[0].key := −maxint;
6     for j := 2 to n do
7       insert(list[j],list,j − 1);
8   end; {of insort}
```

Program 7.7 Insort

One may also obtain an estimate of the computing time of this method based upon the relative disorder in the input file. We shall say that the record R_i is *left out of order* (LOO) iff $R_i < \max_{1 \leq j < i} \{R_j\}$. Clearly, the insertion step has to be carried out only for those records that are LOO. If k is the number of records LOO, then the computing time is $O((k + 1)n)$. The worst case time is still $O(n^2)$. One can also show that the average time is also $O(n^2)$.

Example 7.1: Assume $n = 5$ and the input sequence is (5,4,3,2,1) [note we assume for convenience that the records have only one field which also happens to be the key]. Then, after each insertion we have the following:

$-\infty$, 5, 4, 3, 2, 1	[initial sequence]
$-\infty$, 4, 5, 3, 2, 1	$i = 2$
$-\infty$, 3, 4, 5, 2, 1	$i = 3$
$-\infty$, 2, 3, 4, 5, 1	$i = 4$
$-\infty$, 1, 2, 3, 4, 5	$i = 5$

Note that $-\infty$ denotes **−maxint** and this is an example of the worst case behavior.   □

Example 7.2: $n = 5$ and the input sequence is (2, 3, 4, 5, 1). After each execution of *insert* we have:

$-\infty$, 2, 3, 4, 5, 1	[initial]
$-\infty$, 2, 3, 4, 5, 1	$i = 2$
$-\infty$, 2, 3, 4, 5, 1	$i = 3$
$-\infty$, 2, 3, 4, 5, 1	$i = 4$
$-\infty$, 1, 2, 3, 4, 5	$i = 5$

In this example only R_5 is LOO and the time for each $i = 2,3$ and 4 is $O(1)$ while for $i = 5$ it is $O(n)$.   □

It should be fairly obvious that this method is stable. The fact that the computing time is $O(kn)$ makes this method very desirable in sorting sequences where only a very few records are LOO (i.e., $k \ll n$). The simplicity of this scheme makes it about the fastest sorting method for $n \leq 20 - 25$ elements, depending upon the implementation and machine properties. For variations on this method see exercises 3 and 4.

7.3   QUICKSORT

We now turn our attention to a sorting scheme with a very good average behavior. The quicksort scheme developed by C. A. R. Hoare has the best average behavior among all the sorting methods we shall be studying. In Insertion Sort the key K_i currently controlling the insertion is placed into the right spot with respect to the sorted subfile $(R_1, ...,R_{i-1})$. Quicksort differs from insertion sort in that the key K_i controlling the process is placed at the right spot with respect to the whole file. Thus, if key K_i is placed in position $s(i)$, then $K_j \leq K_{s(i)}$ for $j < s(i)$ and $K_j \geq K_{s(i)}$ for $j > s(i)$. Hence after this positioning has been made, the original file is partitioned into two subfiles, one consisting of records $R_1, ...,R_{s(i)-1}$ and the other of records $R_{s(i)+1}, ...,R_n$. Since in the sorted sequence all records in the first subfile may appear to the left of $s(i)$ and all in the second subfile to the right of $s(i)$, these two subfiles may be sorted independently. The method is best stated recursively as program 7.8. Procedure *interchange* (x,y) performs $t := x; x := y; y := t$.

Example 7.3:   The input file has 10 records with keys (26, 5, 37, 1, 61, 11, 59, 15, 48, 19). The table below gives the status of the file at each call of *qsort*. Square brackets are used to demarcate subfiles yet to be sorted.

R_1	R_2	R_3	R_4	R_5	R_6	R_7	R_8	R_9	R_{10}	m	n
[26	5	37	1	61	11	59	15	48	19]	1	10
[11	5	19	1	15]	26	[59	61	48	37]	1	5
[1	5]	11	[19	15]	26	[59	61	48	37]	1	2
1	5	11	[19	15]	26	[59	61	48	37]	4	5
1	5	11	15	19	26	[59	61	48	37]	7	10
1	5	11	15	19	26	[48	37]	59	[61]	7	8
1	5	11	15	19	26	37	48	59	[61]	10	10
1	5	11	15	19	26	37	48	59	61		□

Analysis of Quicksort

The worst case behavior of this algorithm is examined in exercise 5 and shown to be $O(n^2)$. However, if we are lucky then each time a record is correctly positioned, the subfile to its left will be of the same size as that to its right. This would leave us with the sorting of two subfiles each of size

```
1   procedure qsort(var list: afile; m,n: integer);
2   {sort records list[m], ..., list[n] into nondecreasing
3   order on field key.
4   Key k = list[m].key is arbitrarily chosen as the control key.
5   Pointers i and j are used to partition the subfile so
6   that at any time list[l].key ≤ k, l < i and
7   list[l].key ≥ k, l > j. It is assumed that
8   list[m].key ≤ list[n + 1].key}
9   var i,j,k: integer;
10  begin
11    if m < n
12    then
13    begin
14      i := m; j := n + 1; k := list[m].key;
15      repeat
16        repeat
17          i := i + 1;
18        until list[i].key >= k;
19        repeat
20          j := j - 1;
21        until list[j].key <= k;
22        if i < j
23        then interchange(list[i],list[j]);
24      until i >= j;
25      interchange (list[m],list[j]);
26      qsort(list,m,j - 1);
27      qsort(list,j + 1,n);
28    end; {of if}
29  end; {of qsort}
```

Program 7.8 Qsort

roughly $n/2$. The time required to position a record in a file of size n is $O(n)$. If $T(n)$ is the time taken to sort a file of n records, then when the file splits roughly into two equal parts each time a record is positioned correctly we have

$$T(n) \le cn + 2T(n/2) \quad , \text{ for some constant } c$$

$$\le cn + 2(cn/2 + 2T(n/4))$$

$$\le 2cn + 4T(n/4)$$

$$\vdots$$

$$\le cn \log_2 n + nT(1) = O(n \log_2 n)$$

In our presentation of *qsort*, the record whose position was being fixed with respect to the subfile currently being sorted was always chosen to be the first record in that subfile. Exercise 6 examines a better choice for this control record. Lemma 7.1 shows that the average computing time for Quicksort is $O(n \log_2 n)$. Moreover, experimental results show that as far as average computing time is concerned, it is the best of the internal sorting methods we shall be studying.

Unlike Insertion Sort where the only additional space needed was for one record, Quicksort needs stack space to implement the recursion. In case the files split evenly as in the above analysis, the maximum recursion depth would be log n requiring a stack space of $O(\log n)$. The worst case occurs when the file is split into a left subfile of size $n - 1$ and a right subfile of size 0 at each level of recursion. In this case, the depth of recursion becomes n requiring stack space of $O(n)$. The worst case stack space can be reduced by a factor of 4 by realizing that right subfiles of size less than 2 need not be stacked. An asymptotic reduction in stack space can be achieved by *sorting smaller subfiles first*. In this case the additional stack space is at most $O(\log n)$.

Lemma 7.1: Let $T_{avg}(n)$ be the expected time for *qsort* to sort a file with n records. Then there exists a constant k such that $T_{avg}(n) \leq k\,n \log_e n$ for $n \geq 2$.

Proof: In the call to *qsort* $(1,n)$, K_1 gets placed at position j. This leaves us with the problem of sorting two subfiles of size $j - 1$ and $n - j$. The expected time for this is $T_{avg}(j - 1) + T_{avg}(n - j)$. The remainder of the algorithm clearly takes at most cn time for some constant c. Since j may take on any of the values 1 to n with equal probability we have:

$$T_{avg}(n) \leq cn + \frac{1}{n} \sum_{j=1}^{n} (T_{avg}(j - 1) + T_{avg}(n - j)), \; n \geq 2$$

$$= cn + \frac{2}{n} \sum_{j=0}^{n-1} T_{avg}(j) \tag{7.1}$$

We may assume $T_{avg}(0) \leq b$ and $T_{avg}(1) \leq b$ for some constant b. We shall now show $T_{avg}(n) \leq kn \log_e n$ for $n \geq 2$ and $k = 2(b + c)$. The proof is by induction on n.

Induction Base: For $n = 2$ we have from eq. (7.1):

$$T_{avg}(2) \leq 2c + 2b \leq kn \log_e 2$$

Induction Hypothesis: Assume $T_{avg}(n) \leq kn \log_e n$ for $1 \leq n < m$

Induction Step: From eq. (7.1) and the induction hypothesis we have:

$$T_{avg}(m) \leq cm + \frac{4b}{m} + \frac{2}{m}\sum_{j=2}^{m-1} T_{avg}(j)$$

$$\leq cm + \frac{4b}{m} + \frac{2k}{m}\sum_{j=2}^{m-1} j \log_e j \qquad \cdots \qquad (7.2)$$

Since $j \log_e j$ is an increasing function of j, eq. (7.2) yields:

$$T_{avg}(m) \leq cm + \frac{4b}{m} + \frac{2k}{m}\int_2^m x\log_e x \, dx$$

$$= cm + \frac{4b}{m} + \frac{2k}{m}\left[\frac{m^2 \log_e m}{2} - \frac{m^2}{4}\right]$$

$$= cm + \frac{4b}{m} + km\log_e m - \frac{km}{2}$$

$$\leq km \log_e m \quad , \quad \text{for } m \geq 2. \qquad \qquad \Box$$

7.4 HOW FAST CAN WE SORT?

Both of the sorting methods we have seen have a worst case behavior of $O(n^2)$. It is natural at this point to ask the question: "What is the best computing time for sorting that we can hope for?" The theorem we shall prove shows that if we restrict our question to algorithms for which the only operations permitted on keys are comparisons and interchanges then $O(n \log_2 n)$ is the best possible time.

The method we use is to consider a tree which describes the sorting process by having a vertex represent a key comparison and the branches indicate the result. Such a tree is called a *decision tree*. A path through a decision tree represents a possible sequence of computations that an algorithm could produce.

As an example of such a tree, let us look at the tree obtained for Insertion Sort working on a file with three records in it. The input sequence is 3 records R_1, R_2 and R_3 so the root of the tree is labeled (1,2,3). Depending on the outcome of the comparison between keys K_1 and K_2, this sequence may or may not change. If $K_2 < K_1$, then the sequence becomes (2,1,3), otherwise it stays (1,2,3). The full tree resulting from these comparisons is shown below. The leaf nodes are numbered I-VI and are the only points at which the algorithm may terminate. Hence only six permutations of the input sequence are obtainable from this algorithm. Since all six of these are different and 3! = 6, it follows that this algorithm has enough leaves to constitute a valid sorting algorithm for three records. The maximum depth of this tree is 3. The table below gives six different orderings of key values 7, 9, 10 which show that all six permutations are possible. The tree is not a full binary tree of depth 3 and so it has fewer than $2^3 = 8$ leaves. The possible output permutations are:

LEAF	PERMUTATION	SAMPLE INPUT KEY VALUES WHICH GIVE THE PERMUTATION
I	1 2 3	(7,9,10)
II	1 3 2	(7,10,9)
III	3 1 2	(9,10,7)
IV	2 1 3	(9,7,10)
V	2 3 1	(10,7,9)
VI	3 2 1	(10,9,7)

The decision tree is

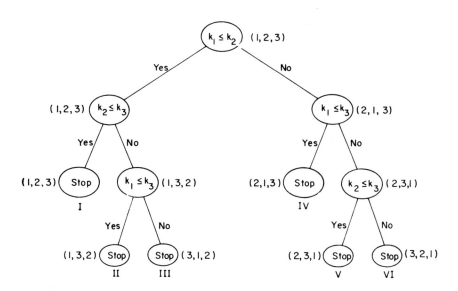

Theorem 7.1: Any decision tree that sorts n distinct elements has a height of at least $\log_2(n!) + 1$.

Proof: When sorting n elements there are $n!$ different possible results.

Thus, any decision tree must have $n!$ leaves. But a decision tree is also a binary tree which can have at most 2^{k-1} leaves if its height is k. Therefore, the height must be at least $\log_2 n! + 1$. $\square$

Corollary: Any algorithm which sorts by comparisons only must have a worst case computing time of at least $O(n \log_2 n)$.
Proof: We must show that for every decision tree with $n!$ leaves there is a path of length $c\ n\log_2 n$, c a constant. By the theorem, there is a path of length $\log_2 n!$. Now

$$n! = n(n - 1)(n - 2) \ ... \ (3)(2)(1)$$
$$\geq (n/2)^{n/2},$$

so $\log_2 n! \geq (n/2) \log_2 (n/2) = O(n\ log_2\ n)$. $\square$

7.5 2-WAY MERGE SORT

Before looking at the merge sort algorithm to sort n records let us see how one may merge two files $(x_l, ...,x_m)$ and $(x_{m+1}, ...,x_n)$ that are already sorted to get a third file $(z_l, ...,z_n)$ that is also sorted. Since this merging scheme is very simple, we directly present the algorithm as program 7.9.

Program on next page

Analysis of Algorithm *merge*

At each iteration of the **while** loop k increases by 1. The total increment in k is $n - l + 1$. Hence the **while** loop is iterated at most $n - l + 1$ times. The **if** statement moves at most one record per iteration. The total time is therefore $O(n - l + 1)$. If records are of length M then this time is really $O(M(n - l + 1))$. When M is greater than 1 we could use linked lists for $(x_1, ...,x_m)$ and $(x_{m+1}, ...,x_n)$ and obtain a new sorted linked list containing these $n - l + 1$ records. Now, we won't need the additional space for $n - l + 1$ records as needed above for Z. Instead only space for $n - l + 1$ links is needed. The merge time becomes independent of M and $O(n - l + 1)$. Note that $n - l + 1$ is the number of records being merged. $\square$

Two-way merge sort begins by interpreting the input as n sorted files each of length 1. These are merged pairwise to obtain $n/2$ files of size 2 (if n is odd, then one file is of size 1). These $n/2$ files are then merged pairwise and so on until we are left with only one file. The example below illustrates the process.

```
1   procedure merge(var x,z : afile; l,m,n : integer);
2   {(x[l], ...,x[m]) and (x[m + 1], ...,x[n]) are
3   two sorted lists with keys
4   such that x[l].key ≤ ... ≤ x[m].key, and
5   x[m + 1].key ≤ ... ≤ x[n].key. These records are merged to
6   obtain the sorted list(z[l], ...,z[n]) such that
7   z[l].key ≤ ... ≤ z[n].key}
8   var i,j,k,t : integer:
9   begin
10    i := l;
11    k := l;
12    j := m + 1; {i, j and k are positions in the three files}
13    while ((i <= m) and (j <= n)) do
14    begin
15     if x[i].key <= x[j].key
16     then
17     begin
18      z[k] := x[i];
19      i := i + 1;
20     end
21     else
22     begin
23      z[k] := x[j];
24      j := j + 1;
25     end;
26     k := k + 1;
27    end; {of while}
28    if i > m
29    then                    {(z_k, ...,z_n) := (x_j, ...,x_n)}
30     for t := j to n do
31      z[k + t - j] := x[t]
32    else                    {(z_k, ...,z_n) := (x_i, ...,x_m)}
33     for t := i to m do
34      z[k + t - i] := x[t];
35   end; {of merge}
```

Program 7.9   Merge

Example 7.4 The input file is (26, 5, 77, 1, 61, 11, 59, 15, 48, 19). The tree below illustrates the subfiles being merged at each pass:

[26]	[5]	[77]	[1]	[61]	[11]	[59]	[15]	[48]	[19]
[5	26]	[1	77]	[11	61]	[15	59]	[19	48]
[1	5	26	77]	[11	15	59	61]	[19	48]
[1	5	11	15	26	59	61	77]	[19	48]
[1	5	11	15	19	26	48	59	61	77]

As is apparent from the example above, merge sort consists of several passes over the records being sorted. In the first pass files of size 1 are merged. In the second, the size of the files being merged is 2. On the i-th pass the files being merged are of size 2^{i-1}. Consequently, a total of $\lceil \log_2 n \rceil$ passes are made over the data. Since two files can be merged in linear time (algorithm *merge*), each pass of merge sort takes $O(n)$ time. As there are $\lceil \log_2 n \rceil$ passes, the total computing time is $O(n \log n)$.

In formally writing the algorithm for 2-way merge, it is convenient to first present an algorithm (program 7.10) to perform one merge pass of the merge sort.

```
1   procedure mpass(var x,y : afile; n,l : integer);
2   {This algorithm performs one pass of the merge sort. It merges
3    adjacent pairs of subfiles of length l from the list x to list
4    y. n is the number of records in x.}
5   var i, t : integer;
6   begin
7     i := 1;
8     while i <= (n − 2*l + 1) do
9     begin
10      merge(x,y,i,i + l − 1, i + 2*l − 1);
11      i := i + 2*l;
12    end;
13    {merge remaining file of length < 2*l}
14    if (i + l − 1) < n then merge(x,y,i,i + l − 1, n)
15    else
16      for t := i to n do
17        y[t] := x[t];
18  end; {of mpass}
```

Program 7.10 Mpass

```
 1  procedure msort(var x : afile; n : integer);
 2  {Sort the file x = (x[1], ....,x[n]) into nondecreasing order on the
 3   keys x[1].key, ...,x[n].key}
 4  var l : integer;
 5       y : afile;
 6  begin
 7    {l is the size of the subfile currently being merged}
 8    l := 1;
 9    while  l < n do
10    begin
11      mpass(x,y,n,l);
12      l := 2 * l;
13      mpass(y,x,n,l); {interchange role of x and y}
14      l := 2 * l;
15    end
16  end; {of msort}
```

Program 7.11   Msort

It is easy to verify that the above algorithm results in a stable sorting procedure. Exercise 10 discusses a variation of the two-way merge sort discussed above. In this variation the prevailing order within the input file is taken into account to obtain initially sorted subfiles of length ≥ 1.

Recursive Formulation of Merge Sort

Merge sort may also be arrived at recursively. In the recursive formulation we divide the file to be sorted into two roughly equal parts called the left and the right subfiles. These subfiles are sorted using the algorithm recursively and then the two subfiles are merged together to obtain the sorted file. First, let us see how this would work on our earlier example.

Example 7.5 The input file (26, 5, 77, 1, 61, 11, 59, 15, 49, 19) is to be sorted using the recursive formulation of 2-way merge sort. If the subfile from l to u is currently to be sorted then its two subfiles are indexed from l to $\lfloor (l + u)/2 \rfloor$ and from $\lfloor (l + u)/2 \rfloor + 1$ to u. The subfile partitioning that takes place is described by the following binary tree. Note that the subfiles being merged are different from those being merged in algorithm *msort*.

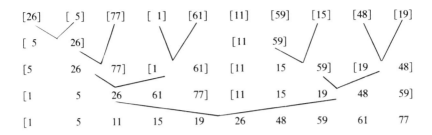

From the preceding example, we may draw the following conclusion. If algorithm *merge* is used to merge sorted subfiles from one array into another, then it is necessary to copy subfiles. For example to merge [5, 26] and [77] we would have to copy [77] into the same array as [5, 26]. To avoid this unnecessary copying of subfiles using sequential allocation, we look to a linked list representation for subfiles. This method of representation will permit the recursive version of merge sort to work efficiently.

Each record is assumed to have three fields: *link, key* and *other*. The record structure is defined as:

type *records* = **record**
            key : **integer**;
            other : *fields*;
            link : **integer**;
        end;
    afile = **array** [0 .. *n*] **of** *records*;

$r[i].link$ and $r[i].key$ are the link and key value fields in record i, $1 \leq i \leq n$. We assume that initially $link[i] = $ **nil**, $1 \leq i \leq n$. Thus each record is initially in a chain containing only itself. Let q and r be pointers to two chains of records. The records on each chain are assumed linked in nondecreasing order of the key field. Let $rmerge(q,r,p)$ be an algorithm to merge the two chains q and r to obtain p which is also linked in nondecreasing order of key values. Then the recursive version of merge sort is given by algorithm *rmsort* (Program 7.12). To sort the file $x_1, ..., x_n$ this algorithm is invoked as $rmsort(x,1,n,p)$. p is returned as the start of a chain ordered as described earlier. In case the file is to be physically rearranged into this order then one of the schemes discussed in section 7.8 may be used. *Rmerge* is given in Program 7.13.

```
1    procedure rmsort(var x : afile; l,u : integer; var p : integer);
2    {The list x = (x[l], ..., x[u]) is to be sorted on the field key.
3    link is a link field in each record and is initially set to 0.
4    The sorted list is a chain beginning at p.
5    x[0] is a record for intermediate results used only in rmerge}
6    var mid,q,r : integer;
7    begin
8      if l >= u then p := l
9      else begin
10       mid := (l + u) div 2;
11       rmsort(x,l,mid,q);
12       rmsort(x,mid+1,u,r);
13       rmerge(x,q,r,p);
14     end; {of if}
15   end; {of rmsort}
```

Program 7.12 Rmsort

```
1    procedure rmerge(x : afile;u,y : integer; var z : integer);
2    {The linked lists u and y are merged to obtain z. In u, y
3    and z the records are linked in order of nondecreasing key
4    values. The file of records is named x of type afile.}
5    var i,j : integer;
6    begin
7      i := u; j := y; z := 0;
8      while ((i < > 0) and (j < > 0)) do
9        if x[i].key <= x[j].key
10       then
11       begin
12         x[z].link := i;
13         z := i; i := x[i].link;
14       end
15       else
16       begin
17         x[z].link := j;
18         z := j; j := x[j].link;
19       end;
20     {move remainder}
21     if i = 0 then x[z].link := j
22             else x[z].link := i;
23     z := x[0].link;
24   end; {of rmerge}
```

Program 7.13 Rmerge

One may readily verify that this linked version of 2-way merge sort results in a stable sorting procedure and that the computing time is $O(n \log n)$.

7.6 HEAP SORT

While the Merge Sort scheme discussed in the previous section has a computing time of $O(n \log n)$ both in the worst case and as average behavior, it requires additional storage proportional to the number of records in the file being sorted. The sorting method we are about to study will require only a fixed amount of additional storage and at the same time will have as its worst case and average computing time $O(n \log n)$. In this method we shall interpret the file to be sorted $R = (R_1, ..., R_n)$ as a binary tree. (Recall that in the sequential representation of a binary tree discussed in Chapter 5 the parent of the node at location i is at $\lfloor i/2 \rfloor$, the left child at $2i$ and the right child at $2i + 1$. If $2i$ or $2i + 1$ is greater than n (the number of nodes), then the corresponding children do not exist. Thus, initially the file is interpreted as being structured as below:

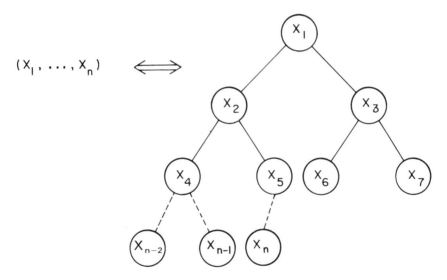

Heap sort may be regarded as a two stage method. First the tree representing the file is converted into a heap. A *heap* is defined to be a complete binary tree with the property that the value of each node is at least as large as the value of its children nodes (if they exist) (i.e., *keys* $K_{\lfloor j/2 \rfloor} \geq K_j$ for $1 \leq \lfloor j/2 \rfloor < j \leq n$). This implies that the root of the heap has the largest key in the tree. In the second stage the output sequence is generated in decreasing order by successively outputting the root and restructuring the remaining tree into a heap.

Essential to any algorithm for Heap Sort is a subalgorithm that takes a binary tree T whose left and right subtrees satisfy the heap property but whose root may not and adjusts T so that the entire binary tree satisfies the heap property. Algorithm *adjust* does this.

```
 1  procedure adjust(var tree : afile; i,n : integer);
 2  {Adjust the binary tree with root i to satisfy the heap property.
 3   The left and right subtrees of i, i.e., with root 2i and 2i + 1,
 4   already satisfy the heap property. No node has index greater
 5   than n.}
 6  var j : integer;
 7      k : integer;
 8      r : records;
 9      done : boolean;
10  begin
11    done := false;
12    r := tree[i];
13    k := tree[i].key;
14    j := 2 * i;
15    while ((j <= n) and not done) do
16    begin {first find max of left and right child}
17      if j < n then if tree[j].key < tree[j + 1].key then j := j + 1;
18      {compare max. child with k. if k is max. then done.}
19      if k >= tree[j].key
20      then
21        done := true
22      else
23      begin
24        tree[j div 2] := tree[j]; {move jth record up the tree}
25        j := 2 * j;
26      end;
27    end;
28    tree[j div 2] := r;
29  end; { of adjust}
```

Program 7.14 Adjust

Analysis of Algorithm Adjust

If the depth of the tree with root i is k, then the **while** loop is executed at most k times. Hence the computing time of the algorithm is $O(k)$. □

The heap sort algorithm may now be stated.

```
1    procedure hsort(var r: afile; n: integer);
2    {the file r = (r[1], ...,r[n]) is sorted into nondecreasing order on
3     the field key}
4    var i : integer;
5        t : records;
6    begin
7      for i := (n div 2) downto 1 do {convert r into a heap}
8        adjust(r,i,n);
9      for i := (n − 1) downto 1 do {sort r}
10     begin
11       t := r[i + 1]; {interchange r₁ and r ᵢ₊₁}
12       r[i + 1] := r[1];
13       r[1] := t;
14       adjust(r,1,i); {recreate heap}
15     end;
16   end; {of hsort}
```

Program 7.15   Hsort

Example 7.6: The input file is (26, 5, 77, 1, 61, 11, 59, 15, 48, 19). Interpreting this as a binary tree we have the following transformations:

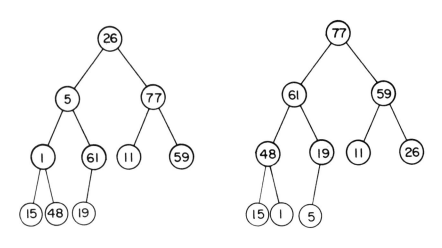

Input File   **Initial Heap**

The figures on pages 353–354 illustrate the heap after restructuring and the sorted part of the file.

Analysis of Algorithm *hsort*

Suppose $2^{k-1} \leq n < 2^k$ so that the tree has k levels and the number of nodes on level i is 2^{i-1}. In the first **for** loop *adjust* is called once for each node that has a child. Hence the time required for this loop is the sum, over each level, of the number of nodes on a level times the maximum distance the node can move. This is no more than

$$\sum_{1 \leq i \leq k} 2^{i-1}(k-i) = \sum_{1 \leq i \leq k-1} 2^{k-i-1}i \leq n \sum_{1 \leq i \leq k-1} i/2^i < 2n = O(n)$$

In the next **for** loop $n - 1$ applications of *adjust* are made with maximum depth $k = \lceil \log_2 (n + 1) \rceil$. Hence the computing time for this loop is $O(n \log n)$. Consequently, the total computing time is $O(n \log n)$. Note that apart from variables, the only additional space needed is space for one record to carry out the interchange in the second **for** loop.

7.7 SORTING ON SEVERAL KEYS

Let us now look at the problem of sorting records on several keys, $K^1, K^2, ..., K^r$ (K^1 is the most significant key and K^r the least). A file of records $R_1, ..., R_n$ will be said to be sorted with respect to the keys $K^1, K^2, ..., K^r$ iff for every pair of records $i, j, i < j$, $(K_i^1, ..., K_i^r) \leq (K_j^1, ..., K_j^r)$. The r-tuple $(x_1, ..., x_r)$ is less than or equal to the r-tuple $(y_1, ..., y_r)$ iff either $x_i = y_i$, $1 \leq i \leq j$ and $x_{j+1} < y_{j+1}$ for some $j < r$ or $x_i = y_i$, $1 \leq i \leq r$.

For example, the problem of sorting a deck of cards may be regarded as a sort on two keys, the suit and face values, with the following ordering relations:

Suits: ♣ < ◇ < ♡ < ♠

and face values: $2 < 3 < 4 ... < 10 < J < Q < K < A$.

There appear to be two popular ways to accomplish the sort. The first is to sort on the most significant key K^1 obtaining several "piles" of records each having the same value for K^1. Then each of these piles is independently sorted on the key K^2 into "subpiles" such that all the records in the same subpile have the same values for K^1 and K^2. The subpiles are then sorted on K^3, etc., and the piles put together. In the example above this would mean first sorting the 52 cards into four piles, one for each of the

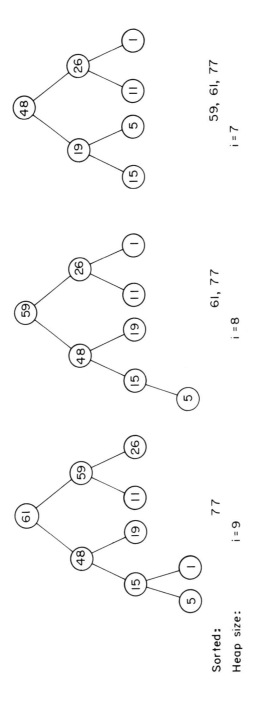

Sorted: 77   61, 77   59, 61, 77

Heap size: i = 9   i = 8   i = 7

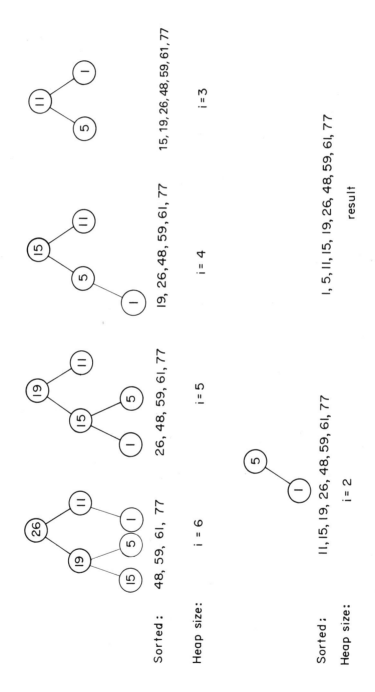

Sorted :   48, 59, 61, 77   26, 48, 59, 61, 77   19, 26, 48, 59, 61, 77   15, 19, 26, 48, 59, 61, 77

Heap size: i = 6   i = 5   i = 4   i = 3

Sorted :   11, 15, 19, 26, 48, 59, 61, 77   1, 5, 11, 15, 19, 26, 48, 59, 61, 77

Heap size: i = 2   result

suit values. Then sort each pile on the face value. Now place the piles on top of each other to obtain the ordering: $2\clubsuit$, ...,$A\clubsuit$, ..., ...,$2\spadesuit$, ...,$A\spadesuit$.

A sort proceeding in this fashion will be referred to as a most significant digit first (MSD) sort. The second way, quite naturally, is to sort on the least significant digit first (LSD). This would mean sorting the cards first into 13 piles corresponding to their face values (key K^2). Then, place the 3's on top of the 2's ..., the kings on top of the queens, the aces on top of the kings; turn the deck upside down and sort on the suit (K^1) using some stable sorting method obtaining four piles, each of which is ordered on K^2; combine the piles to obtain the required ordering on the cards.

Comparing the two procedures outlined above (MSD and LSD) one notices that LSD is simpler as the piles and subpiles obtained do not have to be sorted independently (provided the sorting scheme used for sorting on key K^i, $1 \leq i < r$ is stable). This in turn implies less overhead.

LSD and MSD only specify the order in which the different keys are to be sorted on and not the sorting method to be used within each key. The technique generally used to sort cards is a MSD sort in which the sorting on suit is done by a bin sort (i.e., four "bins" are set up, one for each suit value and the cards are placed into their corresponding "bins"). Next, the cards in each bin are sorted using an algorithm similar to Insertion Sort. However, there is another way to do this. First use a bin sort on the face value. To do this we need thirteen bins, one for each distinct face value. Then collect all the cards together as described above and perform bin sort on the suits using four bins. Note that a bin sort requires only $O(n)$ time if the spread in key values is $O(n)$.

LSD or MSD sorting can be used to sort records on only one logical key by interpreting this key as being composed of several keys. For example, if the keys are numeric, then each decimal digit may be regarded as a key. So if all the keys are in the range $0 \leq K \leq 999$, then we can use either the LSD or MSD sorts for three keys (K^1, K^2, K^3), where K^1 is the digit in the hundredths place, K^2 the digit in the tens place, and K^3 that in the units place. Since all the keys lie in the range $0 \leq K^i \leq 9$, the sort within the keys can be carried out using a bin sort with ten bins. This, in fact, is essentially the process used to sort records punched on cards using a card sorter. In this case using the LSD process would be more convenient as it eliminates maintaining several independent subpiles. If the key is interpreted as above, the resulting sort is called a radix 10 sort. If the key decomposition is carried out using the binary representation of the keys, then one obtains a radix 2 sort. In general, one could choose any radix r obtaining a radix r sort. The number of bins required is r.

Let us look in greater detail at the implementation of an LSD radix r sort. We assume that the records R_1, ...,R_n have keys that are d-tuples

$(x_1, x_2, ..., x_d)$ and $0 \leq x_i < r$. Thus, we shall need r bins. The records are assumed to have a *link* field. The records in each bin will be linked together into a linear linked list with $f[i]$, $0 \leq i \leq r$, a pointer to the first record in bin i and $e[i]$ a pointer to the last record in bin i. These lists will essentially be operated as queues. Algorithm *lrsort* formally presents the LSD radix r method in Program 7.16. This procedure assumes that *rminus*1 is defined as a constant with value $r - 1$. Also it is assumed that the key field of each record is an array $key[1 .. d]$ with $0 \leq key[i] \leq kr = r - 1$.

Analysis of *lrsort*

The algorithm makes d passes over the data, each pass taking $O(n + r)$ time. Hence the total computing time is $O(d(n + r))$. In the sorting of numeric data, the value of d will depend on the choice of the radix r and also on the largest key. Different choices of r will yield different computing times (see Table 7.1).

Example 7.7: We shall illustrate the operation of algorithm *lrsort* while sorting a file of 10 numbers in the range [0,999]. Each decimal digit in the key will be regarded as a subkey. So, the value of d is 3 and that of r is 10. The input file is linked and has the form given on page 358. The nodes are labeled $R_1, ..., R_{10}$. The figures on pages 358-360 illustrate the $r = 10$ case and the list after the queues have been collected from the 10 bins at the end of each phase. By using essentially the method above but by varying the radix, one can obtain (see exercises 13 and 14) linear time algorithms to sort n record files when the keys are in the range $0 \leq K_i < n^k$ for some constant k.

7.8 PRACTICAL CONSIDERATIONS FOR INTERNAL SORTING

Apart from radix sort, all the sorting methods we have looked at require excessive data movement; i.e., as the result of a comparison, records may be physically moved. This tends to slow down the sorting process when records are large. In sorting files in which the records are large it is necessary to modify the sorting methods so as to minimize data movement. Methods such as Insertion Sort and Merge Sort can be easily modified to work with a linked file rather than a sequential file. In this case each record will require an additional link field. Instead of physically moving the record, its link field will be changed to reflect the change in position of that

```
1    procedure lrsort(var r: afile; d,n: integer);
2    {records r = (r[1], ...,r[n]) are sorted on the keys key[1],..., key[d].
3     The range of each key is 0 ≤ key[i] ≤ rminus1. rminus1 is a constant.
4     Sorting within a key is done using a bin sort.}
5    var e,f : array [0 .. rminus1] of integer; {queue pointers}
6        i,j,p,t : integer;
7        k : 0 .. kr; ,
8    begin
9    for i := 1 to n do {link into a chain starting at p}
10       r[i].link := i + 1;
11   r[n].link := 0; p := 1;
12   for i := d downto 1 do {sort on key[i]}
13   begin
14       for j := 0 to rminus1 do {initialize bins to be empty queues}
15       f[j] := 0;
16       while p < > 0 do {put records into queues}
17       begin
18       k := r[p]↑.key[i];
19       if f[k] = 0 then f[k] := p
20                   else r[e[k]]↑.link := p;
21       e[k] := p;
22       p := r[p]↑.link; {get next record}
23       end; {of while}
24       j := 0;
25       while f[j] = 0 do
26           j := j + 1; {find first nonempty queue}
27       p := f[j]; t := e[j];
28       for k := j + 1 to rminus1 do {concatenate remaining queues}
29           if f[k] < > 0
30           then
31           begin
32             r[t]↑.link := f[k];
33             t := e[k];
34           end; {of if  and for}
35       r[t]↑.link := 0;
36   end; {of for of line 12}
37   end; {of lrsort}
```

Program 7.16   Lrsort

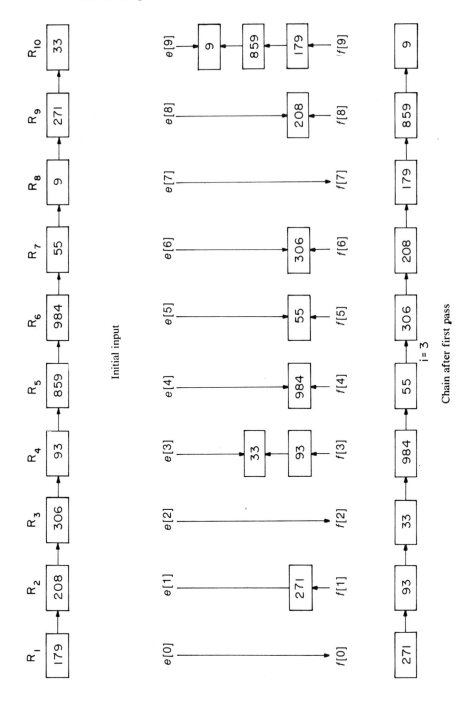

Initial input

Chain after first pass

i = 3

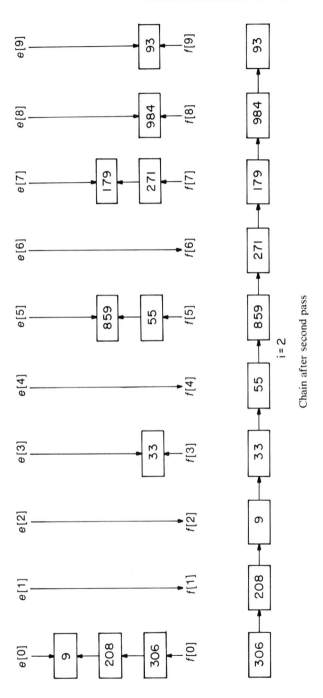

Chain after second pass
i = 2

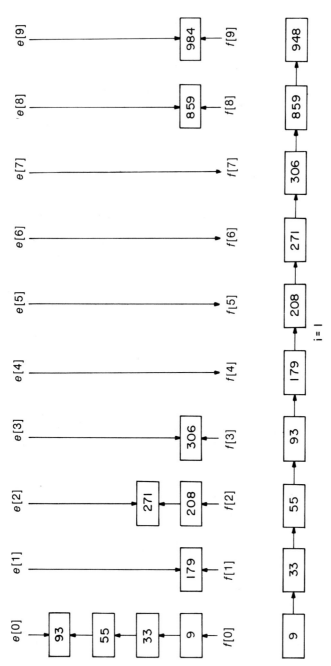

i = 1

Final sorted chain after third pass

record in the file (see exercises 4 and 8). At the end of the sorting process, the records are linked together in the required order. In many applications (e.g., when we just want to sort files and then output them record by record on some external media in the sorted order) this is sufficient. However, in some applications it is necessary to physically rearrange the records *in place* so that they are in the required order. Even in such cases considerable savings can be achieved by first performing a linked list sort and then physically rearranging the records according to the order specified in the list. This rearranging can be accomplished in linear time using some additional space.

If the file, F, has been sorted so that at the end of the sort p is a pointer to the first record in a linked list of records then each record in this list will have a key which is greater than or equal to the key of the previous record (if there is a previous record), see figure 7.1. To physically rearrange these records into the order specified by the list, we begin by interchanging records R_1 and R_p. Now, the record in the position R_1 has the smallest key. If $p \neq 1$ then there is some record in the list with link field $= 1$. If we could change this link field to indicate the new position of the record previously as position 1 then we would be left with records $R_2, ..., R_n$ linked together in nondecreasing order. Repeating the above process will, after $n - 1$ iterations, result in the desired rearrangement. The snag, however, is that in a singly linked list we do not know the predecessor of a node. To overcome this difficulty, our first rearrangement algorithm *list*1, begins by converting the singly linked list p into a doubly linked list and then proceeds to move records into their correct places.

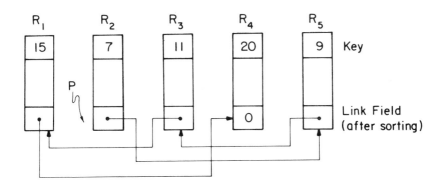

Figure 7.1 List Sort.

```
 1    procedure list1(var r : afile; n : integer; p : integer);
 2    {p is a pointer to a list of n sorted records linked together
 3     by the field link. linkb is assumed to be present in each
 4     record. The records are rearranged so that the resulting
 5     records r[1], ...,r[n] are consecutive and sorted.
 6     Type definitions are as for merge except for an extra link field}
 7    var i,u,s : integer;
 8        a : records;
 9    begin
10        u := 0; s := p;
11        while s < > 0 do {convert p into a doubly linked list using linkb}
12        begin
13          r[s].linkb := u;
14          u := s;
15          s := r[s].link;
16        end;
17        for i := 1 to n − 1 do {move r_p to position i while}
18        begin                        {maintaining the list}
19          if p < > i
20          then
21          begin
22            if r[i].link < > 0 then r[r[i].link].linkb := p;
23            r[r[i].linkb].link := p;
24            a := r[p]; r[p] := r[i]; r[i] := a;
25          end;
26          p := r[i].link;
27        end;
28    end; {of list1}
```

Program 7.17   List1

Example 7.8: After a list sort on the input file (35,18,12,42,26,14) has been made the file is linked as below (only three fields of each record are shown):

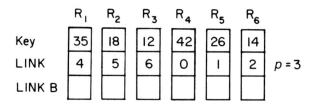

Following the links starting at R_p we obtain the logical sequence of records R_3, R_6, R_2, R_5, R_1 and R_4 corresponding to the key sequence 12, 14, 18, 26, 35, and 42. Filling in the backward links, we have

R_1	R_2	R_3	R_4	R_5	R_6	
35	18	12	42	26	14	
4	5	6	0	1	2	$p = 3$
5	6	0	1	2	3	

The configuration at the end of each execution of the **for** loop is:

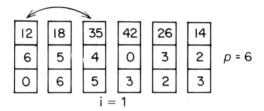

12	18	35	42	26	14	
6	5	4	0	3	2	$p = 6$
0	6	5	3	2	3	

$i = 1$

The logical sequence of the remaining list (*LS*) is: R_6, R_2, R_5, R_3, R_4. The remaining execution yields

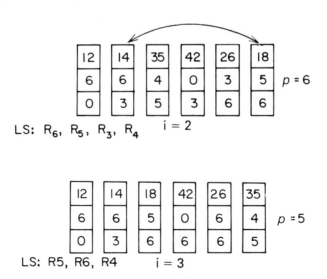

12	14	35	42	26	18	
6	6	4	0	3	5	$p = 6$
0	3	5	3	6	6	

LS: R_6, R_5, R_3, R_4 $i = 2$

12	14	18	42	26	35	
6	6	5	0	6	4	$p = 5$
0	3	6	6	6	5	

LS: R5, R6, R4 $i = 3$

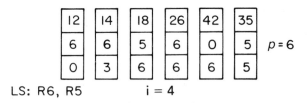

LS: R6, R5   i = 4

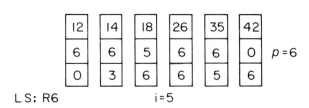

L S: R6   i = 5

Analysis of Algorithm *List*1

If there are n records in the file then the time required to convert the chain P into a doubly linked list is $O(n)$. The **for** loop is iterated $n - 1$ times. In each iteration at most two records are interchanged. This requires 3 records to move. If each record is m words long, then the cost per interchange is $3m$. The total time is therefore $O(nm)$. The worst case of $3(n - 1)$ record moves is achievable. For example consider the input key sequence $R_1, R_2, \ldots, R_n$, with $R_2 < R_3 < \ldots < R_n$ and $R_1 > R_n$. For $n = 4$ and keys 4, 1, 2, 3 the file after each iteration has the following form: $i = 1$: 1,4,2,3; $i = 2$: 1,2,4,3,; $i = 3$: 1,2,3,4. A total of 9 record moves is made.   □

Several modifications to algorithm *list*1 are possible. One that is of interest was given by M. D. MacLaren. This results in a rearrangement algorithm in which no additional link fields are necessary. In this algorithm (Program 7.18), after the record R_p is exchanged with R_i the link field of the new R_i is set to p to indicate that the original record was moved. This, together with the observation that p must always be $\geq i$, permits a correct reordering of the records. The computing time remains $O(nm)$.

```
 1   procedure list2(var r:afile; n:integer; p:integer);
 2   {same function as list1 except that a second link field, linkb,
 3    is not required}
 4   var i,q : integer;
 5        t : records;
 6   begin
 7     for i := 1 to n − 1 do
 8     begin
 9       {find correct record to place into i-th position. The index
10        of this record must be ≥ i as records in positions
11        1, 2,..., i − 1 are already correctly positioned}
12       while p < i do
13         p := r[p].link;
14       q := r[p].link;                {rq is next record with largest key}
15       if p < > i              {interchange ri and rp moving rp to its}
16       then                    {correct spot as rp has i-th smallest key.}
17       begin                   {Also set link from old position of rj to}
18         t := r[i];                              {new one}
19         r[i] := r[p]; r[p] := t; r[i].link := p;
20       end; {of if}
21       p := q;
22     end; {of for}
23   end; {of list2}
```

Program 7.18   List2

Example 7.9: The data is the same as in Example 7.8. After the list sort we have:

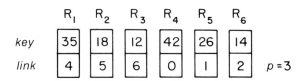

After each iteration of the **for** loop, we have:

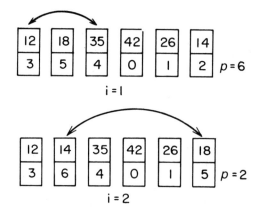

i = 1

i = 2

Now $p < 3$ and so it is advanced to $r[p].link = 6$.

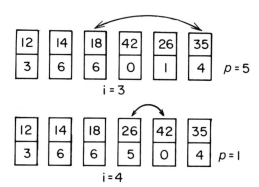

i = 3

i = 4

Again $p < 5$ and following links from $r[p]$ we find $r[6]$ to be the record with fifth smallest key.

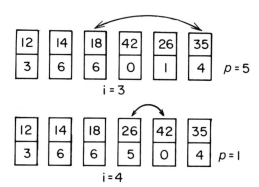

i = 5

Analysis of Algorithm *list2*

The sequence of record moves for *list2* is identical to that for *list1*. Hence, in the worst case $3(n-1)$ record moves for a total cost of $O(n\,m)$ are made. No node is examined more than once in the **while** loop. So the total time for the **while** loop is $O(n)$. While the asymptotic computing time for both *list1* and *list2* is the same and the same number of record moves is made in either case, we would expect *list2* to be slightly faster than *list1* because each time two records are interchanged *list1* does more work than *list2* does. *list1* is inferior to *list2* on both space and time considerations. □

The list sort technique discussed above does not appear to be well suited for use with sort methods such as Quick Sort and Heap Sort. The sequential representation of the heap is essential to Heap Sort. In such cases as well as in the methods suited to List Sort, one can maintain an auxiliary table, *t*, with one entry per record. The entries in this table serve as an indirect reference to the records. Let this table be of type *tablelist* which is defined as *tablelist* = **array** $[1 .. maxn]$ **of integer**. At the start of the sort $t[i] = i$, $1 \leq i \leq n$. If the sorting algorithm requires an interchange of R_i and R_j, then only the table entries need be interchanged, i.e., $t[i]$ and $t[j]$. At the end of the sort, the record with the smallest key is $R_{t[1]}$ and that with the largest $R_{t[n]}$. In general, following a table sort $R_{t[i]}$ is the record with the i'th smallest key. The required permutation on the records is therefore $R_{t[1]}, R_{t[2]}, \ldots, R_{t[n]}$ (see Figure 7.2). This table is adequate even in situations such as binary search, where a sequentially ordered file is needed. In other situations, it may be necessary to physically rearrange the records accord-

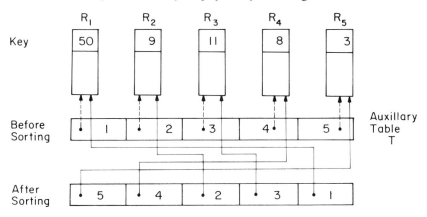

Figure 7.2 Table Sort

ing to the permutation specified by t. The algorithm to rearrange records corresponding to the permutation $t[1]$, $t[2]$,...,$t[n]$ is a rather interesting application of a theorem from mathematics: viz, every permutation is made up of disjoint cycles. The cycle for any element i is made up of i, $t[i]$, $t^2[i]$, ...,$t^k[i]$ (where $t^j[i] = t[t^{j-1}[i]]$ and $t^0[i] = i$) such that $t^k[i] = i$. Thus, the permutation t of figure 7.2 has two cycles, the first involving R_1 and R_5 and the second involving R_4, R_3 and R_2. Algorithm *table* (Program 7.19) utilizes this cyclic decomposition of a permutation. First, the cycle containing R_1 is followed and all records moved to their correct positions. The cycle containing R_2 is the next one examined unless this cycle has already been examined. The cycles for R_3, R_4, ...,R_{n-1} are followed in that order, achieving a reordering of all the records. While processing a trivial cycle for R_1 (i.e., $t[i] = i$), no rearrangement involving record R_i is required since the condition $t[i] = i$ means that the record with the i-th smallest key is R_i. In processing a nontrivial cycle for record R_i (i.e., $t[i] \neq i$), R_i is moved to a temporary position p, then the record at $t[i]$ is moved to $[i]$; next the record at $t[t[i]]$ is moved to $t[i]$, and so on until the end of the cycle $t^k[i]$ is reached and the record at p is moved to $t^{k-1}[i]$.

```
1    procedure table(var r : afile; n : integer; var t : tablelist);
2    {The records r[1], ...,r[n] are rearranged to correspond to the
3      sequence r[t[1]], ...,r[t[n]], n ≥ 1}
4    var i,j,k : integer;
5        p : records;
6    begin
7      for i := 1 to n − 1 do
8      if t[i] < > i
9      then                    {there is a nontrivial cycle starting at i}
10     begin                   {move r[i] to a temporary spot p and follow}
11       p := r[i];    {cycle i, t[i], t[t[i]], ... until the correct spot}
12       j := i;
13       repeat
14         k := t[j];
15         r[j] := r[k];
16         t[j] := j;
17         j := k;
18       until t[j] = i;
19       r[j] := p; {j is position for record p}
20       t[j] := j;
21     end;
22   end; {of table}
```

Program 7.19   Table

Example 7.10: Following a table sort on the file f we have the following values for t (only the key values for the 8 records of f are shown):

	R_1	R_2	R_3	R_4	R_5	R_6	R_7	R_8
f	35	14	12	42	26	50	31	18
t	3	2	8	5	7	1	4	6

There are two nontrivial cycles in the permutation specified by t. The first is R_1, R_3, R_8, R_6 and R_1. The second is R_4, R_5, R_7, R_4. During the first iteration ($i = 1$) of the for loop of algorithm *table*, the cycle R_1, $R_{t[1]}$, $R_{t^2[1]}$, $R_{t^3[1]}$, R_1 is followed. Record R_1 is moved to a temporary spot P. $R_{t[1]}$ (i.e. R_3) is moved to the position R_1; $R_{t^2[1]}$ (i.e. R_8) is moved to R_3; R_6 to R_8 and finally P to R_6. Thus, at the end of the first iteration we have:

f	12	14	18	42	26	35	31	50
t	1	2	3	5	7	6	4	8

For $i = 2,3$, $t[i] = i$, indicating that these records are already in their correct positions. When $i = 4$, the next nontrivial cycle is discovered and the records on this cycle R_4, R_5, R_7, R_4 are moved to their correct positions. Following this we have:

f	12	14	18	26	31	35	42	50
t	1	2	3	4	5	6	7	8

For the remaining values of i ($i = 5$, 6 and 7), $t[i] = i$, and no more nontrivial cycles are found. □

Analysis of Algorithm *table*

If each record uses m words of storage then the additional space needed is m words for p plus a few more for variables such as i, j and k. To obtain an estimate of the computing time we observe that the **for** loop is executed $n - 1$ times. If for some value of i, $t[i] \neq i$ then there is a nontrivial cycle including $k > 1$ distinct records R_i, $R_{t[i]}$ $R_{t^{k-1}[i]}$. Rearranging these records requires $k + 1$ record moves. Following this, the records involved in this cycle are not moved again at any time in the algorithm since $t[j] = j$ for all such records R_j. Hence no record can be in two different nontrivial cycles. Let k_l be the number of records on a nontrivial cycle starting at R_l when $i = l$ in the algorithm. Let $k_l = 0$ for a trivial cycle. Then, the total number of record moves is $\sum_{l=0,k_l \neq 0}^{n-1} (k_l + 1)$. Since the records on nontrivial cycles must be different, $\sum k_l \leq n$. The total record moves is thus maximum when $\sum k_l = n$ and there are $\lfloor n/2 \rfloor$ cycles. When n is even, each cycle contains 2

n →	10	20	50	100	250	500	1000
Quicksort [with median of 3] (File: [N,1,2,3, ..., N − 2, N − 1])	.499	1.26	4.05	12.9	68.7	257.	1018.
Quicksort [without median of 3] (File: [1,2,3, ..., N − 1, N])	.580	1.92	9.92	38.2	226.	856.	3472.
Insertion Sort [with K(0) = −∞] (File: [N,N − 1, ...,2,1])	.384	1.38	8.20	31.7	203.	788.	—
Insertion Sort [without K(0) = −∞] (File: [N,N − 1, ...,2,1])	.382	1.48	9.00	35.6	214.	861.	—
Heap Sort	.583	1.52	4.96	11.9	36.2	80.5	177.
Merge Sort	.726	1.66	4.76	11.3	35.3	73.8	151

(a) Worst case times in milliseconds

n →	10	20	50	100	250	500	1000
Radix Sort (L.S.D.) ($R^D \geq$ 100,000; optimal D & R)	1.82 R = 18; D = 4	3.05 R = 18; D = 4	5.68 R = 47; D = 3	9.04 R = 47; D = 3	20.1 R = 317; D = 2	32.5 R = 317; D = 2	58.0 R = 317; D = 2
Radix Sort (L.S.D.) (R = 10, D = 5)	1.95	3.23	6.97	13.2	32.1	66.4	129.
Quicksort [with median of 3]	.448	1.06	3.17	7.00	20.0	43.1	94.9
Quicksort [without median of 3]	.372	.918	2.89	6.45	20.0	43.6	94.0
Insertion Sort	.232	.813	4.28	16.6	97.1	385.	—
Insertion Sort (without K(0) = −∞)	.243	.885	4.72	18.5	111.	437.	—
Heap Sort	.512	1.37	4.52	10.9	33.2	76.1	166.
Merge Sort	.642	1.56	4.55	10.5	29.6	68.2	144.

(b) Average times in milliseconds

Table 7.1 Computing times for sorting methods. (Table prepared by Randall Istre)

records. Otherwise one contains three and the others two. In either case the number of record moves is $\lfloor 3n/2 \rfloor$. One record moves costs $O(m)$ time. The total computing time is therefore $O(nm)$.   ☐

In comparing the algorithms *list2* and *table* for rearranging records we see that in the worst case *list2* makes $3(n - 1)$ record moves while *table* makes only $\lfloor 3n/2 \rfloor$ record moves. For larger values of *m* it would therefore be worthwhile to make one pass over the sorted list of records creating a table *t* corresponding to a table sort. This would take $O(n)$ time. Then algorithm *table* could be used to rearrange the records in the order specified by *t*.

Of the several sorting methods we have studied there is no one method that is best. Some methods are good for small *n*, others for large *n*. Insertion Sort is good when the file is already partially ordered. Because of the low overhead of the method it is also the best sorting method for "small" *n*. Merge Sort has the best worst case behavior but requires more storage than Heap Sort (though also as an $O(n \log n)$ method it has slighly more overhead than Merge Sort). Quick Sort has the best average behavior but its worst case behavior is $O(n^2)$. The behavior of Radix Sort depends on the size of the keys and the choice of *r*.

These sorting methods have been programmed in FORTRAN and experiments conducted to determine the behavior of these methods. The results are summarized in Table 7.1. Table 7.1(a) gives the worst case sorting times for the various methods while Table 7.1(b) gives the average times. Since the worst case and average times for radix sort are almost the same, only the average times have been reported. Table 7.1(b) contains two rows for Radix Sort. The first gives the times when an optimal radix *r* is used for the sort. The second row gives the times when the radix is fixed at 10. Both tables contain two rows for Insertion Sort. Comparing the two rows gives us an indication of the time saved by using a dummy key, $K(0)$, in the algorithm as opposed to explicitly checking for the left most record (i.e., $R(1)$). In a separate study it was determined that for average times, Quicksort is better than Insertion Sort only when $n \geq 23$ and that for worst case times Merge Sort is better than Insertion Sort only when $n \geq 25$. The exact cut off points will vary with different implementations. In practice, therefore, it would be worthwhile to couple Insertion Sort with other methods so that subfiles of size less than about 20 are sorted using Insertion Sort.

REFERENCES AND SELECTED READINGS

A comprehensive discussion of sorting and searching may be found in:

The Art of Computer Programming: Sorting and Searching, by D. Knuth, vol. 3, Addison-Wesley, Reading, Massachusetts, 1973.

Two other useful references on sorting are:

Sorting and Sort Systems, by H. Lorin, Addison-Wesley, Reading, Massachusetts, 1975.

Internal sorting methods illustrated with PL/1 Programs, by R. Rich, Prentice-Hall, Englewood Cliffs, 1972.

For an in depth study of quicksort and stable merge sort see:

"Quicksort," by R. Sedgewick, STAN-CS-75-492, May 1975, Computer Science Department, Stanford University.

"Stable Sorting and Merging With Optimal Space and Time Bounds," by L. Pardo, STAN-CS-74-470, December 1974, Computer Science Department, Stanford University.

EXERCISES

1. Work through algorithms *binsrch* and *fibsrch* on an ordered file with keys (1,2,3,4,5,6,7,8,9,10,11,12,13,14,15,16) and determine the number of key comparisons made while searching for the keys 2, 10 and 15. For *fibsrch* we need the three Fibonnaci numbers $F_5 = 5$, $F_6 = 8$, $F_7 = 13$.

2. [Count sort] About the simplest known sorting method arises from the observation that the position of a record in a sorted file depends on the number of records with smaller keys. Associated with each record there is a *count* field used to determine the number of records which must precede this one in the sorted file. Write an algorithm to determine the *count* of each record in an unordered file. Show that if the file has n records then all the *counts* can be determined by making at most $n(n-1)/2$ key comparisons.

3. The insertion of algorithm *insert* was carried out by (a) searching for the spot at which the insertion is to be made and (b) making the insertion. If as a result of the search it was decided that the insertion had to be made between R_i and R_{i+1}, then records $R_{i+1}, ..., R_n$ were moved one space to locations $R_{i+2}, ..., R_{n+1}$. This was carried out in parallel with the search of (a). (a) can be sped up using the idea of *binsrch* or *fibsrch*. Write an *insert* algorithm incorporating one of these two searches.

4. Phase (b) (see exercise 3) can be sped up by maintaining the sorted file as a linked list. In this case the insertion can be made without any accompanying movement of the other records. However, now (a) must be carried out sequentially as before. Such an insertion scheme is known as list insertion. Write an algorithm for list insertion. Note that the insertion algorithms of exercises 3 and 4 can be used for a sort without making any changes in *insort*.

5. a) Show that algorithm *qsort* takes $O(n^2)$ time when the input file is already in sorted order.
   b) Why is $K_m \leq K_{n+1}$ required in *qsort*?

6. (a) The quicksort algorithm *qsort* presented in section 7.3 always fixes the position of the first record in the subfile currently being sorted. A better choice for this record is to choose the record with key value which is the median of the keys of the first, middle and last record in the subfile. Thus, using this median of three rule we correctly fix the position of the record R_i with $K_i =$ median $\{K_m, K_{(m+n)/2}, K_n\}$; i.e., K_i is the second largest key, e.g., median $\{10,5,7\}$ $= 7 =$ median $\{10,7,7\}$. Write a nonrecursive version of *qsort* incorporating this median of three rule to determine the record whose position is to be fixed. Also, adopt the suggestion of section 7.8 and use Insertion Sort to sort subfiles of size less than 21. Show that this algorithm takes $O(n \log n)$ time on an already sorted file.
    (b) Show that if smaller subfiles are sorted first then the recursion in algorithm *qsort* can be simulated by a stack of depth $O(\log n)$.

7. Quicksort is an unstable sorting method. Give an example of an input file in which the order of records with equal keys is not preserved.

8. a) Write a nonrecursive merge sort algorithm using linked lists to represent sorted subfiles. Show that if n records each of size m are being sorted then the time required is only $O(n \log n)$ as no records are physically moved.
    b) Use the rules of section 4.8 to automatically remove the recursion from the recursive version of merge sort.
    c) Take the two algorithms written above and run them on random data for n $= 100, 200, ...,1000$ and compare their running times.

9. (i) Prove that algorithm *msort* is stable.
    (ii) Heap sort is unstable. Give an example of an input file in which the order of records with equal keys is not preserved.

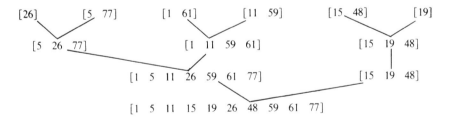

10. In the 2-way merge sort scheme discussed in section 7.5 the sort was stated with n sorted files each of size 1. Another approach would be to first make one pass over the data determining sequences of records that are in order and then using these as the initially sorted files. In this case, a left to right pass over the data of example 7.4 would result in the above partitioning of the data file into sorted subfiles. This would be followed by pairwise merging of the files until only one file remains.

    Rewrite the 2-way merge sort algorithm to take into account the existing order in the records. How much time does this algorithm take on an initially sorted file? Note that the original algorithm took $O(n \log n)$ on such an input file. What is the worst case computing time of the new algorithm? How much additional space is needed? Use linked lists.

11. Does algorithm *lrsort* result in a stable sort when used to sort numbers as in Example 7.7?

12. Write a sort algorithm to sort records $R_1, \ldots, R_n$ lexically on keys $(K^1, \ldots, K^r)$ for the case when the range of each key is much larger than n. In this case the bin sort scheme used in *lrsort* to sort within each key becomes inefficient (why?). What scheme would you use to sort within a key if we desired an algorithm with
   a) good worst case behavior
   b) good average behavior
   c) n is small, say < 15.

13. If we have n records with integer keys in the range $[0, n^2)$, then they may be sorted in $O(n \log n)$ time using heap or merge sort. Radix sort on a single key, i.e., $d = 1$ and $r = n^2$ takes $O(n^2)$ time. Show how to interpret the keys as 2 subkeys so that radix sort will take only $O(n)$ time to sort n records. (Hint: each key, K_i, may be written as $K_i = K_i^1 n + K_i^2$ with K_i^1 and K_i^2 integers in the range $[0,n)$.)

14. Generalize the method of the previous exercise to the case of integer keys in the range $[0,n^p)$ obtaining an $O(pn)$ sorting method.

15. Write the status of the following file F at the end of each phase of the following algorithms;
   a) *insort*
   b) *qsort*
   c) *msort*
   d) *hsort*
   e) *lrsort* — radix 10

$$F = (12,\ 2,\ 16,\ 30,\ 8,\ 28,\ 4\ 10,\ 20,\ 6,\ 18)$$

16. Write a table sort version of quicksort. Now during the sort, records are not physically moved. Instead, $t[i]$ is the index of the record that would have been in position i if records were physically moved around as in algorithm *qsort*. To begin with $t[i] = i$, $1 \leq i \leq n$. At the end of the sort $t[i]$ is the index of the record that should be in the i-th position in the sorted file. So now algorithm *table* of section 7.8 may be used to rearrange the records into the sorted order specified by t. Note that this reduces the amount of data movement taking place when compared to *qsort* for the case of large records.

17. Write an algorithm similar to algorithm *table* to rearrange the records of a file if with each record we have a *count* of the number of records preceding it in the sorted file (see Exercise 2).

18. Under what conditions would an MSD Radix sort be more efficient than an LSD Radix sort?

19. Assume you are given a list of five-letter English words and are faced with the problem of listing out these words in sequences such that the words in each sequence are anagrams, i.e., if x and y are in the same sequence, then word x is a permutation of word y. You are required to list out the fewest such sequences. With this restriction show that no word can appear in more than one sequence. How would you go about solving this problem?

20. Assume you are working in the census department of a small town where the number of records, about 3,000, is small enough to fit into the internal memory of a computer. All the people currently living in this town were born in the United States. There is one record for each person in this town. Each record contains
    (i) the state in which the person was born;
    (ii) county of birth;
    (iii) name of person.
    How would you produce a list of all persons living in this town? The list is to be ordered by state. Within each state the persons are to be listed by their counties, the counties being arranged in alphabetical order. Within each county the names are also listed in alphabetical order. Justify any assumptions you may make.

Chapter 8

EXTERNAL SORTING

In this chapter we consider techniques to sort large files. The files are assumed to be so large that the whole file cannot be contained in the internal memory of a computer, making an internal sort impossible. Before discussing methods available for external sorting it is necessary first to study the characteristics of the external storage devices which can be used to accomplish the sort. External storage devices may broadly be categorized as either sequential access (e.g., tapes) or direct access (e.g., drums and disks). Section 8.1 presents a brief study of the properties of these devices. In sections 8.2 and 8.3 we study sorting methods which make the best use of these external devices.

8.1 STORAGE DEVICES

8.1.1 Magnetic Tapes

Magnetic tape devices for computer input/output are similar in principle to audio tape recorders. The data is recorded on magnetic tape approximately 1/2″ wide. The tape is wound around a spool. A new reel of tape is normally 2400 ft. long (with use, the length of tape in a reel tends to decrease because of frequent cutting off of lengths of the tape). Tracks run across the length of the tape, with a tape having typically 7 to 9 tracks across its width. Depending on the direction of magnetization, a spot on the track can represent either a 0 or a 1 (i.e., a bit of information). At any point along the length of the tape, the combination of bits on the tracks represents a character (e.g., $A - Z,\ 0 - 9, +, :, ;,$ etc.). The number of bits that can be written per inch of track is referred to as the tape density. Examples of standard track densities are 800 and 1600 bpi (bits per inch). Since there are enough tracks across the width of the tape to represent a character, this density also gives the number of characters per inch of tape. Figure 8.1 illustrates this. With the conventions of the figure, the code for the first character on the tape is 10010111 while that for the third character is 00011100. If the tape is written using a density of 800 bpi then the length marked x in the figure is $3/800$ inches.

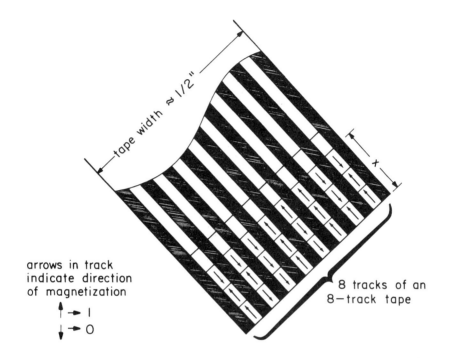

Figure 8.1 Segment of a Magnetic Tape.

Reading from a magnetic tape or writing onto one is done from a tape drive, as shown in figure 8.2. A tape drive consists of two spindles. On one of the spindles is mounted the source reel and on the other the take-up reel. During forward reading or forward writing, the tape is pulled from the source reel across the read/write heads and onto the take-up reel. Some tape drives also permit backward reading and writing of tapes; i.e., reading and writing can take place when tape is being moved from the take-up to the source reel.

If characters are packed onto a tape at a density of 800 bpi, then a 2400 ft. tape would hold a little over 23×10^6 characters. A density of 1600 bpi would double this figure. However, it is necessary to block data on a tape since each read/write instruction transmits a whole block of information into/from memory. Since normally we would neither have enough space in

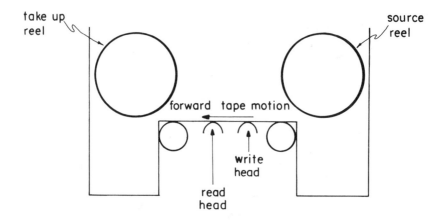

Figure 8.2   A Tape Drive.

memory for one full tape load nor would we wish to read the whole tape at once, the information on a tape will be grouped into several blocks. These blocks may be of a variable or fixed size. In between blocks of data is an interblock gap normally about 3/4 inches long. The interblock gap is long enough to permit the tape to accelerate from rest to the correct read/write speed before the beginning of the next block reaches the read/write heads. Figure 8.3 shows a segment of tape with blocked data.

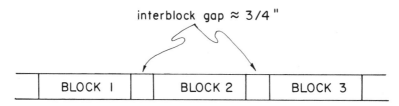

Figure 8.3   Blocked Data on a Tape.

In order to read a block from a tape one specifies the length of the block and also the address, A, in memory where the block is to be transmitted. The block of data is packed into the words $A, A + 1, A + 2, \ldots$ Similarly, in order to write a block of data onto tape one specifies the starting address in memory and the number of consecutive words to be written. These input and output areas in memory will be referred to as buffers. Usually the block size will correspond to the size of the input/output buffers set up in memory. We would like these blocks to be as large as possible for the following reasons:

(i) Between any pair of blocks there is an interblock gap of $3/4''$. With a track density of 800 bpi, this space is long enough to write 600 characters. Using a block length of 1 character/block on a 2400 ft. tape would result in roughly 38,336 blocks or a total of 38,336 characters on the entire tape. Tape utilization is $1/601 < 0.17\%$. With 600 characters per block, half the tape would be made up of interblock gaps. In this case, the tape would have only about 11.5×10^6 characters of information on it, representing a 50% utilization of tape. Thus, the longer the blocks the more characters we can write onto the tape.

(ii) If the tape starts from rest when the input/output command is issued, then the time required to write a block of n characters onto the tape is $t_a + nt_w$ where t_a is the delay time and t_w the time to transmit one character from memory to tape. The delay time is the time needed to cross the interblock gap. If the tape starts from rest then t_a includes the time to accelerate to the correct tape speed. In this case t_a is larger than when the tape is already moving at the correct speed when a read/write command is issued. Assuming a tape speed of 150 inches per second during read/write and 800 bpi the time to read or write a character is 8.3×10^{-6} sec. The transmission rate is therefore 12×10^4 characters/second. The delay time t_a may typically be about 10 milliseconds. If the entire tape consisted of just one long block, then it could be read in $\dfrac{2400 \text{ ft}}{150 \text{ in/sec}} + 10$ msec ≈ 3 min 12 sec, thus effecting an average transmission rate of almost 12×10^4 charac/sec. If, on the other hand, each block were one character long, then the tape would have at most 38,336 characters or blocks. This would be the worst case and the read time would be about 6 min 24 sec or an average of 100 charac/sec. Note that if the read of the next block is initiated soon enough after the read of the present block, then the delay time would be reduced to 5 milliseconds, corresponding to the time needed to get across the interblock gap of $3/4''$ at a tape speed of 150 inches per second. In this case the time to read 38,336 one-character blocks would be 3 min 12 sec, corresponding to an average of about 200 charac/sec.

While large blocks are desirable from the standpoint of efficient tape usage as well as reduced input/output time, the amount of internal memory available for use as input/output buffers puts a limitation on block size.

Computer tape is the foremost example of a sequential access device. If the read head is positioned at the front of the tape and one wishes to read the information in a block 2000 ft. down the tape then it is necessary to forward space the tape the correct number of blocks. If now we wish to read the first block, the tape would have to be rewound 2000 ft. to the front before the first block could be read. Typical rewind times over 2400 ft. of tape could be around one minute.

Unless otherwise stated we will make the following assumptions about our tape drives:
(i)   Tapes can be written and read in the forward direction only.
(ii)   The input/output channel of the computer is such as to permit the following three tasks to be carried out in parallel: writing onto one tape, reading from another and CPU operation.
(iii)   If blocks 1, ...,*i* have been written on a tape, then the tape can be moved backwards block by block using a backspace command or moved to the first block via a rewind command. Overwriting block $i - 1$ with another block of the same size destroys the leading portion of block *i*. While this latter assumption is not true of all tapes drives, it is characteristic of most of them.

8.1.2   Disk Storage

As an example of direct access external storage, we consider disks. As in the case of tape storage, we have here two distinct components: (1) the disk module (or simply disk or disk pack) on which information is stored (this corresponds to a reel of tape in the case of tape storage) and (2) the disk drive (corresponding to the tape drive) which performs the function of reading and writing information onto disks. Like tapes, disks can be removed from or mounted onto a disk drive. A disk pack consists of several platters that are similar to phonograph records. The number of platters per pack varies and typically is about 6. Figure 8.4 shows a disk pack with 6 platters. Each platter has two surfaces on which information can be recorded. The outer surfaces of the top and bottom platters are not used. This gives the disk of figure 8.4 a total of 10 surfaces on which information may be recorded. A disk drive consists of a spindle on which a disk may be mounted and a set of read/write heads. There is one read/write head for each surface. During a read/write the heads are held stationary over the position of the platter where the read/write is to be performed, while the disk itself rotates at high speeds (speeds of 2000-3000 rpm are fairly common). Thus, this device will read/write in concentric circles on each surface. The area that can be read from or written onto by a single stationary head is referred to as a *track*. Tracks are thus concentric circles, and each time the disk completes a revolution an entire track passes a read/write head. There may be from 100 to 1000 tracks on each surface of a platter. The collection of tracks simultaneously under a read/write head on the surfaces of all platters is called a *cylinder*. Tracks are divided into sectors. A *sector* is the smallest addressable segment of a track. Information is recorded along the tracks of a surface in blocks. In order to use a disk, one must specify the track or cylinder number, the sector number which is the start of the block and also the surface. The read/write head assembly is

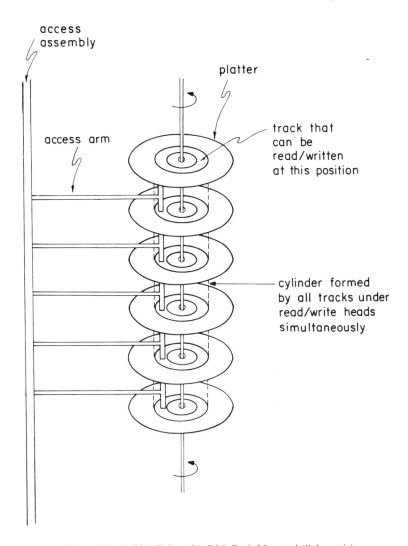

Figure 8.4 A Disk Drive with Disk Pack Mounted (Schematic).

first positioned to the right cylinder. Before read/write can commence, one has to wait for the right sector to come beneath the read/write head. Once this has happened, data transmission can take place. Hence, there are three factors contributing to input/output time for disks:

(i) *Seek time:* time taken to position the read/write heads to the correct cylinder. This will depend on the number of cylinders across which the heads have to move.

(ii)   *Latency time:* time until the right sector of the track is under the read/write head.

(iii)   *Transmission time:* time to transmit the block of data to/from the disk.

Maximum seek times on a disk are around 1/10 sec. A typical revolution speed for disks is 2400 rpm. Hence the latency time is at most 1/40 sec (the time for one revolution of the disk). Transmission rates are typically between 10^5 characters/second and 5×10^5 characters/second. The number of characters that can be written onto a disk depends on the number of surfaces and tracks per surface. This figure ranges from about 10^7 characters for small disks to about 5×10^8 characters for a large disk.

8.2 SORTING WITH DISKS

The most popular method for sorting on external storage devices is merge sort. This method consists of essentially two distinct phases. First, segments of the input file are sorted using a good internal sort method. These sorted segments, known as *runs*, are written out onto external storage as they are generated. Second, the runs generated in phase one are merged together following the merge tree pattern of Example 7.4, until only one run is left. Because the merge algorithm of §7.5 requires only the leading records of the two runs being merged to be present in memory at one time, it is possible to merge large runs together. It is more difficult to adapt the other methods considered in Chapter 7 to external sorting. Let us look at an example to illustrate the basic external merge sort process and analyze the various contributions to the overall computing time. A file containing 4500 records, $A_1, ...,A_{4500}$, is to be sorted using a computer with an internal memory capable of sorting at most 750 records. The input file is maintained on disk and has a block length of 250 records. We have available another disk which may be used as a scratch pad. The input disk is not to be written on. One way to accomplish the sort using the general procedure outlined above is to:

(i) Internally sort three blocks at a time (i.e., 750 records) to obtain six runs R_1-R_6. A method such as heapsort or quicksort could be used. These six runs are written out onto the scratch disk (figure 8.5).

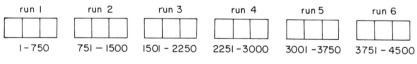

3 blocks per run

Figure 8.5 Blocked Runs Obtained After Internal Sorting.

(ii) Set aside three blocks of internal memory, each capable of holding 250 records. Two of these blocks will be used as input buffers and the third as an output buffer. Merge runs R_1 and R_2. This is carried out by first reading one block of each of these runs into input buffers. Blocks of runs are merged from the input buffers into the output buffer. When the output buffer gets full, it is written out onto disk. If an input buffer gets empty, it is refilled with another block from the same run. After runs R_1 and R_2 have been merged, R_3 and R_4 and finally R_5 and R_6 are merged. The result of this pass is 3 runs, each containing 1500 sorted records of 6 blocks. Two of these runs are now merged using the input/output buffers set up as above to obtain a run of size 3000. Finally, this run is merged with the remaining run of size 1500 to obtain the desired sorted file (figure 8.6).

Let us now analyze the method described above to see how much time is required to sort these 4500 records. The analysis will use the following notation:

t_s = maximum seek time

t_l = maximum latency time

t_{rw} = time to read or write one block of 250 records

$t_{IO} = t_s + t_l + t_{rw}$

t_{IS} = time to internally sort 750 records

$n\ t_m$ = time to merge n records from input buffers to the output buffer

We shall assume that each time a block is read from or written onto the disk, the maximum seek and latency times are experienced. While this is not true in general, it will simplify the analysis. The computing times for the various operations are:

Operation		Time
1) read 18 blocks of input, $18t_{IO}$, internally sort, $6t_{IS}$ write 18 blocks, $18t_{IO}$		$36t_{IO} + 6t_{IS}$
2) merge runs 1-6 in pairs		$36t_{IO} + 4500t_m$
3) merge 2 runs of 1500 records each, 12 blocks		$24t_{IO} + 3000t_m$
4) merge one run of 3000 records with one run of 1500 records		$36t_{IO} + 4500t_m$
	Total Time	$132t_{IO} + 12000t_m + 6t_{IS}$

Note that the contribution of seek time can be reduced by writing blocks on the same cylinder or on adjacent cylinders. A close look at the final computing time indicates that it depends chiefly on the number of passes made over the data. In addition to the initial input pass made over the data

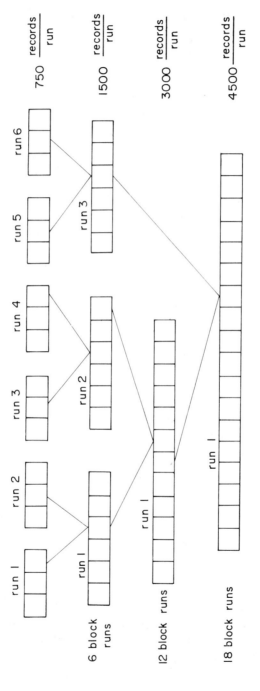

Figure 8.6 Merging the 6 runs.

for the internal sort, the merging of the runs requires 2-2/3 passes over the data (one pass to merge 6 runs of length 750 records, two thirds of a pass to merge two runs of length 1500 and one pass to merge one run of length 3000 and one of length 1500). Since one full pass covers 18 blocks, the input and output time is $2 \times (2\text{-}2/3 + 1) \times 18 \, t_{IO} = 132 \, t_{IO}$. The leading factor of 2 appears because each record that is read is also written out again. The merge time is $2\text{-}2/3 \times 4500 \, t_m = 12,000 \, t_m$. Because of this close relationship between the overall computing time and the number of passes made over the data, future analysis will be concerned mainly with counting the number of passes being made. Another point to note regarding the above sort is that no attempt was made to use the computer's ability to carry out input/output and CPU operation in parallel and thus overlap some of the time. In the ideal situation we would overlap almost all the input/output time with CPU processing so that the real time would be approximately $132 \, t_{IO} \approx 12000 \, t_m + 6t_{IS}$.

If we had two disks we could write on one while reading from the other and merging buffer loads already in memory all at the same time. In this case a proper choice of buffer lengths and buffer handling schemes would result in a time of almost $66 \, t_{IO}$. This parallelism is an important consideration when sorting is being carried out in a non-multi-programming environment. In this situation unless input/output and CPU processing is going on in parallel, the CPU is idle during input/ouput. In a multi-programming environment, however, the need for the sorting program to carry out input/output and CPU processing in parallel may not be so critical since the CPU can be busy working on another program (if there are other programs in the system at the time), while the sort program waits for the completion of its input/output. Indeed, in many multi-programming environments it may not even be possible to achieve parallel input, output and internal computing because of the structure of the operating system.

The remainder of this section will concern itself with: (1) reduction of the number of passes being made over the data and (2) efficient utilization of program buffers so that input, output and CPU processing is overlapped as much as possible. We shall assume that runs have already been created from the input file using some internal sort scheme. Later, we investigate a method for obtaining runs that are on the average about 2 times as long as those obtainable by the methods discussed in Chapter 7.

8.2.1   k-Way Merging

The 2-way merge algorithm of Section 7.5 is almost identical to the merge procedure just described (figure 8.6). In general, if we started with m runs, then the merge tree corresponding to figure 8.6 would have $\lceil \log_2 m \rceil + 1$ levels for a total of $\lceil \log_2 m \rceil$ passes over the data file. The number of passes over the data can be reduced by using a higher order merge, i.e., k-way merge for $k \geq 2$. In this case we would simultaneously merge k runs together. Figure 8.7 illustrates a 4-way merge on 16 runs. The number of

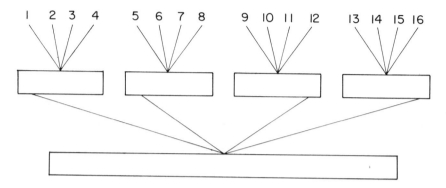

Figure 8.7   A 4-Way Merge on 16 Runs.

passes over the data is now 2, versus 4 passes in the case of a 2-way merge. In general, a k-way merge on m runs requires at most $\lceil \log_k m \rceil$ passes over the data. Thus, the input/output time may be reduced by using a higher order merge. The use of a higher order merge, however, has some other effects on the sort. To begin with, k-runs of size $S_1, S_2, S_3, \ldots, S_k$ can no

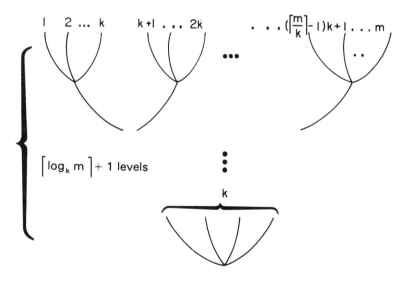

Figure 8.8   A k-Way Merge.

longer be merged internally in $O(\Sigma_1^k S_i)$ time. In a k-way merge, as in a 2-way merge, the next record to be output is the one with the smallest key. The smallest has now to be found from k possibilities and it could be the leading record in any of the k-runs. The most direct way to merge k-runs would be to make $k - 1$ comparisons to determine the next record to output. The computing time for this would be $O((k - 1) \Sigma_1^k S_i)$. Since $\log_k m$ passes are being made, the total number of key comparisons being made is $n(k - 1)\log_k m = n(k - 1)\log_2 m/\log_2 k$ where n is the number of records in the file. Hence, $(k - 1)/\log_2 k$ is the factor by which the number of key comparisons increases. As k increases, the reduction in input/output time will be overweighed by the resulting increase in CPU time needed to perform the k-way merge. For large k (say, $k \geq 6$) we can achieve a significant reduction in the number of comparisons needed to find the next smallest element by using the idea of a selection tree. A *selection tree* is a binary tree where each node represents the smaller of its two children. Thus, the root node represents the smallest node in the tree. Figure 8.9 illustrates a selection tree for an 8-way merge of 8-runs.

The construction of this selection tree may be compared to the playing of a tournament in which the winner is the record with the smaller key. Then, each nonleaf node in the tree represents the winner of a tournament and the root node represents the overall winner or the smallest key. A leaf node here represents the first record in the corresponding run. Since the records being sorted are generally large, each node will contain only a pointer to the record it represents. Thus, the root node contains a pointer to the first record in run 4. The selection tree may be represented using the sequential allocation scheme for binary trees discussed in section 5.3. The number above each node in figure 8.9 represents the address of the node in this sequential representation. The record pointed to by the root has the smallest key and so may be output. Now, the next record from run 4 enters the selection tree. It has a key value of 15. To restructure the tree, the tournament has to be replayed only along the path from node 11 to the root. Thus, the winner from nodes 10 and 11 is again node 11 ($15 < 20$). The winner from nodes 4 and 5 is node 4 ($9 < 15$). The winner from 2 and 3 is node 3 ($8 < 9$). The new tree is shown in figure 8.10. The tournament is played between sibling nodes and the result put in the parent node. Lemma 5.3 may be used to compute the address of sibling and parent nodes efficiently. After each comparison the next takes place one higher level in the tree. The number of levels in the tree is $\lceil \log_2 k \rceil + 1$. So, the time to restructure the tree is $O(\log_2 k)$. The tree has to be restructured each time a record is merged into the output file. Hence, the time required to merge all n records is $O(n \log_2 k)$. The time required to set up the selection tree the first time is $O(k)$. Hence, the total time needed per level of the merge tree of figure 8.8 is $O(n \log_2 k)$. Since the number of levels in this tree is $O(\log_k m)$,

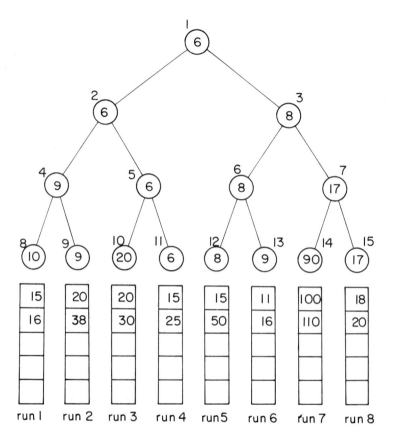

Figure 8.9   Selection tree for 8-way merge showing the first three keys in each of the 8 runs.

the asymptotic internal processing time becomes $O(n \log_2 k \log_k m) = O(n \log_2 m)$. The internal processing time is independent of k.

Note, however, that the internal processing time will be increased slightly because of the increased overhead associated with maintaining the tree. This overhead may be reduced somewhat if each node represents the loser of the tournament rather than the winner. After the record with smallest key is output, the selection tree of figure 8.9 is to be restructured. Since the record with the smallest key value is in run 4, this restructuring involves inserting the next record from this run into the tree. The next record has key value 15. Tournaments are played between sibling nodes along the path from node 11 to the root. Since these sibling nodes represent the losers of tournaments played earlier, we would simplify the restructuring process by placing in each nonleaf node a pointer to the record that loses the tourna-

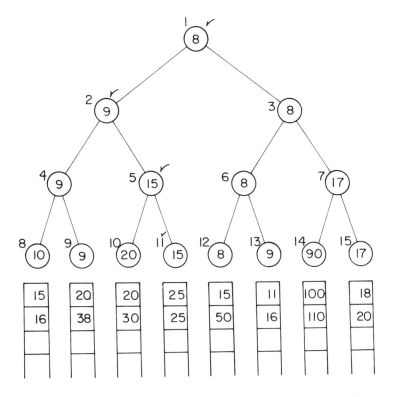

Figure 8.10 Selection tree of Figure 8.9 after one record has been output and tree restructured. Nodes that were changed are marked by √

ment rather than to the winner of the tournament. A tournament tree in which each nonleaf node retains a pointer to the loser is called a *tree of losers*. Figure 8.11 shows the tree of losers corresponding to the selection tree of figure 8.9. For convenience, each node contains the key value of a record rather than a pointer to the record represented. The leaf nodes represent the first record in each run. An additional node, node 0, has been added to represent the overall winner of the tournament. Following the output of the overall winner, the tree is restructured by playing tournaments along the path from node 11 to node 1. The records with which these tournaments are to be played are readily available from the parent nodes. We shall see more of loser trees when we study run generation in section 8.2.3.

In going to a higher order merge, we save on the amount of input/output being carried out. There is no significant loss in internal processing speed. Even though the internal processing time is relatively insensitive to the order of the merge, the decrease in input/output time is not as much as

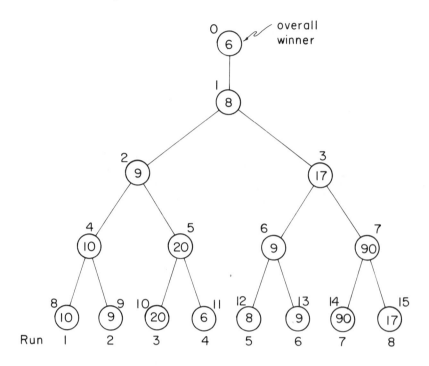

Figure 8.11   Tree of Losers Corresponding to Figure 8.9.

indicated by the reduction to $\log_k m$ passes. This is so because the number
of input buffers needed to carry out a k-way merge increases with k.
Though $k + 1$ buffers are sufficient, we shall see in section 8.2.2 that the
use of $2k + 2$ buffers is more desirable. Since the internal memory available
is fixed and independent of k, the buffer size must be reduced as k
increases. This in turn implies a reduction in the block size on disk. With
the reduced block size each pass over the data results in a greater number
of blocks being written or read. This represents a potential increase in input/
output time from the increased contribution of seek and latency times
involved in reading a block of data. Hence, beyond a certain k value the
input/output time would actually increase despite the decrease in the
number of passes being made. The optimal value for k clearly depends on
disk parameters and the amount of internal memory available for buffers
(exercise 3).

8.2.2   Buffer Handling for Parallel Operation

If k runs are being merged together by a k-way merge, then we clearly
need at least k input buffers and one output buffer to carry out the merge.

This, however, is not enough if input, output and internal merging are to be carried out in parallel. For instance, while the output buffer is being written out, internal merging has to be halted since there is no place to collect the merged records. This can be easily overcome through the use of two output buffers. While one is being written out, records are merged into the second. If buffer sizes are chosen correctly, then the time to output one buffer would be the same as the CPU time needed to fill the second buffer. With only k input buffers, internal merging will have to be held up whenever one of these input buffers becomes empty and another block from the corresponding run is being read in. This input delay can also be avoided if we have $2k$ input buffers. These $2k$ input buffers have to be cleverly used in order to avoid reaching a situation in which processing has to be held up because of lack of input records from any one run. Simply assigning two buffers per run does not solve the problem. To see this, consider the following example.

Example 8.1: Assume that a two way merge is being carried out using four input buffers, $in[i]$, $1 \leq i \leq 4$, and two output buffers, $ou[1]$ and $ou[2]$. Each buffer is capable of holding two records. The first few records of run 1 have key value 1, 3, 5, 7, 8, 9. The first few records of run 2 have key value 2, 4, 6, 15, 20, 25. Buffers $in[1]$ and $in[3]$ are assigned to run 1. The remaining two input buffers are assigned to run 2. We start the merging by reading in one buffer load from each of the two runs. At this time the buffers have the configuration of figure 8.12(a). Now runs 1 and 2 are merged using records from $in[1]$ and $in[2]$. In parallel with this the next buffer load from run 1 is input. If we assume that buffer lengths have been chosen such that the times to input, output and generate an output buffer are all the same then when $ou[1]$ is full we have the situation of figure 8.12(b). Next, we simultaneously output $ou[1]$, input into $in[4]$ from run 2 and merge into $ou[2]$. When $ou[2]$ is full we are in the situation of figure 8.12(c). Continuing in this way we reach the configuration of figure 8.12(e). We now begin to output $ou[2]$, input from run 1 into $in[3]$ and merge into $ou[1]$. During the merge, all records from run 1 get exhausted before $ou[1]$ gets full. The generation of merged output must now be delayed until the inputting of another buffer load from run 1 is completed!   ☐

Example 8.1 makes it clear that if $2k$ input buffers are to suffice then we cannot assign two buffers per run. Instead, the buffers must be floating in the sense that an individual buffer may be assigned to any run depending upon need. In the buffer assignment strategy we shall describe, for each run there will at any time be at least one input buffer containing records from that run. The remaining buffers will be filled on a priority basis; i.e., the run for which the k-way merging algorithm will run out of records first is the one from which the next buffer will be filled. One may easily predict which run's records will be exhausted first by simply comparing the keys of

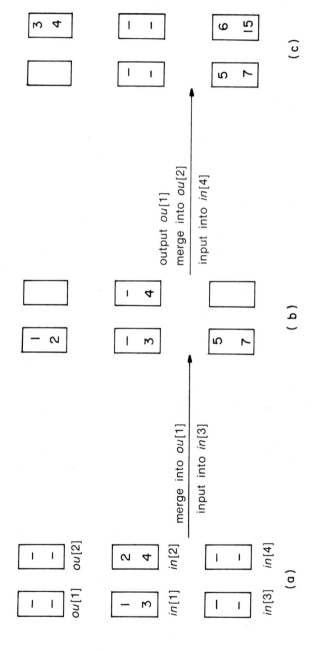

Figure 8.12   Example showing that two fixed buffers per run are not enough for continued parallel operation.

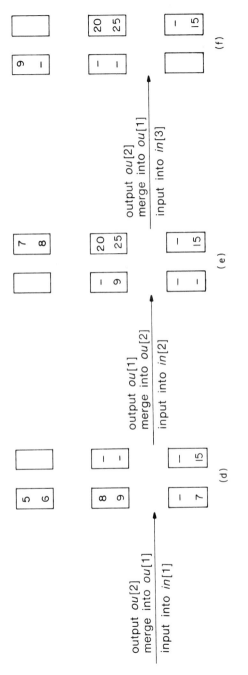

Figure 8.12 (continued)

the last record read from each of the k runs. The smallest such key determines this run. We shall assume that in the case of equal keys the merge process first merges the record from the run with least index. This means that if the key of the last record read from run i is equal to the key of the last record read from run j, and $i < j$, then the records read from i will be exhausted before those from j. So, it is possible that at any one time we might have more than two bufferloads from a given run and only one partially full buffer from another run. All bufferloads from the same run are queued together. Before formally presenting the algorithm for buffer utilization, we make the following assumptions about the parallel processing capabilities of the computer system available:

(i) We have two disk drives and the input/output channel is such that it is possible simultaneously to read from one disk and write onto the other.

(ii) While data transmission is taking place between an input/output device and a block of memory, the CPU cannot make references to that same block of memory. Thus, it is not possible to start filling the front of an output buffer while it is being written out. If this were possible, then by coordinating the transmission and merging rate only one output buffer would be needed. By the time the first record for the new output block was determined, the first record of the previous output block would have been written out.

(iii) To simplify the discussion we assume that input and output buffers are to be the same size.

Keeping these assumptions in mind, we first formally state the algorithm obtained using the strategy outlined earlier and then illustrate its working through an example. Out algorithm merges k-runs, $k \geq 2$, using a k-way merge. $2k$ input buffers and 2 output buffers are used. Each buffer is a contiguous block of memory. Input buffers are queued in k queues, one queue for each run. It is assumed that each input/output buffer is long enough to hold one block of records. Empty buffers are stacked with av pointing to the top buffer in this stack. The stack is a linked list. The following type definitions are made use of:

type
  $buffer = $ **array** $[1..maxbuffsize]$ **of integer**;
  $inputbuffers = $ **array** $[1..twok]$ **of** $buffer$;
  $outputbuffers = $ **array** $[0..1]$ **of** $buffer$;
  $firstbuffers = $ **array** $[1..k]$ **of integer**;
  $endbuffers = $ **array** $[1..k]$ **of integer**;
  $linkfields = $ **array** $[1..twok]$ **of integer**;
  $lastvalues = $ **array** $[1..k]$ **of integer**;
where k is a constant and $twok = 2k$.

The algorithm also assumes that the end of each run has a sentinel record with a very large key, say *maxint*. It is assumed that all records other than the sentinel records have key value less than *maxint*. If block lengths and hence buffer lengths are chosen such that the time to merge one output buffer load equals the time to read a block then almost all input, output and computation will be carried out in parallel. It is also assumed that in the case of equal keys the *k*-way merge algorithm first outputs the record from the run with smallest index.

```
 1  procedure buffering;
 2  var
 3    in : inputbuffers;
 4    out : outputbuffers;
 5    qfront : firstbuffers;
 6    qend : endbuffers;
 7    link : linkfields;
 8    last : lastvalues;
 9    i,j,ou,l,av : integer;
10    lastkeymerged : integer;
11  begin{buffering}
12    for i := 1 to k do {input a block from each run}
13    begin {input first block of run i into in[i]}
14      readbuff(i,i); {arguments are buffer and run number}
15      {readbuff is a procedure that inputs the next block of records}
16    end;
17    while input not complete do
18    begin {wait}
19    end;
20    for i := 1 to k do {initialize queues and free buffers}
21    begin
22      qfront[i] := i; qend[i] := i;
23      last[i] := lastkey(in[i]);
24      {lastkey is a function that returns the last key in a buffer}
25      link[k + i] := k + i + 1; {stack free buffer}
26    end;
27    link[twok] := 0; av := k + 1; ou := 0;
28    {first queue exhausted is the one whose last key is smallest}
29    j := findmin(last,1,k);
30    {findmin is a function that finds j such that last[j] = minimum(last[i]),
          1 ≤ i ≤ k}
31    l := av; av := link[av]; {get next free buffer}
32    if last[j] < > maxint then
```

```
33    {begin to read next block for run j into buffer in[l]}
34    readbuff(l,j);
35    repeat
36    {kwaymerge merges records from the k buffers front[i] into output
37    buffer ou until it is full. If an input buffer beomes empty before
38    ou is filled, the next buffer in the queue for this run is used and
39    the empty buffer is stacked}
40    kwaymerge;
41    while input/output not complete do
42    begin {wait loop}
43    end;
44    if last[j] < > maxint then begin
45            link[end[j]] := l; end[j] := l; last[j] := lastkey(in[l]);
46                                        {queue next block}
47            j := findmin(last,1,k);
48            l := av; av := link[av]; {get next free buffer}
49            end;
50    lastkeymerged := lastkey(out[ou]);
51    if last[j] < > maxint then
52    begin
53        {begin to write out[ou] and read next block of run j into in[l]}
54        writebuff(ou);
55        {writebuff is a procedure that outputs a block of records}
56        readbuff(l,j);
57    end
58    else
59    {begin to write out[ou]}
60    writebuff(ou);
61    ou := 1 − ou;
62    until lastkeymerged = maxint;
63    while output incomplete do
64    begin {wait loop}
65    end;
66  end; {of buffering}
```

Program 8.1   Buffering

Notes: 1) For large k, determination of the queue that will exhaust first can be made in $\log_2 k$ comparisons by setting up a selection tree for $last[i]$, $1 \leq i \leq k$, rather than making $k - 1$ comparisons each time a buffer load is to be read in. The change in computing time will not be significant, since this queue selection represents only a very small fraction of the total time taken by the algorithm.

2) For large k the algorithm *kwaymerge* uses a tree of losers as discussed in section 8.2.1.

3) All input/output except for the initial k blocks that are read and the last block output is done concurrently with computing. Since after k runs have been merged we would probably begin to merge another set of k runs, the input for the next set can commence during the final merge stages of the present set of runs. I.e., when $last[j] = $ **maxint** we begin reading one by one the first blocks from each of the next set of k runs to be merged. In this case, over the entire sorting of a file, the only time that is not overlapped with the internal merging time is the time for the first k blocks of input and that for the last block of output.

4) The algorithm assumes that all blocks are of the same length. This may require inserting a few dummy records into the last block of each run following the sentinel record with key **maxint**.

Example 8.2: To illustrate the working of the above algorithm, let us trace through it while it performs a three-way merge on the following three runs:

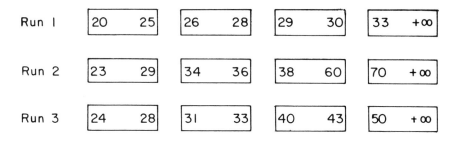

Each run consists of four blocks of two records each; the last key in the fourth block of each of these three runs is **maxint** (shown as $+\infty$). We have six input buffers $in[i]$, $1 \leq i \leq 6$, and 2 output buffers $out[0]$ and $out[1]$.

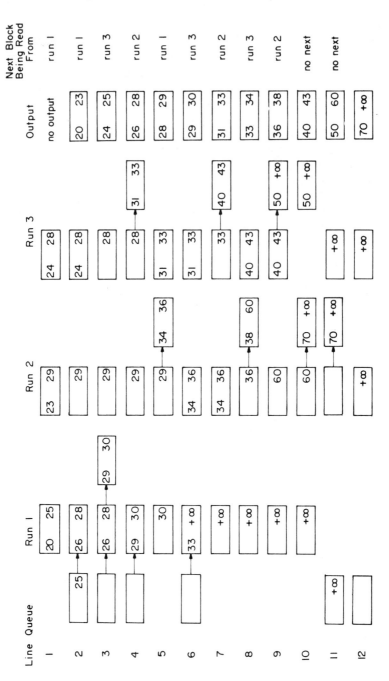

The diagram on page 398 shows the status of the input buffer queues, the run from which the next block is being read and the output buffer being output at the beginning of each iteration of the **repeat-until** of the buffering algorithm.

From line 5 it is evident that during the k-way merge the test for "output buffer full?" should be carried out before the test "input buffer empty?" as the next input buffer for that run may not have been read in yet and so there would be no next buffer in that queue. In lines 3 and 4 all 6 input buffers are in use and the stack of free buffers is empty.   □

We end our discussion of buffer handling by proving that the algorithm *buffering* works. This is stated formally in Theorem 8.1.

Theorem 8.1: The following is true for algorithm *buffering*:

(i) There is always a buffer available in which to begin reading the next block; and

(ii) during the k-way merge the next block in the queue has been read in by the time it is needed.

Proof: (i) Each time we get to line 48 of the algorithm there are at most $k + 1$ buffer loads in memory, one of these being in an output buffer. For each queue there can be at most one buffer that is partially full. If no buffer is available for the next read, then the remaining k buffers must be full. This means that all the k partially full buffers are empty (as otherwise there will be more than $k + 1$ buffer loads in memory). From the way the merge is set up, only one buffer can be both unavailable and empty. This may happen only if the output buffer gets full exactly when one input buffer becomes empty. But $k > 1$ contradicts this. So, there is always at least one buffer available when line 48 is being executed.

(ii) Assume this is false. Let run R_i be the one whose queue becomes empty during *kwaymerge*. We may assume that the last key merged was not the sentinel key **maxint** since otherwise *kwaymerge* would terminate the search rather then get another buffer for R_i . This means that there are more blocks of records for run R_i on the input file and $last[i] \neq$ **maxint**. Consequently, up to this time whenever a block was output another was simultaneously read in (see lines 54 and 56). Input/output therefore proceeded at the same rate and the number of available blocks of data is always k. An additional block is being read in but it does not get queued until line 45. Since the queue for R_i has become empty first, the selection rule for the next run to read from ensures that there is at most one block of records for each of the remaining $k - 1$ runs. Furthermore, the output buffer cannot be full at this time as this condition is tested for before the input buffer empty condition. Thus there are fewer than k blocks of data in memory. This contradicts our earlier assertion that there must be exactly k such blocks of data.   □

8.2.3   Run Generation

Using conventional internal sorting methods such as those of Chapter 7 it is possible to generate runs that are only as large as the number of records that can be held in internal memory at one time. Using a tree of losers it is possible to do better than this. In fact, the algorithm we shall present will on the average generate runs that are twice as long as obtainable by conventional methods. This algorithm was devised by Walters, Painter and Zalk. In addition to being capable of generating longer runs, this algorithm will allow for parallel input, output and internal processing. For almost all the internal sort methods discussed in Chapter 7, this parallelism is not possible. Heap sort is an exception to this. In describing the run generation algorithm, we shall not dwell too much upon the input/output buffering needed. It will be assumed that input/output buffers have been appropriately set up for maximum overlapping of input, output and internal processing. Wherever in the run generation algorithm there is an input/output instruction, it will be assumed that the operation takes place through the input/output buffers. We shall assume that there is enough space to construct a tree of losers for k records, $r[i]$, $0 \le i < k$. This will require a loser tree with k nodes numbered 0 to $k - 1$. Each node, i, in this tree will have one field $l[i]$. $l[i]$ $1 \le i < k$, represents the loser of the tournament played at node i. Node 0 represents the overall winner of the tournament. This node will not be explicitly present in the algorithm. Each of the k record positions $r[i]$ has a run number field $rn[i]$, $0 \le i < k$ associated with it. This field will enable us to determine whether or not $r[i]$ can be output as part of the run currently being generated. Whenever the tournament winner is output, a new record (if there is one) is input and the tournament replayed as discussed in section 8.2.1. Algorithm *runs* is simply an implementation of the loser tree strategy discussed earlier. The variables used in this algorithm have the following significance:

$r[i]$, $0 \le i < k$ ...the k records in the tournament tree
$key[i]$, $0 \le i < k$ ...key value of record $r[i]$
$l[i]$, $0 \le i < k$ ...loser of the tournament played at node i
$rn[i]$, $0 \le i < k$ ...the run number to which $r(i)$ belongs

> rc ...run number of current run
> q ...overall tournament winner
> rq ...run number for $r[q]$
> $rmax$ ...number of runs that will be generated
> $lastkey$ ...key value of last record output

The loop of lines 14-59 repeatedly plays the tournament outputting records. The only interesting thing about this algorithm is the way in which the tree of losers is initialized. This is done in lines 9-12 by setting up a fictitious run numbered 0. Thus, we have $rn[i] = 0$ for each of the k records $r[i]$. Since all but one of the records must be a loser exactly once, the initialization of $l[i] := i$ sets up a loser tree with $r[0]$ the winner. With this initialization the loop of lines 14-59 correctly sets up the loser tree for run 1. The test of line 26 suppresses the output of these k fictitious records making up run 0. The variable $lastkey$ is made use of in line 39 to determine whether or not the new record input, $r[q]$, can be output as part of the current run. If $key(q) < lastkey$ then $r[q]$ cannot be output as part of the current run rc as a record with larger key value has already been output in this run. When the tree is being readjusted (lines 49-58), a record with lower run number wins over one with a higher run number. When run numbers are equal, the record with lower key value wins. This ensures that records come out of the tree in nondecreasing order of their run numbers. Within the same run, records come out of the tree in nondecreasing order of their key values. $rmax$ is used to terminate the algorithm. In line 34, when we run out of input, a record with run number $rmax + 1$ is introduced. When this record is ready for output, the algorithm terminates from line 22. One may readily verify that when the input file is already sorted, only one run is generated. On the average, the run size is almost $2k$. The time required to generate all the runs for an n run file is $O(n \log k)$ as it takes $O(\log k)$ time to adjust the loser tree each time a record is output. The algorithm may be speeded slightly by explicitly initializing the loser tree using the first k records of the input file rather than k fictitious records as in lines 9-12. In this case the conditional of line 26 may be removed as there will no longer be a need to suppress output of certain records. Program 8.2 implements this algorithm in Pascal.

```
type  treerecord = record
                    key : integer
                    {other fields declared here}
                 end;
```

```
1  procedure runs;
2  {generate runs using a tree of losers}
3  label 99;
4  var
5      r : array[0.kminus1] of treerecord;
6      key,l,rn : array[0.kminus1] of integer;
7      rc,q,rq,rmax,lastkey,temp,i,t : integer;
8  begin {runs}
9      for i := 1 to k − 1 do {set up fictitious run 0 to initialize tree}
10     begin
11       rn[i] := 0; l[i] := i; key[i] := 0;
12     end;
13     q := 0; rq := 0; rc := 0; rmax := 0; rn[0] := 0; lastkey := maxint;
14     while true do {output runs}
15     begin
16       if rq < > rc then {end of run}
17       begin
18         if rc < > 0 then
19         begin
20         output end of run marker
21         end;
22         if rq > rmax then goto 99
23                           else rc := rq;
24       end;
25       {output record r[q] if not fictitious}
26       if rq < > 0 then
27       begin
28       writerecord(r[q]);
29       lastkey := key[q];
30       end;
31       {input new record into tree}
32       if no more input then
33       begin
34         rq := rmax + 1; rn[q] := rq;
35       end
36       else
37       begin
38       readrecord(r[q]);
39       if key[q] < lastkey then
40       begin {new record belongs to next run}
41         rq := rq + 1;
42         rn[q] := rq;
43         rmax := rq;
44       end
```

```
45      else
46        rn[q] := rc;
47      end;
48    {adjust losers}
49    t := (k + q) div 2; {t is parent of q}
50    while t < > 0 do
51    begin
52      if (rn[l [t]] < rq) or ((rn[l [t]] = rq) and (key[l [t]] < key[q])) then
53      begin
54        temp := q; q := l[t]; l[t] := temp;
55        rq := rn[q];            {t is the winner}
56      end;
57      t := t div 2; {move up tree}
58    end;
59    end;
60  99: end; {of runs}
```

Program 8.2   Runs

8.3   SORTING WITH TAPES

Sorting on tapes is carried out using the same basic steps as sorting on disks. Sections of the input file are internally sorted into runs which are written out onto tape. These runs are repeatedly merged together until there is only one run. The difference between disk and tape sorting lies essentially in the manner in which runs are maintained on the external storage media. In the case of disks, the seek and latency times are relatively insensitive to the specific location on the disk of the next block to be read with respect to the current position of the read/write heads. (The maximum seek and latency times were about $1/10$ sec and $1/40$ sec respectively.) This is not true for tapes. Tapes are sequential access. If the read/write head is currently positioned at the front of the tape and the next block to be read is near the end of the tape (say $\sim$ 2400 feet away), then the seek time, i.e., the time to advance the correct block to the read/write head, is almost 3 min 2 sec (assuming a tape speed of 150 inches/second). This very high maximum seek time for tapes makes it essential that blocks on tape be arranged in such an order that they will be read in sequentially during the k-way merge of runs. Hence, while in the previous section we did not concern ourselves with the relative position of the blocks on disk, in this section, the distribution of blocks and runs will be our primary concern. We shall study two distribution schemes. Before doing this, let us look at an example to see the different factors involved in a tape sort.

Example 8.3: A file containing 4,500 records, $R_1, ..., R_{4500}$ is to be sorted using a computer with an internal memory large enough to hold only 800 records. The available external storage consists of 4 tapes, *T1*, *T2*, *T3* and *T4*. Each block on the input tape contains 250 records. The input tape is not to be destroyed during the sort. Initially, this tape is on one of the 4 available tape drives and so has to be dismounted and replaced by a work tape after all input records have been read. Let us look at the various steps involved in sorting this file. In order to simplify the discussion, we shall assume that the initial run generation is carried out using a conventional internal sort such as quicksort. In this case 3 blocks of input can be read in at a time, sorted and output as a run. We shall also assume that no parallelism in input, output and CPU processing is possible. In this case we shall use only one output buffer and two input buffers. This requires only 750 record spaces.

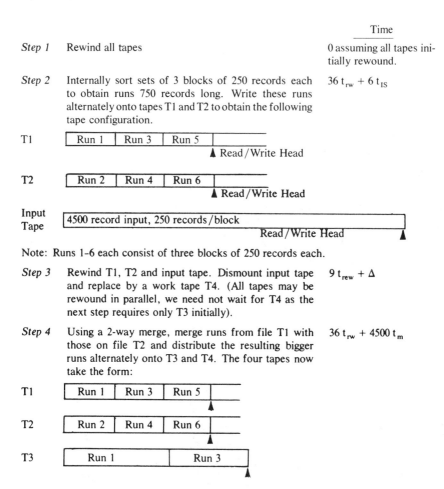

Time

Step 1   Rewind all tapes — 0 assuming all tapes initially rewound.

Step 2   Internally sort sets of 3 blocks of 250 records each to obtain runs 750 records long. Write these runs alternately onto tapes T1 and T2 to obtain the following tape configuration. — $36\,t_{rw} + 6\,t_{IS}$

T1 | Run 1 | Run 3 | Run 5 |
▲ Read/Write Head

T2 | Run 2 | Run 4 | Run 6 |
▲ Read/Write Head

Input Tape | 4500 record input, 250 records/block |
Read/Write Head ▲

Note: Runs 1–6 each consist of three blocks of 250 records each.

Step 3   Rewind T1, T2 and input tape. Dismount input tape and replace by a work tape T4. (All tapes may be rewound in parallel, we need not wait for T4 as the next step requires only T3 initially). — $9\,t_{rew} + \Delta$

Step 4   Using a 2-way merge, merge runs from file T1 with those on file T2 and distribute the resulting bigger runs alternately onto T3 and T4. The four tapes now take the form: — $36\,t_{rw} + 4500\,t_m$

T1 | Run 1 | Run 3 | Run 5 |
▲

T2 | Run 2 | Run 4 | Run 6 |
▲

T3 | Run 1 | Run 3 |
▲

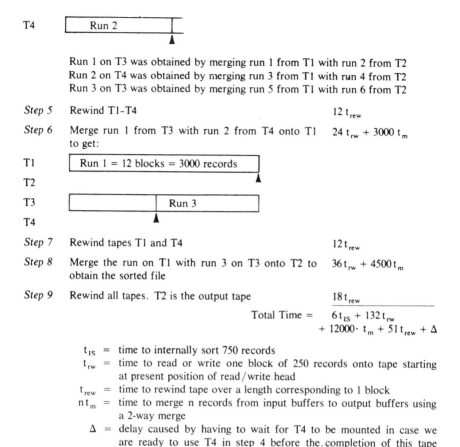

Run 1 on T3 was obtained by merging run 1 from T1 with run 2 from T2
Run 2 on T4 was obtained by merging run 3 from T1 with run 4 from T2
Run 3 on T3 was obtained by merging run 5 from T1 with run 6 from T2

Step 5 Rewind T1-T4 $12\,t_{rew}$

Step 6 Merge run 1 from T3 with run 2 from T4 onto T1 $24\,t_{rw} + 3000\,t_m$
to get:

T1 [Run 1 = 12 blocks = 3000 records]

T2

T3 [Run 3   ]

T4

Step 7 Rewind tapes T1 and T4 $12\,t_{rew}$

Step 8 Merge the run on T1 with run 3 on T3 onto T2 to $36\,t_{rw} + 4500\,t_m$
obtain the sorted file

Step 9 Rewind all tapes. T2 is the output tape $18\,t_{rew}$

$$\text{Total Time} = 6\,t_{IS} + 132\,t_{rw}$$
$$+ 12000 \cdot t_m + 51\,t_{rew} + \Delta$$

t_{IS} = time to internally sort 750 records
t_{rw} = time to read or write one block of 250 records onto tape starting at present position of read/write head
t_{rew} = time to rewind tape over a length corresponding to 1 block
$n\,t_m$ = time to merge n records from input buffers to output buffers using a 2-way merge
Δ = delay caused by having to wait for T4 to be mounted in case we are ready to use T4 in step 4 before the completion of this tape mount.

The above computing time analysis assumes that no operations are carried out in parallel. The analysis could be carried out further as in the case of disks to show the dependence of the sort time on the number of passes made over the data.

8.3.1 Balanced Merge Sorts

Example 8.3 performed a 2-way merge of the runs. As in the case of disk sorting, the computing time here too depends essentially on the number of passes being made over the data. Use of a higher order merge results in a decrease in the number of passes being made without significantly changing the internal merge time. Hence, we would like to use as high an order merge as possible. In the case of disks the order of merge was limited essentially by the amount of internal memory available for use as input/

output buffers. A k-way merge required the use of $2k + 2$ buffers. While this is still true of tapes, another probably more severe restriction on the merge order k is the number of tapes available. In order to avoid excessive tape seek times, it is necessary that runs being merged together be on different tapes. Thus, a k-way tape merge requires at least k tapes for use as input tapes during the merge.

In addition, another tape is needed for the output generated during this merge. Hence, at least $k + 1$ tapes must be available for a k-way tape merge (recall that in the case of a disk, one disk was enough for a k-way merge though two were needed to overlap input and output). Using $k + 1$ tapes to perform a k-way merge requires an additional pass over the output tape to redistribute the runs onto k tapes for the next level of merges (see the merge tree of figure 8.8). This redistribution pass can be avoided through the use of $2k$ tapes. During the k-way merge, k of these tapes are used as input tapes and the remaining k as output tapes. At the next merge level, the role of input-output tapes is interchanged as in example 8.3, where in step 4, $T1$ and $T2$ are used as input tapes and $T3$ and $T4$ as output tapes while in step 6, $T3$ and $T4$ are the input tapes and $T1$ and $T2$ the output tapes (though there is no output for $T2$). These two approaches to a k-way merge are now examined. Algorithms $m1$ and $m2$ perform a k-way merge with the $k + 1$ tapes strategy while algorithm $m3$ performs a k-way merge using the $2k$ tapes strategy.

```
 1   procedure m1;
 2   {sort a file of records from a given input tape using a k-way merge
 3   given tapes t₁, ..., t_{k+1} are available for the sort.}
 4   label 99;
 5   begin
 6     Create runs from the input tape distributing them evenly over
 7     tapes t₁, ...,t_k;
 8     Rewind t₁, ...,t_k and also the input tape;
 9     if there is only 1 run then goto 99; {the sorted file is on t₁}
10     replace input tape by t_{k+1};
11     while true do
12     {repeatedly merge onto t_{k+1} and redistribute back onto t₁, ...,t_k}
13     begin
14       merge runs from t₁, ...,t_k onto t_{k+1};
15       rewind t₁, ...,t_{k+1};
16       if number of runs on t_{k+1} = 1 then goto 99; {output on t_{k+1}}
17       evenly distribute from t_{k+1} onto t₁, ...,t_k;
18       rewind t₁, ...,t_{k+1};
19     end;
20   99: end; {of m1}
```

Program 8.3 $m1$

Analysis of Algorithm $m1$

To simplify the analysis we assume that the number of runs generated, m, is a power of k. Line 6 involves one pass over the entire file. One pass includes both reading and writing. In lines 11-19 the number of passes is $\log_k m$ merge passes and $\log_k m - 1$ redistribution passes. So, the total number of passes being made over the file is $2\log_k m$. If the time to rewind the entire input take is t_{rew}, then the non-overlapping rewind time is roughly $2\log_k m \; t_{rew}$. $\square$

A somewhat more clever way to tackle the problem is to rotate the output tape, i.e., tapes are used as output tapes in the cyclic order, $k + 1, 1, 2, ..., k$. When this is done, the redistribution from the output tape makes less than a full pass over the file. Algorithm $m2$ formally describes the process. For simplicity the analysis of $m2$ assumes that m is a power of k. Program 8.4 is a pseudo-Pascal version of $m2$.

```
1   procedure m2;
2   {Sort a file of records from a given input tape using a k-way merge
3    given tapes t₁,...,tₖ₊₁ are available for the sort.
4    Same type definitions as m1}
5   label 99;
6   begin
7     Create runs from the input file distributing them evenly over
8     tapes t₁,...,tₖ;
9     Rewind t₁,...,tₖ and also the input tape;
10    if there is only 1 run then goto 99; {sorted file on t₁}
11    replace input tape by tₖ₊₁;
12    i := k + 1; {i is index of output tape}
13    while true do
14      begin
15        merge runs from the k tapes tⱼ, 1 <= j <= k + 1 and j <> i
               onto tᵢ;
16        rewind t₁,...,tₖ₊₁;
17        if number of runs on tᵢ = 1 then goto 99; {output on tᵢ}
18        evenly distribute (k − 1)/k of the runs on tᵢ onto tape tⱼ,
19        1<=j<=k + 1 and j<>i and j<>i mod (k + 1)+ 1;
20        rewind tapes tⱼ, 1 <= j <= k + 1 and j <> i;
21        i := i mod (k + 1) + 1;
22      end;
23  99: end; {of m2}
```

Program 8.4 $m2$

Analysis of Algorithm $m2$

The only difference between algorithms $m2$ and $m1$ is the redistributing time. Once again the redistributing is done $\log_k m - 1$ times. m is the number of runs generated in line 7. But now each redistributing pass reads and writes only $(k - 1)/k$ of the file. Hence, the effective number of passes made over the data is $(2 - 1/k) \log_k m + 1/k$. For two-way merging on three tapes this means that algorithm $M2$ will make $3/2 \log_k m + 1/2$ passes while $M1$ will make $2 \log_k m$. If t_{rew} is the rewind time then the non-overlappable rewind time for $M2$ is at most $(1 + 1/k) (\log_k m) t_{rew} + (1 - 1/k) t_{rew}$ as line 20 rewinds only $1/k$ of the file. Instead of distributing runs as in line 18 we could write the first m/k runs onto one tape, begin rewind, write the next m/k runs onto the second tape, begin rewind, etc. In this case we can begin filling input buffers for the next merge level (line 15) while some of the tapes are still rewinding. This is so because the first few tapes written on would have completed rewinding before the distribution phase is complete (for $k > 2$).   □

In case a k-way merge is made using $2k$ tapes, no redistribution is needed and so the number of passes being made over the file is only $\log_k m + 1$. This means that if we have $2k + 1$ tapes available, then a $2k$-way merge will make $(2 - 1/(2k))\log_{2k} m + 1/(2k)$ passes while a k-way merge utilizing only $2k$ tapes will make $\log_k m + 1$ passes. Table 8.13 compares the number of passes being made in the two methods for some values of k.

k	2k-way	k-way
1	$3/2 \log_2 m + 1/2$	—
2	$7/8 \log_2 m + 1/4$	$\log_2 m + 1$
3	$1.124 \log_3 m + 1/6$	$\log_3 m + 1$
4	$1.25 \log_4 m + 1/8$	$\log_4 m + 1$

Table 8.13 Number of passes using a 2k-way merge versus a k-way merge on 2k + 1 tapes.

As is evident from the table, for $k > 2$ a k-way merge using only $2k$ tapes is better than a $2k$-way merge using $2k + 1$ tapes.

Algorithm $M3$ performs a k-way merge sort using $2k$ tapes.

```
 1  procedure m3;
 2  {Sort a file of records from a given input tape using a k-way merge
 3    on 2k tapes t₁,...,t₂ₖ}
 4  begin
 5    Create runs from the input file distributing them evenly
 6    over tapes t₁,...,tₖ;
 7    rewind t₁,...,tₖ; rewind the input tape;
 8    replace the input tape by tape t₂ₖ;
 9    i := 0;
10    while total number of runs on tᵢₖ₊₁,...,tᵢₖ₊ₖ > 1 do
11      begin
12        j := 1 − i;
13        perform a k-way merge from tᵢₖ₊₁,...,tᵢₖ₊ₖ evenly
14        distributing output runs onto tⱼₖ₊₁,...,tⱼₖ₊ₖ;
15        rewind t₁,...,t₂ₖ;
16        i := j; {switch input and output tapes}
17      end;
18    {sorted file is on tᵢₖ₊₁}
19  end; {of m3}
```

Program 8.5 $m3$

Analysis of $m3$

To simplify the analysis assume that m is a power of k. In addition to the initial run creation pass, the algorithm makes $\log_k m$ merge passes. Let t_{rew} be the time to rewind the entire input file. The time for line 7 is t_{rew} and if m is a power of k then the rewind of line 15 takes t_{rew}/k for each but the last iteration of the **while** loop. The last rewind takes time t_{rew}. The total rewind is therefore bounded by $(2 + (\log_k m - 1)/k) \, t_{rew}$. Some of this may be overlapped using the strategy described in the analysis of algorithm $m2$ (exercise 4). ☐

One should note that $m1$, $m2$ and $m3$ use the buffering algorithm of section 8.2.2 during the k-way merge. This merge itself, for large k, would be carried out using a selection tree as discussed earlier. In both cases the proper choice of buffer lengths and the merge order (restricted by the number of tape drives available) would result in an almost complete overlap of internal processing time with input/output time. At the end of each level of merge, processing will have to wait until the tapes rewind. Once again, this wait can be minimized if the run distribution strategy of exercise 4 is used.

8.3.2 Polyphase Merge

Balanced k-way merging is characterized by a balanced or even distribution of the runs to be merged onto k input tapes. One consequence of this is that $2k$ tapes are needed to avoid wasteful passes over the data during which runs are just redistributed onto tapes in preparation for the next merge pass. It is possible to avoid altogether these wasteful redistribution passes when using fewer than $2k$ tapes and a k-way merge, by distributing the "right number" of runs onto different tapes. We shall see one way to do this for a k-way merge utilizing $k + 1$ tapes. To begin, let us see how $m = 21$ runs may be merged using a 2-way merge with 3 tapes $T1$, $T2$ and $T3$. Lengths of runs obtained during the merge will be represented in terms of the length of initial runs created by the internal sort. Thus, the internal sort creates 21 runs of length 1 (the length of initial runs is the unit of measure). The runs on a tape will be denoted by s^n where s is the run size and n the number of runs of this size. If there are six runs of length 2 on a tape we shall denote this by 2^6. The sort is carried out in seven phases. In the first phase the input file is sorted to obtain 21 runs. Thirteen of these are written onto $T1$ and eight onto $T2$. In phase 2, 8 runs from $T2$ are merged with 8 runs from $T1$ to get 8 runs of size 2 onto $T3$. In the next phase the 5 runs of length 1 from $T1$ are merged with 5 runs of length 2 from $T3$ to obtain 5 runs of length 3 on $T2$. Table 8.14 shows the 7 phases involved in the sort.

Phase	T1	T2	T3	Fraction of Total Records Read	
1	1^{13}	1^8	—	1	initial distribution
2	1^5	—	2^8	16/21	merge to T3
3	—	3^5	2^3	15/21·	merge to T2
4	5^3	3^2	—	15/21	merge to T1
5	5^1	—	8^2	16/21	merge to T3
6	—	13^1	8^1	13/21	merge to T2
7	21^1	—	—	1	merge to T1

Table 8.14   Polyphase Merge on 3 Tapes.

Counting the number of passes made during each phase we get $1 + 16/21 + 15/21 + 15/21 + 16/21 + 13/21 + 1 = 5\text{-}4/7$ as a total number of passes needed to merge 21 runs. If algorithm $m2$ of the section 8.3.1 had been used with $k = 2$, then $3/2\lceil \log_2 21 \rceil + 1/2 = 8$ passes would have been made. Algorithm $m3$ using 4 tapes would have made $\lceil \log_2 21 \rceil = 5$ passes. What makes this process work? Examination of Table 8.14 shows that the trick is to distribute the runs initially in such a way that in all phases but the last only one tape becomes empty. In this case we can proceed to the next phase without redistribution of runs as we have two non-empty input tapes and one empty tape for output. To determine what the correct initial distribution is we work backwards from the last phase. Assume there are n phases. Then in phase n we wish to have exactly one run on $T1$ and no runs on $T2$ and $T3$. Hence, the sort will be complete at phase n. In order to achieve this, this run must be obtained by merging a run from $T2$ with a run from $T3$, and these must be the only runs on $T2$ and $T3$. Thus, in phase $n - 1$ we should have one run on each of $T2$ and $T3$. The run on $T2$ is obtained by merging a run from $T1$ with one from $T3$. Hence, in phase $n - 2$ we should have one run on $T1$ and two on $T3$.

Table 8.15 shows the distribution of runs needed in each phase so that merging can be carried out without any redistribution passes. Thus, if we had 987 runs, then a distribution of 377 runs onto $T1$ and 610 onto $T3$ at phase 1 would result in a 15 phase merge. At the end of the fifteenth phase the sorted file would be on $T1$. No redistribution passes would have been made. The number of runs needed for an n phase merge is readily seen to be $F_n + F_{n-1}$ where F_i is the i-th Fibonacci number (recall that $F_7 = 13$ and $F_6 = 8$ and that $F_{15} = 610$ and $F_{14} = 377$). For this reason this method of distributing runs is also known as Fibonacci merge. It can be shown that for three tapes this distribution of runs and resultant merge pattern requires only $1.04 \log_2 m + 0.99$ passes over the data. This compares very favorably with the $\log_2 m$ passes needed by algorithm $M3$ on 4 tapes using a balanced 2-way merge. The method can clearly be generalized to k-way merging on $k + 1$ tapes using generalized Fibonacci numbers. Table 8.16 gives the run distribution for 3-way merging on four tapes. In this case it can be shown that the number of passes over the data is about $0.703 \log_2 m + 0.96$.

Phase	T1	T2	T3
n	1	0	0
n − 1	0	1	1
n − 2	1	0	2
n − 3	3	2	0
n − 4	0	5	3
n − 5	5	0	8
n − 6	13	8	0
n − 7	0	21	13
n − 8	21	0	34
n − 9	55	34	0
n − 10	0	89	55
n − 11	89	0	144
n − 12	233	144	0
n − 13	0	377	233
n − 14	377	0	610

Table 8.15 Run Distribution for 3-Tape Polyphase Merge

Phase	T1	T2	T3	T4
n	1	0	0	0
n − 1	0	1	1	1
n − 2	1	0	2	2
n − 3	3	2	0	4
n − 4	7	6	4	0
n − 5	0	13	11	7
n − 6	13	0	24	20
n − 7	37	24	0	44
n − 8	81	68	44	0
n − 9	0	149	125	81
n − 10	149	0	274	230
n − 11	423	274	0	504
n − 12	927	778	504	0
n − 13	0	1705	1431	927
n − 14	1705	0	3136	2632

Table 8.16 Polyphase Merge Pattern for 3-Way 4-Tape Merging

Example 8.4: The initial internal sort of a file of records creates 57 runs. 4 tapes are available to carry out the merging of these runs. The table below shows the status of the tapes using 3-way polyphase merge.

Phase	T1	T2	T3	T4	Fraction of Total Records Read	
1	1^{13}	—	1^{24}	1^{20}	1	initial distribution
2	—	3^{13}	1^{11}	1^{7}	39/57	merge onto T2
3	5^{7}	3^{6}	1^{4}	—	35/57	merge onto T1
4	5^{3}	3^{2}	—	9^{4}	36/57	merge onto T4
5	5^{1}	—	17^{2}	9^{2}	34/57	merge onto T3
6	—	31^{1}	17^{1}	9^{1}	31/57	merge onto T2
7	57^{1}	—	—	—	1	merge onto T1

The total number of passes over the data is $1 + 39/57 + 35/57 + 36/57 + 34/57 + 31/57 + 1 = 5\text{-}4/57$ compared to $\lceil \log_2 57 \rceil = 6$ passes for 2-way balanced merging on 4 tapes.

Remarks on Polyphase Merging

Our discussion of polyphase merging has ignored altogether the rewind time involved. Before one can begin the merge for the next phase it is necessary to rewind the output tape. During this rewind the computer is essentially idle. It is possible to modify the polyphase merge scheme discussed here so that essentially all rewind time is overlapped with internal processing and read/write on other tapes. This modification requires at least five tapes and can be found in Knuth, Vol. 3. Further, polyphase merging requires that the initial number of runs be a perfect Fibonacci number (or generalized Fibonacci number). In case this is not so, one can substitute dummy runs to obtain the required number of runs.

Several other ingenious merge schemes have been devised for tape sorts. Knuth, Vol. 3, contains an exhaustive study of these schemes.

8.3.3 Sorting with Fewer Than 3 Tapes

Both the balanced merge scheme of section 8.3.1 and the polyphase scheme of section 8.3.2 required at least three tapes to carry out the sort. These methods are readily seen to require only $O(n \log n)$ time where n is the number of records. We state without proof the following results for sorting on one and two tapes.

Theorem 8.2: Any one tape algorithm that sorts n records must take time $\geq O(n^2)$.

Theorem 8.3: n records can be sorted on two tapes in $O(n \log n)$ time if it is possible to perform an inplace rewrite of a record without destroying adjacent records; i.e., if record R_2 in the sequence $R_1 R_2 R_3$ can be rewritten by an equal size record R_2' to obtain $R_1 R_2' R_3$.

REFERENCES AND SELECTED READINGS

See the readings for chapter 7.

The algorithm for theorem 8.3 may be found in:

"A linear time two tape merge," by R. Floyd and A. Smith, *Information Processing Letters*, vol. 2, no. 5, December 1973, pp. 123–

EXERCISES

1. Write an algorithm to construct a tree of losers for records $R_i, 1 \leq i \leq k$, with key values $K_i, 1 \leq i \leq k$. Let the tree nodes be $T_i, 0 \leq i < k$, with $T_i, 1 \leq i < k$ a pointer to the loser of a tournament and T_0 a pointer to the overall winner. Show that this construction can be carried out in time $O(k)$.

2. Write an algorithm, using a tree of losers, to carry out a k-way merge of k runs $k \geq 2$. Show that if there are n records in the k runs together, then the computing time is $O(n \log_2 k)$.

3. a) n records are to be sorted on a computer with a memory capacity of S records ($S \ll n$). Assume that the entire S record capacity may be used for input/output buffers. The input is on disk and consists of m runs. Assume that each time a disk access in made the seek time is t_s and the latency time is t_l. The transmission time is t_t per record transmitted. What is the total input time for phase II of external sorting if a k-way merge is used with internal memory partitioned into I/O buffers so as to permit overlap of input, output and CPU processing as in algorithm *buffering*?

  b) Let the CPU time needed to merge all the runs together be t_{CPU} (we may assume it is independent of k and hence constant). Let $t_s = 80$ *ms*, $t_l = 20$ *ms*, $n = 200{,}000$, $m = 64$, $t_t = 10^{-3}$ sec/record, $S = 2000$. Obtain a rough plot of the total input time, t_{input}, versus k. Will there always be a value of k for which $t_{CPU} \approx t_{input}$?

4. a) Modify algorithm $m2$ using the run distribution strategy described in the analysis of this algorithm.

  b) Let t_{rw} be the time to read/write a block and t_{rew} the time to rewind over one block length. If the initial run creation pass generates m runs for m a power of k, what is the time for a k-way merge using your algorithm? Compare this with the corresponding time for algorithm $m2$.

5. Obtain a table corresponding to Table 8.16 for the case of a 5-way polyphase merge on six tapes. Use this to obtain the correct initial distribution for 497 runs so that the sorted file will be on $T1$. How many passes are made over the data in achieving the sort? How many passes would have been made by a 5-way balanced merge sort on six tapes (algorithm $m2$)? How many passes would have been made by a 3-way balanced merge sort on six tapes (algorithm $m3$)?

6. In this exercise we shall investigate another run distribution strategy for sorting on tapes. Let us look at a 3-way merge on four tapes of 157 runs. These runs are initially distributed according to: 70 runs on $T1$, 56 on $T2$ and 31 on $T3$. The merging takes place according to the table below.

Line	Phase	T1	T2	T3	T4	
1	1	1^{70}	1^{56}	1^{31}	—	initial distribution
2	2	1^{39}	1^{25}	—	3^{31}	merge on to T4
3	2	1^{14}	—	2^{25}	3^{31}	merge T1, T2 to T3
4	3	—	6^{14}	2^{11}	3^{17}	merge T1, T3, T4 to T2
5		5^{11}	6^{14}	—	3^{6}	merge T3, T4 to T1
6		5^{5}	6^{8}	14^{6}	—	merge T1, T2, T4 to T3
7	4	—	6^{3}	14^{6}	11^{5}	merge T1, T2 to T4
8	5	31^{3}	—	14^{3}	11^{2}	merge T2, T3, T4 to T1
9		31^{3}	25^{2}	14^{1}	—	merge T3, T4 to T2
10		31^{2}	25^{1}	—	70^{1}	merge T1, T2, T3 to T4
11	6	31^{1}	—	56^{1}	70^{1}	merge T1, T2 to T3
12	7	—	157^{1}	—	—	merge T1, T3, T4 to T2

i.e., each phase consists of a 3-way merge followed by a 2-way merge and in each phase almost all the initial runs are processed.

a) Show that the total number of passes made to sort 157 runs is 6-62/157.

b) Using an initial distribution from Table 8.16 show that Fabonacci merge on four tapes makes 6-59/193 passes when the number of runs is 193.

The distribution required for the process discussed above corresponds to the cascade numbers which are obtained as below for a k-way merge: Each phase (except the last) in a k-way cascade merge consists of a k-way merge followed by a $(k - 1)$-way merge followed by a $(k - 2)$-way merge...a 2-way merge. The last phase consists of only a k-way merge. The table below gives the cascade numbers corresponding to a k-way merge. Each row represents a starting configuration for a merge phase. If at the start of a phase we have the distribution n_1, n_2, ...,n_k where $n_i > n_{i+1}$, $1 \leq i < k$, then at the start of the previous phase we need $\sum_1^k n_i$, $\sum_1^{k-1} n_i$, ..., $n + n_2$, n_1 runs on the k input tapes respectively.

						Number of Runs
1	0	0	...	0	0	1
1	1	1	...	1	1	k
$\vdots$	$\vdots$	$\vdots$		$\vdots$	$\vdots$	
n_1	n_2	n_3	...	n_{k-1}	n_k	$\sum_1^k n_i$
$\sum_1^k n_i$	$\sum_1^{k-1} n_i$	$\sum_1^{k-2} n_i$	...	$n_1 + n_2$	n_1	

Initial Distribution for a k-way Cascade Merge

It can be shown that for a 4-way merge Cascade merge results in more passes over the data than a 4-way Fibonacci merge.

7. a) Generate the first 10 rows of the initial distribution table for a 5-way Cascade merge using six tapes (see exercise 6).

b) Observe that 671 runs corresponds to a perfect 5-way Cascade distribution. How many passes are made in sorting the data using a 5-way Cascade merge? $\left(\text{Ans: } 5\dfrac{561}{671} \right)$

c) How many passes are made by a 5-way Fibonacci merge starting with 497 runs and the distribution 120, 116, 108, 92, 61? $\left(\text{Ans: } 5\ \dfrac{400}{497} \right)$

The number of passes is almost the same even though Cascade merge started with 35% more runs! In general, for ≥ 6 tapes Cascade merge makes fewer passes over the data than does Fibonacci merge.

8. List the runs output by algorithm *runs* using the following input file and $k = 4$.

   100, 50, 18, 60, 2, 70, 30, 16, 20, 19, 99, 55, 20

9. For the example of figure 8.14 compute the total rewind time. Compare this with the rewind time needed by algorithm *m2*.

Chapter 9

SYMBOL TABLES

The notion of a symbol table arises frequently in computer science. When building loaders, assemblers, compilers, or any keyword driven translator a symbol table is used. In these contexts a symbol table is a *set of name-value pairs*. Associated with each name in the table is an attribute, a collection of attributes, or some directions about what further processing is needed. The operations that one generally wants to perform on symbol tables are (i) ask if a particular name is already present, (ii) retrieve the attributes of that name, (iii) insert a new name and its value, and (iv) delete a name and its value. In some applications, one wishes to perform only the first three of these operations. However, in its fullest generality we wish to study the representation of a structure which allows these four operations to be performed efficiently.

Is a symbol table necessarily a *set* of names or can the same name appear more than once? If we are translating a language with block structure (such as ALGOL or Pascal) then the variable X may be declared at several levels. Each new declaration of X implies that a new variable (with the same name) must be used. Thus we may also need a mechanism to determine which of several occurrences of the same name is the most recently introduced.

These considerations lead us to a specification of the structure *symbol table*. A set of axioms is shown on the next page.

Imagine the following set of declarations for a language with block structure:

procedure $x(a,b$: **integer**);
  var i,j : **integer**;
  procedure y $(c,d$: **real**);
    var x, i : **real**;
  begin
  end;
  begin
  end;

structure *SYMBOL—TABLE*
  declare *CREATE( )* → *symtb*
          INSERT(symtb,name, value) → *symtb*
          DELETE(symtb,name) → *symtb*
          FIND(symtb,name) → *value*
          HAS(symtb,name) → *Boolean*
          ISMTST(symtb) → *Boolean;*
  for all *S* ϵ *symt*b, *a*,*b* ϵ *name*, *r* ϵ *value* **let**
   ISMTST(CREATE) :: = **true**
   ISMTST(INSERT(S,a,r)) :: = **false**
   HAS(CREATE,a) :: = **false**
   HAS(INSERT(S,a,r),b) :: =
    if *EQUAL(a,b)* **then true else** *HAS(S,b)*
   DELETE(CREATE,a) :: = *CREATE*
   DELETE(INSERT(S,a,r),b) :: =
    if *EQUAL(a,b)* **then** *S*
    else *INSERT(DELETE(S,b),a,r)*
   FIND(CREATE,a) :: = *error*
   FIND(INSERT(S,a,r),b) :: = **if** *EQUAL(a,b)* **then** *r*
                              else *FIND(S,b)*
  end
end *SYMBOL—TABLE*

The representation of part of the symbol table (ignoring procedure names and parameters) for these declarations would look like $S =$

$$INSERT(INSERT(INSERT(INSERT(CREATE,i,\textbf{integer}),$$
$$j,\textbf{integer}),x,\textbf{real}),i,\textbf{real})$$

Notice the identifier *i* which is declared twice with different attributes. Now suppose we apply FIND(*S,i*). By the axioms EQUAL(*i,i*) is tested and has the value **true**. Thus the value **real** is returned as a result. If the function DELETE(*S,i*) is applied then the result is the symbol table

$$INSERT(INSERT(INSERT(CREATE,i,\textbf{integer}),j,\textbf{integer}),x,\textbf{real})$$

If we wanted to change the specification of DELETE so that it removes all occurrences of *i* then one axiom needs to be redefined, namely

DELETE(INSERT(S,a,r),b) :: =
  if *EQUAL(a,b)* **then** *DELETE(S,b)*
  else *INSERT(DELETE(S,b),a,r)*

The remaining sections of this chapter are organized around different ways to implement symbol tables. Different strategies are preferable given different assumptions. The first case considered is where the identifiers are known in advance and no deletions or insertions are allowed. Symbol tables with this property are called *static*. One solution is to sort the names and store them sequentially. Using either the binary search or Fibonacci search method of section 7.1 allows us to find any name in $O(\log_2 n)$ operations. If each name is to be searched for with equal probability then this solution, using an essentially balanced binary search tree, is optimal. When different identifiers are searched for with differing probabilities and these probabilities are known in advance this solution may not be the best. An elegant solution to this problem is given in section 9.1.

In section 9.2 we consider the use of binary trees when the identifiers are not known in advance. Sequential allocation is no longer desirable because of the need to insert new elements. The solution which is examined is AVL or height balanced trees. Finally in section 9.3 we examine the most practical of the techniques for dynamic search and insertion, hashing.

9.1 STATIC TREE TABLES

Definition: A *binary search tree t* is a binary tree; either it is empty or each node in the tree contains an identifier and:
   (i)   all identifiers in the left subtree of *t* are less (numerically or alphabetically) than the identifier in the root node *t*;
   (ii)   all identifiers in the right subtree of *t* are greater than the identifier in the root node *t*;
   (iii) the left and right subtrees of *t* are also binary search trees.

For a given set of identifiers several binary search trees are possible. Figure 9.1 shows two possible binary search trees for a set of words. To determine whether an identifier *x* is present in a binary search tree, *x* is compared with the root. If *x* is less than the identifier in the root, then the search continues in the left subtree; if *x* equals the identifier in the root, the search terminates successfully; otherwise the search continues in the right subtree. This is formalized in algorithm *search* (Program 9.1). The data types used by the algorithm are defined as:

type *identifier* = **packed array** [1 .. *maxchar*] **of char**;
        treepointer = ↑*treerecord*;
        treerecord = **record**
                            leftchild : *treepointer*;
                            ident : *identifier*;
                            rightchild : *treepointer*;
                        end;

where *maxchar* is of type **const**.

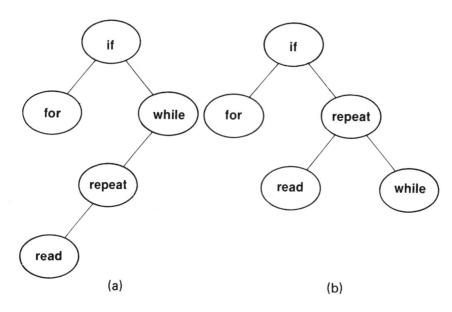

(a)   (b)

Figure 9.1 Two possible binary search trees.

```
 1  procedure search(t:treepointer; x:identifier; var retpointer:treepointer);
 2  {Search the binary search tree t for x. Each node has fields
 3  leftchild, ident, rightchild. Return retpointer = nil if x is not
 4  in t. Otherwise, return retpointer such that retpointer↑.ident = x.}
 5  var found : boolean;
 6  begin
 7    retpointer := t; found := false;
 8    while (retpointer < > nil) and (not found) do
 9      if x < retpointer↑.ident then {search left subtree}
10        retpointer := retpointer↑.leftchild
11      else if x > retpointer↑.ident then {search rightsubtree}
12        retpointer := retpointer↑.rightchild
13      else                           {We've found x}
14        found := true;
15  end; {of search}
```

Program 9.1 Search

In our study of binary search in chapter 7, we saw that every sorted file corresponded to a binary search tree. For instance, a binary search on the file **(do, if, read)** corresponds to using algorithm *search* on the binary search tree of figure 9.2. While this tree is a full binary tree, it need not be optimal over all binary search trees for this file when the identifiers are searched for with different probabilities. In order to determine an optimal binary search tree for a given static file, we must first decide on a cost measure for search trees. In searching for an identifier at level k using algorithm *search*, k iterations of the **while** loop of lines 2–8 are made. Since this loop determines the cost of the search, it is reasonable to use the level number of a node as its cost.

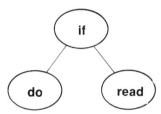

Figure 9.2 Binary search tree corresponding to a binary search on the file (**do**, **if**, **read**).

Consider the two search trees of figure 9.1. As names are encountered a match is searched for in the tree. The second binary tree requires at most three comparisons to decide whether there is a match. The first binary tree may require four comparisons, since any identifier which alphabetically comes after **if** but precedes **repeat** will test four nodes. Thus, as far as worst case search time is concerned, this makes the second binary tree more desirable than the first. To search for an identifier in the first tree takes one comparison for the **if**, two for each of **for** and **while**, three for **repeat** and four for **loop**. Assuming each is searched for with equal probability, the average number of comparisons for a successful search is 2.4. For the second binary search tree this amount is 2.2. Thus, the second tree has a better average behavior, too.

In evaluating binary search trees, it is useful to add a special "square" node at every place there is a null link. Doing this to the trees of figure 9.1 yields the trees of figure 9.3. Remember that every binary tree with n nodes has $n + 1$ null links and hence it will have $n + 1$ square nodes. We shall call these nodes *external* nodes because they are not part of the original tree. The remaining nodes will be called *internal* nodes. Each time a binary search tree is examined for an identifier which is not in the tree, the search terminates at an external node. Since all such searchers represent unsuccessful searches, external nodes will also be referred to as *failure* nodes. A binary tree with external nodes added is an *extended binary tree*. Figure 9.3

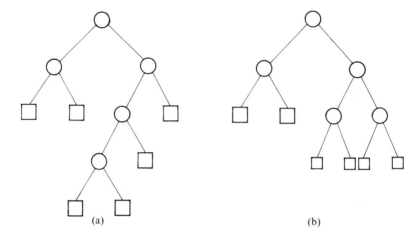

Figure 9.3 Extended binary trees corresponding to search trees of figure 9.1.

shows the extended binary trees corresponding to the search trees of figure 9.1. We define the *external path length* of a binary tree to be the sum over all external nodes of the lengths of the paths from the root to those nodes. Analogously, the *internal path length* is defined to be the sum over all internal nodes of the lengths of the paths from the root to those nodes. For the tree of figure 9.3(a) we obtain its internal path length, I, to be:

$$I = 0 + 1 + 1 + 2 + 3 = 7$$

Its external path length, E, is:

$$E = 2 + 2 + 4 + 4 + 3 + 2 = 17.$$

Exercise 1 shows that the internal and external path lengths of a binary tree with n internal nodes are related by the formula $E = I + 2n$. Hence, binary trees with the maximum E also have maximum I. Over all binary trees with n internal nodes what are the maximum and minimum possible values for I? The worst case, clearly, is when the tree is skewed (i.e., when the tree has a depth of n). In this case,

$$I = \sum_{i=0}^{n-1} i = n(n-1)/2.$$

To obtain trees with minimal I, we must have as many internal nodes as close to the root as possible. We can have at most 2 nodes at distance 1, 4 at distance 2, and in general the smallest value for I is

$$0 + 2 \cdot 1 + 4 \cdot 2 + 8 \cdot 3 + \ \ldots.$$

This can be more compactly written as

$$\sum_{1 \leq k \leq n} \lfloor \log_2 k \rfloor = O(n \log_2 n).$$

One tree with minimal internal path length is the complete binary tree defined in section 5.2.

Before attempting to use these ideas of internal and external path lengths to obtain optimal binary search trees, let us look at a related but simpler problem. We are given a set of $n + 1$ positive weights $q_1, \ldots, q_{n+1}$. Exactly one of these weights is to be associated with each of the $n + 1$ external nodes in a binary tree with n internal nodes. The *weighted external path length* of such a binary tree is defined to be $\sum_{1 \leq i \leq n+1} q_i k_i$ where k_i is the distance from the root node to the external node with weight q_i. The problem is to determine a binary tree with minimal weighted external path length. Note that here no information is contained within internal nodes.

For example, suppose $n = 3$ and we are given the four weights: $q_1 = 15$, $q_2 = 2$, $q_3 = 4$ and $q_4 = 5$. Two possible trees would be:

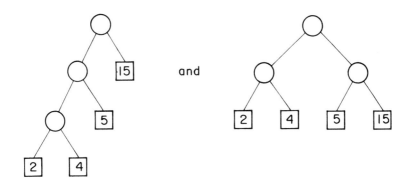

and

Their respective weighted external path lengths are:

$$2 \cdot 3 + 4 \cdot 3 + 5 \cdot 2 + 15 \cdot 1 = 43$$

and

$$2 \cdot 2 + 4 \cdot 2 + 5 \cdot 2 + 15 \cdot 2 = 52.$$

Binary trees with minimal weighted external path length find application in several areas. One application is to determine an optimal merge pattern for $n + 1$ runs using a 2-way merge. If we have four runs R_1-R_4 with q_i being the number of records in run R_i, $1 \leq i \leq 4$, then the skewed binary tree above defines the following merge pattern: merge R_2 and R_3; merge the result of this with R_4; and finally merge with R_1. Since two runs with n and m records each can be merged in time $O(n + m)$ (cf. section 7.5), the merge time following the pattern of the above skewed tree is proportional to $(q_2 + q_3) + \{(q_2 + q_3) + q_4\} + \{q_1 + q_2 + q_3 + q_4\}$. This is just the weighted external path length of the tree. In general, if the external node for run R_i is at a distance k_i from the root of the merge tree, then the cost of the merge will be proportional to $\Sigma q_i k_i$ which is the weighted external path length.

Another application of binary trees with minimal external path length is to obtain an optimal set of codes for messages $M_1, ..., M_{n+1}$. Each code is a binary string which will be used for transmission of the corresponding message. At the receiving end the code will be decoded using a decode tree. A decode tree is a binary tree in which external nodes represent messages. The binary bits in the code word for a message determine the branching needed at each level of the decode tree to reach the correct external node. For example, if we interpret a zero as a left branch and a one as a right branch, then the decode tree corresponds to codes 000, 001, 01 and 1 for messages M_1, M_2, M_3 and M_4, respectively. These codes are called Huffman codes. The cost of decoding a code word is proportional to the number of bits in the code. This number is equal to the distance of the corresponding external node from the root node. If q_i is the relative frequency with which

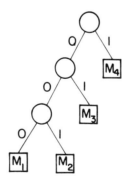

message M_i will be transmitted, then the expected decode time is $\Sigma_{1 \leq i \leq n+1} q_i d_i$ where d_i is the distance of the external node for message M_i from the root node. The expected decode time is minimized by choosing code words resulting in a decode tree with minimal weighted external path length!

A very nice solution to the problem of finding a binary tree with minimum weighted external path length has been given by D. Huffman. We simply state his algorithm and leave the correctness proof as an exercise. The following type declarations are assumed:

```
type   treepointer = ↑treerecord;
       treerecord = record
                       leftchild : treepointer;
                       weight : integer;
                       rightchild : treepointer;
                    end;
```

The algorithm *huffman* makes use of a list *l* of extended binary trees. Each node in a tree has three fields: *weight, leftchild* and *rightchild*. Initially, all trees in *l* have only one node. For each tree this node is an external node, and its weight is one of the provided q_i's. During the course of the algorithm, for any tree in *l* with root node *t* and depth greater than 1, $t \uparrow.weight$ is the sum of weights of all external nodes in *t*. Algorithm *huffman* uses the subalgorithms *least* and *insert*. *least* determines a tree in *l* with minimum *weight* and removes it from *l*. *insert* adds a new tree to the list *l*.

```
1   procedure huffman (var l : listpointer; n : integer);
2   {l is a list of n single node binary trees as described above.}
3   var t : treepointer;
4       i : integer;
5   begin
6     for i := 1 to n − 1 do        {loop n − 1 times}
7       begin
8         new(t);                    {create a new binary tree}
9         t↑.leftchild := least(l);  {by combining the trees}
10        t↑.rightchild := least(l); {with the two smallest weights}
11        t↑.weight := t↑.leftchild↑.weight + t↑.rightchild↑.weight;
12        insert(l,t);
13      end;
14  end; {of huffman}
```

Program 9.2   Huffman

We illustrate the way this algorithm works by an example. Suppose we have the weights $q_1 = 2$, $q_2 = 3$, $q_3 = 5$, $q_4 = 7$, $q_5 = 9$, $q_6 = 13$. Then the sequence of trees we would get is (the number in a circular node represents the sum of the weights of external nodes in that subtree):

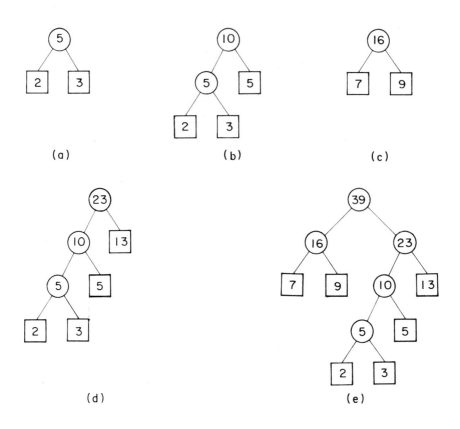

(a)   (b)   (c)

(d)   (e)

The weighted external path length of this tree is

$$2 \cdot 4 + 3 \cdot 4 + 5 \cdot 3 + 13 \cdot 2 + 7 \cdot 2 + 9 \cdot 2 = 93$$

In comparison, the best complete binary tree has weighted path length 95.

Analysis of Algorithm *huffman*

The main loop is executed $n - 1$ times. If l is maintained as a heap (section 7.6) then each call to *least* and *insert* requires only $O(\log n)$ time. Hence, the asymptotic computing time for the algorithm is $O(n \log n)$.   □

Let us now return to our original problem of representing a symbol table as a binary search tree. If the binary search tree contains the identifiers $a_1, a_2, ..., a_n$ with $a_1 < a_2 < ... < a_n$ and the probability of searching for each a_i is p_i, then the total cost of any binary search tree is $\sum_{1 \leq i \leq n} p_i \cdot$ level(a_i) when only successful searches are made. Since unsuccessful searches, i.e., searches for identifiers not in the table, will also be made, we should include the cost of these searches in our cost measure, too. Unsuccessful searches terminate with *retpointer* := **nil** in algorithm *search*. Every node with a null subtree defines a point at which such a termination can take place. Let us replace every null subtree by a failure node. The identifiers not in the binary search tree may be partitioned into $n + 1$ classes E_i, $0 \leq i \leq n$. E_0 contains all identifiers X such that $X < a_1$. E_i contains all identifiers X such that $a_i < X < a_{i+1}$, $1 \leq i < n$ and E_n contains all identifiers X, $X > a_n$. It is easy to see that for all identifiers in a particular class E_i, the search terminates at the same failure node and it terminates at different failure nodes for identifiers in different classes. The failure nodes may be numbered 0 to n with i being the failure node for class E_i, $0 \leq i \leq n$. If q_i is the probability that the identifier being searched for is in E_i, then the cost of the failure nodes is $\sum_{0 \leq i \leq n} q_i \cdot$ (level (failure node i) $- 1$). The total cost of a binary search tree is therefore:

$$\sum_{1 \leq i \leq n} p_i \cdot \text{level } (a_i) + \sum_{0 \leq i \leq n} q_i \cdot (\text{level (failure node } i) - 1) \quad (9.1)$$

An *optimal binary search tree* for the identifier set $a_1, ..., a_n$ is one which minimizes eq. (9.1) over all possible binary search trees for this identifier set. Note that since all searches must terminate either successfully or unsuccessfully we have $\sum_{1 \leq i \leq n} p_i + \sum_{0 \leq i \leq n} q_i = 1$.

Example 9.1: The possible binary search trees for the identifier set (a_1, a_2, a_3) = (**do, if, read**) are:

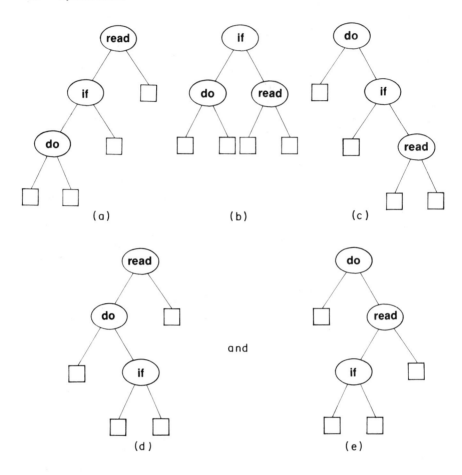

With equal probabilities $p_i = a_j = 1/7$ for all i and j we have:

cost (tree a) = 15/7; cost (tree b) = 13/7
cost (tree c) = 15/7; cost (tree d) = 15/7
cost (tree e) = 15/7.

As expected, tree b is optimal. With $p_1 = .5$, $p_2 = .1$, $p_3 = .05$, $q_0 = .15$, $q_1 = .1$, $q_2 = .05$, and $q_3 = .05$ we have

cost (tree a) = 2.65; cost (tree b) = 1.9
cost (tree c) = 1.5; cost (tree d) = 2.05
cost (tree e) = 1.6

Tree c is optimal with this assignment of p's and q's. ☐

From among all the possible binary search trees how does one determine the optimal tree? One possibility would be to proceed as in example 9.1 and explicitly generate all possible binary search trees. The cost of each such tree could be computed and an optimal tree determined. The cost of each of the binary search trees can be determined in time $O(n)$ for an n node tree. If $N(n)$ is the total number of distinct binary search trees with n identifiers, then the complexity of the algorithm becomes $O(n\ N(n))$. From section 5.9 we know that $N(n)$ grows too rapidly with increasing n to make this brute force algorithm of any practical significance. Instead we can find a fairly efficient algorithm by making some observations regarding the properties of optimal binary search trees.

Let $a_1 < a_2 < \ldots < a_n$ be the n identifiers to be represented in a binary search tree. Let us denote by T_{ij} an optimal binary search tree for $a_{i+1}, \ldots, a_j$, $i < j$. We shall adopt the convention that T_{ii} is an empty tree for $0 \le i \le n$ and that T_{ij} is not defined for $i > j$. We shall denote by c_{ij} the cost of the search tree T_{ij}. By definition c_{ii} will be 0. r_{ij} will denote the root of T_{ij} and $w_{ij} = q_i + \Sigma_{k=i+1}^{j} (q_k + p_k)$ will denote the weight of T_{ij}. By definition we will have $r_{ii} = 0$ and $w_{ii} = q_i$, $0 \le i \le n$. An optimal binary search tree for $a_1, \ldots, a_n$ is therefore T_{on}, its cost is c_{on}, its weight w_{on} and its root r_{on}.

If T_{ij} is an optimal binary search tree for $a_{i+1}, \ldots, a_j$ and $r_{ij} = k$, $i < k \le j$, then T_{ij} has two subtrees L and R. L is the left subtree and contains the identifiers $a_{i+1}, \ldots, a_{k-1}$ and R is the right subtree and contains the identifiers $a_{k+1}, \ldots, a_j$ (figure 9.4). The cost c_{ij} of T_{ij} is

$$c_{i,j} = p_k + \text{cost } (L) + \text{cost } (R) + w_{i,k-1} + w_{k,j} \qquad (9.2)$$

$$\text{weight } (L) = \text{weight } (T_{i,k-1}) = w_{i,k-1}$$

$$\text{weight } (R) = \text{weight } (T_{k,j}) = w_{k,j}$$

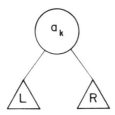

Figure 9.4 An optimal binary search tree T_{ij}.

From eq. (9.2) it is clear that if c_{ij} is to be minimal, then cost $(L) = c_{i,k-1}$ and cost $(R) = c_{k,j}$ as otherwise we could replace either L or R by a subtree of lower cost, thus getting a binary search tree for $a_{i+1}, ...,a_j$ with lower cost than c_{ij}. This would violate the assumption that T_{ij} was optimal. Hence, eq. (9.2) becomes:

$$c_{ij} = p_k + w_{i,k-1} + w_{k,j} + c_{i,k-1} + c_{k,j}$$
$$= w_{i,j} + c_{i,k-1} + c_{k,j} \qquad (9.3)$$

Since T_{ij} is optimal it follows from eq. (9.3) that $r_{ij} = k$ is such that

$$w_{ij} + c_{i,k-1} + c_{k,j} = \min_{i<l\leq j} \{w_{ij} + c_{i,l-1} + c_{l,j}\}$$

or

$$c_{i,k-1} + c_{k,j} = \min_{i<l\leq j} \{c_{i,l-1} + c_{l,j}\} \qquad (9.4)$$

Equation (9.4) gives us a means of obtaining T_{on} and c_{on} starting from the knowledge that $T_{ii} = \phi$ and $c_{ii} = 0$.

Example 9.2: Let $n = 4$ and $(a_1,a_2,a_3,a_4) = $ (**do, if, read, while**). Let $(p_1,p_2,p_3,p_4) = (3,3,1,1)$ and $(q_0,q_1,q_2,q_3,q_4) = (2,3,1,1,1)$. The p's and q's have been multiplied by 16 for convenience. Initially, we have $w_{i,i} = q_i$, $c_{ii} = 0$ and $r_{ii} = 0$, $0 \leq i \leq 4$. Using eqs. (9.3) and (9.4) we get:

$$w_{01} = p_1 + w_{00} + w_{11} = p_1 + q_1 + w_{00} = 8$$
$$c_{01} = w_{01} + \min \{c_{00} + c_{11}\} = 8$$
$$r_{01} = 1$$
$$w_{12} = p_2 + w_{11} + w_{22} = p_2 + q_2 + w_{11} = 7$$
$$c_{12} = w_{12} + \min \{c_{11} + c_{22}\} = 7$$
$$r_{12} = 2$$
$$w_{23} = p_3 + w_{22} + w_{33} = p_3 + q_3 + w_{22} = 3$$
$$c_{23} = w_{23} + \min \{c_{22} + c_{33}\} = 3$$
$$r_{23} = 3$$
$$w_{34} = p_4 + w_{33} + w_{44} = p_4 + q_4 + w_{33} = 3$$
$$c_{34} = w_{34} + \min \{c_{33} + c_{44}\} = 3$$
$$r_{34} = 4$$

Knowing $w_{i,i+1}$ and $c_{i,i+1}$, $0 \le i < 4$ we can again use equations (9.3) and (9.4) to compute $w_{i,i+2}$, $c_{i,i+2}$, $r_{i,i+2}$, $0 \le i < 3$. This process may be repeated until w_{04}, c_{04} and r_{04} are obtained. The table of figure 9.5 shows the results of this computation. From the table we see that $c_{04} = 32$ is the minimal cost of a binary search tree for a_1 to a_4. The root of tree T_{04} is a_2. Hence, the left subtree is T_{01} and the right subtree T_{24}. T_{01} has root a_1 and subtrees T_{00} and T_{11}. T_{24} has root a_3; its left subtree is therefore T_{22} and right subtree T_{34}. Thus, with the data in the table it is possible to reconstruct T_{04}. Figure 9.6 shows T_{04}.   □

	0	1	2	3	4
0	$w_{00} = 2$ $c_{00} = 0$ $r_{00} = 0$	$w_{11} = 3$ $c_{11} = 0$ $r_{11} = 0$	$w_{22} = 1$ $c_{22} = 0$ $r_{22} = 0$	$w_{33} = 1$ $c_{33} = 0$ $r_{33} = 0$	$w_{44} = 1$ $c_{44} = 0$ $r_{44} = 0$
1	$w_{01} = 8$ $c_{01} = 8$ $r_{01} = 1$	$w_{12} = 7$ $c_{12} = 7$ $r_{12} = 2$	$w_{23} = 3$ $c_{23} = 3$ $r_{23} = 3$	$w_{34} = 3$ $c_{34} = 3$ $r_{34} = 4$	
2	$w_{02} = 12$ $c_{02} = 19$ $r_{02} = 1$	$w_{13} = 9$ $c_{13} = 12$ $r_{13} = 2$	$w_{24} = 5$ $c_{24} = 8$ $r_{24} = 3$		
3	$w_{03} = 14$ $c_{03} = 25$ $r_{03} = 2$	$w_{14} = 11$ $c_{14} = 19$ $r_{14} = 2$			
4	$w_{04} = 16$ $c_{04} = 32$ $r_{04} = 2$				

Figure 9.5 Computation of c_{04}, and r_{04}. The computation is carried out row wise from row 0 to row 4.

The above example illustrates how equation (9.4) may be used to determine the c's and r's and also how to reconstruct T_{on} knowing the r's. Let us examine the complexity of this procedure to evaluate the c's and r's. The evaluation procedure described in the above example requires us to compute c_{ij} for $(j - i) = 1,2, ...,n$ in that order. When $j - i = m$ there are $n - m + 1$ c_{ij}'s to compute. The computation of each of these c_{ij}'s requires us to

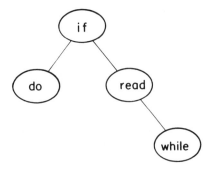

Figure 9.6 Optimal search tree for example 9.2.

find the minimum of m quantities (see equation (9.4)). Hence, each such c_{ij} can be computed in time $O(m)$. The total time for all c_{ij}'s with $j - i = m$ is therefore $O(nm - m^2)$. The total time to evaluate all the c_{ij}'s and r_{ij}'s is therefore

$$\Sigma_{1 \le m \le n} (nm - m^2) = O(n^3).$$

Actually we can do better than this using a result due to D. E. Knuth which states that the optimal l in equation (9.4) may be found by limiting the search to the range $r_{i,j-1} \le l \le r_{i+1,j}$. In this case the computing time becomes $O(n^2)$ (exercise 4). Algorithm *obst* (Program 9.3) uses this result to obtain in $O(n^2)$ time the values of w_{ij}, r_{ij} and c_{ij}, $0 \le i \le j \le n$. The actual tree T_{on} may be constructed from the values of r_{ij} in $O(n)$ time. The algorithm for this is left as an exercise. The datatypes used by *obst* are as:

> **type** *identifier* = **packed array** [1..*maxchar*] **of char**;
> *identarray* = **array**[1..*n*] **of** *identifier*;
> *parray* = **array**[1..*n*] **of integer**;
> *qarray* = **array**[0..*n*] **of integer**;
> *carray* = **array**[0..*n*,0..*n*] **of integer**;

```
1  procedure obst (p:parray; q:qarray; a:identarray; var c,r,w:carray);
2  {Given n distinct identifiers a₁ < a₂ < ... < aₙ and probabilities
3   pⱼ, 1 ≤ i ≤ n and qᵢ, 0 ≤ i ≤ n this algorithm computes the
4   cost cᵢⱼ of optimal binary search trees tᵢⱼ for identifiers aᵢ₊₁, ...,aⱼ.
5   It also computes rᵢⱼ, the root of tᵢⱼ. wᵢⱼ is the weight of tᵢⱼ.}
6  var i,j,k,l,m : integer;
7  begin
8    for i := 0 to n − 1 do
9      begin
10       w[i,i] := q[i]; r[i,i] := 0; c[i,i] := 0; {initialize}
11       w[i, i + 1] := q[i] + q[i + 1] + p[i + 1]; {optimal trees with one
                                                                node}
12       r[i, i + 1] := i + 1;
13       c[i, i + 1] := q[i] + q[i + 1] + p[i + 1];
14     end;
15   w[n,n] := q[n]; r[n,n] := 0; c[n,n] := 0;
16   for m := 2 to n do {find optimal trees with m nodes}
17     for i := 0 to n − m do
18       begin
19         j := i + m;
20         w[i,j] := w[i, j − 1] + p[j] + q[j];
21         k := knuthmin (c,r,i,j);
22         {knuthmin returns a value k in the range [r[i, j − 1],
23          r[i + 1,j] minimizing c[i, k − 1] + c[k,j]}
24         c[i,j] := w[i,j] + c[i, k − 1] + c[k,j]; {eq. (9.3)}
25         r[i,j] := k
26       end;
27   end; {of obst}
```

Program 9.3   Obst

9.2 DYNAMIC TREE TABLES

Dynamic tables may also be maintained as binary search trees. An identifier x may be inserted into a binary search tree t by using the search algorithm of the previous section to determine the failure node corresponding to x. This gives the position in t where the insertion is to be made. Figure 9.7 shows the binary search tree obtained by entering the months JANUARY to DECEMBER in that order into an initially empty binary search tree. Algorithm *bst*, program 9.4 is a more formal rendition of the insertion process just described.

```
1   procedure bst (x : identifier; var t,retpointer : treepointer);
2   {Search the binary search tree t for the node pointed to by
3   retpointer such that retpointer↑.ident = x. If x is not already
4   in the tree then it is entered at the appropriate point.
5   The data types are as defined for Program 7.1.}
6   var trailpointer : treepointer;
7        found : boolean;
8   begin
9     trailpointer := nil; {trailpointer will trail retpointer through the tree}
10    retpointer := t;
11    found := false;
12    while (retpointer < > nil) and (not found ) do
13       begin
14         if x < retpointer↑.ident then {search left subtree}
15            begin
16              trailpointer := retpointer;
17              retpointer := retpointer↑.leftchild;
18            end
19         else if x > retpointer↑.ident then {search right subtree}
20            begin
21              trailpointer := retpointer;
22              retpointer := retpointer↑.rightchild;
23            end
24         else
25            found := true;
26       end;
27    if not found then
28       begin {x not in tree and can be entered as child of trailpointer}
29         new (retpointer); retpointer↑.ident := x;
30         retpointer↑.leftchild := nil;
31         retpointer↑.rightchild := nil;
32         if t = nil then {insert into empty tree}
33            t := retpointer
34         else if x < trailpointer↑.ident then
35            trailpointer↑.leftchild := retpointer
36         else
37            trailpointer↑.rightchild := retpointer;
38       end;
39   end; {of bst}
```

Program 9.4   Bst

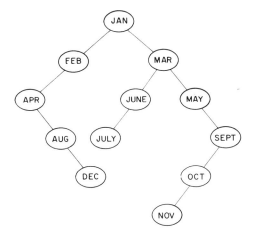

Figure 9.7 Binary search tree obtained for the months of the year.

The maximum number of comparisons needed to search for any identifier in the tree of figure 9.7 is six for NOVEMBER. The average number of comparisons is (1 for JANUARY + 2 each for FEBRUARY and MARCH + 3 each for APRIL, JUNE and MAY + ... + 6 for NOVEMBER)/12 = $42/12 = 3.5$. If the months are entered in the order JULY, FEBRUARY, MAY, AUGUST, DECEMBER, MARCH, OCTOBER, APRIL, JANUARY, JUNE, SEPTEMBER and NOVEMBER then the tree of figure 9.8 is obtained. This tree is well balanced and does not have any paths to a node with a null link that are much longer than others. This is not true of the tree of figure 9.7 which has six nodes on the path from the root to NOVEMBER and only two nodes, JANUARY and FEBRUARY, on another path to a null link. Moreover, during the construction of the tree of figure 9.8 all intermediate trees obtained are also well balanced. The maximum number of identifier comparisons needed to find any identifier is now 4 and the average is $37/12 \approx 3.1$. If instead the months are entered in lexicographic order, the tree degenerates to a chain as in figure 9.9. The maximum search time is now 12 identifier comparisons and the average is 6.5. Thus, in the worst case, binary search trees correspond to sequential searching in an ordered file. When the identifiers are entered in a random order, the tree tends to be balanced as in figure 9.8. If all permutations are equiprobable then it can be shown the average search and insertion time is $O(\log n)$ for an n node binary search tree.

From our earlier study of binary trees, we know that both the average and maximum search time will be minimized if the binary search tree is

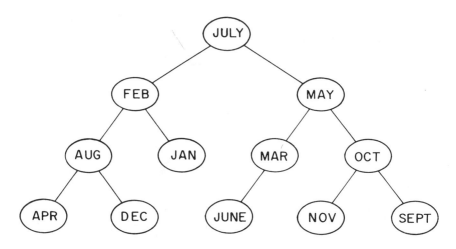

Figure 9.8 A balanced tree for the months of the year.

maintained as a complete binary tree at all times. However, since we are dealing with a dynamic situation, identifiers are being searched for while the table is being built and so it is difficult to achieve this ideal without making the time required to add new entries very high. This is so because in some cases it would be necessary to restructure the whole tree to accommodate the new entry and at the same time have a complete binary search tree. It is, however, possible to keep the trees balanced so as to ensure both an average and worst case retrieval time of $O(\log n)$ for a tree with n nodes. We shall study one method of growing balanced binary trees. These balanced trees will have satisfactory search and insertion time properties.

Height Balanced Binary Trees

Adelson-Velskii and Landis in 1962 introduced a binary tree structure that is balanced with respect to the heights of subtrees. As a result of the balanced nature of this type of tree, dynamic retrievals can be performed in $O(\log n)$ time if the tree has n nodes in it. At the same time a new identifier can be entered or deleted from such a tree in time $O(\log n)$. The resulting tree remains height balanced. The tree structure introduced by them is given the name AVL-tree. As with binary trees it is natural to define AVL trees recursively.

Definition: An empty tree is height balanced. If T is a nonempty binary tree with T_L and T_R as its left and right subtrees, then T is *height balanced* iff (i) T_L and T_R are height balanced and (ii) $|h_L - h_R| \leq 1$ where h_L and h_R are the heights of T_L and T_R, respectively.

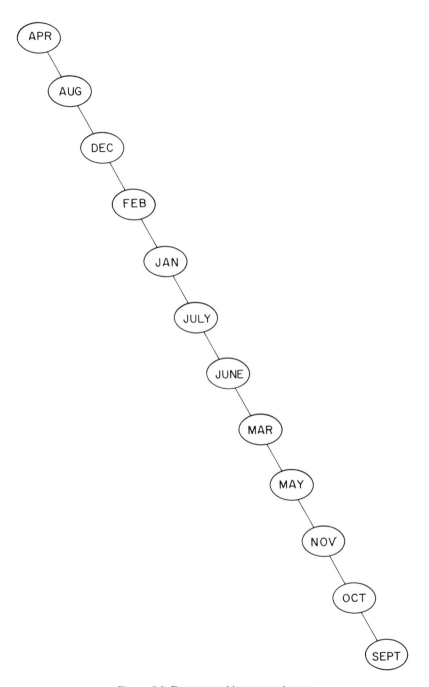

Figure 9.9 Degenerate binary search tree.

The definition of a height balanced binary tree requires that every subtree also be height balanced. The binary tree of figure 9.7 is not height balanced since the height of the left subtree of the tree with root 'APRIL' is 0 while that of the right subtree is 2. The tree of figure 9.8 is height balanced while that of figure 9.9 is not. To illustrate the processes involved in maintaining a height balanced binary search tree, let us try to construct such a tree for the months of the year. This time let us assume that the insertions are made in the order MARCH, MAY, NOVEMBER, AUGUST, APRIL, JANUARY, DECEMBER, JULY, FEBRUARY, JUNE, OCTOBER and SEPTEMBER. Figure 9.10 shows the tree as it grows and the restructuring involved in keeping the tree balanced. The numbers within each node represent the difference in heights between the left and right subtrees of that node. This number is referred to as the balance factor of the node.

Definition: The *balance factor, BF(T)*, of a node T in a binary tree is defined to be $h_L - h_R$ where h_L and h_R are the heights of the left and right subtrees of T. For any node T in an AVL tree $BF(T) = -1, 0$ or 1.

Inserting MARCH and MAY results in the binary search trees (i) and (ii) of figure 9.10. When NOVEMBER is inserted into the tree, the height of the right subtree of MARCH becomes 2, while that of the left subtree is 0. The tree has become unbalanced. In order to rebalance the tree, a rotation is performed. MARCH is made the left child of MAY and MAY becomes the root. The introduction of AUGUST leaves the tree balanced. However, the next insertion, APRIL, causes the tree to become unbalanced again. To rebalance the tree, another rotation is performed. This time, it is a clockwise rotation. MARCH is made the right child of AUGUST and AUGUST becomes the root of the subtree (figure 9.10(v)). Note that both the previous rotations were carried out with respect to the closest parent of the new node having a balance factor of ±2. The insertion of JANUARY results in an unbalanced tree. This time, however, the rotation involved is somewhat more complex than in the earlier situations. The common point, however, is that it is still carried out with respect to the nearest parent of JANUARY with balance factor ±2. MARCH becomes the new root. AUGUST together with its left subtree becomes the left subtree of MARCH. The left subtree of MARCH becomes the right subtree of AUGUST. MAY and its right subtree, which have identifiers greater than MARCH, become the right subtree of MARCH. If MARCH had a nonempty right subtree, this could have become the left subtree of MAY since all identifiers would have been less than MAY. Inserting DECEMBER and JULY necessitates no rebalancing. When FEBRUARY is inserted the tree again becomes unbalanced. The rebalancing process is very similar to that used when JANUARY was inserted. The nearest parent with balance factor ±2 is AUGUST. DECEMBER becomes the new root of that subtree.

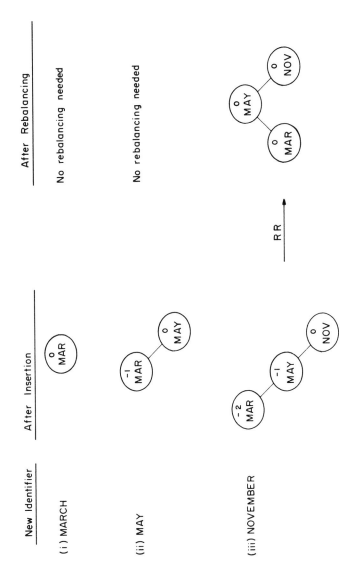

Figure 9.10 Balanced trees obtained for the months of the year.

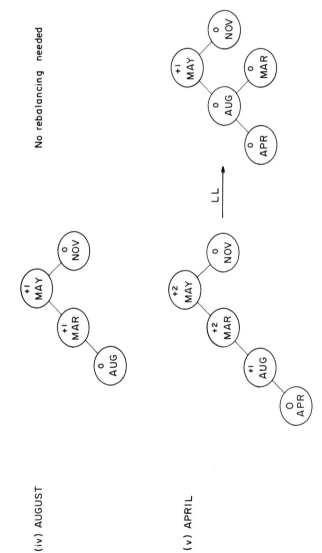

No rebalancing needed

(iv) AUGUST

(v) APRIL

Figure 9.10 (continued)

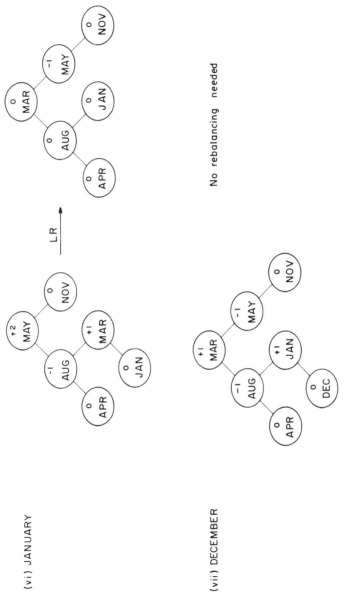

(vi) JANUARY

LR →

No rebalancing   needed

(vii) DECEMBER

Figure 9.10 (continued)

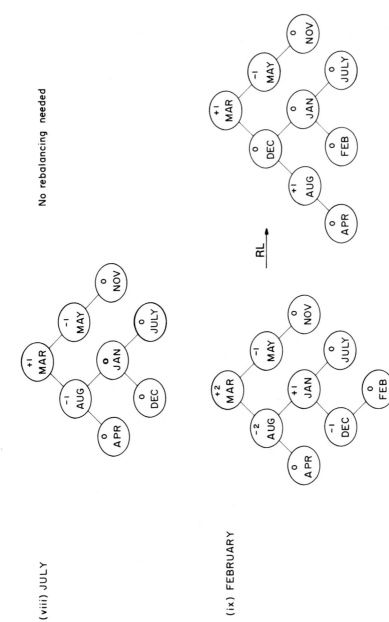

No rebalancing needed

(viii) JULY

(ix) FEBRUARY

RL

Figure 9.10 (continued)

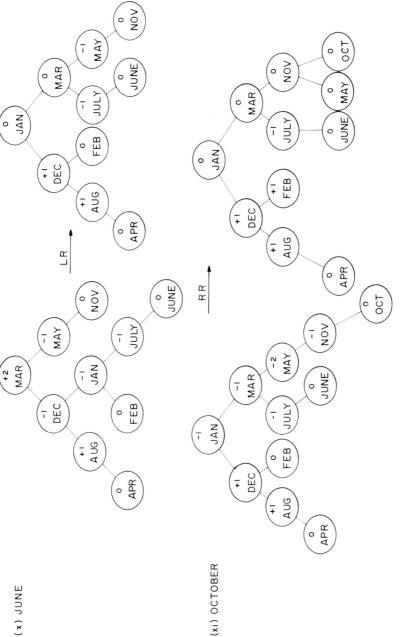

(x) JUNE

(xi) OCTOBER

Figure 9.10 (continued)

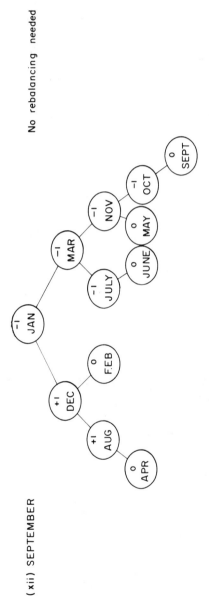

(xii) SEPTEMBER

No rebalancing needed

Figure 9.10 (continued)

AUGUST with its left subtree becomes the left subtree. JANUARY and its right subtree becomes the right subtree of DECEMBER, while FEBRUARY becomes the left subtree of JANUARY. If DECEMBER had had a left subtree, it would have become the right subtree of AUGUST. The insertion of JUNE requires the same rebalancing as in figure 9.10(vi). The rebalancing following the insertion of OCTOBER is identical to that following the insertion of NOVEMBER. Inserting SEPTEMBER leaves the tree balanced.

In the preceding example we saw that the addition of a node to a balanced binary search tree could unbalance it. The rebalancing was carried out using essentially four different kinds of rotations LL, RR, LR and RL (figure 9.10 (v), (iii), (vi) and (ix) respectively). LL and RR are symmetric as are LR and RL. These rotations are characterized by the nearest ancestor, A, of the inserted node, Y, whose balance factor becomes ± 2. The following characterization of rotation types is obtained:

LL: new node Y is inserted in the left subtree of the left subtree of A
LR: Y is inserted in the right subtree of the left subtree of A
RR: Y is inserted in the right subtree of the right subtree of A
RL: Y is inserted in the left subtree of the right subtree of A

Figures 9.11 and 9.12 show these rotations in terms of abstract binary trees. The root node in each of the trees of the figures represents the nearest ancestor whose balance factor has become ± 2 as a result of the insertion. A moment's reflection will show that if a height balanced binary tree becomes unbalanced as a result of an insertion then these are the only four cases possible for rebalancing (if a moment's reflection doesn't convince you, then try exercise 6). In both the example of figure 9.10 and the rotations of figures 9.11 and 9.12, notice that the height of the subtree involved in the rotation is the same after rebalancing as it was before the insertion. This means that once the rebalancing has been carried out on the subtree in question, it is not necessary to examine the remaining tree. The only nodes whose balance factors can change are those in the subtree that is rotated.

In order to be able to carry out the rebalancing of figures 9.11 and 9.12 it is necessary to locate the node A around which the rotation is to be performed. As remarked earlier, this is the nearest ancestor of the newly inserted node whose balance factor becomes ± 2. In order for a node's balance factor to become ± 2, its balance factor must have been ± 1 before the insertion. Furthermore, the nearest ancestor whose balance factor becomes ± 2 is also the nearest ancestor with balance factor ± 1 before the insertion. Therefore, before the insertion, the balance factors of all nodes on the path from A to the new insertion point must have been 0. With this information, the node A is readily determined to be the nearest ancestor of the new node

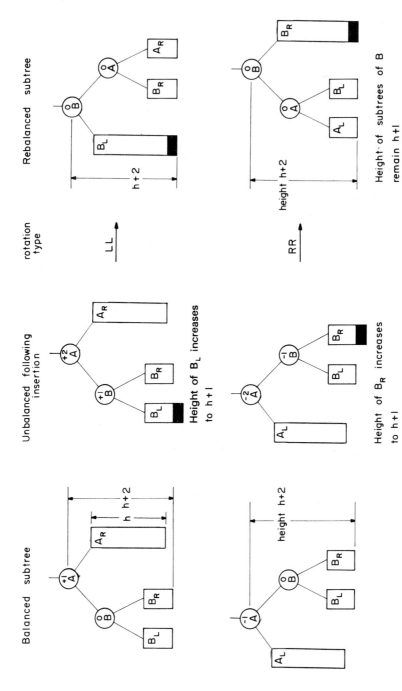

Figure 9.11 Rebalancing rotations of type *LL* and *RR*.

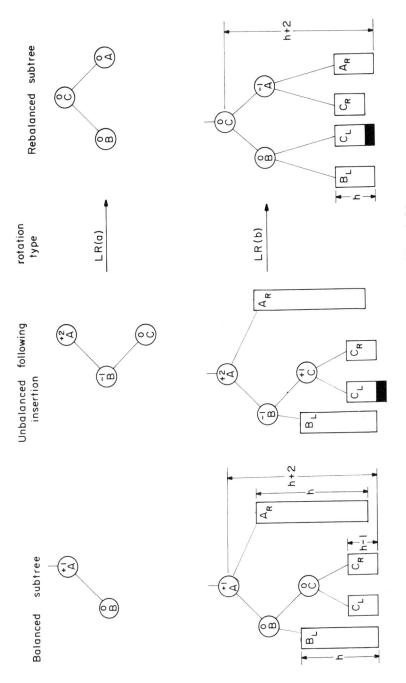

Figure 9.12 Rebalancing rotations of type *LR* and *RL*.

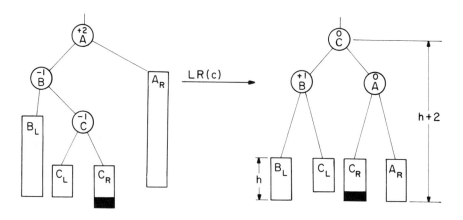

RL a,b and c are symmetric to LR a,b and c (see exercise (6))

Figure 9.12 (continued)

having a balance factor ± 1 before insertion. To complete the rotations the address of F, the parent of A, is also needed. The changes in the balance factors of the relevant nodes are shown in figures 9.11 and 9.12. Knowing F and A, all these changes can easily be carried out. What happens when the insertion of a node does not result in an unbalanced tree (figure 9.10 (i), (ii), (iv), (vii), (viii) and (xii))? While no restructuring of the tree is needed, the balance factors of several nodes change. Let A be the nearest ancestor of the new node with balance factor ± 1 before insertion. If as a result of the insertion the tree did not get unbalanced even though some path length increased by 1, it must be that the new balance factor of A is 0. In case there is no ancestor A with balance factor ± 1 (as in figure 9.10 (i), (ii), (iv), (vii) and (xii)), let A be the root. The balance factors of nodes from A to the parent of the new node will change to ± 1 (see figure 9.10 (viii), $A =$ JANUARY). Note that in both cases the procedure for determining A is the same as when rebalancing is needed. The remaining details of the insertion-rebalancing process are spelled out in algorithm *avlinsert*, program 9.5. The type definitions in use are:

type *identifier* = **packed array** [1..*maxchar*] **of char**;
    treepointer = ↑*treerecord*;
    treerecord = **record**
                leftchild : *treepointer*;
                ident : *identifier*;
                rightchild : *treepointer*;
                bf : $-1..1$;
        end;

In order to really understand the insertion algorithm, the reader should try it out on the example of figure 9.10. Once you are convinced that it does keep the tree balanced, then the next question is how much time does it take to make an insertion? An analysis of the algorithm reveals that if h is the height of the tree before insertion, then the time to insert a new identifier is $O(h)$. This is the same as for unbalanced binary search trees, though the overhead is significantly greater now. In the case of binary search trees, however, if there were n nodes in the tree, then h could in the worst case be n (figure 9.9) and the worst case insertion time was $O(n)$. In the case of AVL trees, however, h can be at most $O(\log n)$ and so the worst case insertion time is $O(\log n)$. To see this, let N_h be the minimum number of nodes in a height balanced tree of height h. In the worst case, the height of one of the subtrees will be $h-1$ and of the other $h-2$. Both these subtrees are also height balanced. Hence, $N_h = N_{h-1} + N_{h-2} + 1$ and $N_0 = 0$, $N_1 = 1$ and $N_2 = 2$. Note the similarity between this recursive definition for N_h and that for the Fibonacci numbers $F_n = F_{n-1} + F_{n-2}$, $F_0 = 0$ and $F_1 = 1$. In fact, we can show (exercise 16) that $N_h = F_{h+2} - 1$ for $h \geq 0$. From Fibonacci number theory it is known that $F_h \approx \phi^h / \sqrt{5}$ where $\phi = (1 + \sqrt{5})/2$. Hence, $N_h \approx \phi^{h+2} / \sqrt{5} - 1$. This means that if there are n nodes in the tree, then its height, h, is at most $\log\phi\,(\sqrt{5}\,(n+1)) - 2$. The worst case insertion time for a height balanced tree with n nodes is, therefore, $O(\log n)$.

```
1   procedure avlinsert(x : identifier; var y,t : treepointer);
2   {the identifier x is inserted into the AVL tree with root t.
3    Each node is assumed to have an identifier field ident, left
4    and right child fields leftchild and rightchild and a two bit
5    balance factor field bf. p↑.bf = height of p↑.leftchild -
6    height of p↑.rightchild. y is set such that y↑.ident = x.}
7   var a,b,c,f,p,q,clchild,crchild : treepointer;
8       found, unbalanced : boolean;
9       d : integer;
10  begin {avlinsert}
11    if t = nil then {special case: empty tree t = 0}
12      begin
13        new(y); y↑.ident := x; t := y; t↑.bf := 0;
14        t↑.leftchild := nil; t↑.rightchild := nil;
15      end
16    else
17      begin
18        {phase 1: Locate insertion point for x. a keeps track of
19         most recent node with balance factor ± 1 and f is the
20         parent of a. q follows p through the tree.}
```

```
21        f := nil; a := t; p := t; q := nil; found := false;
22        while (p < > nil) and (not found) do
23            begin {search t for insertion point for x}
24                if p↑.bf < > 0 then
25                begin
26                    a := p; f := q;
27                end;
28                if x < p↑.ident then {take left branch}
29                    begin
30                        q := p; p := p↑.leftchild;
31                    end
32                else if x > p↑.ident then {take right branch}
33                    begin
34                        q := p; p := p↑.rightchild;
35                    end
36                else                        {x is in t}
37                    begin
38                        y := p; found := true;
39                    end;
40            end; {of while}
41        if not found then
42            begin
43                {phase 2: insert and rebalance. x is not in t and
44                may be inserted as the appropriate child of q.}
45                new(y); y↑.ident := x; y↑.leftchild := nil;
46                y↑.rightchild := nil; y↑.bf := 0;
47                if x < q↑.ident then {insert as leftchild}
48                                q↑.leftchild := y
49                            else {insert as rightchild}
50                                q↑.rightchild := y;
51                {adjust balance factors of nodes on path from a to q.
52                note that by the definition of a, all nodes on this
53                path must have balance factors of 0 and so will change
54                to ±1. d = + 1 implies x is inserted in left subtree
55                of a. d = − 1 implies x is inserted in right subtree of a.}
56                if x > a↑.ident then
57                    begin
58                        p := a↑.rightchild; b := p; d := −1;
59                    end
60                else
61                    begin
62                        p := a↑.leftchild; b := p; d := +1;
63                    end;
```

```
64      while p < > y do
65          if x > p↑.ident then {height of right increases by 1}
66              begin
67                  p↑.bf := −1; p := p↑.rightchild;
68              end
69          else                        {height of left increases by 1}
70              begin
71                  p↑.bf := +1; p := p↑.leftchild;
72              end;
73      {Is tree unbalanced?}
74      unbalanced := true;
75      if a↑.bf = 0 then {tree still balanced}
76          begin
77              a↑.bf := d; unbalanced := false;
78          end;
79      if a↑.bf + d = 0 then {tree still balanced}
80          begin
81              a↑.bf := 0; unbalanced := false;
82          end;
83      if unbalanced then {tree unbalanced, determine rotation
                                                            type}
84          begin
85              if d = +1 then {left imbalance}
86                  begin
87                      if b↑.bf = +1 then {rotation type LL}
88                          begin
89                              a↑.leftchild := b↑.rightchild;
90                              b↑.rightchild := a; a↑.bf := 0; b↑.bf := 0;
91                          end
92                      else
93                          begin
94                              c := b↑.rightchild;
95                              b↑.rightchild := c↑.leftchild;
96                              a↑.leftchild := c↑.rightchild;
97                              c↑.leftchild := b;
98                              c↑.rightchild := a;
99                              case c↑.bf of
100                                 +1 : begin {LR(b)}
101                                         a↑.bf := −1; b↑.bf := 0;
102                                     end;
103                                 −1 : begin {LR(c)}
104                                         b↑.bf := 1; a↑.bf := 0;
105                                     end;
```

```
106                                 0 : begin {LR(a)}
107                                       b↑.bf := 0; a↑.bf := 0;
108                                     end;
109                                 end;
110                                 c↑.bf := 0; b := c; {b is a new root}
111                               end; {of if b↑.bf = +1}
112                             end {of then left imbalance}
113                         else {right imbalance; this is symmetric to left
114                               imbalance and is left as an exercise.}
115                           begin
116                           end;
117                         {Subtree with root b has been rebalanced and
118                         is the new subtree.}
119                         if f = nil then
120                           t := b
121                         else if a = f↑.leftchild then
122                                       f↑.leftchild := b
123                         else if a = f↑.rightchild then
124                                       f↑.rightchild := b;
125                   end; {of if unbalanced}
126           end; {of if not found}
127       end; {of if t = nil}
128   end; {of avlinsert}
```

Program 9.5   Avlinsert

Exercises 9-13 show that it is possible to find and delete a node with identifier X and to find and delete the k-th node from a height balanced tree in $O(\log n)$ time. Results of an empirical study of deletion in height balanced trees may be found in the paper by Karlton, et.al. (see the references). Their study indicates that a random insertion requires no rebalancing, a rebalancing rotation of type LL or RR and a rebalancing rotation of type LR and RL with probabilities .5349, .2327 and .2324, respectively. Table 9.12 compares the worst case times of certain operations on sorted sequential lists, sorted linked lists and AVL-trees. Other suitable balanced tree schemes are studied in Chapter 10.

9.3   HASH TABLES

In tree tables, the search for an identifier key is carried out via a sequence of comparisons. Hashing differs from this in that the address or location of an identifier, X, is obtained by computing some arithmetic function, f, of

Operation	Sequential List	Linked List	AVL-Tree
Search for X	O(log n)	O(n)	O(log n)
Search for k^{th} item	O(1)	O(k)	O(log n)
Delete X	O(n)	O(1) (doubly linked list and position of X known)	O(log n)
Delete k^{th} item	O(n − k)	O(k)	O(log n)
Insert X	O(n)	O(1) (if position for insertion is known)	O(log n)
Output in order	O(n)	O(n)	O(n)

Table 9.12   Comparison of various structures

X. $f(X)$ gives the address of X in the table. This address will be referred to as the hash or home address of X. The memory available to maintain the symbol table is assumed to be sequential. This memory is referred to as the hash table, ht. The hash table is partitioned into b buckets, $ht[0]$, ...,$ht[b−1]$. Each bucket is capable of holding s records. Thus, a bucket is said to consist of s slots, each slot being large enough to hold one record. Usually $s = 1$ and each bucket can hold exactly one record. A hashing function, $f(X)$, is used to perform an identifier transformation on X. $f(X)$ maps the set of possible identifiers onto the integers 0 through $b − 1$. If the identifiers were drawn from the set of all legal Fortran variable names then there would be $T = \Sigma_{0 \le i \le 5} 26 \times 36^i > 1.6 \times 10^9$ distinct possible values for X. Any reasonable program, however, would use far less than all of these identifiers. The ratio n/T is the *identifier density*, while $\alpha = n/(sb)$ is the *loading density* or *loading factor*. Since the number of identifiers, n, in use is usually several orders of magnitude less than the total number of possible identifiers, T, the number of buckets, b, in the hash table is also much less than T. Therefore, the hash function f must map several different identifiers into the same bucket. Two identifiers I_1, I_2 are said to be *synonyms* with respect to f if $f(I_1) = f(I_2)$. Distinct synonyms are entered into the same bucket so long as all the s slots in that bucket have not been used. An *overflow* is said to occur when a new identifier I is mapped or hashed by f into a full bucket. A *collision* occurs when two nonidentical identifiers are hashed into the same bucket. When the bucket size s is 1, collisions and overflows occur simultaneously.

As an example, let us consider the hash table ht with $b = 26$ buckets, each bucket having exactly two slots, i.e., $s = 2$. Assume that there are $n = 10$ distinct identifiers in the program and that each identifier begins with a letter. The loading factor, α, for this table is $10/52 = 0.19$. The hash function f must map each of the possible identifiers into one of the numbers 1-26. If the internal binary representation for the letters A-Z corresponds to the numbers 1-26, respectively, then the function f defined by $f(X) =$ the first character of X will hash all identifiers X into the hash table. The identifiers GA, D, A, G, L, $A2$, $A1$, $A3$, $A4$ and E will be hashed into buckets 7, 4, 1, 7, 12, 1, 1, 1, 1 and 5, respectively, by this function. The identifiers A, $A1$, $A2$, $A3$ and $A4$ are synonyms. So also are G and GA. Figure 9.13 shows the identifiers GA, D, A, G, and $A2$ entered into the hash table. Note that GA and G are in the same bucket and each bucket has two slots. Similarly, the synonyms A and $A2$ are in the same bucket. The next identifier, $A1$, hashes into the bucket $ht[1]$. This bucket is full and a search of the bucket indicates that $A1$ is not in the bucket. An overflow has now occurred. Where in the table should $A1$ be entered so that it may be retrieved when needed? We will look into overflow handling strategies in section 9.3.2. In the case where no overflows occur, the time required to enter or search for identifiers using hashing depends only on the time required to compute the hash function f and the time to search one bucket. Since the bucket size s is usually small (for internal tables s is usually 1) the search for an identifier within a bucket is carried out using sequential search. The time, then, is independent of n, the number of identifiers in use. For tree tables, this time was, on the average, $\log n$. The hash function in the above example is not very well suited for the use we have in mind because of the very large number of collisions and resulting overflows that occur. This is so because it is not unusual to find programs in which many of the variables begin with the same letter. Ideally, we would like to choose a function f which is both easy to compute and results in very few colli-

	SLOT 1	SLOT 2
1	A	A2
2	0	0
3	0	0
4	D	0
5	0	0
6	0	0
7	GA	G
⋮	⋮	⋮
26	0	0

Zeros indicate empty slots

Figure 9.13 Hash table with 26 buckets and two slots per bucket.

sions. Since the ratio b/T is usually very small, it is impossible to avoid collisions altogether.

In summary, hashing schemes perform an identifier transformation through the use of a hash function f. It is desirable to choose a function f which is easily computed and also minimizes the number of collisions. Since the size of the identifier space, T, is usually several orders of magnitude larger than the number of buckets b, and s is small, overflows necessarily occur. Hence a mechanism to handle overflows is also needed.

9.3.1 Hashing Functions

A hashing function, f, transforms an identifier X into a bucket address in the hash table. As mentioned earlier the desired properties of such a function are that it be easily computable and that it minimize the number of collisions. A function such as the one discussed earlier is not a very good choice for a hash function for symbol tables even though it is fairly easy to compute. The reason for this is that it depends only on the first character in the identifier. Since many programs use several identifiers with the same first letter, we expect several collisions to occur. In general, then, we would like the function to depend upon all the characters in the identifiers. In addition, we would like the hash function to be such that it does not result in a biased use of the hash table for random inputs; i.e., if X is an identifier chosen at random from the identifier space, then we want the probability that $f(X) = i$ to be $1/b$ for all buckets i. Then a random X has an equal chance of hashing into any of the b buckets. A hash function satisfying this property will be termed a *uniform hash function*.

Several kinds of uniform hash functions are in use. We shall describe four of these.

(i) Mid-Square

One hash function that has found much use in symbol table applications is the 'middle of square' function. This function, f_m, is computed by squaring the identifier and then using an appropriate number of bits from the middle of the square to obtain the bucket address; the identifier is assumed to fit into one computer word. Since the middle bits of the square will usually depend upon all of the characters in the identifier, it is expected that different identifiers would result in different hash addresses with high probability even when some of the characters are the same. Figure 9.14 shows the bit configurations resulting from squaring some sample identifiers. The number of bits to be used to obtain the bucket address depends on the table size. If r bits are used, the range of values is 2^r, so the size of hash tables is chosen to be a power of 2 when this kind of scheme is used.

IDENTIFIER	INTERNAL REPRESENTATION	
X	X	X²
A	1	1
A1	134	20420
A2	135	20711
A3	136	21204
A4	137	21501
A9	144	23420
B	2	4
C	3	11
G	7	61
DMAX	4150130	21526443617100
DMAX1	415013034	5264473522151420
AMAX	1150130	1345423617100
AMAX1	115013034	3454246522151420

Figure 9.14   Internal representations of X and X^2 in octal notation. X is input right justified, zero filled, six bits or 2 octal digits per character.

(ii) Division

Another simple choice for a hash function is obtained by using the modulo (**mod**) operator. The identifier X is divided by some number M and the remainder is used as the hash address for X.

$$f_D(X) = X \bmod M$$

This gives bucket addresses in the range $0 - (M - 1)$ and so the hash table is at least of size $b = M$. The choice of M is critical. If M is a power of 2, then $f_D(X)$ depends only on the least significant bits of X. For instance, if each character is represented by six bits and identifiers are stored right justified in a 60-bit word with leading bits filled with zeros (figure 9.15) then with $M = 2^i$, $i \le 6$ the identifiers $A1$, $B1$, $C1$, $X41$, $DNTXY1$, etc. all have the same bucket address. With $M = 2^i$, $i \le 12$ the identifiers AXY, BXY, $WTXY$, etc. have the same bucket address. Since programmers have a tendency to use many variables with the same suffix, the choice of M as a power of 2 would result in many collisions. This choice of M would have

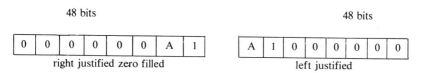

Figure 9.15 Identifier Al right and left justified and zero filled. (6 bits per character).

even more disastrous results if the identifier X is stored left justified zero filled. Then, all 1 character identifiers would map to the same bucket, 0, for $M = 2^i$, $i \le 54$; all 2 character identifiers would map to the bucket 0 for M

$= 2^i$, $i \leq 48$ etc. As a result of this observation, we see that when the division function f_D is used as a hash function, the table size should not be a power of 2 while when the "middle of square" function f_m is used the table size is a power of 2. If M is divisible by 2 then odd keys are mapped to odd buckets (as the remainder is odd) and even keys are mapped to even buckets. The use of the hash table is thus biased.

Let us try some other values for M and see what kind of identifiers get mapped to the same bucket, the goal being that we wish to avoid a choice of M that will lead to many collisions. This kind of analysis is possible as we have some idea as to the relationships between different variable names programmers tend to use. For instance, the knowledge that a program tends to have variables with the same suffix led us to reject $M = 2^i$. For similar reasons even values of M prove undesirable. Let $X = x_1 x_2$ and $Y = x_2 x_1$ be two identifiers each consisting of the characters x_1 and x_2. If the internal binary representation of x_1 has value $C(x_1)$ and that for x_2 has value $C(x_2)$ then if each character is represented by 6 bits, the numeric value of X is $2^6 C(x_1) + C(x_2)$ while that for Y is $2^6 C(x_2) + C(x_1)$. If p is a prime number dividing M then $(f_D(X) - f_D(Y)) \bmod p = (2^6 C(x_1) \bmod p + C(x_2) \bmod p - 2^6 C(x_2) \bmod p - C(x_1) \bmod p) \bmod p$. If $p = 3$, then

$$
\begin{aligned}
(f_D(X) - f_D(Y)) \bmod p \\
= (64 \bmod 3 \ C(x_1) \bmod 3 + C(x_2) \bmod 3 \\
- 64 \bmod 3 \ C(x_2) \bmod 3 - C(x_1) \bmod 3) \bmod 3 \\
= C(x_1) \bmod 3 + C(x_2) \bmod 3 - C(x_2) \bmod 3 - C(x_1) \bmod 3 \\
= 0 \bmod 3.
\end{aligned}
$$

i.e., permutations of the same set of characters are hashed at a distance a factor of 3 apart. Programs in which many variables are permutations of each other would again result in a biased use of the table and hence result in many collisions. This happens because 64 mod 3 = 1. The same behavior can be expected when 7 divides M as 64 mod 7 = 1. These difficulties can be avoided by choosing M as a prime number. Then, the only factors of M are M and 1. Knuth has shown that when M divides $r^k \pm a$ where k and a are small numbers and r is the radix of the character set (in the above example $r = 64$), then $X \bmod M$ tends to be a simple superposition of the characters in X. Thus, a good choice for M would be: M *a prime number such that M does not divide* $r^k \pm a$ *for small k and a.* In section 9.3.2 we shall see other reasons for choosing M as a prime number. In practice it has been observed that it is sufficient to choose M such that it has no prime divisors less than 20.

(iii) Folding

In this method the identifier X is partitioned into several parts, all but the last being of the same length. These parts are then added together to obtain the hash address for X. There are two ways of carrying out this addition. In the first, all but the last part are shifted so that the least significant bit of each part lines up with the corresponding bit of the last part (figure 9.16(a)). The different parts are now added together to get $f(X)$. This method is known as *shift folding*. The other method of adding the parts is *folding at the boundaries*. In this method, the identifier is folded at the part boundaries and digits falling into the same position are added together (figure 9.16(b)) to obtain $f(X)$.

P_1	P_2	P_3	P_4	P_5

$P_1 = 123$ $P_2 = 203$ $P_3 = 241$ $P_4 = 112$ $P_5 = 20$

P_1	123
P_2	203
P_3	241
P_4	112
P_5	20
	699

P_1	123
P_2^r	302
P_3	241
P_4^r	211
P_5	20
	897

(a) shift folding

(b) folding at the boundaries $P_i^r =$ reverse of P_i

Figure 9.16 Two methods of folding.

(iv) Digit Analysis

This method is particularly useful in the case of a static file where all the identifiers in the table are known in advance. Each identifier X is interpreted as a number using some radix r. The same radix is used for all the identifiers in the table. Using this radix, the digits of each identifier are examined. Digits having the most skewed distributions are deleted. Enough digits are deleted so that the number of digits left is small enough to give an address in the range of the hash table. The criterion used to find the digits to be used as addresses, based on the measure of uniformity in the distribution of values in each digit, is to keep those digits having no abnormally high peaks or valleys and those having small standard deviation. The same digits are used for all identifiers.

Experimental results presented in §9.3.2 suggest the use of the division method with a divisor M that has no prime factors less than 20 for general purpose applications.

9.3.2.   Overflow Handling

In order to be able to detect collisions and overflows, it is necessary to initialize the hash table, *ht*, to represent the situation when all slots are empty. Assuming that no record has identifier zero, then all slots may be initialized to zero.† When a new identifier gets hashed into a full bucket, it is necessary to find another bucket for this identifier. The simplest solution would probably be to find the closest unfilled bucket. Let us illustrate this on a 26-bucket table with one slot per bucket. Assume the identifiers to be *GA*, *D*, *A*, *G*, *L*, *A*2, *A*1, *A*3, *A*4, *Z*, *ZA*, *E*. For simplicity we choose the hash function $f(X)$ = first character of *X*. Initially, all entries in the table are zero. $f(GA) = 7$, this bucket is empty, so *GA* and any other information making up the record are entered into *ht*[7]. *D* and *A* get entered into the buckets *ht*[4] and *ht*[1], respectively. The next identifier *G* has $f(G) = 7$. This slot is already used by *GA*. The next vacant slot is *ht*[8] and so *G* is entered there. *L* enters *ht*[12]. *A*2 collides with *A* at *ht*[1], the bucket over-flows and *A*2 is entered at the next vacant slot *ht*[2]. *A*1, *A*3 and *A*4 are entered at *ht*[3], *ht*[5] and *ht*[6], respectively. *Z* is entered at *ht*[26], *ZA* at *ht*[9] (the hash table is used circularly), and *E* collides with *A*3 at *ht*[5] and

1	A
2	A2
3	A1
4	D
5	A3
6	A4
7	GA
8	G
9	ZA
10	E
11	0
12	L
13	0
	0
≈	⋮ ≈
	0
26	Z

Figure 9.17 Hash table with linear probing. 26 buckets, 1 slot per bucket.

†A clever way to avoid initializing the hash table has been discovered by T. Gonzalez (see exercise 22).

is eventually entered at $ht[10]$. Figure 9.17 shows the resulting table. This method of resolving overflows is known as *linear probing* or *linear open addressing*.

In order to search the table for an identifier, x, it is necessary to first compute $f(x)$ and then examine keys at positions $ht[f(x)]$, $ht[f(x) + 1]$, ...,$ht[f(x) + j]$ such that $ht[f(x) + j]$ either equals x (x is in the table) or *blankident* (x is not in the table) or we eventually return to $ht[f(x)]$ (the table is full). The resulting algorithm is Program 9.7. The data types used are:

> **type** *identifier* = **packed array**[1..*maxchar*] **of char**;
> *hashtable* = **array**[1..*maxsize*] **of** *identifier*;

```
1  procedure linsrch (x : identifier; ht : hashtable; var j : integer; b :
                                                        integer);
2    {Search the hash table ht[0..b − 1] (each bucket has exactly 1
3    slot) using linear probing. If ht[j] = blankident then the j-th bucket
4    is empty and x can be entered into the table. Otherwise ht[j] = x
5    which is already in the table. f is the hash function.}
6    var i : integer
7    begin
8      i := f(x); j := i;
9      while (ht[j] < > x) and (ht[j] < > blankident) do
10       begin
11         j := (j + 1) mod b; {treat the table as circular}
12         if j = i then {no empty slots}
13                       tablefull;
14       end;
15   end; {of linsrch}
```

Program 9.6   Linsrch

Our earlier example shows that when linear probing is used to resolve overflows, identifiers tend to cluster together, and moreover, adjacent clusters tend to coalesce, thus increasing the search time. To locate the identifier, ZA, in the table of figure 9.17, it is necessary to examine $ht[26]$, $ht[1]$, ...,$ht[9]$, a total of ten comparisons. This is far worse than the worst case behavior for tree tables. If each of the identifiers in the table of figure 9.12 was retrieved exactly once, then the number of buckets examined would be 1 for A, 2 for $A2$, 3 for $A1$, 1 for D, 5 for $A3$, 6 for $A4$, 1 for GA, 2 for G, 10 for ZA, 6 for E, 1 for L and 1 for Z for a total of 39 buckets examined. The average number examined is 3.25 buckets per identifier. An analysis of the method shows that the expected average number of identifier comparisons, P, to look up an identifier is approximately $(2 - \alpha)/(2 - 2\alpha)$ where

α is the loading density. This is the average over all possible sets of identifiers yielding the given loading density and using a uniform function f. In the above example $\alpha = 12/26 = .47$ and $P = 1.5$. Even though the average number of probes is small, the worst case can be quite large.

One of the problems with linear open addressing is that it tends to create clusters of identifiers. Moreover, these clusters tend to merge as more identifiers are entered, leading to bigger clusters. Some improvement in the growth of clusters and hence in the average number of probes needed for searching can be obtained by *quadratic probing*. Linear probing was characterized by searching the buckets $(f(x) + i)$ mod b, $0 \leq i \leq b - 1$ where b is the number of buckets in the table. In quadratic probing, a quadratic function of i is used as the increment. In particular, the search is carried out by examining buckets $f(x)$, $(f(x) + i^2)$ mod b and $(f(x) - i^2)$ mod b for $1 \leq i \leq (b - 1)/2$. When b is a prime number of the form $4j + 3$, for j an integer, the quadratic search described above examines every bucket in the table. The proof that when b is of the form $4j + 3$, quadratic probing examines all the buckets 0 to $b - 1$, relies on some results from number theory. We shall not go into the proof here. The interested reader should see Radke [1970] for a proof. Table 9.18 lists some primes of the form $4j - 3$. Another possibility is to use a series of hash functions $f_1, f_2, \ldots, f_m$. This method is known as *rehashing*. Buckets $f_i(x)$, $1 \leq i \leq m$ are examined in that order. An alternate method for handling bucket overflow, random probing, is discussed in exercise 19.

One of the reasons linear probing and its variations perform poorly is that searching for an identifier involves comparison of identifiers with different hash values. In the hash table of figure 9.17, for instance, searching for the identifier ZA involved comparisons with the buckets $ht[1]$ to $ht[8]$, even though none of the identifiers in these buckets had a collision with $ht[26]$ and so could not possibly be ZA. Many of the comparisons being made could be saved if we maintained lists of identifiers, one list per bucket, each list containing all the synonyms for that bucket. If this were done, a search would then involve computing the hash address $f(x)$ and examining only those identifiers in the list for $f(x)$. Since the sizes of these

Prime	j	Prime	j
3	0	43	10
7	1	59	14
11	2	127	31
19	4	251	62
23	5	503	125
31	7	1019	254

Table 9.18   Some primes of the form $4j + 3$.

lists is not known in advance, the best way to maintain them is as linked chains. Additional space for a link is required in each slot. Each chain will have a head node. The head node, however, will usually be much smaller than the other nodes since it has to retain only a link. Since the lists are to be accessed at random, the head nodes should be sequential. We assume they are numbered 1 to M if the hash function f has range 1 to M.

Using chaining to resolve collisions and the hash function used to obtain figure 9.17, the hash chains of figure 9.19 are obtained. When a new identifier, x, is being inserted into a chain, the insertion can be made at either end. This is so because the address of the last node in the chain is known as a result of the search that determined x was not in the list for $f(x)$. In the example of figure 9.19 new identifiers were inserted at the front of the chains. The number of probes needed to search for any of the identifiers is now 1 for each of $A4$, D, E, G, L, and ZA; 2 for each of $A3$, GA and Z; 3 for $A1$; 4 for $A2$ and 5 for A for a total of 24. The average is now 2 which is considerably less than for linear probing. Additional storage, however, is needed for links. The algorithm that results when chaining is used is given in Program 9.7. The data types are:

```
type identifier = packed array[1..maxchar] of char;
     listpointer = ↑listnode;
     listnode = record
                      ident : identifier;
                      link : listpointer;
                end;
     hashtable = array[1..maxsize] of listpointer;
```

```
1  procedure chnsrch (x : identifier; var ht : hashtable;
2                          b : integer; var j : listpointer);
3    {Search the hash table ht[0..b − 1] for x. Either ht[i] = nil or
4     it is a pointer to the list of identifiers x:f(x) = i. List
5     nodes have field ident and link. Either j points to the node
6     already containing x or j = nil.}
7    var found : boolean;
8      begin
9      j := ht[f(x)]; {compute head node address}
10         {search the chain starting at j}
11     found := false;
12       while (j <> nil) and not found do
13         if j↑.ident = x then found := true
14                         else j :=j↑.link;
15     end; {of chnsrch}
```

Program 9.7   Chnsrch

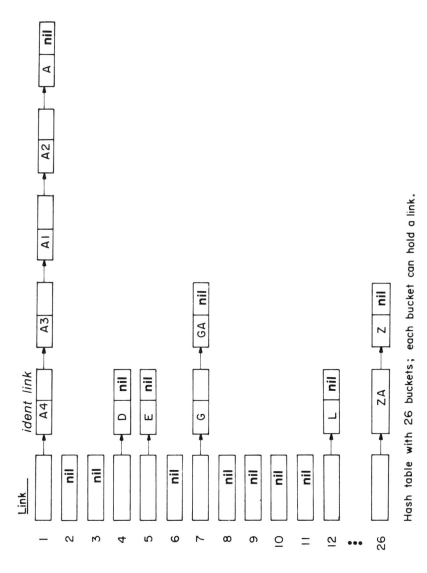

Hash table with 26 buckets; each bucket can hold a link.

Figure 9.19 Hash chains corresponding to Figure 9.17.

The expected number of identifier comparisons can be shown to be $\approx 1 + \dfrac{\alpha}{2}$ where α is the loading density n/b (b = number of head nodes). For $\alpha = 0.5$ this figure is 1.25 and for $\alpha = 1$ it is about 1.5. This scheme has the additional advantage that only the b head nodes must be sequential and reserved at the beginning. Each head node, however, will be at most 1/2 to 1 word long. The other nodes will be much bigger and need be allocated only as needed. This could represent an overall reduction in space required for certain loading densities despite the links. If each record in the table is five words long, $n = 100$ and $\alpha = 0.5$, then the hash table will be of size 200 $\times$ 5 = 1000 words. Only 500 of these are used as $\alpha = 0.5$. On the other hand, if chaining is used with one full word per link, then 200 words are needed for the head nodes ($b = 200$). Each head node is one word long. One hundred nodes of six words each are needed for the records. The total space needed is thus 800 words, or 20% less than when no chaining was being used. Of course, when α is close to 1, chaining uses more space than linear probing. However, when α is close to 1, the average number of probes using linear probing or its variations becomes quite large and the additional space used for chaining can be justified by the reduction in the expected number of probes needed for retrieval. If one wishes to delete an entry from the table, then this can be done by just removing that node from its chain. The problem of deleting entries while using open addressing to resolve collisions is tackled in exercise 17.

The results of this section tend to imply that the performance of a hash table depends only on the method used to handle overflows and is independent of the hash function so long as a uniform hash function is being used. While this is true when the identifiers are selected at random from the identifier space, it is not true in practice. In practice, there is a tendency to make a biased use of identifiers. Many identifiers in use have a common suffix or prefix or are simple permutations of other identifiers. Hence, in practice we would expect different hash functions to result in different hash table performance. The table of figure 9.20 presents the results of an empirical study conducted by Lum, Yuen and Dodd. The values in each column give the average number of bucket accesses made in searching eight different tables with 33,575; 24,050; 4909; 3072; 2241; 930; 762 and 500 identifiers each. As expected, chaining outperforms linear open addressing as a method for overflow handling. In looking over the figures for the various hash functions, we see that division is generally superior to the other types of hash functions. For a general application, it is therefore recommended that the division method be used. The divisor should be a prime number, though it is sufficient to choose a divisor that has no prime factors less than

hash function type	α = n/b .5		.75		.9		.95	
	C	L	C	L	C	L	C	L
MIDSQ	1.26	1.73	1.40	9.75	1.45	27.14	1.47	37.53
DIV	1.19	4.52	1.31	7.20	1.38	22.42	1.41	25.79
FOLD S	1.33	21.75	1.48	65.10	1.40	77.01	1.51	118.57
FOLD B	1.39	22.97	1.57	48.70	1.55	69.63	1.51	97.56
DA	1.35	4.55	1.49	30.62	1.52	89.20	1.52	125.59
THEO	1.25	1.50	1.37	2.50	1.45	5.50	1.48	10.50

Number of slots per bucket = 1

C = chaining
L = linear open addressing
α = loading density
MIDSQ = middle of square
DIV = division
FOLD S = shift folding
FOLD B = folding at boundaries
DA = digit analysis
THEO = theoretical expectation based on random keys

Figure 9.20 Average number of bucket accesses per identifier retrieved (condensed from Lum, Yuen and Dodd, "Key-to-Address Transform Techniques: A Fundamental Performance Study on Large Existing Formatted Files," CACM, April 1971, Vol. 14, No. 4, pp. 228-239.

20. The table also gives the theoretical expected number of bucket accesses based on random keys.

9.3.3 THEORETICAL EVALUATION OF OVERFLOW TECHNIQUES

The experimental evaluation of hashing techniques indicates a very good performance over conventional techniques such as balanced trees. The worst case performance for hashing can, however, be very bad. In the worst case an insertion or a search in a hash table with n identifiers may take $O(n)$ time. In this section we present a probabilistic analysis for the expected performance of the chaining method and state without proof the results of similar analyses for the other overflow handling methods. First, we formalize what we mean by expected performance.

Let $HT(0: b - 1)$ be a hash table with b buckets, each bucket having one slot. Let f be a uniform hash function with range $[0, b - 1]$. If n identifiers $X_1, X_2, ..., X_n$ are entered into the hash table then there are b^n distinct hash sequences $f(X_1), f(X_2), ..., f(X_n)$. Assume that each of these is equally likely to occur. Let S_n denote the expected number of identifier comparisons needed to locate a randomly chosen X_i, $1 \le i \le n$. Then, S_n is the average number of comparisons needed to find the j-th key X_j; averaged over $1 \le j \le n$ with each j equally likely and averaged over all b^n hash sequences assuming each of these to also be equally likely. Let U_n be the expected number of identifier comparisons when a search is made for an identifier not in the hash table. This hash table contains n identifiers. The quantity U_n may be defined in a manner analogous to that used for S_n.

Theorem 9.1   Let $\alpha = n/b$ be the loading density of a hash table using a uniform hashing function f. Then:

(i)   for linear open addressing

$$U_n \approx \frac{1}{2} \left(1 + \frac{1}{(1 - \alpha)^2} \right)$$

$$S_n \approx \frac{1}{2} \left(1 + \frac{1}{1 - \alpha} \right)$$

(ii)   for rehashing, random probing and quadratic probing

$$U_n \approx 1/(1 - \alpha)$$

$$S_n \approx - \left(\frac{1}{\alpha} \right) \log_e (1 - \alpha)$$

(iii)   for chaining

$$U_n \approx \alpha$$

$$S_n \approx 1 + \alpha/2$$

Proof   Exact derivations of U_n and S_n are fairly involved and can be found in Knuth's book *The Art of Computer Programming: Sorting and Searching*. Here, we present a derivation of the approximate formulas for chaining. First, we must make clear our count for U_n and S_n. In case the identifier X being searched for has $f(X) = i$ and chain i has k nodes on it (not including the head node) then k comparisons are needed if X is not on the chain. If X is j nodes away from the head node, $1 \le j \le k$, then j comparisons are needed.

When the n identifiers distribute uniformly over the b possible chains, the expected number in each chain is $n/b = \alpha$. Since $U_n =$ expected number of identifiers on a chain, we get $U_n = \alpha$.

When the i-th identifier, X_i, is being entered into the table, the expected number of identifiers on any chain is $(i - 1)/b$. Hence, the expected number of comparisons needed to search for X_i after all n identifiers have been entered is $1 + (i - 1)/b$ (this assumes that new entries will be made at the end of the chain). We therefore get:

$$S_n = \frac{1}{n} \sum_{i=1}^{n} \{1 + (i - 1)/b\} = 1 + \frac{n - 1}{2b} \approx 1 + \frac{\alpha}{2} \qquad \square$$

REFERENCES AND SELECTED READINGS

The $O(n^2)$ optimum binary search tree algorithm is from:

"Optimum Binary Search Trees," by D. Knuth, *Acta Informatica*, vol. 1, Fasc 1, 1971, pp. 14–25.

For a discussion of heuristics that obtain in $O(n \log n)$ time nearly optimal binary search trees see:

"Nearly Optimal Binary Search Trees," by K. Melhorn, *Acta Informatica*, vol. 5, 1975, pp. 287–295.

"Binary Search Trees and File Organization," by J. Nievergelt, *ACM Computing Surveys*, vol. 6, no. 3, Sept. 1974, pp. 195–207.

For more on Huffman codes see: "An Optimum Encoding with Minimum Longest Code and Total Number of Digits," by E. Schwartz, *Information and Control*, vol. 7, 1964, pp. 37–44.

Additional algorithms to manipulate AVL trees may be found in:

"Linear lists and priority queues as balanced binary trees," by C. Crane, STAN-CS-72-259, Computer Science Department, Stanford University, February 1972.

The Art of Computer Programming: Sorting and Searching by D. Knuth, Addison-Wesley, Reading, Massachusetts, 1973 (section 6.2.3).

Results of an empirical study on height balanced trees appear in:

"Performance of Height-Balanced Trees," by P. L. Karlton, S. H. Fuller, R. E. Scroggs and E. B. Koehler, *CACM*, vol. 19, no. 1, Jan. 1976, pp. 23–28.

Several interesting and enlightening works on hash tables exist. Some of these are:

"Scatter storage techniques," by R. Morris, *CACM*, vol. 11, no. 1, January 1968, pp. 38–44.

"Key to Address Transform Techniques: A Fundamental Performance Study on Large Existing Formatted Files," by V. Lum, P. Yuen and M. Dodd, *CACM*, vol. 14, no. 4, April 1971, pp. 228–239.

"The quadratic quotient method: a hash code eliminating secondary clustering," by J. Bell, *CACM*, vol. 13, no. 2, February 1970, pp. 107–109.

"Full table quadratic searching for scatter storage," by A. Day, *CACM*, vol. 13, no. 8, August 1970, pp. 481–482.

"Identifier search mechanisms: a survey and generalized model," by D. Severence, *ACM Computing Surveys*, vol. 6, no. 3, September 1974, pp. 175–194.

"A practitioner's guide to addressing algorithms: a collection of reference tables and rules-of-thumb," by D. Severence and R. Duhne, Technical Report No. 240, Department of Operations Research, Cornell University, November 1974.

"Hash table methods," by W. Mauer and T. Lewis, *ACM Computing Surveys*, vol. 7, no. 1, March 1975, pp. 5–20.

"The quadratic hash method when the table size is not prime," by V. Batagelj, *CACM*, vol. 18, no. 4, April 1975, pp. 216–217.

The Art of Computer Programming: Sorting and Searching, by D. Knuth, Addison-Wesley, Reading, Massachusetts, 1973.

"Reducing the retrieval time of scatter storage techniques," by R. Brent, *CACM*, vol. 16, no. 2, February 1973, pp. 105–109.

"General performance analysis of key-to-address transformation methods using an abstract file concept," by V. Lum, *CACM*, vol. 16, no. 10, October 1973, pp. 603–612.

"The use of quadratic residue research," by C. E. Radke, *CACM*, vol. 13, no. 2, Feb. 1970, pp. 103–105.

A method to avoid hash table initialization may be found in:

"Algorithms for sets and related problems," by T. Gonzalez, University of Oklahoma, Nov. 1975.

EXERCISES

1. (a) Prove by induction that if T is a binary tree with n internal nodes, I its internal path length and E its external path length, then $E = I + 2n, n \geq 0$.
   (b) Using the result of (a) show that the average number of comparisons s in a successful search is related to the average number of comparisons, u, in an unsuccessful search by the formula

$$s = (1 + 1/n)u - 1, \ n \geq 1.$$

2. (a) Show that algorithm *huffman* correctly generates a binary tree of minimal weighted external path length.
   (b) When n runs are to be merged together using an m-way merge. Huffman's method generalizes to the following rule: "First add $(1 - n)$ mod $(m - 1)$ runs of length zero to the set of runs. Then repeatedly merge together the m shortest remaining runs until only one run is left." Show that this rule yields an optimal merge pattern for m-way merging.

3. Using algorithm *obst* compute w_{ij}, r_{ij} and c_{ij}, $0 \leq i < j \leq 4$ for the identifier set $(a_1, a_2, a_3, a_4) = $ (**end, goto, print, read**) with $p_1 = 1/20$, $p_2 = 1/5$, $p_3 = 1/10$, $p_4 = 1/20$, $q_0 = 1/5$, $q_1 = 1/10$, $q_2 = 1/5$, $q_3 = 1/20$, $q_4 = 1/20$. Using the r_{ij}'s construct the optimal binary search tree.

4. (a) Show that the computing time of algorithm *obst* is $O(n^2)$.
   (b) Write an algorithm to construct the optimal binary search tree T_{on} given the roots r_{ij}, $0 \leq i < j \leq n$. Show that this can be done in time $O(n)$.

5. Since, often, only the approximate values of the p's and q's are known, it is perhaps just as meaningful to find a binary search tree that is nearly optimal; i.e., its cost, eq. (9.1), is almost minimal for the given p's and q's. This exercise explores an $O(n \log n)$ algorithm that results in nearly optimal binary search trees. The search tree heuristic we shall study is:

   Choose the root A_k such that $| w_{0,k-1} - w_{k,n}|$ is as small as possible. Repeat this procedure to find the left and right subtrees of A_k.

   (a) Using this heuristic obtain the resulting binary search tree for the data of exercise 3. What is its cost?
   (b) Write a Pascal algorithm implementing the above heuristic. Your algorithm should have a time complexity of at most $O(n \log n)$.

   An analysis of the performance of this heuristic may be found in the paper by Melhorn.

6. (a) Convince yourself that Figures 9.11 and 9.12 take care of all the possible situations that may arise when a height balanced binary tree becomes unbalanced as a result of an insertion. Alternately come up with an example that is not covered by any of the cases in Figure 9.11 and 9.12.
    (b) Complete Figure 9.12 by drawing the tree configurations for the rotations *RL* (a), (b) and (c).

7. Complete algorithm *avlinsert* by filling in the steps needed to rebalance the tree in case the imbalance is of type *RL*.

8. Obtain the height balanced trees corresponding to those of Figure 9.10 using algorithm *avlinsert*, starting with an empty tree, on the following sequence of insertions:
    DECEMBER, JANUARY, APRIL, MARCH, JULY, AUGUST, OCTOBER, FEBRUARY, NOVEMBER, MAY, JUNE.
    Label the rotations according to type.

9. Assume that each node in an AVL tree t has the field *lsize*. For any node, a, $a\uparrow.lsize$ is the number of nodes in its left subtree $+1$. Write an algorithm *avlfind(t,k)* to locate the k-th smallest identifier in the subtree t. Show that this can be done in $O(\log n)$ time if there are n nodes in t.

10. Rewrite algorithm *avlinsert* with the added assumption that each node has a *lsize* field as in exercise 9. Show that the insertion time remains $O(\log n)$.

11. Write an algorithm to list the nodes of an AVL-tree T in ascending order of *ident* fields. Show that this can be done in $O(n)$ time if T has n nodes.

12. Write an algorithm to delete the node with identifier x from an AVL tree t. The resulting tree should be restructured if necessary. Show that the time required for this is $O(\log n)$ when there are n nodes in t.

13. Do exercise 12 for the case when each node has a *lsize* field and the k-th smallest identifier is to be deleted.

14. Write an algorithm to merge the nodes of the two AVL trees T_1 and T_2 together to obtain a new AVL tree. What is the computing time of your algorithm?

15. Write an algorithm to split an AVL tree, T, into two AVL trees T_1 and T_2 such that all identifiers in T_1 are $\leq x$ and all those in T_2 are $> x$.

16. Prove by induction that the minimum number of nodes in an AVL tree of height h is $N_h = F_{h+2} - 1$, $h \geq 0$.

17. Write an algorithm to delete identifier x from a hash table which uses hash function f and linear open addressing to resolve collisions. Show that simply setting the slot previously occupied by x to *blankident* does not solve the

problem. How must algorithm *linsrch* be modified so that a correct search is made in the situation when deletions are permitted? Where can a new identifier be inserted?

18. (i) Show that if quadratic searching is carried out in the sequence $(f(x) + q^2), (f(x) + (q - 1)^2), ..., (f(x) + 1), f(x), (f(x) - 1, ..., (f(x) - q^2)$ with $q = (b - 1)/2$ then the address difference mod b between successive buckets being examined is

$$b - 2, b - 4, b - 6, ..., 5, 3, 1, 1, 3, 5, ..., b - 6, b - 4, b - 2$$

(ii) Write an algorithm to search a hash table $ht[0: b - 1]$ of size b for the identifier x. Use f as the hash function and the quadratic probe scheme discussed in the text to resolve. In case x is not in the table, it is to be entered. Use the results of part (i) to reduce the computations.

19. [Morris 1968] In random probing, the search for an identifier, X, in a hash table with b buckets is carried out by examining buckets $f(x), f(x) + S(i), 1 \leq i \leq b - 1$ where $S(i)$ is a pseudo random number. The random number generator must satisfy the property that every number from 1 to $b - 1$ must be generated exactly once. (i) Show that for a table of size 2^r, the following sequence of computations generates numbers with this property:

   Initialize R to 1 each time the search routine is called.
   On successive calls for a random number do the following:
   $R \leftarrow R * 5$
   $R \leftarrow$ low order $r + 2$ bits of R
   $S(i) \leftarrow R/4$
   (ii) Write an algorithm, incorporating the above random number generator, to search and insert into a hash table using random probing and the middle of square hash function, f_m.

   It can be shown that for this method, the expected value for the average number of comparisons needed to search for X is $-(1/\alpha) \log (1 - \alpha)$ for large table sizes. α is the loading factor.

20. Write an algorithm to list all the identifiers in a hash table in lexicographic order. Assume the hash function f is $f(X) =$ first character of X and linear probing is used. How much time does your algorithm take?

21. Let the binary representation of identifier X be $x_1 x_2$. Let $|x|$ denote the number of bits in x and let the first bit of x_1 be 1. Let $|x_1| = \lceil |x|/2 \rceil$ and $|x_2| = \lfloor |x|/2 \rfloor$. Consider the following hash function.

$$f(X) = \text{middle } k \text{ bits of } (x_1 \; XOR \; x_2)$$

where XOR is exclusive or. Is this a uniform hash function if identifiers are drawn at random from the space of allowable Pascal identifiers? What can you say about the behavior of this hash function in a real symbol table usage?

22. [T. Gonzalez] Design a symbol table representation which allows one to search, insert and delete an identifier x in $O(1)$ time. Assume that $1 \leq X \leq m$ and that $m +$ n units of space are available where n is the number of insertions to be made. (Hint: use two arrays $a[1..n]$ and $b[1..m]$ where $a[i]$ will be the i-th identifier inserted into the table. If X is the i-th identifier inserted then $b[x] = i$.) Write algorithms to search, insert and delete identifiers. Note that you cannot initialize either a or b to zero as this would take $O(n + m)$ time. Note that x is an integer.

23. [T. Gonzalez] Let $S = \{x_1, x_2, \ldots, x_n\}$ and $T = \{y_1, y_2, \ldots, y_r\}$ be two sets. Assume $1 \leq x_i \leq m$, $1 \leq i \leq n$ and $1 \leq y_i \leq m$, $1 \leq i \leq r$. Using the idea of exercise 22 write an algorithm to determine if $S \subseteq T$. Your algorithm should work in $O(r + n)$ time. Since $S \equiv T$ iff $S \subseteq T$ and $T \subseteq S$, this implies that one can determine in linear time if two sets are equivalent. How much space is needed by your algorithm?

24. [T. Gonzalez] Using the idea of exercise 22 write an $O(n + m)$ time algorithm to carry out the function of algorithm *verify2* of section 7.1. How much space does your algorithm need?

25. Complete table 9.12 by adding a column for hashing.

26. For a fixed k, $k \geq 1$, we define a height balanced tree $HB(k)$ as below:

Definition An empty binary tree is a $HB(k)$ tree. If T is a non-empty binary tree with T_L and T_R as its left and right subtrees, then T is $HB(k)$ iff (i) T_L and T_R are $HB(k)$ and (ii) $|h_L - h_R| \leq k$ where h_L and h_R are the heights of T_L and T_R, respectively.

For the case of $HB(2)$ trees obtain the rebalancing transformations.

27. Write an insertion algorithm for $HB(2)$ trees.

28. Using the notation of §9.3.3 show that when linear open addressing is used:

$$S_n = \frac{1}{n} \sum_{i=0}^{n-1} U_i$$

Using this equation and the approximate equality:

$$U_n \approx \frac{1}{2} \left(1 + \frac{1}{(1 - \alpha)^2} \right) \quad \text{where } \alpha = \frac{n}{b}$$

show that $S_n \approx \dfrac{1}{2} \left(1 + \dfrac{1}{(1 - \alpha)} \right)$

29. [Guttag] The following set of operations defines a symbol table which handles a language with block structure. Give a set of axioms for these operations:

INIT—creates an empty table;

ENTERB—indicates a new block has been entered;

ADD—places an identifier and its attributes in the table;

LEAVEB—deletes all identifiers which are defined in the innermost block;

RETRIEVE—returns the attributes of the most recently defined identifier;

ISINB—returns true if the identifier is defined in the innermost block else false.

Chapter 10

FILES

10.1 FILES, QUERIES AND SEQUENTIAL ORGANIZATIONS

A file, as described in earlier chapters (and as distinct from the **file** type in Pascal), is a collection of records where each record consists of one or more fields. For example, the records in an employee file could contain these fields:

Employee Number (E#)
Name
Occupation
Degree (Highest Degree Obtained)
Sex
Location
Marital Status (MS)
Salary

Sample data for such a file is provided in figure 10.1.

Record	E#	Name	Occupation	Degree	Sex	Location	MS	Salary
A	800	HAWKINS	programmer	B.S.	M	Los Angeles	S	10,000
B	510	WILLIAMS	analyst	B.S.	F	Los Angeles	M	15,000
C	950	FRAWLEY	analyst	M.S.	F	Minneapolis	S	12,000
D	750	AUSTIN	programmer	B.S.	F	Los Angeles	S	12,000
E	620	MESSER	programmer	B.S.	M	Minneapolis	M	9,000

Figure 10.1 Sample Data for Employee File.

The primary objective of file organization is to provide a means for record retrieval and update. The update of a record could involve its deletion, changes in some of its fields or the insertion of an entirely new record. Certain fields in the record are designated as key fields. Records may be

474

retrieved by specifying values for some or all of these keys. A combination of key values specified for retrieval will be termed a *query*. Let us assume that in the employee file of figure 10.1 the fields Employee Number, Occupation, Sex and Salary have been designated as key fields. Then, some of the valid queries to the file are:

Retrieve the records of all employees with

Q1:   Sex = M

Q2:   Salary > 9,000

Q3:   Salary > average salary of all employees

Q4:   (Sex = M *and* Occupation = Programmer) *or* (Employee Number > 700 and Sex = F)

One invalid query to the file would be to specify location = Los Angeles, as the location field was not designated as a key field. While it might appear that the functions one wishes to perform on a file are the same as those performed on a symbol table (chapter 9), several complications are introduced by the fact that the files we are considering in this chapter are too large to be held in internal memory. The tables of chapter 9 were small enough that all processing could be carried out without accessing external storage devices such as disks and tapes.

In this chapter we are concerned with obtaining data representations for files on external storage devices so that required functions (e.g. retrieval, update) may be carried out efficiently. The particular organization most suitable for any application will depend upon such factors as the kind of external storage device available, type of queries allowed, number of keys, mode of retrieval and mode of update. Let us elaborate on these factors.

Storage Device Types

We shall be concerned primarily with direct access storage devices (DASD) as exemplified by disks. Some discussion of tape files will also be made.

Query Types

The examples Q1-Q4 above typify the kinds of queries one may wish to make. The four query types are:

Q1: Simple Query: The value of a single key is specified.

Q2: Range Query: A range of values for a single key is specified.

Q3: Functional Query: Some function of key values in the file is specified (e.g., average or median).

Q4: Boolean Query: A boolean combination of Q1-Q3 being logical operators *and, or, not*.

Number of Keys

The chief distinction here will be between having only one key and files with more than one key.

Mode of Retrieval

The mode of retrieval may be either real time or batched. In real time retrieval the response time for any query should be minimal (say a few seconds from the time the query is made). In a bank the accounts file has a mode of retrieval which is real time since requests to determine a balance must be satisfied quickly. Similarly, in an airline reservation system we must be able to determine the status of a flight (i.e., number of seats vacant) in a matter of a few seconds. In the batched mode of retrieval, the response time is not very significant. Requests for retrieval are batched together on a "transaction file" until either enough requests have been received or a suitable amount of time has passed. Then all queries on the transaction file are processed.

Mode of Update

The mode of update may, again, be either real time or batched. Real time update is needed, for example, in a reservation system. As soon as a seat on a flight is reserved, the file must be changed to indicate the new status. Batched update would be suitable in a bank account system where all deposits and withdrawals made on a particular day could be collected on a transaction file and the updates made at the end of the day. In the case of batched update one may consider two files: the Master File and the Transactions File. The Master File represents the file status after the previous update run. The transactions file holds all update requests that haven't yet been reflected in the master file. Thus, in the case of batched update, the master file is always 'out of date' to the extent that update requests have been batched on the transaction file. In the case of a bank file using real time retrieval and batched update, this would mean that only account balances at the end of the previous business day could be determined, since today's deposits and withdrawals haven't yet been incorporated into the master file.

The simplest situation is one in which there is only one key, the only queries allowed are of type Q1 (simple query), and all retrievals and updates are batched. For this situation tapes are an adequate storage medium. All the required functions can be carried out efficiently by maintaining the master file on a tape. The records in the file are ordered by the key field. Requests for retrieval and update are batched onto a transaction tape. When it is time to process the transactions, the transactions are sorted into order by the key field and an update process similar to algorithm *verify2* of section 7.1 is carried out, creating a new master file. All records in the old master file are examined, changed if necessary and then written out onto a new master file. The time required for the whole process is essentially $O(n + m \log m)$ where n and m are the number of records in the master and transaction files, respectively (to be more accurate this has to be multiplied by the record length). This procedure is good only when the number of transactions that have been batched is reasonably large. If $m = 1$ and $n = 10^6$ then clearly it is very wasteful to process the entire master file. In the case of tapes, however, this is the best we can do since it is usually not possible to alter a record in the middle of a tape without destroying information in an adjacent record. The file organization described above for tape files will be referred to as *sequentially ordered*.

In this organization, records are placed sequentially onto the storage media, (i.e., they occupy consecutive locations and in the case of a tape this would mean placing records adjacent to each other). In addition, the physical sequence of records is ordered on some key, called the *primary key*. For example, if the file of figure 10.1 were stored on a tape in the sequence A, B, C, D, E then we would have a sequential file. This file, however, is unordered. If the primary key is Employee Number then physical storage of the file in the sequence B, E, D, A, C would result in an ordered sequential file. For batched retrieval and update, ordered sequential files are preferred over unordered sequential files since they are easier to process (compare *verify2* with *verify1* of 7.1).

Sequential organization is also possible in the case of a DASD such as a disk. Even though disk storage is really two dimensional (cylinder $\times$ surface) it may be mapped down into a one dimensional memory using the technique of §2.4. If the disk has c cylinders and s surfaces, one possibility would be to view disk memory sequentially as in figure 10.2. Using the notation t_{ij} to represent the j-th track of the i-th surface, the sequence is $t_{1,1}$, $t_{2,1}$, $t_{3,1}$, ...,$t_{s,1}$, $t_{1,2}$, ...,$t_{s,2}$ etc.

If each employee record in the file of figure 10.1 were on track long, then a possible sequential organization would store the records A, B, C, D, E onto tracks $t_{3,4}$, $t_{4,4}$, $t_{5,4}$, $t_{6,4}$, and $t_{7,4}$, respectively (assuming $c \geq 4$ and $s \geq 7$). Using the interpretation of figure 10.2 the physical sequence in which the records have been stored is A, B, C, D, E. If the primary key is Employee Number then the logical sequence for the records is B, E, D, A, C as $E\#(B) < E\#(E) < ... < E\#(C)$. This would thus correspond to an unordered sequential file. In case the records are stored in the physical sequence B, E, D, A, C, then the file is ordered on the primary key, the logical and physical record sequences are the same, and the organization is that of a sequentially

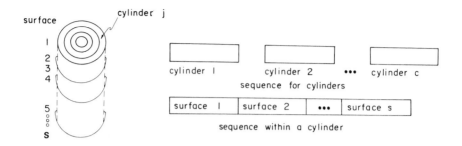

Figure 10.2 Interpreting Disk Memory as Sequential Memory.

ordered file.Batched retrieval and update can be carried out essentially in the same way as for a sequentially ordered tape file by setting up input and output buffers and reading in, perhaps, one track of the master and transaction files at a time (the transaction file should be sorted on the primary key before beginning the master file processing). If updates do not change the size of records and no insertions are involved then the updated track may be written back onto the old master file. The sequential interpretation of figure 10.2 is particularly efficient for batched update and retrieval as the tracks are to be accessed in the order: all tracks on cylinder 1 followed by all tracks on cylinder 2, etc. As a result of this the read/write heads are moved one cylinder at a time and this movement is necessitated only once for every s tracks read (s = number of surfaces). The alternative sequential interpretation (figure 10.3) would require accessing tracks in the order: all tracks on surface 1, all tracks on surface 2, etc. In this case a head movement would be necessitated for each track being read (except for tracks 1 and c).

surface 1	surface 2	...	surface s

track 1	track 2	...	track c	Odd surfaces
track c	track c − 1	...	track 1	Even surfaces

Figure 10.3 Alternative Sequential Interpretation of Disk Memory.

Since in batched update and retrieval the entire master file is scanned (typical files might contain 10^5 or more records), enough transactions must be batched for this to be cost effective. In the case of disks it is possible to extend this sequential ordered organization for use even in situations where the number of transactions batched is not enough to justify scanning the entire master file. First, take the case of a retrieval. If the records are of a fixed size then it is possible to use binary search to obtain the record with the desired key value. For a file containing n records, this would mean at most $\lceil \log_2 n \rceil$ accesses would have to be made to retrieve the record. For a file with 10^5 records of length 300 characters this would mean a maximum of 17 accesses. On a disk with maximum seek time $1/10$ sec, latency time $1/40$ sec and a track density of 5000 characters/track this would mean a retrieval time of at most $17 \left(1/10 + 1/40 + \dfrac{300}{5000} \times \dfrac{1}{40} \right)$ sec $\simeq 2.15$ sec. Retrieving an arbitrary record from the same file stored on a tape with density 1600 bpi and a tape speed of 150 in/sec would in the worst case require 125 sec as the entire file must be read to access the last record (this does not include the time to cross interblock gaps and to restart tape motion, etc. The actual time needed will be more than 125 sec).

When records are of variable size, binary search can no longer be used, as, given the address of the first and last records in a file, one can no longer calculate the address of the middle record. The retrieval time can be considerably reduced by maintaining an index to guide the search. An index is just a collection of key value and address pairs. In the case of the file of figure 10.1 stored in the physical sequence B, E, D, A, C at addresses $t_{1,2}$, $t_{2,2}$, $t_{3,2}$, $t_{4,2}$ and $t_{5,2}$ the index could contain five entries, one for each record in the file. The entries would be the pairs $(510, t_{1,2})$, $(620, t_{2,2})$, $(750, t_{3,2})$, $(800, t_{4,2})$, and $(900, t_{5,2})$. An index which contains one entry for every record in the file will be referred to as a *dense index*. If a dense index is maintained for the primary key then retrieval of a record with primary key $= x$ could be carried out by first looking into the index and finding the pair $(x, addr)$. The desired record would then be retrieved from the location $addr$. The total number of accesses needed to retrieve a record would now be one plus the number of accesses needed to locate the tuple $(x, addr)$ in the index. In §10.2 we shall look at efficient indexing techniques that allow index searches to be carried out using at most three accesses even for reasonably large files. This means that a retrieval from the file of 10^5 records discussed earlier could be carried out making at most four accesses rather than the seventeen accesses needed by a binary search. Since all addresses are kept in the index, it is not necessary to have fixed size records.

Sequential file organizations on a disk suffer from the same deficiencies as sequential organizations in internal memory. Insertion and deletion of records require moving large amounts of data in order to create space for the new record or to utilize the space used by the record being deleted. In practice these difficulties can be overcome to some extent by marking deleted records as having been deleted and not physically deleting the record. If a record is to be inserted, it can be placed into some "overflow" area rather than in its correct place in the sequentially ordered file. The entire file will have to be periodically reorganized. Reorganization will take place when a sufficient number of overflow records have accumulated and when many "deletions" have been made. While this method of handling insertions and deletions results in a degradation of system performance as far as further retrievals and updates is concerned, it is preferable to copying over large sections of the file each time an update is made. In situations where the update rate is very high or when the file size is too large to allow for periodic file reorganization (which would require processing the whole file), other organizations are called for. These will be studied in a later section.

So far, we have discussed only file organization when the number of keys is one. What happens when there is more than one key? A sequential file, clearly, can be ordered on only one key, the primary key. If an employee file is maintained on a disk using sequential organization with Employee Number as the primary key then how does one retrieve all records with occupation = programmer? One obvious, and inefficient, way would be to process the entire file, outputting all records that satisfy this query. Another, possibly more efficient way would be to maintain a dense index on the occupation field, search this index and retrieve the necesary records. In fact one could maintain a dense index on every key. This and other possibilities will be studied in §10.3.

Let us summarize the ideas we have discussed. File organization is concerned with representing data records on external storage media. The choice of a representation depends on the environment in which the file is to operate, e.g., real time, batched, simple query, one key, multiple keys, etc. When there is only one key, the records may be sorted on this key and stored sequentially either on tape or disk. This results in a sequentially ordered file. This organization is good for files operating in batched retrieval and update mode when the number of transactions batched is large enough to make processing the entire file cost effective. When the number of keys is more than one or when real time responses are needed, a sequential organization in itself is not adequate. In a general situation several indexes may have to be maintained. In these cases, file organization breaks down into two more or less distinct aspects: (i) the directory (i.e. collection of indexes) and (ii) the physical organization of the records themselves. This will be referred to as the physical file. We have already discussed one possible physical organization, i.e., sequential (ordered and unordered). In this general framework, processing a query or update request would proceed in two steps. First, the indexes would be interrogated to determine the parts of the physical file that are to be searched. Second, these parts of the physical file will be searched. Depending upon the kinds of indexes maintained, this second stage may involve only the accessing of records satisfying the query or may involve retrieving nonrelevant records too.

10.2 INDEX TECHNIQUES

One of the important components of a file is the directory. A directory is a collection of indexes. The directory may contain one index for every key or may contain an index for only some of the keys. Some of the indexes may be dense (i.e., contain an entry for every record) while others may be nondense (i.e., contain an entry for only some of the records). In some cases all the indexes may be integrated into one large index. Whatever the situation, the index may be thought of as a collection of pairs of the form (key value, address). If the records A,B,C,D,E of figure 10.1 are stored on disk addresses a_1, a_2, ...,a_5, respectively, then an index for the key Employee Number would have entries $(800,a_1)$; $(510,a_2)$; $(950,a_3)$; $(750,a_4)$ and $(620,a_5)$. The index would be dense since it contains an entry for each of the records in the file. We shall assume that all the key values in an index are distinct. This may appear to be restrictive since several records may have the same key value as in the case of the Occupation key in figure 10.1. Records A,D,E all have the value 'programmer' for the Occupation key. This difficulty can be overcome easily by keeping in the address field of each distinct key value a pointer to another address where we shall maintain a list of addresses of all records having this value. If at address b_1 we stored the list of addresses of all programmer records, i.e., a_1, a_4, and a_5, and at b_2 stored the address list for all analysts, i.e., a_2 and a_3, then we could achieve the effect of a dense index for Occupation by maintaining an index with entries ('programmer', b_1) and ('analyst', b_2). Another alternative would be to change the format of entries in an index to (key value, address 1, address 2, ...address n). In both cases, different entries will have distinct key values. The second alternative would require the use of variable size nodes. The use of variable size nodes calls for complex storage management schemes (see §4.8), and so we would normally prefer the first alternative. An index, then, consists of pairs of the type (key value, address), the key values being distinct. The functions one wishes to perform on an index are: search for a key value; insert a new pair; delete a pair from the index; modify or update an existing entry. These functions are the same as those one had to perform on a dynamic table (§9.2). An index differs from a table essentially in its size. While a table was small enough to fit into available internal memory, an index is too large for this and has to be maintained on external storage (say, a disk). As we shall see, the techniques for maintaining an index are rather different from those used in chapter 9 to maintain a table. The reason for this is the difference in the amount of time needed to access information from a disk and that needed to access information from internal memory. Accessing a word of information from internal memory takes typically about 10^{-8} seconds while accessing the same word from a disk could take about 10^{-1} seconds.

10.2.1   Cylinder-Surface Indexing

The simplest type of index organization is the cylinder-surface index. It is useful only for the primary key index of a sequentially ordered file. It assumes that the sequential interpretation of disk memory is that of figure 10.2 and that records are stored sequentially in increasing order of the primary key. The index consists of a cylinder index and several surface indexes. If the file requires c cylinders (1 through c) for storage then the cylinder index contains c entries. There is one entry corresponding to the largest key value in each cylinder. Figure 10.4 shows a sample file together with its cylinder index (figure 10.4(b)). Associated with each of the c cylinders is a surface index. If the disk has s usable surfaces then each surface index has s entries. The i-th entry in the surface index for cylinder j is the value of the largest key on the j-th track of the i-th surface. The total number of surface index entries is therefore $c \cdot s$. Figure 10.4(c) shows the surface index for cylinder 5 of the file of figure 10.4(a). A search for a record with a particular key value X is carried out by first reading into memory the cylinder index. Since the number of cylinders in a disk is only a few hundred the cylinder index typically occupies only one track. The cylinder index is searched to determine which cylinder possibly contains the desired record. This search can be carried out using binary search in case each entry requires a fixed number of words. If this is not feasible, the cylinder index can consist of an array of pointers to the starting point of individual key values as in figure 10.5. In either case the search can be carried out in $O(\log c)$ time. Once the cylinder index has been searched and the appropriate cylinder determined, the surface index corresponding to that cylinder is retrieved from the disk.

The number of surfaces on a disk is usually very small (say 10) so that the best way to search a surface index would be to use a sequential search. Having determined which surface and cylinder is to be accessed, this track is read in and searched for the record with key X. In case the track contains only one record, the search is trivial. In the example file, a search for the record corresponding to the Japanese torpedo bomber Nakajima B5N2 which was used at Pearl Harbor proceeds as follows: the cylinder index is accessed and searched. It is now determined that the desired record is either in cylinder 5 or it is not in the file. The surface index to be retrieved is that

#	Aircraft	Nation	Type	Speed Max mph	Cruising mph	Range miles	Max Altitude feet	Crew	Guns	Bombs	C	S
1	Amiot 143	France	NB	193	155	746	25,920	5	4	y	1	1
2	Avenger	USA	TB	271	145	2530	22,400	3	3	y	1	1
3	Avro Lancaster	GB	HB	287	210	1660	24,500	7	10	y	1	2
4	Barracuda Mk II	GB	TB	228	—	686	16,600	3	2	y	1	2
5	Black Widow	USA	NF	366	—	2500	33,100	3	8	y	1	3
6	Bloch MB-152	France	Fr	302	279	398	33,000	1	4	N	1	3
7	Boomerang	Aus.	Fr	295	—	932	29,000	1	6	y	1	4
8	Bregeut 691	France	AB	298	186	839	13,100	2	5	y	1	4
9	Caproni	Italy	MB	165	143	839	18,000	3	4	y	2	1
10	Caudron	France	Fr	303	199	559	29,855	1	4	N	2	1
11	Devastator	USA	TB	266	128	1000	19,700	3	2	y	2	2
12	Droop Snoot	USA	FB	414	290	450	44,000	1	5	y	2	2
13	Fiat Centauro	Italy	Fr	385	348	1025	42,650	1	5	N	2	3
14	Flying Fortress	USA	Br	317	210	2400	36,600	10	13	y	2	3
15	Hawker Tempest	GB	FB	436	391	740	36,500	1	4	y	2	4
16	Heinkel III H	Ger.	MB	252	211	1280	27,900	5	7	y	2	4
17	Heinkel 162A	Ger.	Fr	553	—	606	39,370	1	2	N	3	1
18	Heinkel 177 A-1	Ger.	HB	317	267	3480	22,970	5	6	y	3	1
19	Heinkel 219 A-5	Ger.	NF	416	336	1243	39,600	2	6	N	3	2
20	Helldiver	USA	Br	295	158	1925	29,100	2	4	y	3	2
21	Ilushin II-4	USSR	MB	277	—	1616	33,000	4	3	y	3	3

Figure 10.4(a) World War II aircraft.

#	Aircraft	Nation	Type	Speed Max mph	Cruising mph	Range miles	Max Altitude feet	Crew	Guns	Bombs	C	S
22	Ilyushin Shturmovik	USSR	AB	251	199	466	24,600	2	5	y	3	3
23	Invader	USA	LB	355	284	1400	22,100	3	10	y	3	4
24	Junkers 188 E-1	Ger.	MB	311	233	1209	30,660	4	5	y	3	4
25	Kawanishi N1K2-J	Japan	Fr	370	230	1065	35,300	1	4	N	4	1
26	Kingcobra	USA	FB	408	378	450	43,000	1	5	y	4	1
27	Lavochkin La-9	USSR	Fr	429	311	1078	36,515	1	4	N	4	2
28	Macchi Veltro	Italy	Fr	391	—	612	36,910	1	5	N	4	2
29	Marauder	USA	LB	283	216	1100	19,800	7	11	y	4	3
30	Messerschmitt Hornisse	Ger.	HF	388	367	1050	33,000	2	8	N	4	3
31	Messerschmitt Komet	Ger.	Fr	597	—	—	39,500	1	2	N	4	4
32	Messerschmitt Sturmvogel	Ger.	Fr	541	—	652	37,565	1	4	N	4	4
33	MIG-5	USSR	FB	370	—	—	—	1	4	y	5	1
34	Mitsubishi G4M1	Japan	MB	267	196	3750	29,000	7	5	y	5	1
35	Mitsubishi Ki-67	Japan	HB	378	249	2361	31,070	6	5	y	5	2
36	Mosquito Mk VI	GB	FB	378	255	1855	33,000	2	8	y	5	2
37	Mustang P-51D	USA	Fr	437	362	950	41,900	1	6	y	5	3
38	Nakajima B5N2	Japan	TB	236	162	1237	27,100	3	2	y	5	3
39	Petlyakov Pe-8	USSR	HB	276	224	2300	25,920	11	6	y	5	4
40	Spitfire Mk XVI	GB	Fr	405	328	980	42,500	1	6	N	5	4
41	Superfortress	USA	HB	357	230	3250	31,850	10	13	y	6	1
42	Sykhoi Su-2	USSR	LB	302	—	746	28,870	2	5	y	6	1

Figure 10.4(a)   World War II aircraft (continued).

#	Aircraft	Nation	Type	Speed Max mph	Cruising mph	Range miles	Max Altitude feet	Crew	Guns	Bombs	C	S
43	Tupolev Tu-2	USSR	Br	345	258	1555	33,000	4	7	y	6	2
44	Vengeance	USA	Br	279	230	2000	22,300	2	6	y	6	2

Abbreviations

Aus.	Australia	HF	heavy fighter
AB	attack bomber	LB	light bomber
Br	bomber	MB	medium bomber
C	cylinder	NB	night bomber
FB	fighter bomber	NF	night fighter
Fr	fighter	N	no
GB	Great Britain	S	surface
Ger.	Germany	y	yes
HB	heavy bomber		

Figure 10.4(a) World War II aircraft (continued).

(Condensed from *Airplanes* by Enzo Angelucci, McGraw-Hill Book Co., New York, 1971.) Cylinder/surface indexing is for a disk with four surfaces and assuming two records per track. The organization is that of a sequential file ordered on the field—Aircraft.

cylinder	highest key value
1	Bregeut 691
2	Heinkel III H
3	Junkers 188 E-1
4	Messerschmitt Sturmvogel
5	Spitfire Mk XVI
6	Vengeance

Figure 10.4(b)   Cylinder index for file of figure 10.4(a).

surface	highest key value
1	Mitsubishi G 4M1
2	Mosquito MkV1
3	Nakajima B5N2
4	Spitfire MkXVI

Figure 10.4(c)   Surface index for cylinder 5.

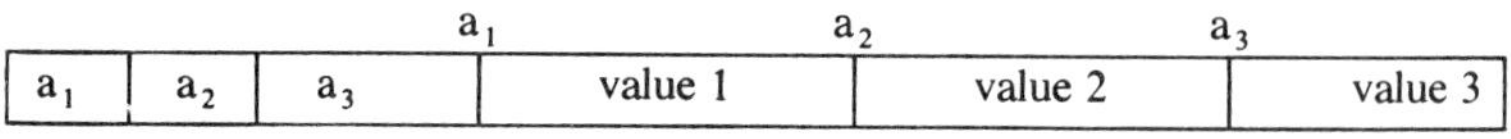

Track Layout

Figure 10.5 Using an Array of Pointers to Permit Binary Search
with Variable Length Key Values.

for cylinder 5. A search of this index results in the information that the correct surface number is 3. Tract $t_{5,3}$ is now input and searched. The desired record is found on this track. The total number of disk accesses needed for retrieval is three (one to access the cylinder index, one for the surface index and one to get the track of records). When track sizes are very large it may not be feasible to read in the whole track. In this case the disk will usually be sector addressable and so an extra level of indexing will be needed: the sector index. In this case the number of accesses needed to retrieve a record will increase to four. When the file extends over several disks, a disk index is also maintained. This is still a great improvement over the seventeen accesses needed to make a binary search of the sequential file.

This method of maintaining a file and index is referred to as ISAM (Indexed Sequential Access Method). It is probably the most popular and simplest file organization in use for single key files. When the file contains more than one key, it is not possible to use this index organization for the remaining keys (though it can still be used for the key on which the records are sorted in case of a sequential file).

10.2.2   Hashed Indexes

The principles involved in maintaining hashed indexes are essentially the same as those discussed for hash tables §9.3. The same hash functions and overflow handling techniques are available. Since the index is to be maintained on a disk and disk access times are generally several orders of magnitude larger than internal memory access times, much consideration must be given to hash table design and the choice of an overflow handling technique. Let us reconsider these two aspects of hash system design, giving special consideration to the fact that the hash table and overflow area will be on a disk.

Overflow Handling Techniques

The overflow handling techniques discussed in §9.3.2 are:
(i)   rehashing
(ii)   open addressing (a)   random
                                (b)   quadratic
                                (c)   linear
(iii) chaining.
The expected number of bucket accesses when $s = 1$ is roughly the same for methods (i), (iia) and (iib). Since the hash table is on a disk, and these overflow techniques tend to randomize the use of the hash table, we can expect each bucket access to take almost the maximum seek time. In the case of (iic), however, overflow buckets are adjacent to the home bucket and so their retrieval will require minimum seek time. While using chaining we can minimize the tendency to randomize use of the overflow area by designating certain tracks as overflow tracks for particular buckets. In this case successive buckets on a chain may be retrieved with little or no additional seek time. To the extent that this is possible, we may regard one bucket access to be equally expensive using methods (iic) and (iii). Bucket accesses using the other methods are more expensive, and since the average number of buckets retrieved isn't any better than (iii), we shall not discuss these further.

Hash Table

Let b, s, α and n be as defined in §9.3. For a given α and n we have $\alpha = n/(bs)$, and so the product bs is determined. In the case of a hash table maintained in internal memory we chose the number of slots per bucket, s, to be 1. With this choice of s, the expected number of buckets accessed when open linear addressing is used is $(2 - \alpha)/(2 - 2\alpha)$, and $1 + \alpha/2$ when chaining is used to resolve overflows. Since individual bucket accesses from a disk are expensive, we wish to explore the possibility of reducing the number of buckets accessed by increasing s. This would of necessity decrease b, the number of buckets, as bs is fixed. We shall assume that when chaining is used, the home bucket can be retrieved with one access. The hash table for chaining is similar to that for linear open addressing. Each bucket in the hash table, i.e., each home bucket, has s slots. Each such bucket also has a link field. This differs from the organization of §9.3.2 where $s = 0$ for home buckets using chaining. Remaining buckets on individual chains have only one slot each and require additional accesses. Thus, if the key value X is in the i-th node on a chain (the home bucket being the first node in the chain), the number of accesses needed to retrieve X is i. In the case of linear open addressing if X is i buckets away from the home bucket, $f(x)$, then the number of accesses to retrieve X is $1 + i$.

By way of example, consider the hash function $f(x) =$ first character of X and the values B, $B1$, $B2$, $B3$, A. Using a hash table with $b = 6$ and $s = 1$, the assignment of figure 10.6(a) is obtained if overflows are handled via linear open addressing. If each of the values is searched for once then the total number of bucket retrievals is 1(for A) + 1(for B) + 2(for $B1$) + 3(for $B2$) + 4(for $B3$) = 11. When the same table space is divided into three buckets each with two slots and $f'(X) = [f(X)/2]$ the assignment of key values to buckets is as in figure 10.6(b). The number of bucket retrievals needed now is 1 (for each of B and $B1$) + 2(for each of $B2$ and $B3$) + 3(for A) = 9. Thus the average number of buckets retrieved is reduced from 11/5 per search to 9/5 per search. The buckets of figure 10.6(b) are twice as big as those of figure 10.6(a). However, unless the bucket size becomes very large, the time to retrieve a bucket from disk will be dominated largely by the seek and latency time. Thus, the time to retrieve a bucket in each of the two cases discussed above would be approximately the same. Since the total average search time is made up of two components—first, the time, t_r,

bucket 1	A
2	B
3	B1
4	B2
5	B3
6	

$s = 1$
(a)

Slot 1	Slot 2
B	B1
B2	B3
A	

$s = 2$
(b)

Figure 10.6 Hash Tables With $s = 1$ and 2.

to read in buckets from disk and second, the time, t_p, to search each bucket in internal memory—we should choose b and s so as to minimize $a(t_r + t_p)$ where a = average number of buckets retrieved. Using a sequential search within buckets, the time t_p is proportional to s. Thus the average t_p for figure 10.6(b) is one and a half times that for figure 10.6(a). When s is small and the hash table is on a disk, we have $t_r \gg t_p$ and it is sufficient to minimize $a \cdot t_r$. Let us contrast this to the situation in 9.3 where t_r and t_p are comparable. The table of figure 10.6(a) can be searched with an average of $11/5$ key comparisons and accesses. The table of figure 10.6(b) requires one comparison to find B, 2 for $B1$, 3 for $B2$, 4 for $B3$ and 5 for A for a total of 15 comparisons. This implies an average of three comparisons per search. In this case the search time has actually increased with the increase in s. But, when the table is on disk, the average times are roughly $11t_r/5$ and $9t_r/5$, and the table with $s = 2$ gives better performance. In general, we can conclude that increasing s while maintaining $b \cdot s$ fixed reduces a (see figure 10.7). The table of figure 10.8 shows the results of some experiments conducted on existing hashed files maintained on disk. As is evident from this table, for a fixed α, the average number of bucket accesses decreases with increasing s. Moreover, for $s \geq 10$, the average number of accesses for open linear addressing is roughly the same as for chaining. This, together with our earlier observation that unless care is taken while using chaining, successive accesses will access random parts of the disk, while in the case of open linear addressing consecutive disk segments would be accessed, leads

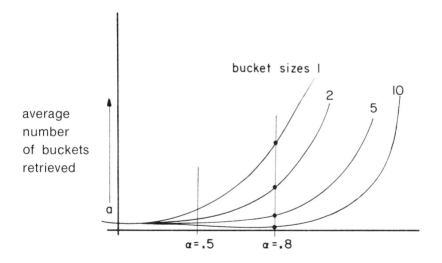

Figure 10.7 $\alpha = .5$

Bucket size, s →		1		2		5		10		20		50	
Hash function →		D	M	D	M	D	M	D	M	D	M	D	M
Loading factor α ↓													
α = .5	C	1.19	1.26	1.09	1.14	1.02	1.03	1	1.01	1	1	1	1
	L	4.52	1.73	1.17	1.20	1.02	1.03	1	1	1	1	1	1
α = .75	C	1.31	1.40	1.19	1.29	1.11	1.16	1.07	1.09	1.03	1.03	1	1.03
	L	7.2	9.75	3.35	1.80	1.29	1.20	1.04	1.06	1.01	1.02	1	1
α = .9	C	1.38	1.45	1.30	1.37	1.24	1.27	1.16	1.28	1.09	1.15	1.03	1.07
	L	22.42	27.14	4.80	6.54	1.94	1.81	1.32	1.30	1.08	1.11	1.01	1.03
α = .95	C	1.41	1.47	1.34	1.39	1.25	1.32	1.20	1.28	1.17	1.28	1.08	1.15
	L	25.79	37.53	10.80	10.80	4.47	2.62	2.32	1.29	1.25	1.29	1.03	1.08

D = division
M = middle of square
C = chaining
L = linear open addressing
α = loading factor = (number of entries)/(number of slots in hash table)

Note For the same α C uses more space than L as overflows are handled in a separate area.

Figure 10.8 Observed average number of bucket accesses for different α and s. (Condensed from Lum, Yuen and Dodd: Key to Address Transform techniques. A fundamental performance study on large existing formatted files. CACM, Vol. 14, No. 4, April 1971.)

us to the conclusion that with suitable α and s linear addressing will outperform chaining (contrast this with the case of internal tables).

While both the data of figures 10.7 and 10.8 might suggest a choice for b = 1 (thus maximizing the value of s), such a choice for s clearly is not best. The optimal value of s will depend very much on the values of the latency time, seek time and transmission rates of the disk drive in use. We may rewrite the retrieval time per bucket, t_r, as $t_s + t_l + s \cdot t_t$ where t_s, t_l and t_t are the seek time, latency time and transmission time per slot, respectively. When the seek time is very large relative to t_t the optimal s would tend to be larger than when t_s is very small compared to t_t (as in the case of a drum). Another consideration is the size of the input buffer available. Since the bucket has to be read into some part of internal memory, we must set aside enough space to accommodate a bucket load of data.

Loading Order

As in the case of internal tables, the order in which key values are entered into the hash table is important. To the extent possible, an attempt should be made to enter these values in order of nonincreasing frequency of search. When this is done, new entries should be added to the end of the overflow chain rather than at the front.

10.2.3 Tree Indexing—B-Trees

The AVL tree of §9.2 provided a means to search, insert and delete entries from a table of size n using at most $O(\log n)$ time. Since these same functions are to be carried out in an index, one could conceivably use AVL trees for this application too. The AVL tree would itself reside on a disk. If nodes are retrieved from the disk, one at a time, then a search of an index with n entries would require at most $1.4 \log n$ disk accesses (the maximum depth of an AVL tree is $1.4 \log n$). For an index with a million entries, this would mean about 28 accesses in the worst case. This is a lot worse than the cylinder sector index scheme of §10.2.1. In fact, we can do much better than 28 accesses by using a balanced tree based upon an m-way search tree rather than one based on a binary search tree (AVL trees are balanced binary search trees).

Definition: An m-way search tree, T, is a tree in which all nodes are of degree $\leq m$. If T is empty, (i.e., $T = $ **nil**) then T is an m-way search tree. When T is not empty it has the following properties:
  (i) T is a node of the type

$$n, \ A_0, \ (K_1, A_1), \ (K_2, A_2), \ ..., \ (K_n, A_n)$$

where the A_i, $0 \leq i \leq n$ are pointers to the subtrees of T and the K_i, $1 \leq i \leq n$ are key values; and $1 \leq n < m$.

(ii) $K_i < K_{i+1}$, $1 \leq i < n$

(iii) All key values in the subtree A_i are less than K_{i+1}, and greater than K_i, $0 < i < n$.

(iv) All key values in the subtree A_o are less than K_l and those in A_n are greater than K_n.

(v) The subtrees A_i, $0 \leq i \leq n$ are also m-way search trees.

As an example of a 3-way search tree consider the tree of figure 10.9 for key values 10, 15, 20, 25, 30, 35, 40, 45 and 50. One may easily verify that it satisfies all the requirements of a 3-way search tree. In order to search for any key value x in this tree, we first "look into" the root node t at address a and determine the value of i for which $K_i \leq x < K_{i+1}$ (for convenience we use $K_0 = minint$ and $K_{n+1} = maxint$ where $minint$ is smaller than all legal key values and $maxint$ is larger than all legal key values). In case $x = K_i$ then the search is complete. If $x \neq K_i$ then by the definition of an m-way search tree x must be in subtree A_i if it is in the tree. When n (the number of keys in a node) is "large," the search for the appropriate value of i above may be carried out using binary search. For "small" n a sequential search is more appropriate. In the example if $x = 35$ then a search in the root node indicates that the appropriate subtree to be searched is the one with root A_1

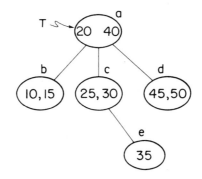

node	schematic format
a	2,b,(20,c),(40,d)
b	2,0,(10,0),(15,0)
c	2,0,(25,0),(30,e)
d	2,0,(45,0),(50,0)
e	1,0,(35,0)

Figure 10.9 Example of a 3-way search tree.

at address c. A search of this root node indicates that the next node to search is at address e. The key value 35 is found in this node and the search terminates. If this search tree resides on a disk then the search for $x = 35$ would require accessing the nodes of addresses a, c and e for a total of three disk accesses. This is the maximum number of accesses needed for a search in the tree of figure 10.9. The best binary search tree for this set of key values requires four disk accesses in the worst case. One such binary tree is shown in figure 10.10.

Algorithm *msearch* searches an m-way search tree t for key value x using the scheme described above. In practice, when the search tree represents an index, the tuples (K_i, A_i) in each of the nodes will really be 3-tuples (K_i, A_i, B_i) where B_i is the address in the file of the record with key K_i. This address would consist of the cylinder and surface numbers of the track to be accessed to retrieve this record (for some disks this address may also include the sector number). The A_i, $0 \leq i \leq n$ are the addresses of root nodes of subtrees. Since these nodes are also on a disk, the A_i are cylinder and surface numbers. We assume that $A_i = 0$ is a null address.

```
1   procedure msearch(t:mtree; x:integer; var p:mtree; var i,j:integer);
2   {Search the m-way search tree t residing on disk for the key value x.
3    Individual node format is n,A₀,(K₁,A₁),...,(Kₙ,Aₙ), n < m. A triple
4    (p,i,j) is returned. j = 1 implies x is found at node location p with key Kᵢ.
5    Else j = 0 and p is the location of the node into which x can be inserted.}
6   label 99;
7   begin
8   p := t; K₀ := −maxint; q := nil; j := 1; {q is the parent of p}
9   while p < > 0 do
10     begin
11     input node located at p from disk;
12     Let this node define n,A₀,(K₁,A₁),...,(Kₙ,Aₙ);
13     Kₙ₊₁ := maxint;
14     Let i be such that Kᵢ <=x < Kᵢ₊₁;
15     if x = Kᵢ then {x has been found; return (p,i,1)} goto 99;
16     q := p; p := Aᵢ;
17     end;
18     {x is not in t; return location of node into which insertion can take
            place}
19   p := q; j := 0; {return q,i,0;}
20   99: end; {of msearch}
```

Program 10.1 Msearch

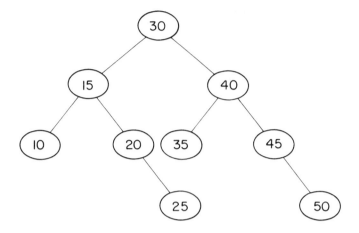

Figure 10.10   Best AVL-tree for data of figure 10.9.

Analyzing algorithm *msearch* is fairly straightforward. The maximum number of disk accesses made is equal to the height of the tree t. Since individual disk accesses are very expensive relative to the time needed to process a node (i.e., determine the next node to access lines 14–16) we are concerned with minimizing the number of accesses needed to carry out a search. This is equivalent to minimizing the height of the search tree. In a tree of degree m and height $h \geq 1$ the maximum number of nodes is $\sum_{0 \leq i \leq h-1} m^i = (m^h - 1)/(m - 1)$. Since each node has at most $m - 1$ keys, the maximum number of entries in an m-way tree index of height h would be $m^h - 1$. For a binary tree with $h = 3$ this figure is 7. For a 200-way tree with $h = 3$ we have $m^h - 1 = 8 \times 10^6 - 1$.

Clearly, the potentials of high order search trees are much greater than those of low order search trees. To achieve a performance close to that of the best m-way search trees for a given number of entries n, it is necessary that the search tree be balanced. The particular variety of balanced m-way search trees we shall consider here is known as a B-tree. In defining a B-tree it is convenient to reintroduce the concept of failure nodes as used for optimal binary search trees in §9.1. A failure node represents a node which can be reached during a search only if the value x being searched for is not in the tree. Every subtree with root $=$ nil is a point that is reached during the search iff x is not in the tree. For convenience, these empty subtrees will be replaced by hypothetical nodes called failure nodes. These nodes will be drawn square and marked with an F. The actual tree structure does not contain any such nodes but only the value **nil** where such a node occurs. Figure 10.11 shows the 3-way search tree of figure 10.9 with failure nodes. Failure nodes are the only nodes that have no children.

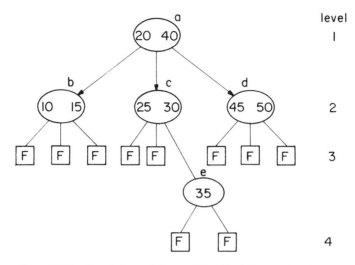

Figure 10.11   Search tree of figure 10.9 with failure nodes shown.

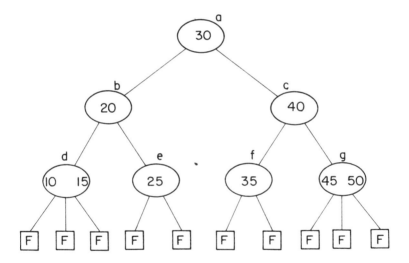

Figure 10.12   B-tree of order 3 for data of figure 10.9.

Definition: A *B*-tree, *t*, of order *m* is an *m*-way search tree that is either
empty or is of height ≥ 1 and satisfies the following properties:
  (i)   the root node has at least 2 children
  (ii)   all nodes other than the root node and failure nodes have at least
         $\lceil m/2 \rceil$ children
  (iii) all failure nodes are at the same level.

The 3-way search tree of figure 10.11 is not a B-tree since it has failure nodes at levels 3 and 4. This violates requirement (iii). One possible B-tree of order 3 for the data of figure 10.9 is shown in figure 10.12. Notice that all nonfailure nodes are either of degree 2 or 3. In fact, for a B-tree of order 3, requirements (i), (ii) and the definition of an m-way search tree together imply that all nonfailure nodes must be of degree 2 or 3. For this reason, B-trees of order 3 are also known as 2-3 trees.

While the total number of nonfailure nodes in a B-tree of a given order may be greater than the number of such nodes in the best possible search tree of that order (the 2-3 tree of figure 10.12 has seven nodes while the 3-way search tree of figure 10.9 has only five), we shall see later that it is easier to insert and delete nodes into a B-tree retaining the B-tree properties than it is to maintain the best possible m-way search tree at all times. Thus, the reasons for using B-trees rather than optimal m-way search trees for indexes are the same as those for using AVL trees as opposed to optimal binary search trees when maintaining dynamic internal tables.

Number of Key Values in a B-Tree

If t is a B-tree of order m in which all failure nodes are at level $l + 1$ then we know that the maximum number of index entries in t is $m^l - 1$. What is the minimum number, N, of entries in t? From the definition of a B-tree we know that if $l > 1$, the root node has at least two children. Hence, there are at least two nodes at level 2. Each of these nodes must have at least $\lceil m/2 \rceil$ children. Thus there are at least $2\lceil m/2 \rceil$ nodes at level 3. At level 4 there must be at least $2\lceil m/2 \rceil^2$ nodes, and continuing this argument, we see that there are at least $2\lceil m/2 \rceil^{l-2}$ nodes at level l when $l > 1$. All of these nodes are nonfailure nodes. If the key values in the tree are $K_1, K_2, ..., K_N$ and $K_i < K_{i+1}$, $1 \le i < N$, then the number of failure nodes is $N + 1$. This is so because failures occur for $K_i < X < K_{i+1}$, $0 \le i \le N$ and $K_0 = minint$, $K_{N+1} = maxint$. This results in $N + 1$ different nodes that one could reach while searching for a key value x not in t. Therefore, we have,

$$N + 1 = \text{number of failure nodes in } t$$
$$= \text{number of nodes at level } l + 1$$
$$\ge 2\lceil m/2 \rceil^{l-1}$$

and so, $$N \ge 2\lceil m/2 \rceil^{l-1} - 1, \; l \ge 1$$

This in turn implies that if there are N key values in a B-tree of order m then all nonfailure nodes are at levels less than or equal to l, $l \le \log_{\lceil m/2 \rceil} \{(N + 1)/2\} + 1$. The maximum number of accesses that have to be made for a search is l. Using a B-tree of order $m = 200$, an index with

$N \leq 2 \times 10^6 - 2$ will have $l \leq \log_{100}\{(N+1)/2\} + 1$. Since l is integer, we obtain $l \leq 3$. For $n \leq 2 \times 10^8 - 2$ we get $l \leq 4$. Thus, the use of a high order B-tree results in a tree index that can be searched making a very small number of disk accesses even when the number of entries is very large.

Choice of m

B-trees of high order are desirable since they result in a reduction in the number of disk accesses needed to search an index. If the index has N entries then a B-tree of order $m = N + 1$ would have only one level. This choice of m clearly is not reasonable, since by assumption the index is too large to fit in internal memory. Consequently, the single node representing the index cannot be read into memory and processed. In arriving at a reasonable choice for m, we must keep in mind that we are really interested in minimizing the total amount of time needed to search the B-tree for a value x. This time has two components, one, the time for reading in the node from the disk and two, the time needed to search this node for x. Let us assume that each node of a B-tree of order m is of a fixed size and is large enough to accomodate n, A_0 and $m - 1$ values for (K_i, A_i, B_i), $1 \leq j < m$. If the K_i are at most α characters long and the A_i and B_i each β characters long, then the size of a node is approximately $m(\alpha + 2\beta)$ characters. The time, t_i, required to read in a node is therefore:

$$
\begin{aligned}
t_i &= t_s + t_l + m(\alpha + 2\beta)\, t_c \\
&= a + bm
\end{aligned}
$$

where $a = t_s + t_l =$ seek time + latency time
$\qquad b = (\alpha + 2\beta)t_c$ and $t_c =$ transmission time per character

If binary search is used to carry out the search of line 14 of algorithm *msearch* then the internal processing time per node is $c \log_2 m + d$ for some constants c and d. The total processing time per node is thus,

$$\tau = a + bm + c \log_2 m + d \qquad (10.1)$$

For an index with N entries, the number of levels, l, is bounded by:

$$
\begin{aligned}
l &\leq \log_{\lceil m/2 \rceil}\{(N+1)/2\} + 1 \\
&\leq f\,\frac{\log_2\{(N+1)/2\}}{\log_2 m} \quad \text{for some constant } f
\end{aligned}
$$

The maximum search is therefore given by (10.2).

$$\text{maximum search time} = g \left\{ \frac{a + d}{\log_2 m} + \frac{bm}{\log_2 m} + c \right\} \text{seconds} \qquad (10.2)$$

$$\text{where} \quad g = f \cdot \log_2 \{(N + 1)/2\}.$$

We therefore desire a value of m that minimizes (10.2). Assuming that the disk drive available has a $t_s = 1/100$ sec and $t_l = 1/40$ sec we get $a = 0.035$ sec. Since d will typically be a few microseconds, we may ignore it in comparison with a. Hence, $a + d \approx a = 0.035$ sec. Assuming each key value is at most six characters long and that each A_i and B_i is three characters long, $\alpha = 6$ and $\beta = 3$. If the transmission rate $t_c = 5 \times 10^{-6}$ sec/character (corresponding to a track capacity of 5000 characters), $b = (\alpha + 2\beta)t_c = 6 \times 10^{-5}$ sec. The right hand side of equation (10.2) evaluates to

$$g \left\{ \frac{35}{\log_2 m} + \frac{0.06m}{\log_2 m} + 1000 \, c \right\} \text{milliseconds} \qquad (10.3)$$

Plotting this function gives us the graph of figure 10.13. From this plot it is evident that there is a wide range of values of m for which nearly optimal performance is achieved. This corresponds to the almost flat region $m \, \epsilon$ [50,400]. In case the lowest value of m in this region results in a node size greater than the allowable capacity of an input buffer, the value of m will be determined by the buffer size.

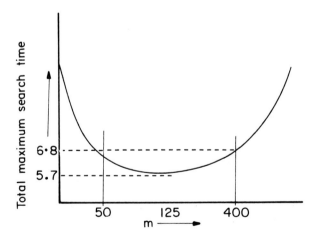

Figure 10.13   Plot of $(35+.06m)/\log_2 m$

Insertion

In addition to searching an index for a particular key value x, we also wish to insert and delete entries. We shall now focus attention on the problem of inserting a new key value x into a B-tree. The insertion is to be carried out in such a way that the tree obtained following the insertion is also a B-tree. As we shall see, the algorithm for doing this is conceptually much simpler than the corresponding insertion algorithm for AVL trees.

In attempting to discover the operations needed to carry out the insertion, let us insert $x = 38$ into the 2-3 tree of figure 10.12. First, a search of the tree is carried out to determine where the 38 is to be inserted. The failure node that is reached during this search for $x = 38$ is the fourth from the right. Its parent node is f. The node f contains only one key value and thus has space for another. The 38 may therefore be entered here, and the tree of figure 10.14(a) is obtained. In making this insertion, the tree nodes a, c and f were accessed from the disk during the search. In addition the new node f had to be written back onto the disk. The total number of accesses is therefore four. Next, let us insert $x = 55$. A search into the B-tree of figure 10.14(a) indicates that this key value should go into the node g. There is no space in this node, since it already contains $m - 1$ key values. Symbolically inserting the new key value at its appropriate position in a node that previously had $m - 1$ key values would yield a node, p, with the following format

$$m, A_0, (K_1, A_1) \ldots, (K_m, A_m)$$
$$\text{and} \quad K_i < K_{i+1}, \ 1 \le i < m.$$

This node may be split into two nodes p and p' with the following formats

$$\text{node } p: \ \lceil m/2 \rceil - 1, A_0, (K_1, A_1), \ \ldots, (K_{\lceil m/2 \rceil - 1}, A_{\lceil m/2 \rceil - 1}) \quad (10.4)$$
$$\text{node } p': \ m - \lceil m/2 \rceil, A_{\lceil m/2 \rceil}, (K_{\lceil m/2 \rceil + 1}, A_{\lceil m/2 \rceil + 1}), \ \ldots, (K_m, A_m)$$

The remaining value $K_{\lceil m/2 \rceil}$ and the new node p' form a tuple $(K_{\lceil m/2 \rceil}, p')$, and an attempt is made to insert this tuple into the parent of p. In the current example the node g splits into two nodes g and h. The tuple $(50, h)$ is inserted into the parent of g, i.e., node c. Since c has only one key value in it, this insertion can be carried out easily. This time, three accesses were made to determine that $x = 55$ should be inserted into g. Since node g was changed, it had to be written out onto disk. The node h had also to be written out onto disk. Assuming that node c is still in internal memory, another disk access is needed to write out the new node c. The total number of accesses is therefore six. The tree obtained is that of figure

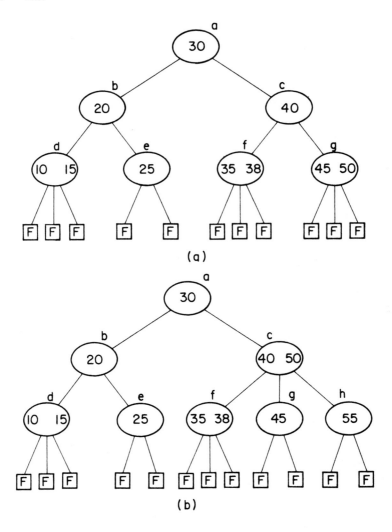

Figure 10.14   Insertion into a *B*-tree of order 3.

10.14(b). Insertion of *x* = 37, 5, and 18 results in the trees of figure 10.14(c), (d) and (e). Into this final tree let us insert *x* = 12. The appropriate node for insertion is node *k*. In determining this, the nodes *a*, *b* and *k* were accessed from the disk. We shall assume that there is enough internal memory available to hold these three nodes in memory. Insertion into node *k* requires that it be split into two nodes *k* and *l*. The tuple (15,*l*) is to be inserted into the parent node *b*. The new nodes *k* and *l* are written out onto the disk. Insertion into *b* results in this node splitting into two nodes *b*

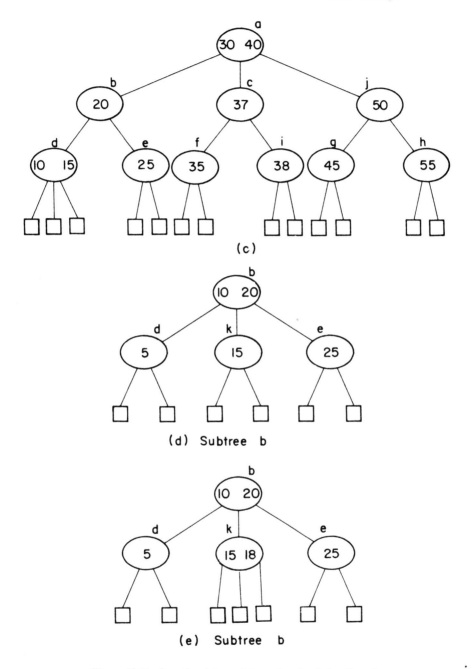

(c)

(d) Subtree b

(e) Subtree b

Figure 10.14 Insertion into a B-tree of order 3 (continued).

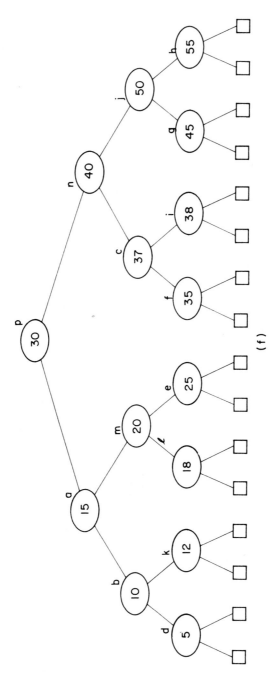

Figure 10.14   Insertion into a *B*-tree of order 3 (continued).

(f)

and m. These two nodes are written onto the disk. The tuple $(15, m)$ is to be inserted into the parent node a which also splits. The new nodes a and n are written out, leaving us to insert the tuple $(30, n)$ into the parent of a. Node a is the root node and thus has no parent. At this point, a new root node, p, with subtrees a and n is created. The height of the B-tree increases by 1. The total number of accesses needed for this insertion is ten.

One may readily verify that the insertion transformations described above preserve the index as a B-tree and take care of all possibilities. The resulting algorithm for insertion assumes all nodes on the path from the root to the insertion point are stacked. If enough memory is unavailable then only the addresses need be stacked and $parent[p]$ can be used.

```
1   procedure insertb(var t : mtree; x : integer);
2   {Key value x is inserted into the B-tree, t, of order m. t
      resides on a disk}
3   label 99;
4   var A,p,p',t:mtree; i,j,K: integer;
5   begin
6     A := nil; K := x; {(K,A) is tuple to be inserted}
7     msearch(t,x,p,i,j); {p is location of node for insertion}
8     if j < > 0 then goto 99; {x is already in t}
9     while p < > 0 do
10      begin
11        insert (K,A) into appropriate position in node at location p;
12        Let the resulting node have the form: n,A₀,(K₁,A₁),...,(Kₙ,Aₙ);
13        if n <= m − 1 then begin
14          {resulting node is not too big}
15          output node located at p onto disk; goto 99; end;
16        {node located at p has to be split}
17        Let node p and node p' be defined as in equation 10.4;
18        output(p,p') onto the disk;
19        K := K|m/2|; A := p'; p := parent[p];
20      end;
21      {a new root is to be created}
22      Create a new node r with format 1,t,(K,A);
23      t :=r; output t onto disk;
24  99: end; {of insertb}
```

Program 10.2   Insertb

Analysis of *insertb*

In evaluating algorithm *insertb*, we shall use as our performance measure the number of disk accesses that are made. If the B-tree t originally has l levels then the search of line 7 requires l accesses since x is not in t. Each time a node splits (line 17), two disk accesses are made (line 18). After the final splitting, an additional access is made either from line 15 or from line 23. If the number of nodes that split is k then the total number of disk accesses is $l + 2k + 1$. This figure assumes that there is enough internal memory available to hold all nodes accessed during the call of *msearch* in line 7. Since at most one node can split at each of the l levels, k is always $\leq l$. The maximum number of accesses needed is therefore $3l + 1$. Since in most practical situations l will be at most 4, this means about thirteen accesses are needed to make an insertion in the worst case.

In the case of algorithm *insertb*, this worst case figure of $3l + 1$ accesses doesn't tell the whole story. The average number of accesses is considerably less than this. Let us obtain an estimate of the average number of accesses needed to make an insertion. If we start with an empty tree and insert N values into it then the total number of nodes split is at most $p - 2$ where p is the number of nonfailure nodes in the final B-tree with N entries. This upper bound of $p - 2$ follows from the observation that each time a node splits, at least one additional node is created. When the root node splits, two additional nodes are created. The first node created results from no splitting, and if a B-tree has more than one node then the root must have split at least once. Figure 10.15 shows that $p - 2$ is the best possible upper bound on the number of nodes split in the creation of a p node B-tree when $p > 2$ (note that there is no B-tree with $p = 2$). A B-tree of order m with p nodes has at least

$$1 + (\lceil m/2 \rceil - 1)(p - 1)$$

key values as the root has at least one key value and remaining nodes have at least $\lceil m/2 \rceil - 1$ key values. The average number of splittings, s, may now be determined

$$\begin{aligned} s &= (\text{total number of splittings})/N \\ &\leq (p - 2)/\{1 + (\lceil m/2 \rceil - 1)(p - 1)\} \\ &< 1/(\lceil m/2 \rceil - 1). \end{aligned}$$

For $m = 200$ this means that the average number of splittings is less than $1/99$ per key inserted. The average number of disk accesses is therefore only $l + 2s + 1 < l + 101/99 \approx l + 1$.

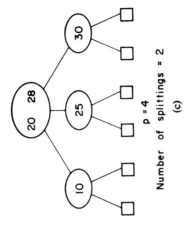

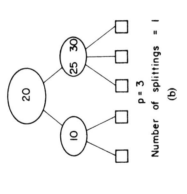

Figure 10.15 *B*-trees of order 3.

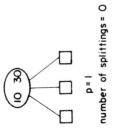

Deletion

Key values may be deleted from the B-tree using an algorithm that is almost as simple as the one for insertion. To illustrate the transformations involved, let us consider the B-tree of order 3 in figure 10.16(a). First, we shall consider the problem of deleting values from leaf nodes (i.e., nodes with no children). Deletion of the key value $x = 58$ from node f is easy, since the removal of this key value leaves the node with 1 key value which is the minimum every nonroot node must have. Once it has been determined that $x = 58$ is in node f, only one additional access is needed to rewrite the new node f onto disk. This deletion leaves us with the tree of figure 10.16(b). Deletion of the key value $x = 65$ from node g results in the number of keys left behind falling below the minimum requirement of

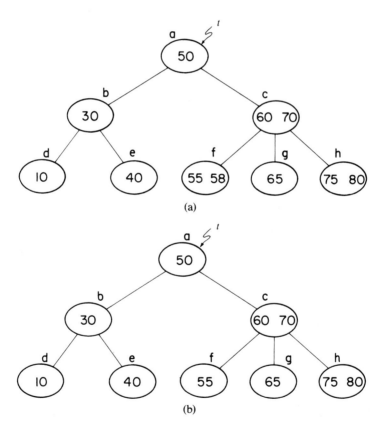

(a)

(b)

Figure 10.16 Deletion from a B-tree of order 3. (Failure nodes have been dispensed with).

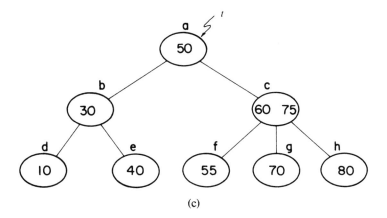

(c)

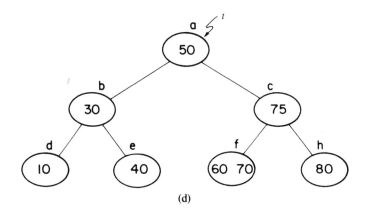

(d)

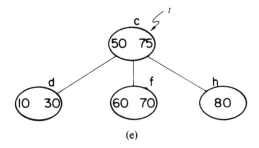

(e)

Figure 10.16 Deletion from a *B*-tree of order 3. (Continued).

$\lceil m/2 \rceil - 1$. An examination of g's nearest right sibling, h, indicates that it has $\geq \lceil m/2 \rceil$ keys, and the smallest key value in h, i.e., 75 is moved up to the parent node c. The value 70 is moved down to the child node g. As a result of this transformation, the number of key values in g and h is $\geq \lceil m/2 \rceil - 1$, the number in c is unchanged and the tree retains its B-tree properties. In the search for $x = 65$, the nodes a, c and g had to be accessed. If all three nodes are retained in memory then from c the address of h, the nearest right sibling of g, is readily determined. Node h is then accessed. Since three nodes are altered (g,c, and h), three more accesses are to be made to rewrite these nodes onto disk. Thus, in addition to the accesses made to search for $x = 65$, four more accesses need to be made to effect the deletion of $x = 65$. In case g did not have a nearest right sibling or if its nearest right sibling had only the minimum number of key values, i.e., $\lceil m/2 \rceil - 1$, we could have done essentially the same thing on g's nearest left sibling. In deleting $x = 55$ from the tree of figure 10.16(c), we see that f's nearest right sibling, g, has only $\lceil m/2 \rceil - 1$ key values and that f does not have a nearest left sibling. Consequently, a different transformation is needed. If the parent node of f is of the form $n, A_0, (K_1, A_1), \ldots (K_n, A_n)$ and $A_i = g$ then we can combine the remaining keys of f with the keys of g and the key K_i into one node, g. This node will have $(\lceil m/2 \rceil - 2) + (\lceil m/2 \rceil - 1) + 1 = 2\lceil m/2 \rceil - 2 \leq m - 1$ key values which will at most fill the node. Donig this with the nodes f, g and c results in the B-tree of figure 10.16(d). Three additional accesses are needed (one to determine that g was too small, one to rewrite each of g and c). Finally, let us delete $x = 40$ from node e of figure 10.16(d). Removal of this key value leaves e with $\lceil m/2 \rceil - 2$ key values. Its nearest left sibling d does not have any extra key values. The keys of d are combined with those remaining in e and the key value 30 from the parent node to obtain the full node d with values 10 and 30. This however leaves b with one value too few. Its right sibling c has no extra values and so the remaining keys of b are combined with the value 50 from a and the $\lceil m/2 \rceil - 1$ values of c to obtain a new node c. The root node a becomes empty and is discarded. This takes a total of four additional accesses (one to fetch each of d and c, one to rewrite each of the altered nodes c and d).

When the key value x being deleted is not in a leaf node, a simple transformation reduces this deletion to the case of deletion from a leaf node. Suppose that $K_i = x$ in the node p and p is of the form $n, A_0, (K_1, A_1), \ldots, (K_n, A_n)$ with $1 \leq i \leq n$. Since p is not a leaf node, $A_i \neq 0$. We can determine y, the smallest key value in the subtree A_i. This will be in a leaf node Q. Replace K_i in p by y and write out the new p. This leaves us with the problem of deleting y from q. Note that this retains the search properties of the tree. For example the deletion of $x = 50$ from the tree of figure 10.16(a) can be accomplished by replacing the 50 in node a by the 55 from node f and then proceeding to delete the 55 from node f (see figure 10.17).

The details are provided in algorithm *deleteb* on page 515. To reduce the worst case performance of the algorithm, only either the nearest left or right sibling of a node is examined.

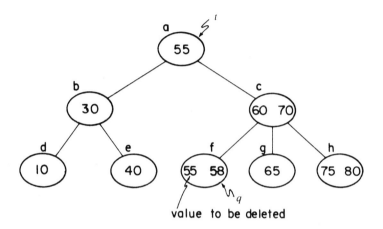

Figure 10.17 Deleting 50 from node a of figure 10.16(a).

Analysis of *deleteb*

The search for x in line 5 together with the search for the leaf q in lines 11-17 requires l accesses if l is the number of levels in t. In case p is not a leaf node at line 7 then it is modified and written out in line 18. Thus, the maximum number of accesses made in lines 5-20 is $l + 1$. Starting from a leaf, each iteration of the **while** loop of lines 24-59 moves p one level up the tree. So, at most $l - 1$ iterations of this loop may be made. Assuming that all nodes from the root t to the leaf P are in internal memory, the only additional accesses needed are for sibling nodes and for rewriting nodes that have been changed. The worst case happens when $l - 1$ iterations are made and the last one results in termination at line 44 or the corresponding point in line 56. The maximum number of accesses for this loop is therefore $(l - 1)$

```
1   procedure deleteb (var t:mtree; x:integer);
    {delete x from B-tree t of order m. t resides on a disk}
2   label 99;
3   var i,j: integer; t,p,q,y,z:mtree;
4   begin
5     msearch(t,x,p,i,j);
6     if j < > 1 then goto 99; {x is not in t}
7     Let p be of the form: n,A₀,(K₁,A₁),...,(Kₙ,Aₙ) and Kᵢ = x
8     if A₀ < > 0 then
9     {deletion from a nonleaf, find key to move up}
10      begin
11        q := Aᵢ; {move to right subtree}
12        while q is not a leaf node do
13          begin
14            let q be of the form: n',A₀',(K₁',A₁'),...,(Kₙ',Aₙ,');
15            q := A₀';
16          end;
17        Let q be of the form n',A'₀,(K'₁,A'₁),...,(K'ₙ,A'ₙ);
18        replace Kᵢ in node p by K₁' and write the altered node p onto
                disk
19        p := q; i := 1;
20        Let n,A₀,(K₁,A₁),...,(Kₙ,Aₙ) be as defined by the new node p
21      end; {of if A₀ < > 0}
22    {delete Kᵢ from node p, a leaf}
23    from node p:n,A₀,(K₁,A₁),...,(Kₙ,Aₙ) delete (Kᵢ,Aᵢ) and replace n by
            n − 1;
24    while (n < ⌈m/2⌉ − 1) and p < > t do
25      if p has a nearest right sibling y then
26        begin
27          let y: n'',A''₀,(K''₁,A''₁),...,(K''ₙ',A''ₙ) and
28          let z: n',A'₀,(K'₁,A'₁),...,(K'ₙ',A'ₙ') be the
29                parent of p and y;
30          let A'ⱼ = y and A'ⱼ₋₁ = p;
31          if n'' > = ⌈m/2⌉ then
32            {redistribute key values}
33              begin
34              {update node p}
35              (Kₙ₊₁,Aₙ₊₁) := (Kⱼ'A₀'');
36              n := n + 1;
37              {update node z}
38              Kⱼ' := K₁'';
39              {update node y}
```

```
40              (n",A₀",(K₁",A₁"),....) :=
41                              (n"-1,A₁",(K₂",A₂",...);
42              output nodes p,y,z onto disk
43              goto 99;
44            end; {of if n" > = ⌈m/2⌉}
45            {combine nodes p,Kⱼ' and y}
46              r := 2* ⌈m/2⌉ − 2;
47              output r,A₀,(K₁,A₁),...,(Kₙ,Aₙ),(Kⱼ',A₀"),
48              (K"₁,A"₁),....,(K"ₙ,A"ₙ) onto disk at location p
49              {update}
50              (n,A₀...) := ( n'-1,A'₀,...,(K'ⱼ₋₁,A'ⱼ₋₁),(K'ⱼ₊₁,A'ⱼ₊₁)...)
51              p := z;
52            end {of if P has a nearest right sibling}
53          else {node p must have a left sibling}
54            begin
55              {this is symmetric to lines 28–52 and
56              is left as an exercise}
57            end; {of if and while}
58          if n < > 0 then
59            output p: (n, A₀, ... , (Kₙ,Aₙ)
60          else {change root}
61              t := A₀;
62  99: end; {of deleteb}
```

Program 10.3   Deleteb

for siblings, plus $(l − 2)$ updates at line 47 and the corresponding point in line 55, plus 3 updates at line 42 or the corresponding point in line 55 for termination. This figure is $2l$. The maximum number of accesses required for a deletion is therefore $3l + 1$.

The deletion time can be reduced at the expense of disk space and a slight increase in node size by including a delete bit, F_i, for each key value k_i in a node. Then we can set $F_i = 1$ if $K_i...$ has not been deleted and $F_i = 0$ if it has. No physical deletion takes place. In this case a delete requires a maximum of $l + 1$ accesses (l to locate the node containing x and 1 to write out this node with the appropriate delete bit set to 0). With this strategy, the number of nodes in the tree never decreases. However, the space used by deleted entries can be reused during further insertions (see exercises). As a result, this strategy would have little effect on search and insert times (the number of levels increases very slowly with increasing n when m is large).

Insert times may even decrease slightly due to the ability to reuse deleted entry space. Such reuses would not require us to split any nodes. For a variation of *B*-trees see exercises 10.14 through 10.20.

Variable Size Key Values

With a node format of the form $n, A_0, (K_1, A_1), ..., (K_n, A_n)$, the first problem created by the use of variable size key values, K_i, is that a binary search can no longer be carried out since given the location of the first tuple (K_1, A_1) and n, we cannot easily determine K_n or even the location of $K_{(1+n)/2}$. When the range of key value size is small, it is best to allocate enough space for the largest size key value. When the range in sizes is large, storage may be wasted and another node format may become better, i.e., the format $n, A_0, \alpha_1, \alpha_2, ..., \alpha_n, (K_1, A_1), ..., (K_n, A_n)$ where α_i is the address of K_i in internal memory, i.e., K_i = memory (α_i). In this case a binary search of the node can still be made. The use of variable size nodes is not recommended since this would require a more complex storage management system. More importantly, the use of variable size nodes would result in degraded performance during insertion. For example, insertion of $x = 85$ into the 2–3 tree of figure 10.16(e) would require us to request a larger node, j, to accomodate the new value being added to the node h. As a result, node c would also be changed since it contains a pointer to h. This pointer must be changed to j. Consequently, nodes of a fixed size should be used. The size should be such as to allow for at least $m - 1$ key values of the largest size. During insertions, however, we can relax the requirement that each node have $\leq m - 1$ key values. Instead, a node will be allowed to hold as many values as can fit into it and will contain at least $\lceil m/2 \rceil - 1$ values. The resulting performance will be at least as good as that of a *B*-tree of order m. Another possibility is to use some kind of key sampling scheme to reduce the key value size so as not to exceed some predetermined size d. Some possibilities are prefix and suffix truncation, removing vowels, etc. Whatever the scheme used, some provision will have to be made for handling synonyms (i.e., distinct key values that have the same sampled value). Key sampling is discussed further in §10.2.4.

10.2.4   Trie Indexing

An index structure that is particularly useful when key values are of varying size is the trie. A *trie* is a tree of degree $m \geq 2$ in which the branching at any level is determined not by the entire key value but by only a portion of it. As an example consider the trie of figure 10.18. The trie contains two types of nodes. The first type we shall call a *branch node* and the second contains 27 link fields. All characters in the key values are assumed to be one of the 26 letters of the alphabet. A blank is used to terminate a key value. At level 1 all key values are partitioned into 27 disjoint classes depending on their first character. Thus, $t1.link[i]$ points to a subtrie containing all key values beginning with the i-th letter (t is the root of the trie). On the j-th level the branching is determined by the j-th character. When a subtrie contains only one key value, it is replaced by a node of type information. This node contains the key value, together with other relevant information such as the address of the record with this key value, etc. In the figure, branch nodes are represented by rectangles while ovals are used for information nodes.

Searching a trie for a key value x requires breaking up x into its constituent characters and following the branching patterns determined by these characters. The algorithm *trie*, program 10.4, assumes that $p = $ **nil** is not a branch node and that $p1.key$ is the key value represented in p if p is an information node.

Analysis of Algorithm *trie*

The search algorithm for tries is very straightforward and one may readily verify that the worst case search time is $O(l)$ where l is the number of levels in the trie (including both branch and information nodes). In the case of an index, all these nodes will reside on disk and so at most l accesses will have to be made to effect the search. (Also, note that in this case the pointer type cannot be used as Pascal does not allow input/output of pointers. The link field will now be implemented as an integer.) Given a set of key values to be represented in an index, the number of levels in the trie will clearly depend on the strategy or key sampling technique used to determine the branching at each level. This can be defined by a sampling function $sample(x,i)$ which appropriately samples x for branching at the i-th level. In the example trie of figure 10.18 and in the search algorithm *trie* this function was

(a) $sample(x,i) = i$-th character of x.

Some other possible choices for this function are ($x = x_1x_2 \ldots x_n$)

(b) $sample(x,i) = x_{n-i+1}$

(c) $sample(x,i) = x_{r(x,i)}$ for $r(x,i)$ a randomization function

(d) $sample(x,i) \begin{cases} x_{i/2} & \text{if } i \text{ is even} \\ x_{n-(i-1)/2} & \text{if } i \text{ is odd} \end{cases}$

```
 1  function trie(var t,p: trieptr; x: integer):trieptr;
 2  {Search a trie t for key value x. It is assumed that branching on
 3   the i-th level is determined by the i-th character of the key value}
 4  var c: char; i,k : integer;
 5  begin
 6  {assume we can always concatenate at least 1 trailing blank to x}
 7  k := x; concatenate (k,' ');
 8  i := 1; p := t;
 9  while p is a branch node do
10     begin
11        c := i-th character of k;
12        p := p↑.link[c];
13        i := i + 1;
14     end;
15  if p = nil or p↑.key < > x then trie := nil
16                              else trie := p
17  end; {of trie}
```

Program 10.4   Trie

For each of these functions one may easily construct key value sets for which that particular function is best, i.e. it results in a trie with the fewest number of levels. The trie of figure 10.18 has five levels. Using the function (b) on the same key values yields the trie of figure 10.20, which has only three levels. An optimal sampling function for this data set will yield a trie that has only two levels (figure 10.21). Choosing the optimal sampling function for any particular set of values is very difficult. In a dynamic situation, with insertion and deletion, we wish to optimize average performance. In the absence of any further information on key values, probably the best choice would be (c). Even though all our examples of sampling have involved single character sampling we need not restrict ourselves to this. The key value may be interpreted as consisting of digits using any radix we desire. Using a radix of 27^2 would result in 2 character sampling. Other radixes would give different samplings. The maximum number of levels in a trie can be kept low by adopting a different strategy for information nodes. These nodes can be designed to hold more than one key value. If the maximum number of levels allowed is l then all key values that are synonyms up to level $l - 1$ are entered into the same information node. If the sampling function is chosen correctly, there will be only a few synonyms in each information node. The information node will therefore be small and can be processed in internal memory. Figure 10.22 shows the use

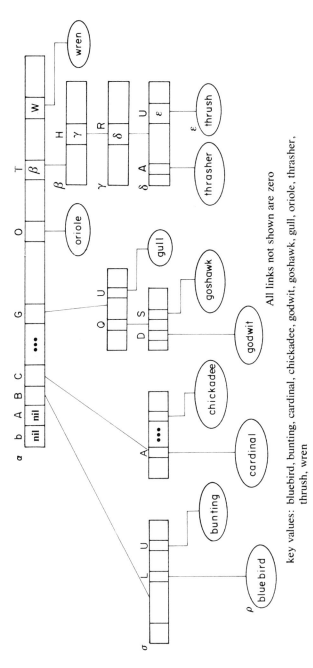

key values: bluebird, bunting, cardinal, chickadee, godwit, goshawk, gull, oriole, thrasher, thrush, wren

All links not shown are zero

Figure 10.18 Trie created using characters of key value left to right, one at a time.

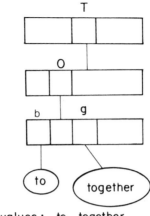

key values: to, together

Figure 10.19 Trie showing need for a terminal character (in this case a blank).

of this strategy on the trie of figure 10.18 with $l = 3$. In further discussion we shall, for simplicity, assume that the sampling function in use is (a) and that no restriction is placed on the number of levels in the trie.

Insertion

Insertion into a trie is straightforward. We shall indicate the procedure by means of two examples and leave the formal writing of the algorithm as an exercise. Let us consider the trie of figure 10.18 and insert into it the two entries: bobwhite and bluejay. First, we have $x =$ bobwhite and we attempt to search for 'bobwhite' in t. This leads us to node σ, where we discover that $\sigma.link['O'] = $ **nil**. Hence x is not in t and may be inserted here (see figure 10.23). Next, $x = $ bluejay and a search of t leads us to the information node ρ. A comparison indicates that $p.key <> x$. Both $\rho.key$ and x will form a subtrie of σ. The two values $\rho.key$ and x are sampled until the sampling results in two different values. The happens when the 5th letter of $p.key$ and x are compared. The resulting trie after insertion is in figure 10.23.

Deletion

Once again, we shall not present the deletion algorithm formally but we will look at two examples to illustrate some of the ideas involved in deleting entries from a trie. From the trie of figure 10.23 let us first delete

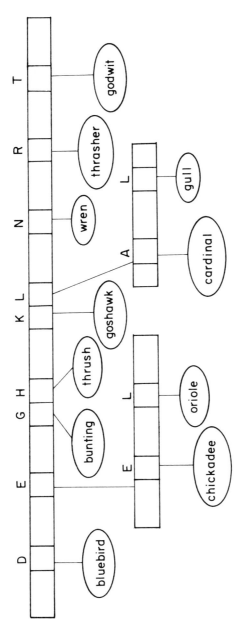

Figure 10.20 Trie constructed for data of figure 10.18 sampling one character at a time, right to left.

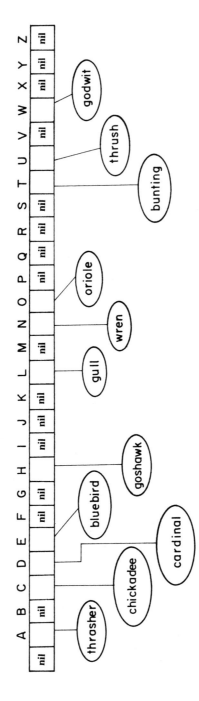

Figure 10.21 An optimal trie for data of figure 10.18 sampling on first level done by using 4th character of key values.

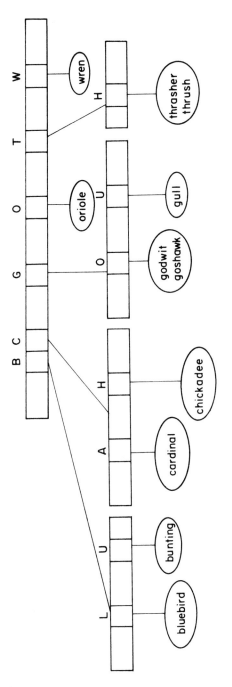

Figure 10.22 Trie obtained for data of figure 10.18 when number of levels is limited to 3. Key has been sampled left to right one character at a time.

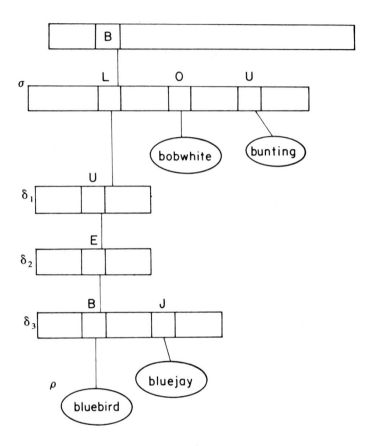

Figure 10.23 Section of trie of figure 10.18 showing changes resulting from inserting bobwhite and bluejay.

'bobwhite.' To do this we just set $\sigma.link['O'] := $ **nil**. No other changes need be made. Next, let us delete 'bluejay.' This deletion leaves us with only one key value in the subtrie, δ_3. This means that the node δ_3 may be deleted and ρ moved up one level. The same can be done for nodes δ_1 and δ_2. Finally, the node σ is reached. The subtrie with root σ has more than one key value. Therefore ρ cannot be moved up any more levels and we set $\sigma.link['L'] := \rho$. In order to facilitate deletions from tries, it is useful to add a *count* field in each branch node. This count field will at all times give us the number of information nodes in the subtree for which it is the root. See exercise 26 for more on tries.

10.3   FILE ORGANIZATIONS

10.3.1   Sequential Organizations

The problems associated with sequential organizations were discussed earlier. The most popular sequential organization scheme is ISAM, in which a cylinder-surface index is maintained for the primary key. In order to efficiently retrieve records based on other keys, it is necessary to maintain additional indexes on the remaining keys (i.e., secondary keys). The structure of these indexes may correspond to any of the alternative index techniques discussed in the previous section. The use of secondary key indexes will be discussed in greater detail in connection with inverted files.

10.3.2   Random Organization

In this organization, records are stored at random locations on disks. This randomization could be achieved by any one of several techniques. Some of these techniques are direct addressing, directory lookup and hashing.

Direct Addressing

In direct addressing with equal size records, the available disk space is divided out into nodes large enough to hold a record. The numeric value of the primary key is used to determine the node into which a particular record is to be stored. No index on this key is needed. With primary key = Employee #, the record for Employee # = 259 will be stored in node 259. With this organization, searching and deleting a record given its primary key value requires only one disk access. Updating a record requires two (one to read and another to write back the modified record). When variable size records are being used an index can be set up with pointers to actual records on disk (see figure 10.24). The number of accesses needed using this scheme is one more than for the case when memory was divided into fixed size nodes. The storage management scheme becomes more complex (§10.4). The space efficiency of direct accessing depends on the identifier density n/T (n = number of distinct primary key values in the file, T = total number of possible primary key values). In the case of internal tables, this density is usually very low and direct addressing was very space inefficient.

Directory LookUp

This is very similar to the scheme of figure 10.24 for the case of direct addressing with variable size records. Now, however, the index is not of direct access type but is a dense index maintained using a structure suitable

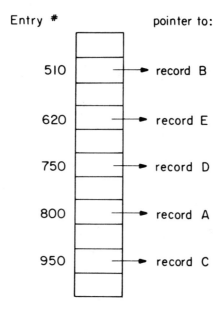

Figure 10.24 Direct Access Index for Data of Figure 10.1.

for index operations. Retrieving a record involves searching the index for the record address and then accessing the record itself. The storage management scheme will depend on whether fixed size or variable size nodes are being used. Except when the identifier density is almost 1, this scheme makes a more efficient utilization of space than does direct addressing. However it requires more accesses for retrieval and update, since index searching will generally require more than one access. In both direct addressing and directory lookup, some provision must be made for collisions (i.e., when two or more records have the same primary key value). In many applications the possibility of collisions is ruled out since the primary key value uniquely identifies a record. When this is not the case, some of the schemes to be discussed in §10.3.3 and §10.3.4 may be used.

Hashing

The principles of hashed file organization are essentially the same as those for a hashed index. The available file space is divided into buckets and slots. Some space may have to be set aside for an overflow area in case chaining is being used to handle overflows. When variable size records are present, the number of slots per bucket will be only a rough indicator of the number of records a bucket can hold. The actual number will vary dynamically with the size of records in a particular bucket.

Random organization on the primary key using any of the above three techniques overcomes the difficulties of sequential organizations. Insertions and deletions become relatively trivial operations. At the same time, random organizations lose the advantages of a sequential ordered organization. Batch processing of queries becomes inefficient as the records are not maintained in order of the primary key. In addition, handling of range queries becomes exceedingly inefficient except in the case of directory look-up with a suitable index structure. For example, consider these two queries: (i) retrieve the records of all employees with Employee Number > 800 and (ii) retrieve all records with $301 \leq$ employee number ≤ 800. To do (i) we will need to know the maximum employee number in the file or else examine every node. If the maximum employee number is known then (i) becomes similar to (ii), so let's look at (ii). With direct addressing and hashing, we would have to search for records with employee number = 301, 302, ... 800, a total of 500 independent searches. The number of records satisfying the query may be much smaller (even 0). In the case of ISAM we could in three accesses locate the record (if one exists) having the smallest employee number satisfying the query and retrieve the remaining records one at a time. The same is possible when a search tree type directory (index) is maintained.

10.3.3   Linked Organization

Linked organizations differ from sequential organizations essentially in that the logical sequence of records is generally different from the physical sequence. In a sequential organization, if the i-th record of the file is at location l_i then the $(i + 1)$-th record is in the next physical position $l_i + c$ where c may be the length of the i-th record or some constant that determines the inter-record spacing. In a linked organization the next logical record is obtained by following a link value from the present record. Linking records together in order of increasing primary key value facilitates easy insertion and deletion once the place at which the insertion or deletion to be made is known. Searching for a record with a given primary key value is difficult when no index is available, since the only search possible is a sequential search. To facilitate searching on the primary key as well as on secondary keys it is customary to maintain several indexes, one for each key. An employee number index, for instance, may contain entries corresponding to ranges of employee numbers. One possibility for the example of figure 10.1 would be to have an entry for each of the ranges 501-700, 701-900 and 901-1100. All records having $E \#$ in the same range will be linked together as in figure 10.25. Using an index in this way reduces the length of the lists and thus the search time. This idea is very easily generalized to allow for easy secondary key retrieval. We just set up indexes for each key and allow records to be in more than one list. This leads to the *multilist* structure for file representation. Figure 10.26 shows the indexes and lists corresponding to a multilist representation of the data of figure 10.1. It is assumed that the only fields designated as keys are: $E\#$, Occupation, Sex and Salary. Each record in the file, in addition to all the relevant information fields, has one link field for each key field.

The logical order of records in any particular list may or may not

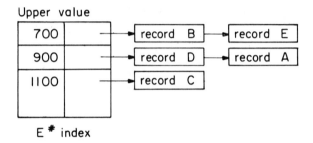

Upper value

700		→ record B → record E
900		→ record D → record A
1100		→ record C

$E\#$ index

Figure 10.25

be important depending upon the application. In the example file, lists corresponding to $E\#$, Occupation and Sex have been set up in order of increasing $E\#$. The salary lists have been set up in order of increasing salary within each range (record A precedes D and C even though $E\#(C)$ and $E\#(D)$ are less than $E\#(A)$).

Notice that in addition to key values and pointers to lists, each index entry also contains the length of the corresponding list. This information is useful when retrieval on boolean queries is required. In order to meet a query of the type, retrieve all records with Sex = female and Occupation = analyst, we search the Sex and Occupation indexes for female and analyst, respectively. This gives us the pointers B and B. The length of the list of analysts is less than that of the list of females, so the analyst list starting at B is searched. The records in this list are retrieved and the Sex key examined to determine if the record truly satisfies the query. Retaining list lengths enables us to reduce search time by allowing us to search the smaller list. Multilist structures provide a seemingly satisfactory solution for simple and range queries. When boolean queries are involved, the search time may bear no relation to the number of records satisfying the query. The query $K1 = XX$ *and* $K2 = XY$ may lead to a $K1$ list of length n

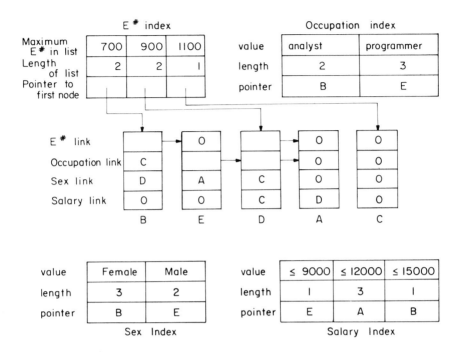

value	Female	Male
length	3	2
pointer	B	E

Sex Index

value	≤ 9000	≤ 12000	≤ 15000
length	1	3	1
pointer	E	A	B

Salary Index

Figure 10.26 Multilist representation for figure 10.1.

and a $K2$ list of length m. Then, $\min\{n,m\}$ records will be retrieved and tested against the query. It is quite possible that none or only a very small number of these $\min\{n,m\}$ records have both $K1 = XX$ and $K2 = XY$. This situation can be remedied to some extent by the use of *compound keys*. A compound key is obtained by combining two or more keys together. We could combine the Sex and Occupation keys to get a new key Sex-Occupation. The values for this key would be: female analyst, female programmer, male analyst and male programmer. With this compound key replacing the two keys Sex and Occupation, we can satisfy queries of the type, all male programmers or all programmers, by retrieving only as many records as actually satisfy the query. The index size, however, grows rapidly with key compounding. If we have ten keys $K_1, ..., K_{10}$, the index for K_i having n_i entries, then the index for the compound key K_1-K_2- ...-K_{10} will have $\pi_{i=1}^{10} \, n_i$ entries while the original indexes had a total of $\Sigma_{i=1}^{10} \, n_i$ entries. Also, handling simple queries becomes more complex if the individual key indexes are no longer retained (see the exercises).

Inserting a new record into a multilist structure is easy so long as the individual lists do not have to be maintained in some order. In this case the record may be inserted at the front of the appropriate lists (see exercise 27). Deletion of a record is difficult since there are no back pointers. Deletion may be simplified at the expense of doubling the number of link fields and maintaining each list as a doubly linked list (see exercises 28 and 30). When space is at a premium, this expense may not be acceptable. An alternative is the coral ring structure described below.

Coral Rings

The coral ring structure is an adaptation of the doubly linked multilist structure discussed above. Each list is structured as a circular list with a headnode. The headnode for the list for key value $K_i = x$ will have an information field with value x. The field for key K_i is replaced by a link field. Thus, associated with each record, y, and key, K_i, in a coral ring there are two link fields: $y\uparrow.alink[i]$ and $y\uparrow.blink[i]$. The *alink* field is used to link together all records with the same value for key K_i. The *alinks* form a circular list with a headnode whose information field retains the value of K_i for the records in this ring. The *blink* field for some records is a back pointer and for others it is a pointer to the head node. To distinguish between these two cases another field $y\uparrow.flag[i]$ is used. $y\uparrow.flag[i] = 1$ if $y\uparrow.blink[i]$ is a back pointer and $y\uparrow.flag[i] = 0$ otherwise. In practice the *flag* and *blink* fields may be combined with $y\uparrow.blink[i] > 0$ when it is a back pointer and < 0 when it is a pointer to the head node. When the *blink* field of a record $y\uparrow.blink[i]$ is used as a back pointer, it points to the nearest record z, preceding it in its circular list for K_i having $z\uparrow.blink[i]$ also a back pointer. In any given circular list, all records with back pointers form another circular list in the reverse direction (see figure 10.27). The presence of these back pointers makes it possible to carry out a deletion without having to start at the front of each list containing the record being deleted in order to determine the preceding records in these lists (see exercise 32). Since these *blink* fields will usually be smaller than the original key fields they replace, an overall saving in space will ensue. This is, however, obtained at the expense of increased retrieval time (exercise 31). Indexes are maintained as for multilists. Index entries now point to head nodes. As in the case of multilists, an individual node may be a member of several rings on different keys.

10.3.4 Inverted Files

Conceptually, inverted files are similar to multilists. The difference is that while in multilists records with the same key value are linked together with link information being kept in individual records, in the case of inverted files this link information is kept in the index itself. Figure 10.28

node α

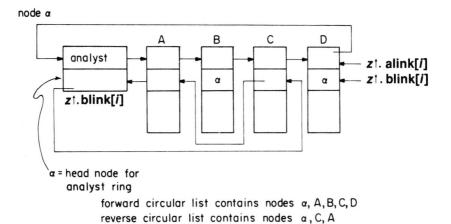

α = head node for
    analyst ring

forward circular list contains nodes α, A, B, C, D
reverse circular list contains nodes α, C, A

Figure 10.27 Coral ring for analysts in a hypothetical file.

shows the indexes for the file of figure 10.1. A slightly different strategy has
been used in the $E\#$ and salary indexes than was used in figure 10.26,
though the same strategy could have been used here too. To simplify
further discussion, we shall assume that the index for every key is dense
and contains a value entry for each distinct value in the file. Since the index
entries are variable length (the number of records with the same key value
is variable), index maintenance becomes more complex than for multilists.
However, several benefits accrue from this scheme. Boolean queries require
only one access per record satisfying the query (plus some accesses to process the indexes). Queries of the type $K1 = XX \; or \; K2 = XY$ can be processed by first accessing the indexes and obtaining the address lists for all
records with $K1 = XX$ and $K2 = XY$. These two lists are then merged to
obtain a list of all records satisfying the query. $K1 = XX \; and \; K2 = XY$ can
be handled similarly by intersecting the two lists. $K1 = $ .not. XX can be
handled by maintaining a universal list, U, with the addresses of all
records. Then, $K1 = $ .not. XX is just the difference between U and the list
for $K1 = XX$. Any complex boolean query may be handled in this way.
The retrieval works in two steps. In the first step, the indexes are processed
to obtain a list of records satisfying the query and in the second, these
records are retrieved using this list. The number of disk accesses needed is
equal to the number of records being retrieved plus the number to process
the indexes. Exercise 34 explores the time savings that can result using this
structure rather than multilists.

Inverted files represent one extreme of file organization in which only the
index structures are important. The records themselves may be stored in any
way (sequentially ordered by primary key, random, linked ordered by primary

E# index

510	B
620	E
750	D
800	C
950	A

Occupation index

analyst	B,C
programmer	A,D,E

Sex index

female	B,C,D
male	A,E

Salary index

9,000	E
10,000	A
12,000	C,D
15,000	B

A,B,C,D,E indicate addresses of the records in the file.

Figure 10.28 Indexes for fully inverted file.

key etc). Inverted files may also result in space saving compared with other file structures when record retrieval does not require retrieval of key fields. In this case the key fields may be deleted from the records. In the case of multilist structures, this deletion of key fields is possible only with significant loss in system retrieval performance (why?). Insertion and deletion of records requires only the ability to insert and delete within indexes.

10.3.5 Cellular Partitions

In order to reduce file search times, the storage media may be divided into cells. A cell may be an entire disk pack or it may simply be a cylinder. Lists are localized to lie within a cell. Thus if we had a multilist organization in which the list for $key1 = prog$ included records on several different cylinders then we could break this list into several smaller lists where each *prog* list included only those records in the same cylinder. The index entry for *prog* will now contain several entries of the type (*addr, length*), where *addr* is a pointer to the start of a list of records with *key 1 = prog* and *length* is the number of records on this list. By doing this, all records in the same cell (i.e., cylinder) may be accessed without moving the read/write heads. In case a cell is a disk pack then using cellular partitions it is possible to search different cells in parallel (provided the system hardware permits simultaneous reading/writing from several disk drives).

It should be noted that in any real situation a judicious combination of the techniques of this section would be called for, i.e., the file may be inverted on certain keys, ringed on others, and a simple multilist on yet other keys.

10.4 STORAGE MANAGEMENT

The functions of a storage management system for an external storage device (such as a disk) are the same as those for a similar system for internal memory. The storage management system should be able to allocate and free a contiguous block of memory of a given size. In chapter 4 we studied several memory management schemes. For fixed size nodes we used a linked stack together with the routines *ret* and *getnode* of §4.3. For variable size nodes the boundary tag method of §4.7 was good. We also studied a general purpose management scheme involving garbage collection and compaction in §4.9. When the storage to be managed is on an external device, the management scheme used should be such as to minimize the time needed to allocate and free storage. This time will to a large extent depend on the number of external storage accesses needed to effect allocation or freeing. In this section we shall review and reevaluate the storage management schemes of chapter 4 with emphasis on the number of device accesses required.

Fixed Size Nodes

All nodes that are free may be linked together into an available space list as in §4.3 and §4.7. Assuming that the value of *av* is always in memory, the allocate and free algorithms take the form:

```
1  procedure getnode (var i : integer);
2  {Get a free node on disk. i is the address of this node
3  Assume that av is global}
4  begin
5    if av = 0 then begin
6                   writeln ('no more nodes');
7                   goto 999; {999 is program end}
8                 end;
9    i := av;
10   {get(x); reads the link field in a node n on disk}
11   av := get (av);
12 end; {of getnode}
```

```
1  procedure ret(i : integer);
2  {free the disk node at address i}
3  begin
4    {out(n,y) sets the link field of node n on disk to y}
5    out (i, av);
6    av := i ;
7  end; {of ret}
```

Program 10.5   Getnode and Ret

Each algorithm requires one access to carry out its function. In case the total number of free nodes at all times is small, this access can be eliminated altogether by maintaining the available space list in the form of a stack which contains the addresses of all free nodes. This stack would not be maintained in place as in the case of §4.3, where the free space itself made up the stack. Instead, the stack could reside permanently in memory and no accesses would be needed to free or allocate nodes.

Variable Size Nodes

In the boundary tag method, the use of boundary tags made it possible to free a block while coalescing adjacent blocks in a constant amount of time. In order to do this it is essential that the free space be maintained in place as we need to test the tags at $p - 1$ and $p + n$ (cf. §4.7). Such a scheme would therefore require several accesses (exercise 35) in order to free and allocate nodes. These accesses can again be eliminated by maintaining in memory a list of all blocks of storage that are free. Allocation can be made using first fit, and nodes can be freed in time $O(n)$ if n is the number of blocks in free space (exercise 36). Since the cost of a disk access is several orders of magnitude more than the cost of internal processing, this scheme will be quicker than the boundary tag method even when free space consists of several thousand blocks. When free space contains many nodes it may not be possible to keep the list of free nodes in memory at all times. In this case the list will have to be read in from disk whenever needed and written back onto disk when modified. Still, the number of accesses will be fewer than when an in place free list is maintained (as is required by the boundary tag method).

Garbage Collection and Compaction

The principles for this technique stay essentially the same. The process was seen to be rather slow for the case of internal memory management. It is even slower for external storage because of the increased access times. In file systems that have a heavy activity rate (i.e., frequent real time update, etc.), it is not possible to allocate a continuous chunk of time large enough to permit garbage collecton and compaction. It is necessary, therefore, to devise these algorithms so that they can work with frequent interruptions, leaving the file in a usable state whenever interrupted.

REFERENCES AND SELECTED READINGS

For additional material on file structures and data base management systems see:

File structures for on line systems, by D. Lefkovitz, Hayden Book Co., New Jersey, 1969.

Data Management for on line systems, by D. Lefkovitz, Hayden Book Co., New Jersey, 1974.

Computer data base organization, by J. Martin, Prentice-Hall, Englewood Cliffs, 1975.

An introduction to data base management systems, by C. Date, Addison-Wesley, Reading, Massachusetts, 1975.

Additional material on indexes can be found in:

The Art of Computer Programming: Sorting and Searching, by D. Knuth, Addison-Wesley, Reading, Massachusetts, 1973.

"Binary search trees and file organization," by J. Nievergelt, *ACM Computing Surveys*, vol. 6, no. 3, September 1974, pp. 195–207.

EXERCISES

1. A file of employee records is being created. Each record has the following format:

E#	NAME	Occupation	Location

All four fields have been designated as keys. The file is to consist of the following 5 records:

A	10	JAMES	PROG	MPLS
B	27	SHERRY	ANAL	NY
C	39	JEAN	PROG	NY
D	50	RODNEY	KEYP	MPLS
E	75	SUSAN	ANAL	MPLS

Draw the file and index representations for the following organizations (assume that an entry in an index is a tuple (value, pointer 1, pointer 2, ...,pointer k) and these tuples are kept sequentially).
a) Multilist File
b) Fully Inverted File
c) Ring File
d) Sequential ordered by name, inverted on E# and location, ringed on occupation.

2. Write an algorithm to process a tape file in the batched mode. Assume the master file is ordered by increasing primary key value and that all such values are distinct. The transaction file contains transactions labeled update, delete and insert. Each such transaction also contains the primary key value of the record to be updated, deleted or inserted. A new updated master file is to be created. What is the complexity of your algorithm?

3. Show that all B-trees of order 2 are full binary trees.

4. (a) Into the following 2-3 tree insert the key 62 using algorithm *insertb*.

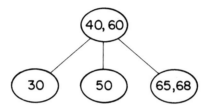

Assuming that the tree is kept on a disk and one node may be fetched at a time, how many disk accesses are needed to make this insertion? State any assumptions you make.

(b) From the following B-tree of order 3 delete the key 30 (use algorithm *deleteb*). Under the same assumptions as in (a), how many disk accesses are needed?

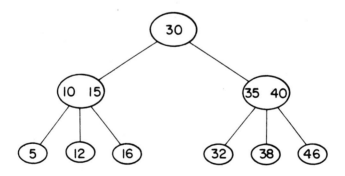

5. Complete line 55 of algorithm *deleteb*.

6. Write insertion and deletion algorithms for B-trees assuming that with each key value is associated an additional field f such that $f = 1$ iff the corresponding key value has not been deleted. Deletions should be accomplished by

simply setting the corresponding $f = 0$ and insertions should make use of deleted space whenever possible without restructuring the tree.

7. Write algorithms to search and delete keys from a B-tree by position; i.e., $search(k)$ finds the k-th smallest key and $delete(k)$ deletes the k-th smallest key in the tree. (*Hint:* In order to do this efficiently additional information must be kept in each node. With each pair (K_i, A_i) keep $N_i = \sum_{j=0}^{i-1}$ (number of key values in the subtree $A_j + 1$).) What are the worst case computing times of your algorithms?

8. Program the AVL tree insertion algorithm of §9.2 and also the B-tree insertion algorithm with $m = 3$. Evaluate the relative performance of these two methods for maintaining dynamic internal tables when only searches and insertions are to be made. This evaluation is to be done by obtaining real computing times for various input sequences as well as by comparing storage requirements.

9. Modify algorithm *insertb* so that in case $n = m$ in line 16 then we first check to see if either the nearest left sibling or the nearest right sibling of p has fewer than $m - 1$ key values. If so, then no additional nodes are created. Instead, a rotation is performed moving either the smallest or largest key in p to its parent. The corresponding key in the parent together with a subtree is moved to the sibling of p which has space for another key value.

10. [Bayer and McCreight] The idea of exercise 9 can be extended to obtain improved B-tree performance. In case the nearest sibling, P', of P already has $m - 1$ key values then we can split both P and P' to obtain three nodes P, P' and P'' with each node containing $\lfloor (2m - 2)/3 \rfloor$, $\lfloor (2m - 1)/3 \rfloor$ and $\lfloor 2m/3 \rfloor$ key values. Figure 10.29 below describes this splitting procedure when P' is P's nearest right sibling.

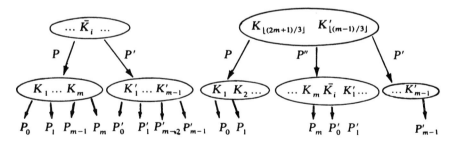

(a) Node P overflows   (b) After Splitting P and P'

Figure 10.29 Splitting P and nearest right sibling P'.

Rewrite algorithm *insertb* so that node splittings occur only as described above.

11. A B^*-tree, t, of order m is a search tree that is either empty or is of height ≥ 1. When t is not empty then the extended tree t (i.e., t with failure nodes added) satisfies the following conditions:

   (i)   The root node has at least 2 and at most $2\lfloor(2m - 2)/3\rfloor + 1$ children.

   (ii)   The remaining nonfailure nodes have at most m and at least $\lceil(2m - 1)/3\rceil$ children each.

   (iii) All failure nodes are on the same level.

   For a B^*-tree of order m and containing N key values show that if $x = \lceil(2m - 1)/3\rceil$ then

   (a) The depth, d of t satisfies:

$$d \leq 1 + \log_x\{(N + 1)/2\}$$

   (b) the number of nodes p in t satisfies:

$$p \leq 1 + (N - 1)/(x - 1)$$

   What is the average number of splittings if t is built up starting from an empty B^*-tree?

12. Using the splitting technique of exercise 10 write an algorithm to insert a new key value x into a B^*-tree, t, of order m. How many disk accesses are made in the worst case and on the average? Assume that t was initially of depth l and that t is maintained on a disk. Each access retrieves or writes one node.

13. Write an algorithm to delete the identifier x from the B^*-tree, t, of order m. What is the maximum number of accesses needed to delete x from a B^*-tree of depth l? Make the same assumptions as in exercise 12.

14. The basic idea of a B-tree may be modified differently to obtain a B'-tree. A B'-tree of order m differs from a B-tree of order m only in that in a B'-tree identifiers may be placed only in leaf nodes. If P is a nonleaf node in a B'-tree and is of degree j then the node format for P is: j, $L(1)$, $L(2)$, ... $L(j - 1)$ where $L(i)$ $1 \leq i < j$ is the value of the largest key in the i-th subtree of P. Figure 10.30 shows two B'-trees of order 3. Notice that in a B'-tree the key values in the leaf nodes will be increasing left to right. Only the leaf nodes contain such information as the address of records having that key value. If there are n key values in the tree then there are n leaf nodes. Write an algorithm to search for x in a B'-tree t of order 3. Show that the time for this is $O(\log n)$.

15. For a B'-tree of order 3 write an algorithm to insert x. Recall that all non-leaf nodes in a B'-tree of order 3 are of degree 2 or 3. Show that the time for this is $O(\log n)$.

16. Write an algorithm to delete x from a B'-tree, t, of order 3. Since all key values are in leaf nodes, this always corresponds to a deletion from a leaf. Show that if t has n leaf nodes then this requires only $O(\log n)$ time.

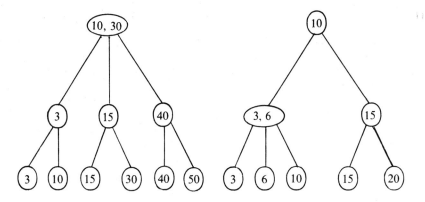

Figure 10.30 Two B'-trees of order 3.

17. Let T and T' be two B'-trees of order 3. Let T'' be a B'-tree of order 3 containing all key values in T and T''. Show how to construct T'' from T and T' in $O(\log n)$ time.

18. Write computer programs to insert key values into AVL trees, B-trees of order 3, $B*$-trees of order 3 and B'-trees of order 3. Evaluate the relative performance of these four representations of internal tables.

19. Do exercise 18 when the required operations are search for x, insert x and delete x.

20. Obtain *search, insert* and *delete* algorithms for B'-trees of order m. If the tree resides on disk, how many disk accesses are needed in the worst case for each of the three operations? Assume the tree has n leaf nodes.

21. Draw the trie obtained for the following data: Sample the keys left to right one character at a time. Using single character sampling obtain an optimal trie for the above data (an optimal trie is one with the fewest number of levels).

AMIOT, AVENGER, AVRO, HEINKEL, HELLDIVER, MACCHI,
MARAUDER, MUSTANG, SPITFIRE, SYKHOI

22. Write an algorithm to insert a key value x into a trie in which the keys are sampled left to right, one character at a time.

23. Do exercise 22 with the added assumption that the trie is to have no more than six levels. Synonyms are to be packed into the same information node.

24. Write an algorithm to delete x from a trie t under the assumptions of exercise 22. Assume that each branch node has a count field equal to the number of information nodes in the subtrie for which it is the root.

25. Do exercise 24 for the trie of exercise 23.

26. In the trie of Figure 10.23 the nodes δ_1 and δ_2 each have only one child. Branch nodes with only one child may be eliminated from tries by maintaining a *skip* field with each node. The value of this field equals the number of characters to be skipped before obtaining the next character to be sampled. Thus, we can have $skip[\delta_3] = 2$ and delete the nodes δ_1 and δ_2. Write algorithms to search, insert and delete from tries in which each branch node has a skip field.

In exercises 27–34 records have n keys. The i-th key value for record z is $z\uparrow.key[i]$. The link field for the i-th key is $z.link[i]$. The number of accesses required by an algorithm should be given as a function of list lengths.

27. Write an algorithm to insert a record, z, into a multilist file with n keys. Assume that the order of records in individual lists is irrelevant. Use the primitives *search(x)* and *update(x,a)* to search and update an index. *update(x,a)* changes the address pointer for x to a. How many disk accesses (in addition to those needed to update the index) are needed?

28. Write an algorithm to delete an arbitrary record z from a multilist file (see exercise 27). How many disk accesses are needed?

29. Write an algorithm to insert record z into a multilist file assuming that individual lists are ordered by the primary key $z\uparrow.key[1]$. How many accesses are needed for this (exclude index accesses)?

30. Assuming that each list in a multilist file is a doubly linked list, write an algorithm to delete an arbitrary record z. The forward link for key i is $z\uparrow.alink[i]$ while the corresponding backward link is $z\uparrow.blink[i]$.

31. Write an algorithm to output all key values for record z in a ring structure. How many accesses are needed for this? How many accesses are needed to do the same in a multilist file?

32. Write an algorithm to delete an arbitrary record z from a ring file.

33. Describe briefly how to do the following:
- (i) In a multilist organization: (a) output all records with $key1 = \text{PROG}$ and key $2 = \text{NY}$. How many accesses are needed to carry this out? (b) Output all records with $key1 = \text{PROG}$ or $key2 = \text{NY}$. How many accesses are needed for this? Assume that each access retrieves only one record.
- (ii) If a ring organization is used instead, what complications are introduced into (a) and (b) above?
- (iii) How could the following be carried out using an inverted organization: a) output all records with $key1 = \text{PROG}$ *and* $key2 = \text{NY}$

b) output all records with $key1 = \text{PROG}$ *or* $key2 = \text{NY}$

c) output all records with $key1 = \text{PROG}$ *and* $key2 \neq \text{NY}$

How many accesses are needed in each case (exclude accesses to get indexes)?

34. A 10^5 record file is maintained as an inverted file on a disk with track capacity 5000 characters. This disk has 200 tracks on each of its 10 surfaces. Each record in the file is 50 characters long and has five key fields. Each key is binary (i.e., has only two distinct values) and so the index for each key can be maintained as a binary bit string of length 10^5 bits. If one character is six bits long, then each index takes about four tracks. How should the five indexes be stored on disk so as to minimize total seek time while processing the indexes in order to determine which records satisfy a given boolean query Q? This processing involves reading in one track of each index and testing the query against records represented by this track. Then the next set of index tracks is input and so on. How much time does it take to process all the indexes in order to determine which records are to be retrieved? Assume a seek time of $1/10$ sec and a latency time of $1/40$ sec. Also assume that only the input time is significant. If k records satisfy this query, how much more time is needed to retrieve these k records? Using other file structures it may be necessary to read in the whole file. What is the minimum time needed to read in the entire file of 10^5 records? How does this compare with the time needed to retrieve k records using an inverted file structure?

35. Determine how many disk accesses are needed to allocate and free storage using algorithms *allocate* and *free* of §4.7 for the boundary tag method when the storage being managed is disk storage.

36. Write storage management algorithms for disk storage maintaining a list of free blocks in internal memory. Use first fit for allocation. Adjacent free blocks should be coalesced when a block is freed. Show that both these tasks can be accomplished in time $O(n)$ where n is the number of free blocks.

Index